LYSTER'S INTERNATIONAL WILDLIFE LAW

The development of international wildlife law has been one of the most significant exercises in international law-making during the last fifty years. This second edition of *Lyster's International Wildlife Law* coincides with both the UN Year of Biological Diversity and the twenty-fifth anniversary of Simon Lyster's first edition. The risk of wildlife depletion and species extinction has become even greater since the 1980s. This new edition provides a clear and authoritative analysis of the key treaties which regulate the conservation of wildlife and habitat protection, and of the mechanisms available to make them work. The original text has also been significantly expanded to include analysis of the philosophical and welfare considerations underpinning wildlife protection, the cross-cutting themes of wildlife and trade, and the impact of climate change and other anthropogenic interferences with species and habitat. *Lyster's International Wildlife Law* is an indispensable reference work for scholars, practitioners and policy-makers alike.

MICHAEL BOWMAN is Associate Professor at the School of Law, University of Nottingham, where his principal teaching and research interests lie in public international law, particularly international environmental and treaty law.

PETER DAVIES is Associate Professor at the School of Law, University of Nottingham, where his main teaching and research interests lie in international environmental law and European Union environmental law.

CATHERINE REDGWELL is Professor of International Law at University College London, where her main teaching and research interests lie in international environmental and energy law.

LYSTER'S INTERNATIONAL WILDLIFE LAW

SECOND EDITION

by

MICHAEL BOWMAN

PETER DAVIES

and

CATHERINE REDGWELL

CAMBRIDGE
UNIVERSITY PRESS

CAMBRIDGE
UNIVERSITY PRESS

University Printing House, Cambridge CB2 8BS, United Kingdom

One Liberty Plaza, 20th Floor, New York, NY 10006, USA

477 Williamstown Road, Port Melbourne, VIC 3207, Australia

314-321, 3rd Floor, Plot 3, Splendor Forum, Jasola District Centre, New Delhi - 110025, India

79 Anson Road, #06-04/06, Singapore 079906

Cambridge University Press is part of the University of Cambridge.

It furthers the University's mission by disseminating knowledge in the pursuit of education, learning and research at the highest international levels of excellence.

www.cambridge.org
Information on this title: www.cambridge.org/9780521527293

First published 2010

A catalogue record for this publication is available from the British Library

Library of Congress Cataloging in Publication data
Bowman, Michael.
Lyster's international wildlife law. – 2nd ed. / by Michael Bowman, Peter Davies, and Catherine Redgwell.
p. cm.
Rev. ed. of: International wildlife law / by Simon Lyster. 1985. Includes bibliographical references.
ISBN 978-0-521-82029-5 (hardback) – ISBN 978-0-521-52729-3 (pbk.)
1. Wildlife conservation (International law) I. Davies, Peter G. G. II. Redgwell, Catherine. III. Lyster, Simon. International wildlife law. IV. Title.
V. Title: International wildlife law.
K3525.B69 2010
346.04′69516–dc22
2010037291

ISBN 978-0-521-82029-5 Hardback
ISBN 978-0-521-52729-3 Paperback

CONTENTS

FOREWORD

I am thrilled and delighted that a second edition of *Lyster's International Wildlife Law* has been written and published, and I feel very privileged to have been asked to write this foreword.

When I first wrote *International Wildlife Law* in the early 1980s, it was the most comprehensive book on the subject available – indeed pretty much the only one available! It reflected the growing concern at the time for threatened species and their habitats, and the emerging body of regional and global agreements to protect them. However, so much has changed since the early 1980s. Then the word 'biodiversity', to describe the variety of species and genetic material within species, had scarcely been invented, and there was no Biodiversity Convention. That was only signed in 1992, at the Earth Summit in Rio de Janeiro. Climate change was a subject that a few visionaries were starting to express concern about, but was nothing like the headline issue it is today.

And it is only in the last twenty-five years that the concept of sustainable development has taken centre stage. In the early days, wildlife conservation was seen as a sensible and moral thing to do to prevent species extinction. But the deep and strong interdependence between people and wildlife – the idea that meeting human development aspirations and wildlife conservation are dependent on each other, that you cannot save wildlife without taking account of human needs – was nothing like as widely accepted as it is today.

However, even if new concepts have emerged, the threats to wildlife, the importance of conserving wildlife and the need for international co-operation to achieve effective conservation are greater than ever. Indeed, with exploding human population increases and emerging threats from climate change, there is an even higher risk of wildlife depletion and species extinction now than there was in the early 1980s. And the consequences of failing to tackle threats such as climate change, habitat loss and unsustainable use of natural resources are, frankly, terrifying as they threaten both wildlife and our own survival.

So we desperately need a new edition of *International Wildlife Law*. We need a clear and widely understood explanation of the international agreements that exist and the mechanisms available to make them work. Just as the first edition was used by the students, practitioners and policy-makers of yesterday to guide them in their work, I really hope the second edition will be even more influential.

Congratulations to all three authors for having written it!

Simon Lyster

PREFACE

From amongst the vast array of specialist textbooks, casebooks and monographs which have been written within the general area of international law, certain examples stand out as having made a seminal contribution. In some cases, their excellence lies in the sheer clarity, precision and thoroughness of their exposition of relevant principles, whereas in others their distinction lies in the fact that they have explored previously uncharted waters, or offered a wholly new perspective on more familiar territory. Yet surely few have combined these attributes to such impressive effect as Simon Lyster's *International Wildlife Law*, published in 1985.

Although academic interest in international environmental law was beginning to burgeon at that time, the bulk of the attention which had been devoted to it focused upon pollution issues, with the importance of conservation of species and ecosystems scarcely recognised in the literature. As a result, there was very little prior scholarship to draw upon when preparing a monograph on international wildlife law. In these circumstances, to produce a text of such breadth, depth and lucidity that it would for so long serve the purposes of expert practitioners, students and lay readers alike represented an extraordinary achievement for which Simon Lyster has attracted well-earned acclaim.

The idea of preparing an updated edition of this valued work was hatched long ago, and it is only the patience and forbearance of our publishers, Cambridge University Press, that has allowed it ultimately to come to fruition. That said, it is something of a happy coincidence that the manuscript should finally have been submitted in 2010, the International Year of Biodiversity, not to mention the twenty-fifth anniversary of the publication of the original edition.

The authors have attempted to capture the spirit and style of the original as far as possible, though the vast accretion of practice arising out of implementation of the treaties covered, not to mention the adoption of several more recent instruments of fundamental significance, has inevitably added to the bulk of detail. Also, the ready contemporary availability of treaty texts via the Internet has enabled us to replace the documentary Appendix with additional substantive sections covering background and cross-cutting themes.

The three authors have all read and commented upon each other's contributions, though each chapter remains essentially the work of one of us, as follows:

Michael Bowman – Chapters 1, 2, 3, 7, 10, 13, 16, 20 and 22;
Peter Davies – Chapters 5 (section 4), 6, 8, 9, 12, 15 and 21;
Catherine Redgwell – Chapters 4, 5 (sections 1–3 and 5), 11, 14, 17, 18 and 19.

Many people have assisted in the preparation of this edition, and we would like in particular to thank the following: Finola O'Sullivan, Richard Woodham and the editorial team at Cambridge University Press; the following for responding to requests for information – Claudia de Windt (Senior Legal Specialist, OAS), Stella Duff (IWC), Richard Huber (Principal Environmental Specialist, OAS), Dwight Peck (Communications Officer, Ramsar Secretariat), Clark Peteru (Environmental Legal Adviser, SPREP), Marina Sansostri Ratchford (US Fish and Wildlife Service), and Willem Wijnstekers (Secretary-General, CITES); former colleague Karen Scott, now of the University of Canterbury, New Zealand; our many wildlife law students at undergraduate, LL M and PhD levels, especially Maeve Hall for her assistance in relation to the chapter on wildlife and pollution, and Al Gillespie for many stimulating conversations on the philosophical basis of the law; Gareth Bowman, Fiona Hayes and Helen Wade, for their invaluable technical expertise and practical assistance. Peter Davies would additionally like to give a personal vote of thanks to Jennie Hale for all her invaluable encouragement during the writing of this book.

We have endeavoured to state the law as at January 2010 (although on rare occasions it has been possible to refer to later developments in 2010).

Michael Bowman
Peter Davies
Catherine Redgwell

18 February 2010

ABBREVIATIONS

ACAP	2001 Agreement for the Conservation of Albatrosses and Petrels (CMS agreement); or Arctic Contaminants Action Program Working Group of the Arctic Council
ACB	ASEAN Centre for Biodiversity
ACCOBAMS	1996 Agreement on the Conservation of Cetaceans of the Black Sea, Mediterranean Sea and Contiguous Atlantic Area
ACPB	1973 Agreement on the Conservation of Polar Bears
AEPS	Arctic Environmental Protection Strategy
AEWA	1995 Agreement on the Conservation of African–Eurasian Migratory Waterbirds (CMS agreement)
AFDI	Annuaire français de droit international
AJIL	*American Journal of International Law*
ALIDES	Central American Alliance for Sustainable Development
ALR	*Australian Law Reports*
AMAP	Arctic Monitoring and Assessment Programme
AMCEN	African Ministerial Conference on the Environment
Apia Convention	1976 Convention on Conservation of Nature in the South Pacific
ASCOBANS	1992 Agreement on the Conservation of Small Cetaceans of the Baltic, North East Atlantic, Irish and North Seas
ASEAN	Association of Southeast Asian Nations
ASMA	Antarctic Specially Managed Area
ASPA	Antarctic Specially Protected Area
AT	1959 Antarctic Treaty
ATCM	Antarctic Treaty Consultative Meeting
ATCP	Antarctic Treaty Consultative Party
AT-NCP	Antarctic Treaty Non-consultative Party
ATS	Antarctic Treaty System
AU	African Union (formerly the OAU)

Barcelona Convention	1995 Convention for the Protection of the Marine Environment and the Coastal Region of the Mediterranean (replacing 1976 Convention)
Barcelona SPA Protocol	1995 Protocol concerning Specially Protected Areas and Biological Diversity in the Mediterranean
Basel Convention	1989 Basel Convention on the Control of Transboundary Movements of Hazardous Wastes and Their Disposal
BCIS	Biodiversity Conservation Information System
BFSP	*British Foreign and State Papers*
BLG	Biodiversity Liaison Group
Brundtland Report	World Commission on Environment and Development, *Our Common Future* (1987)
BYIL	*British Yearbook of International Law*
CAFF	Conservation of Arctic Flora and Fauna Working Group of the Arctic Council
Cartagena Convention	1983 Convention for the Protection and Development of the Marine Environment of the Wider Caribbean Region
CBD	1992 United Nations Convention on the Conservation of Biological Diversity
CCAD	Central American Commission of Environment and Development
CCAMLR	1980 Convention on the Conservation of Antarctic Marine Living Resources
CCAS	1972 Convention on the Conservation of Antarctic Seals
CCD	Convention to Combat Desertification (see also UNCCD)
CCSBT	Commission for the Conservation of Southern Bluefin Tuna
CDM	Clean Development Mechanism (under the Kyoto Protocol)
CEC	Commission for Environmental Co-operation (NAFTA)
CEMP	Comprehensive Ecosystem Monitoring Programme (CCAMLR)
CEP	Caribbean Environment Programme
CEP (EP)	Committee on Environmental Protection (Environmental Protocol to the Antarctic Treaty)

CEPA	Communication, Education and Public Awareness Programme (Ramsar)
CETS	*Council of Europe Treaty Series* (see also *ETS*)
CHM	Clearing House Mechanism
CIDA	Canadian International Development Agency
CIPRA	International Commission for the Protection of Alpine Regions
CITES	1973 Convention on International Trade in Endangered Species
Climate Change Convention	1992 United Nations Framework Convention on Climate Change
CLP	*Current Legal Problems*
Cm	Command Paper (UK) 5th series
Cmd	Command Paper (UK) 3rd series
Cmnd	Command Paper (UK) 4th series
CMS	1979 Bonn Convention on the Conservation of Migratory Species of Wild Animals (see also Bonn Convention)
COFI	Committee on Fisheries (FAO)
Colorado JIntLP	*Colorado Journal of International Law and Policy*
COM	Commission (of the European Union)
CONCAUSA	1994 Central American–US Joint Accord on Biodiversity, Energy, Environmental Legislation and Trade and Investment
CoP	Conference of the Parties
CPAN	Circumpolar Protected Areas Network
CPPS	Permanent Commission for the South Pacific
CRAMRA	Antarctic Minerals Convention
CRIC	Committee for Review of Implementation of the Convention (UNCCD)
CSD	Commission on Sustainable Development
CST	Committee on Science and Technology (of the UNCCD)
CTE	Committee on Trade and Environment (WTO)
CYbIL	Canadian Yearbook of International Law
Denv. J. Int'L L. & Pol'y	*Denver Journal of International Law and Policy*
DSB	Dispute Settlement Body (WTO)
EC	European Community
ECJ	European Court of Justice
ECR	*European Court Reports*
EEZ	exclusive economic zone
EFZ	exclusive fishery zone

EIA	environmental impact assessment
EJIL	*European Journal of International Law*
ELQ	*Ecology Law Quarterly*
EMEP	Co-operative Programme for the Monitoring and Evaluation of the Long-Range Transmission of Air Pollutants in Europe
ENB	*Earth Negotiations Bulletin* (of the IIED)
Env LR	*Environmental Law Reports* (UK)
EP	Environmental Protocol (to Antarctic Treaty)
EPL	*Environmental Policy and Law*
EPPR	Emergency Prevention, Preparedness and Response Working Group of the Arctic Council
ETIS	Elephant Trade Information System (under CITES)
ETS	*Europe Treaty Series* (later *CETS*)
EU	European Union
EUROBATS	1991 Agreement on the Conservation of Populations of European Bats (CMS agreement)
FAO	United Nations Food and Agriculture Organisation
FFI	Fauna and Flora International
GATT	General Agreement on Tariffs and Trade (WTO)
GEF	Global Environmental Facility (IBRD/UNEP/UNDP)
GEO	Global Environmental Outlook (of UNEP)
Georgetown IELR	*Georgetown International Environmental Law Review*
GoE	Group of Experts (of the UNCCD)
GROMS	Global Registry of Migratory Species
GTI	Global Taxonomic Initiative (of the CBD)
Harv. ILJ	*Harvard International Law Journal*
IAEA	International Atomic Energy Agency
IABIN	Inter-American Biodiversity Information Network
IATF	Summit of the Americas Inter-Agency Task Force
IATTC	Inter-American Tropical Tuna Commission
IBPOW	Island Biodiversity Programme of Work (of the CBD)
IBRD	International Bank for Reconstruction and Development (or World Bank)
ICBP	International Committee for Bird Protection
ICCAT	International Commission for the Conservation of Atlantic Tuna
ICJ	International Court of Justice
ICJ Rep	*International Court of Justice Reports*
ICLQ	*International and Comparative Law Quarterly*

ICOMOS	International Council on Monuments and Sites
ICRAN	International Coral Reef Action Network (managed by ICRI)
ICRI	International Coral Reef Initiative
ICRW	International Convention for the Regulation of Whaling
IELMT	*International Environmental Legal Material and Treaties*
IFAD	International Fund for Agricultural Development
IFAW	International Fund for Animal Welfare
IFF	Intergovernmental Forum on Forests
IIED	International Institute for Environment and Development
IISD	International Institute for Sustainable Devlopment
IJECL	*International Journal of Estuarine and Coastal Law*
IJMCL	*International Journal of Marine and Coastal Law*
ILC	International Law Commission
ILM	*International Legal Materials*
ILR	*International Law Reports*
IMO	International Maritime Organisation
IOPN	International Office for the Protection of Nature
IOTC	Indian Ocean Tuna Commission
IP	Intellectual Property
IPCC	Intergovernmental Panel on Climate Change
IPPC	International Plant Protection Convention
IPE	B. Ruster, B. Simma and M. Bock (eds.), *International Protection of the Environment: Treaties and Related Documents*, 30 vols. + Index (Oceana Publications, 1975–83)
IPOA	International Plan of Action (FAO)
ITLOS	International Tribunal for the Law of the Sea
ITTO	International Tropical Timber Organisation
IUCN	International Union for the Conservation of Nature
IUU	illegal, unregulated and unreported fishing
IWC	International Whaling Commission
IWFEA	International Wolf Foundation – Environment Action
IWRB	International Waterfowl Research Board (now Wetlands International)
JAMBA	1974 Agreement for the Protection of Migratory Birds and Birds in Danger of Extinction and Their Environment

JARPA	Japanese Whale Research Program under Special Permit in the Antarctic
JARPN	Japanese Whale Research Program under Special Permit in the North Pacific
JEL	*Journal of Environmental Law*
JERL	*Journal of Energy and Natural Resources Law*
JI	Joint Implementation (under the Kyoto Protocol)
JIEL	*Journal of International Economic Law*
JIWLP	*Journal of International Wildlife Law and Policy*
Kingston SPAW Protocol	1990 Protocol Concerning Specially Protected Areas and Wildlife in the Wider Caribbean Region
Kyoto Protocol	1997 Kyoto Protocol to the Climate Change Convention
LADA	Land Degradation Assessment in Drylands
Lima Convention	1981 Lima Convention for the Protection of the Marine Environment and Coastal Areas of the South-East Pacific
LMOs	living modified organisms
LNTS	*League of Nations Treaty Series*
LOSC	1982 United Nations Convention on the Law of the Sea (see also UNCLOS)
LRTAP	1979 Convention on Long-Range Transboundary Air Pollution
MAB	Man and Biosphere Programme (UNESCO)
MAR	Mesoamerican Reef Alliance (of ICRI)
MARPOL 73/78	International Convention for the Prevention of Pollution from Ships, 1973, as amended by the Protocol of 1978 relating thereto
MBTA	1918 Migratory Bird Treaty Act
MEA	multilateral environmental agreement
MEDASSET	Mediterranean Association to Save the Sea Turtle
Melb. JIL	*Melbourne Journal of International Law*
MEY	maximum economic yield
Mich. J Int'l L	*Michigan Journal of International Law*
MIKE	Monitoring of Illegal Killing of Elephants (under CITES)
MoC	memorandum of co-operation
MoP	meeting of the parties
MoU	memorandum of understanding
MSY	maximum sustainable yield
MUP	Manchester University Press
NABCI	North American Bird Conservation Initiative
NAFO	Northwest Atlantic Fisheries Organisation

NAFTA	North American Free Trade Agreement
Nairobi Convention	1985 Convention for the Protection, Management and Development of the Marine and Coastal Environment of the Eastern African Region
Nairobi SPAW Protocol	1985 Protocol Concerning Protected Areas and Wild Fauna and Flora in the Eastern African Region
NAMMCO	North Atlantic Marine Mammal Commission
NASCO	North Atlantic Salmon Conservation Organization
Nat. Resources J	*Natural Resources Journal*
NAWMP	North American Waterfowl Management Plan
NEPAD	New Partnership for Africa's Development
NGO	non-governmental organisation
NMP	New Management Procedure (of the IWC)
OAS	Organization of American States
OAU	Organisation of African Unity (now the AU)
Ocean & Coastal LJ	*Ocean and Coastal Law Journal*
ODIL	*Ocean Development and International Law*
OIE	Office International des Epizooties/International Office for Epizootics, now more commonly known as the World Organisation for Animal Health
OPRC	1990 International Convention on Oil Pollution Preparedness, Response and Cooperation
OPRC-HNS Protocol	2000 Protocol on Preparedness, Response and Cooperation to Pollution Incidents by Hazardous and Noxious Substances
OY	optimum yield
OSPAR Convention	1992 Convention for the Protection of the Marine Environment of the North East Atlantic
Paipa SPA Protocol	1989 Protocol for the Conservation and Management of Protected Marine and Coastal Areas of the South-East Pacific
PAME	Protection of the Arctic Marine Environment Working Group of the Arctic Council
PCBs	polychlorinated biphenyls
PCIJ	Permanent Court of International Justice
PERSGA	Regional Organization for the Conservation of the Environment of the Red Sea and Gulf of Aden
PIC	prior informed consent
POPs	persistent organic pollutants
PPM	process and production method
RECIEL	*Review of European Community and International Environmental Law*

REDPARQUES	Latin American Cooperation Network of National Parks
Rep. Int. Whal. Commn	*Report of the International Whaling Commission*
Res.	resolution
RFMO	Regional Fisheries Management Organization
RGDIP	*Revue générale de droit international public*
RMP	Revised Management Procedure (of the IWC)
RMS	Revised Management Scheme (of the IWC)
ROKAMBA	2006 Agreement on the Conservation of Migratory Birds
Rotterdam Convention	1998 Rotterdam Convention on the Prior Informed Consent Procedure for Certain Hazardous Chemicals and Pesticides in International Trade
RSPB	Royal Society for the Protection of Birds
SBSTTA	Subsidiary Body for Scientific, Technical and Technological Advice (CBD)
SCAR	Scientific Committee for Antarctic Research
SDWG	Sustainable Development Working Group of the Arctic Council
SEA	Strategic Environmental Assessment
SEAFO	South East Atlantic Fisheries Organisation
SIOFA	Southern Indian Ocean Fisheries Agreement
SOCER	State of the Cetacean Environment Report
SOLAS	1974 International Convention for the Safety of Life at Sea (as amended)
SOWER	Southern Ocean Whale and Ecosystem Research programme
SPA	specially protected area
SPAMI List	List of Specially Protected Areas of Mediterranean Importance (under the Barcelona SPA Protocol)
SPAW	1990 Kingston Protocol Concerning Specially Protected Areas and Wildlife
SPREP	South Pacific Regional Environment Programme
SPS	Agreement on Sanitary and Phytosanitary Measures (WTO)
SSA	1995 Agreement on Highly Migratory and Straddling Fish Stocks
STAC	Scientific and Technical Advisory Committee (of the Kingston SPAW Protocol)
Stat.	Statute

Stockholm Convention	2001 Stockholm Convention on Persistent Organic Compounds
STRP	Scientific and Technical Review Panel (of Ramsar)
TAC	total allowable catch
TBT	Agreement on Technical Barriers to Trade (WTO)
TIAS	*Treaties and Other International Acts Series* (of the US)
TRAFFIC NGO	Monitoring Trade in Endangered Species
TREMs	trade-related environmental measures
TRIPs	Agreement on Trade-Related Aspects of Intellectual Property Rights (WTO)
UKTS	*United Kingdom Treaty Series*
UNCC	United Nations Compensation Commission
UNCCD	2004 United Nations Convention to Combat Desertification (see also CCD)
UNCED	United Nations Conference on Environment and Development, Rio de Janeiro, 1992
UNCHE	1972 UN Conference on the Human Environment
UNCLOS	1982 United Nations Convention on the Law of the Sea (see also LOSC)
UNCTAD	United Nations Conference on Trade and Development
UNDP	United Nations Development Programme
UNECE	United Nations Economic Commission for Europe
UNEP	United Nations Environment Programme
UNESCO	United Nations Educational, Scientific and Cultural Organisation
UNF	UN Foundation
UNFCCC	1992 United Nations Framework Convention on Climate Change
UNGA	United Nations General Assembly
UNJYB	*United Nations Juridical Year Book*
UNTS	*United Nations Treaty Series*
USAID	US Agency for International Development
USC	United States Code
USTS	*United States Treaty Series*
UTLR	*University of Tasmania Law Review*
VCLT	1969 Vienna Convention on the Law of Treaties
VMS	vessel monitoring system
WCED	World Commission on Environment and Development
WCMC	World Conservation Monitoring Centre (of UNEP)

WCPFC	Western and Central Pacific Ocean Fisheries Commission
WCS	World Conservation Strategy
WHC	World Heritage Convention
WHMSI	Western Hemisphere Migratory Species Initiative
WIPO	World Intellectual Property Organisation
WMO	World Meteorological Organisation
WSPA	World Society for the Protection of Animals
WSSD	United Nations World Summit on Sustainable Development (Johannesburg, 2002)
WTO	World Trade Organisation
WWF	World Wide Fund for Nature
Yale JIL	*Yale Journal of International Law*
Yb. Int'l Env. L	*Yearbook of International Environmental Law*
ZaöRV	*Zeitschrift für Ausländisches öffentliches Recht und Völkerrecht*

PART I

Foundations of international wildlife law

Chapter 1

The historical evolution of international wildlife law

1. Introduction

It is difficult to obtain a clear understanding of any legal topic without some sense of the chronology of key developments and the wider historical context out of which they emerged. Areas of legal regulation tend to evolve not in a meticulously planned, orderly fashion, but as an unstructured series of responses to perceived problems, and against the backdrop of the social and political realities of the day. Early attempts to regulate whaling and sealing, for example, must be viewed in light of the considerable economic importance such industries once held, which may be difficult to credit from a purely contemporary perspective. More generally, the political emphasis placed on conservation policy and legal regulation has fluctuated significantly over time, reflecting the prevailing preoccupations of the international community during successive eras. This chapter presents a broad overview of the evolution of international wildlife law against the background of such considerations.

2. Early developments

The enactment of national legislation to protect wildlife and the environment generally can be traced back to antiquity, with forestry conservation laws adopted in Babylon in 1900 BC and a law for the establishment of nature reserves promulgated in Egypt in 1370 BC. The use of international legal instruments for this purpose is a much more recent phenomenon, however, dating essentially from the final quarter of the nineteenth century. By this time, the process of colonial expansion had stimulated a great deal of scientific interest, shared to some extent by the general public, in the world's wildlife. The voyages of Charles Darwin, as recorded in his subsequent writings, had proved particularly influential in that regard, and national societies concerned with ornithology and wildlife generally began to proliferate in western Europe and the United States. At the same time, the development of heavy industry and the expansion of human settlements began to pose threats to nature on a significant scale.

The inescapable interdependence of national communities with regard to natural resources had become apparent from much earlier times through their shared reliance upon the vast international watercourses, in particular the Rhine and the Danube, that flowed through the territories of many major European powers. Initially, the question of navigation was paramount, but inevitably the issue of water resources also emerged as an important concern.[1] In due course, more overtly environmental issues came to the fore: in 1868, regulations were first adopted concerning the transport of inflammable, corrosive and poisonous substances along the Rhine;[2] and in 1885, a convention was concluded for the regulation of fishing in that river.[3] During that same period, the near destruction of European viticulture by the accidental introduction of the aphid-like insect *Phylloxera vastatrix* prompted the adoption of a succession of treaties to control the spread of plant pests and diseases.[4]

Around the turn of the century, however, there occurred a series of legal developments of much more fundamental significance for present purposes. In 1892, following unsuccessful attempts to regulate exploitation of the North Pacific fur seal fishery by means of bilateral arrangements,[5] the United States and Great Britain (on behalf of Canada) agreed to submit their differences to arbitration.[6] To this day the *Bering Sea Fur Seals* arbitration remains one of the very few instances of judicial or arbitral determination of an international conservation dispute.[7] It was not wholly successful in resolving matters, however, and further treaties regarding the fur seal fishery were concluded in 1911 and subsequently.[8]

[1] See generally S. C. McCaffrey, *The Law of International Watercourses* (Oxford University Press, 2001).

[2] 9 *IPE* 4689. [3] 25 *IPE* 200, following earlier, bilateral, arrangements.

[4] 1881 International Convention Respecting Measures to be Taken against *Phylloxera vastatrix*, 73 *BFSP* 323, and 1889 Additional Convention, 81 *BFSP* 1311.

[5] 1891 Agreement for a Modus Vivendi in Relation to Fur Seal Fisheries in the Bering Sea, 8 *IPE* 3655.

[6] 1892 Treaty Submitting to Arbitration the Questions Relating to the Fur Seal Fisheries in the Bering Sea, 176 *CTS* 447.

[7] (1898) 1 *Moore's International Arbitral Awards* 755.

[8] 1911 Convention for the Preservation and Protection of Fur Seals, 8 *IPE* 3682; 1957 Interim Convention on Conservation of North Pacific Fur Seals, 314 *UNTS* 105, and later amendments.

Meanwhile, in 1900, the major powers then controlling the continent of Africa adopted the first regional conservation treaty of general scope, the Convention for the Preservation of Wild Animals, Birds and Fish in Africa,[9] which sought to regulate the exploitation of wildlife and encouraged the creation of nature reserves. The convention never formally entered into force, though some parties took steps to implement its provisions within their own jurisdictions.[10] Two years later, following decades of lobbying by the agricultural community, European governments concluded a treaty for the protection of birds which were valued by farmers as predators upon insects and other pest species that diminished crop yields.[11]

Although significant historical milestones in the evolution of international wildlife law, neither of these conventions achieved a great deal in practice, nor could they be judged particularly enlightened by modern standards. First, each resulted, at least in part, from political pressure to protect some particular, narrowly conceived human interest – in the latter case, agricultural productivity; in the former, the preservation of a sufficient supply of wildlife to satisfy the hunting community. This nakedly utilitarian perspective was apparent from the very title of the birds treaty and made explicit in the preamble to the African Convention, which spoke of the conservation of species which were 'useful to man or inoffensive'. This point alone might not be judged too serious a deficiency, since modern concepts of sustainable utilisation are also primarily anthropocentric in character, but the extreme narrowness of their focus was evident in the recognition in both treaties of a category of 'noxious' species (*nuisibles* in the French text), which were not merely excluded from the scope of protection but positively targeted for persecution. Ironically, these species included many which are nowadays recognised to require the very strictest protection, such as eagles and hawks in the birds convention and various crocodiles, snakes and birds of prey under the African treaty. Equally, the agreements in question were deficient in a structural sense, in that they incorporated no institutional mechanisms to ensure their effective implementation. This is scarcely surprising given the generally primitive nature of international treaty arrangements of the day, but time has shown the incorporation of such mechanisms to be vital if international conservation agreements are to prosper in the longer term.

[9] 94 *BFSP* 75. [10] See ibid., introductory note.

[11] 1902 Convention for the Protection of Birds Useful to Agriculture, 102 *BFSP* 969.

Aside from the absence of institutional machinery within early treaty regimes, this era was also characterised by a dearth of international organisations to service the broader needs of the international community. Following the rapid proliferation of nature conservation societies at the national level, however, and the inevitable trend towards greater international collaboration amongst these groups, a proposal was made at the Eighth International Congress of Zoology for the creation by states of a permanent international organisation in this field.[12] The Swiss conservationist Paul Sarasin was a prominent advocate of this idea, which led to the elaboration in 1913 of an Act of Foundation of a Consultative Commission for the International Protection of Nature,[13] to assume responsibility for collecting and disseminating information on conservation matters. Unfortunately, the outbreak of hostilities in 1914 meant that the commission never commenced its functions, and other ambitious plans for international conservation activities were likewise abandoned.

3. The interwar period

The period between the Great War and the Second World War saw environmental protection slip back down the international agenda,[14] as diplomatic efforts became concentrated upon the restoration and preservation of peaceful relations, alongside urgent labour, maritime and commercial concerns and the continuing problem of trafficking in women and children.[15] The League of Nations devoted some attention to the problem of marine pollution, but declined to make a priority of nature conservation generally. Attempts to activate the pre-war Consultative Commission proved unsuccessful.

It was, in fact, largely at the non-governmental level that the most promising developments were occurring. In 1922, at the prompting of an American ornithologist, T. Gilbert Pearson, the International Committee for Bird Protection (ICBP) was founded to serve as a co-ordinating

[12] See R. Boardman, *International Organisation and the Conservation of Nature* (Macmillan, 1981), pp. 26–30.

[13] 219 *CTS* 32. The Act took the form of a conference resolution; signatories were Argentina, Austria/Hungary, Belgium, Denmark, France, Germany, Great Britain, Italy, the Netherlands, Norway, Portugal, Russia, Spain, Sweden, Switzerland and the US.

[14] On this period generally, see Boardman, *supra* n. 12, pp. 30–5.

[15] For the major multilateral treaties of the period, see M. J. Bowman and D. J. Harris, *Multilateral Treaties: Index and Current Status* (Butterworths, 1984).

agency for national associations concerned with avian conservation.[16] During the 1920s, the ICBP was instrumental in setting the agenda for the protection of birds internationally and more recently it has re-emerged as a potent force, not least through its involvement in the elaboration and implementation of contemporary conservation treaties.[17] Nevertheless, there remained a need to expand transnational collaboration on a wider front. Following the creation in 1925 of the Netherlands Commission for International Nature Protection, its founder, P. G. van Tienhoven, spearheaded a movement for the creation of an international counterpart through the forum of the International Union of Biological Sciences. This new organisation, which obtained financial support from the Dutch government, was formally constituted in 1934 as the International Office for the Protection of Nature (IOPN). Among the many tasks it identified to foster progress in nature conservation internationally were the collection and dissemination of both scientific studies and legislative texts. Meanwhile, in the United States, the American Committee for International Wild Life Protection (ACIWLP) was established in 1930 as an umbrella group for existing national conservation organisations. The ACIWLP not only provided additional funding for the IOPN, but also helped to maintain international momentum behind the conservation issue when Europe again became distracted by the scourge of war.

The activities of these new non-governmental agencies also served as catalysts for some of the relatively few significant inter-governmental developments which occurred during this period. For example, the colonial powers revisited the question of wildlife conservation in Africa by concluding the 1933 International Convention for the Protection of Flora and Fauna,[18] which was intended to replace the 1900 convention. It was primarily concerned with the creation of protected areas, but also provided for the protection of species listed in an Annex. The concept of 'noxious' species disappeared. Shortly afterwards, the Pan American Union adopted the 1940 Convention on Nature Protection and Wildlife Preservation in the Western Hemisphere.[19] The main emphasis

[16] The ICBP was subsequently renamed the International *Council* for Bird *Preservation* and recently reconstituted as BirdLife International.

[17] As to which, see Chapter 7 below.

[18] 172 *LNTS* 241. Of the colonial powers, Belgium, France (without formally ratifying), Italy, Portugal and the UK became parties, as did Egypt, South Africa, Sudan and (much later) Tanzania amongst African states. Interestingly, the convention was also extended to India (see Articles 1 and 13).

[19] 161 *UNTS* 229. See further Chapter 8 below.

of this agreement was similarly upon the establishment of protected areas, within which human activities were to be subject to graduated levels of restriction. It also contained provisions for the protection of wildlife generally, especially migratory birds (already the subject of bilateral arrangements between the United States and its immediate neighbours)[20] and species requiring urgent protection. A prominent feature of agreements covering the western hemisphere has been their strong emphasis upon aesthetic considerations as a justification for conservation, always a significant strand in the fabric of North American environmental ethics.[21] Within that region, the United States and Canada once again found themselves resorting to arbitration during this period, this time over the problem of transboundary air pollution.[22]

Other noteworthy developments of the era included the adoption of the 1920 Convention regarding the Organisation of the Campaign against Locusts,[23] and the introduction of the first, faltering efforts to regulate the exploitation of whales. The 1931 Convention for the Regulation of Whaling was followed by further agreements later in the decade,[24] but these treaties suffered from major deficiencies and were soon superseded.

4. The immediate postwar period

Once again, nature conservation was not high on the international agenda in the years immediately following the formal cessation of hostilities in 1945, and relatively few major environmental initiatives occurred during this period. Nevertheless, this was a time of fundamental organisational change for the international community generally, and a number of major institutional innovations proved significant to the cause of environmental protection in the longer term.

The key development was the establishment of the United Nations as the major global political institution, soon followed by the creation of the various specialised agencies, designed to undertake responsibility for the more detailed, technical problems facing postwar international

[20] See further Chapter 7 below. [21] For further discussion, see Chapter 3 below.

[22] *Trail Smelter* Arbitration (1939) 33 *AJIL* 182; (1941) 35 *AJIL* 684.

[23] 4 *IPE* 1642. This topic has also been addressed in many later treaties.

[24] 1931 Convention for the Regulation of Whaling, 155 *LNTS* 349; the 1937 International Agreement for the Regulation of Whaling, 190 *LNTS* 79, and its subsequent protocols.

society. Although there was no environmental agency as such, several of these new bodies found themselves increasingly preoccupied with environmental questions as time progressed, in particular the Food and Agriculture Organisation (FAO – crop diversity, fisheries conservation), the United Nations Educational, Scientific and Cultural Organisation (UNESCO – habitat conservation), the World Meteorological Organisation (WMO – climate change) and the International Maritime Organisation (IMO – marine pollution).[25] The necessity for some kind of supra-national institution devoted specifically to conservation issues was still keenly felt in some quarters, however, and led to the creation under UNESCO's auspices of the International Union for the Protection of Nature (IUPN), incorporating the earlier IOPN. It was later renamed the IUCN – the International Union for the *Conservation* of Nature *and Natural Resources* – and continues to play a vital role in this field, not least through publication of its *Red List of Threatened Species*, a comprehensive guide to the current conservation status of plants and animals. IUCN is an unusual institution in that, although technically classed as a non-governmental organisation, it numbers governments and government agencies amongst its membership alongside scientific, professional and conservation bodies. In that sense it represents a microcosm of international activity in the environmental field as a whole, where the role of NGOs is particularly prominent and there are now relatively well-established lines of communication and co-operation between the governmental and non-governmental sectors.

The following year, the UN itself demonstrated its concern for conservation issues by convening the first global conference on this question – the 1949 Conference on the Conservation and Utilisation of Resources (UNCCUR).[26] Essentially a 'talking shop' with no mandate to adopt resolutions for substantive action, UNCCUR was nonetheless an indicator of growing recognition of the importance of nature conservation, as well as of its crucial relationship with economic development, which has become such a pervasive theme of international policy in subsequent years. Another significant milestone was the adoption a decade later of the 1959 Antarctic Treaty by the major powers and

[25] On the specialised agencies generally, see P. Sands and P. Klein, *Bowett's Law of International Institutions* (Sweet and Maxwell, 6th ed., 2009) and, for surveys of their current activities in the environmental field, the *Yearbook of International Environmental Law*.

[26] The process was initiated by the Economic and Social Council, one of the six original 'principal organs' of the UN.

claimants to the southern continent.[27] Although overtly more concerned with scientific co-operation than with environmental protection as such, this agreement laid the foundations for what has come to be known as the Antarctic Treaty System, a network of measures which have become increasingly centred around conservation over the years.[28]

The immediate postwar era was, moreover, not entirely devoid of legal instruments dedicated specifically to conservation objectives. The whaling question was revisited via the 1946 International Convention for the Regulation of Whaling,[29] which, despite its many deficiencies, remains to this day the primary vehicle for the conservation of the larger cetacean species.[30] This was immediately followed by the establishment, usually under the auspices of the FAO, of a number of regional fisheries arrangements.[31] 1950 saw the adoption by various European nations of the International Convention for the Protection of Birds,[32] which was designed to replace the 1902 convention but was again hamstrung from the outset by the failure to incorporate institutional mechanisms for its implementation. The following years witnessed the conclusion of various plant protection agreements,[33] and the first treaty to tackle the pollution of marine ecosystems, specifically that caused by routine discharges of oil in the course of shipping operations.[34] An important manifestation of the early work of the UN's own law reform agency, the International Law Commission,[35] emerged in 1958 in the four Geneva Conventions on the Law of the Sea,[36] though

[27] 402 *UNTS* 71. [28] See further Chapter 11 below. [29] 161 *UNTS* 72.

[30] For further discussion, see Chapter 6 below.

[31] See, e.g., the 1948 Agreement for the Establishment of the Indo-Pacific Fisheries Commission, 120 *UNTS* 59; and the 1949 Agreement for the Establishment of a General Fisheries Council for the Mediterranean, 126 *UNTS* 237.

[32] 638 *UNTS* 186.

[33] See, e.g., the 1951 International Convention for the Protection of Plants and Plant Products, 220 *UNTS* 121 (superseding the old *Phylloxera vastatrix* conventions, *supra* n. 4); and the 1951 Convention for the Establishment of the European and Mediterranean Plant Protection Organisation, *UKTS* no. 44 (1956), Cmd. 9878.

[34] 1954 International Convention for the Prevention of Pollution of the Sea by Oil, 327 *UNTS* 3.

[35] The Commission was established by the UN General Assembly in 1948, acting under Article 13, UN Charter. See further the *Yearbook of the International Law Commission*; I. Sinclair, *The International Law Commission* (Cambridge University Press, 1987); M. Anderson and A. E. Boyle (eds.), *International Law Commission and the Future of International Law* (BIICL, 1998).

[36] 1958 Conventions on (i) the Territorial Sea and Contiguous Zone, 516 *UNTS* 205; (ii) the High Seas, 450 *UNTS* 82; (iii) Fishing and Conservation of the Living Resources of the High Seas, 559 *UNTS* 285; (iv) the Continental Shelf, 499 *UNTS* 311.

(despite the inclusion of one concerned with fisheries conservation) these are noteworthy more for the absence than for the presence of detailed environmental provision. Growing preoccupation with the potential hazards, as well as benefits, of nuclear power led to the creation in 1956 of the International Atomic Energy Agency (IAEA),[37] followed by various treaties concerned with legal liability and security control in the nuclear field.[38] Two disputes concerning interference with the natural flow of international watercourses were submitted to arbitration.[39] The real heyday of international wildlife law was, however, still to come.

5. The age of environmental awareness

Any attempt to allocate a precise date to the final consolidation of environmental protection, and wildlife conservation in particular, as serious and enduring issues on the global political agenda would plainly be arbitrary. There can, however, be little doubt that it occurred at some point during the 1960s, when a discernible change in the climate of public opinion began to have its effect upon those who wielded political power. Some commentators attribute particular significance to the impact of literary works such as Rachel Carson's *Silent Spring*, published in 1962,[40] though the first stirrings of popular consciousness had already become evident the previous year with the creation of the World Wildlife Fund (WWF),[41] a campaigning and fund-raising organisation closely linked to IUCN. Subsequently, particular incidents captured the headlines and generated major political repercussions, as when, in 1967, the Liberian oil tanker *Torrey Canyon* ran aground off the south-western tip of the United Kingdom, vividly bringing home the threat posed by shipping

[37] See the 1956 Statute of the International Atomic Energy Agency, 276 *UNTS* 3.

[38] See, e.g., the 1957 Convention on the Establishment of a Security Control in the Field of Nuclear Energy, 5 *European Yearbook* 282; 1960 Convention on Third Party Liability in the Field of Nuclear Energy, 8 *European Yearbook* 203, and 1963 Supplementary Convention, 523 *UNTS* 93; 1962 Convention on the Liability of Operators of Nuclear Ships, 1 *IPE* 405; 1963 Vienna Convention on Civil Liability for Nuclear Damage and Optional Protocol, 1963 *UNJYB* 148.

[39] *Lac Lanoux* Arbitration (1957) 24 *ILR* 101 (Spain/France); *Gut Dam* Arbitration (1968) 8 *ILM* 118 (US/Canada).

[40] R. F. Nash, *The Rights of Nature* (University of Wisconsin Press, 1989), p. 78; W. Fox, *Towards a Transpersonal Ecology* (SUNY Press, 1995), pp. 4–5.

[41] The WWF was subsequently renamed the World Wide Fund for Nature, while retaining its original initials.

accidents to the marine and coastal environment and prompting a series of urgent measures in response.[42]

At the inter-governmental level, the UN Conference on the Human Environment (UNCHE), convened in Stockholm in 1972, was undoubtedly a seminal event, marking the beginnings of an organised system of international environmental policy and law through its adoption of a Declaration of key environmental principles, together with an Action Plan to implement them, and the creation of the first global agency with a specifically environmental brief, the United Nations Environment Programme (UNEP).[43] The scope of the Stockholm Declaration extended far beyond the issue of conservation, though several of its principles were relevant in that regard. Principles 2 and 3, for example, provided that natural resources (including flora, fauna and representative samples of natural ecosystems) must be safeguarded for the benefit of present and future generations and that the Earth's capacity to produce renewable resources must be maintained and, where possible, restored or improved. In addition, Principle 4 provided that

> Man has a special responsibility to safeguard and wisely manage the heritage of wildlife and its habitat which are now gravely imperilled by a combination of adverse factors. Nature conservation, including wildlife, must therefore receive importance in planning for economic development.

Despite the importance of the UNCHE, it should be noted that many significant initiatives in the conservation field had already occurred prior to that time. Indeed, UNESCO's Man and the Biosphere Conference,[44] held in Paris during 1968, was an important forerunner to Stockholm, reflecting growing concern over species and habitat conservation, and the need for formal international action to achieve such objectives. A succession of such initiatives bore fruit over this period, several even before the Stockholm Conference.

[42] The RAF was instructed to bomb the tanker, even though it was on the high seas, in order to contain the pollution threat. Several marine pollution conventions followed in 1969. See further P. W. Birnie, A. E. Boyle and C. J. Redgwell, *International Law & the Environment* (Oxford University Press, 3rd ed., 2009), Chapter 7; and Chapter 21 of this work.

[43] See generally L. B. Sohn, 'The Stockholm Declaration on the Human Environment' (1973) 14 *Harv. ILJ* 423.

[44] Formally entitled the Conference on the Conservation and Rational Use of the Biosphere, it led in 1970 to the inauguration of UNESCO's Man and the Biosphere Programme.

The earliest of these was the 1968 African Convention on the Conservation of Nature and Natural Resources,[45] the first such agreement to have been concluded by the independent African nations themselves, under the auspices of the newly established Organisation of African Unity.[46] Unfortunately, the Convention was afflicted by the same institutional shortcomings as its regional predecessors and consequently failed to deliver major practical benefits to the conservation cause. A pivotal event occurred some three years later, however, with the adoption of the 1971 Ramsar Convention on the Conservation of Wetlands of International Importance,[47] which signalled the beginnings of a transition to a more modern approach to the multilateral regulation of environmental issues. First, in terms of participation, it represents a striking example of the partnership between governmental and non-governmental actors which has become characteristic of treaties in this area. NGOs have been prominent throughout the history of the Convention, from its original conception and drafting to its ongoing implementation and development, and across the entire spectrum of activities, whether promotional, administrative or scientific. Second, from a substantive point of view, it was the first such agreement to focus upon protection of a particular habitat type, paving the way for a more ecologically based approach to conservation, whereby species are considered not merely in isolation but as part of the wider ecosystem in which they function. Finally, from a structural perspective, it pioneered the incorporation of key institutional elements, such as a secretariat, a conference of the parties and supporting administrative infrastructure.[48] This ensured that implementation of the commitments undertaken by the parties could be kept under continuous review, an element conspicuously lacking from earlier conservation treaties.[49] Admittedly, the form in which these institutional arrangements were initially established was relatively primitive, but that is commonly the case with prototypes. Later treaties were quick to learn from both its strengths and its weaknesses,

[45] 1001 *UNTS* 3.

[46] The OAU (now the African Union) was created by its 1963 Charter, 479 *UNTS* 39, which entered into force in September of that year. Note also its 1967 Phyto-sanitary Convention for Africa, OAU Doc.CAB/LEG/24.4/11.

[47] 996 *UNTS* 245. Ramsar is the Iranian town where the convention was adopted.

[48] Much of its present committee structure has actually been established subsequently, but the original institutions undoubtedly laid the foundations for these developments.

[49] With the exception of fisheries conservation agreements, where the underlying political dynamic is markedly different. See further Chapter 5 below.

and the Ramsar Convention itself has had occasion to borrow back ideas from such treaties in order to remedy some of its own original shortcomings.[50]

From then on, the pace of developments accelerated to such an extent that it is possible only to record them in the barest outline. The following decade witnessed the adoption of many of the key global treaties in the field, notably the 1972 Convention for the Protection of the World Cultural and Natural Heritage,[51] the 1973 Convention on International Trade in Endangered Species (CITES)[52] and the 1979 Bonn Convention on the Conservation of Migratory Species of Wild Animals.[53] The many notable features of these agreements included, respectively, (i) the creation of an international fund to be used for the protection of globally important natural heritage sites; (ii) the potentially fruitful interaction between national and international agencies, procedures and laws for the regulation of trade in wildlife; and (iii) the proposed network of ancillary agreements to flesh out the provisions of the parent convention for the collaborative protection of migratory species. Each of these innovations has proved capable of translation from its particular original context to the broader field of environmental regulation, thereby helping to shape a coherent corpus of law with its own distinctive array of principles, practices and procedures.

At the regional level, too, significant developments were occurring. In relation to Antarctica, treaties were adopted for the conservation of seals,[54] and of marine living resources generally,[55] especially the krill resource which lies at the heart of the Antarctic food web. Indeed, the 'ecosystem' focus of the 1980 CCAMLR Convention was much heralded for its visionary approach at the time.[56] A conservation convention for the South Pacific was adopted in 1976,[57] followed by one for the European region in 1979.[58] It is, perhaps, ironic to note that it was not until this belated stage that the European nations, having demonstrated so much interest in the fate of the biota of other regions, finally got

[50] For discussion, see Chapter 13 below.

[51] 1972 *UNJYB* 89; see further Chapter 14 below.

[52] 993 *UNTS* 443; see further Chapter 15 below.

[53] 19 *ILM* 15; see further Chapter 16 below. [54] 11 *ILM* 251. [55] 19 *ILM* 841.

[56] See generally Chapter 11 below.

[57] 1976 Convention on Conservation of Nature in the South Pacific, 1 *SMTE* 463; see further Chapter 12 below.

[58] 1979 Convention on the Conservation of European Wildlife and Natural Habitats, 1284 *UNTS* 209; see further Chapter 10 below.

around to adopting protective measures for their own, now vastly depleted, wildlife resources.

Beyond the specific realm of wildlife conservation, there was ample evidence of international environmental activity across a broad front. The International Court of Justice delivered judgment in the *Nuclear Tests* cases,[59] though, to the disappointment of environmentalists, ultimately declined to address the substantive legal issues raised by the French government's programme of weapons testing in the South Pacific. There was, however, a vast proliferation during this period of treaties designed to tackle the problem of pollution, particularly of the marine environment,[60] while the first multilateral convention concerned with protection of the atmosphere was adopted at the end of the decade.[61]

Yet it would be misguided to regard the mere adoption of treaties, however innovative, as constituting in itself a reason for celebration. Rather, it is the incorporation of rigorous and appropriate substantive provisions, coupled with the willingness of governments to commit themselves not merely to participation but to scrupulous compliance with those provisions, which represents the true yardstick of progress. Here the picture was at this stage decidedly mixed. Several of the crucial instruments discussed above, most notably the Ramsar and Bonn conventions, not only appeared thin on substantive commitments, but were initially slow to attract governmental adherence, particularly from developing countries, while others, such as CITES, found many parties ill-prepared to discharge the responsibilities which they had undertaken, even down to such basic aspects as the designation of national agencies to perform key functions in the trade-regulation process.[62]

It was clearly essential to increase the urgency with which states were prepared to address such problems and, by enhancing environmental awareness generally, to dispel the notion that nature conservation was simply a luxury they could ill afford. With those aims in mind, a number of organisations collaborated to produce the World Conservation Strategy, promulgated in 1980.[63] A central theme of the Strategy was its emphasis upon the importance of living resource conservation for

[59] (1974) *ICJ Rep* 253, 457. [60] See generally Chapter 21 below.

[61] 1979 Convention on Long-Range Transboundary Air Pollution, 18 *ILM* 1442.

[62] For more detailed discussion, see Part IV of this work.

[63] World Conservation Strategy: Living Resource Conservation for Sustainable Development (1980), prepared by IUCN, with the involvement of UNEP, WWF, the FAO and UNESCO.

human survival and sustainable development, and the need to displace traditional assumptions that nature conservation and economic development were inherently inimical to one another. It accordingly identified three basic objectives, namely the maintenance of essential ecological processes and life-support systems, the preservation of genetic diversity and the sustainable utilisation of species and ecosystems. It expressly acknowledged the potential contribution of international treaties in that regard,[64] but at the same time recognised the danger of 'weak conventions' which might 'permit the illusion that problems are being tackled when in fact they are not'.[65] Examination of the extent to which the international community has successfully absorbed and responded to these lessons represents a pervasive aim of this work.

The Strategy was essentially a policy document, intended to educate and inform, rather than one importing any specific legal effects, but for several years attempts had been under way to secure the adoption of a normative instrument embodying many of the same basic principles.[66] This aspiration was fulfilled in 1982 with the adoption by the UN General Assembly of the World Charter for Nature,[67] co-sponsored by Zaire and some thirty-five other nations, and approved by a vote of 111 to one.[68] Although its status as a General Assembly resolution denies the Charter formal binding force, a noteworthy feature is that its provisions are couched in unambiguously normative style:[69] thus paragraph 1 of the section headed 'General Principles' states that 'Nature shall be respected and its essential processes shall not be impaired.' Further principles provide for the safeguarding of the Earth's genetic viability; the protection of unique areas, representative ecosystems and natural habitats; the sustainable utilisation of natural resources; and the protection of nature in times of war. Principle 2 expressly states that the 'population levels of all life forms, wild and domesticated, must be at least sufficient for their

64 See ibid., section 15.3. 65 Ibid.

66 The process had been initiated by General Mobutu of Zaire at the 12th General Assembly of the IUCN, held in Kinshasa during 1975.

67 UNGA Res. 37/7, 37 UNGAOR Suppl. No. 51, at 17, UN Doc.A/37/51 (1982). See generally W. E. Burhenne and W. A. Irwin, *The World Charter for Nature* (Erich Schmidt, 2nd rev. ed., 1986).

68 Only the US voted against. There were eighteen abstentions, mainly by Amazonian states.

69 This feature plainly influenced the US position, their delegate indicating that 'if all the "shalls" that are in the document could have been changed to "shoulds" we would have been much more likely to have gone along with it'. See Burhenne and Irwin, *supra* n. 67, at p. 39.

survival'. Although occasionally overlooked, the World Charter for Nature represents a considered attempt by the international community to deal comprehensively and exclusively with the question of man's relationship with nature, and is therefore properly to be counted as one of the main foundation stones of international wildlife law.[70]

Further attempts to cement the relationship between environmental protection and economic development were then undertaken by the UN General Assembly through its establishment of the World Commission on Environment and Development (WCED), chaired by former Norwegian prime minister Gro Harlem Brundtland. The Commission's report,[71] published in 1987, provided strong endorsement of the objective of sustainable development. In addition, it stressed the importance of the maintenance of biological diversity, calling for the adoption of a new convention embodying collective responsibility for the conservation of wildlife species, to be reflected in the creation of an international trust fund to benefit those states which were to bear the brunt of conservation obligations.

The process culminated in 1992 with the convening at Rio de Janeiro of the UN Conference on Environment and Development (UNCED), also known as the Rio Earth Summit. By this time, however, developing states had formed themselves into an effective negotiating force, and the Conference Declaration is marked by its heavy, anthropocentric bias towards developmental issues.[72] Nature itself does not receive prominent mention.[73] At the same time, it is not to be forgotten that the Rio Declaration specifically states in its preamble that its intention is to 'build upon' its 1972 counterpart, the principles of which are expressly reaffirmed. Furthermore, it has been observed that the Rio document

> also introduces important new principles, including precautionary action, environmental impact assessment, the polluter pays principle, and public participation, which had not previously secured such widespread support, but which have gradually become more widely evidenced in treaties and state practice.[74]

[70] Note its recent recognition as such in the preamble to the 2003 African Nature Conservation Convention, *infra* n. 89.

[71] WCED, *Our Common Future* (Oxford University Press, 1987).

[72] See generally M. Pallemaerts and I. Porras, Chapters 1 and 2 respectively, in P. Sands (ed.), *Greening International Law* (Earthscan, 1993).

[73] Indeed, the only reference appears to be in Principle 1, which declares that human beings 'are entitled to a healthy and productive life *in harmony with nature*' (emphasis added).

[74] P.W. Birnie and A.E. Boyle, *Basic Documents on International Law and the Environment* (Oxford University Press, 1995), p. 9.

Given this preoccupation with the establishment of fundamental themes, policies and principles of environmental protection, and the clarification of their relationship with economic development, there were fewer examples of treaties focusing specifically on issues of wildlife conservation during the 1980s. Nevertheless, several seminal agreements were of major indirect significance in that regard. The UN Convention on the Law of the Sea,[75] finally adopted in 1982 after years of negotiations, is characterised by its heavy emphasis upon environmental matters, certainly by comparison with its 1958 counterparts. The International Tropical Timber Agreement,[76] concluded the following year and essentially a commodities treaty, is noteworthy for its innovative incorporation of references to conservation, sustainable utilisation and the maintenance of ecological balance,[77] though the extent to which this has impacted upon traditional approaches to exploitation is debatable.[78] The question of ozone layer depletion was addressed through the medium of the 1985 Vienna Convention and its 1987 Montreal Protocol,[79] while the Chernobyl incident prompted the adoption in 1986 of conventions concerning both notification and assistance in the event of nuclear accidents.[80] A further series of protracted negotiations culminated in the adoption of the 1988 Antarctic Minerals Convention (CRAMRA),[81] designed to establish a comprehensive regime for the regulation of the exploitation of mineral resources in Antarctica. Yet within just a couple of years, the climate of international opinion on this question had shifted so dramatically that a fifty-year moratorium was placed on all such activities by the 1991 Antarctic Environmental Protocol,[82] marginalising CRAMRA entirely.

The year 1992 witnessed arguably the most momentous event in the history of international wildlife law with the opening for signature at the Rio Earth Summit of the UN Convention on Biological Diversity (CBD).[83] Responding to the call of the Brundtland Commission, this represented the first attempt by the international community to enshrine

[75] 21 *ILM* 1621. [76] UNCTAD Doc TD/TIMBER/11.

[77] See, e.g., the preamble (third recital), Articles 1(h), 23, 25(2).

[78] For further discussion of forests, see Chapter 18 below. [79] 26 *ILM* 1529; 26 *ILM* 1550.

[80] 1986 Convention on Early Notification of a Nuclear Accident, 25 *ILM* 1370; 1986 Convention on Assistance in the Case of a Nuclear Accident or Radiological Emergency, 25 *ILM* 1377.

[81] 1988 Convention on the Regulation of Antarctic Mineral Resource Activities, 27 *ILM* 868.

[82] 1991 Protocol on Environmental Protection to the Antarctic Treaty, 30 *ILM* 1461.

[83] 31 *ILM* 818; see further Chapter 17 below.

in legally binding form a comprehensive regime governing the management of global biological resources, both wild and domesticated. It embraces the issues of jurisdiction, conservation (both *in situ* and *ex situ*), sustainable utilisation and the equitable sharing of the resulting benefits, access to genetic resources, technical and scientific co-operation (including access to and transfer of technology), and the handling of biotechnology. Inevitably, this breadth of coverage is obtained at a price, with many provisions expressed in vague and uncertain form, or hedged around with substantial qualifications. Greater specification is, however, envisaged through the adoption of later protocols.[84] Crucially, the Convention is not intended to affect rights and obligations arising under earlier treaties, except where their exercise 'would cause a serious damage or threat to biological diversity'.[85] Prior agreements will accordingly remain in operation, though increasing attention will doubtless have to be paid to the harmonisation of policy and practice within the network of biodiversity-related treaties generally.[86] The creation of a liaison group embracing the major conventions in the field is accordingly a most welcome development.[87]

The CBD was not intended to inhibit the development of future treaties on the subject of the conservation and management of natural resources, and was indeed followed in relatively short order by a sequence of major global initiatives launched under the aegis of the FAO with regard to the exploitation and conservation of fisheries and of plant genetic resources.[88] A revised nature conservation agreement for the African region, designed to replace the 1968 instrument, was adopted in 2003.[89] After a slow start, ancillary agreements to the CMS designed to address the needs of particular migratory birds and animals have begun to proliferate.[90] Meanwhile, the first protocol to the CBD itself, concerning biosafety,[91] was concluded in the year 2000.

The fate of wildlife species will be dictated not only by agreements such as these, however, but by instruments in which they are not the overt focus of concern. Central amongst these is a treaty opened for signature alongside the

[84] Article 28. [85] Article 22(1).

[86] On the legal significance of later developments on the interpretation of treaties, see the discussion below in Chapter 2, Section 3(iv).

[87] See further Chapter 17 below.

[88] 2001 International Treaty on Plant Genetic Resources for Food and Agriculture, text available at www.planttreaty.org/texts_en.htm. On fisheries, see further Chapter 5 below.

[89] Text available from the African Union website at www.africa-union.org; see further Chapter 9 below.

[90] See further Chapters 7 and 16 below. [91] 39 *ILM* 1027.

CBD at Rio, namely the UN Framework Convention on Climate Change.[92] The disruption of ecological processes attributable to anthropogenic intensification of the 'greenhouse effect' threatens serious problems for conservation, not least through its impacts upon protected areas,[93] and the international community undoubtedly faces a major challenge if it is to co-ordinate its efforts to confront the twin problems of climate change and the diminution of biological diversity. The detailed regime to tackle the former was established in the Kyoto Climate Change Protocol,[94] and is currently the subject of further intense debate.

Amongst other substantive issues which have been confronted by conventions adopted since the early 1990s are the utilisation and protection of freshwater resources (not only globally,[95] but also at the regional and local levels)[96] and also of marine areas and mountain regions;[97] the regulation of hazardous chemicals,[98] organic pollutants,[99] transboundary consequences of industrial accidents and disposal of ballast water from ships;[100] and, finally, the process of desertification.[101] Significant procedural questions addressed include environmental impact assessment in a transboundary context and public participation and access to environmental information and justice,[102]

[92] 31 *ILM* 848.

[93] For discussion of these aspects specifically, see Chapter 21 below. [94] 37 *ILM* 22.

[95] 1997 UN Convention on the Non-navigational Uses of International Watercourses, 36 *ILM* 710.

[96] See, e.g., the 1992 UNECE Convention on the Protection and Use of Transboundary Watercourses and International Lakes, 31 *ILM* 1312 (Europe); 1995 Protocol on Shared Watercourses in the SADC, and 2000 Revised Protocol, 40 *ILM* 321 (Africa). Major international watercourses which have become the subject of treaty regimes over this period include the Elbe, Rhine, Danube, Jordan, Mekong and Ganges, joining earlier arrangements relating to, e.g., lakes Constance and Geneva, the Great Lakes, and the Mosel, Indus, Plate, Niger and Zambezi rivers, though the extent to which environmental issues have been addressed within these regimes has varied considerably. For an overview, see Birnie, Boyle and Redgwell, *supra* n. 42, Chapter 10.

[97] Marine examples include the North East Atlantic, the Baltic, the Mediterranean, the Black Sea, the Caspian Sea and the Gulf: see further Birnie, Boyle and Redgwell, *supra* n. 42, Chapter 7, Part 3. Key examples of mountain regions are the Alps and the Carpathians (see further Chapter 18 of this work).

[98] 1998 Convention on Prior Informed Consent Procedure for Certain Hazardous Chemicals and Pesticides, 38 *ILM* 1.

[99] 2001 Convention on Persistent Organic Pollutants, 40 *ILM* 531.

[100] 1992 Convention on the Transboundary Effects of Industrial Accidents (1992) 31 *ILM* 1330; 2004 Convention for the Control and Management of Ships' Ballast Water, viewable at www.imo.org/conventions/mainframe.asp?topic_id=867.

[101] 1994 Convention on Desertification, 33 *ILM* 1328.

[102] 1991 Espoo Convention on Environmental Impact Assessment in a Transboundary Context, 30 *ILM* 802; 1998 Aarhus Convention on Access to Information, Public Participation in Decision-Making and Access to Justice in Environmental Matters, 38 *ILM* 517.

while attempts have also been made within the European region both to develop the role of criminal law in the cause of environmental protection and to tackle the vexed question of civil liability for environmental harm.[103]

Most efforts to establish principles of international environmental liability in treaty form have in fact struggled to command the support of states, and it is noteworthy that the two codification exercises recently completed by the International Law Commission which have implications in this field have not ultimately been cast in that medium: significantly, they have reflected a relatively expansive approach to the scope of compensable environmental harm, both in the realm of civil liability and (less obviously) for the purposes of state responsibility.[104] An unprecedented opportunity to explore the latter body of principles in an environmental context occurred in the aftermath of the Iraqi invasion of Kuwait in 1990, when the UN Security Council utilised its powers not only to ensure the expulsion of the occupying forces but to establish a Compensation Commission charged with the task of securing compensation from the Iraqi government for victims of the conflict. The catalogue of claims presented included a number relating to environmental harm suffered by states, in respect of which a total of just over US$5 billion was ultimately awarded. The expert panel that processed these claims, recognising that it was traversing relatively uncharted waters, ultimately contrived to balance a relatively expansive formulation of the fundamental norms of state responsibility in the environmental context with a more cautious and conservative approach towards their application to the facts.[105]

The growing importance of environmental concerns within the purview of international law generally has, moreover, been clearly reflected in the docket of the International Court of Justice in recent years.[106] An advisory opinion was delivered by the Court in 1996 regarding the question of the legality of nuclear weapons,[107] while conservation issues constituted a background aspect of cases concerning sovereignty over

[103] 1999 Convention on the Protection of the Environment through Criminal Law, *ETS* 172; 38 *ILM* 505; 1993 Lugano Convention on Civil Liability for Damage Resulting from Activities Dangerous to the Environment, 32 *ILM* 1228. Regarding the EU, see also Council Directive 2004/35 on Environmental Liability with Regard to the Prevention and Remedying of Environmental Damage, OJ 2004 L143/56.

[104] For further discussion, see below, Chapter 3, Section 4(c).

[105] See further ibid.

[106] Pursuant to Article 26(1) of the Court's Statute, a specialist chamber (the first of its kind) was created in 1993 to deal with environmental cases, but it was never activated and was effectively dissolved in 2006.

[107] (1996) *ICJ Rep* 226.

Kasikili/Sedudu Island[108] and *Pulau Ligitan and Pulau Sipadan*.[109] Of the cases where ecological issues ostensibly featured more centrally, the *Phosphate Lands* case was, in fact, eventually settled out of court,[110] while the *Gabcikovo-Nagymaros Project* case ultimately turned more on principles of treaty law than of environmental law.[111] In the *Pulp Mills* case,[112] Uruguay was found to be in breach of its procedural obligations under relevant treaty provisions to notify and negotiate with Argentina regarding the construction of pulp mills on a transboundary watercourse, but not of its substantive obligations regarding environmental protection. The court seemed ill at ease, however, in its handling of the evidential issues. Two potentially more instructive cases are currently pending concerning Japanese Whaling in Antarctica and the alleged transboundary impacts of Colombian aerial spraying of toxic herbicides.[113]

The recent revitalisation of the long-established Permanent Court of Arbitration has provided an alternative forum for the resolution of environmental disputes,[114] while yet further opportunities have presented themselves through the emergence of the International Tribunal for the Law of the Sea (ITLOS) and the dispute settlement mechanisms of the World Trade Organisation (WTO). The prospect of the latter institution doing full justice to the environmental dimension of disputes appears uncertain, however, given the particular focus and orientation of the treaty pursuant to which it was established.[115]

Yet it remains the case that the fate of the world's wildlife species ultimately depends less on these eye-catching, but generally narrowly focused, instances of dispute settlement than upon considerations of a more mundane, but broader and more pervasive, significance. The first concerns the extent to which conservation thinking becomes truly entrenched both in the articulated aspirations of the international community as a whole and in the policy and practice of individual governments. Little can be taken for granted here, notwithstanding the

[108] (1999) *ICJ Rep* 1045. [109] (2002) *ICJ Rep* 625.

[110] For the preliminary objections phase in this case, see (1992) *ICJ Rep* 240; and, for its subsequent removal from the Court's list following the settlement, (1993) *ICJ Rep* 322.

[111] (1997) *ICJ Rep* 7.

[112] Judgment of 20 April 2010, (2010) *ICJ Rep*.

[113] Information regarding the progress of these two cases may be obtained from the ICJ website at www.icj-cij.org.

[114] Prominent examples include the 2003 *OSPAR* Arbitration and the 2008 *MOX Plant* case: see generally www.pca-cpa.org.

[115] On the WTO system generally, see Chapter 19 below.

recognition of the need to ensure environmental sustainability as Goal 7 of the eight Millennium Development Goals: history demonstrates all too clearly the ease with which conservation concerns tend to become sidelined whenever the overt focus is on economic advance. Potentially more promising was the integration within this Goal, at the 2002 Johannesburg World Summit on Sustainable Development, of the more specific CBD commitment 'to achieve a significant reduction in the current rate of biodiversity loss' by the year 2010.[116] In recognition of the importance of this goal, the UN designated the year 2010 the International Year of Biodiversity. Yet the prospects of ever making real progress towards such targets will depend ultimately upon a second crucial factor, namely the urgency, dedication and ingenuity displayed in the routine, day-to-day implementation of the many treaties already adverted to in this chapter. It will, accordingly, be desirable to examine the question of treaty implementation in more detail, but first it is necessary to consider the legal, institutional and philosophical backdrop on to which these arrangements are projected.

Recommended further reading

R. Boardman, *International Organisation and the Conservation of Nature* (Macmillan, 1981)

S. S. Hayden, *The International Protection of Wildlife* (Columbia University Press, 1942; reprinted Kolthoff, 2007)

T. Kuokkanen, *International Law and the Environment: Variations on a Theme* (Kluwer Law International, 2002)

P. H. Sand, Chapter 2 in D. Bodansky, J. Brunnée and E. Hey (eds.), *The Oxford Handbook of International Environmental Law* (Oxford University Press, 2007)

P. Sands, *Principles of International Environmental Law* (Cambridge University Press, 2nd ed., 2003), Chapter 2

[116] See CBD Decision VI/26 and WSSD Plan of Implementation, para. 42. For later developments, see www.countdown2010.net.

Chapter 2

Wildlife and the international legal system

1. Introduction

Since this work focuses specifically upon the use of international legal measures for the conservation, management and protection of wildlife, it will be helpful to begin with a brief overview of the international legal system generally, contrasting it with other legal regimes. *Public international law* is the body of legal principles that governs states and other international persons in their dealings with one another on the international plane.[1] Its scope extends far beyond the realms of environmental regulation to embrace peaceful co-operation and the conduct of diplomatic relations generally, prohibitions on the use of force in international affairs and the protection of human rights, to name but a few major areas of concern.[2] This system is to be contrasted with the collection of norms – known variously as *national, domestic* or *municipal law* – that operates within each nation to regulate the activities of ordinary human beings and other entities (such as limited companies and public corporations) that are recognised as possessing rights and duties under the system in question. Public international law must also be distinguished from other supra-national systems, of which the most conspicuous current example is the law of the *European Union* – a regional intergovernmental organisation created by a succession of treaties which, while themselves governed by international law, have the effect of generating a distinct legal order, with its own institutions, law-making procedures and mechanisms for enforcement, which is applicable to

1 Or, simply, 'international law'. The label 'public' serves to distinguish this system from 'private international law' – the body of principles through which each municipal legal system seeks to resolve conflicts of jurisdiction with other such systems in cases involving transnational elements. All references to 'international law' in this work are to the 'public' variety, unless otherwise indicated.

2 For a more comprehensive indication, see M. D. Evans (ed.), *International Law* (Oxford University Press, 3rd ed., 2010).

and within member states.[3] This work is not concerned with national law or with that of the European Union except incidentally, and then only to the extent that these various systems interact in the field of wildlife protection.[4] For example, international treaties create obligations which are binding upon those states which accept them, and that will frequently require the enactment of measures at the national or regional levels in order to implement the duties in question.

Although public international law is quite properly considered as law,[5] what cannot be denied is that it represents law of a relatively primitive kind. This reflects the nature of the political community it serves, which is characterised by the absence of strong, centralised institutions and a heavy emphasis on the individual sovereignty of member states. There is no supra-national legislature empowered to create laws binding on the global community, nor any international police force to ensure compliance with such rules as have been established.[6] Though there is a World Court,[7] its role is primarily dispute settlement rather than enforcement as such,[8] and is in any event limited to controversies in respect of which the states involved have by some means consented to its jurisdiction. Even where governments are willing in principle to comply with legal norms, the technical expertise and financial resources needed to transform this aspiration into reality are often lacking. Finally, the mechanisms which are available for the authoritative generation of legal obligations struggle to keep pace with the ever more sophisticated social,

3 On the law of the European Union generally, see P. P. Craig and G. De Burca, *EU Law: Text, Cases and Materials* (Oxford University Press, 4th ed., 2008); and, for environmental protection specifically, J. H. Jans and H. H. B. Vedder, *European Environmental Law* (Europa, 3rd ed., 2008); L. Kramer, *EC Environmental Law* (Sweet & Maxwell, 6th ed., 2007).

4 On the relationship between international law and municipal law, see M. N. Shaw, *International Law* (Cambridge University Press, 6th ed., 2008), Chapter 4; D. J. Harris, *Cases and Materials on International Law* (Sweet & Maxwell, 7th ed., 2010), Chapter 3.

5 See generally Harris, *supra* n. 4, Chapter 1.

6 The UN Security Council is empowered under the UN Charter to take enforcement action to maintain or restore international peace and security. Even then, it is dependent upon UN members to provide the necessary forces.

7 'World Court' is the title commonly applied to both the current International Court of Justice (ICJ), created along with the UN in 1945, and its predecessor, the Permanent Court of International Justice (PCIJ), established in 1920.

8 Note that prosecutions in the International Criminal Court, and other similar tribunals which the international community has from time to time established, are of individuals, rather than of states.

political and technical demands imposed upon them by the international community.

With these considerations in mind, this chapter begins with a description of the principal law-creating mechanisms, or sources of international law, followed by an overview of the rules governing the adoption and implementation of treaties, the predominant mechanism for the generation of international legal obligations. It concludes with an examination of certain legal principles which are of particular relevance to the conservation of wildlife and its habitats.

2. Sources of international law

The various mechanisms by which international legal norms may be created are itemised in Article 38(1) of the Statute of the International Court of Justice (ICJ).[9] This provision instructs the Court, in adjudicating international disputes, to apply

(a) international conventions, whether general or particular, establishing rules expressly recognised by the contesting states;
(b) international custom, as evidence of a general practice accepted as law;
(c) the general principles of law recognised by civilised nations; and
(d) subject to the provisions of Article 59, judicial decisions and the teachings of the most highly qualified publicists of the various nations, as subsidiary means for the determination of rules of law.

Although the term is not expressly used, these elements are generally understood to constitute the principal 'sources' of international law.[10] It will be convenient to deal with custom first.

a) Custom

In legal systems which serve political communities of a relatively primitive character, custom tends to assume a primary role,[11] and international law constitutes no exception. The term 'custom' refers to the normative traditions which have evolved over time within the community in question to

[9] The Statute is appended to the UN Charter, 1 *UNTS* xvi.
[10] See generally Shaw, *supra* n. 4, Chapter 3; Harris, *supra* n. 4, Chapter 2; A. E. Boyle and C. Chinkin, *The Making of International Law* (Oxford University Press, 2007).
[11] See, e.g., C. K. Allen, *Law in the Making* (Clarendon Press, 7th ed., 1964).

regulate the conduct of its individual members. In international law, this is reflected in the requirement, specified by the ICJ in the *North Sea Continental Shelf* cases,[12] that for any principle to qualify as a customary rule it must be of a 'fundamentally norm-creating character'.[13] Beyond that, the essence of custom as a source of international law is captured in the phrase 'a general practice accepted as law', which alludes to two critical elements, one factual and one psychological. The former, indicated by the words 'general practice', is understood to require such widespread adherence to a particular pattern of behaviour as to amount to a 'constant and uniform usage' to that effect.[14] Various criteria have been laid down in order to determine whether sufficient consistency exists for this purpose.[15] Yet no amount of practice can of itself be sufficient to establish a customary rule of a mandatory character: it may be that the practice has been followed purely for reasons of comity or convenience, and it must therefore also be shown that the necessary psychological element is present. This is referred to as *opinio juris* – usually translated as a sense, or feeling, of legal obligation. In the *Nuclear Weapons* case, for example, it was held that the non-use of such weapons by states that possessed them could not of itself establish a customary prohibition on use, which required proof that such restraint was attributable to a sense of compliance with a legal duty, rather than merely an exercise of political choice.[16]

Commonly, customary principles are of global application, but they may alternatively be purely regional in scope,[17] or applicable amongst groups of states linked by ideological, religious or other considerations.[18] This underlines the fact that custom is broadly grounded in consent, a further consequence of which is that states may effectively opt out of its

[12] (1969) *ICJ Rep* 3. [13] See para. 72 of the Judgment.

[14] *Asylum* case (1950) *ICJ* Rep 266.

[15] See in particular the *Asylum* case, ibid.; *Anglo-Norwegian Fisheries* case (1951) *ICJ Rep* 116; *North Sea Continental Shelf* cases (1969) *ICJ Rep* 3; *Nicaragua* case (1986) *ICJ Rep* 14.

[16] (1996) *ICJ Rep* 226. See especially paras. 64–7 of the Judgment.

[17] In the *Asylum* case, the ICJ recognised in principle the possibility of a regional custom amongst Latin American states, but found its existence not to have been proved.

[18] Religious considerations might be relevant in the case of, e.g., Islamic states, as to which, see W. B. Hallaq, *An Introduction to Islamic Law* (Cambridge University Press, 2009). Also, certain customs were formerly claimed by the USSR to apply amongst socialist states. Regarding other considerations, in the *Right of Passage* case, (1960) *ICJ Rep* 6, the Court upheld the existence of a custom applicable between just two states.

applicability through a process of 'persistent objection'.[19] Such dissent must, however, be manifest during the formative period of the custom in question; once it is firmly established it will be too late to seek exemption. This means that newly independent states must take existing law as they find it – a cause of no little tension in international affairs, as formerly dependent territories find themselves bound by rules which they had no part in formulating. An element of flexibility remains, however, in that customs may be changed by the same processes as those by which they were created: the original rule restricting the exclusive fishing rights of coastal states to their three-mile territorial sea, for example, has been progressively relaxed in the light of persistent demands by states for zones extending up to 200 miles.[20] Nevertheless, such changes are likely to result in long periods of uncertainty while the process of reform unfolds, and states which seek to act as 'law-makers' may initially have to endure a period of being regarded as 'law-breakers'.[21]

Custom has, however, played a relatively minor part in the development of international wildlife law specifically. Although certain commentators argued even prior to the 1992 Earth Summit that state practice supported the recognition of a general customary duty to take appropriate steps to protect endangered species,[22] others have responded that, even if this were true, the detailed application of any such duty could only feasibly be specified through the medium of particular, internationally agreed, treaty arrangements.[23] It is therefore to treaties as a source of international obligations that we must turn.

b) *International conventions*

Although the term 'convention' may be employed in a variety of senses, here it refers to international treaties or agreements concluded among states or other international persons, and having binding force in international law. Such agreements also appear under a wide variety of other labels, including pacts, charters, accords, arrangements, protocols and even declarations or memoranda of understanding, though many of

[19] Recognised, e.g., in the *Asylum* and the *Anglo-Norwegian Fisheries* cases, *supra* n. 15.
[20] For the current position, see Part V of the 1982 UN Convention on the Law of the Sea, 21 *ILM* 1261 and Chapter 5 below.
[21] See on this point the *Fisheries Jurisdiction* cases (1974) *ICJ Rep* 3 and 175.
[22] M. J. Glennon, 'Has International Law Failed the Elephant?' (1990) 84 *AJIL* 30.
[23] P. W. Birnie, A. E. Boyle and C. J. Redgwell, *International Law and the Environment* (Oxford University Press, 3rd ed., 2009), pp. 698–701.

these terms are also applied to instruments that lack binding force. The true legal status of any particular instrument depends upon matters of substance and intention, rather than nomenclature.

i) The nature and role of treaties in international affairs

Given the cumbersome nature of custom as a source of law, there is a need for a more malleable and sophisticated mechanism for the generation of legal obligations of the intricacy currently required in international affairs. This is particularly so with respect to the regulation of environmental problems, which are commonly of a technically complex and constantly evolving character. In domestic law, this role is largely fulfilled by legislation, but the absence of any such mechanism on the international plane means that the relevant regulatory standards have to be painstakingly negotiated by governments and embodied in formal agreements. International treaties are highly diverse in nature, ranging from those of a purely bilateral character to those potentially applicable to the entire global community, and from essentially contractual arrangements to those with quasi-legislative effect.

Yet even where treaties are described as having a 'law-making' character, it must be understood that this is 'legislation' of a very special kind, since its applicability rests entirely upon consent: no state can be compelled to participate in an international treaty against its will. Naturally, this imposes significant constraints upon the establishment of an effective conservation regime: no environmental problem, however urgent, may be addressed by this means unless the requisite political will is evident on the part of governments. Furthermore, even if negotiations succeed, there is a danger that the regime ultimately agreed will represent simply the lowest common denominator of governmental commitment, perhaps creating a mere illusion of progress.[24] At the same time, the elaboration of a treaty which is so rigorous that it outstrips the ultimate willingness of governments to commit to it represents no less a pitfall.[25] This confirms that the effectiveness of international agreements is a function of three major variables, namely the range, rigour and appropriateness of the substantive provisions; the effectiveness of the machinery for implementation and enforcement;

[24] See on this point IUCN/UNEP/WWF, World Conservation Strategy (1980), Section 15, para. 3.

[25] The 1985 ASEAN Nature Conservation Agreement, (1985) 15 *EPL* 64, represents a striking example of this phenomenon.

and the level of participation by states.[26] Given the obvious tension between the first two and the last of these factors, it is vital to ensure that an appropriate balance is struck.

Fortunately, the international community has displayed considerable ingenuity in refining the treaty as a law-making mechanism, developing models of ever-increasing sophistication. One well-tried approach involves using the main body of the text for the elaboration of general commitments, with the technical detail consigned to accompanying annexes or appendices. This has the advantage of allowing differentiated arrangements for the amendment of these two elements, with streamlined procedures for the more technical aspects. In conservation treaties, appendices are commonly utilised for the listing of particular species to which the obligations in the main body of the text are applicable,[27] or for the promulgation of more detailed action plans for their conservation.[28] Changes to these details can be made with minimal bureaucratic complication, whereas amendment of the basic obligations themselves is neither as straightforward nor as common.[29]

A still more elaborate approach has seen the emergence of so-called 'framework' conventions, of particular value where the subject matter of regulation is controversial, or where work on the detailed resolution of problems is further from fruition. Such agreements characteristically contain substantive obligations of a relatively vague and generalised kind, but include a commitment to negotiate more elaborate regulatory provision through the medium of ancillary agreements (commonly labelled 'protocols') to deal with more specialised aspects. The 'parent' convention usually provides for the creation of technical and/or administrative institutions to take responsibility for this follow-up work. Since either or both of these levels of agreement may incorporate technical annexes, there is scope for provision of an extremely elaborate, multilayered nature. Framework agreements have been extensively used with regard to the regulation of pollution,[30] and also occasionally in relation

[26] M. J. Bowman, 'The Effectiveness of International Nature Conservation Agreements', in H. T. Anker and E. M. Basse (eds.), *Land Use and Nature Protection: Emerging Legal Aspects* (DJOF Publishing, 2000).

[27] For examples of this technique, see Chapters 7, 10, 15 and 16 below.

[28] As in the case of the 1995 African–Eurasian Waterbirds Agreement (AEWA), (1995) 6 *YBIEL* 909, which envisages two tiers of action plans.

[29] Compare, for example, the various amendment procedures established by Articles 15–17 of the 1973 Convention on International Trade in Endangered Species (CITES), 993 *UNTS* 243.

[30] For examples, see the discussion in Chapter 21 below.

to conservation. The Biodiversity Convention represents an example,[31] as does the 1979 Migratory Species Convention, which has spawned a prolific and diverse family of 'daughter' agreements.[32]

Factors which typically affect the willingness of states to commit themselves to international conservation regimes include the ability of the instrument in question to accommodate divergent national preoccupations and capacities, and the possibility of obtaining assistance or benefits to offset the demands of participation. Where developing countries are concerned, the tailoring of treaty obligations to recognise their particular stage of development, along with the prospects of financial support or technology transfer, represent important inducements which have now been extensively employed. Another device to facilitate participation in multilateral standard-setting instruments is to permit the making of reservations by states upon their acceptance, allowing them to evade the effect of certain provisions which would otherwise have discouraged them from committing to the treaty in question. Allowing participation on this restricted basis is commonly judged preferable to precluding it entirely.[33]

ii) Relationship between custom and treaties

The legislative character of treaties is most clearly apparent in those which seek to overcome the limitations of custom as a source of law by restating, clarifying and amplifying customary principles in written form, or filling the void where no such principles exist. The importance of this process was underlined in 1948 by the creation of the International Law Commission (ILC) as the official UN body charged with responsibility for the codification and progressive development of international law.[34] Although most of its output to date has concerned traditional core areas of international law (such as the law of treaties, diplomatic relations and state responsibility), some has related more closely to environmental protection, such as the 1997 International Watercourses Convention.[35] Work on the codification of technically specialised areas of law has also been undertaken by other permanent bodies,[36] or accomplished through purely ad hoc processes.[37]

[31] See Chapter 17 below. [32] See Chapter 16 below.

[33] See further Section 3(iii) below in this chapter. [34] See Article 13, UN Charter.

[35] 36 *ILM* 700.

[36] Work on human rights and outer space, for example, has generally been undertaken by other, more specialised UN organs, such as the Human Rights Commission or the Committee on Outer Space.

[37] Both the CBD and UNCLOS were the product of specially constituted processes. The earlier 1958 Geneva Conventions on the Law of the Sea were, however, the result of ILC studies.

The intricacies of the relationship between custom and treaties were explored by the ICJ in the *North Sea Continental Shelf* cases,[38] where three possibilities were recognised. First, a treaty provision might simply be declaratory of existing custom; second, it might have the effect of crystallising an emerging customary rule; finally, the treaty might serve as the historical source of a principle that subsequently achieves customary status through general recognition by states.[39] Many codification efforts reflect a combination of all these possibilities, the ILC's work on the law of treaties, discussed below, representing a notable example.

c) General principles of law

The third category of norms identified by the Court's Statute comprises 'general principles of law recognised by civilised nations'. While a great many rules of conduct may be discernible from a consideration of custom and treaties alone, it is unlikely that these will enable a court or tribunal to resolve every issue that might arise in litigation. General principles of law of the kind that would be recognised by jurists everywhere, regardless of their individual legal background, accordingly serve as an additional source to facilitate the filling of any lacunae which might otherwise appear in the law. Thus, in the *Chorzow Factory* case,[40] the Permanent Court of International Justice (PCIJ) observed that it had long been accepted, both in international arbitration and by municipal courts, that no party could complain of another's non-performance of a legal obligation if it had itself rendered compliance impossible; subsequently, it referred also to a 'general conception of law' that every violation of a legal engagement involved an obligation to make reparation.[41] The concept of *res judicata* and the admissibility of circumstantial evidence constitute other judicially recognised examples of general principles of law.[42]

[38] *Supra* n. 15. See also the *Nicaragua* case, *supra* n. 15.

[39] In the case itself, the treaty provision in question – Article 6(2) of the 1958 Geneva Convention on the Continental Shelf, 499 *UNTS* 311 – was judged not to reflect customary international law on any of these bases.

[40] Indemnity, Jurisdiction phase (1927) *PCIJ Rep*, Series A, No. 9, p. 31.

[41] Merits phase (1928) *PCIJ Rep*, Series A, No. 17, p. 29. See now the ILC's 2001 Articles on Responsibility of States for Internationally Wrongful Acts, Articles 1 and 31.

[42] See, respectively, the *UN Administrative Tribunal* case (1954) *ICJ Rep* 47, p. 53; and the *Corfu Channel* case (1949) *ICJ Rep* 4, p. 18.

Although the point is not entirely uncontroversial, this term is probably broad enough to embrace general principles both of international and of municipal law. As to the former, such principles might at first sight appear hard to distinguish from customary rules, but it should be remembered that, in order to qualify for customary status, a principle must be of a 'fundamentally norm-creating character' – i.e. embody a specific rule of conduct. 'General principles of law', by contrast, may include certain broader notions and informing ideas, such as *good faith*, *equity*, *proportionality* and *reciprocity*, which permeate international legal rules generally. Although such principles cannot be invoked as free-standing rules of law in their own right, they constitute components of numerous other legal norms, such as those governing the interpretation of legal instruments, the lawfulness of countermeasures or the exercise of the right of self-defence. Accordingly, they may be recruited by analogy into the judicial solution of novel problems in respect of which definitive rules have yet to emerge.

What is beyond doubt is that such lacunae may be filled by recourse to principles widely encountered in national legal systems. In view of the vast number of such systems that now exist in the world, the identification of such principles might appear to demand a formidable research effort, but the approach actually adopted by the World Court in this context has never been especially rigorous.[43] Rather, it has been recognised that these systems can be grouped into several major families – the common law, civil law and Islamic systems,[44] for example – and judges typically seek evidence of these principles at that level of generality, rather than conducting an exhaustive survey of some 200 national legal orders. It is also clear that the emphasis has been placed upon the broad flavour of the principle, rather than on the intricate detail.[45]

The striking incongruity of the reference to 'civilised nations' is explicable on the basis that the phrase was imported unchanged into Article 38(1) from the Statute of the old Permanent Court, which was drafted in 1920. In the modern context, it is conventionally understood to refer simply to independent states, though an alternative slant was

[43] See H. Waldock, 'General Course on Public International Law' (1962-II) 106 *Hague Recueil* 54.

[44] See generally R. David and J. E. C. Brierley, *Major Legal Systems in the World Today* (Stevens, 3rd ed., 1985); H. P. Glenn, *Legal Traditions of the World* (Oxford University Press, 2000).

[45] Note especially the individual opinions of Judge Hudson in the *Diversion of Water from the Meuse* case (1937) *PCIJ Rep*, Series A/B, No. 70, at pp. 76–7; and Lord McNair in the *South-West Africa* case (1950) *ICJ Rep* 128, at p. 148.

recently offered by the vice-president of the ICJ, Judge Weeramantry, in his separate opinion in the *Gabcikovo-Nagymaros Project* case.[46] In his view, the Court was entitled to have regard not only to principles common to the major legal families today, but also to certain fundamental ideals embraced by all the major cultures and civilisations throughout history. The avowed aim was to overcome the inherent formalism of the law, and revitalise it through the reintegration of certain 'pristine and universal values which command international recognition'.[47] Interestingly, the principle he found to be endorsed in numerous cultural traditions, including those of ancient, tribal and indigenous communities, was that of sustainable development. Although the phrase 'civilised nations' might originally have been employed primarily in order to exclude supposedly primitive traditions,[48] his approach has much to commend it, as there has been widespread recognition in recent years of the need to harness the wisdom of indigenous cultures in order to facilitate the task of reconfiguring man's relations with the natural world into a less destructive pattern.[49]

d) *Judicial decisions*

Following the itemisation of these *formal* sources of international law, judicial decisions and the writings of publicists are referred to in Article 38(1)(d) as 'subsidiary means for the determination of rules of law', i.e. as *material* sources.[50] This means that while judges and writers do not make the law as such, their pronouncements may provide authoritative evidence as to its content. As regards judicial decisions, pride of place is undoubtedly accorded to those of the World Court itself, though assistance may also be gleaned from other sources, as specialist courts and tribunals empowered to adjudicate between states have proliferated in recent years. In addition, there is a long tradition of arbitration of international disputes,[51] whether through

[46] (1997) *ICJ Rep* 7. [47] Ibid., p. 109. [48] To this effect, see Waldock, *supra* n. 43.

[49] See, e.g., the Rio Declaration, Principle 22; Biodiversity Convention, 12th preambular recital and Article 8(j).

[50] On this distinction, see G. Schwarzenberger, *International Law* (Stevens, 3rd ed., 1957), Volume I, pp. 26–7, where a formal source is defined as 'that from which a rule of law derives its force and validity'. In international law (in contrast to English law, for example), judicial decisions are not of that character, there being no system of binding precedent. See Article 59, ICJ Statute.

[51] Like judicial settlement, arbitration involves the delivery of a binding decision on the basis of law; it differs primarily in the degree of freedom allowed to the parties in the selection of the adjudicators.

the Permanent Court of Arbitration,[52] through the various claims commissions and similar standing bodies which have been established over the last two centuries, or through the succession of ad hoc tribunals convened to deal with particular cases.[53]

Yet the guidance available from this body of case law remains limited for present purposes, since environmental issues are so seldom the subject of international litigation. Even the few decisions which have arisen have established comparatively little in terms of fundamental legal norms.[54] In the area of wildlife law specifically, the paucity of decisions is particularly pronounced, and those that have occurred relate primarily to fisheries jurisdiction, which has not always been treated as falling within the field at all.[55] The *Bering Sea Fur Seals* arbitration does address some significant issues, however, which are discussed below.[56]

Judicial guidance upon questions of international law may, however, sometimes be available from national litigation. In the *Tasmanian Dam* case,[57] for example, the High Court of Australia had occasion to analyse the nature of that country's commitments under the 1972 World Heritage Convention in the course of determining the respective areas of competence of the federal and state governments in conservation matters. In *Count Lippens v Etat Belge*[58] and *Defenders of Wildlife v Endangered Species Scientific Authority*,[59] environmental activists instituted proceedings before Belgian and US courts respectively in order to challenge their government's compliance with international conservation obligations. Such challenges are most likely to be encountered in jurisdictions like Belgium and the US in which international treaties are accorded a legal status comparable to that of national legislation.[60] In the UK and many Commonwealth countries, by contrast, treaties produce no internal legal effects unless 'transformed' by national legislation, in

[52] As to which, see P. Hamilton et al. (eds.), *The Permanent Court of Arbitration* (Kluwer, 1999).

[53] See generally A. M. Stuyt (ed.), *Survey of International Arbitration, 1794–1989* (Kluwer, 3rd ed., 1990).

[54] For discussion, see P. Sands, *Principles of International Environmental Law* (Cambridge University Press, 2nd ed., 2003), Chapter 5.

[55] This topic was excluded from the 1st edition of this work, though primarily on the grounds that it was so extensive, and already well covered by other studies. See now, however, Chapter 5 below.

[56] See Section 4(a)(i) of this chapter.

[57] *Commonwealth of Australia v State of Tasmania* (1983) 46 *ALR* 625; 68 *ILR* 266.

[58] (1964) 47 *ILR* 336. [59] 659 F.2d 168 (1981).

[60] Though this will usually only be the case where the treaty in question is 'self-executing'. See generally Shaw, *supra* n. 4, pp. 135–62, and Chapter 4 below.

which circumstances recourse to the text of the treaty itself may sometimes be appropriate for interpretational purposes.[61]

e) Writings of publicists

The writings of publicists constitute the second category of material sources referred to in the Court's Statute and, for many practical purposes, textbooks, monographs and journal articles undoubtedly represent the most readily accessible repositories of information and guidance on questions of international law. During the formative period of the modern system in the seventeenth century, legal writers played a preeminent role in its development,[62] and fainter echoes of such influence tend to be manifest whenever new subdisciplines establish themselves in the international legal order. The particular contribution of writers lies in their identification and elaboration of underlying themes and principles, evaluation of different methodological approaches and highlighting of cases of concern. International wildlife law has certainly benefited from such scholarship.[63] Accordingly, although they are unlikely ever to reclaim the predominance that they once enjoyed, the contribution of writers to the development of the law remains vital.

f) 'Soft' law

In addition to the mechanisms through which norms of binding legal effect may be established, the phenomenon of 'soft' law should be noted. This is the term applied to the mass of recommendations, declarations and related measures addressed to states which, while lacking mandatory force, are nevertheless intended to influence their conduct. The expression 'soft law' is a curious one, suggesting an elusive middle ground between provisions which are and provisions which are not legally

[61] Ibid. [62] For a helpful overview of this process, see ibid., Chapter 1.

[63] See, e.g., S. S. Hayden, *The International Protection of Wildlife* (Columbia University Press, 1942); R. Boardman, *International Organisation and the Conservation of Nature* (Macmillan, 1981); S. Lyster, *International Wildlife Law* (Grotius, 1985); S. Bilderbeek, *Biodiversity and International Law* (IOS Press, 1992); C. de Klemm and C. Shine, *Biological Diversity Conservation and the Law* (IUCN, 1993); M. J. Bowman and C. J. Redgwell (eds.), *International Law and the Conservation of Biological Diversity* (Kluwer, 1996); P. van Heijnsbergen, *International Legal Protection of Wild Fauna and Flora* (IOS Press, 1997); J. Beer-Gabel and B. Labat, *La protection internationale de la faune et de la flore sauvages* (Bruylant, 1999). For a specialist academic journal, note the *Journal of International Wildlife Law and Policy* (Taylor & Francis).

binding, but it is designed to acknowledge the powerful practical significance of measures the effect of which is essentially persuasive. In reality, indeed, the distinction between hard and soft law in terms of its effect upon conduct is sometimes difficult to discern; as noted above, there is no absolute guarantee of performance even of strict legal duties, while the moral force of some soft law may create an inducement to conform which is virtually as powerful. In the environmental field, soft-law measures have been especially significant – indeed, it is fair to say that the main principles and parameters of the subject have been largely established through such mechanisms.

Soft law is characteristically cast in written form, but plainly not every legal document, even of an official nature, falls within its scope. In order to do so, the instrument must be of an essentially normative character, so that those which are purely descriptive or argumentative, or of a policy-oriented nature, cannot qualify.[64] Even so, the instruments in which it is manifest are extremely diverse, ranging from

> treaties, but which include only soft obligations ... to non-binding or voluntary resolutions and codes of conduct formulated and accepted by international and regional organisations ... to statements prepared by individuals in a non-governmental capacity, but which purport to lay down international principles.[65]

The 'softness' in question may therefore derive from various factors, including the essential juridical nature of the instrument in question, the legal status of the entities which have devised or subscribed to it, and the precise way in which it is worded.

As regards treaties, their capacity to generate legally binding effects ultimately depends upon the specific wording employed, since 'the use of a treaty form does not of itself ensure a hard obligation'.[66] Typically, the phrase 'the parties *shall* ...' is used for this purpose, whereas '*should*' is indicative of mere exhortation. Even in the former case, however, it is necessary to examine the substantive content of the commitments undertaken: a statement that the parties 'shall formulate and implement their planning so as to promote ... as far as possible the wise use of

[64] Thus it is doubtful whether even a document as important as the World Conservation Strategy is correctly described as soft law.

[65] C. M. Chinkin, 'The Challenge of Soft Law: Development and Change in International Law' (1989) 38 *ICLQ* 850.

[66] Ibid., p. 851.

wetlands in their territory' may involve a duty, but it is plainly one of an extremely vague and diluted kind.[67] Similarly, it may be possible to establish a legal duty to 'endeavour' to take certain action,[68] but this is clearly very different from requiring that such action be taken.

Even if an instrument employs mandatory language and is cast in treaty form, it cannot qualify as such unless it has been concluded amongst entities which possess treaty-making capacity and intend it to be so regarded. For the most part, only states or inter-governmental organisations enjoy such capacity. Some documents ostensibly in treaty form are in fact the work of purely private bodies and therefore cannot represent hard law.[69] The International Law Association (ILA) has undertaken numerous unofficial codification projects, its 1966 Helsinki Rules on the Uses of the Waters of International Rivers representing perhaps the best-known example.[70] Given that these rules have been widely cited in the literature, and sometimes by governments, they could be regarded as having achieved soft-law status, but the principles they contain can only become legally binding upon states through some extraneous means, e.g. to the extent that they reflect customary law or are translated into formal treaty commitments.

Perhaps the commonest manifestation of soft law, however, lies in the mass of resolutions, recommendations and codes of conduct which have been adopted by states at international conferences or through other deliberative processes. In the environmental field, these range from the most generalised and wide-ranging statements of principle – including the declarations adopted at the 1972 Stockholm Conference (UNCHE) and the 1992 Rio Earth Summit (UNCED) – to the most specialised and particular, such as the elaborate code of practice governing the return to the wild of confiscated wildlife specimens under Article 8(4) of CITES.[71] If the juridical status of the instrument in question is such as to render it non-binding, no amount of usage of the word 'shall' can create a legally binding obligation, though it may carry considerable moral or political significance. The 1982 World Charter for Nature, for example, uses 'shall' throughout – a factor that was of itself sufficient to cause the United States to vote against it,[72] despite its absence of mandatory effect.

[67] See Article 3(1) of the Ramsar Convention, discussed in Chapter 13 below.

[68] See, e.g., the discussion of the *Tasmanian Dam* case in Chapters 14 and 16 below.

[69] Note, for example, the Harvard Research Draft Conventions on various aspects of international law, which represent the unofficial work of academic lawyers in the US.

[70] 2 *IPE* 5741. [71] CITES Resolution Conf. 10.7.

[72] See W. E. Burhenne and W. A. Irwin (eds.), *The World Charter for Nature* (Erich Schmidt, 2nd ed., 1986), p. 39.

3. The law of treaties

The existence of a body of principles to govern the adoption and application of legal agreements is plainly vital to the effective conduct of international relations. Inevitably, such principles evolved over time from state practice to form an important element of customary law, and once the International Law Commission was created the codification of this body of rules was assigned to it as a priority task. Following extensive deliberations, the Vienna Convention on the Law of Treaties (the 'Vienna Convention' – although this title will be employed here for convenience, it should be noted that there are two further Vienna Conventions concerning treaty law, both of which are referred to below) was duly adopted in 1969.[73] The law of treaties represents a challenging topic of study in its own right, and all that can be attempted here is to highlight certain key issues and refer the reader to resources for further research.[74] An important preliminary point is that the rules set out in the Convention to govern the operation of treaties are, for the most part, essentially residual in character; that is, they apply only in default of specific agreement amongst the parties as to how the treaty is to be adopted, interpreted, applied or terminated.

a) Treaty-making capacity

For practical reasons, the substantive scope of the Vienna Convention was limited to *written* agreements *between states*, but the treaty-making capacity of inter-governmental organisations was never in doubt and was confirmed in a later codification.[75] *Non-governmental* organisations, by contrast, have never been recognised as possessing formal treaty-making capacity and no agreement to which they are party can therefore be treated as binding under international law.[76] Within the Bonn Convention system, for example, appropriately qualified NGOs have frequently been involved as front-line participants in ancillary

[73] 1969 *UNJYB* 140.

[74] See especially A. Aust, *Modern Treaty Law and Practice* (Cambridge University Press, 2nd ed., 2007). For the ILC's own invaluable commentary to its draft of the 1969 Vienna Convention (hereinafter the *ILC Commentary*), see *Yearbook of the ILC*, 1966, Volume II, pp. 177–274.

[75] 1986 Vienna Convention on the Law of Treaties between States and International Organizations or between International Organizations (1978) *UNJYB* 106.

[76] The status and effect of such instruments under *other* legal systems – e.g. domestic law – requires separate consideration, however.

agreements adopted for the conservation of particular migratory species,[77] but in such cases the form adopted has always been that of the non-binding memorandum of understanding, rather than a formally binding treaty. This does not mean that NGOs have no part to play in the practical implementation of hard-law instruments; on the contrary, their contribution is often recognised to be vital,[78] but is characteristically delivered in the capacity of observers or consultants, rather than as parties with formal obligations or voting rights in any associated decision-making process.

b) Negotiation and participation

Multilateral treaties of the kind considered in this work result from diplomatic negotiating processes which sometimes require many years for their successful completion. The adoption of the 1982 UN Convention on the Law of the Sea, for example, represented the culmination of a process which began in 1973. Sometimes these negotiations are free-standing, while in other cases they occur under the auspices of some existing international organisation with responsibilities concerning the subject matter of the proposed treaty.[79] Formal records of these deliberations – the so-called *travaux préparatoires* – will normally be maintained, and are often published or made available to researchers. Naturally, they may be instructive for those who later seek to interpret the treaty or understand its origins and objectives.

When a final draft of the treaty has been agreed, it will usually be signed by the negotiating states, which serves to endorse it as the authentic expression of that agreement.[80] In most cases, however, signature is not of itself sufficient to render the treaty binding upon the states in question, an outcome which requires completion of a distinct process known as 'expression of consent to be bound'.[81] Generally, this entails the further step of ratification,[82] which involves the deposit of a formal instrument with the body designated as the depositary for the agreement.[83] This two-stage

[77] See further Chapter 16 below.

[78] See, for example, Chapter 13 below on the bestowal of formal 'partnership' status upon certain NGOs under the Ramsar Convention.

[79] Numerous environmental treaties have, for example, been concluded within the framework of UN bodies such as the UNEP, the FAO, IMO or UNESCO.

[80] 1969 Vienna Convention, Article 10. [81] Ibid., Article 11.

[82] The Vienna Convention refers additionally to 'acceptance' or 'approval' (see Articles 2(1)(b) and 14) to signify alternative means by which signature may be perfected.

[83] The functions of depositaries are dealt with in Articles 76–8.

process allows time for reflection, as well as the completion of any procedures required of particular governments by virtue of their own domestic constitutions, such as submission of the treaty to the national legislature for its approval. While treaties may allow for the expression of consent through signature alone, this is relatively unusual in the case of multilateral law-making treaties.[84]

Plainly, therefore, great care must be taken with the term 'signatory', which, when used accurately, may well refer to states that are not yet bound by the obligations set out in the treaty. Those that have expressed their consent to be bound are more correctly known as *contracting states*, or, once the treaty has actually entered into force for them, *(contracting) parties*.[85] Unfortunately, there is no guarantee that such terms will always be used in accordance with the definitions laid down in the Vienna Convention itself.

Many treaties also allow non-signatory states to become parties, usually by depositing a formal instrument of *accession* or *adherence*.[86] This possibility is sometimes made subject to conditions or restrictions, however, such as obtaining the consent of the negotiating states or, perhaps, the institution under whose aegis the treaty was adopted; any such conditions will normally be established by the terms of the treaty itself. Rights of participation may also be extended to regional economic integration organisations, such as the EU,[87] and occasionally to other international institutions.[88]

A corollary of the notion of consent to be bound, and of the sovereignty and autonomy of states generally, is that treaties have no binding force except as between those that have expressed such consent (though rights may be conferred on third parties if that is the clear intention). Where treaty obligations restate customary law, however, they may be applicable to non-party states on that basis.[89]

The Vienna Convention establishes a residual rule that acceptance of a treaty by a state is effective in respect of its entire territory,[90] which

[84] For an example, see the 1971 Ramsar Convention, Article 9(2).

[85] 1969 Vienna Convention, Article 2.

[86] The Vienna Convention itself employs the former term, without specific definition but in a separate provision (Article 15) from that governing ratification. The sense is clearly that indicated in the text above; see the *ILC Commentary* at p. 199.

[87] See, e.g., the Biodiversity Convention, Articles 33–5.

[88] One obvious example is the 1986 Vienna Convention, *supra* n. 75 (see Articles 82–4), since its very purpose is to establish rules to govern treaties to which international organisations are parties.

[89] Vienna Convention, Articles 34–8. [90] Ibid., Article 29.

includes any overseas possessions. In practice, however, states with dependent territories tend to specify those to which their acceptance relates, and most modern multilateral conventions contain provisions to govern the making of such declarations. Should such territories subsequently gain their independence, it will be pertinent to consider whether they have succeeded to the obligations in question – i.e. whether the treaty remains applicable to them. This complex and controversial issue was addressed in the 1978 Vienna Convention on Succession of States in respect of Treaties,[91] which broadly favours a 'clean-slate' approach in this context,[92] but has not been widely ratified.[93]

c) Entry into force and duration

Given its contractual foundations, the entry into force of a treaty would seem to require, as a juridical minimum, acceptance by two states (or other eligible entities), but multilateral treaties generally set a higher threshold, the precise level of which depends upon the balance to be struck between such factors as the urgency of its coming into effect and the need for widespread participation. In the case of conservation treaties aiming at global applicability, the thresholds chosen have varied greatly,[94] with the Law of the Sea Convention fixing the figure as high as sixty.[95] To enable states to make any necessary preparations, it is common to require that the achievement of such thresholds be followed by a brief delay – usually a few months or a year – before the treaty enters into force. Attainment of the conditions specified for entry into force often takes a considerable time, and in some cases may never be achieved – the 1985 ASEAN Nature Conservation Agreement currently stands as a notable example.[96]

Once in force, a treaty remains operational until any conditions stipulated for its termination are satisfied, or the parties simply agree to bring it to an end.[97] Treaties may also be terminated at the instance of one or more parties on account of material breach by another,

[91] 25 *ILM* 543.

[92] In fact, problems of succession arise wherever a break in the continuity of legal personality occurs – e.g. through the dissolution of entities such as Czechoslovakia, Yugoslavia and the USSR, or through the merger or reunification of states, as in the case of Germany, Vietnam and Yemen.

[93] See Shaw, *supra* n. 4, Chapter 17.

[94] See, e.g., the Ramsar Convention, Article 13 (seven acceptances required); CITES, Article 23 (ten); CMS, Article 18 (fifteen); World Heritage Convention, Article 33 (twenty); CBD, Article 36 (thirty).

[95] Article 308. [96] See Chapter 12 below. [97] Vienna Convention, Article 54.

fundamental change of circumstances or impossibility of performance.[98] These grounds are rarely invoked successfully, however; significant procedural hurdles have to be surmounted,[99] and the tendency of courts and tribunals has been to uphold the continuation of the treaty wherever possible.[100] Nevertheless, an agreement for the conservation of a particular species could in principle be regarded as terminated in the event of the extinction of that species notwithstanding the best efforts of the parties. In practice, the most likely basis for termination of a multilateral conservation treaty is the conclusion of a later treaty relating to the same subject matter.[101] Even here, however, it is usually provided that the earlier version will be superseded only for states that become parties to both. The 1950 International Convention for the Protection of Birds, for example, makes such provision in relation to its predecessor,[102] as do the 1968 and 2003 African regional conservation treaties in respect of theirs.[103] In such cases, the earlier treaty is likely to dwindle into progressive insignificance, particularly where it is formally denounced by those that accept the later version.

Indeed, even treaties which technically remain in force for all their parties may gradually become devoid of practical influence; this is particularly true of older instruments, which usually made no provision for regular meetings of the parties and could therefore easily slip from their attention over time. The 1950 Birds Convention has itself been described as 'moribund' for all practical purposes, the main focus of attention for avian conservation having switched to other fora.[104] More recent treaties have tended to avoid such problems by incorporating suitable arrangements for ongoing implementation.

Although most law-making treaties are in themselves of unspecified or unlimited duration, it is standard practice to allow for the withdrawal of individual parties through the process of denunciation.[105] This is achieved through formal notification to the depositary, and takes effect in accordance with any period of notice (most commonly one year) or

[98] Ibid., Articles 60–2. [99] See ibid., Articles 65–8.

[100] Note, for example, the *Gabcikovo-Nagymaros Project* case, *supra* n. 46.

[101] Either by express agreement, or by operation of law under Article 59, Vienna Convention (i.e. if the two are so incompatible as to be incapable of simultaneous performance).

[102] Concluded in 1902. For discussion of these treaties, see Chapter 7 below.

[103] See respectively Article 21(3), and Articles 34 and 38; see further Chapter 9 below.

[104] See generally Chapter 7 below.

[105] Note that this term does not necessarily imply moral disapproval, merely a desire to cease participation.

other conditions specified in the treaty itself.[106] In point of fact, the denunciation of conservation treaties has been relatively infrequent, albeit not entirely unknown. The United Arab Emirates withdrew from CITES, for example, following trenchant criticism of its initial failure to take effective measures for implementation, but has subsequently resumed participation. The intensely politicised nature of the whaling issue has led to an unusually high incidence of denunciation of the 1946 Whaling Convention. In several cases, however, the country in question either withdrew the notification before it took effect, or resumed participation subsequently.[107]

d) Reservations

The possibility of a state formulating a reservation to its acceptance of a treaty has already been mentioned. A reservation is a unilateral statement (however phrased or named) whereby a state purports to exclude or to modify the legal effect of certain provisions of the treaty.[108] Its effect is generally that the state becomes a party to the treaty in question, but excluding some element or obligation which it finds unacceptable. By virtue of the principle of reciprocity, however, it will then be disabled from demanding performance of that same obligation by other parties. Whether reservations are permissible at all depends essentially on the intention manifest in the treaty in question, and is usually now the subject of express provision. In any event, a reservation may not be made if it is contrary to the object and purpose of the treaty.[109] Naturally, the attitude of other parties is important in this context, and complex provision is made in the Vienna Convention to allow for the effects of this.[110]

In wildlife conservation treaties, the use of 'general' reservations (i.e. those excluding the effect of entire provisions) is in fact quite often prohibited,[111] though their deployment in relation to particular species covered by those provisions is, by contrast, frequently allowed.[112] In many cases, the use of such powers is permitted not only at the time of

106 Vienna Convention, Articles 54 and 56.

107 For details, see M. J. Bowman and D. J. Harris, *Multilateral Treaties: Index and Current Status* (Butterworths, 1984), Treaty 200; see further Chapter 6 below.

108 Vienna Convention, Article 2(d). 109 Ibid., Article 19.

110 The issues are too complex to pursue here; see Articles 20 and 21; and Aust, *supra* n. 74, Chapter 8.

111 Note in that regard the Biodiversity Convention, Article 37.

112 See, e.g., CITES, Article 23; CMS, Articles 11 and 14; Bern Convention, Article 22.

initial acceptance of the treaty but also subsequently, in respect of amendments bringing additional species within its coverage.[113]

e) *Implementation and interpretation*

Obviously it is not the mere adoption but the effective implementation of treaty obligations which is necessary to achieve the goals originally set by the negotiating states. The Vienna Convention has little to say about this issue beyond the basic principle that 'every treaty in force is binding upon the parties to it and must be performed by them in good faith':[114] *pacta sunt servanda*. In the event of non-compliance, however, certain defences applicable to breaches of international obligation generally may be available by virtue of the rules of state responsibility – these include consent, self-defence, force majeure, distress, necessity and the withholding of performance as a permissible countermeasure to prior unlawful action.[115] Each of these defences is narrow in scope, however, and difficult to establish.[116] The expression of consent to be bound by a treaty represents a serious commitment which is not to be easily evaded.

The Vienna Convention deals more extensively, however, with the vital question of treaty interpretation.[117] The provisions in question, which the ICJ has repeatedly declared to reflect customary international law,[118] represent a synthesis of the divergent approaches to interpretation which had previously been evident from academic discourse.[119] The basic rule is laid down in Article 31(1), which provides:

> A treaty shall be interpreted in good faith in accordance with the ordinary meaning to be given to the terms of the treaty[120] in their context and in the light of its object and purpose.

This requires that each provision be interpreted in the light of the treaty as a whole, including its preamble and annexes. The preamble is likely to be of particular value in elucidating the motivations which prompted the

113 See, e.g., CITES, Article 15(3), CMS, Article 11(6), Bern Convention, Article 17(3).
114 Vienna Convention, Article 26.
115 See the International Law Commission's 2001 Articles on Responsibility of States for Internationally Wrongful Acts, Part One; Chapter V; Part Three, Chapter II.
116 See, e.g., the *Rainbow Warrior* arbitration (1990) 82 *ILR* 499.
117 See generally Aust, *supra* n. 74, Chapter 13.
118 See, e.g., *Libya v Chad* (1994) *ICJ Rep* 4, para. 41.
119 See on this point F. G. Jacobs, 'Varieties of Approach to Treaty Interpretation' (1969) 18 *ICLQ* 318.
120 A special meaning may be given to a term, however, if the parties so intended: Vienna Convention, Article 31(4).

treaty's adoption. The 'context' also includes any agreement or instrument relating to the treaty which was accepted by all the parties in connection with its conclusion.[121] Due account must also be taken of any subsequent agreement or practice amongst the parties regarding the interpretation of the treaty or the application of its provisions.[122] Since modern wildlife treaties tend to be supported by regular formal meetings of the parties, they commonly generate a wealth of material of the kind envisaged by this article.

Article 32, headed 'Supplementary means of interpretation', provides:

> Recourse may be had to supplementary means of interpretation, including the preparatory work of the treaty and the circumstances of its conclusion, in order to confirm the meaning resulting from the application of Article 31, or to determine the meaning when the interpretation according to Article 31:
> (a) leaves the meaning ambiguous or obscure; or
> (b) leads to a result which is manifestly absurd or unreasonable.

Thus the *travaux préparatoires* are relegated to an ancillary role, to be resorted to only for the avoidance of impenetrability or absurdity. This, again, is in keeping with contemporary notions of the treaty as a 'living instrument', where more attention is to be focused on ongoing developments than upon the mindsets of the parties back when the treaty was negotiated.

International law also recognises a number of more detailed rules or canons of interpretation, many of which are mirrored in national law.[123] The Vienna Convention does not refer to these specifically, but they unquestionably remain applicable to the contemporary interpretation process. One of the best known is the principle of effectiveness, *ut res magis valeat quam pereat*.[124] As the ILC has recognised, this is in a general sense embodied in the Article 31 requirements to interpret the treaty in good faith and in the light of its object and purpose, but the principle also has more specific ramifications. One of these takes the form of a presumption that no individual provision should be

[121] Ibid., Article 31(2). The Final Act to the Ramsar Convention, for example, affirmed the parties' entitlement to specify any dependent territories to which their acceptance extended, notwithstanding the omission of any such clause from the Convention itself.

[122] Vienna Convention, Article 31(3) (a), (b).

[123] For examples, see Aust, *supra* n. 74, at 200–1.

[124] Literally, interpretation 'so that the instrument flourishes rather than perishes'. See Lord McNair, *The Law of Treaties* (Clarendon Press, 2nd ed., 1961), pp. 383–5.

construed in such a way as to deprive it of all practical effect where an alternative interpretation allowing it some meaning is possible.[125]

Article 33 then addresses the widespread practice of concluding treaty texts in multiple language versions,[126] providing that in such cases all texts are equally authentic (unless otherwise agreed) and are presumed to have the same meaning. In reality, the goal of achieving exactly the same nuance in several languages throughout a wide array of complex regulatory provisions is all but unattainable, and discrepancies are virtually certain to occur. In these circumstances, it may seem attractive to agree that one of the texts will prevail, but this option is seldom exercised in practice and, when it is, may well backfire. A stipulation in the 1971 Ramsar Wetlands Convention that the English text would prevail in the event of divergence discouraged many Francophone countries from ratifying the convention at all, and the clause was eventually amended to make all the language texts equally authentic.[127]

The need to resolve discrepancies amongst the various language texts is therefore a recurrent problem. To assist, Article 33(4) provides that

> when a comparison of the authentic texts discloses a difference of meaning which the application of articles 31 and 32 does not remove, the meaning which best reconciles the texts, having regard to the object and purpose of the treaty, shall be adopted.

One final point to note here arises from the provisions of Article 31(3)(c), which stipulates that the interpretation process must also take into account 'any relevant rules of international law applicable in the relations between the parties'. This confirms that the task of treaty interpretation must be undertaken not merely in the light of the surrounding factual circumstances, but also with regard to the broader legal context. Although *any* rule of international law may potentially prove relevant in this sense, those which bear specifically upon the issue of environmental protection are likely to assume particular significance in the interpretation of wildlife-related treaties, and it is therefore desirable to provide a brief overview of the rules in question.

[125] *Cayuga Indian Claims* case, *AD* 1925–26, No. 271.

[126] UN treaties, for example, are now customarily concluded in six languages – Arabic, Chinese, English, French, Russian and Spanish.

[127] See the 1982 Protocol, 22 *ILM* 698.

4. Key principles of international environmental law

While international environmental law largely involves the application of ordinary legal rules in an environmental context, it is clear that certain principles have acquired a specialised flavour and significance in this field, and that some genuinely novel concepts have also emerged. This network of principles represents the backcloth against which treaty regimes concerning wildlife conservation must necessarily be viewed.[128]

a) Sovereignty over natural resources

'Sovereignty' concerns the allocation and exercise of supreme power and authority within a given legal order. As seen above, the international legal system is founded not upon the concentration of such authority in centralised institutions, but upon its distribution across the entire global community of states. The fundamental principle that each independent state enjoys full sovereignty over all natural resources within its territory has duly been confirmed in a sequence of legal instruments adopted since the 1960s.[129] It applies not only to the mineral and water resources which have traditionally been at the forefront of governmental concerns, but to the living resources represented by flora and fauna found within national frontiers.

i) Limitations of traditional conceptions of sovereignty

In this context, however, application of the concept of sovereignty generates unusual complication, stemming principally from the interaction of two factors, namely (i) the pervasive lack of congruity between *ecological* and *geopolitical* realities and (ii) the very special character of living things generally. Thus political boundaries commonly slice through landscape features such as lakes, rivers, forests and mountain ranges without regard to the operation of natural ecological processes. Such habitats are therefore prone to be affected by the adoption of divergent,

[128] For more detailed discussion, see Birnie, Boyle and Redgwell, *supra* n. 23, esp. Chapters 3, 4 and 11; and Sands, *supra* n. 54, esp. Chapter 6.

[129] Note particularly the 1962 General Assembly Resolution on Permanent Sovereignty over Natural Resources, GA Res. 1803, GAOR, 17th Sess., Supp. 17, p. 15; 1974 Charter of Economic Rights and Duties of States, GA Res. 3281 (XXIX), (1975) 14 *ILM* 251 (Article 2); 1972 Declaration of the Stockholm Conference on the Human Environment (Principle 21); 1992 Declaration of the UN Conference on Environment and Development (Principle 2).

and sometimes incompatible, approaches to conservation by neighbouring states. To complicate the matter further, wildlife resources are commonly not static but mobile, with many animals undertaking migratory peregrinations that extend over thousands of miles and numerous legal jurisdictions. In these circumstances, uncontrolled exploitation in just one country along a migration route might have the effect of sabotaging even the most scrupulous conservation efforts of many others.

The political and economic significance of these issues became apparent long ago in the *Bering Sea Fur Seals* arbitration.[130] Pursuant to the cession of Alaska by Russia in 1867, the United States acquired sovereignty over the Pribilov Islands, breeding grounds of the highly valued and intensively exploited stock of North Pacific fur seals. When agreement amongst interested states on a conservation regime for the fishery proved impossible, the US opted for unilateral action, seizing certain British vessels that were engaged in sealing in the Bering Sea beyond the limits of national jurisdiction. It defended these actions by reference to the need to conserve seal stocks, claiming to have inherited from Russia certain historic rights of exclusive jurisdiction in the Bering Sea. It also claimed special proprietary or protective rights over the herds, to be exercised as trustee for the international community as a whole, by virtue of the unique relationship established through their regular return to its territory for breeding purposes.

The arbitrators rejected these claims, however, and reasserted the traditional principles governing jurisdiction over living resources. On the high seas, fur seals represented a resource open to exploitation by any state, and interference with vessels lawfully engaged in such activities could not be justified. Claims of exclusive jurisdiction in the Bering Sea had neither been asserted in recent times by Russia nor recognised by Great Britain, and the location of the seals' breeding grounds gave rise to no special rights on the part of the US. Nevertheless, the risks inherent in a 'free-for-all' approach to exploitation were all too evident. At the parties' request, the arbitrators accordingly devised a comprehensive conservation regime for the seals, entailing closed seasons and protected waters, the licensing of sealing vessels, the prohibition of indiscriminate methods of capture and the recording of catch levels. These arrangements were not wholly successful, however, not least because they were not accepted by other states engaged in exploitation, and it proved

[130] (1893) 1 *Moore's International Arbitration Awards* 755.

necessary to reactivate efforts to establish a formal multilateral treaty regime for the fishery.[131]

This case neatly encapsulates the problems posed for conservation by traditional principles of international law. On the one hand, the sovereign rights of states within their own territories entitle them to exploit wildlife resources without restraint, even in such a way as to undermine the conservation measures adopted by other states along natural migration routes. On the other, the *res communis* status of areas beyond national jurisdiction,[132] such as the high seas, precipitates an unedifying scramble for exploitation on a 'first-come, first-served' basis, leading to the much-discussed 'tragedy of the commons'.[133] Attempts have therefore been made to revisit the basic concepts of jurisdiction in order to restrain excessive exploitation. A number of possible approaches have emerged.[134]

ii) Shared sovereignty

There is no legal requirement that sovereignty be exclusive, and certain areas both of land and of sea have from time to time fallen under regimes of joint sovereignty.[135] Furthermore, in the *River Oder* case in 1929,[136] the World Court recognised the existence of a 'community of interest' amongst riparian states in international watercourses, a concept which has subsequently been extended from the navigational context to that of environmental protection.[137] During the 1970s, there were signs of the emergence of a distinct legal regime to govern 'shared natural resources',[138] such as river systems, internal seas, mountain chains, forests and migratory species, but the idea ultimately attracted only muted endorsement from the General Assembly.[139] Governmental reservations, however, appeared to relate more to the

[131] See the 1911 Convention for the Preservation and Protection of Fur Seals, 8 *IPE* 3682; and the 1957 Interim Convention on the Conservation of North Pacific Fur Seals, 314 *UNTS* 105, and subsequent amendments.

[132] *Res communis* refers to common property: no state may appropriate areas of the high seas to its own exclusive use or control in the absence of general acquiescence on the part of other states.

[133] See G. Hardin, 'The Tragedy of the Commons' (1968) 162 *Science* 1243.

[134] See further D. Bodansky, J. Brunnée and E. Hey (eds.), *The Oxford Handbook of International Environmental Law* (Oxford University Press, 2007), Chapter 23.

[135] For examples, see Shaw, *supra* n. 4, pp. 206–7.

[136] (1929) *PCIJ Rep*, Series A, No. 23.

[137] *Gabcikovo-Nagymaros Project* case, *supra* n. 46; see especially para. 85 of the judgment.

[138] See, e.g., UNGA Resolution 3129 (XXVIII), 1973; Article 3, Charter of Economic Rights and Duties of States, UNGA Resolution 3281 (XXIX), 1974; 1978 UNEP Principles on Conservation and Harmonious Utilisation of Natural Resources Shared by Two or More States (1978) 17 *ILM* 1091.

[139] UNGA Resolution 34/186 (1979).

nomenclature than to the actual legal implications, which revolved around equitable utilisation, co-operation, information exchange and avoidance of harm to the interests of others. These ideas have continued to gain recognition in environmental law generally,[140] while all of them featured prominently in the final draft of the 1997 Watercourses Convention.[141]

iii) The common heritage of mankind

Even the notion of shared sovereignty, however, fails to allow much recognition to the *global* dimension of concern regarding wildlife and natural ecosystems, and there has been recurrent pressure for the elaboration of conceptual devices to reflect this broader community of interest. One concept which envisages the effective 'internationalisation' of natural resources is that of the 'common heritage of mankind'.[142] Although this expression is widely (and loosely) used for rhetorical purposes, in a legal sense it has a clearly defined meaning. Specifically, it refers to a regime whereby a resource may not be exploited for individual advantage, but must be conserved and utilised for the benefit of the international community at large. Plainly, this is unlikely to be possible without elaborate institutional apparatus to undertake, or at least supervise, the tasks of exploitation and distribution of benefits. As a result, it has made limited headway in international affairs, the only instances of its adoption so far being in relation to the resources of outer space and the deep-sea bed.[143] Even here, it has not been enthusiastically embraced by nations best placed actually to engage in exploitation, encountering opposition from the United States in particular. In a similar way, states whose wildlife has so far escaped the worst ravages of urbanisation and industrialisation have seen little virtue in relinquishing sovereignty over these potentially valuable resources in favour of some international management regime. The concept of common heritage has therefore made little impact in relation to wildlife, and is, in fact, not actually reflected even in the World Heritage Convention itself.[144]

140 See generally Birnie, Boyle and Redgwell, *supra* n. 23, pp. 192–4.

141 1997 Convention on the Non-navigational Uses of International Watercourses, 36 *ILM* 719.

142 See generally K. Baslar, *The Concept of Common Heritage of Mankind in International Law* (Martinus Nijhoff, 1998).

143 See respectively the 1979 Agreement Concerning the Activities of States on the Moon and Other Celestial Bodies (1979) 18 *ILM* 1434; and the 1982 UN Convention on the Law of the Sea (1982) 21 *ILM* 1261, Part XI. As to the latter, see further the 1994 Agreement Relating to the Implementation of Part XI (1994) 33 *ILM* 1309.

144 See further Chapter 14 below.

iv) Common interest or concern

Plainly, some less revolutionary device was needed to reflect the general idea of community interest, but without undermining state authority too severely, and that device has proved to be the concept of 'common interest' or 'common concern'. Thus both 'change in the earth's climate and its adverse effects' and 'the conservation of biological diversity' have been declared to represent 'the common concern of humankind'.[145] The essential implications are that, while existing conceptions of sovereignty are left formally undisturbed, all such matters are to be considered legitimate topics for international debate, precluding complaints of unwarranted intrusion into the reserved sphere of domestic jurisdiction.[146] Rather, an element of international accountability is involved, whereby sovereignty must be exercised in accordance with a regime of conservation obligations owed to the community as a whole, and in respect of which other states undertake duties of support and assistance. In retrospect, both the Wetlands and World Heritage Conventions can be seen to have evolved in accordance with this schema.

The quest for a suitable normative framework to reflect the distribution and balance of interests in global wildlife resources is itself indicative of a wider concern for the achievement of harmony in the relations between each state, its immediate neighbours and the wider community, an objective which is reflected in the emergence of various other important principles of international environmental law.

b) The principle of good neighbourliness

The maintenance of peaceful relations amongst its members represents a key objective of every political community, and is reflected internationally in, inter alia, the principle of good neighbourliness, referred to in Article 74 of the UN Charter. This principle is in turn manifest in a number of more specific, interconnected, duties to which states are subject in the environmental context.

i) The duty to prevent, control and reduce environmental harm

In the *Corfu Channel* case,[147] the ICJ recognised a duty on the part of every state 'not to allow knowingly its territory to be used for acts

[145] See the first and third preambular recitals of the Climate Change and Biodiversity Conventions respectively.
[146] See Article 2(7), UN Charter. [147] (1949) *ICJ Rep* 4, 22.

contrary to the rights of other states', a principle already familiar to environmental lawyers from the *Trail Smelter* arbitration.[148] These decisions effectively represent applications of the Roman law maxim *sic utere tuo ut alienum non laedas*,[149] and indicate the limitations upon each state's sovereignty over its own territory and natural resources which are necessary to preserve the rights of others. This trade-off is formally recognised in Principle 2 of the Rio Declaration,[150] which provides:

> States have, in accordance with the Charter of the United Nations and the principles of international law, the sovereign right to exploit their own resources pursuant to their own environmental and developmental policies, and the responsibility to ensure that activities within their jurisdiction or control do not cause damage to the environment of other states or of areas beyond the limits of national jurisdiction.

States have, however, been slow to heed the Stockholm Declaration's related call, repeated with greater urgency at Rio, to 'develop further the international law regarding liability and compensation for the victims of pollution and other environmental damage'.[151] There are accordingly still uncertainties regarding the substantive scope of the customary duty of prevention, the standard of liability it entails, the kind of harm it is designed to prevent, and the threshold of seriousness this must cross before becoming actionable.[152] As a result, the importance of developing liability regimes under *national* law has been emphasised,[153] with increasing recognition afforded to the 'polluter-pays' principle.[154] Although there is still widespread reluctance to pursue this notion with full rigour, there is at least an increasing readiness to consider the need for compensation in respect of harm *to* the environment itself – i.e. to species and ecosystems – rather than simply harm caused *through* the environment to traditionally recognised interests in property or personal security.[155]

148 (1941) 35 *AJIL* 716.
149 'Use your own property in such a way as to avoid injury to anyone else's.'
150 Essentially restating Principle 21 of the Stockholm Declaration.
151 See Stockholm Declaration, Principle 22; Rio Declaration, Principle 13.
152 See generally Birnie, Boyle and Redgwell, *supra* n. 23, Chapter 3.
153 Rio Declaration, Principle 13; 2006 ILC Draft Principles on the Allocation of Loss in the case of Transboundary Harm Arising out of Hazardous Activities, at http://untreaty.un.org/ilc/texts/9_10.htm.
154 Rio Declaration, Principle 16.
155 See further Chapter 3 below, and, generally, M. J. Bowman and A. E. Boyle (eds.), *Environmental Damage in International and Comparative Law* (Oxford University Press, 2002).

Even more importantly, there has been a shift of emphasis away from liability and towards regulation. This is evident both in the proliferation of legal regimes designed to control environmentally hazardous activities and in a growing insistence upon the conduct of environmental impact assessments prior to the generation of such risks.[156] The need to err on the side of caution in this regard is also recognised in the form of the 'precautionary approach', so that, for example, 'where there are threats of serious or irreversible damage, lack of full scientific certainty shall not be used as a reason for postponing cost-effective measures to prevent environmental degradation'.[157]

ii) Duties of co-operation

Neighbourliness can scarcely be pursued in isolation, and Principle 7 of the Rio Declaration duly requires states to 'co-operate in a spirit of global partnership to conserve, protect and restore the health and integrity of the Earth's ecosystem'.[158] Similarly, Article 5 of the Biodiversity Convention requires co-operation 'in respect of areas beyond national jurisdiction and on other matters of mutual interest, for the conservation and sustainable use of biological diversity'. Comparable provisions occur in other wildlife treaties.[159]

Duties of co-operation also appear in more specific guises, such as the obligation to 'provide prior and timely notification and relevant information to potentially affected States on activities that may have a significant adverse transboundary effect and . . . consult with those States at an early stage and in good faith'.[160] Such obligations are long-established in relation to the use of international watercourses,[161] and have progressively been recognised in other areas,[162] arguably merging into a

[156] See, on this point, the Rio Declaration, Principle 17; 1991 Espoo Convention on Environmental Impact Assessment in a Transboundary Context, 30 *ILM* 802.

[157] Rio Declaration, Principle 15. See further A. Trouwborst, *Evolution and Status of the Precautionary Principle in International Law* (Kluwer, 2002); R. Cooney and B. Dickson (eds.), *Biodiversity and the Precautionary Principle* (Earthscan, 2005).

[158] For further references to co-operation, see Principles 5, 9, 12, 13, 14 and 27.

[159] E.g., Ramsar, Article 5; CMS, Articles 2(1), 4 and 5; Bern Convention, Articles 1(1), 4(4), 10(1) and 11(1).

[160] Rio Declaration, Principle 19.

[161] See especially the *Lac Lanoux* arbitration (1957) 24 *ILR* 101.

[162] See, e.g., Principles 6 and 7 of the 1978 UNEP Principles, *supra* n. 138; Article 6, 1989 Convention on the Control of Transboundary Movements of Hazardous Wastes and Their Disposal (1989) 28 *ILM* 657; Article 4, 1992 Convention on the Transboundary Effects of Industrial Accidents (1992) 31 *ILM* 1330.

general customary duty to initiate such procedures wherever there is a significant risk of transboundary harm.[163] Procedural obligations of this kind have also been incorporated into environmental impact assessment arrangements in cases of transboundary risk,[164] and therefore feed directly back into the general duty of the prevention of harm discussed above. Duties of notification become particularly urgent in cases of environmental emergency, which is the subject of separate provision in the Rio Declaration and elsewhere.[165] On a broader front, there is considerable inherent virtue in the pooling of environmental information and expertise, the development of co-operative research programmes and the fostering of best practice, and provision is now routinely made for the cultivation of such co-operation.[166]

iii) The equitable utilisation of resources

Since natural resources are frequently in heavy demand, there is an obvious need for the exercise of restraint in their exploitation, together with recognition of the just claims of all stakeholders. At the broadest level, these considerations are reflected in Principle 8 of the Rio Declaration, which provides:

> To achieve sustainable development and a higher quality of life for all people, States should reduce and eliminate unsustainable patterns of production and consumption and promote appropriate demographic policies.

In some cases, more specific duties of equitable utilisation have been recognised, most notably in relation to the exploitation of international watercourses, where a series of particular factors which bear upon equitability has been identified.[167]

c) *The principle of sustainable development*

The perception that conservation and environmental protection represent unwarranted impediments to human development has yielded ground of late to a recognition that the two objectives are not inimical

[163] See further Birnie, Boyle and Redgwell, *supra* n. 23, pp. 177–80.

[164] Articles 3 and 5, 1991 Espoo Convention, *supra* n. 156.

[165] Rio Declaration, Principle 18. See also, e.g., the 1986 Convention on Early Notification of a Nuclear Accident (1986) 25 *ILM* 1370.

[166] See, e.g., the CBD, Article 18; Antarctic Environmental Protocol, Article 10; Ramsar, Article 4(2), CMS, Article 2(3)(a).

[167] 1966 ILA Helsinki Rules, Article 5; 1997 Watercourses Convention, Article 6.

but interdependent.[168] In consequence, sustainable development has become one of the dominant themes of the modern era. As a principle of international law, it contains a number of distinct but interrelated strands.

i) The principle of integration

At its heart lies the principle of integration, encapsulated in Principle 4 of the Rio Declaration:

> In order to achieve sustainable development, environmental protection shall constitute an integral part of the development process and cannot be considered in isolation from it.

While considerable theoretical controversy exists regarding the extent to which this principle serves to prioritise the pursuit of development goals over environmental protection,[169] there is little doubt that the practical reality in many countries is that environmental advocacy struggles to make itself heard amidst the clamour of the energy, transport, trade and industrial lobbies, and that merely maintaining the place of conservation issues on the domestic political agenda represents a major challenge for governments. The extent to which international treaty arrangements succeed in strengthening the hand of environment ministries in restraining ecologically damaging development projects therefore represents one important measure of their value.

Integration is essentially an organisational matter, and in itself conveys little regarding the substance of the policies which are to be integrated. The duty of good neighbourliness, discussed above, points the way on this issue, however, and is supplemented by the currently evolving duties of natural-resource conservation. Yet if the ongoing support of governments is to be secured, the overall justice and propriety of proposed conservation measures will have to be clearly demonstrable, highlighting the importance of the concept of equity as a component of the sustainable-development paradigm. It has emerged in two distinct guises.

ii) Inter-generational equity

Acknowledging the need for development to be sustainable not merely over the short term but in perpetuity, the preamble to the Stockholm

[168] Note especially WCED, *Our Common Future* (Oxford University Press, 1987); and the successive versions of the World Conservation Strategy.

[169] For a range of interpretations, see P. Sands (ed.), *Greening International Law* (Earthscan, 1996).

Declaration identifies its intended beneficiaries as being both *present* and *future* generations.[170] Although by no means unprecedented in an international legal instrument,[171] this represents a particularly forthright recognition of the claims of generations to come as key stakeholders in the sustainable-development process, and has been echoed in numerous later texts.[172] Consequently, the notion of preserving options and opportunities for the benefit of posterity has become a central objective of international environmental law.

With regard to wildlife, the guiding principle is that of *sustainable utilisation*, which has been defined for the purpose of one convention as

> human use of a [resource] so that it may yield the greatest continuous benefit to present generations while maintaining its potential to meet the needs and aspirations of future generations.[173]

This principle is, however, easier to state in general terms than to particularise in any concrete context, and the history of attempts to regulate the exploitation of fisheries, for example, gives little cause for optimism regarding the strength of global commitment to meaningful conservation.[174] Even where exploitation is essentially recreational rather than commercial, powerful emotions and long-standing cultural traditions are often engaged,[175] rendering the pursuit of sustainability an extremely challenging task.

iii) Intra-generational equity

A further factor is that the dependence of governments upon contemporary public support means that they cannot afford to focus exclusively upon the interests of generations to come; consequently, the principle of sustainable development also seeks to enhance fairness *within the present generation*. Here, the primary focus is upon the reduction of inequities between states,[176] reflecting the protracted struggle of developing countries for the achievement of an international economic order which

[170] Para. 6 (emphasis added).
[171] See, e.g., the preamble to the 1946 Whaling Convention.
[172] See, e.g., the World Charter for Nature, preamble; Rio Declaration, Principle 3; preambles to CITES and the Bern, Bonn and Biodiversity Conventions.
[173] The Ramsar Convention; see further Chapter 13 below.
[174] See Chapters 5 and 6 below. [175] In relation to hunting, for example.
[176] Though attention is also focused on individuals, through calls for improved access to information, participation in decision-making and availability of legal redress: see Principle 10. The special role of women, youth and indigenous communities is also stressed: Principles 20–2.

reflects their interests more fairly. Planetary life-support systems clearly cannot be maintained, or biological diversity conserved, without their active support, and this has considerably strengthened their hand in the global negotiating process. Thus a number of key provisions of the Rio Declaration accord special priority to the needs of developing states in the quest for sustainable development.[177] In particular, all states are to co-operate in the tasks of eradicating poverty and reducing global disparities in living standards, and strengthening endogenous capacity building through technology transfer and exchanges of scientific knowledge.[178]

Such exhortations may be translated into legal obligations through the notion of *common but differentiated responsibility*, in accordance with which developed countries acknowledge a special responsibility 'in view of the pressures their societies place on the global environment and of the technologies and financial resources they command'.[179] Accordingly, many modern conservation treaties make provision for technical and financial assistance to developing and transitional economies, with the Biodiversity Convention expressing the significance of this responsibility in particularly forthright terms.[180] In addition, the substantive obligations it imposes are characteristically qualified by phrases indicating the need for individual circumstances, especially developmental status, to be taken into account. Customary obligations regarding the equitable utilisation of resources, also grounded in the need for justice between states, can also to some extent be tailored to reflect individual needs and capacities.

iv) The juridical character of the principle of sustainable development

Despite widespread recognition of the principle of sustainable development, fundamental difficulties arise out of its lack of precision, especially regarding the precise balance to be struck between development and sustainability. Inevitably, considerable discretion must be left to individual states regarding its detailed application, making it difficult to discern any formal duty to ensure that development is pursued sustainably. In the *Gabcikovo-Nagymaros* case, the ICJ endorsed the concept of sustainable development only to the extent of describing it as an apt expression of the need to reconcile economic development with environmental protection.[181] Even

177 Principle 6. 178 Principles 5 and 9. 179 Principle 7. 180 See Article 20(4).
181 Para. 140 of the Judgment.

Judge Weeramantry's more expansive individual opinion did not go beyond describing it as a 'principle of normative value' to be taken into account 'not merely in a general way, but with reference to specific principles, concepts and aspirational standards'.[182] Bearing these observations in mind, perhaps the most plausible explanation of the current state of the law is that 'although international law may not require development to be sustainable, it does require development decisions to be the outcome of a process which promotes sustainable development'.[183]

On this view, the function of the concept is primarily procedural, rendering national decisions liable to international scrutiny but reserving appropriate discretion to governments. This is arguably reflected in the outcome in the *Gabcikovo* case itself, where the parties were required to 'look afresh' at the environmental consequences of their arrangements and to implement such monitoring and abatement measures as they judged to be necessary in the light of sustainable-development considerations.[184] Insofar as sustainable development has a substantive role, it might assume the form of a 'meta-principle' relevant to the interpretation and elaboration of norms established by other means,[185] after the fashion, perhaps, of 'equity', 'reciprocity' or 'proportionality'. That is, while there is no general duty to develop sustainably (or to behave equitably, reciprocally or proportionally), such considerations may be factored into the specification of particular duties generated by custom or treaty.

d) Conservation, protection and related concepts

Despite the undoubted importance of the concept of sustainable development, it would be unwise to assume that it tells the full story of modern environmental law, particularly insofar as it relates to wildlife. The majority of wildlife treaties speak in terms of 'conservation' rather than of sustainable utilisation, but this expression is seldom defined and might carry a variety of nuances of meaning.[186] It is true that the World Conservation Strategy, which does provide a definition, employs a

[182] See the opening and concluding passages of Section A of his Opinion.
[183] Birnie, Boyle and Redgwell, *supra* n. 23, p. 96.
[184] See para. 140 of the Judgment. See further the 'Introduction' to A. E. Boyle and D. A. C. Freestone (eds.), *International Law and Sustainable Development* (Oxford University Press, 1999).
[185] See V. Lowe, Chapter 2 in Boyle and Freestone, *supra* n. 184.
[186] See especially Birnie, Boyle and Redgwell, *supra* n. 23, pp. 550–4.

formula which is difficult to distinguish from that commonly used to define sustainable utilisation, namely 'management of human use of the biosphere so that it may yield the greatest sustainable benefit to present generations while maintaining its potential to meet the needs and aspirations of future generations',[187] yet many wildlife species have no direct utility, and the most that this definition could require would be that *where such resources are used*, such use should be sustainable.[188] Conservation may therefore *entail* sustainable utilisation, rather than *equate to* it. The Strategy itself identifies sustainable utilisation as only one of the objectives of conservation, the others being the maintenance of ecological processes and life-support systems and the preservation of genetic diversity.[189] Furthermore, fleeting acknowledgement is also given to the *ethical* case for conservation,[190] a point that is significantly expanded in the revised version of the Strategy published in 1991.[191] Finally, it is noticeable that some treaties speak in terms of the *protection* of wildlife, which has on occasion been seen to involve not only *rational* but also *humane* use.[192]

This complex and in some respects confusing picture must therefore be examined more closely in order to identify the precise philosophical underpinnings of contemporary wildlife law, and it is that issue which forms the subject matter of Chapter 3.

Recommended further reading

A. Aust, *Modern Treaty Law and Practice* (Cambridge University Press, 2nd ed., 2007)

P. W. Birnie, A. E. Boyle and C. J. Redgwell, *International Law and the Environment* (Oxford University Press, 3rd ed., 2009)

D. Bodansky, J. Brunnee and E. Hey (eds.), *The Oxford Handbook of International Environmental Law* (Oxford University Press, 2007)

D. J. Harris, *Cases and Materials in International Law* (Sweet & Maxwell, 7th ed., 2010)

P. Sands, *Principles of International Environmental Law* (Cambridge University Press, 2nd ed., 2003)

M. N. Shaw, *International Law* (Cambridge University Press, 7th ed., 2008)

[187] World Conservation Strategy, Section 1.4. Compare the Ramsar definition of sustainable utilisation cited in Section 4(c)(ii) above.

[188] This point is expressly articulated in the preamble to the Bonn Convention.

[189] Section 1.7 of the Strategy. [190] Ibid., Sections 3.1 and 3.2.

[191] See further Chapter 3 below.

[192] Cf., e.g., the preamble (final recital) and Article 3(1), 1972 Antarctic Seals Convention, 11 *ILM* 251.

Chapter 3

The philosophical foundations of international wildlife law

1. Introduction

Although it would be unrealistic to claim that international wildlife law has evolved in accordance with any grand philosophical strategy, all legislative initiatives are plainly intended to advance some significant underlying policy, and over time the sheer proliferation of treaty regimes has highlighted the need to establish some broader, overall direction and coherence in the system, based upon the developing aspirations and values of the international community. As it happens, wildlife law is nourished by a particularly rich tradition of theorising about the relationship between humankind and 'nature', and in recent decades environmental ethics have become a central concern of moral philosophy.[1] Underpinning these deliberations is the recognition that the natural world embodies significant value, and should therefore be protected.

This chapter accordingly explores the question of natural value, first examining the various forms of value that have been identified within the natural world, before seeking to identify more precisely the specific entities in which such value resides. It concludes by analysing the mechanisms through which these various values may be quantified and compared. In each case, attention is given to the extent to which philosophical concepts and arguments have exerted any practical influence upon the evolution of international wildlife law.

[1] For a valuable anthology, see A. Light and H. Rolston III (eds.), *Environmental Ethics: An Anthology* (Blackwell, 2003), and for an extensive online bibliography prepared by the International Society for Environmental Ethics, see www.cep.unt.edu/bib. On the relationship between international law and environmental ethics specifically, see A. Gillespie, *International Environmental Law, Policy and Ethics* (Clarendon, 1997).

2. The nature of value

Although there is no absolute consistency in the use of terminology, there is widespread agreement that nature exhibits various forms of value, of which the most widely recognised categories are *instrumental*, *inherent* and *intrinsic*.[2] It is clear, moreover, that many natural entities, including humans, may exhibit all of these simultaneously.

a) Forms of value

The instrumental value of any particular entity lies in the material purpose it serves or the use to which it may be put, as in the case of a fish consumed for food or a tree cut down for timber. It is sometimes labelled *commodity* value,[3] particularly when applied to direct human consumption of natural resources. Instrumental value may, however, be either direct or indirect, anthropocentric or non-anthropocentric. Species exploited for human sustenance, for example, will in turn be ecologically dependent upon other plants and animals, which must therefore themselves be conserved if human food sources are to be maintained. Ultimately, all human existence depends upon perpetuation of the life-support systems of the planet, and the instrumental values which permeate the mass of ecological relationships amongst wildlife species generally. Each one contributes to the maintenance of the ecosystem in which it is found, and those whose *contributory* value is judged especially significant are known as *keystone* species,[4] identifying them as particular targets for conservation concern.

Inherent value, by contrast, is that which an entity possesses of itself, by virtue not of its utility, but of its mere existence. Thus nature, like works of art, is commonly valued for aesthetic reasons, such considerations having been especially prominent within the North American

[2] The terms 'inherent' and 'intrinsic', for example, are commonly confused or conflated: see E. C. Hargrove's contributions to E. C. Hargrove (ed.), *The Animal Rights/Environmental Ethics Debate* (SUNY Press, 1992). See further R. Attfield, *The Ethics of Environmental Concern* (University of Georgia Press, 2nd ed., 1991); W. Fox, *Towards a Transpersonal Ecology* (SUNY Press, 1995); F. Mathews, *The Ecological Self* (Routledge, 1991); H. Rolston III, *Conserving Natural Value* (Columbia University Press, 1994); G. E. Varner, *In Nature's Interests?* (Oxford University Press, 1998).

[3] B. G. Norton, 'Commodity, Amenity and Morality: The Limits of Quantification in Valuing Biodiversity', in E. O. Wilson (ed.), *Biodiversity* (National Academy Press, 1988).

[4] Ibid., p. 203; see also E. O. Wilson, *The Diversity of Life* (Penguin, 1992), esp. Chapter 9.

tradition of environmental ethics.[5] In view of its recreational associations, inherent value is sometimes labelled *amenity* value,[6] but it may equally derive from cultural or religious perspectives which accord symbolic or totemic significance to particular life forms, where the terminology of amenity seems less appropriate. Plants and animals have in fact played a crucial role in the myths, stories and cultural traditions of all societies at all times, including the present.[7] The aesthetic or cultural appeal of the natural world is, of course, capable of being exploited for financial gain – through such activities as seaside holidays, mountaineering or whalewatching – and is routinely treated as a form of utility by economists, albeit one of a non-consumptive character.[8] To that extent, inherent value may sometimes be difficult to distinguish from the instrumental variety.

Intrinsic value, finally, is that which an entity possesses of itself, for itself, regardless of the interests or utility of others.[9] It is sometimes referred to as *moral* value,[10] indicating that all entities which exhibit such value can be said to have a good of their own, and therefore to fall within the scope of moral considerability.[11] While humans have always recognised themselves as possessing such value, the question of its existence in other entities has provoked acute controversy. One approach widely accepted amongst contemporary environmental ethicists, however, grounds intrinsic value specifically in the property of *autopoiesis* (meaning self-production or self-renewal),[12] a characteristic of all living things, and of living things exclusively. These are accordingly seen as *ends in themselves*, rendering them worthy of moral consideration in their own right.[13] Autopoietic intrinsic-value theory therefore represents

[5] See Hargrove, *supra* n. 2. [6] Norton, *supra* n. 3.

[7] J. Frazer, *The Golden Bough* (1922; Wordsworth ed., 1993); L. Daston and G. Mitman (eds.), *Thinking with Animals* (Columbia University Press, 2005).

[8] D. Pearce and D. Moran, *The Economic Value of Biodiversity* (Earthscan, 1994); N. Hanley, 'The Economic Value of Environmental Damage', in M. J. Bowman and A. E. Boyle (eds.), *Environmental Damage in International and Comparative Law* (Oxford University Press, 2002).

[9] In addition to the works cited at n. 2, *supra*, see N. Agar, *Life's Intrinsic Value* (Columbia University Press, 2001).

[10] Norton, *supra* n. 3.

[11] See K. Goodpaster, 'On Being Morally Considerable' (1978) 75 *Journal of Philosophy* 308.

[12] Autopoiesis – from the Greek *autos* (self) and *poiein* (to produce) – is in origin a biological concept: see L. Margulis and D. Sagan, *What Is Life?* (Weidenfeld & Nicholson, 1995), Chapter 1; S. Rose, *Lifelines* (Penguin, 1997), Chapter 1. See further Section 3(b) below in this chapter.

[13] R. Eckersley, *Environmentalism and Political Theory* (UCL Press, 1992), p. 60.

a more fully reasoned version of earlier approaches based on 'respect' or 'reverence' for life.[14]

Although the concept of intrinsic value has come under fire from certain philosophers, economists and development theorists,[15] these attacks do not seem to have significantly undermined it as a theoretical construct.[16] In any event, the reservations of individual commentators are comfortably outweighed by the fact that the value of other life forms in their own right is widely recognised (though perhaps with varying degrees of commitment) by all the major cultures and religions, a point confirmed in 1993 by the Council for a Parliament of the World's Religions.[17] Its affirmation of 'respect for the community of living beings' – people, animals and plants – had been foreshadowed in declarations made by representatives of several major faiths at WWF's 25th Anniversary Conference, held at Assisi in 1986.[18] In addition, notions of the community and continuity of all life are apparent within the earlier tribal traditions of the world,[19] recourse to which has frequently been proposed in recent times as a means of restoring humanity's fractured relationship with nature. More importantly still for present purposes, the concept of intrinsic value (along with the instrumental and inherent varieties) appears to have secured recognition in international law.

b) Recognition of natural values in international law

Early attempts at the international regulation of human relations with nature were undoubtedly prompted by utilitarian considerations, generally of a narrowly anthropocentric character. Thus the conservation of

[14] See generally Gillespie, *supra* n. 1, Chapter 9.

[15] See, e.g., J. B. Callicott, 'Animal Liberation: A Triangular Affair' (1980) 2 *Envtl. Ethics* 311; Pearce and Moran, *supra* n. 8, Chapter 1; S. Sarkar, *Biodiversity and Environmental Philosophy: An Introduction* (Cambridge University Press, 2005).

[16] For refutation of these various criticisms, see Fox, *supra* n. 2, pp. 184–96. See further T. Ronnow-Rasmussen and M. J. Zimmerman (eds.), *Recent Work on Intrinsic Value* (Springer, 2005).

[17] See 'Towards a Global Ethic: An Initial Declaration', in J. Beversluis (ed.), *Sourcebook of the World's Religions* (New World Library, 3rd ed., 2000), Chapter 22. The 'global ethic' reflects a 'common set of core values' found in the teachings of the world's religions. See further P. Morgan and M. Braybrooke (eds.), *Testing the Global Ethic* (CoNexus Press, 1998).

[18] For the texts of these declarations, see (1987) 17 *EPL* 47, 87.

[19] See Beversluis, *supra* n. 17, Chapters 1, 6; A. L. Peterson, *Being Human* (University of California Press, 2001), Chapter 4; H. P. Glenn, *Legal Traditions of the World* (Oxford, 2000), pp. 68–73.

resources for direct human consumption provided the motivation for the succession of treaties concerning seals, whales and fish that were adopted from the late nineteenth century onwards. The concerns underlying the 1900 African Convention and the 1902 Birds Convention were equally self-serving,[20] a point re-emphasised by the provisions encouraging persecution of the widely drawn category of 'nuisance' species. It is noteworthy, however, that most of these treaties ultimately contributed little to the attainment even of their own limited objectives, the urge for exploitation invariably tending to outstrip the willingness of states to accept meaningful constraints upon their activities.

Later conservation measures have also reflected instrumental values, though of a broader kind than those which motivated these early treaties. Thus the Biodiversity Convention defines 'biological resources' as including all biotic entities 'with *actual or potential* use or value for humanity',[21] while the many forms of utility recognised in this context embrace the ecological, genetic, social, economic, scientific, educational, cultural and recreational.[22] The first of these specifically acknowledges the contributory value of species to the functioning of the ecosystems in which they are found, a point confirmed in other treaties: the preamble to CITES, for example, describes wild fauna and flora as 'an irreplaceable part of the natural systems of the earth'.

Inherent values have also long been recognised. The preamble to the 1940 Western Hemisphere Convention, for example, proclaimed the desire to preserve both 'scenery of extraordinary beauty' and 'regions and natural objects of aesthetic value'. Aesthetic considerations also featured in the definitions of national parks and nature monuments, and as a reason for the protection of migratory birds. Subsequently, similar considerations provided the inspiration for the 1972 World Heritage Convention, in which the 'natural heritage' was defined to include natural sites and landscape features of outstanding universal value from the point of view of aesthetics or natural beauty.[23]

In addition, references to aesthetic values as a justification for conservation now commonly occur in treaty preambles[24] – a prime example being the Biodiversity Convention itself – while enjoyment of natural beauty may also sometimes underpin the recognition of 'recreational'

[20] For the full titles of treaties referred to in this chapter, and their text location references, see Chapter 1 above.
[21] Article 2 (emphasis added). [22] Preamble, first recital. [23] Article 2.
[24] See, e.g., the 1968 African Convention, 1973 CITES, 1979 Bonn and Bern Conventions.

values.[25] Furthermore, as explained above, inherent value may alternatively be manifest in the attribution of symbolic or totemic significance to wildlife, as reflected in preambular references to 'cultural' and 'religious' – or even to 'social' and 'educational' – values.[26]

As regards intrinsic value, the earlier instruments tend to be silent. Even in the modern era, anthropocentric motivations have plainly predominated and have, indeed, been deliberately accentuated with a view to persuading developing countries in particular that their own long-term interests are best served by a commitment to conservation, rather than by unrestrained exploitation. Affirming this approach, the World Conservation Strategy proclaimed that 'conservation, like development, is for people'.[27]

Yet, at the same time, alternative perspectives were never jettisoned entirely, and both the Strategy itself and the subsequent Brundtland Report contain fleeting recognition of the moral case for conservation.[28] More importantly, legal instruments have displayed a growing commitment to the notion of intrinsic value. Following a veiled reference in the Stockholm Declaration,[29] the first overt recognition occurred in the preamble to the Bern Convention, a European regional arrangement.[30] Shortly afterwards, the principle received unequivocal endorsement at the global level, when the preamble to the World Charter for Nature proclaimed, 'Every form of life is unique, warranting respect regardless of its worth to man, and to accord other organisms such recognition, man must be guided by a moral code of action'. The Charter's first substantive paragraph duly stipulated that nature must be respected and its essential processes not impaired. This theme was further elaborated in the 1991 revision of the World Conservation Strategy, *Caring for the Earth*,[31] which established a number of 'interrelated and mutually supporting principles' for a sustainable society. The first of these – 'Respect and Care

[25] See generally Gillespie, *supra* n. 1, Chapter 5.

[26] For a helpful survey, see ibid., Part V.

[27] World Conservation Strategy, Chapter 1, para. 5.

[28] See IUCN, World Conservation Strategy (1980), Chapter 3, para. 2 ('We are morally obliged – to our descendants *and to other creatures* – to act prudently'; emphasis added); WCED, *Our Common Future* (Oxford, 1987), pp. 147, 155.

[29] Principle 4, which adds little to Principles 2 and 3 unless interpreted as a recognition of the need to preserve wildlife for its own sake. On the drafting history, see L. B. Sohn, 'The Stockholm Declaration on the Human Environment' (1973) 14 *Harv ILJ* 423, p. 459.

[30] Though several African states also now participate; see Chapter 10 below.

[31] IUCN/UNEP/WWF, *Caring for the Earth: A Strategy for Sustainable Living* (IUCN, 1991).

for the Community of Life' – is described as the founding principle which provides the ethical basis for all the rest. It not only reaffirms that every form of life 'warrants respect independently of its worth to people', but adds that human development 'should not threaten the integrity of nature or the survival of other species'.

Finally, the Biodiversity Convention, in the opening recital of its preamble, expressly recognises the 'intrinsic value of biological diversity', alongside its many expressions of instrumental and inherent value. The precise wording, in which intrinsic value is not merely itemised as one in a catalogue of motivations, but set apart from the list of anthropocentric justifications which follow, seems to give particular emphasis to this moral dimension.[32] The near-universal acceptance of the Convention strongly underlines the extent to which the intrinsic value of non-human life forms has achieved international recognition.[33]

Additional support for this approach can be found in substantive treaty provisions. Article 3(1) of the 1991 Environmental Protocol to the Antarctic Treaty acknowledges the intrinsic value of Antarctica, though the wording of this provision arguably fails to convey the distinction between this and other forms of value.[34] In the Biodiversity Convention itself, substantive conservation commitments are usually expressed to be applicable not to biological *resources*, but to biological *diversity* as such,[35] implying the need to maintain the variability of life forms generally, regardless of their actual or potential utility to humans.[36] Even the CBD's Addis Ababa Guidelines on Sustainable Use confirm that 'intrinsic and other non-economic values of biological diversity' should be taken into account in the formulation of policy.[37] The 2003 African Nature Conservation Convention, despite its predominantly utilitarian flavour, lists 'environmental protection' as a key objective alongside conservation and sustainable use of resources in Article 2, while Article 4 requires that these objectives be pursued 'with due regard to ethical and traditional values'.

32 For a more sceptical view, see P. W. Birnie, A. E. Boyle and C. J. Redgwell, *International Law and the Environment* (Oxford University Press, 3rd ed., 2009), p. 618.

33 By January 2010, the Convention boasted 193 parties. US non-ratification is attributable to other considerations.

34 It refers to 'the intrinsic value of Antarctica, *including* its wilderness and aesthetic values and its value as an area for scientific research' (emphasis added).

35 See, e.g., Articles 1, 5–7, 8(a), 8(b), 8(g), 8(i), 8(j), 11–14. By contrast, the reference is to biological resources in Articles 8(c), 9(d), 10, 15.

36 Since that represents the CBD definition of biological resources, as noted above.

37 CBD Decision VII/12; see Practical Principle 10.

In the light of human nature, there is little doubt that anthropocentric concerns will continue to provide the strongest practical impetus for international conservation efforts, but the need for a more expansive and pluralistic approach seems also to have gained clear recognition.

3. The locus of value

Although each of the various forms of value specified above has secured recognition in international law, the precise identification of the entities which exhibit such value has proved a significantly more difficult question, both for philosophers and for lawyers.

a) Instrumental and inherent values

As regards instrumental value, although reference is commonly made to the exploitation of wildlife species or of natural ecosystems, it is clear that this is merely a form of shorthand, since in reality neither species nor ecosystems can be eaten, burned for fuel or converted into garments. Rather, it is individual plants and animals that are utilised for these purposes. Often, indeed, it is primarily some specific part or derivative of the organism in question that has traditionally been prized – the horn of the rhino or the elephant's ivory, for example – but continued access to such commodities plainly depends upon the survival of the plants or animals which produce them. Instrumental value is not, of course, confined to living things, but resides also in the abiotic elements of natural ecosystems – indeed, the importance of soil, air and water both for direct human utilisation and in relation to the maintenance of ecological processes generally can hardly be overstated.

The location of inherent value is more complex. From an aesthetic point of view, such value may reside in any entity capable of being the subject of sensual appreciation. Clearly, plants and animals may satisfy this criterion, either individually or collectively, though the emphasis in the latter case is likely to fall upon aesthetically appreciable assemblages (notably flocks, herds, landscapes and vistas), rather than upon ecologically significant collectivities such as species, communities or ecosystems. Once again, such value is not restricted to living entities, but extends to inanimate features of the landscape, including mountains, lakes and rivers, and even to transient or intangible elements such as clouds, sunsets and rainbows. Where inherent value derives from cultural or religious considerations, the entities which exhibit it can only be identified empirically, though individual plants and animals again seem likely candidates, albeit often as representatives of their kind.

In all these cases, however, it will obviously be impossible to preserve the anthropocentrically valued elements in isolation, without a firm commitment to the conservation of species, ecosystems and natural processes generally.

b) Intrinsic value

Most complex of all, however, is the question of the precise locus of intrinsic value. As this concept is defined to mean the value which an entity possesses of itself, for itself, it is plain that it postulates an entity of a rather special kind, since, while a mountain or a rainbow might be said to be valuable *in* or *of* itself, it is unlikely to be judged to have value *for* itself. Fortunately, the process by which such entities may be identified has been the subject of extensive philosophical analysis.

i) Organisms

The Australian philosopher Freya Mathews,[38] for example, has argued that autopoietic entities have value for themselves precisely because they are 'self-realising' – i.e. they function in accordance with their own, internally generated, biological programme, or *telos*: 'A self-realizing being . . . is one which through its nature, defines a self-interest. What happens to it matters because it is actively seeking to preserve its own integrity, its identity.'[39] Plainly, the prime exemplar of self-realisation is the individual organism, which characteristically 'satisfies its own energy requirements, grows, repairs or renews its own tissues and reproduces itself'.[40] By contrast, inanimate features of the environment, such as air, rocks or pools of water, cannot satisfy this definition, since they do not *function* so much as merely *exist*, and do not actively strive to do anything, least of all perpetuate themselves. Even mechanical devices and similar artefacts, such as bicycles, computers, or guided missiles, which might appear to embody a purpose, do not in reality exhibit or pursue any goals of their own, since their purpose is superimposed from outside by their human creators. According to Mathews,

> Organisms differ from such systems in as much as they do embody their purpose in themselves; for an organism, to exist is to possess self-interest.

[38] Mathews, *supra* n. 2. [39] Ibid., p. 103. [40] Ibid., p. 98.

> Unlike the machine, which can exist as a durable, material structure independently of fulfilling the purpose for which it is made, the existence of an organism coincides with its purpose, for its purpose is to exist.[41]

Similar arguments have been embraced by other environmental ethicists, amongst whom the intrinsic value of individual organisms is widely recognised.[42] Yet this claim has not gone completely unchallenged, and the case has been made for the recognition of such value at both higher and lower levels of biological organisation.

ii) Genes

Thus the rapid development in recent decades of the disciplines of molecular biology and genetics has caused many scientists to focus their attention at the level of the gene, rather than the organism, with some specifically deprecating the adoption of any outlook which

> overstates the importance of individuals in the hierarchy of life ... An individual's relevance is in its Darwinian fitness, its capacity to transmit its genes to the next generation ... When considered across generations, individuals are little more than temporary vesicles that express and replicate genes.[43]

From this perspective, even humans may be considered mere 'survival machines – robot vehicles blindly programmed to preserve the selfish molecules known as genes'.[44]

Yet this gene-centred view of life, associated particularly with the biologist Richard Dawkins, has also attracted much criticism,[45] and it may be that the heyday of belief in the causal significance of *individual* genes is now passing. Genes are not, in reality, selfish in anything but the most extended metaphorical sense,[46] and it is only in the specialised

[41] Ibid., p. 101. There is, of course, no suggestion that this purpose need be conscious.

[42] See especially P. Taylor, 'The Ethics of Respect for Nature', in Hargrove, *supra* n. 2; the other works there cited, and the chapters by Naess and Sessions, Rodman and Rothenberg in A. Drengson and Y. Inoue (eds.), *The Deep Ecology Movement* (North Atlantic Books, 1995).

[43] R. Vrijenhoek, 'Natural Processes, Individuals and Units of Conservation', in B. G. Norton et al., *Ethics on the Ark* (Smithsonian Institution Press, 1995).

[44] R. Dawkins, *The Selfish Gene* (Oxford University Press, rev. ed., 1989), Preface.

[45] See, e.g., Rose, *supra* n. 12; G. Dover, 'Anti-Dawkins', in H. Rose and S. Rose (eds.), *Alas Poor Darwin* (Vintage, 2001); S. J. Gould, 'Evolution of Organisms', in C. A. R. Boyd and D. Noble (eds.), *The Logic of Life* (Oxford University Press, 1993); L. Moss, *What Genes Can't Do* (MIT Press, 2004).

[46] Even the metaphor itself is scarcely ideal: C. Tudge, *The Engineer in the Garden* (Pimlico, 1993), at p. 111.

environment of the cell in which it is embedded that DNA can actually perform its function of replication.[47] Furthermore, the essential concept of the gene is still surprisingly problematic, resisting easy definition.[48] Finally, opinions differ as to whether genes are actually necessary for life at all,[49] or have ever existed as independent entities.[50] It is, however, common ground that they have not done so for at least 500 million years,[51] opting instead to 'swarm in huge colonies' in the form of organisms.[52] These are, moreover, not mere passive reflections of particular patterns of genes,[53] but dynamic entities which 'influence their own destiny in interesting, complex and comprehensible ways'.[54] All these considerations are therefore said to demand the urgent rehabilitation of the concept of organism in evolutionary biology.[55]

Dawkins himself long ago conceded that 'there really is something pretty impressive about individual organisms',[56] and has also emerged as an articulate advocate of the extension of moral considerability from humans to members of other species.[57] Accordingly, there seems to be no scientific reason to displace organisms from the central place they have been accorded within many philosophical theories of intrinsic value. As far as genes themselves are concerned, however, the case may as yet be regarded as unproven.

iii) Species

Given the strong emphasis upon holism in almost all ecological theories, a further challenge to the moral primacy of organisms comes from the higher levels of biological organisation, namely species and ecosystems. Rolston, for example, has called for recognition of the intrinsic value of the species, as a

47 Rose, *supra* n. 12, pp. 254–5.

48 See P. R. Sloan (ed.), *Controlling Our Destinies* (University of Notre Dame Press, 2000), Preface; Moss, *supra* n. 45, Chapter 1; A. Woolfson, *An Intelligent Person's Guide to Genetics* (Duckworth Overlook, 2004), p. 18.

49 See, e.g., A. Woolfson, *Life without Genes* (HarperCollins, 2000).

50 Cf. Dawkins, who speaks (*supra* n. 44, at p. 19) of them once 'floating loose in the sea', with those who doubt that there ever was 'a self-sufficient, naked gene on the beach'. C. Wills and J. Bada, *The Spark of Life* (Oxford University Press, 2000), p. 130.

51 D. Noble and C. A. R. Boyd, 'The Challenge of Integrative Physiology', in Boyd and Noble, *supra* n. 45, p. 5.

52 Dawkins, *supra* n. 44, p. 19.

53 Rose, *supra* n. 12, p. 306.

54 Gould, *supra* n. 45, p. 37.

55 Ibid.

56 R. Dawkins, *The Extended Phenotype* (Oxford University Press, 1982), p. 250.

57 See, e.g., his 'Gaps in the Mind', in P. Cavalieri and P. Singer (ed.), *The Great Ape Project* (Fourth Estate, 1993).

> level of biological identity reasserted genetically over time . . . The species line is the *vital* living system, the whole, of which individual organisms are the essential parts. The species defends a particular form of life, pursuing a pathway through the world, resisting death (extinction), by regeneration maintaining a normative identity over time. The value resides in the dynamic form . . .[58]

Yet however attractive this view may initially appear,[59] it is open to serious objections. As Ferré has rightly pointed out,[60]

> species do not literally . . . 'use' individuals, 'defend' a form of life or 'resist' extinction. Particular organisms defend their lives, and in so doing enhance the possibility that future organisms like them will continue enjoying the good of their kind. Species, however, do not defend themselves. To say they do commits . . . the fallacy of 'misplaced concreteness'.[61]

Mathews agrees that species are abstract rather than concrete entities, classes rather than systems, and that 'their continuity of form is the *outcome* of the strivings of individual organisms' rather than of the species itself.[62] Species, therefore, do not possess intrinsic value.

iv) Ecosystems

Where ecosystems are concerned, there is again widespread disagreement. In particular, the intrinsic value exhibited by individual organisms might also be recognised in ecosystems if, as some ecologists believe, it is appropriate to think of ecosystems as a kind of 'super-organism'. According to Rolston,

> An ecosystem generates a spontaneous order that envelops and produces the richness, beauty, integrity and dynamic stability of the component parts. Though these organized interdependencies are loose in comparison with the tight connections within an organism, all these metabolisms are as vitally linked as are liver and heart. The equilibrating ecosystem is not merely push–pull forces. It is an equilibrating of values.[63]

[58] H. Rolston III, 'Value in Nature and the Nature of Value', in R. Attfield and A. Belsey (eds.), *Philosophy and the Natural Environment* (Cambridge University Press, 1994), p. 21, original emphasis.
[59] See further Eckersley, *supra* n. 13, p. 61.
[60] F. Ferré, 'Highlights and Connections', in Attfield and Belsey, *supra* n. 58, p. 229.
[61] This concept is attributed to A. N. Whitehead, *The Function of Reason* (1929; Beacon Press ed., 1971).
[62] Mathews, *supra* n. 2, pp. 179–80, original emphasis. See further Attfield, *supra* n. 2, pp. 150–1.
[63] Rolston, *supra* n. 58, p. 23.

Mathews offers qualified support for the idea that ecosystems possess intrinsic value, largely on the basis that '*by their own efforts*, they procure the energy for their self-maintenance'.[64] Others remain unconvinced, however,[65] generally on the grounds that an ecosystem 'does not have the integrated unity that one expects from a true system'.[66] Even Rolston ultimately seems reluctant to label the 'systemic' value manifested by ecosystems as 'intrinsic', though he is adamant that it is foundational, in the sense that no intrinsic values could exist without it. This is undeniable, but equally consistent with the hypothesis that ecosystems are of instrumental value to the organisms which inhabit them. Further doubts regarding the possession of intrinsic value by ecosystems relate to problems of identification and demarcation: how is it to be determined precisely where one ecosystem ends and another begins? Such uncertainty is arguably less problematic, however, with respect to the biosphere as a whole, to which 'deep' ecologists are certainly inclined to ascribe intrinsic value.[67] Yet the objection regarding looseness of organisation remains. Attfield concludes,

> Certainly everything which is of value . . . is located within the biosphere, and the systems of the biosphere are necessary for the protection of all these creatures. But that does not give the biosphere or its systems intrinsic value. Rather, it shows them to have instrumental value, since what is of value in its own right is causally dependent on them.[68]

Given this divergence of views regarding the degree of integrated unity which ecosystems exhibit, by comparison with that of truly autopoietic entities, they must be regarded as at best contentious candidates for recognition as repositories of intrinsic value.

c) *Practical implications*

The discussion above suggests that intrinsic value resides primarily in individual organisms, and arguably in ecosystems, but not in genes or species. Yet it might be objected that any value theory which accords

[64] Mathews, *supra* n. 2, pp. 129–35, original emphasis.
[65] Attfield, *supra* n. 2, Chapter 8. [66] E. Mayr, *This Is Biology* (Belknap, 1997), p. 222.
[67] See A. Naess, 'The Shallow and the Deep, Long-Range Ecology Movement' (1973) 16 *Inquiry* 95; W. Devall and G. Sessions, *Deep Ecology: Living as if Nature Mattered* (Gibbs Smith, 1985); Drengson and Inoue, *supra* n. 42.
[68] Attfield, *supra* n. 2, p. 159.

pride of place to individual organisms rather than species flies in the face of all contemporary conservation policy, which is targeted almost exclusively at the higher levels of biological organisation, with little overt concern for the fate of individuals. It is therefore important to explain why such an objection would be mistaken. At the heart of this issue lies the recognition that the intrinsic value of individual organisms manifests itself in two distinct, albeit related, forms. Specifically, each organism embodies both a *good-of-its-own* and a *good-of-its-kind*. Although both expressions are widely utilised in the literature, they are, unfortunately, not always clearly distinguished.[69]

Essentially, the good-of-its-kind of any organism embraces those aspects of its nature that are shared with all others of its kind, regardless of their location in space and time. The concept of a 'kind' for this purpose equates most readily with that of the species, though it is also exemplified in a progressively more generalised sense at each of the higher taxonomic categories of genus, family, order, class and so on. Ultimately, all living things are 'of a kind' in the sense that they share the characteristic of autopoiesis, which, as seen above, represents the source of their intrinsic value. Nevertheless, the species represents the closest and arguably most meaningful manifestation of kinship. Any traits which are common to all conspecifics must *ex hypothesi* be capable of transmission across the generations, and, since it is now accepted that characteristics acquired during the lifetime of an organism cannot usually be so transmitted,[70] it follows that the 'essence' of each species[71] is determined principally by genetics and perpetuated by reproduction.[72] This conclusion, indeed, faithfully reflects the basic conception of the species as a reproductively isolated aggregate of populations of individuals.[73] Accordingly, the particular form of intrinsic value encapsulated

[69] See, e.g., Rolston, *supra* n. 2, at p. 172.

[70] The contrary theory is associated particularly with the nineteenth-century biologist Lamarck.

[71] Strictly, since even conspecifics are not genetically identical, it may be preferable to think in terms of a 'cluster' of genetically derived traits, a broad array of which will be exhibited by each individual: R. A. Wilson, *Genes and the Agents of Life* (Cambridge University Press, 2005).

[72] Emerging theories do, however, allow for the trans-generational transmission of certain traits not only by genetic, but also by epigenetic, cultural or symbolic means. See, e.g., E. Jablonka and M. J. Lamb, *Evolution in Four Dimensions* (MIT Press, 2005).

[73] This is known as the *biological* species concept (there are several competing definitions). See generally Mayr, *supra* n. 66, Chapter 7.

by the notion of the good-of-its-kind must derive principally from the *genotype* of each organism.[74]

The good-of-its-own of any organism constitutes a broader concept, however. The fact that each member of a sexually reproducing species is genetically unique provides the foundation for the individuality underlying this good,[75] but is by no means the exclusive factor. While its genetic make-up undoubtedly establishes the parameters for its development as an individual, that will also be profoundly conditioned by the process of continuous interaction with its environment, making each organism much more than the sum total of its genes. Thus the availability of light, warmth, shelter, nutrition and social support may effectively determine whether, and to what extent, individual organisms ultimately flourish. Indeed, the incidence of such factors at critical phases of development can decisively influence such crucial features as gender, body shape and sociability itself in some species.[76] In addition, the life experiences of many animals are captured in the form of learning processes which profoundly affect the path of their individual development. The significance of such matters for present purposes suggests that the good-of-its-own which each organism exhibits corresponds more closely to its *phenotype*.[77]

The relationship between these two manifestations of intrinsic value is by no means straightforward. The good-of-its-kind of each organism is reflected in a series of broad, genetically determined characteristics, dispositions and potentials, whereas the good-of-its-own manifests itself in its specific attributes and realised capacities, as shaped environmentally. Thus the propensity to form social relationships which typifies many species forms part of the good-of-their-kind, whereas the good-of-its-own includes also the benefits derived by an individual from relationships actually formed. Equally, the capacity to feel pain forms part of the good-of-its-kind of any sentient species, since it provides an adaptive mechanism whereby animals may protect themselves from

[74] The genotype is the totality of the genes contained within the cells of an organism.

[75] With the exception of clones, such as identical twins, which develop from a single fertilised egg.

[76] For examples, see M. Hall and T. Halliday, *Behaviour and Evolution* (Open University, 1992), pp. 72, 117.

[77] That is, the 'totality of the characteristics of an individual, resulting from the interaction of the genotype with the environment' (Mayr, *supra* n. 66, Glossary). The phenotype accordingly includes all aspects of an organism's morphology, physiology and behaviour.

harm. At the same time, the interests of the individual obviously lie in avoiding pain as much as possible, at least if there are no important lessons to be learned from it.

Furthermore, when determining the practical measures needed to protect these various forms of value, a clear distinction is apparent. Although the good-of-its-kind is a property of individual organisms, it is essentially shared by all representatives of that kind, and may therefore (indeed, *can only*) be maintained in perpetuity by ensuring the survival of the species (or higher taxon) in question. The fate of individuals as such recedes in importance, because the good-of-their-kind is perpetuated through reproduction, and passed on to members of future generations. In the case of species which are at risk of extinction, however, the fate of individuals assumes greater importance, since each one may represent an indispensable vehicle for preserving the good-of-its-kind. In every case, effective conservation will require the maintenance of an adequate population, exhibiting sufficient genetic variation, to guarantee the species' viability in the face of the ever-changing challenges which the environment may present. Equally, attention must be focused upon maintenance of all the natural life-support systems upon which each species is dependent, and this inevitably entails the conservation of *ecosystems* for instrumental reasons, regardless of whether they are themselves regarded as exhibitors of intrinsic value.

Since, however, the intrinsic value of every living thing embraces also the good-of-its-own, rendering each organism morally considerable in its own right, any acceptable normative code must in addition pay due regard to the protection of individuals for their own sake. This may involve the establishment of appropriate restraints upon the infliction of cruelty, unnecessary suffering or premature death. Obviously, however, this does not require that *all* harm to individuals be prevented; there is, for example, no cause for human intervention in natural ecological processes, such as predation, with a view to eliminating the suffering of prey animals.[78] Furthermore, even in the case of purely anthropogenic harm, it is important to note that intrinsic value affords only a prima-facie claim to protection. Accordingly, the need to defend such value may be overridden by other considerations, including the respective needs

[78] Amongst the more obvious reasons for avoiding such interventions are (i) that they would, without justification, merely privilege the interests of prey species over those of predators; (ii) that they would subvert the processes by which natural selection, over time, shapes and refines the good of both kinds and (iii) that in any event we lack the expertise and resources to do so successfully on any systematic basis.

and interests of humans and other life forms. Everything therefore depends upon the relative weighting to be given to these various interests.[79] At the very least, however, a moral code should be taken to require controls upon the *wanton* infliction of cruelty.

Seen in this light, intrinsic-value theory may pose less of a challenge to current policies regarding the conservation of species and ecosystems, though it may well require that greater attention be paid to the needs and interests of individual organisms than in the past.

d) The locus of value in international law

Given the philosophical complexities surrounding the question of locus of value, it is scarcely surprising that this question has not been explored in any depth within the international legal system. For most practical purposes, relatively little turns upon it, as the key response required of states – the conservation of species, ecosystems and basic ecological processes – remains the same regardless of the precise view taken on this underlying ethical issue. Nevertheless, some endorsement of the points made above is occasionally evident in the detailed formulation of conservation obligations. As regards instrumental values, for example, the Convention on International Trade in Endangered Species, notwithstanding its title, makes clear throughout its substantive provisions that trade is actually conducted in 'specimens' of such species,[80] i.e. in individual plants or animals or their parts and derivatives.

By far the greatest uncertainty, however, concerns the locus of intrinsic value, since here the relevant instruments are largely uninformative. The Bern Convention, for example, rather vaguely attributes intrinsic value to 'wild flora and fauna'.[81] The World Charter for Nature's demand for 'nature' to be respected is scarcely more precise, though the preambular assertion that 'to accord other *organisms* such recognition, man must be guided by a moral code of action'[82] might be read, consistently with the philosophical arguments outlined above, to demand some concern at least for the fate of individuals.[83] This is certainly evident in the revised version of the World Conservation Strategy, *Caring for the Earth*, which elaborates these underlying moral principles in the following terms:

[79] See Section 4 of this chapter below. [80] The first such reference is in Article 2(1).
[81] Fourth preambular paragraph. [82] Fourth preambular paragraph (emphasis added).
[83] Cf., however, the unofficial commentary to the Charter: W. E. Burhenne and W. A. Irwin, *World Charter for Nature* (Erich Schmidt, 2nd rev. ed., 1986), p. 136.

> Every form of life warrants respect independently of its worth to people. Human development should not threaten the integrity of nature or the survival of other species. People should treat all creatures decently, and protect them from cruelty, avoidable suffering and unnecessary killing.

Although the Strategy itself has no legally binding effects, there are many examples of formal treaty provisions which require the protection of individual organisms within particular regulatory contexts. What is more controversial is whether any universal principle to that effect has yet emerged within the public international legal system, a question which is explored more fully in Chapter 20 below.

Even legal instruments which refer expressly to intrinsic value shed little light on the specific question of locus. The Antarctic Environmental Protocol, despite recognising the intrinsic value of the Antarctic ecosystem, confusingly adds that this *includes* certain other values which are plainly instrumental or inherent. The leading treaty in the field, the Biodiversity Convention, is scarcely clearer. The preamble actually ascribes intrinsic value to 'biological diversity', even though 'diversity' as such would not seem to be a 'self' capable of exhibiting such value. Possibly this should be understood as a form of shorthand, signifying that intrinsic value resides in all those entities the diversity of which the Convention seeks to secure. Since this is defined to include diversity 'within species, between species and of ecosystems',[84] the CBD might be thought to recognise such value at all the major levels of biological organisation – namely ecosystems, species, organisms and genes. On the other hand, the CBD definition does refer initially to 'the variability of living *organisms* from all sources',[85] possibly intending to confirm the primacy of individual plants and animals in that regard. Plainly the matter cannot be taken to have been resolved in any definitive sense. The Addis Ababa Guidelines do, however, call for the promotion of 'more efficient, ethical and humane use of components of biodiversity', thereby echoing the fundamental principle laid down in *Caring for the Earth*, and referred to above.

4. The measure of value

The fact that several distinct types of value exist, often concurrently, in so many diverse entities, generates the need for reliable methods of comparison and quantification. Thus, at the broad policy level, pursuit of

[84] Article 2. [85] Ibid., emphasis added.

sustainable development will entail the continual determination of priorities between economic and environmental considerations: should mining or logging activities, for example, be authorised in areas which constitute prime habitat for endangered species?[86] At the other end of the spectrum, more precise financial valuations of nature may be required in circumstances where compensation is sought in litigation concerning unlawful environmental damage – an oil spill, for example, resulting in harm to coastal ecosystems. Some sense of the measure of value lost may also be reflected in criminal penalties or administrative charges exacted in respect of environmental harm.[87] Needless to say, great controversy attaches to all these questions.

a) Economic valuation

One possible response lies in the approach adopted by economists to questions of valuation generally:[88] i.e. that the value of any given item is determined by the amount that people would be prepared (i) to pay in order to acquire or preserve it or (ii) to accept by way of compensation for its loss or diminution. The choice between these two methods, known respectively as WTP (willingness to pay) and WTAC (willingness to accept compensation), is determined essentially by the current incidence of property rights in the item in question. Where commodities are bought and sold on the market, as in the case of wildlife specimens traded commercially, an indication of their values can be obtained from an examination of market prices. In many cases, however, the utility that people derive from the environment – from visiting beaches or walking in the countryside, for example – may not be directly expressed in terms of commodity prices, yet they may certainly feel worse off if the beaches are contaminated by pollution or the fields carved up by motorways. Many people, moreover, value the environment for reasons other than immediate self-interest, and will pay to preserve a

[86] The apparent incommensurability of such considerations may be resolved by conducting a detailed cost–benefit analysis to inform the policy process – see Pearce and Moran, *supra* n. 8, Chapter 3 – but this will only prove reliable if the methodology is sufficiently robust to capture all the various elements of value involved.

[87] Though here other factors, such as the defendant's state of mind and the incidence of previous infractions, may intrude.

[88] For an accessible introduction, see Hanley, *supra* n. 8. For fuller treatments, see Pearce and Moran, *supra* n. 8; L. Tacconi, *Biodiversity and Ecological Economics* (2000); J. Rietbergen-McCracken and H. Abaza (eds.), *Environmental Valuation* (2000).

pristine area (Antarctica, for example) or an endangered species regardless of any expectation of direct personal benefit. Due account should therefore also be taken of these *non-use* or *existence* values in the quantification process.[89]

Accordingly, economists have devised various methods for valuing non-market goods generally on the basis of *stated* or *revealed preferences*. One well-tried example of the former is *contingent valuation*, which might involve, for example, a survey to establish how much people would be prepared to pay to avoid future environmental disasters, such as the contamination of rivers. For this purpose, the cost might be envisaged, say, in the form of a hypothetical increase in water bills to cover the expense of purification. Yet there are obvious disadvantages in relying on mere assertions of hypothetical willingness to pay, and many economists accordingly place greater emphasis on *revealed preferences*, which are grounded in actual behaviour. Established approaches include the *travel cost method*, which assesses how much people have actually expended in visiting particular places, such as beaches or wildlife reserves, and the extent to which their willingness to pay is affected by any deterioration in environmental quality. Another method is *hedonic pricing*, in which environmental degradation may be measured, for example, in terms of its effect upon house prices in the locality.

Imaginative as these various approaches undoubtedly are within the context of their own discipline, and important as it is that they be pursued, the overall impression generated by economic approaches to environmental valuation is that they display considerable shortcomings.[90] First, there is often considerable uncertainty regarding both the choice of valuation methods and the precise details of their application. Controversy may be evident even at the primary stage of selection between WTP and WTAC: the environment, unfortunately, does not fit neatly into established concepts of property ownership. A significant minority of people, indeed, refuse on principle to attribute a monetary value to environmental deterioration, usually on account of 'rights-based beliefs which are at odds with the utilitarian views implicit in the economic concept of value'.[91] Furthermore, any argument based upon willingness to pay inevitably has to take account of ability to do so, with

[89] Such elements of course reflect the *inherent* value of nature, in the terminology discussed above.

[90] See generally Gillespie, *supra* n. 1, Chapter 3.

[91] Hanley, *supra* n. 8, p. 37. See further Section 2(b) above.

the consequence that the preferences of the affluent are likely to be accorded priority, given their ability simply to outbid their competitors.[92] Even if such inequity must be tolerated, it is far from clear that existing methods are capable of capturing all aspects of environmental degradation. This problem is particularly acute in cases of disruption of fundamental ecological functions, such as climate change, where either the technical means to calculate the loss or the political willingness to exact payment for it may be lacking.[93] Finally, it is generally conceded that economic valuation, being entirely anthropocentric in orientation, cannot capture intrinsic values.

In view of these considerations, economic methodology should probably be restricted to an ancillary role in the valuation of nature and the determination of the specific priorities demanded by the principle of sustainable development. While it might be regarded as providing prima-facie guidance with respect to anthropocentric forms of value, a more comprehensive assessment may need to draw upon broader philosophical approaches.

b) Philosophical approaches to valuation

Here again, however, clear answers prove elusive. First of all, the very fact that the notion of intrinsic value – that which an entity possesses of itself, *for itself* – is auto-referential seems to exclude the possibility of any common currency in accordance with which such values could be compared. Each manifestation of such value is by definition total, and the respective totalities are incommensurable. Yet the practical necessity of making the various kinds of evaluation highlighted above remains inescapable, and some means must be found to facilitate this process.

Essentially, two main approaches are evident from the literature, sometimes labelled the *qualified* and *unqualified* perspectives on intrinsic value.[94] The former draws a distinction between moral *standing*, which is an inevitable concomitant of such value, and moral *significance*,[95] which concerns the relative weight to be attached to the interests of those with standing. On this view, intrinsic value is seen as being

[92] Gillespie, *supra* n. 1, pp. 54–7. [93] Hanley, *supra* n. 8, p. 33.
[94] T. Hayward, *Ecological Thought* (Polity, 1994), p. 65.
[95] Goodpaster, *supra* n. 11; Attfield, *supra* n. 2, Chapter 8.

distributed differentially throughout the natural world,[96] the criterion most commonly proposed for determining the quantum of value exhibited by any given organism being the *complexity* of the entity in question.[97] Accordingly,

> If the value of a being resides in its self-maintaining activity, then the measure of its intrinsic value would seem to be the degree of its power of self-maintenance . . . [which] is in general linked with degree of complexity. Complexity of organization in a living system tends to indicate the capacity of the organism in question to survive in a wider range of environmental conditions than less complex organisms could accommodate. It tends to indicate the capacity of an organism to utilize resources, make the most of opportunities and get out of trouble.[98]

On this view, grass, for example, 'may have some modicum of intrinsic value . . . but not very much',[99] since the range of responses available to plants is decidedly limited.

While this approach has powerful intuitive appeal – not least because it provides a plausible basis for prioritising human interests over those of other species – it is open to serious objections. First, it is redolent of outmoded concepts such as the *Scala natura*, or Great Chain of Being, which saw humanity as occupying the higher rungs of an evolutionary ladder heading towards heavenly perfection. Such notions have, however, been authoritatively dismissed as mere 'snobbery', lacking any basis in biological science.[100] The evolutionary process in truth bears no resemblance to a linear ascent towards greater complexity, and references to 'higher' or 'lower' life forms make little scientific sense.[101] In particular, the power of self-maintenance of every extant life form has by definition proved adequate for its survival to the present, and the future survival prospects of any given species are most unlikely to be dependent on complexity alone, which might just as easily precipitate its

[96] That is, it acknowledges *grades* of value, as well as *types*. 'The universe is full of intrinsic values . . . [which] all deserve ethical respect *to the degrees appropriate to the intensity of the values concerned*': F. Ferré, 'Personalistic Organicism: Paradox or Paradigm?', in Attfield and Belsey, *supra* n. 58, p. 72 (emphasis added).

[97] See, e.g., P. Schaber (ed.), *The Dignity of Non-human Organisms*, Special Issue, (2000) 13(1/2) *Journal of Agricultural and Environmental Ethics*.

[98] Mathews, *supra* n. 2, p. 122. Note that Mathews is merely explaining, rather than endorsing, this approach.

[99] Ferré, *supra* n. 96, p. 69.

[100] R. Dawkins, *The Blind Watchmaker* (Penguin, 1988), p. 261.

[101] M. Midgley, *Beast and Man* (Routledge, rev. ed., 1995), Chapter 7; S. J. Gould, *Life's Grandeur* (Jonathan Cape, 1996), Chapter 2.

downfall.[102] After all, the great apes represent some of the most complex life forms on the planet, but they are all under threat of extinction in the wild. Indeed, whether judged in terms of species longevity or diversity, current gross biomass or the likelihood of surviving the multitude of environmental changes or catastrophes which might conceivably occur, a plausible claim may be made that it is in reality the *simplest* life forms – e.g. bacteria – which are the most successful.[103]

A second, 'unqualified', perspective on intrinsic value has therefore emerged. This 'biocentric egalitarianism' posits the equal worth of all life forms;[104] on this view, humans are merely members of Earth's community of life, holding their membership on similar terms to all other species.[105] The key distinction between humans and others resides in the realms not of *value*, but rather of *moral agency*, which generates the uniquely human responsibility to ensure that the equal worth of other species is duly respected. Inter-specific conflicts of interest are therefore to be resolved by reference to the importance of the particular interests at issue, and the seriousness of the harm that threatens them, rather than by assuming that any one species (humans included) is entitled to automatic priority over others.[106] This approach may well appear less palatable to many, although the possibility that this is attributable simply to 'irrational bias in our own favor'[107] certainly cannot be excluded.

In the absence of any current consensus on these matters, an approach should be sought which encapsulates the major strengths of each theory, while avoiding either impracticability or serious internal inconsistency. Clearly, the task is formidable, but it may help to recall the distinction drawn earlier between the good-of-its-own and the good-of-its-kind which each organism exhibits. As regards the good-of-its-kind, the egalitarian approach has much to commend it, since no plausible reason is apparent for attributing priority to the survival of any one species over any other: each has contrived to establish an ecological niche for itself, and each forms a unique part of the overall web of relationships which collectively comprise the biosphere. The moral commitment should therefore be to strive to ensure the survival of *every* species, at least where such threats as they face are essentially anthropogenic in nature. Even from this egalitarian

[102] To put it another way, an 'increase in immediate "fitness" . . . may be achieved by losing eyes or legs as well as by gaining them'. J. Maynard Smith and E. Szathmary, *The Major Transitions in Evolution* (W. H. Freeman, 1995), p. 4.

[103] Gould, *supra* n. 101, pp. 175–95; Margulis and Sagan, *supra* n. 12, Chapter 1.

[104] Hargrove, *supra* n. 2, p. xvii. [105] Taylor, *supra* n. 42, pp. 105ff.

[106] See generally Varner, *supra* n. 2, Chapter 4. [107] Taylor, *supra* n. 42, p. 115.

perspective, however, a plausible case could be made for according conservation priority to life forms which embody the *good of a greater kind* (i.e. a higher biological taxon) than that of the species. Since the extermination of Steller's sea cow in the eighteenth century, for example, the dugong (*Dugong dugon*) has been the sole representative of the entire biological family Dugongidae, so securing *its* survival might justifiably be favoured over that of every single one of the innumerable species of beetle.

Of course, conservation decisions in the real world have to take account of all forms of value, not merely the intrinsic variety, and human attention will doubtless continue to be drawn in practice towards the conservation of especially charismatic or commercially valuable species, as well as those which perform keystone functions for the ecosystems in which they are found. One key virtue of intrinsic-value theory, however, is that it provides a sound basis for arguing that the good uniquely embodied in each individual life form deserves equal consideration, thereby providing a counterweight to these powerful anthropocentric pressures.

When it comes to evaluating the good-of-its-own of each individual organism, however, the strictly egalitarian approach seems intuitively more difficult to sustain. Attributing the same degree of moral significance to an amoeba as to a dolphin or a human simply seems inappropriate, even if that might ultimately help to curb our more exploitative tendencies. A partial answer is that even under a notionally egalitarian approach, whereby the *quantity* of value of each individual organism is treated as identical regardless of species, the *quality* of that value should be seen as different. That is, more care and attention would inevitably be required to enable a complex organism such as a human being to flourish in accordance with its nature than would be necessary in the case of a gnat. For the simplest organisms, indeed, where advanced consciousness is ostensibly lacking, and the 'life plan' of each revolves essentially around simple self-perpetuation, that interest will largely have been secured through assiduous attention to the objective of preserving the good-of-its-kind, as explained above. In the case of sentient species, by contrast, the avoidance of pain and suffering and the advancement of welfare generally become additional considerations to be taken into account. Precise quantification of the intrinsic value of wild-living organisms in *financial* terms remains a formidable task, however, and difficult to conceive on any basis other than a rough-and-ready tariff system of the kind encountered in some domestic legal systems.[108]

[108] See Bowman and Boyle, *supra* n. 8, esp. Chapters 4, 12 and 13.

In the case of ecosystems, there are fewer psychological obstacles to acceptance of equal value, and conservation policy is duly geared towards the preservation of representative examples of all the major habitat types. Even here, however, awareness-raising programmes have occasionally proved necessary to counteract traditionally unfavourable perceptions of ecosystems such as bogs and swamps. Where precise quantification is required, some assessment of the economic value of ecosystem services may be possible: one recent estimate of the benefits provided by wetland ecosystems globally, for example, amounted to US$14 trillion per annum.[109] Usually, however, the evaluation of damage caused to ecosystems will be assessed by reference to the cost of remediation, in respect of which there is now a substantial body of literature.[110] Focusing at the level of the ecosystem might indeed be more appropriate in the case of incidents involving environmental damage on a macro scale, insofar as assessment of the harm to particular species or individual organisms might prove impractical.[111] Plainly, these questions are extremely challenging, and no clear consensus has yet emerged as to their precise answers.

c) *The measure of value in international law*

Not surprisingly, such issues have not been extensively explored in international law. There has, however, been a gradual extension to all forms of life of recognition in principle of their moral and legal significance. Undoubtedly, there has been less practical emphasis in the past on floral species and fungi, and little or none on micro-organisms, but the Biodiversity Convention makes no such distinction itself, referring instead to the need to preserve the variability of organisms generally. The World Charter for Nature states categorically that 'the population levels of *all* life forms . . . must be at least sufficient for their survival',[112] though this does not, of course, represent a hard-law obligation. Egalitarianism evidently has its limits, however, as the preamble to the Stockholm Declaration specifically affirms that 'Of all things in the world, *people* are the most precious'.[113]

[109] See Chapter 13 below.

[110] For a recent introduction, see J. Van Andel and J. Aronson (eds.), *Restoration Ecology* (Blackwell, 2006).

[111] Note here the Saudi Arabian claim to the UN Compensation Commission discussed in the section immediately following.

[112] Principle 2 (emphasis added). [113] Preambular Paragraph 5 (emphasis added).

This does not mean that immediate human interests are invariably to prevail over those of other species, however. Indeed, the statement cited actually appears in a paragraph recognising the need to control human numbers,[114] so evidently there can be too much even of the best thing! Furthermore, some treaty provisions do expressly prioritise ecological requirements over the economic and recreational interests of humans.[115] Finally, even where treaties permit the culling of endangered species in defence of fundamental human interests, it must often be established that this will not be detrimental to the ultimate survival of the species concerned.[116]

The presently underdeveloped condition of international law is particularly apparent in respect of the quantification of damage in environmental disputes,[117] since principles of state responsibility are rarely invoked in this context, and, even where claims have been pursued, they have usually concentrated upon the harm suffered to familiar human interests.[118] Support for the actionability of harm to the environment itself can be found in the framing of certain international claims,[119] and implicitly in the dicta of international courts and tribunals,[120] Sands suggests,[121] but unambiguous and authoritative confirmation has until recently been lacking. In recognition of these uncertainties, both the Stockholm and Rio Declarations called for further development of the law regarding liability and compensation for environmental damage.[122]

114 Principle 8 of the Rio Declaration likewise recognises the need 'to promote appropriate demographic policies'.

115 The Bern Convention, Article 2. For discussion, see Chapter 10 and, with regard to parallel provisions in EU instruments, Chapter 7 below.

116 Bern Convention, Article 9; CMS, Article 3(5).

117 See generally Bowman and Boyle, *supra* n. 8.

118 Consider, e.g., the *Trail Smelter* and *Gut Dam* arbitrations, (1939) 33 *AJIL* 182; (1941) 35 *AJIL* 684; and (1968) 8 *ILM* 118.

119 E.g. those of Australia and New Zealand in the *Nuclear Tests* cases (1974) *ICJ Rep* 253, 457, and Nauru in the *Phosphate Lands Case* (1993) ICJ Rep 322. Neither claim was ultimately resolved by the ICJ, the former being declared moot and the latter settled by agreement.

120 E.g. the *Lac Lanoux* arbitration (1957) 24 *ILR* 101, and the *Gabcikovo-Nagymaros* case (1997) *ICJ Rep* 7.

121 P. Sands, *Principles of International Environmental Law* (Cambridge University Press, 2nd ed., 2003), pp. 877–8.

122 See Principles 22 and 13, respectively; the latter plea extends to national, as well as international, law.

A glimmer of light is cast by the International Law Commission's 2001 Articles on Responsibility of States for Internationally Wrongful Acts,[123] Article 36 of which provides that compensation for international wrongdoing may cover 'any financially assessable damage'. As suggested in the accompanying Commentary, this might in principle include claims for the degradation of an ecosystem or the extinction/diminution of wildlife species,[124] though the proper approach to quantification of such claims is not addressed. What seems increasingly clear, however, is that environmental 'clean-up' costs, or other restoration expenses reasonably incurred, should be recoverable as compensation: this point is endorsed both by state practice regarding the question of liability for damage caused by space objects,[125] and in the awards in respect of environmental loss made by the United Nations Compensation Commission (UNCC), established to process claims concerning damage occasioned by the Iraqi invasion of Kuwait in 1990.[126]

These UNCC awards are, indeed, instructive in several respects. Pursuant to the resolution which established the Commission,[127] a number of substantial claims were made by governments in respect of 'environmental damage and the depletion of natural resources' resulting from the Iraqi action.[128] The panel which processed the claims expressly confirmed that the denial under certain treaty-based regimes of compensation for pure environmental damage lent no support to the contention that such loss was excluded in international law generally.[129] On the other hand, it is not easy to detect unequivocal examples of

[123] Report of the 53rd Session, ILC (2001), GAOR 56th Session, Supp. 10. See further J. Crawford, *The ILC's Articles on State Responsibility: Introduction, Text and Commentaries* (Cambridge, 2002).

[124] Earlier drafts had referred to 'economically assessable' harm, which might more readily have been interpreted to exclude such claims.

[125] On the Canadian claim regarding the disintegration of the Soviet satellite *Cosmos 954* over its territory in 1978, see L. de La Fayette, Chapter 9 in Bowman and Boyle, *supra* n. 8, pp. 171–3. The Soviet government paid Cdn$3 million in compensation, approximately half the sum spent on an environmental clean-up operation.

[126] For details of awards regarding environmental ('F4') claims, which were processed in five instalments, see the UNCC website at www.unog.ch/uncc/reports.htm#_F4; and for discussion, see P. H. Sand, 'Compensation for Environmental Damage from the 1991 Gulf War' (2005) 35 *EPL* 244.

[127] Security Council Resolution 687 (1991).

[128] The former included claims regarding damage to groundwater aquifers, wetlands, rangelands, forests, mangroves and intertidal zones and the latter to loss of fish, water resources, timber and agricultural land.

[129] See, e.g., the *Panel Report* on the 5th instalment, paras. 55–8.

compensation for such harm from amongst its findings. Jordan was awarded almost US$250,000 to finance the reintroduction of threatened ungulates into the wild after its original programme was disrupted by the war, though this sum reflected not the value of the specimens themselves but rather the cost of their reintroduction. Another Jordanian claim, for damage to the Azraq Ramsar site, seemingly included elements of pure environmental loss, but foundered at the stage of proving a causal connection with Iraqi action.[130] A Saudi Arabian claim for US$127 million in respect of the deaths of ninety-three marine mammals and almost 100,000 seabirds as a result of oil spills also failed, partly on causation grounds but also for lack of adequate information on costing.[131] Unfortunately, therefore, the opportunity to quantify a claim for pure environmental harm was missed, though, interestingly, Iraq did concede that the number of animals lost was in principle an appropriate metric for valuation.[132] It also asserted, however, that seabirds were a regional rather than a national resource.[133] The panel suggested that compensation awarded under another head for the development of various shoreline reserves would help to offset the waterfowl losses in question.[134] Another intriguing concession made more than once by Iraq was that ecosystems such as coral reefs do indeed exhibit intrinsic value, though again the implications remained unexplored as the claims in question also failed for lack of proof.[135] Most of the successful claims concerned expenses attributable to the restoration of degraded ecosystems and therefore (while instructive as quantifications of conventional compensation in a novel context)[136] shed little light upon the *terra incognita* of compensating lost intrinsic values. Rather, they illustrate how such questions might in the future be sidestepped, since simply financing a successful restoration programme might ultimately serve to reinstate all the natural values – whether instrumental, inherent or intrinsic – found in degraded ecosystems, provided always that no species has actually become extinct.

130 Ibid., paras. 375–82.

131 Ibid., paras. 650–63. The Saudis had broadly relied on a 1996 guidance document on restocking costs prepared by the US National Oceanic and Atmospheric Administration.

132 Ibid., para. 656. 133 Ibid., para. 654. 134 Ibid., para. 662.

135 See, e.g., the *Panel Reports* on the 4th instalment (Part I), paras. 152–4; and 5th instalment, paras. 386–8.

136 The panel were generally unsympathetic to expensive, 'high-tech' solutions, preferring to reimburse the costs of restoring basic ecosystem functions, and leaving the rest to natural regeneration.

Plainly, these awards arose out of a highly untypical situation. The general reluctance of governments to pursue international claims concerning environmental damage has seen the focus of environmental litigation shift to the domestic level.[137] Here again, however, the law tends to be underdeveloped,[138] with recovery often limited to traditional forms of tort loss, such as personal injury, property damage, and, in some jurisdictions, pure economic loss. Damage to the environment itself is often not actionable at all, so opportunities to ascribe a value to elements of the natural world in their own right scarcely arise. Only rarely, it seems, have national liability regimes been adopted which are potentially, or actually, applicable to such losses.[139]

International law may sometimes impact upon claims before national tribunals, however, typically in situations where the legal principles or procedures to be applied have been specified or influenced by international agreement.[140] In some cases, special funds and institutions have been created to compensate environmental harm. Here again, however, the tendency has been to exclude claims for damage to the environment per se, although a more progressive attitude is occasionally evident and there is certainly a growing trend to allow compensation for the costs of remediation.[141] More promising still is the International Law Commission's recent adoption of Draft Principles on the Allocation of Loss in the Case of Transboundary Harm Arising out of Hazardous Activities.[142] Essentially, these recommend that a strict liability to pay prompt and adequate compensation to victims should be channelled under national law to those in control of the activity that caused the harm. Principle 2(a)(iii) is progressive in envisaging liability for damage to the environment per se,[143] without restriction to the cost of response

137 Note, however, *Pulp Mills* (2010) *ICJRep*, and the *Aerial Herbicide Spraying* case currently before the ICJ.

138 Bowman and Boyle, *supra* n. 8.

139 See, e.g., the chapters concerning the Nordic countries, Poland, Mauritius and Brazil, in ibid.

140 Notable examples include nuclear activities and marine oil pollution. See generally de La Fayette, *supra* n. 125. See further Chapter 21 of this work.

141 For discussion, see Parts V and VI of Ong's chapter in Bowman and Boyle, *supra* n. 8; Sands, *supra* n. 121, pp. 915–22; Birnie, Boyle and Redgwell, *supra* n. 32, pp. 437–40.

142 For current text, with Commentary, see the 2006 ILC Report, GAOR A/61/10, pp. 110–82. For discussion, see Birnie, Boyle and Redgwell, *supra* n. 32, pp. 319–22.

143 Accordingly, Principle 3 expressly indicates that the victims of such harm may include states themselves.

or restoration measures. It remains to be seen what impact, if any, this proposal produces on actual compensation practice.

A further opportunity for elaboration of the legal regime governing the quantification and compensation of harm to wildlife arises out of the process initiated in the year 2000 under Article 14(2) of the Biodiversity Convention,[144] since this enables the matter to be considered in a forum which has conservation as a principal concern.[145] Progress to date has been slow, however, and the outcome cannot yet be predicted with any confidence.[146] The need for further work in this area will be considered at the 10th Meeting of the CoP.[147] A parallel process initiated under the Biosafety Protocol has reached the more advanced stage of a draft operational text for a supplementary protocol, but many issues remain to be resolved.[148]

5. Conclusions

A considerable variety of motivations may be found for the protection of nature, with instrumental, inherent and intrinsic values all widely recognised in philosophical writings. Each of these, moreover, receives some degree of recognition in international law, though the emphasis placed upon them has tended to vary at different times and over different contexts. Less clearly identified for legal purposes are the precise elements of the natural world which exhibit such values, though ethical analysis suggests that the answer may vary as between categories. As regards intrinsic value, autopoietic value theory proposes that it resides primarily in organisms, and possibly in ecosystems, but not in genes or species. The implications of this view for conservation policy are less dramatic than might be supposed, however, since the intrinsic value of each organism embraces not only the good-of-its-own, but also the good-of-its-kind, which cannot be preserved other than through the conservation of its species, and of the ecosystems upon which it is dependent. In fact, the main practical implication of this view lies in the need for greater

[144] Decision V/18 of the CBD CoP.

[145] There is, however, no guarantee that damage to *wildlife* and damage to *biological diversity* will necessarily be treated as identical.

[146] See the CBD Executive Secretary's recent report on *Liability and Redress*, UNEP/CBD/COP/9/20/ Add. 1. See further Chapter 17 below.

[147] Decision IX/23.

[148] See CBD Decisions V/1 and V/18; and Decision BS-IV/12, Annex.

attention to be paid to the wellbeing of individual creatures, a matter which international law has as yet addressed in only a desultory fashion.

A final crucial issue concerns the quantification of such values. While formal assertions of the need to ensure the survival of all life forms may be treated as acknowledgements of universal value in nature, the real test lies in the way such considerations are balanced against human interests. It is, however, in relation to the more precise, financial calculation of environmental values that the greatest difficulty has been encountered. While economic approaches may assist with the determination of anthropocentric values, they fail to capture intrinsic values and tend generally to understate the true cost of environmental damage. Neither national nor international compensation regimes have effectively resolved these issues as yet, and therefore risk exacerbating the problem of environmental degradation, through allowing nature to be treated as a free resource.

Recommended further reading

R. Attfield, *The Ethics of Environmental Concern* (University of Georgia Press, 2nd ed., 1991)

M. J. Bowman and A. E. Boyle (eds.), *Environmental Damage in International and Comparative Law* (Oxford University Press, 2002)

A. Gillespie, *International Environmental Law, Policy and Ethics* (Clarendon, 1997)

A. Light and H. Rolston III (eds.), *Environmental Ethics: An Anthology* (Blackwell, 2003)

F. Mathews, *The Ecological Self* (Routledge, 1991)

R. Nash, *The Rights of Nature* (University of Wisconsin Press, 1989)

D. Pearce and D. Moran, *The Economic Value of Biodiversity* (Earthscan, 1994)

H. Rolston III, *Conserving Natural Value* (Columbia University Press, 1994)

S. Sarkar, *Biodiversity and Environmental Philosophy: An Introduction* (Cambridge University Press, 2005)

Chapter 4

Implementation and enforcement of international wildlife law

1. Introduction

Implementation constitutes a key element in ensuring compliance with international wildlife law.[1] It plays a dominant role in ensuring non-state actors' compliance with international norms, particularly where international obligations have been translated, directly or indirectly, into national law. It may also afford opportunities for non-state actors successfully to challenge national implementation of wildlife law through judicial review – national rules on standing and remedies permitting. Although international wildlife law is less developed than, say, human rights law in terms of individual enforcement of rights through national courts, there is significant case law upon which to draw where courts have invoked, directly or indirectly, general international environmental norms. Although an exhaustive survey of such invocation is beyond the scope of this chapter, it will consider the trends in domestic judicial enforcement, and the role that national courts play in both developing and enforcing international wildlife law. It will also consider the nature of the international norms in question and the impact this exerts on national implementation (both legislative and judicial). The impact of instrument choice at the national level will also be observed.

As part of the discussion of national implementation and enforcement of international wildlife law, this chapter will address how international wildlife law treaties and institutions ensure effective implementation and compliance with wildlife norms. While there is an abundant literature on

[1] See, generally, P. W. Birnie, A. E. Boyle and C. J. Redgwell, *International Law and the Environment* (Oxford University Press, 3rd ed., 2009), Chapters 2 and 3; P. Sands, *International Law and the Environment* (Cambridge University Press, 2nd ed., 2003), Chapter 5; and C. Redgwell, 'National Implementation', in D. Bodansky, J. Brunnee and E. Hey (eds.), *The Oxford Handbook of International Environmental Law* (Oxford University Press, 2007), Chapter 40, with this chapter drawing on this last in particular.

implementation, enforcement and compliance with international environmental law, there has been a tendency to focus on pollution treaties and to overlook the significant contribution of international wildlife treaties to our understanding of the 'compliance pull' of international norms.[2] This chapter, and the discussion of implementation of specific wildlife treaties found elsewhere in this volume, is a further step towards redressing this imbalance.

A natural threshold question in a chapter addressed to national implementation is 'What is implementation?' UNEP Guidelines on multilateral environmental agreement compliance and enforcement define implementation as encompassing, '*inter alia*, all relevant laws, regulations, policies, and other measures and initiatives, that contracting parties adopt and/or take to meet their obligations under a multilateral environmental agreement and its amendments, if any'.[3] This chapter will adopt a shorthand definition of national implementation as 'measures parties take to make international agreements operative in their domestic law',[4] though attention will also be paid to NGO involvement with implementation at the national and supra-national levels.

The chapter is divided into several sections. Following this introduction, section 2 addresses the domestic constitutional law context. Section 3 addresses national implementation of international wildlife law, embracing legislative, administrative and judicial methods of implementation. Enforcement is principally the focus of this last method, be it direct or indirect enforcement of wildlife law through the courts. Direct enforcement includes the exercise of police powers by the state in prosecuting environmental offences. Indirect judicial implementation and enforcement of international wildlife law may occur in numerous ways, including through the invocation of international wildlife law principles in private litigation or as a defence invoked by the state in judicial review of a decision to revoke a licence or permit. Section 3 addresses both, before concluding with reference to procedural issues of jurisdiction, standing and remedies.

All three types of implementation mechanism addressed in section 3 – legislative, administrative and judicial – might be termed 'hard' or 'legal'

2 A tendency noted by Goodwin in his analysis of compliance under the World Heritage Convention: E. J. Goodwin, 'The World Heritage Convention, the Environment, and Compliance' (2009) 20(2) *Colo. J. Int'l Envt'l L. & Pol'y* 157.

3 UNEP Governing Council Decision SS.VII/4, 'Compliance with and enforcement of multilateral environmental agreements', UNEP(DEPI)/MEAs/WBG.1/3, annex II (Feb. 2002).

4 R. Reeve, *Policing International Trade in Endangered Species: The CITES Treaty and Compliance* (Earthscan, 2002), p. 16, citing the definition contained in the Nordic Research Project on the Effectiveness of International Environmental Agreements: Draft Report (Finnish Ministry of the Environment, 1995), p. 6.

enforcement in that they engage the public institutions of the state (legislature, bureaucracy, courts) in the implementation and enforcement of international law. Increasingly, however, there are 'softer' mechanisms of implementation and compliance control, which are actively encouraged under international wildlife treaties. This development draws on the role of major groups in the implementation of international environmental law addressed in Chapters 23–32 of Agenda 21, and may be seen in the context of the development of public participation in environmental decision-making more generally. Stakeholder involvement in implementation has been actively encouraged under a number of international wildlife law treaties,[5] including the Ramsar and World Heritage Conventions, the Convention to Combat Desertification and the revised 2003 African Convention. Such encouragement extends not only to ensuring public participation in decision-making by public authorities, but also to less formal methods of communication with all affected stakeholders, and to processes of consultation between private parties, such as natural-resources companies and stakeholders.

Following from this consideration of national implementation, section 4 shifts the focus to the role accorded national implementation *in* international wildlife law. Here specific national implementation and enforcement techniques mandated or encouraged by specific wildlife treaty texts are identified. Monitoring and reporting obligations are now common in wildlife treaty arrangements, and this international oversight of national implementation is addressed in section 5. [6] Obstacles to effective national implementation, and the international response thereto (in particular financial and technical support), are examined in section 6, before the final section seeks to offer some conclusions.

2. The constitutional law context for implementation

A further threshold issue is the extent to which the domestic constitutional legal order impacts upon the implementation of international wildlife law. The challenge of effective national implementation through legislative,

[5] See generally D. Zillman, A. Lucas and R. Pring (eds.), *Human Rights in Natural Resources Management: Public Participation in the Sustainable Development of Mining and Energy Resources* (Oxford University Press, 2001); and Principle 10 of the Rio Declaration.

[6] See generally J. Wettestad, 'Monitoring and Verification', in D. Bodansky, Brunnee and Hey, *supra* n. 1, Chapter 42.

administrative and judicial measures is one faced by all states, regardless of constitutional system. Even for constitutional systems that recognise the possibility of direct effect of international law through constitutional provision or a doctrine of self-executing treaty obligations, there are few international wildlife obligations that are capable of such execution.[7] Yet differences will clearly arise in consequence of the different constitutional accommodations of international law within the domestic legal order, be it through direct effect or judicial receptivity to international law arguments. Nonetheless, such studies as have taken place on judicial enforcement of international environmental law have not found appreciable differences between common and civil law jurisdictions in this regard.[8]

One key difference that does arise concerns legislative competence with respect to environmental matters, an issue particularly for federal states. There are examples of constitutional challenge to federal legislative competence that have arisen explicitly in wildlife law enforcement. For example, the well-known 1983 *Tasmanian Dam* case in the High Court of Australia involved a legal challenge to a proposed dam development affecting a site in Tasmania that had been designated under the World Heritage Convention (WHC).[9] Tasmania wished to go ahead with a project that impacted on a federally designated wilderness park and had been rendered illegal by federal legislation; the case arose from constitutional challenge to the federal legislation. Here the Australian High Court was willing to find that acceptance of an international obligation was sufficient to confer upon the Commonwealth of Australia the power to make laws implementing such obligations. In a close decision (4–3) the Court also held that there was a legal duty under the World Heritage Convention to protect designated world heritage sites. However, the courts in other federal states have been more reluctant to conflate external treaty-making powers and internal subject-matter competence to legislate. Thus in a challenge to the federal Ocean Dumping Control Act involving federal competence to

[7] For example, Article 2 of the 1950 International Convention for the Protection of Birds, held to be non-self-executing by the Belgian Conseil d'État in *Count Lippens v État Belge, Ministre de l'Agriculture* 47 *ILR* 336.

[8] See D. Bodansky and J. Brunnee, 'Introduction: The Role of National Courts in the Field of International Environmental Law', in M. Anderson and P. Galizzi (eds.), *International Environmental Law in National Courts* (BIICL, 2002), Chapter 1.

[9] *Commonwealth of Australia v State of Tasmania* (*Tasmanian Dam* case) (1983) *CLR* 1; reproduced in A. Palmer and C. Robb (eds.) *International Environmental Reports* (Cambridge University Press, 2004), Volume II, at p. 13. See further Chapter 11 below.

implement the 1972 London (Dumping) Convention, the Canadian Supreme Court found the statute to fall within federal competence but did so on the basis of the 'national' importance of reducing and eliminating marine pollution, and expressly rejected a general principle of federal jurisdiction to implement international agreements.[10] In the US by contrast, a case concerning federal legislation giving effect to a migratory bird treaty with Canada established that the federal government has authority to adopt legislation to implement treaties – although some have recently questioned this result.[11] One of the controversial features of the case is that the treaty was concluded only after federal legislation was held unconstitutional on the basis that the US Constitution does not provide an expressly enumerated federal power to regulate the hunting of migratory birds.

These cases highlight one of the difficulties of national implementation for federal states, where the competence to conclude international agreements is not necessarily matched by competence to legislate. Such constitutional impediments may not be relied upon, however, to justify breach of an international obligation assumed by the state.[12] In reality, the practice of federal states of including provincial/state representatives in their negotiating teams, and (where extant) a constitutional requirement of a role for the national legislative body in the ratification process, mitigate many of the worst effects of these constitutional obstacles.[13] Exceptionally the matter may be one raised for inclusion in the text of the environmental instrument itself. Article 34 WHC is one such 'federalism clause', addressed to state parties that 'have a federal or non-unitary constitutional system' and requiring federal governments to discharge their obligations, and to ensure that their constituent units do so where implementation of the WHC comes under their jurisdiction. However,

[10] *R v Crown Zellerbach* [1988] 1 *SCR* 401, reproduced in Palmer and Robb, *supra* n. 9, p. 67, applying the 'national-concern' test of the residual peace, order and good-government clause in the constitution.

[11] *Missouri v Holland* (1920) 252 US 416, reproduced in Palmer and Robb, *supra* n. 9, p. 492.

[12] See Article 27 of the 1969 Vienna Convention on the Law of Treaties; on manifest violation of internal law, see Article 46.

[13] States may also attach a federalism clause to their instrument of ratification; see, for example, the federalism understanding of the United States attached to its 1992 ratification of the 1966 International Covenant on Civil and Political Rights, and the Canadian federalism reservation (objected to by a number of other parties) accompanying its ratification of the 1991 Espoo Convention on Environmental Impact Assessment in a Transboundary Context.

Boer's 1992 analysis of the Australian experience under the WHC suggests a lack of co-operation between the federal, state and territorial governments – and a 'lack of political maturity in relations between the elements of the Australian federation in environmental management' which 'seems to be contrary to the spirit of Article 34'.[14]

Constitutional issues of the relationship between legislative competence and the exercise of external-relations powers are likewise confronted in the European Union. There are few areas of exclusive EU competence of relevance to international wildlife law; much more frequently encountered is shared or mixed competence, reflected in participation clauses in recent international treaties such as the CBD, which provides for the participation of both the EU and its member states. Some treaties do not, of course, provide for the direct treaty participation of non-state entities – the original text of CITES, for example (and a 1983 amendment so providing has yet to enter into force) – but this has not prevented the EU from giving effect to CITES by regulation directly binding on the member states and subject to the full enforcement powers of EU law.[15] Moreover, a rare instance of the direct effect of an environmental treaty provision is found in the European Court of Justice's 2004 judgment on a preliminary ruling reference from the Cour de cassation in France. There the ECJ held that Article 6(3) of the 1980 Athens Protocol for the Protection of the Mediterranean Sea against Pollution from Land-Based Sources (now Article 6(1) of the amended Protocol, 1996) has direct effect 'so that any interested party is entitled to rely on those provisions before national courts'.[16] Such regional reinforcement is a potent additional tool in the implementation of international wildlife law. As noted in Chapters 7 and 10, birds and sea turtles have been particular beneficiaries of EU enforcement action, with EU law serving almost as a form of surrogate mechanism for the implementation of the conservation principles contained in international treaties for their protection.

3. National implementation

As indicated above, national implementation may be divided into three separate yet clearly related and overlapping aspects: legislative,

[14] B. Boer, 'World Heritage Disputes in Australia' (1992) 7 *Envtl L. & Litig.* 247, p. 256.

[15] Council Regulation EC/338/97, OJ 1997 L61/1, replacing an earlier (1982) regulation. See further discussion in Chapter 15 below.

[16] Case C-213/03, Judgment of the Court (Second Chamber) of 15 July 2004 (*Syndicat professionnel coordination des pêcheurs de l'Etang de Berre et de la région v Electricité de France*), para. 47.

administrative, and judicial implementation. National laws and regulations implementing substantive treaty obligations have the advantage over administrative and judicial implementation of greater transparency and, generally, clarity in the application of the legal principles, whether as a guide to conduct or in the application of the law by the courts in the event of violation. Legislative implementation of a state's international obligations performs a 'delegated normativity' function, conditioning not only state but also non-state actors' behaviour. It can also demonstrate a preventive, even precautionary, approach to the implementation of environmental measures.

a) Legislative implementation

There is increasing sophistication in international wildlife treaties regarding methods of implementation. 'Is legislation necessary?' – a familiar question in the EU context regarding directives, for example – resonates in international wildlife law as well. There are two aspects to this question. The first concerns the extent to which domestic law already fulfils the obligations assumed. If no legislative implementation takes place, there is the risk that overarching treaty objectives will not be achieved. This is particularly problematic with the CBD, with its soft obligations: (i) it has no listing obligations (unlike many other conservation treaties); (ii) its substantive provisions are peppered with qualifying language (e.g. 'as far as possible and as appropriate'); and (iii) it leaves the detailed regulation of conservation to other, more specifically worded, biodiversity-related treaties (Ramsar, Bonn, Bern, CITES). Yet, as indicated above, Article 6 requires states to 'develop . . . or adapt for this purpose' existing national strategies, plans or programmes, suggesting that at least a degree of legislative implementation will be required to fulfil these CBD obligations. Moreover, it is difficult to see how the *in situ* conservation obligations of Article 8, such as the requirement to establish a system of protected areas, can be accomplished without legislative implementation (or the adaptation of existing legislative measures).

The second aspect of the question is whether the treaty permits non-legislative (soft) implementation, e.g. through devolved codes of conduct or similar mechanisms. Under a number of wildlife treaties, there are a range of measures indicated, including administrative. But in carrying out the obligation to implement in good faith, it may prove necessary to legislate effectively to regulate the activities of territorial subunits (e.g. the Australian example with Tasmania and the WHC) and effectively to control the activities of non-state actors within and beyond the state (e.g. regulating high-seas fisheries). Legislation is most likely to be necessary when implementation obligations require the state to exercise due diligence in respect of the activities of non-state actors – inspection powers of the flag state, for example – and where adequate deterrent sanctions are to be imposed. It is difficult to imagine how, for example, CITES or any of the fisheries agreements considered in Chapter 5 could properly be implemented without, inter alia, a legislative framework for the issuance of permits and the sanctioning of breach of permit conditions. Liability regimes, as yet not extensively developed under international wildlife law, perhaps most clearly underscore the necessity for a legislative response.[17]

In addition, national constitutional and/or legislative provisions may directly mandate implementation of treaty obligations. We find something along these lines in South Africa's National Environmental Management Act 107 of 1998, which empowers the minister to pass domestic legislation or regulations to give effect to any international instrument to which South Africa is a party; it also requires the minister to report on 'the international environmental instruments for which he or she is responsible' and to submit 'an Annual Performance Report on Sustainable Development' as part of South Africa's commitment to implementing Agenda 21 (section 26).

b) Administrative implementation

In 1990, Sand identified a new phenomenon in international (environmental) law – transnational administrative implementation and enforcement[18] – emerging from the development of national focal points and implementation authorities and enhanced co-operation between them. In fact, a number of wildlife treaties require the designation of national focal points to facilitate, inter alia, information exchange (e.g. the revised 2003 African Convention). Under its current strategic plan, the Ramsar parties have set the year 2015 as the deadline for the designation of national focal points both for CEPA and STRP purposes. Other examples of transnational administrative

[17] The 2003 African Convention (Article XXIV) and the CBD (Article 14(2)) and Biosafety Protocol (Article 27) each provide for future consideration of liability; see Chapters 9 and 17 respectively.

[18] P. H. Sand, 'Lessons Learned in Global Environmental Governance' (1990–1) 18 *B.C. Envt'l Aff. L. Rev.* 213.

implementation are co-operation between customs authorities under CITES (e.g. for the 'mutual recognition' of permits) and exchange of information and notification obligations between port authorities under CCAMLR (co-operating in, inter alia, 'alert diffusion'). Thus, whilst it may be the foreign ministries that are most actively engaged in the negotiation of the treaty text, it is the administrative authorities of the state upon which fall many of the practical issues of implementation and enforcement. This raises acutely the issue of capacity, both financial and technical, which is considered further below.

c) Judicial enforcement

The role of the judiciary in the implementation and enforcement of international environmental law was recognised in UNEP's Montevideo Programme III, adopted in 2001, which identifies judges as a key group for capacity building. A UNEP Global Judges Symposium was held on the eve of the Johannesburg World Summit on Sustainable Development in 2002 which adopted the 'Johannesburg principles on the role of law and sustainable development'. These affirm, inter alia, 'that an independent judiciary and judicial process is vital for the implementation, development and enforcement of international environmental law'.[19] There have been a number of studies of judicial implementation of international environmental law, including a three-volume compendium of summaries of environment-related cases by UNEP (see www.unep.org). Whilst this underlines the potential of the judicial role in implementing key international environmental principles such as the precautionary principle and the principle of inter-generational equity, only seven of the sixty-nine cases discussed therein overtly address international environmental law, principally in cases relating to issues of competing land use and nature conservation or involving principles such as precaution or polluter-pays.[20]

[19] For discussion of these principles, and subsequent developments, see Lord Justice Carnwath, 'Judicial Protection of the Environment: At Home and Abroad' (2004) 16 *JEL* 315.

[20] Volume I examines issues of standing, environmental impact assessment, choice of forum, public-trust doctrine, the precautionary principle, the polluter-pays principle, and riparian right to water; Volume II summarises cases on planning control, police power and compulsory acquisition in environmental management, and the place of culture in environmental management (mainly New Zealand and Australian cases); and Volume III addresses forum and jurisdiction, physical planning, pollution control, enforcement, rights of local community to use local natural resources, and animal protection.

Of course, many national cases that are concerned with implementation and enforcement of domestic planning and environmental laws will serve to implement key treaty and customary obligations. The difficulty lies in tracing the connection in these cases to implementation of international obligations, in the absence of an express link (such as explicit reference to the treaty obligation sought to be implemented or enforced). It also should be recognised that the courts play a role supplemental to the state's political organs, with whom the principal implementation obligation resides. The success of this supplemental role will depend on a variety of factors, not the least of which is the perceived desirability of judicial law-making, and the competence or expertise of the judiciary in the environmental sphere. Only a few states have taken the step of establishing specially designated environmental courts, such as New Zealand's Environment Court and the Land and Environment Court of the Australian state of New South Wales.[21] According to one recent survey of twelve jurisdictions, 'the role of national courts in implementing international environmental law has been rather limited to date [2002]'.[22] If one obstacle to more active involvement of national courts is indeed judicial *horror juris non domestici* in some instances,[23] then UNEP's judicial capacity building, promotion of judicial networking and sharing of information should produce dividends – but these are for the long term.

It is important also to acknowledge that, unlike in the fields of human rights law and trade law, for example, there is no dedicated central dispute settlement mechanism for international wildlife (or environmental) law, nor any specialised regional or international court competent to apply and enforce international environmental law along the lines of the European, African, or Inter-American Courts of Human Rights, with access for non-state actors. Thus, unlike human rights plaintiffs, environmental plaintiffs face domestic legal obstacles to enforcement of environmental rights or interests that cannot generally be surmounted by recourse to a supranational body. Even at the inter-state level, proposals for an international environmental court have not prospered, and the Environmental Chamber of the International Court of Justice, first designated in 1993, was never used, and was abolished in 2006. In consequence, plaintiffs'

[21] See further www.justice.govt.nz/courts/environment-court and www.lawlink.nsw.gov.au/lec; and, generally, G. Pring and K. Pring, *Greening Justice: Creating and Improving Environmental Courts and Tribunals* (WRI, 2010).

[22] Bodansky and Brunnee, *supra* n. 8, p. 9.

[23] Ibid., p. 21.

only recourse may be national judicial implementation and enforcement measures.

As already indicated, direct enforcement by domestic courts of international wildlife law is rare. In dualist states, there is no possibility for the direct enforcement of treaty obligations (save for EU law) without domestic legislative implementation. Wildlife treaty obligations are rarely of sufficient precision to give rise to direct effect even in monist states. Direct application and enforcement of customary international law is possible in both systems, but again specific instances are relatively rare. One such instance is the Indian Supreme Court's adventurous decision in *Vellore Citizens' Welfare Forum v Union of India* (1996), where it found the concept of sustainable development, the precautionary principle and the polluter-pays principle to be part of customary international law and hence applicable as part of Indian domestic law.[24] A decision of the 'Green Bench' of the Court,[25] the judgment reviewed a plethora of both hard-law (UNFCCC, CBD) and soft-law (Stockholm, Rio, Brundtland Report, Agenda 21) instruments in determining that sustainable development is part of customary international law and thus part of domestic law (and also found no conflict with statute law or with the Indian Constitution). This bold decision has been followed in a number of subsequent cases in India.[26] It is unusual in its reliance on customary international (environmental) law, since many other courts that invoke environmental principles, especially the polluter-pays principle, the precautionary principle, sustainable development and intergenerational equity, choose to avoid discussion of their legal status. Thus, for example, in the celebrated case of *In Re Minors Oposa* (1993) before the Philippines Supreme Court,[27] which involved a legal challenge to the grant of timber licences in remaining rainforest brought by the legal representatives of minors, the Court held that the plaintiffs had standing

[24] (1996) 5 SCC 647, discussed by M. Anderson, 'International Environmental Law in Indian Courts', in Anderson and Galizzi, *supra* n. 8, p. 156, and reproduced in Palmer and Robb, *supra* n. 9, p. 270.

[25] The Indian Supreme Court persuaded High Courts in several states – the Bombay, Calcutta, Madras and Gujarat High Courts, for example – to devote greater judicial resources to environmental cases through the designation of a 'green bench'. See S. Divan and A. Rosencranz, *Environmental Law and Policy in India* (Oxford University Press, 2nd ed., 2001), p. 4.

[26] For critical analysis see L. Rajamani, 'Public Interest Environmental Litigation in India: Exploring Issues of Access, Participation, Equity, Effectiveness and Sustainability' (2007) 19(3) *JEL* 293.

[27] Extracted in Palmer and Robb, *supra* n. 9, p. 382.

to challenge the award of the licences, since the resulting deforestation would cause harm to both present and future generations. Inter-generational equity was relied upon, yet it is far from clear that the Court applied inter-generational equity as a rule of *international* law. Similar conclusions may be drawn regarding the concept of inter-generational equity before the Canadian courts.[28] An excellent further example of judicial 'dodging' of the international legal status of an environmental principle is the application of the precautionary principle by the Land and Environmental Court of New South Wales as a 'statement of common sense'.[29]

More frequently encountered in domestic judicial decisions is the application of international wildlife law in the interpretation and application of domestic law. This indirect application typically arises in the use of international environmental norms as an aid to interpretation, especially where recourse to the treaty or other instrument assists the interpretation of the implementing domestic legislation. Thus, for example, in the Dutch case of *GJP Ziers*[30] an administrative decision to approve hotel construction with adverse impact on badger habitat was adjudged 'unreasonable' because of incompatibility with the requirements of the 1979 Bern Convention on the Conservation of European Wildlife and Natural Habitats. In seeking standing for judicial review of the United Kingdom Secretary of State's decision to offer offshore blocks for petroleum licensing in the North East Atlantic region, Greenpeace relied successfully upon the EU Habitats Directive as influenced by, inter alia, the CBD, in arguing that the Secretary of State had failed to take account of the impact of petroleum activities upon coral and cetaceans in the area.[31] There is nothing unique to the use of international wildlife law in these techniques; rather, they are a reflection of the general relationship between domestic and international law. As such, other doctrines may come into play,

[28] J. V. DeMarco, 'Case Note: *Imperial Oil Ltd v Quebec (Minister of the Environment)*' (2004) 13(1) *RECIEL* 108; for broader discussion see J. V. DeMarco and M. L. Campbell, 'The Supreme Court of Canada's Progressive Use of International Environmental Law and Policy in Interpreting Domestic Legislation' (2004) 13(3) *RECIEL* 320.

[29] *Leatch v National Parks and Wildlife Service*, 23 November 1993 (Stein J.), reproduced in Palmer and Robb, *supra* n. 9, p. 57.

[30] Afd G RvS 30 December 1993, AB 1995, no. 24, discussed in A. Nollkaemper, 'International Environmental Law in the Courts of the Netherlands', in Anderson and Galizzi, *supra* n. 8, p. 187, and extracted in Palmer and Robb, *supra* n. 9, p. 359.

[31] *R v Secretary of State for Trade and Industry, ex parte Greenpeace Ltd.* [2000] 2 *CMLR* 94 (Q. B. Div.), also reproduced in Palmer and Robb, *supra* n. 9, p. 462.

including the widely applied presumption that legislators do not intend to legislate inconsistently with the international obligations of the state. The opportunities for such application are, however, few and far between when contrasted with other fields such as human rights. This is in part a reflection of the many difficult procedural issues arising for environmental plaintiffs (see below).

The Dutch and UK cases cited above are both examples of successful individual/NGO judicial challenge to state action using international wildlife law instruments and principles. There are further examples where the state invokes the provisions of international environmental law to resist challenges by individuals to regulatory or other measures adopted by the state to implement its international environmental obligations. Most common are challenges to refusals of planning consent or planning enforcement measures that affect individuals' ability commercially or otherwise to develop land.[32] Thus, for example, the World Heritage Convention was successfully relied upon by the United Kingdom in a challenge to a refusal of planning consent for coal mining activities in Northumberland,[33] and by Egypt in a challenge to the revocation of hotel building permits near the Great Pyramids.[34]

Apart from direct challenges to state action, in a few cases private parties have invoked international environmental law in litigation against other private parties. This approach runs the risk that the obligation relied upon will be held to apply only as between states. In general, courts have been reluctant to give horizontal direct effect to international environmental law principles in the absence of legislative implementation. Thus, both in *Beneal v Freeport-McMoran*[35] and in *Amlon Metals v FMC*,[36] attempts to apply international environmental principles (polluter-pays, precaution, proximity) to non-state actors were unsuccessful on the basis that these principles apply only to states. In consequence, the state continues to play an important intermediary role in the application of such principles within domestic law, highlighting once again the importance especially of legislative implementation.

[32] See also the examples cited in the UNEP Volume III, *supra* n. 20.

[33] *Coal Contractors Limited v Secretary of State for the Environment and Northumberland County Council* [1993] *EGCS* 218.

[34] In ICSID arbitration: see *Southern Pacific Properties (Middle East) Ltd v Egypt* (1993), available at (1993) 32 *ILM* 933.

[35] 1997 US Dist Lexis 4767 (10 April 1997).

[36] (SDNY, 1991) 775 F Supp 668.

d) Procedural issues

Among the reasons frequently cited for the relative paucity of domestic case law on international wildlife issues are the procedural obstacles to litigation. These are familiar arguments both in domestic law, which has seen significant legal developments in terms of access to information, justice and decision-making, and on the international plane. Judicial resolution of environmental disputes may encounter three particular difficulties: (i) jurisdiction, (ii) standing and (iii) remedies. It is rare for these issues to be directly addressed by international law, thus leaving them largely for domestic courts to resolve.

i) Jurisdiction

Where the defendant is an international corporation, and/or the damage alleged is transboundary in nature, issues of conflict of laws may well arise. Domestic courts may decline jurisdiction on the basis that courts in another state are better placed to adjudicate the matter (*forum non conveniens*). Such was the fate of Ecuadorian indigenous groups challenging Texaco's oil development activities in Ecuador before US courts pursuant to, inter alia, the Alien Tort Claims Act.[37] Indeed, a number of individuals and groups have sought unsuccessfully to launch Alien Tort Claims Act proceedings in the US against US multinationals arising from natural resource activities abroad alleged to infringe international human rights and environmental standards. Jurisdiction may also be declined on the basis that the plaintiff is suing the 'wrong' defendant, as discussed above.

ii) Standing

There is no level – domestic, regional, international – where the issue of standing does not loom large for environmental litigants. Even the progressive 1998 Aarhus Convention fails to harmonise this thorny issue, with its access to justice provisions (Article 9) requiring the demonstration of a 'sufficient interest' (or impairment of a right if such is required for standing under domestic administrative law) yet relying to a significant extent upon national legislation. Article 9(2) recognises that non-governmental organisations may constitute 'the public concerned' with a sufficient interest for standing (further defined in Article 2(5)),

[37] *Aguinda v Texaco* (SDNY 2001) 142 F Supp 2d 534, upheld by the US Court of Appeals (Second Circuit), 16 August 2002, 303 F.3d 470. Court proceedings have since been launched in Ecuador.

and deems such organisations to have rights capable of being impaired where the administrative procedural law of a state party to the Convention requires this as a precondition for standing.

It is certainly the case that restrictive rules on standing are frequently identified as the most significant barrier to domestic implementation of international environmental law through the courts, preventing suitable cases from reaching the judicial domain. As indicated above, the principle of inter-generational equity was famously relied upon by the Philippines Court to confer standing on minors wishing to oppose the grant of timber licences in one of the last remaining areas of untouched forest in the Philippines. *In re Minors Oposa* finds an echo in progressive decisions of the Indian Supreme Court,[38] yet these cases remain on the whole exceptional. Nor is it the case that domestic jurisdictions readily acknowledge the standing of plaintiffs to claim on behalf of wildlife or of the environment, a domestic echo of the international judicial reluctance to develop *actio popularis*.[39] Nonetheless there have been some progressive developments, including the recognition of standing of NGOs such as the Sierra Club and Greenpeace to challenge private and public action detrimental to the environment at the national and regional levels. Moreover, where permitted, public-interest intervention in cases before domestic courts can be an effective method for introducing international environmental law and policy arguments. A recent survey of six major environmental cases before the Canadian Supreme Court concludes that in four of these cases such issues were considered only because of the arguments of public-interest interveners.[40]

iii) Remedies

Linked to the problems of standing are remedies, especially where plaintiffs seek to bring an *actio popularis*. The Indian case of *Vellore* is unusual in the award of compensation not only to individuals directly suffering harm from the pollution of the watercourse, but also in directing that an Environmental Trust Fund be established, by the polluter, to finance general ecological clean-up. Generally speaking there is no harmonisation of remedies under international wildlife law, save for the few

[38] See further Anderson, *supra* n. 24.

[39] The *locus classicus* on standing for the natural environment is C. Stone, 'Should Trees Have Standing?', published in the course of proceedings in *Sierra Club v Morton* (1972) 45 *Southern California Law Review* 450. Other judicial techniques include recourse to public trust and related doctrines.

[40] DeMarco and Campbell, *supra* n. 28, p. 330.

examples of liability and compensation regimes established principally in connection with hazardous activities in the pollution context (such as nuclear and hazardous waste and maritime transport of petroleum). Of the wildlife law treaties considered here, only three – the 1991 Environmental Protocol to the Antarctic Treaty, the 2000 Cartagena Biosafety Protocol and the 2003 African Convention – have made provision for the subsequent adoption of liability provisions, with only the Antarctic liability protocol operational.[41]

4. Requirements of national implementation under wildlife agreements

a) Soft-law instruments

The importance of national implementation for international environmental law generally is recognised in key soft-law instruments such as the 1972 Stockholm Declaration, which in Principles 11–17 places significant emphasis upon domestic policy and planning. The 1982 UN General Assembly Resolution 37/7 on a World Charter for Nature reaffirms in its preamble 'the need for appropriate measures, at the national and international, individual and collective, and private and public levels, to protect nature and to promote international co-operation in the field'. Such measures include implementation of the applicable international legal provisions for the conservation of nature and protection of the environment (para. 21(c)). Here again the importance of national policies and strategies is emphasised but, unlike the Stockholm Declaration, implementation is not made the sole purview of states. The World Charter for Nature mandates wider participation by other public authorities, international organisations, individuals, groups and corporations, to the extent that they are able. This theme is continued in the 1992 Rio Declaration on Environment and Development, especially in the accompanying Agenda 21, though Principle 11 of the Rio Declaration places squarely on states the obligation to enact 'effective' environmental legislation.

Annual national reporting on the implementation of Agenda 21 has occurred through the Commission on Sustainable Development (CSD), established as a result of Rio. Annual national reports are supplemented by a five-year cycle of country profiles, the purpose of which is to help

[41] See further discussion in Chapters 9, 11 and 17 below.

countries monitor their own implementation progress, whilst facilitating information exchange and serving 'as institutional memory to track and record national actions undertaken to implement Agenda 21'.[42] The World Summit on Sustainable Development saw the further production of 'national assessment reports', a form of self-appraisal of ten years' implementation of Agenda 21 and of the further issues developed by the CSD.

b) Treaty implementation requirements

Despite the growing importance of soft law, the principal focus of this chapter is upon national implementation of 'hard' obligations, in particular treaty obligations. This reflects the reality that the vast majority of binding international wildlife obligations are grounded in treaty instruments. It is axiomatic that every treaty generates an obligation to implement, as expressed in the maxim *pacta sunt servanda*. The strength of this obligation was underscored by the International Court of Justice in the 1997 *Gabcikovo-Nagymaros* case,[43] while, as noted above, the High Court in Australia drew upon it in elaborating the Commonwealth of Australia's obligations under the World Heritage Convention.

Requirements of national/regional implementation are frequently spelled out in treaty texts, with varying degrees of specificity. Implementation obligations may include:

- The development of policies and strategies for implementation. For example, Article 6 of the CBD requires each contracting party to develop national strategies, plans or programmes for the conservation and sustainable use of biological diversity, or to adapt existing strategies, etc., for this purpose.
- The requirement to adopt laws, regulations and other measures that take into account internationally agreed rules and standards and recommended practices and procedures, or that are no less effective than such global rules and standards. An example of the former, a type of indirect standard setting, is found in Article 60(3) of the 1982 Law of the Sea Convention (LOSC). An example of the latter – an obligation of result – is found in Article 210 LOSC, which requires that

[42] According to the Division for Sustainable Development in the UN Department of Economic and Social Affairs. The WSSD in 2002 produced a plan of implementation, and stimulated the conclusion of further partnership arrangements with the private sector, which are also being monitored by the CSD.

[43] *Gabcikovo-Nagymaros Dam* Case (Hungary/Slovakia), (1997) *ICJ Reports* 7.

'[n]ational laws, regulations and measures shall be no less effective in preventing, reducing and controlling ... pollution [from dumping] than the global rules and standards'.

- The requirement to designate an appropriate authority to issue permits, maintain records and monitor compliance/environmental conditions. Such obligations are commonly found in wildlife treaties, such as Article VI of CITES and Article X of the revised 2003 African Convention.
- The requirement that states take 'appropriate measures' to prevent and punish contraventions of the treaty. An example is found in Article VIII of CITES. Appropriate measures may be more precisely spelled out, as in the requirement that states shall prohibit violations and shall establish sanctions in respect thereof (Article 4).
- The requirement that states undertake monitoring, control and surveillance, including through observer schemes. Many examples may be found here, especially in respect of treaties regulating living resources, such as the 1995 Straddling Stocks Agreement, the 1946 Whaling Convention, the 1980 CCAMLR and the 1978 Convention on Future Multilateral Co-operation in the North West Atlantic Fisheries.
- The possibility of upward derogation; that is, setting national standards higher than required by the treaty instrument. This is generally permissible and, indeed, frequently exhorted: see, for example, Article 5 of the WHC.
- Encouragement to conclude bilateral, regional and/or multilateral agreements. This is a marked feature of many wildlife instruments, especially of the Bonn Convention and Ramsar. The 2000 Cartagena Biosafety Protocol to the 1992 CBD directly encourages such agreements consistent with its objectives, as does Article 197 of the 1982 LOSC.

Certain implementation techniques contain elements of substantive obligation, such as requirements to conduct a prior environmental impact assessment which are widespread in wildlife treaties, particularly where protected-areas designation is utilised.[44]

Another common technique in wildlife treaties is to set forth specific prohibitions, which states are required to implement through the application of specific 'measures', but leaving the method and means to the state. Virtually all of the wildlife treaties considered here adopt such an

[44] See Article 8 CBD.

approach. Such prohibitions are essentially obligations of result. This regulatory approach is a reflection both of the essentially horizontal and decentralised character of international law-making, and of the specific bargains and compromises embedded in specific environmental treaty-making. In consequence, regulatory or non-regulatory techniques may be employed, including soft implementation through codes of conduct, industry voluntary agreements and the like. The latter are of particular import in 'regulating' behaviour of non-state actors.

Since Rio, some wildlife implementation obligations are also conditioned by the principle of common but differentiated responsibility. This is enunciated in Principle 7 of the Rio Declaration. Article 6 of the CBD also conditions implementation of the obligations of each party 'in accordance with its particular conditions and capabilities'. Such language leads to different standards in national laws; parties undertake common obligations but these are differentiated in respect of precise implementation. Implementation standards are thus conditioned by context, taking into account the particular capabilities and circumstances of developing state parties.

5. Reporting, monitoring and compliance review

As indicated in Chapter 1, the first generation of international wildlife treaties rarely provided for any degree of monitoring or oversight of national implementation. Increasingly, however, modern wildlife treaties provide for a comprehensive feedback loop, from implementation to monitoring to reporting to international review to non-compliance mechanisms. The latter are now sometimes referred to as 'review institutions'. For example, Raustiala, in his 2001 study for UNEP on reporting and reviewing institutions in ten multilateral environmental agreements (MEAs), defines review institutions broadly to embrace

> specific institutions, formal or informal, that gather, assess, and take decisions based on information relevant to the implementation of, compliance with, adjustment of, and effectiveness of obligations contained in MEAs, as well as in subsidiary agreements and authoritative decisions of the parties.[45]

This underscores the evolutionary nature of many wildlife treaty instruments and the dynamic effect of decision-making by the conference of

[45] K. Raustiala, *Reporting and Review Institutions in 10 Multilateral Environmental Agreements* (UNEP, 2001), at p. 2.

the parties, as well as the impact of the work of treaty subsidiary bodies and secretariats. Perhaps the most striking example of monitoring and reporting obligations giving rise to new prescriptions is the evolution of the Bonn Convention, a major framework agreement with a number of 'daughter' agreements addressed to specific species, one of which (EUROBATS) is already 'second-generation'.[46]

Under most international wildlife agreements, states party not only have the obligation to implement but also an express obligation to report upon such implementation. Through reporting, it is possible to obtain a snapshot of overall implementation and enforcement patterns. Such reporting obligations might include supplying the text of implementing laws and measures (e.g. Bonn); transmission of specimens of the documentation employed when implementing the permitting or certification system required (e.g. CITES); supplying the results of monitoring environmental conditions (e.g. the 1991 Environmental Protocol to the AT); and publication of records kept, and of the results of monitoring, as well as the compilation of official reports, or summaries thereof, reflecting application and enforcement of the treaty (e.g. CITES). A number of wildlife treaties have had, and continue to have, problems with non-submission of reports,[47] and with inaccuracies in them, sometimes deliberately so.[48] Non-state actors can play an important role here, as a source of additional information on national implementation, such as TRAFFIC under CITES and BirdLife International under Ramsar.

The link between reporting, implementation and compliance has also given rise to a relatively new phenomenon in the context of national implementation of international wildlife obligations, and that is compliance review. This type of review occurs through scrutiny of implementation performance by a standing (or implementation or compliance) committee (e.g. the 1991 Alps Convention and Protocols, the 2000 Cartagena Protocol, the 'files' procedure of the Bern Convention, and the role of the World Heritage Committee under the WHC) and/or

[46] And the Siberian Crane MoU substantially revised; see further discussion in Chapter 10 below.

[47] See, for example, compliance review of non-reporting under CITES, discussed in Chapters 15 and 21 below.

[48] Such as deliberate Russian misreporting of whaling effort: A. Chayes and A. Handler Chayes, *The New Sovereignty: Compliance with International Regulatory Agreements* (Harvard University Press, 1995), p. 155; see also discussion in Chapter 6 below.

by the Conference of the Parties (e.g. CITES). Some recent instruments make some provision for the future establishment of an implementation review procedure, such as the compliance mechanism envisaged under the 2000 Cartagena Protocol to the 1992 CBD. Typically, compliance procedures are designed to ensure a return to compliance through a range of techniques, including the possibility of facilitative and/or coercive measures (e.g. access to facilitative financing, or the suspension of trading privileges).[49]

To an extent, non-state actors may play an informal role in treaty compliance mechanisms. Thus, for example, a representative of the Mirrar Traditional Owners challenging Australian authorisations for the Jabiluka uranium mine in Kakadu National Park was permitted to appear before a supra-national body, the World Heritage Committee (which was considering the impact of the expanded mine on the natural and cultural heritage of the park in 1999); a number of other non-profit organisations and NGOs were in attendance as observers. Energy Resources of Australia Inc. was not allowed to appear because of its profit-making status, but a letter from the chief executive was circulated to participants and annexed to the Report. In the event, the Committee did not 'danger-list' the site, and the mine expansion did not proceed (owing, inter alia, to a downturn in the price of uranium, which rendered it unprofitable). Recourse to the WHC arose when domestic legal proceedings had been exhausted – and proved ineffective (from the viewpoint of Mirrar Traditional Owners) – even though the company had complied with extant legal requirements under Australian law. However, until recently, direct access by non-state actors to formal non-compliance procedures was rare. This is because these mechanisms make no provision for the indirect invocation against a state party, by a non-state actor, but rather rely on state complaints, referrals by the treaty secretariat, or 'self-incrimination'. However, such provision has been made under the compliance procedure of the 1998 Aarhus Convention, where eleven of the first twelve complaints lodged were by NGOs against state parties (the twelfth being inter-state).[50] A particularly striking example of a mechanism permitting complaints by individuals and NGOs to its Standing Committee is the 'files' procedure of the Bern Convention, operational since 1993.[51]

[49] See discussion in Chapter 19 below.
[50] See further www.unece/environment.
[51] See further Chapter 10 below.

6. Facilitating implementation

A number of obstacles to effective implementation may arise, and come to be highlighted under treaty-based non-compliance or other procedures. Under CITES, Ramsar and the Bonn Convention, for example, a number of non-compliance cases have arisen from an inability of states effectively to carry out their reporting obligations. For developing-country parties, this is often a consequence of lack of financial resources and lack of technical expertise. Harmonising of reporting obligations, as has occurred under Ramsar, is one method for streamlining the reporting burden and enhancing compliance. Lack of scientific knowledge and expertise is another issue, evident for example in the implementation of the CBD, where developing-country parties especially are hampered by inadequate scientific knowledge of the full extent of biodiversity contained within their borders. This is exacerbated by the fact that much of the taxonomic research is carried out by developed countries, a fact recognised and sought to be redressed by the treaty bodies through the Global Taxonomic Initiative. *In situ* conservation obligations under the CBD may require the designation of protected areas, with the need consequently to enforce such designation, an issue also under a number of other wildlife treaties. CITES is dependent on the issuance of certificates and careful monitoring of points of entry for illegally traded flora and fauna, as indeed is the 2000 Cartagena Protocol to the CBD regulating the transboundary movement of living modified organisms. In general, there are six types of obstacles to national implementation, which may operate individually or collectively: (i) financial, (ii) technical, (iii) scientific, (iv) legal and administrative, (v) political and (vi) textual (i.e. the treaty text itself may be insufficiently clear and precise to give rise to precise obligations for national implementation). In recognition of these barriers to implementation, implementation facilitation is now a key feature of contemporary wildlife treaty arrangements.

A consistent theme throughout these chapters is the need for adequate financing of wildlife treaties.[52] For example, Article XXVIII of the revised 2003 African Convention recognises the 'central importance of financing to the achievement of the purposes of the Convention' and calls on each state party, 'taking into account its capability', to 'make every effort to ensure that adequate financial resources are available for the

[52] See also L. Boisson de Chazournes, 'Technical and Financial Assistance', in Bodansky, Brunnee and Hey, *supra* n. 1, Chapter 41.

implementation of the Convention'.[53] Funding is central to effectiveness, whether it is the cost of the bodies supporting the treaty system, of implementation, or of participation at meetings of the parties. Most of the agreements considered in this work contain a funding mechanism, generally based on contributions set in accordance with UN 'tariffs', and referred to under 'institutional arrangements' or 'implementation' in each chapter. Additional contributions may be forthcoming from specially designated funds, such as the trust fund arrangements under the World Heritage, Bonn and Ramsar conventions. The CBD is in a different position as the 'beneficiary' of the Global Environmental Facility (GEF); indeed, the the Biodiversity Liaison Group has expressed the view that the GEF should provide support for all five biodiversity-related conventions.[54] The GEF was established in 1991 and, in addition to being the financial mechanism for the CBD, CCD and UNFCCC, grants support to developing countries for projects related to biodiversity, climate change, international waters, land degradation, the ozone layer and persistent organic pollutants. Particularly pertinent for habitat conservation is its Small Grant Programme (SGP), which, in partnership with the UN Foundation,[55] provides funding for 'Community Management of Protected Areas for Conservation' (COMPACT), including designated World Heritage sites, Ramsar sites and biosphere reserves.[56] External support has also been obtained from the GEF for a major capacity-building initiative for critical sites along AEWA flyways.[57]

Attracting additional, external sources of financial support is of increasing importance for wildlife treaties. Trust funds and other forms of ad hoc financing are now an important source of revenue, above and beyond 'regular' contributions.[58] This has been particularly evident in fund-raising for emergency response to threats to wildlife and habitat such as the Rapid Response Facility under the WHC and the Great Apes Survival Project (GRASP), a public–private partnership launched in 2001 and led by UNESCO and UNEP. It now involves twenty-three range states, several donor nations, thirty non-governmental organisations, and four wildlife

[53] See further discussion in Chapter 9 below.

[54] BLG-3, para. 9, available at www.biodiv.org.

[55] See further n. 60 below.

[56] See further www.sgp.undp.org.

[57] The 'Wings Over Wetlands' project (WOW): see www.wingsoverwetlands.org.

[58] See, for the request by the CITES New Delhi CoP that the Secretariat seek external funding to meet the cost of appropriate technical assistance for developing countries, Resolution Conf. 3.4, discussed in Chapter 15 below.

treaties (the World Heritage Convention, the CBD, Bonn and CITES).[59] Another significant source of external funding is the UNF,[60] which has funded, inter alia, the International Corporate Wetlands Restoration Partnership, a joint initiative with the Nature Conservancy and the Gillette Company designed to leverage private financial contributions to match existing international mechanisms under conventions such as Ramsar and the World Heritage Convention.[61]

International financial institutions also have a role to play in facilitating wildlife conservation, especially bearing in mind the role of the World Bank as the trustee of the GEF, which it administers jointly with the UNDP and UNEP. Implementation facilitation also occurs through the ordinary loan arrangements of the World Bank, which have 'mainstreamed' the environment and which peg project compliance measures to international standards, including international agreements for the conservation of wildlife.[62] Other international institutions have a role to play in capacity building, such as the Commonwealth Secretariat and its involvement in financing legal expertise in the drafting of maritime legislation for the implementation of the 1982 LOSC in Africa and the Caribbean region in particular.

International wildlife law has also responded to the problem of lack of scientific knowledge and expertise impeding national action. Where lack of scientific certainty arises from the nature of the environmental problem itself, such as the precise impacts of marine pollutants, the precautionary principle has evolved. Lack of scientific knowledge may also relate to lack of indigenous expertise linked to finance and capacity. The Global Taxonomic Initiative under the CBD aims at closing the developing-country knowledge gap in respect of biological diversity through species identification. It is also designed to plug general scientific knowledge gaps which exist regarding the nature and extent of biological diversity; the GROMS system under the Bonn Convention is a further example of capacity building of general scientific knowledge. In

[59] See www.grasp.org.

[60] An independent public charity under US law founded in 1998 after Ted Turner's gift of US$1 billion to the United Nations. It encourages public–private partnerships.

[61] See www.icwrp.org and further discussion in Chapter 14 below.

[62] See, inter alia, Environmental Assessment Sourcebook Updates No. 10, March 1996 (International Agreements on Environment and Natural Resources: Relevance and Application in Environmental Assessment); and No. 20, October 1997 (Biodiversity and Environmental Assessment). See also No. 28, June 2002 (Wetlands and Environment Assessment). Full text is available at www.worldbank.org.

addition, the clearing-house mechanisms established under a number of wildlife agreements are Web-based systems to facilitate the exchange of knowledge and expertise through the parties themselves, including examples of implementing legislation.

Ultimately, the question is one of the allocation of scarce national resources in the face of competing national demands. The political will to ensure effective implementation of existing and future wildlife obligations is a crucial factor. This may be influenced by external pressures, such as regular meetings of the conference of the parties and compliance review, and by internal pressures generated by civil society and the role of major groups in the sustainable development process, which was acknowledged at Rio in Agenda 21.

7. Conclusion

Notwithstanding very significant evolution in international wildlife law during the past forty years in particular, we still do not have a complete picture of the extent to which it is implemented by legislative/executive action at the domestic level. A recent trend in general international environmental law doctrine is to emphasise the need for effective implementation and enforcement of the existing rules, rather than the promulgation of further substantive norms. This emphasis upon national implementation is evident in the influence of the Rio Conference – 'Think Globally, Act Locally'. Yet the techniques available for assessing the extent – not to mention the effectiveness – of such implementation are still rudimentary and incomplete. In consequence, it is difficult to examine, say, the relative paucity of cases, and to draw from it conclusions regarding the effectiveness of national implementation. Is national legislation so well designed and implemented that few cases arise in practice? Or is this relative paucity a result of judicial restraint or aversion to international wildlife law? Or is a record of poor implementation – coupled with very restrictive standing requirements, deterrent cost rules or the like – effectively deterring potential litigants? Or is it that there are cases we simply do not know about – a general problem of the dissemination of state practice in the environmental context? What is clear is that, as a relatively new area of international law, international wildlife law will be increasingly invoked in horizontal and vertical proceedings before national courts, and legislative implementation and enforcement will continue to be scrutinised by supra-national bodies via national reporting and monitoring obligations, as well as (in some cases) via non-compliance procedures. It is unlikely that international wildlife law will achieve as high a profile as international human rights law before national courts, but there is some cause for optimism in the extent to which international wildlife law is permeating national policy discourse, legal instruments and (slowly) judicial decision-making.

Recommended further reading

M. Anderson and P. Galizzi (eds.), *International Environmental Law in National Courts* (BIICL, 2002)

E. J. Goodwin, 'The World Heritage Convention, the Environment, and Compliance' (2009) 20(2) *Colo. J. Int'l Envt'l L. & Pol'y* 157

A. Palmer and C. Robb (eds.), *International Environmental Reports Volume 4: International Environmental Law in National Courts* (Cambridge University Press, 2004)

C. Redgwell, 'National Implementation', in D. Bodansky, J. Brunnee and E. Hey (eds.), *The Oxford Handbook of International Environmental Law* (Oxford University Press, 2007)

R. Reeve, *Policing Trade in Endangered Species: The CITES Treaty and Compliance* (RIIA/Earthscan, 2002)

P. Sand, 'Lessons Learned in Global Environmental Governance' (1990–1) 18 *B.C. Envt'l Aff. L. Rev.* 213

UNEP, Compendium of National Decisions on Matters Related to Environment (Vol. I, 1998; Vols. II–III, 2001)

PART II

Species regulation

Chapter 5

Fish

1. Background

The need for international regulation of marine fisheries is self-evident given that many fish species spend some or all of their life cycle crossing national maritime zones and/or in areas beyond national jurisdiction.[1] Traditionally, international law recognised freedom of fishing beyond the territorial sea, with legal title to the resource arising only on capture. This led Garrett Hardin in a seminal article in the 1960s to note the 'tragedy of the commons':[2] in the absence of ownership and of international co-operation with respect to high-seas fish stocks in particular, the oceans had become a 'free for all'. Sharks, rays, turtles and tuna are amongst the high-seas stocks which have suffered serious depredation, with several species now listed on CITES Appendices.[3]

As with many other forms of wildlife regulation, the initial impetus for international regulation of fish stocks was conservation of commercially exploited species for economic benefit. Increasingly, however, the conservation of fish stocks as an ultimately exhaustible natural resource and of fish species as part of marine ecosystem management has emerged as an additional objective, and is found reflected in more recent instruments such as the sustainable-use obligations of the 1995 Agreement on Straddling and Highly Migratory Fish Stocks (SSA), considered further below.

[1] See, generally, R. R. Churchill and A. V. Lowe, *The Law of the Sea* (Manchester University Press, 3rd ed., 1999), Chapter 14, p. 281. As they also observe, most fish stocks are interrelated, either in a predator–prey relationship or because they inhabit the same area so that fishing effort with respect to a target species leads to by-catch of other species.

[2] G. Hardin, 'Tragedy of the Commons' (1968) *Science* 162. For more recent treatment of property rights and marine fisheries see R. Barnes, *Property Rights and Natural Resources* (Hart Publishing, 2009), Chapter 8.

[3] On the application of CITES to marine fisheries see E. Franckx, 'The Protection of Biodiversity and Fisheries Management: Issues Raised by the Relationship between CITES and LOSC', in D. Freestone, R. Barnes and D. Ong (eds.) *The Law of the Sea: Progress and Prospects* (Oxford University Press, 2006), Chapter 12, and n. 12 below.

Fishing intensity has steadily increased since total world catch was first recorded in 1938 at 15 million tonnes, with total capture production of 92 million tonnes in 2006,[4] an estimated first-sale value of US$91.2 billion and some 43.5 million people directly engaged in primary fish production.[5] In addition, the top ten species were the same in 2006 as in 2004, constituting 30 per cent of total capture production, and most of which are fully exploited or overexploited.[6] Fish stocks remain a significant food source for much of the world's population and form the mainstay of both artisanal and large-scale commercial fishing operations. Fishing methods, if unregulated, can deplete fish stocks, cause habitat modification through destructive fishing practices, unbalance marine ecosystems and threaten other species.[7] Collapse of heavily fished stocks, such as the Peruvian anchovy and California sardine fisheries, and the near collapse of the Atlantic cod fishery have ecological as well as economic and social consequences.

Given the extent, and often highly technical character, of fisheries regulation, the purpose of this chapter is to provide an overview of international and regional approaches to marine fisheries conservation.[8] Particular attention will be paid to the linkages between the instruments discussed here and the key treaties explored elsewhere in this volume,[9] and to the regulatory techniques (e.g. open and close seasons, net size) and approaches (e.g. precautionary, ecosystem) employed in the fisheries context.

2. Institutional framework

As will become evident below, one key element missing from the institutional landscape of fisheries regulation is an overarching institution responsible for

[4] 'World Capture Production 2001–2007', in *FAO Yearbook of Fishery Statistics Summary Tables*, available at www.fao.org. Total capture production for 2007 was just over 90 million tonnes.

[5] FAO, *The State of World Fisheries and Aquaculture 2008* (FAO, 2009), pp. 5 and 23.

[6] Ibid., pp. 12 and 30. Over 80 per cent of the 523 selected world fish stocks for which assessment information is available are fully exploited or overexploited – or depleted, and recovering from depletion – and the conclusion, as of previous reports, is that maximum wild fishery capture potential from the oceans has probably been reached. Ibid., p. 35.

[7] For example, the impact on albatross of long-line fishing for Patagonian toothfish led to the adoption, inter alia, of CCAMLR Conservation Measure 29/XV to Minimise the Catch of Seabirds.

[8] Our focus here is the international and regional regulation of marine fisheries, with freshwater fisheries addressed where pertinent in other chapters, e.g. Chapters 15 (CITES) and 17 (biodiversity).

[9] Other marine living resources are addressed in Chapters 11 (polar regions), 14 (whaling) and 15 (CITES), for example.

co-ordination of the range of international and regional fisheries instruments and institutions. The United Nations body with responsibility for fisheries matters, the Food and Agriculture Organisation (FAO), does not exercise this oversight authority.[10] Nonetheless it has a significant role to play in fisheries regulation, and in the gathering and dissemination of crucial information about the state of global fishing stocks and the extent of fishing effort. Established in 1945, its purpose is 'to promote and where appropriate to recommend national and international action with respect to the conservation of natural resources'.[11] In addition, FAO provides specialist technical advice to other treaty bodies, such as in respect of the listing of marine species on CITES Appendices.[12]

Of particular note is the Committee on Fisheries (COFI), which was established in 1965 as a subsidiary body of the FAO Council. It remains the only global inter-governmental forum where major international fisheries issues are examined and recommendations addressed to various stakeholders (e.g. governments, regional fishery bodies, NGOs, fishery workers).[13] It now meets biennially, most recently in 2009.[14] It has two subcommittees, on fish trade and on aquaculture. COFI has also been used as a forum for the negotiation of global agreements and non-binding instruments such as the 1993 Agreement to Promote Compliance with International Conservation and Management Measures by Fishing Vessels on the High Seas (1993 Compliance Agreement),[15] the 1995 Code of

[10] P. W. Birnie, A. E. Boyle and C. J. Redgwell, *International Law and the Environment* (Oxford University Press, 3rd ed., 2009), p. 713.

[11] And improved methods of agricultural production: Article I(2) FAO Constitution.

[12] For example, in December 2009, using CITES criteria, independent fisheries experts meeting under FAO auspices proposed CITES Appendix II listing of the oceanic whitetip shark (*Carcharhinus longimanus*), porbeagle (*Lamna nasus*) and scalloped hammerhead shark (*Sphyrna lewini*); in addition, the proposed listing of 'lookalike' shark species to help enforcement for scalloped hammerhead shark was found to be justified in two of the four cases, the great hammerhead shark (*Sphyrna mokarran*) and smooth hammerhead shark (*Sphyrna zygaena*). There was consensus on Appendix II listing for Atlantic bluefin tuna (*Thunnus thynnus*), but not for Appendix I listing. At CITES CoP 15 in Doha in 2010 these proposals, put forward by Palau, the United States and Sweden, were adopted with respect to sharks; *Thunnus thynnus* was placed on Appendix I (proposal by Monaco). See further discussion of CITES below in Chapter 15.

[13] See further www.fao.org.

[14] See FAO Fisheries and Aquaculture Report No. 902, *Report of the Twenty-Eighth Session of the Committee on Fisheries* (2009) FIEL/R902.

[15] (1994) 33 *ILM* 968. Amongst other things, the Agreement requires flag states effectively to exercise responsibility over their fishing vessels and (facilitated by the FAO) exchange information on vessels authorised by them to fish on the high seas, which should improve identification of illegal fishing vessels. See further W. Edeson, D. Freestone and

Conduct for Responsible Fisheries[16] and the voluntary International Plans of Action (IPOAs) concluded thereunder,[17] and the 2008 International Guidelines for the Management of Deep-Sea Fisheries in the High Seas. Such instruments may have a significant effect on state practice. For example, a recent analysis commissioned by the FAO of the impact of the 1995 non-binding Code of Conduct concludes that it 'has become a broadly accepted "one-stop-shop" international reference for principles of best management practice in fisheries' and has contributed to wide acceptance of key concepts for the management of fisheries resources embedded in the Code such as 'sustainable', 'precautionary' and 'ecosystem-based'.[18] Certainly its influence may be detected in the provisions of the SSA concluded in the same year and considered further below. Yet the report also acknowledges the continuing deterioration of world fish stocks, continued overcapacity, and key governance challenges particularly at the national and Regional Fisheries Management Organisation (RFMO) levels.[19]

3. General law of the sea framework

The 1982 UN Convention on the Law of the Sea (LOSC)[20] provides 'the foundation for the modern law relating to international fisheries'.[21] In particular, the LOSC attributes jurisdiction over conservation and use of

E. Gudmundsdottir, *Legislating for Sustainable Fisheries: A Guide to Implementing the 1993 FAO Compliance Agreement and 1995 UN Fish Stocks Agreement* (World Bank, 2001).

[16] See further G. Moore, 'The Code of Conduct for Responsible Fisheries', in E. Hey (ed.), *Developments in International Fisheries Law* (Brill, 1999), Chapter 5.

[17] Four IPOAs have been developed to date: three in 1999, for Reducing Incidental Catch of Seabirds in Longline Fisheries, for the Conservation and Management of Sharks, and for the Management of Fishing Capacity; and one adopted in 2001, to Prevent, Deter and Eliminate Illegal, Unreported and Unregulated Fishing (IUU), though significant reservations were expressed by some states when adopting this last with respect to provisions on, inter alia, boarding and inspection and the use of trade sanctions. FAO Fisheries Report No. 655, *Report of the Twenty-Fourth Session of the Committee on Fisheries* (2001) FIPL/R655, pp. 15–17. For analysis of the impact of IPOAs, see G. Lutgen, 'Soft Law with Hidden Teeth: The Case for a FAO International Plan of Action on Sea Turtles' (2006) 9(2) *IJWLP* 155.

[18] G. Hosch, 'Analysis of the Implementation and Impact of the FAO Code of Conduct for Responsible Fisheries since 1995', FAO Fisheries and Aquaculture Circular No. 1038 (FAO, 2009), pp. 75–6.

[19] Ibid., section 4, 'Impact of the Code'.

[20] 21 *ILM* (1982) 1261. Concluded in 1982, the LOSC entered into force on 16 November 1994 and presently has 160 parties.

[21] Birnie, Boyle and Redgwell, *supra* n. 10, p. 714; for what the LOSC does *not* achieve, see ibid., pp. 715 and 751–2. Two obvious gaps are the absence of a co-ordinating institutional framework for the various international and regional initiatives, and ecosystem/biodiversity conservation principles.

marine living resources within the various maritime zones, and also sets forth certain basic conservation principles applicable therein. Within the territorial sea, states have traditionally enjoyed exclusive rights to fisheries as part of the exercise of sovereignty there. Under the 1982 LOSC, a twelve-mile limit is established for the territorial sea, within which foreign vessels must refrain from unauthorised fishing activities and where the coastal state may adopt laws and regulations to prevent infringement of its fishery laws.[22] However, since most major fish stocks exist further seawards, coastal state fisheries regulation within the territorial sea 'does not offer any great potential for control and protection in regard to the major fishery resources'.[23]

Beyond the territorial sea,[24] the LOSC recognises the exclusive sovereign rights of the coastal state over the EEZ for the purpose of exploring and exploiting, conserving and managing the living and non-living resources of the zone, which extends out 188 miles beyond the twelve-mile territorial sea.[25] With an estimated 90 per cent of commercially exploited living resources located within the 200-mile coastal belt,[26] this extension of coastal state rights and jurisdiction has had profound consequences for fisheries exploitation and conservation. These rights are exclusive, though dependent on express proclamation, and are recognised as customary international law.[27] It is for the coastal state to determine the total allowable catch (TAC) for marine living resources in the EEZ.[28]

[22] See Articles 3, 19(2)(i) and 42(1)(c). Such laws and regulations must be consistent with the LOSC and any conservation agreements to which the coastal state is party.

[23] C. A. Fleisher, 'Fisheries and Biological Resources', in R.-J. Dupy and D. Vignes (eds.), *A Handbook on the Law of the Sea* (Martinus Nijhoff, 1991), Volume II, p. 997.

[24] The concept of an exclusive fishing zone adjacent to the territorial sea emerged in the 1960s in particular, with a number of states extending exclusive fishing rights up to twelve miles. Iceland's fifty-mile exclusive fishery zone was successfully challenged by the UK and the Federal Republic of Germany, though the ICJ nonetheless recognised that a coastal state specially dependent on fisheries had certain preferential rights over fisheries resources in adjacent areas. *Fisheries Jurisdiction* cases (*United Kingdom v Iceland*) (Merits) (1974) *ICJ Rep.* 3; (*Federal Republic of Germany v Iceland*) (Merits) (1974) *ICJ Rep.* 175.

[25] Articles 56 and 57.

[26] P. A. Driver, 'International Fisheries', in R. P. Barston and P. W. Birnie (eds.), *The Maritime Dimension* (George Allen & Unwin, 1980), p. 44.

[27] As acknowledged by the ICJ in the *Libya/Malta Continental Shelf* case [1985] *ICJ Rep.* 13, at 33. However, as Churchill and Lowe observe, 'It is much more doubtful whether the detailed obligations in the articles relating to the exercise of coastal State jurisdiction over fisheries', inter alia, have passed into customary law. Churchill and Lowe, *supra* n. 1, pp. 161–2.

[28] Article 61(1).

Most importantly from a fisheries conservation perspective, these exclusive rights are accompanied by duties with respect to the conservation and utilisation of the living resources of the EEZ. Thus coastal states are required to take management and conservation measures to ensure that stocks are not endangered by overexploitation, and to maintain stocks at, or restore them to, 'levels which can produce the maximum sustainable yield [MSY], as qualified by relevant environmental and economic factors ... taking into account fishing patterns, the interdependence of stocks and any generally recommended international standards' at the subregional, regional or international level.[29] These fisheries management duties of the coastal state are excluded from the compulsory dispute settlement provisions of the LOSC save for compulsory conciliation where, for example, the coastal state has manifestly failed to ensure that the maintenance of EEZ fish stocks is not seriously endangered.[30] This wedding of environmental and economic criteria in Article 61, and the absence of effective international oversight of coastal state fisheries management, has led to criticism that these EEZ conservation obligations are 'largely illusory'.[31] In addition, the MSY approach of Article 61 to the conservation of living resources has been heavily criticised.[32] It is supplemented by the optimum sustainable yield (OSY) approach to utilisation of living resources in Article 62, which permits the coastal state in regulating access to its EEZ fisheries to take measures setting, inter alia, the type, age and size of species that may be harvested; quotas; open and close seasons and area(s) of fishing activity; the type, size and amount of gear; the type, size and number of vessels; the information required on, for example, catch size and effort; the placing of observers onboard; the landing of the catch in the ports of the coastal state; and enforcement procedures.[33]

[29] Article 61(2) and (3). This includes taking into account effects on associated or dependent species: Article 61(4). See also Article 194(5), where measures for the protection and preservation of the marine environment include those 'necessary to protect and preserve rare or fragile ecosystems as well as the habitat of depleted, threatened or endangered species and other forms of marine life'.

[30] Article 297(3); nor does the FAO have the authority to exercise oversight of coastal-state fisheries management. See further R. R. Churchill, 'The Jurisprudence of the International Tribunal for the Law of the Sea Relating to Fisheries: Is there Much in the Net?' (2007) 22 *IJMCL* 383.

[31] R. Barnes, 'The Convention on the Law of the Sea: An Effective Framework for Domestic Fisheries Conservation?', in Freestone, Barnes and Ong, *supra* n. 3, Chapter 13, p. 234.

[32] Birnie, Boyle and Redgwell, *supra* n. 10, pp. 590–3.

[33] Article 62(4).

With respect to high-seas fisheries,[34] the LOSC provides that the freedom of the high seas is exercised under the conditions laid down by the Convention and by 'other rules of international law'.[35] In addition to the general requirement that all high-seas freedoms must be exercised with due regard for the interests of other states in their exercise of the freedom of the high seas,[36] freedom of fishing is further subject to provisions in Articles 116–20 on the 'conservation and management of the living resources of the high seas'. Article 117 requires all states 'to take, or to co-operate with other States in taking, such measures for their respective nationals as may be necessary for the conservation of the living resources on the high seas'. The duty to co-operate is further elaborated in Article 118 in respect of states whose nationals exploit the same resources, or different resources in the same area, with recognition of subregional or regional fisheries organisations as possible vehicles for such co-operation.[37] Examples of such arrangements are considered further below. However, there is no express obligation to continue negotiating until agreement, nor are the consequences of a failure to reach agreement stipulated. Finally, Article 119 stipulates the measures that states shall take in determining the allowable catch of high-seas resources and the criteria to be taken into account in establishing other conservation measures for high-seas living resources.[38] These draw to a

[34] Sedentary species are considered part of the natural resources of the coastal state's continental shelf: Article 77(4). This provision makes no mention of conservation, and by virtue of Article 68 the EEZ provisions expressly do not apply to sedentary species. This has led some commentators to conclude that the coastal state has no obligation to manage or conserve such species. Churchill and Lowe, *supra* n. 1, p. 320; contra D. Ong, 'Towards an International Law for the Conservation of Offshore Hydrocarbon Resources within the Continental Shelf?', in Freestone, Barnes and Ong, *supra* n. 3, Chapter 6. In any event, since most sedentary species are located within the 200-mile limit it seems likely that EEZ management and conservation measures adopted there should also improve conservation of sedentary species. Birnie, Boyle and Redgwell, *supra* n. 10, p. 719.

[35] Article 87(1). On high-seas fisheries management and enforcement see D. Guilfoyle, *Shipping Interdiction and the Law of the Sea* (Cambridge University Press, 2009), Chapter 6.

[36] Article 87(2).

[37] Hey appears to suggest that there is an obligation under Article 118 to enter into such arrangements: E. Hey, *The Regime for the Exploitation of Transboundary Marine Fisheries Resources* (Martinus Nijhoff, 1989), at p. 83, n. 2; contra D. Freestone, 'The Effective Conservation and Management of High Seas Living Resources: Towards a New Regime?' (1994) 5(3) *Canterbury Law Review* 341.

[38] However, security of food supply is also an objective of the 1995 FAO Code on Responsible Fisheries, *supra* n. 15; while the SSA refers to the conservation and sustainable use of straddling and highly migratory fish stocks (see below).

very considerable extent upon the principles set forth in Article 61 regarding conservation of the living resources of the EEZ, discussed above.[39]

In addition to the general provisions outlined above, the LOSC also articulates special rules for certain marine living resources,[40] namely anadromous (e.g. salmon), catadromous (e.g. eels)[41] and highly migratory species,[42] and marine mammals (for which stricter rules, established by other competent international organisations – such as the IWC – may be established or maintained).[43] This is implicit recognition that the living resources of the oceans governed by the LOSC (and other agreements) include, in addition to fish, marine mammals (e.g. cetaceans), reptiles (e.g. turtles), seabirds (e.g. albatross), crustacea (e.g. lobster), corals (both soft corals and deep-ocean coldwater corals) and vegetation (e.g. seaweed).[44]

4. Straddling and Highly Migratory Fish Stocks Agreement

The objective of the UN Agreement Relating to the Conservation and Management of Straddling Fish Stocks and Highly Migratory Fish Stocks (SSA),[45] the first global agreement to regulate high-seas fisheries, 'is to ensure the long-term conservation and sustainable use of straddling fish stocks and highly migratory fish stocks through effective implementation

[39] With the additional Article 119(3) requirement that conservation measures and their implementation be non-discriminatory. See further B. Kwiatkowska, *The 200 Mile Exclusive Economic Zone in the New Law of the Sea* (Martinus Nijhoff, 1989), p. 67.

[40] While this is beyond the scope of the present chapter, for further discussion see Churchill and Lowe, *supra* n. 1, pp. 311–20; Birnie, Boyle and Redgwell, *supra* n. 10, pp. 722–9; and W. T. Burke, *The New International Law of Fisheries: UNCLOS 1982 and Beyond* (Clarendon Press, 1994), Chapters 4 and 5.

[41] Articles 66 and 67 LOSC.

[42] Governed by the EEZ provisions, in particular Article 64, and listed in Annex I LOSC. These provisions must now be read in the light of the 1995 SSA.

[43] See Article 65, extended to the high seas by Article 120; and P. W. Birnie, 'Marine Mammals: Exploring the Ambiguities of Article 65 of the Convention on the Law of the Sea and Related Provisions: Practice under the International Convention for the Regulation of Whaling', in Freestone, Barnes and Ong, *supra* n. 3, Chapter 14.

[44] D. Freestone and S. M. A. Salman, 'Ocean and Freshwater Resources', in D. Bodansky, J. Brunnee and E. Hey (eds.), *The Oxford Handbook of International Environmental Law* (Oxford University Press, 2007), Chapter 15, p. 340.

[45] 34 *ILM* (1995) 1542. Concluded in 1995, it entered into force on 11 November 2001 and presently has seventy-seven parties. See, generally, P. G. G. Davies and C. Redgwell, 'The International Legal Regulation of Straddling Fish Stocks' (1996) *BYIL* 199.

of the relevant provisions of the [LOSC]'.[46] It sets forth principles which apply to conservation and management of such stocks both within and beyond areas of national jurisdiction. Drawing on existing good practice codified in, for example, the FAO Code of Conduct for Responsible Fisheries, and new environmental concepts, the SSA embodies 'international minimum standards on how to run a good fishery'.[47] It reinforces new environmental concepts[48] through the recognition in Article 5 of the precautionary principle,[49] the ecosystem approach,[50] conservation of biological diversity,[51] and the objective of sustainable development of straddling stocks.[52]

In keeping with growing concerns regarding fishing techniques and high levels of incidental catches, there is also the obligation to minimise the catch of non-target species through measures including, 'to the extent practicable, the development and use of selective, environmentally safe and cost-effective fishing gear and techniques'.[53] Obligations to collect and share data, and to implement and enforce conservation and management measures through effective monitoring, control and surveillance, are also found in Article 5 and then amplified in later provisions of the SSA, particularly Annex I.

With respect to conservation measures, the SSA requires coastal and fishing states to 'adopt measures to ensure long-term sustainability of straddling fish stocks and highly migratory fish stocks and promote the

[46] Article 2. Straddling fish stocks cross a zone of national jurisdiction and the high seas; highly migratory fish stocks include species such as tuna.

[47] See further D. Anderson, 'The Straddling Stocks Agreement of 1995 – An Initial Assessment' (1996) 45 *ICLQ* 463. These could constitute 'generally recommended international minimum standards' for the purposes of Articles 61(3) and 119(1) LOSC. Ibid.

[48] Anderson emphasises recognition of the precautionary principle and of large marine ecosystems. Ibid., at pp. 466 and 469. Gherari emphasises sustainability and precaution. H. Gherari 'L'accord de 4 août 1995 sur les stocks chevauchants et les stocks de poissons grands migrateurs' (1996) 100 *RGDIP* 367, pp. 373–4.

[49] The precautionary approach is identified as a general principle in Article 5(c) which is further elaborated in Article 6 ('application of the precautionary approach') and in Annex II, which sets forth 'Guidelines for the Application of the Precautionary Reference Points in Conservation and Management of Straddling Fish Stocks and Highly Migratory Fish Stocks'. Essentially the SSA provides for the establishment of 'stock-specific reference points' which, if approached, should not be exceeded; if exceeded, then action to restore the stocks is to be taken pursuant to Article 6(3)(b) which requires states to determine the reference points and to determine the action to be taken if they are exceeded. Thus it is left to states, co-operating through RFMOs where extant and competent, to determine the consequences of exceeding predetermined precautionary reference points, and not regulated by the SSA.

[50] Article 5(d) and (e). [51] Article 5(g). [52] See Article 5(a) and (h). [53] Article 5(f).

objective of their optimum utilization'.[54] The basis for setting such measures is not new, but relies on the approach taken in Articles 61 and 119 LOSC discussed above. With respect to straddling stocks, the relevant coastal and fishing states are to co-operate in order to agree upon measures necessary for the conservation of the stocks in the adjacent high-seas area.[55] Such co-operation may be direct or through the co-operation procedures contained in the SSA.[56]

The criteria for determining compatibility of conservation and management measures within and beyond areas of national jurisdiction include the obligations to take into account measures adopted within national jurisdiction,[57] and to 'ensure that measures adopted in respect of such stocks for the high seas do not undermine the effectiveness of such measures'.[58] In respect of previously agreed high-seas measures, and of those agreed by the relevant RFMO, there is merely the obligation to take such measures into account – if they exist.[59] Further evidence of the priority accorded coastal-state interests is found in the obligation to take into account the biological unity of the stocks (a clear application of the ecosystem approach), 'including the extent to which the stocks occur and are fished in areas under national jurisdiction'.[60] The final criteria relate to the dependence of coastal and fishing states upon the stocks concerned, and the obligation to ensure that any measures agreed do not result in harmful impact on the living marine resources as a whole.[61]

The SSA also elaborates upon the duty to co-operate, whether directly or through the relevant RFMO. Where an RFMO has the competence to establish management and conservation measures for relevant stocks, the duty to co-operate of states fishing those stocks includes joining the relevant RFMO or agreeing to apply its measures.[62] If no regional

54 Article 5(a). 55 Article 7(1).

56 Articles 8–16. See further discussion in Davies and Redgwell, *supra* n. 45.

57 Coastal states are obliged to inform relevant fishing states directly or through an RFMO of measures adopted in respect of straddling and highly migratory stocks: Article 7(7). High-seas states have a similar obligation to other states in respect of measures adopted regulating their fishing vessels on the high seas: Article 7(8).

58 Article 7(2)(a). A requirement that high-seas measures be 'no less stringent' than national measures was dropped due to opposition from, inter alia, Poland and Korea. See further D. A. Balton, 'Strengthening the Law of the Sea: The New Agreement on Straddling Fish Stocks and Highly Migratory Fish Stocks' (1996) 27 *ODIL* 143, at 163.

59 Article 7(2)(b) and (c). 60 Article 7(2)(d). 61 Article 7(2)(e) and (f).

62 In this connection, Article 8(3) further provides: 'The terms for participation in such organization or arrangement shall not preclude such States from membership or participation; nor shall they be applied in a manner which discriminates against any State or

organisation or arrangement exists, interested states are obliged to co-operate in the creation of such organisation or arrangement.[63] There is particular urgency attached to negotiations to this end where stocks are under threat of overexploitation or where a new fishery is being developed for such stocks.[64]

Thus the key to accessing fishery resources to which regional conservation and management measures apply is through co-operative arrangements; otherwise contracting states do not have access to high-seas stocks conserved and managed through an RFMO or other arrangement.[65] These provisions are clearly aimed at the problems of new entrants to the fishery,[66] and of reflagging in non-parties to an RFMO; both problems have been experienced under NAFO, the RFMO which, generally speaking, was the Conference's model for such organisations.[67] Furthermore, states which are non-members and non-participants are obliged to ensure that their fishing vessels are not authorised to engage in fishing activities in respect of those stocks to which regional conservation measures apply.[68]

Enforcement measures may be taken by the flag,[69] coastal[70] or port state.[71] Of particular note is Article 21, which contains innovative

group of States having a real interest in the fisheries concerned.' The participation clauses of some RFMOs may require reassessment in the light of this provision.

63 Article 8(5).

64 Article 8(2), which further provides that, 'Pending agreement on such arrangements, States shall observe the provisions of this Agreement and shall act in good faith and with due regard to the rights, interests and duties of other States.'

65 Article 8(4). Nor does the failure to join or reach agreement free non-members/non-participants from the duty to co-operate in the conservation and management of straddling fish stocks and highly migratory fish stocks: Article 17(1).

66 Article 11 SSA addresses the nature and extent of participatory rights for new entrants, listing criteria designed to balance coastal and distant-water fishing-nation interests in the stocks.

67 Anderson, *supra* n. 47, p. 470.

68 Article 17(2).

69 Article 18 on flag-state enforcement mirrors the 1993 FAO Agreement to Promote Compliance with International Conservation and Management Measures by Fishing Vessels on the High Seas, *supra* n. 15. Flag states are to ensure compliance by their fishing vessels with RFMO conservation measures for straddling stocks. The Agreement requires enforcement irrespective of where the violation occurs, immediate investigation of any alleged violations, and prompt report to the state or RFMO alleging the violation.

70 The coastal state may, with flag-state authorisation, board and inspect on the high seas a vessel which is suspected of having been engaged in unauthorised fishing within an area under the jurisdiction of a coastal state: Article 20(6).

71 Including the inspection of gear and record books and the prohibition of landing and transhipments of catch 'where it has been established that the catch has been taken in a manner which undermines the effectiveness of sub-regional, regional or global conservation and management measures on the high seas': Article 23(3).

provisions permitting coastal-state enforcement action in respect of violations of RFMO measures on the high seas. A state party to the SSA and also a member of an RFMO may enforce the conservation provisions of that RFMO against the fishing vessels of another party to the SSA even where that party is not a member of the relevant RFMO. Basic procedures for boarding and inspection are set out in Article 22, and include obligations for both the inspecting and flag states.[72] Since the ability of the coastal state to exercise inspection powers on the high seas in connection with suspected fisheries violations is limited to the enforcement of multilaterally adopted conservation measures, this should be a strong incentive to pursue agreement for the regulation of stocks in regions or subregions not presently subject to such international regulation.[73] This is a significant advance on international co-operation regarding the enforcement of conservation measures on the high seas;[74] a measure of its importance is the safeguard built into Article 22, the inspection and enforcement provisions of which apply if an RFMO fails to adopt boarding and inspection procedures within two years of the entry into force of the SSA.

The novel provisions of the SSA are thus dependent for their effective implementation upon co-operation between states, in particular through RFMOs. While the SSA constitutes an amplification of the LOSC, it in turn will require further amplification and implementation by states at the regional level. The result is a three-tiered structure of LOSC, SSA and RFMO, with mutual reinforcement and dependence. Although the SSA does provide in certain limited instances for automatic supplement of RFMO measures (e.g. Article 22 on boarding and inspection), the success of the SSA will ultimately be judged in the tier below. It is to this tier that we now turn.

5. The role of regional fisheries management organisations or arrangements (RFMO/As)

The SSA therefore supplemented the provisions of the LOSC by establishing the principles and mechanisms applicable to the conservation

[72] See further Guilfoyle, *supra* n. 35.

[73] Mfodwo, Tsaymeni and Blay note that the desire jointly to manage shared and highly migratory stocks in the region led to the conclusion of the Gulf of Guinea Convention and an agreement establishing the Sub-Regional Commission on Fisheries in the North West African coastal area. K. Mfodwo, M. Tsaymeni and S. Blay, 'The Exclusive Economic Zone: State Practice in the African Atlantic Region' (1989) 20 *ODIL* 445, p. 461.

[74] Anderson, *supra* n. 47, p. 471.

and management of straddling and highly migratory stocks. Whilst the LOSC placed responsibility on coastal states to manage fish stocks within their respective EEZs, the SSA envisages that regional fisheries management organisations or arrangements will bear responsibility for the effective conservation and management of straddling and highly migratory fish stocks in relation to the high seas.[75] Various regional fisheries management organisations with responsibilities for the management of high-seas fish stocks already existed at the time of the adoption of the SSA.[76] Some were established to manage high-seas fish stocks generally in a given region, while others manage a type of species (such as tuna or salmon). New organisations and arrangements have been established in both these categories since the adoption of the SSA in 1995.

a) Organisations with general responsibilities for high-seas fisheries management in a given region

Four organisations already existed back in 1995 and continue to perform their management responsibilities today:[77] the Commission for the Conservation of Antarctic Marine Living Resources (CCAMLR);[78] the then General Fisheries Council for the Mediterranean (now the General Fisheries Commission for the Mediterranean (GFCM));[79] the Northwest Atlantic Fisheries Organization (NAFO);[80] and the North East Atlantic Fisheries Commission (NEAFC).[81] CCAMLR, NAFO and NEAFC

[75] See B. Applebaum and A. Donohue, 'The Role of Fisheries Management Organizations', in E. Hey (ed.) *Developments in International Fisheries Law* (Kluwer, 1999), p. 236; and the SSA, Articles 8–10, which emphasise the key role of RFMO/As to encourage co-operation between states with a view to ensuring effective conservation and management.

[76] Discussion is limited to organisations which actually manage fisheries. Numerous additional bodies have been established to provide advice (scientific and/or relating to management) on fisheries management: see the Food and Agriculture Organization's website on regional fishery bodies at www.fao.org/fi/body/rfb/index.htm.

[77] See Churchill and Lowe, *supra* n. 1, at 297, where reference is also made to organisations which are now defunct.

[78] See Chapter 11 below.

[79] Established by the 1949 Agreement for the Establishment of the General Fisheries Council for the Mediterranean, 126 *UNTS* 237 (amended in 1963, 1976 and 1997; amended version available at www.fao.org/Legal/treaties/003t-e.htm).

[80] Established by the 1978 Convention on Future Multilateral Cooperation in the Northwest Atlantic Fisheries, Cmnd 7569 297. See NAFO's website at www.nafo.int.

[81] Established by the 1980 Convention on Future Multilateral Co-operation in the North East Atlantic, Cmnd 8474 297. See NEAFC's website at www.neafc.org.

manage both straddling stocks and discrete high-seas stocks, while the GFCM manages a variety of species including east Atlantic tuna, swordfish, hake, mullet, shrimp, lobster and sardine.

Other agreements establishing a regional organisation or arrangement have been adopted since the signing of the SSA, with a view to exercising general responsibilities for the management of high-seas fisheries. In 2001 the Convention on the Conservation and Management of Fisheries Resources in the South East Atlantic Ocean became the first treaty to establish a regional fisheries management body since the adoption of the Straddling and Highly Migratory Fish Stocks Agreement – the 2001 Convention entered into force in April 2003 and established the South East Atlantic Fisheries Organisation (SEAFO).[82] SEAFO manages both straddling and discrete high-seas stocks. An agreement was also adopted in July 2006 to manage high-seas fish stocks (apart from tuna)[83] in the South Indian Ocean; once it has entered into force,[84] the Meeting of the Parties to the 2006 Southern Indian Ocean Fisheries Agreement (SIOFA) will meet at least once a year and be responsible for the setting of conservation and management measures.[85] More recently, in November 2009 the Convention on the Conservation and Management of the High Seas Fishery Resources of the South Pacific Ocean was adopted,[86] which, once in force, will fill the 'gap that exists in the international conservation and management of non-highly migratory species' in the area in question.[87]

[82] 2001 Convention on the Conservation and Management of the Fishery Resources in the Southeast Atlantic Ocean (2002) 41 *ILM* 257 and available at SEAFO's website at www.seafo.org.

[83] Tuna is managed by the Indian Ocean Tuna Commission; see *infra* n. 119.

[84] As at January 2010 the Cook Islands, the EU and the Seychelles have become contracting states. However, the agreement will only enter into force on receipt of the fourth instrument of ratification, acceptance or approval (at least two of which must be deposited by coastal states bordering the area of application); Article 24.

[85] See the Food and Agriculture Organisation (FAO) website at fao.org/fi/nems/news/detail_news.asp?lang=en&event_id=34553. The 2006 Southern Indian Ocean Fisheries Agreement is available from the FAO on request. See also www.fao.org/legal/treaties/035s-e.htm.

[86] Available at www.southpacificrfmo.org/assets/Convention-and-Final-Act/2010Feb01-2284949-v1-SPRFMOConvention-preparedforcertification+signature.pdf.

[87] See www.southpacificrfmo.org. The area of application of this 2009 Convention covers part of the area regulated under the 2000 Convention on the Conservation and Management of Highly Migratory Fish Stocks in the Western and Central Pacific Ocean ((2001) 40 *ILM* 277). The latter entered into force in June 2004 establishing the Commission for the Conservation and Management of Highly Migratory Fish Stocks in the Western and Central Pacific Ocean (WCPFC). WCPFC manages highly migratory stocks only and will therefore be addressed later in section 5(b)(i) below.

This 2009 Convention will establish the South Pacific Regional Fisheries Management Organisation (SPRFMO).

In an overview chapter of this nature, it is simply not possible to deliberate upon the functioning of all these RFMO/As. Instead, an introduction will be given to two of these organisations: the long-established NAFO and the much more recently launched SEAFO. The reader is also reminded that a discussion of CCAMLR appears below in Chapter 11.

i) NAFO

NAFO was established in 1979 and currently has twelve members.[88] The organisation aims to 'contribute through consultation and cooperation to the optimum utilisation, rational management and conservation of the fishery resources' in the North West Atlantic.[89] It has the capacity to regulate all fish stocks in the region apart from salmon, tuna and marlins; whales regulated by the IWC; and sedentary species.[90] NAFO comprises four main institutions: the General Council, the Scientific Council, the Fisheries Commission and the Secretariat, which is located in Dartmouth, Nova Scotia.[91] The General Council manages NAFO's internal and external affairs. NAFO's Fisheries Commission has responsibility for the management and conservation of fish stocks in the NAFO 'Regulatory Area', which is that area of the region situated outside waters in which coastal states exercise their own jurisdiction. The four coastal states in question are Canada, Denmark (in respect of the Faroes and Greenland), France (in respect of St Pierre et Miquelon), and the USA. In carrying out its functions, the Fisheries Commission takes into account scientific advice provided by the Scientific Council. It is also obliged to 'seek to ensure consistency' between its proposals and those taken by the relevant coastal state in respect of straddling stocks.[92]

Conservation and management measures adopted by NAFO include the allocation of catch quotas to specific parties, a rebuilding programme for Greenland halibut, bans on the taking of certain stocks in given areas, the setting of by-catch, and fishing gear and minimum fish-size requirements, as well as the adoption of a precautionary approach in the setting

[88] Canada, Cuba, Denmark (concerning the Faroes and Greenland), the European Union, France (concerning St Pierre et Miquelon), Iceland, Japan, the Republic of Korea, Norway, the Russian Federation, Ukraine, and the USA. NAFO's predecessor was the International Commission of the Northwest Atlantic Fisheries (ICNAF).

[89] 1978 Convention on Future Multilateral Cooperation in the Northwest Atlantic Fisheries, Article II(1).

[90] Article I(4). [91] NAFO's website is at www.nafo.int. [92] Article XI(3).

of some quotas. Control and monitoring measures adopted include the establishment of a vessel register and an obligation to record and report catches. A vessel monitoring system and an observer programme have also been introduced. In addition, a Joint Inspection and Surveillance Scheme has been implemented. This allows for the boarding and inspection of vessels by authorised NAFO inspectors to ensure compliance with NAFO conservation and management measures, and the citing of serious offences by such inspectors. The scheme endorses flag-state jurisdiction for the prosecution of alleged offences. NAFO has also introduced an inspection procedure which places the onus on port states to carry out inspections on vessels which use their ports to land fish. Port states must carry out a number of checks, including the checking of species caught, the size of the catch and the type of fishing gear utilised. Measures adopted in 2009 allow parties to designate those of its ports at which landings and transhipment of catches must take place.[93]

NAFO in 2010 had in place moratoria on the taking of cod, American plaice, witch flounder and capelin in given parts of the Regulatory Area. The need for such moratoria suggests that NAFO must continue to improve its ability to regulate fish stocks in the North West Atlantic region.[94] A particular concern has been illegal, unregulated and unreported fishing (IUU),[95] and a scheme has been adopted with a view to promoting compliance with NAFO measures in this regard. For example, any non-contracting party vessels fishing in the Regulatory Area will be regarded as engaging in activities which undermine the effectiveness of NAFO measures. The flag state concerned will be informed and asked to take steps to ensure such vessels desist from such activities. Vessels involved in IUU can be placed on a NAFO blacklist and will not then be allowed to land, tranship or refuel in any port of a NAFO member. Similar schemes to encourage non-parties to comply with RFMO conservation measures have been adopted by a number of other organisations, including CCAMLR and NEAFC.

[93] On NAFO conservation and enforcement measures see www.nafo.int/about/frames/activities.html.

[94] NAFO now reviews general compliance with its conservation and management measures. The first review in 2004 highlighted a number of incidents of non-compliance: the taking of stocks under moratoria, violations of mesh specifications, VMS specification infringements, catch misreporting, and the lack of an independent observer presence on fishing vessels. NAFO, Annual Compliance Review - 2003, NAFO/FC/ Doc. 04/13.

[95] Defined in the voluntary 2001 International Plan of Action to Prevent, Deter and Eliminate Illegal, Unreported and Unregulated Fishing, at section II(3.1–3) (available at www.fao.org/DOCREP/003/y1224e/y1224e00.htm). See *supra* n. 17.

A factor which has undermined NAFO's effectiveness in conserving fish stocks has been the ability of parties to register objections to its decisions. This ability to lodge objections is a common feature of early efforts to manage fishing activities.[96] The lodging of an objection by a given party would render the measure non-binding as far as that particular party is concerned.[97] Continued resort to the use of objections by the European Community to NAFO conservation measures in the late 1980s and early 1990s led in part to the *Estai* incident in March 1995 in which four fifty-millimetre rounds were fired across the bows of a Spanish trawler, the *Estai*, by Canadian fisheries protection officers.[98] While fishing on the high seas in the NAFO Regulatory Area, the *Estai* was then boarded and towed to St John's, Newfoundland. Canada justified what the EC Fisheries Commissioner regarded as an 'act of organized piracy',[99] claiming that there was no other way to stop the overfishing of a straddling stock, the Greenland Halibut, by EC-registered vessels. Concerned at the severe depletion of fish stocks in the region, Canada had by the early 1990s introduced domestic measures to reduce overfishing in waters within its exclusive fishery zone (EFZ). However, it took the view that these measures were being constantly undermined by continued overexploitation of straddling fish stocks within NAFO's Regulatory Area adjacent to its EFZ. Having objected to NAFO conservation and management measures, the EC habitually set its own unilateral catch quotas. Canada perceived these unilateral quotas as a hindrance to steps it had taken to conserve fish stocks. Additionally, Canada had been frustrated by a lack of enforcement action taken by other NAFO flag states in respect of alleged violations of NAFO decisions, and to fishing on the high seas by vessels registered in countries which were non-parties to the NAFO agreement. This incident underlined the urgent need for an international regime to foster international co-operation in relation to the conservation and management of straddling fish stocks; the Straddling and Highly Migratory Fish Stocks Agreement was adopted just under five months after the arrest of the *Estai*. Use of the objection

[96] For example, similar voting procedures allowing parties to opt out of decisions were established in NEAFC, IOTC and ICCAT.

[97] Article XII(1).

[98] See, generally, Davies and Redgwell, *supra* n. 45, at 202–17 and 253–7. Spain commenced an action before the International Court of Justice in March 1995 following the incident. The Court ruled on 4 December 1998 that it did not enjoy jurisdiction to adjudicate in this matter.

[99] Emma Bonino, quoted in *The Times*, 11 March 1995, p. 15.

procedure within NAFO still persists, although not to the same extent as in the late 1980s and 1990s when on average ten objections every year were made.[100] More recently, the number of objections lodged has averaged two per year.[101]

NAFO was, of course, founded before the adoption of the SSA. It has taken some steps to draw itself into line with certain features of the latter and of the 1993 Compliance Agreement. For example, some NAFO measures have been introduced adopting a precautionary approach to fisheries management,[102] and steps have been taken to tackle the problem of free riders (fishing in the NAFO Regulatory Area by vessels registered in non-member states), and also to establish a more effective system of enforcement (mutual boarding, a system of inspection at sea and port-state inspection). However, NAFO has accepted that more radical reform is required to bring the operation of the organisation into line with the approach of the SSA. In September 2005 it commenced a review process in which its management approach and decision-making procedures have in particular come under scrutiny. On 28 September 2007 NAFO adopted an amendment to the Convention.[103] This has not as yet come into force and will require ratification by three-quarters of the NAFO parties before it does so. The amendment will change the name of the treaty to the Convention on Cooperation in the Northwest Atlantic Fisheries, and its stated objective will be to 'ensure the long term conservation and sustainable use of the fishery resources' in the treaty's area of application and to 'safeguard the marine ecosystems in which these resources are found'.[104] Parties will 'apply the precautionary approach' in accordance with the SSA.[105] Additionally, they will take into account 'the impact of fishing activities on other species and marine ecosystems and in doing so, adopt measures to minimize harmful impact on living resources and marine ecosystems'.[106] Levels of fishing must 'not exceed those commensurate with the sustainable use of the fishery resource'.[107]

Objections to measures will still be allowed under the proposed amended treaty but, importantly, in future an explanation will be

[100] Fisheries and Oceans Canada, 'The NAFO Objection Procedure' (2004), at www.dfo-mpo.gc.ca/media/backgrou/2004/hq-ac90a_e.htm.
[101] Ibid.
[102] NAFO in 2004, for example, agreed to apply a precautionary approach to yellowtail flounder and shrimp in particular divisions of the Regulatory Area.
[103] Available at www.nafo.int/about/frames/about.html. [104] Amended Article II.
[105] Amended Article III(c). [106] Amended Article III(d). [107] Amended Article III(f).

required for any such objection, as will an indication of alternative measures the state in question will take to conserve and manage the fishery resource.[108] These improvements will certainly improve transparency in the process. In addition, the objecting state can submit the issue to an ad hoc panel, comprising a group of experts, which will review the explanation of the objecting state and also the alternative measures noted by the latter. If the objecting state fails to submit the issue to the ad hoc panel, the Commission itself can do so if a simple majority of commissioners vote in favour. The Commission will then meet to consider the ad hoc panel's recommendations. Unresolved issues can then be taken to dispute settlement, which may ultimately involve submission of the issue to compulsory proceedings under the LOSC or the SSA.[109] It is to be hoped that this improved system will enhance accountability, facilitate the settlement of disagreements between the parties, and bring NAFO more into line with more recently established RFMOs.[110]

Attention will now briefly turn to SEAFO, an RFMO founded since the adoption of the SSA.

ii) SEAFO

SEAFO was established by the 2001 Convention on the Conservation and Management of Fisheries Resources in the South East Atlantic Ocean.[111] The aim of this agreement is to 'ensure the long-term conservation and sustainable use of the fishery resources in the Convention Area'.[112] SEAFO's area of application comprises a large part of the South East Atlantic beyond areas of national jurisdiction in the region. The RFMO comprises the SEAFO Commission, the Scientific Committee, the Compliance Committee and the Secretariat. The latter is located in Walvis Bay, Namibia. The Commission is the main decision-making body of the organisation, and is to receive support in this task from its subsidiary bodies, the Compliance and Scientific Committees. The coastal states in the region are Angola, Namibia, the Republic of South

108 Amended Article XIV. 109 Amended Article XV.

110 This need to provide reasons for any opt-outs is also endorsed, for example, within SEAFO. Any reasons provided are circulated and a review meeting can be called by any other SEAFO Party: 2001 Convention on the Conservation and Management of Fisheries Resources in the South East Atlantic Ocean, Article 23. If the review meeting fails to settle the issue, a formal dispute settlement procedure could be invoked by any party; see Article 24. The text of the treaty is reproduced at www.seafo.org.

111 (2002) 41 *ILM* 257.

112 2001 Convention on the Conservation and Management of Fisheries Resources in the South East Atlantic Ocean, Article 2.

Africa and the United Kingdom (in respect of St Helena, Tristan da Cunha and the Ascension Islands). Angola, the EU, Japan, Namibia, Norway and South Africa are current members of the Commission.

The text of the 2001 Convention on the Conservation and Management of Fisheries Resources in the South East Atlantic Ocean has been much influenced by recently negotiated international instruments. It is particularly in tune with the SSA (especially in relation to the applicable general principles of fisheries management, the specific adoption of the precautionary and ecosystem approaches, reporting, monitoring, inspection, compliance and enforcement).[113] In line with the general approach endorsed in the SSA, the special requirements of developing states must also be taken into account. In this regard, co-operation with such states is to include the provision of financial, technical and training assistance, as well as the transfer of appropriate technology. Assistance must also be given to ensure that coastal developing states are in a position to fulfil their reporting requirements; develop an effective observer scheme; implement monitoring, control, and surveillance requirements; and enforce SEAFO measures.[114]

In addition to facilitating the ability of coastal developing states to fulfil their obligations, the success of SEAFO will ultimately depend on enticing those distant-water fishing states still active in the region to become members of SEAFO or otherwise to agree to abide by its conservation and management measures. At one time or other since the mid-1990s fishing vessels of numerous non-parties to SEAFO (including vessels from China, Cuba, Iceland, Korea, Russia, Taiwan, Poland, Ukraine and Uruguay) have all carried out fishing operations in the Convention Area.[115] It is noteworthy, however, that Japan became the latest state to ratify the treaty in January 2010. An additional issue faced by SEAFO is a lack of accurate data as to fishing activities and fish stocks. The status of stocks in the area is largely unknown – as indeed is the extent of IUU. Important measures already adopted by SEAFO to address IUU include a system of port-state control for vessels,[116] and the establishment of a SEAFO record of authorised vessels.[117]

[113] The 2000 Convention on the Conservation and Management of Highly Migratory Fish Stocks in the Western and Central Pacific Ocean (which established WCPFC) and the 2006 SIOFA agreement are also similarly influenced.

[114] Article 21. [115] SEAFO, First Annual Commission Report 2004, Annex 8.

[116] SEAFO Conservation measure 09/07. [117] SEAFO Conservation measure 07/06.

b) *Organisations established to manage specific species in a given region*

(i) Tuna and other highly migratory species The LOSC refers to certain species as being 'highly migratory' in nature.[118] A number of RFMOs have been established to manage such highly migratory stocks, particularly tuna and tuna-like species: the International Commission for the Conservation of Atlantic Tuna (ICCAT),[119] the Indian Ocean Tuna Commission (IOTC),[120] the Commission for the Conservation of Southern Bluefin Tuna (CCSBT)[121] and the Inter-American Tropical Tuna Commission (IATTC).[122] In addition, and since the adoption of the SSA, the Commission for the Conservation and Management of Highly Migratory Fish Stocks in the Western and Central Pacific Ocean (WCPFC) has been established following the entry into force in June 2004 of the 2000 Convention on the Conservation and Management of Highly Migratory Fish Stocks in the Western and Central Pacific Ocean.[123] The WCPFC's inaugural meeting was held in December 2004. These five tuna commissions have begun to share relevant information, including details of vessels licensed to fish in waters under their management, and lists of those vessels deemed to have been involved in IUU fishing.[124]

It is of interest to note that it was a dispute within the CCSBT which led to the ITLOS ruling in the *Southern Bluefin Tuna* cases in 1999.[125] Japan had proposed increases in the total allowable catch set by CCSBT and, when these proposals failed to achieve the consensus needed, unilaterally implemented a quota for experimental fishing in 1998. In Japan's view this

118 A list of migratory species is provided in Annex I, LOSC.

119 Established by the 1966 International Convention for the Conservation of Atlantic Tuna, 673 UNTS 63, and available at ICCAT's website at www.iccat.es.

120 Established by the 1993 Agreement for the Establishment of the Indian Ocean Tuna Commission, Cm. 2695 (1994) 313. Text also available at the IOTC's website at www.iotc.org.

121 Established by the 1993 Convention for the Conservation of Southern Bluefin Tuna, 1819 *UNTS* 360. Text also available at CCSBT's website at www.ccsbt.org.

122 Established by the 1949 Convention for the Establishment of the Inter-American Tropical Tuna Commission, 80 *UNTS* 3. Text also available at the IATTC's website at www.iattc.org. Note now the 2003 Antigua Convention addressed in n. 145 and accompanying text.

123 Established by the 2000 Convention on the Conservation and Management of Highly Migratory Fish Stocks in the Western and Central Pacific Ocean, 40 *ILM* 277 (2001). Text also available at the WCPFC's website at www.wcpfc.int.

124 See www.tuna-org.org/#.

125 *Southern Bluefin Tuna* cases (*New Zealand v Japan*; *Australia v Japan*) (Request for provisional measures) 38 *ILM* 1624 (1999).

quota was necessary to collect scientific data on the southern bluefin tuna stock. On the other hand, New Zealand and Australia pointed to evidence from the CCSBT's Scientific Committee to the effect that the low abundance of the stock was reason for serious biological concern, and argued that the setting of the unilateral quota was simply an attempt by Japan to take more than its allocated quota of the total allowable catch. New Zealand and Australia asked ITLOS to prescribe provisional measures pending the findings of the Arbitral Tribunal in this matter to be constituted under Annex VII LOSC.[126] The ITLOS ruling in August 1999 stipulated that all three states should 'refrain from conducting an experimental fishing programme ... except with the agreement of the other parties or unless the experimental catch is counted against its annual national allocation', and also that the three countries should resume negotiations 'with a view to reaching agreement' on conservation and management measures. In reaching its determination, ITLOS considered that 'measures should be taken as a matter of urgency to ... avert further deterioration of the southern bluefin tuna stock', and that the three parties should 'act with prudence and caution to ensure effective measures are taken to prevent serious harm' to the southern bluefin tuna stock.

Despite the efforts of RFMOs established to conserve and manage highly migratory species, there is real concern as to the status of many tuna stocks. A report prepared for the Review Conference of the Straddling and Highly Migratory Fish Stocks Agreement indicates that the bluefin tuna stock in the West Atlantic and stocks of southern bluefin tuna are a long way below historical optimal yields and are regarded as depleted.[127] Additionally, there is evidence that certain tuna fisheries are overexploited:[128] the bluefin tuna fishery in the East Atlantic, albacore in the North Atlantic, and the bigeye tuna fishery in the East Pacific provide examples.[129] A number of tuna and tuna-like species are fully

[126] The Arbitral Tribunal subsequently found on 4 August 2000 that it did not enjoy jurisdiction in this matter and lifted the provisional measures; see this ruling at http://untreaty.un.org/cod/riaa/cases/vol_XXXIII/1-57.pdf.

[127] In the sense that 'catches are well below historical optimal yields, irrespective of the amount of fishing effort exerted'; UN General Assembly, Report submitted in accordance with para. 17 of General Assembly resolution 59/25, to assist the Review Conference to implement its mandate under para. 2, article 36 of the UN Fish Stocks Agreement, document A/CONF.210/2006/1 (4 January 2006), paras. 18 and 37.

[128] In the sense that 'the fishery is being exploited above the optimal yield/effort which is believed to be sustainable in the long-term, with no potential room for further expansion and a higher risk of stock depletion/collapse'; ibid., paras. 18 and 37–42.

[129] Ibid.

exploited:[130] the Pacific bluefin tuna, albacore in the South Atlantic and in the North and South Pacific, bigeye and yellowfin tuna in most regions of the world, and swordfish in the Pacific and Atlantic.[131] Only a few highly migratory fish stocks can now be classified as providing a potential for limited further expansion in terms of production of the fishery: skipjack tuna in the Pacific and maybe in the Indian Ocean, and perhaps albacore in the Indian Ocean.[132]

In relation to the most recently established RFMO managing highly migratory species, the decision-making structure within the WCPFC deserves special mention. Wherever possible, decisions will be made by consensus. However, when this is not possible, some decisions, such as the determination of total allowable catch and the total level of fishing effort, can nonetheless be taken by a three-fourths majority.[133] No party has the right to opt out under an objection procedure. An internal review procedure can, however, be invoked by an aggrieved party, but if the review panel finds that the decision need not be changed or revoked then it will become binding on all parties. This could be seen as an important alternative to the approach adopted under many of the older RFMO/As in relation to decision-making where use of objection procedures has frustrated their ability to function. It should, however, be noted that certain WCPFC decisions must always be taken by consensus, and these include the actual allocation of the agreed total allowable catch.[134]

(ii) Salmon and other anadromous species Anadromous species begin life in fresh water, then live in the sea but swim back into fresh water to reproduce. The salmon fishery represents the most significant commercial fishery of this type of species. Relevant RFMOs include the North Atlantic Salmon Conservation Organization (NASCO),[135] the North

[130] 'Fishery is operating at or close to optimal yield/effort, with no expected room for further expansion'; ibid., paras. 18 and 37–42.

[131] Ibid., paras. 37–42. [132] Ibid., paras. 38 and 42.

[133] 2000 Convention on the Conservation and Management of Highly Migratory Fish Stocks in the Western and Central Pacific Ocean, Article 20. The three-fourths majority must include a three-fourths majority of South Pacific Forum Fisheries Agency (FFA) members and a three-fourths majority of FFA non-members.

[134] Ibid., Article 10(4).

[135] See the NASCO website at www.nasco.int. Canada, Denmark (with regard to the Faroes and Greenland), the EU, Norway, the Russian Federation and the USA are party to the 1982 Convention for the Conservation of Salmon in the North Atlantic Ocean, Cmnd. 8839 315. Iceland withdrew from the end of 2009.

Pacific Anadromous Fish Commission (NPAFC),[136] and the Pacific Salmon Commission (PSC).[137]

(iii) Pollock The case of the Alaska pollock in the Central Bering Sea provides a notorious example of the overexploitation of an important straddling fish stock. The so-called Donut Hole is an area of high seas which is surrounded by waters that fall within the national jurisdiction of the Russian Federation and the USA. In the North Pacific, catches of Alaska Pollock rose from '300,000 tonnes in the 1950s to about 4 million tonnes in the early 1970s and 6.7 million tonnes in the late 1980s'.[138] Approximately 25 to 30 percent of the catch in the Bering Sea was made in the Donut Hole,[139] and the fishery was severely overexploited. The 1994 Convention on the Conservation and Management of Pollock Resources in the Central Bering Sea (the 'Donut Hole Convention')[140] was specifically designed to restore and maintain Pollock resources at a level which will permit their maximum sustainable yield, and has been ratified by six parties (China, Japan, Poland, the Republic of Korea, the Russian Federation and the USA). A moratorium on commercial Pollock fishing has been in place for over ten years. No Commission has been established but the parties meet on an annual basis. The Scientific and Technical Committee advises the parties on stock levels.

(iv) Halibut In 1923 Canada and the USA adopted the Convention for the Preservation of the Halibut Fishery of the Northern Pacific Ocean,[141] thereby establishing the International Fisheries Commission (now known as the International Pacific Halibut Commission (IPHC)). The IPHC manages the taking of Pacific halibut in the Northern Pacific Ocean and the Bering Sea. Halibut in the regulated area is caught

[136] In addition to a variety of salmon, the treaty seeks to manage the taking of steelhead trout. Canada, Japan, the Republic of Korea, the Russian Federation and the USA are party to the 1992 Convention for the Conservation of Anadromous Stocks in the North Pacific Ocean, which is available at the NPAFC website at www.npafc.org.

[137] Canada and the USA are parties to the 1985 Treaty for the Conservation, Management and Optimum Production of Pacific Salmon, available at the PSC website at www.psc.org.

[138] FAO, World Review of Highly Migratory Species and Straddling Stocks (1994), FAO Fisheries Technical Paper No. 337, Chapter 3.1.

[139] Ibid.

[140] (1995) 34 *ILM* 67 306, and available at www.afsc.noaa.gov/refm/cbs/default.htm.

[141] 32 *LNTS* 93. Original treaty and subsequent amendments can be found at the IPHC's website at www.iphc.washington.edu/halcom.

predominantly by the commercial fishing industry, but a significant amount of catch is also taken by sport fishing.

c) *Improving the performance of RFMO/As*

Progress has been made by certain RFMO/As in incorporating principles and approaches endorsed in the SSA, as was recognised at the 2005 Conference on the Governance of High Seas Fisheries and the UN Fish Agreement. However, the Conference noted that further progress was required:

> while the governance of some RFMO/As have been improved by incorporating the principles and provisions of newly developed international instruments and tools, including, *inter alia*, those related to ecosystem considerations in fisheries management, other RFMO/As remain to be so improved and, to that end, there is a need for political will to further strengthen and modernise RFMO/As to ensure that such challenges and responsibilities are effectively addressed.[142]

The call for reform of existing RFMO/As was endorsed by the Task Force on Illegal, Unreported and Unregulated Fishing on the High Seas,[143] and the 2006 Review Conference on the Straddling and Highly Migratory Fish Stocks Convention noted that 'additional work is needed to advance the implementation of the [SSA] through RFMOs'.[144] NAFO became the first RFMO/A to institute a formal reform process in this regard and was followed by CCAMLR, NEAFC and ICCAT. Furthermore, members of the IATTC negotiated the Antigua Convention,[145] which, having entered

[142] Ministerial Declaration of the 2005 Conference on the Governance of High Seas Fisheries and the UN Fish Agreement, St John's, Newfoundland, Canada, 1–5 May 2005. Report available at www.dfo-mpo.gc.ca/fgc-cgp/conf_report_e.htm#d. On the need to improve practice in RFMO/As and for proposals to that end, see the report published by WWF International and TRAFFIC International: A. Willock and M. Lack, *Follow the Leader: Learning from Experience and Best Practice in Regional Fisheries Management Organizations* (TRAFFIC International, 2006).

[143] High Seas Task Force, *Closing the Net: Stopping Illegal Fishing on the High Seas* (Sadag SA, 2006). Governments participating in this Task Force included Australia, Canada, Chile, Namibia, New Zealand and the UK.

[144] UN General Assembly, Report of the Review Conference on the Agreement for the Implementation of the Provisions of the United Nations Convention on the Law of the Sea of 10 December 1982 Relating to the Conservation and Management of Straddling Fish Stocks and Highly Migratory Fish Stocks, Annex, para. 5 (document A/CONF.210/2006/15).

[145] 2003 Convention for the Strengthening of the Inter-American Tropical Tuna Commission Established by the 1949 Convention between the United States of America and the Republic of Costa Rica, available at the IATTC's website at www.iattc.org/HomeENG.htm.

into force on 27 August 2010, prevails over the original IATTC Convention for ratifying parties, and introduces a range of approaches intended to implement the SSA (including utilisation of the precautionary approach and the ecosystem approach).

There is a particular need to ensure that fisheries management decisions are taken within RFMO/As in line with best data and independent scientific advice. Determination of total allowable catch should also be made in accordance with the precautionary approach.[146] An early criticism of the WCPFC has been that, having been advised by its Scientific Committee to reduce bigeye and yellowfin tuna mortality rates, it did not do so in 2005 but instead determined that 'fishing effort for bigeye and yellowfin tuna . . . shall not be increased beyond current levels'.[147] Furthermore, the CCSBT and the IOTC have been criticised for failing to adopt measures to reduce catch quotas where accurate data on fish populations have been lacking or uncertain.[148] Despite warnings from their own scientific committees, there have been situations where they have preferred simply to call for further information or analysis of the issue rather than to take immediate action.[149] In common with many other RFMOs in such situations, no doubt concerns as to the impact on the fishing industry have at times outweighed the need to take prompt action to reduce allowable catches.[150]

Decisions within RFMO/As need to take into account the impact of fishing on the ecosystem as a whole.[151] While CCAMLR endorses an ecosystem approach in which modifications to the marine ecosystem should be prevented or minimised, not enough consideration in the past has been given in some other organisations to the impact made by fishing on the wider ecosystem. Such impacts include effects on non-target fisheries and food chains, by-catch of endangered species (sea turtles, cetaceans and seabirds), pollution of the marine environment and the destruction of vital and sensitive habitats (such as coral reefs) through contact with gear of fishing vessels. Encouraging developments

[146] Ministerial Declaration of the 2005 Conference on the Governance of High Seas Fisheries and the UN Fish Agreement, *supra* n. 142, para. 4A; UN General Assembly Report, *supra* n. 144, para. 36. On the ecosystem approach see FAO, The Ecosystem Approach to Fisheries (FAO Technical Guidelines for Responsible Fisheries, No. 4(2)) (2003).

[147] Willock and Lack, *supra* n. 142, p. 13; and WCPFC Conservation and Management Measure 2005–1 (WCPFC Second Session, 12–16 December 2005).

[148] Willock and Lack, *supra* n. 142, pp. 12–13. [149] Ibid. [150] Ibid., p. 12.

[151] Ministerial Declaration of the 2005 Conference on the Governance of High Seas Fisheries and the UN Fish Agreement, *supra* n. 142, para. 4A; UN General Assembly Report, *supra* n. 144, para. 36.

endorsing a move to an ecosystem approach have, however, recently been taken by a number of RFMOs including, for example, NAFO (as addressed above), NEAFC,[152] and also the IATTC in endorsing the Antigua Convention.[153]

In relation to monitoring, control and surveillance techniques, it is encouraging that registers of licensed fishing vessels and blacklists of vessels involved in IUU are more commonplace within RFMOs, as are procedures of inspection both at sea and in port states.[154] In addition, all RFMOs have taken action or are mandated to take action to ensure vessel monitoring systems are placed on vessels within their respective areas of management.[155] However, in relation to compliance and enforcement, the UN Review Conference on the Straddling and Highly Migratory Fish Stocks Convention noted that 'problems of non-compliance by members and co-operating members and fishing by non-members continue to undermine the effectiveness of adopted conservation and management measures within RFMO convention areas'.[156] There is still a need, therefore, to renew efforts to combat IUU and the problems caused by reflagging. Additionally, states must take action to reduce overcapacity in their fishing fleets, and to ensure effective penalties are imposed on vessels involved in illegal fishing.[157]

Necessary improvements in the performance of RFMOs, of course, presuppose that a RFMO/A actually exists in a given geographical area. This is not, however, always the case and there is therefore an obvious need for appropriate arrangements to be made to ensure this situation is remedied. Positive steps have, however, been noted with regard to, for example, the Southern Indian Ocean (SIOFA) and the Southern Pacific Ocean (WCPFC). However, more states must be encouraged to join RFMO/As if they have a coastal-state interest and/or they fish in a given area,[158] or at the very least such states should indicate a willingness to abide by the relevant RFMO's conservation and management measures as non-parties. More widespread ratification of the SSA must also be

[152] A new text to the Convention agreed in 2006 endorses not only a precautionary but also an ecosystem approach; see www.neafc.org/system/files/%252Fhome/neafc/drupal2_files/london-declaration_and_new_convention.pdf. The parties also agreed to provisionally apply this so-called 'New Convention' pending its ratification.

[153] The 2003 Antigua Convention endorses the application of the precautionary approach as described in the Straddling and Highly Migratory Fish Stocks Agreement. Article 6(3)(d) of the latter endorses an ecosystem approach.

[154] UN General Assembly Report, *supra* n. 144, para. 47.

[155] Ibid. [156] Ibid., para. 29. [157] Ibid., paras. 50 and 62.

[158] UN General Assembly Report, *supra* n. 144, paras. 39–40.

encouraged, as should efforts to increase the ability of developing states to implement this agreement effectively.[159]

6. Conclusion

Given the 'tragedy of the commons' with respect to high-seas fishing, it might have been expected that the extension of coastal-state jurisdiction over a 200-mile EEZ would lead to more sustainable fishing. To the contrary, fish stocks continue to be overexploited in many regional areas, including the North Pacific, the Bering Sea, the Antarctic, the North Atlantic and the North Sea.[160] Competition for high-seas stocks has intensified, with adverse consequences for highly migratory and straddling stocks in particular. The SSA, despite containing a 'code of good practice' for sustainable fishing, has not yet succeeded in addressing depletion of such stocks, in which IUU fishing and overcapacity continue to play a significant adverse role. Institutional failure at regional and international levels in achieving effective sustainable use of fisheries resources remains a weakness in the international regulation of fisheries, with a 2005 study confirming that NAFO, CCAMLR and other post-UNCLOS fisheries commissions continue to exhibit deficiencies first identified in the 1970s.[161] A recent EU report pessimistically concludes that '[f]isheries management in the European Union is not working as it should and the objective of achieving long-term sustainability is not being reached'.[162] There is little case for optimism with respect to fisheries management in other regions of the oceans.

Recommended further reading

W. T. Burke, *The New International Law of Fisheries: UNCLOS 1982 and Beyond* (Clarendon Press, 1994)

R. R. Churchill and A. V. Lowe, *The Law of the Sea* (Manchester University Press, 3rd edn, 1999)

[159] In this regard there is a particular need to encourage the participation of developing states in RFMOs by, inter alia, enhancing their capacity to undertake research, to collect data, and to engage in effective monitoring, control and surveillance, as well as their ability to introduce port-state controls. Ibid., para. 79.

[160] For assessment see Birnie, Boyle and Redgwell, *supra* n. 10, Chapter 13; and Burke, *supra* n. 40.

[161] M. W. Lodge and S. N. Nandan, 'Some Suggestions towards Better Implementation of the 1995 UN Fish Stocks Agreement' (2005) 20 *IJMCL* 345.

[162] Fishing Opportunities for 2009: Policy Statement from the European Commission (COM (2008) 331 final), p. 5.

P. G. G. Davies and C. Redgwell, 'The International Legal Regulation of Straddling Fish Stocks' (1996) *BYIL* 199

D. Freestone, R. Barnes and D. Ong (eds.), *The Law of the Sea: Progress and Prospects* (Oxford University Press, 2006)

D. Freestone and S. M. A. Salman, 'Ocean and Freshwater Resources', in D. Bodansky, J. Brunnee and E. Hey (eds.), *The Oxford Handbook of International Environmental Law* (Oxford University Press, 2007)

Chapter 6

Cetaceans

1. Background

The history of man's depletion of one species of great whale after another is perhaps the most infamous example of human mismanagement of the Earth's natural resources. As early as the thirteenth century, Basque whalers had so overexploited right whales (*Eubalaena glacialis*) in the Bay of Biscay that they were forced to look further afield for their prey. Since then, the whaling industry has proceeded in a series of booms and slumps as the discovery of new whaling techniques and new whaling grounds has been invariably followed by rapid depletion of one population after another. Great whales and whalers now survive in numbers which are a small fraction of their former abundance, and the commercial whaling industry, which once employed over 70,000 people in the USA alone, is almost non-existent.[1]

The need for international co-operation in preventing their overexploitation is self-evident since so many whales inhabit waters beyond national jurisdiction. Nonetheless, it was not until 1931 that the first whaling treaty, the Convention for the Regulation of Whaling,[2] was concluded. The 1931 Convention went some way towards controlling the worst whaling practices, but it only scratched the surface of the real problem. It prohibited commercial hunting of right whales,[3] and tried to prevent excessive wastage of other species by requiring whalers to make full use of all carcasses and by banning the killing of calves or suckling whales, immatures and female whales which were accompanied

[1] For a more comprehensive analysis of the history of whaling and its early regulation, see J. Scarff, 'The International Management of Whales, Dolphins, and Porpoises: An Interdisciplinary Assessment' (1977) 6(2) *ELQ* 343.

[2] 155 *LNTS* 349. The Convention came into force on 16 January 1935.

[3] Article 4. However, Article 3 of the Convention exempted aboriginal whaling from the application of the treaty (provided that native craft propelled by oars or sails were used, no firearms were carried, aboriginal people only were involved and they were not under contract to deliver the products of their whaling to a third person).

by calves or sucklings.[4] However, it had limited practical value because five whaling states – Argentina, Chile, Germany, Japan and the USSR – refused to accede to it. The 1931 Convention was followed by the 1937 International Agreement for the Regulation of Whaling.[5] This agreement prohibited the taking of grey (*Eschrichtius robustus*) and right whales[6] and the taking of blue (*Balaenoptera musculus*), fin (*Balaenoptera physalus*), humpback (*Megaptera novaeangliae*) or sperm whales (*Physeter macrocephalus*) below certain minimum lengths;[7] set closed seasons in relation to certain species located in particular geographical areas;[8] prohibited the taking of calves and of females accompanied by calves;[9] endorsed the fullest possible utilisation of whales taken;[10] and required every factory ship to have at least one inspector on board.[11] However, the agreement failed to reduce the numbers of whales being taken,[12] and was not ratified by Japan.

These agreements were soon superseded by the International Convention for the Regulation of Whaling (the 'Whaling Convention'),[13] which was signed in Washington, DC on 2 December 1946 and came into force on 10 November 1948. Originally signed by most of the major whaling states, the Convention has since been left by some and joined by others,[14] but it has overseen most of the world's whaling activities from its entry into force to the present day. The Whaling Convention established the International Whaling Commission (IWC),[15] which meets annually and adopts regulations on catch quotas, protected species and whaling methods. These regulations are contained in a Schedule which is an integral part of the

[4] See Articles 5 and 6.

[5] 1937 International Agreement for the Regulation of Whaling (190 *LNTS* 79) as amended by the 1938 Protocol (196 *LNTS* 131) and the 1945 Protocol (148 *UNTS* 114).

[6] Article 4. [7] Article 5. [8] Article 9.

[9] Article 6. [10] Article 11. [11] Article 1.

[12] P. W. Birnie, *International Regulation of Whaling: From Conservation of Whaling to Conservation of Whales and Regulation of Whale Watching* (Oceana Publications, 1985), Volume I, p. 126.

[13] 161 *UNTS* 72; *TIAS* No. 1849; *UKTS* No. 5 (1949), Cmd. 7604; and *UKTS* No. 68 (1959), Cmnd. 849.

[14] Japan, for example, did not become a party until 1951. Canada left the Whaling Convention in 1982. Iceland withdrew in 1992 but rejoined in 2002. Peru and Chile were among the original signatories to the Whaling Convention but in 1952, together with Ecuador, they established their own Permanent Commission for the Exploitation and Conservation of the Marine Resources of the South Pacific (CPPS) to, inter alia, regulate whaling in waters within 200 miles of their respective coastlines (see http://cpps-int.org; Colombia joined the CPPS in 1979). Peru and Chile finally ratified the Whaling Convention in 1979, as did Ecuador in 1991. Ecuador left the Whaling Convention in 1994 but rejoined in 2007.

[15] Whaling Convention, Article 3(1).

Whaling Convention.[16] The most significant amendment to the Schedule was made in 1982 when the IWC introduced a moratorium on commercial whaling from the 1986 coastal and 1985–6 pelagic whaling seasons. Commercial catch quotas have since remained set at zero.

This chapter addresses the objectives of the Whaling Convention and its scope. This is followed by an examination of the IWC and of key conservation and management issues that have been addressed within it by the parties. The controversial ability of parties to issue special permits for scientific research and the issue of small-type coastal whaling are then examined. Attention then turns to the important issue of enforcement, and finally to the relationship between the legal regime and other international treaties and organisations.

2. Objectives

The Whaling Convention has mixed objectives. On the one hand it aims to protect whales from overexploitation. The preamble to the Convention recognises that 'the history of whaling has seen over-fishing of one area after another and of one species of whale after another to such a degree that it is essential to protect all species of whales from further over-fishing'. Additionally, the preamble recognises 'the interest of the nations of the world in safeguarding for future generations the great natural resources represented by the whale stocks'. It goes on to state that the parties desire to 'establish a system of international regulation for the whale fisheries to ensure proper and effective conservation and development of whale stocks'. On the other hand, the Convention is by no means a protectionist treaty. Its preamble also states that it is in the common interest to achieve the optimum level of whale stocks 'without causing widespread economic and nutritional distress' and that the parties have 'decided to conclude a convention to provide for the proper conservation of whale stocks and thus make possible the orderly development of the whaling industry'. The Convention clearly aims to achieve a situation where stocks have recovered sufficiently to be able to sustain controlled exploitation. However, the phrase 'and thus make possible the orderly development of the whaling industry' makes it quite clear that the primary purpose of the Convention is conservation of whale stocks for the secondary objective of enabling the whaling industry to develop in an orderly fashion. Conservation is the top priority; orderly development of

[16] Ibid., Article 1(1).

the whaling industry comes next. Indeed, one recent study[17] concludes that development of the industry as such was not an essential part of the Convention's objectives at all,[18] which centred rather upon the proper and effective conservation of whales for the benefit of future generations, and as a means of ensuring the preservation of good order in the process of their exploitation.[19]

An important resolution was adopted by a majority of the parties in 2003 to strengthen the IWC's conservation agenda further by establishing a Conservation Committee.[20] However, although twenty-five voted in favour, a considerable minority (twenty states) voted against. Many of those parties not in favour of the resolution had sympathy with pro-whaling state parties (who also voted against the resolution), who argue that treating the Convention as a predominantly conservationist instrument is wholly inappropriate bearing in mind that the role of the IWC is to strike a balance between conservation and the orderly development of the whaling industry. The pro-whaling lobby is led by Japan, Iceland and Norway,[21] who take the view that the commercial harvesting of certain

17 M. J. Bowman '"Normalizing" the International Convention for the Regulation of Whaling' (2008) 29(3) *Mich.J.Int'l L* 293.

18 It notes in particular that the element of continuity with the earlier 1937 Agreement envisaged by the sixth recital of the Whaling Convention's preamble extended only to the 'principles embodied *in the provisions*' (emphasis added) of that agreement (which concerned methods of regulation) rather than to those indicated in its *preamble*, where the objective of securing industrial profitability was declared. This downgrading of the emphasis upon profitability to the status of only an ancillary concern (especially Article 5 (2)d of the Whaling Convention) may seem less surprising when it is realised that all the preliminary drafting work for the Whaling Convention was undertaken by the US, where whaling had ceased to be an economically significant industry.

19 It is to be remembered that the bulk of exploitation was inevitably to be conducted in the waters of Antarctica – an area of immense political controversy at the time – by states that had only months earlier been at war (indeed the peace treaty with Japan had still to be finalised) and in circumstances of acute world shortages of oils and fats. The need for *orderly* development could scarcely have been stronger.

20 IWC Resolution 2003–1; Annual Report of the International Whaling Commission 2003, pp. 58–9 (the Berlin Initiative on Strengthening the Conservation Agenda of the IWC).

21 Norway has, for example, noted that 'instead of serving its purpose of being an organization to provide for the management of whaling activities, [the IWC] has turned into an instrument for activists seeking to prohibit whaling as a matter of principle'; Opening Statement to the 53rd IWC meeting by the Norwegian delegation, July 2001 (London). For Japanese perspectives, see K. Sumi, 'The Whale War between Japan and the United States: Problems and Prospects' (1989) 17(2) *Denv. J. Int'L L and Policy* 317, and K. Hirata, 'Why Japan Supports Whaling' (2005) 8(2–3) *JIWLP* 129.

whales, particularly the Atlantic, North Pacific and Antarctic minke (*Balaenoptera acutorostrata, B. bonaerensis*), should now be allowed in accordance with the principle of sustainable utilisation. The deliberations within the IWC in recent years have served to underline the real tensions that exist between these pro-whaling states and other countries, such as Australia, the Netherlands, New Zealand, the UK and the USA, who adopt a protectionist stance towards cetaceans. As a consequence, much of the debate within the IWC has been polarised in recent years.

3. Scope of the Whaling Convention

a) Types of whaling operations covered by the Whaling Convention

The Whaling Convention applies to 'factory ships, land stations and whale catchers' under the jurisdiction of parties to the Convention.[22] A factory ship is defined as 'a ship in which or on which whales are treated whether wholly or in part', a land station means 'a factory on the land at which whales are treated wholly or in part', and a whale catcher is defined as 'a ship used for the purpose of hunting, taking, towing, holding on to or scouting for whales'.[23] By a protocol to the Whaling Convention adopted in 1956, the definition of 'whale catcher' was extended to include helicopters and other aircraft.[24]

The Convention cannot, of course, apply to whaling ships operating under the jurisdiction of non-parties. This has resulted in periodic upsurges of 'pirate' whaling – whaling by vessels often manned by nationals of party states which fly the flag of a non-party as a flag of convenience in order to escape IWC controls.[25] It will be noted later in this chapter that both the IWC and individual parties have taken measures to thwart 'pirate' whaling and have enjoyed some success in this regard. Nonetheless, this type of unregulated whaling remains a potential obstacle in the future to the ability of the IWC to supervise all

[22] Whaling Convention, Article 1(2). [23] Ibid., Article 2(1)–(3).

[24] Protocol to the International Convention for the Regulation of Whaling, 1956, 338 *UNTS* 366; in force 4 May 1959.

[25] See R. L. Brownell and A. V. Yablokov, 'Illegal and Pirate Whaling', in W. F. Perrin, B. Wursig and J. G. M Thewissen (eds.), *Encyclopaedia of Marine Mammals* (Academic Press, 2002), pp. 608–12, at p. 611. This is a problem in the context of high-seas fisheries as well, further explored in Chapter 5 above.

whaling operations should the commercial whaling moratorium be lifted.

b) *Waters covered by the Whaling Convention*

The Whaling Convention applies to 'all waters' in which whaling is carried on by factory ships, land stations or whale catchers.[26] This is potentially very wide, and could embrace not only the high seas but also the exclusive economic zone (EEZ) (or exclusive fishing zone if an EEZ is not proclaimed) and the territorial seas of state parties. Such a reading would extend the geographic scope of the Convention beyond what is contemplated in most international fisheries agreements. Moreover, it appears to run contrary to the sovereign rights which the 1982 Law of the Sea Convention (UNCLOS) accords the coastal state 'for the purposes of . . . exploiting, conserving and managing the natural resources, whether living or non-living' within the EEZ.[27] This concept of sovereign rights over natural resources within EEZs is widely accepted to have attained customary status, and UNCLOS does not acknowledge the right of organisations to interfere with the exercise of a coastal state's rights within its EEZ.[28] The question has thus been raised whether 'all waters' should in fact be limited to the high seas beyond these coastal zones. Some Latin American states have argued against the competence of the IWC to regulate in their 200-mile coastal zones, but most parties accept the application of the Whaling Convention in their respective maritime zones.[29]

c) *Whales covered by the Whaling Convention*

The main text of the Convention refers only to 'whales' and without definition. Since the distinction between 'whales', 'small whales' and

26 Whaling Convention, Article 1(2).

27 Article 56(1)(a) UNCLOS. The EEZ extends up to 188 nautical miles measured beyond the twelve-mile territorial sea, to an overall maximum breadth of 200 nautical miles.

28 See R. Gambell, 'International Management of Whales and Whaling: An Historical Review of the Regulation of Commercial and Aboriginal Subsistence Whaling' (1993) 46(2) *Arctic* 97, at p. 105.

29 See P. W. Birnie, 'International Legal Issues in the Management and Protection of the Whale: A Review of Four Decades of Experience' (1989) 29 *Natural Resources Law* 903, at pp. 916–17, where it is noted that Latin American states (Argentina, Brazil, Chile, Mexico, Peru and Panama) have 'strongly resisted any attempt to argue that the [Whaling Convention's] scope extends to these areas'.

'dolphins and porpoises' is ambiguous from a taxonomic viewpoint, the jurisdiction of the IWC over smaller cetaceans is unclear. The question of jurisdiction is particularly important because large numbers of small cetaceans are killed each year either as a result of direct exploitation or incidentally to other fishing operations.[30] Yellowfin tuna tend to swim beneath large schools of porpoises, and fishermen have adopted the practice of encircling large schools of porpoises with nets in order to catch the tuna underneath. Some porpoises inevitably become entangled and drown. The European Commission has noted that, in relation to by-catch in the North Sea alone, it is estimated that 'each year several thousand harbour porpoises are caught in bottom-set gillnets'.[31]

The Annex on Nomenclature of whales affixed to the Final Act of the Convention listed the names of certain cetaceans and, for the most part, confined such reference to large cetaceans.[32] Some members of the IWC, such as Denmark, Japan and Norway, have taken the view that the Commission only enjoys regulatory competence in relation to the catching of these named whales. The IWC has indeed traditionally limited the scope of its regulations, with a few exceptions, to the larger baleen and toothed whales. However, others, such as New Zealand, the UK and Australia, have noted that the Annex is not an integral part of the Convention (unlike, for example, the Schedule), and have supported the view that, as it was produced simply for guidance purposes, the Annex 'should not be used to restrict the range of the Commission's activities'.[33] We will note later in this chapter that, despite the lack of agreement as to competence in relation to the management of small cetaceans, the IWC has agreed that international co-operation is needed to conserve small cetaceans.

[30] See Scarff, *supra* n. 1, p. 379; see also E. Mitchell, *Porpoises, Dolphins and Small Whale Fisheries of the World*, Monograph No. 3 (IUCN, 1973), pp. 87–9.

[31] European Commission, Proposal for a Council Regulation Laying down Measures Concerning Incidental Catches of Cetaceans in Fisheries and Amending Regulation (EC) No. 88/98 COM 2003 451.

[32] The Annex makes reference to the right, bowhead, humpback, blue, fin, northern minke, sei, Bryde's, grey, pigmy right and sperm whales. Reference is also made to both the northern and southern bottlenose dolphins.

[33] See Chairman's Report of the Thirty-Eighth Annual Meeting (1986), p. 5. On the IWC and competence in relation to small cetaceans, see P. W. Birnie, 'Small Cetaceans and the IWC' (1997) 10(1) *Georgetown IELR* 1, and A. Gillespie, 'Small Cetaceans, International Law and the IWC' (2000) 2(2) *Melb. JIL* 257.

4. The International Whaling Commission

The IWC has to date met annually and is composed of one voting representative of each party who may be accompanied by experts and advisers.[34] The IWC is serviced by the IWC Secretariat.[35]

a) *Membership*

Eighty-eight states are party to the Whaling Convention at the time of writing.[36] Each state party is represented by a commissioner. Any state which did not originally sign the Convention, whether or not it is involved in whaling, may become a party to the treaty simply by notifying the depositary government in writing.[37] The fifteen original signatories all historically had interests in whaling, but the vast majority of parties are not now whaling states. Indeed, voting records at IWC meetings suggest that most of the eighteen states which joined the Convention between March 1979 and the IWC meeting in 1982 did so with the express object of bringing commercial whaling to an end. A moratorium on commercial whaling was considered and rejected by several IWC meetings prior to 1982. The fact that the 1982 meeting finally agreed to halt commercial whaling, at least temporarily, from 1986 is as much an indication of the voting power of these new parties as of any change of heart by the whaling states.[38]

b) *Committees*

The International Whaling Commission is authorised to establish 'such committees as it considers desirable to perform such functions as it may authorise'.[39] The most important committees have traditionally

[34] Whaling Convention, Article 3(1). See further section 4 below, which, inter alia, notes that the IWC comprises one voting representative of each party who may be accompanied by experts and advisers.

[35] The Secretariat is located at 'The Red House', Station Road, Impington, Cambridgeshire, UK.

[36] Details can be obtained from the IWC's website: www.iwcoffice.org.

[37] Whaling Convention, Article 10(2). The US government is the depositary government.

[38] The vote for zero catch limits for commercial whaling for the 1985–6 pelagic and 1986 coastal seasons and thereafter was twenty-five in favour, seven against and five abstentions. Fifteen of the parties who voted in favour were non-whaling states which had acceded to the Whaling Convention since March 1979.

[39] Whaling Convention, Article 3(4).

been the permanent Finance and Administration, Scientific, and Technical Committees. The Finance and Administration Committee is responsible for the provision of advice to the IWC on issues relating to budget, expenditure, financial contributions from parties and staffing questions.[40] The Scientific Committee, on which all parties have the right to be represented if they so wish, is responsible for studying available scientific and statistical information on whale stocks and whaling, for reviewing national scientific research programmes, and for making appropriate recommendations to the IWC.[41] In the past, one of its most important tasks was to advise on the appropriate classification of whale stocks under the New Management Procedure, to be discussed later, and on the size of commercial quotas to be set. It has additionally been importantly engaged in the 'comprehensive assessment', also to be discussed later. The Scientific Committee will always meet immediately prior to annual IWC meetings. The Technical Committee, on which all parties also have the right to be represented if they so elect, advises the IWC on management principles and non-scientific matters such as aboriginal whaling, whale-killing methods, and whaling outside the jurisdiction of the IWC.[42]

In addition to these three key committees, the Conservation Committee was established by IWC resolution in 2003.[43] Its establishment was not without controversy.[44] This committee has the responsibility to prepare a Conservation Agenda and make recommendations to the IWC on the Conservation Agenda. It will also implement those aspects of the agenda which the IWC refers to it, and make general recommendations to the IWC on the updating of the agenda. The committee will additionally explore the manner in which the IWC can best co-ordinate its research with other international organisations and legal regimes, such as the Convention on Migratory Species (CMS), the Convention on Conservation and Management of Antarctic Marine Living Resources (CCAMLR), the International Maritime Organisation, IUCN, and UNEP.

[40] Rules of Procedure and Financial Regulations of the International Whaling Commission, para. M(8).

[41] Ibid., para. M(4). [42] Ibid., para. M(7). [43] IWC Resolution 2003–1, *supra* n. 20.

[44] The *Japan Times* on 25 June 2003 commented that Resolution 2003–1 was to be seen as 'a vote against the resumption of commercial whaling. It is difficult to escape the impression that the IWC is becoming increasingly like an "international antiwhaling commission".'

Subcommittees have also been established (on aboriginal subsistence whaling and infractions). Additionally, ad hoc working groups are established to assist the IWC and its committees in its deliberations.

c) Research programmes

The Whaling Convention authorises the IWC to:

> (a) encourage, recommend, or if necessary, organise studies and investigations relating to whales and whaling;
> (b) collect and analyse statistical information concerning the current condition and trend of the whale stocks and the effects of whaling activities thereon;
> (c) study, appraise, and disseminate information concerning methods of maintaining and increasing the populations of whale stocks.[45]

The Convention encourages the IWC to publish reports and other information relevant to whales and whaling.[46] Substantial research has been done and continues to be carried out. The Scientific Committee has been engaged in the 'comprehensive assessment' of the impact of the commercial ban on whaling.[47] The decision to proceed with this assessment reflected the fact that data on cetacean population levels lacked accuracy and detail. A resumption of commercial whaling could not be contemplated until the Scientific Committee had been given the opportunity to examine the status of all whale stocks. Research has in particular addressed stock size, population trends, carrying capacity and productivity.

In addition, note should be made of the Antarctic research programme known as SOWER (Southern Ocean Whale and Ecosystem Research programme), which has been promoted by the IWC. SOWER has had a focus on the estimation of the krill, minke whale and blue whale (*Balaenoptera musculus*) populations in the southern hemisphere. Work within this programme has involved sighting cruises in Antarctic waters, the taking of skin samples from living whales, and the recording of blue whales with a view to facilitating the estimation of rare populations.

Importantly, the Scientific Committee also continues to research into the threats to cetaceans caused by marine environmental changes. It is

[45] Whaling Convention, Article 4(1). [46] Ibid., Article 4(2).
[47] Articles and papers of particular relevance to the work of the Scientific Committee have been published in the *Journal of Cetacean Research and Management* since 1999.

now recognised that any system of whale stock management which failed to take into account the impact on cetaceans of environmental factors would be inadequate. The impact of incidental catches, noise pollution (especially in relation to military sonar),[48] ozone layer depletion, climate change,[49] habitat degradation and chemical pollutants (e.g. organochlorines and heavy metals) on cetaceans have provided particular focus for attention. In 1999, for example, a programme of research entitled POLLUTION 2000+ was endorsed by the Scientific Committee with a view to assessing the impact of PCBs (polychlorinated biphenyls) on whales, and to create a model for further research on other pollutants and their effect on cetaceans.[50]

Research has additionally addressed the issue of habitat destruction. A State of the Cetacean Environment Report (SOCER) is published annually by the Scientific Committee, providing a focus on pressures on those habitats of crucial importance to cetaceans. Other work has concentrated on the impact of noise on whales, and there are IWC-endorsed plans for research on the interaction between fish stocks and whales.[51] Too often research programmes have, however, suffered from a lack of funding. The POLLUTION 2000+ programme, for example, has been sponsored in part by the IWC with additional contributions from state parties; although some contracting parties have indeed contributed financially, difficulties have been encountered in raising adequate funding for this programme.[52]

d) Observers

The Whaling Convention makes no provision for the admission of observers to IWC meetings, but the IWC's Rules of Procedure allow non-parties and inter-governmental organisations to be represented by observers if they have previously attended an IWC meeting, or if they submit a written request to the Commission sixty days prior to the meeting, or if

[48] On the issue of noise and the marine environment see K. Scott, 'International Regulation of Undersea Noise' (2004) 53(2) *ICLQ* 287.

[49] See W. Burns, 'From the Harpoon to the Heat: Climate Change and the IWC in the 21st Century' (2000) 3(1) *JIWLP* 50.

[50] See Chapter 21 below for further discussion of the impact of pollution on wildlife.

[51] Japan has for some considerable time asserted that whales have a detrimental impact on fish stocks; see J. W. Young, 'Do Large Whales Have an Impact on Commercial Fishing in the South Pacific Ocean?' (2000) 3(3) *JIWLP* 253.

[52] See IWC Resolution 2000–7.

the Commission invites them to attend.[53] National or international non-governmental organisations (NGOs) may also be given observer status but any such organisation must submit its request in writing sixty days before the IWC meeting. The Commission may then subsequently issue an invitation.[54] The large number of observers who have attended IWC meetings in recent years to lobby for the positions they espouse demonstrates the widespread public interest in the work of the Commission.[55]

e) Decision-making

The IWC has the power to amend the Schedule, although it is important to note that, in the absence of consensus, such an amendment requires a three-quarters majority of state parties voting to be adopted.[56] The Schedule contains the detailed regulations governing the protection and exploitation of whales. It very importantly provides flexibility by allowing quotas to be set taking into account current estimates of whale stocks. The IWC has the power to amend the Schedule in order to fix:

(a) protected and unprotected species;
(b) open and closed seasons;
(c) open and closed waters, including the designation of sanctuary areas;
(d) size limits for each species;
(e) time, methods and intensity of whaling (including the maximum catch of whales to be taken in any one season);
(f) types and specifications of gear and apparatus and appliances which may be used;
(g) methods of measurement; and
(h) catch returns and other statistical and biological records.[57]

The Whaling Convention stipulates that amendments to the Schedule 'shall be based on scientific findings', that amendments shall only be made when 'necessary to carry out the objectives and purposes of this Convention' and that 'the interests of the consumers of whale products

[53] Rules of Procedure and Financial Regulations of the International Whaling Commission (as amended at the IWC's Fifty-Ninth Annual Meeting, May 2007), para. C(1)(a).
[54] Ibid., para. C(1)(b).
[55] At the IWC meeting in 2008 observers included, for example, the Alaskan Eskimo Whaling Commission, the Japanese Fisheries Association and Greenpeace International.
[56] Whaling Convention, Article 3(2). [57] Ibid., Article 5(1).

and the whaling industry' shall be considered.[58] The Convention prohibits the IWC from allocating catch quotas among the parties or from restricting the number or nationality of factory ships or land stations.[59] The fact that amendments shall be based on scientific findings has caused complications within the IWC and its Scientific Committee. There has often proved to be a lack of agreement on the best ways to estimate stock size, and therefore in reaching agreement on 'those species best able to sustain exploitation'.[60]

Only formal amendments to the Schedule require a three-quarters majority of those states voting; other decisions require a simple majority of Commission members voting in the absence of consensus. In addition to regulating whaling by means of the Schedule, the IWC is authorised to 'make recommendations to any or all contracting Governments on any matters which relate to whales or whaling and to the objectives and purposes of this Convention'.[61] Pursuant to this authority, the IWC has made recommendations on a number of different issues in the form of resolutions. These recommendations do not, of course, have the same legal force as amendments to the Schedule, and they require only a simple majority of parties voting to be adopted. However, they are examples of 'soft law' intended to influence the conduct of parties. Resolutions over the years have varied from inviting Japan to reconsider the level of its domestic quota for Dall's porpoises,[62] to urging Canada to refrain from issuing a license to take a bowhead whale (*Balaena mysticetus*) from the Hudson Bay–Foxe Basin population.[63] We will note in later discussion that other examples of IWC resolutions include those adopted to address the issues of 'pirate' whaling, humane killing, whaling under special permit and whalewatching.

f) Use of the objection procedure

Any amendment to the Schedule adopted by the IWC can be avoided by a state party by the registering of an objection by that party within ninety

[58] Ibid., Article 5(2). [59] Ibid., Article 5(2).

[60] Ibid., Preamble. See P. W. Birnie, 'IWC-Bargaining and Compromise' (1981) 5 *Marine Policy* 79, at pp. 83–4, and D. M. Wilkinson, 'The Use of Domestic Measures to Enforce International Whaling Agreements: A Critical Perspective' (1989) 17(2) *Denv. J. Int. L and Policy* 271, at p. 274.

[61] Whaling Convention, Article 6.

[62] IWC Resolution 1999–9; Annual Report of the International Whaling Commission 1999, pp. 55–6.

[63] IWC Resolution 2000–2; Annual Report of the International Whaling Commission 2000, p. 55.

days of notification of its adoption.[64] In effect, the objecting party will not then be bound by the relevant Schedule amendment. If a party registers an objection within the prescribed ninety-day period, an additional period of up to 120 days is allowed for other parties to withdraw their previously registered approval of the amendment.

Use of the objection procedure has undermined decisions of the International Whaling Commission on a number of occasions. As early as 1954, Canada, Japan, the USA and the USSR objected to a five-year prohibition on the taking of blue whales in the North Pacific – one of the IWC's first real conservationist initiatives. Since these four were the only states hunting blue whales in the North Pacific, their objection rendered the IWC action totally ineffective.[65] Perhaps the most significant objection has proved to be Norway's in relation to the commercial whaling moratorium. Japan, Norway, Peru and the USSR registered objections to the amendment of the Schedule which introduced the moratorium. Japan and Peru have subsequently withdrawn their objections and are therefore now bound by the amendment to the Schedule bringing the ban into force. However, by registering an objection in accordance with the terms of the Convention, the ban on commercial whaling is not binding on Norway, nor indeed on the Russian Federation (the successor to the USSR under the Convention) should it choose to resume commercial whaling operations in the future. Norway has taken the view that the North East Atlantic minke whale stock is not threatened with extinction and can be sustainably harvested.[66] In May 1993 Norway announced its intention to recommence commercial whaling operations by taking 160 minke whales from the North East Atlantic in 1993. Norwegian commercial whaling operations have continued despite numerous calls in the form of resolutions by the majority in the IWC requesting that Norway reconsider its objection and halt commercial whaling activities.[67]

64 Whaling Convention, Schedule, Article 5(3). An objection procedure is also found in a number of international fisheries agreements, as discussed in Chapter 5 above.

65 See Sixth Report of the International Whaling Commission (1955), p. 5.

66 Abundance estimates agreed by the Scientific Committee in 1996 put the population of North Eastern Atlantic minke whale at over 67,000 in 1989, risen to over 118,000 in 1995; *Rep. Int. Whal. Commn* 47:30 (1997).

67 See, for example, IWC Resolution 1995–5 (*Rep. Int. Whal. Commn* 46:44, 1996), IWC Resolution 1996–5 (*Rep. Int. Whal. Commn* 47:50, 1997), IWC Resolution 1997–3 (*Rep. Int. Whal. Commn* 48:46, 1998), and IWC Resolution 2001–5 (Annual Report of the International Whaling Commission 2001, p. 56).

5. Conservation and management

a) Early management methods

For over twenty years, the IWC used the 'blue whale unit' as its yardstick for annual catch limits. This device regulated the total amount of whales that could be taken in a given year by all those states actively engaged in whaling; the latter in effect 'competed for the quota'.[68] This blunt regulatory instrument failed to control the harvest of individual species and was based on the amount of oil a species might typically produce when compared to another type of whale; one blue whale unit was considered to be either one blue whale or two fin whales or two and a half humpbacks or six sei whales (*Balaenoptera borealis*) (or an appropriate combination).[69] Until the mid-1960s, when the most important whaling product changed from oil to meat, the system of blue whale units hastened the decline of blue and fin whales because whalers preferred to hunt these two oil-rich species notwithstanding they could catch larger numbers of smaller whales.[70]

For the first fifteen years of the Convention's existence the Schedule in fact imposed few restrictions on whaling.[71] An unprecedented number of whales were killed during that time, reaching a peak of approximately 60,000 in the 1960–1 season.[72] Since then, faced with grossly depleted stocks of several whale species and an increasingly powerful anti-whaling lobby, the IWC has adopted a more conservationist approach. Continuing concern as to overexploitation of whale stocks prompted the 1972 Stockholm United Nations Conference on the Human Environment to recommend the introduction of a ten-year moratorium on commercial whaling.[73]

The inept blue whale unit was abandoned in 1972 in favour of quotas on a species-by-species basis, but the non-binding recommendation of the Stockholm Conference was not endorsed at the twenty-fourth IWC meeting held in London that year. Instead, in 1974 the IWC adopted

[68] S. Oberthur, 'The ICRW: From Over-Exploitation to Total Prohibition', in H. O. Bergesen, G. Parmann and Ø. B. Thommessen, *Yearbook of International Co-operation on Environment and Development 1998/99* (Earthscan, 1998), p. 30.

[69] See para. 8(b) of the Schedule as it was in 1949, published in the IWC's first report in 1950 at p. 16.

[70] See Scarff, *supra* n. 1, p. 352.

[71] The Schedule set an overall quota of 16,000 'blue whale units' (see para. 8(a) of the Schedule as it was in 1949), and there were no restrictions on the methods of killing whales.

[72] See Twelfth Report of the International Whaling Commission (1961), pp. 4–5.

[73] UN Doc.A/CONF.48/14, recommendation 33.

a new system of control known as the New Management Procedure (NMP), which pinpoints quotas still further and was introduced in 1976. Under the NMP each species is divided into anything up to twenty different stocks, and quotas are set on a stock-by-stock basis. Each stock is classified as an 'initial management stock', a 'sustained management stock' or a 'protection stock', depending upon the relationship between the population level of the stock and the level of its 'maximum sustainable yield'.[74] Commercial harvesting of protection stocks is prohibited,[75] and exploitation of stocks in the other two categories must be sustainable.[76] Classification frequently varies for different stocks of the same species. Most fin whale stocks, for example, have protection-stock status, although the East Greenland–Iceland stock is currently designated sustained management stock.[77] In addition, the minke Northeastern Atlantic stock is currently a protection stock, whilst the minke Northern Indian Ocean stock has been declared an initial management stock.[78]

b) The introduction of the commercial whaling moratorium

The adoption of the NMP did not, however, ensure effective protection of whale stocks; particular difficulties were experienced in establishing maximum sustainable yield and stock sizes. Concerned at the perceived overexploitation of whale stocks, the lack of accurate data on whale population levels and the ineffectiveness of management procedures to regulate commercial whaling, the IWC in 1982 agreed to a moratorium on commercial whaling from the 1986 coastal and 1985–6 pelagic whaling seasons. Since this time, catch quotas in the Schedule have been set at zero in relation to commercial whaling. The historic amendment to the Schedule introducing the moratorium reads as follows:

> Notwithstanding the other provisions of paragraph 10, catch limits for the killing for commercial purposes of whales from all stocks for the 1986 coastal and the 1985/86 pelagic seasons and thereafter shall be zero. This provision will be kept under review, based upon the best scientific advice, and by 1990 at the latest the Commission will undertake a comprehensive assessment of the effects of this decision on whale stocks and consider modification of this provision and the establishment of other catch limits.

Notwithstanding the classification of a particular whale stock under the NMP, the effect of this amendment was to prohibit commercial

[74] Whaling Convention, Schedule, para. 10. [75] Ibid., para. 10(c).
[76] Ibid., para. 10(a)–(b). [77] Ibid., Table 1. [78] Ibid.

whaling from 1985–6 in Antarctica and from 1986 elsewhere until the IWC decides otherwise. Of course, a party which has objected to this Schedule amendment would not be bound by it. As indicated above, four states initially did so, with two states, Norway and the Russian Federation, still not bound by the amendment.

c) *The 'comprehensive assessment' and the development of the Revised Management Scheme*

An important aspect of the amendment to the Schedule introducing the moratorium was the need to carry out a 'comprehensive assessment' of the impact of the commercial ban on whaling by 1990. More accurate data on population levels was needed before any possible resumption of commercial whaling could be contemplated. Since the decision to set catch quotas at zero, the IWC's Scientific Committee has engaged in this comprehensive assessment by examining the status of all whale stocks. This work involves the assessment of current stock size, population trends, carrying capacity and productivity.[79] Concluded examinations over time have included assessments of the southern hemisphere, North Atlantic and North Pacific minke whale populations, North Atlantic fin whale and North Pacific Bryde's whale (*Balaenoptera edeni, B. brydei*) stocks, southern and northern hemisphere right whale populations, North Atlantic humpback populations, southern hemisphere blue whales and the Bering–Chukchi–Beaufort Seas bowhead whale stock. Completion of abundance estimates for the Antarctic minke whales remains of key importance.

The comprehensive assessment process includes the development of a Revised Management Procedure (RMP) designed to replace the NMP. Following endorsement of the RMP by the Scientific Committee in 1991, the IWC finally accepted a revised specification of the RMP in 1994.[80] One of the clear failings of the NMP was its failure to take into account the scientific uncertainties involved in estimating population sizes. The RMP seeks to factor in such uncertainties in the setting of stable catch limits. After extensive testing by the Scientific Committee over a number of years, the RMP is designed to establish catch limits which take into account not only uncertainties in our knowledge of population stocks,

[79] See Report of the 1986 Special Meeting of the Scientific Committee on Planning for a Comprehensive Assessment of Whale Stocks; *Rep. Int. Whal. Commn* 37:147–57, 1987.
[80] IWC Resolution 1994–5, *Rep. Int. Whal. Commn* 45:43–4, 1995.

but also potentially imperfect data on a number of issues such as environmental change. As such, it has been described by one commentator as 'a very conservative regime',[81] and by others as 'the most conservatory of any system currently existing for setting quota'.[82] The objective is to ensure all stocks reach 72 per cent of their initial stock level. Where stocks have been overexploited, they will be allowed to recover; if stocks are below 54 per cent of their initial abundance before exploitation, no catch limits will be set. The RMP has been designed to take into account a variety of factors, including historic catch underestimation and environmental pollution impacting on cetaceans. Guidelines have been established for conducting surveys and analysing data, and the IWC has agreed that abundance estimates which are not endorsed by the Scientific Committee should not be 'used in the implementation of the RMP'.[83] The RMP offers some hope that the regulation of whaling will be more effective if commercial whaling ever resumes in the future. Of course, much will still depend on the accuracy of state party reports on annual catches. In the past, there have been instances when such reports have not accurately portrayed the level of takes. The most notorious example came to light in the mid-1990s when Soviet catch records were found to have been considerably falsified for the period from 1947 to 1972.[84] In the southern hemisphere alone, unreported takes by Soviet whaling vessels totalled over 100,000 whales in this period.[85]

The RMP has not yet been implemented as the IWC has recognised that a comprehensive Revised Management Scheme (RMS) must be adopted beforehand.[86] The RMS will incorporate the RMP as its key

[81] R. Gambell, 'The International Whaling Commission Today', in G. Petursdottir (ed.), *Whaling in the North Atlantic* (University of Iceland Fisheries Research Institute, 1997), pp. 51–2. Ray Gambell served as secretary to the IWC from 1976 to 2000.

[82] P. W. Birnie, A. E. Boyle and C. J. Redgwell, *International Law and the Environment* (Oxford University Press, 3rd ed., 2009), p. 726.

[83] IWC Resolution 1995–7, *Rep. Int. Whal. Commn* 46:45–6, 1996.

[84] In early 1994, the IWC was informed by the Russian Federation of considerable inaccuracies in catch data supplied by the USSR over a number of years (particularly regarding takes of blue, right and humpback whales); see generally V. A. Zemsky, A. A. Berzin, Yu. A. Mikhalyev and D. D. Tormosov, *Soviet Antarctic Whaling Data (1947–1972)* (Center for Russian Environmental Policy, 1995). See generally on this issue and on the need for accurate reporting Gambell, *supra* n. 81, p. 52; and W. C. G. Burns and G. Wandsforde-Smith, 'The International Whaling Commission and the Future of Cetaceans in a Changing World' (2002) 11(2) *RECIEL* 199, at pp. 200–1.

[85] See Brownell and Yablokov, *supra* n. 25, p. 609.

[86] The RMP will not be implemented until all aspects of the Revised Management System have been incorporated into the Schedule; IWC Resolution 1994–5, *Rep. Int. Whal. Commn* 45:43–4, 1995. On efforts to find agreement on the RMS see A. Gillespie, 'The Search for a New Compliance Mechanism within the IWC' (2003) 34 *ODIL* 349.

scientific element, but work remains to be completed on non-scientific aspects of the RMS, particularly the necessary inspection and observation programme intended to ensure any future commercial whaling operations comply with IWC requirements.[87] Progress on unresolved issues has been very protracted. Indeed, some pro-whaling countries have taken the view that anti-whaling states are delaying the implementation of the RMS, and thereby any possible resumption of commercial whaling, by failing to reach agreement on the inspection and observation issue. They also point out that paragraph 10(e) of the Schedule (introducing the moratorium) was due to be reviewed by the latest in 1990, but that little progress has been made to date to reintroduce commercial whaling operations of those populations of minke whales which they believe are capable of being sustainably harvested.[88] In the year 2000, the IWC acknowledged the importance 'that the process of completion of the RMS proceed expeditiously',[89] and the fifty-third IWC meeting in 2001 subsequently highlighted a number of unresolved issues, which included:

- the level of coverage by international observers,
- the frequency of reporting by observers,
- whether a state party had the right to object to the appointment of an observer,
- the matter of DNA catch verification and collection of animal welfare data,
- issues concerning the monitoring of the origins of whale products once on the market and
- questions relating to the funding of any inspection and observer scheme.

Significant progress has remained elusive and the 2006 IWC meeting acknowledged that a stalemate had been reached in this respect. This apparent deadlock has already had repercussions. Although Iceland withdrew from the Convention in 1992, it rejoined in 2002 at a Special Meeting of the IWC held in Cambridge (UK) in October 2002. Iceland had not lodged a formal objection under Article 5(3) to the introduction of the ban on commercial whaling in 1982. On rejoining Iceland was of

[87] IWC Resolution 1994–5, *Rep. Int. Whal. Commn* 45:44, 1995, and Gambell, *supra* n. 81, p. 52–3.

[88] See the view of Japan expressed at the fifty-first IWC meeting, Annual Report of the International Whaling Commission 1999, p. 27.

[89] IWC Resolution 2000–3; Annual Report of the International Whaling Commission 2000, p. 55.

course unable to lodge any such objection under the Whaling Convention as the window for this possibility (within ninety days of notification of the moratorium's adoption) had long expired. However, and controversially,[90] Iceland entered a legal reservation to the moratorium on rejoining. In effect, Iceland has rejoined the Convention but purports to exclude the application of the commercial moratorium to its whaling operations. The Whaling Convention makes no express provision as to the ability of parties to make reservations, and in these circumstances general international law allows a state to make a reservation unless 'the reservation is incompatible with the object and purpose of the treaty'.[91] The Icelandic reservation made it clear that no Icelandic whaling vessel would engage in commercial whaling before 2006 and that commercial whaling operations would not be authorised in 2006 or thereafter if progress was indeed being made in negotiations on the RMS. Due to the lack of progress in RMS negotiations within the IWC, Iceland in October 2006 announced its intention to recommence commercial whaling, utilising its reservation, and currently continues to sanction commercial whaling by its whaling fleet.

d) Aboriginal whaling

Since the implementation of the moratorium, all commercial catch quotas have been set at zero. However, catch quotas above zero are still set for certain aboriginal catches.[92] The setting of quotas for this type of whaling reflects an appreciation of the particular needs of certain indigenous or native peoples, such as the Inuit.[93] Under IWC regulation

[90] The legal status under general public international law of this reservation remains a matter of contention within the IWC. See A. Gillespie, 'Iceland's Reservation at the International Whaling Commission' (2003) 14(5) *EJIL* 977. Nineteen states have lodged objections to Iceland's reservation.

[91] 1969 Vienna Convention on the Law of Treaties, 1155 *UNTS* 331, Article 19(c). Although Article 4 of the Vienna Convention notes that it 'applies only to treaties which are concluded by States after the entry into force of the present convention with regard to such States', it is arguable that its provisions on reservations are representative of customary international law and would therefore apply in the context of Iceland's reservation; see Gillespie, *supra* n. 90, p. 987. The Vienna Convention entered into force on 27 January 1980.

[92] Whaling Convention, Schedule, para. 13.

[93] On aboriginal whaling, see N. Doubleday, 'Aboriginal Subsistance [*sic*] Whaling: The Right of Inuit to Hunt Whales and Implications for International Law' (1989) 17(2) *Denv. J. Int. L and Policy* 373, and J. Firestone and J. Lilley, 'Aboriginal Subsistence Whaling and the Right to Practice and Revitalize Cultural Traditions and Customs' (2005) 8(2–3) *JIWLP* 177.

aboriginal subsistence whaling is allowed by natives in Greenland (for mainly fin and minke whales), the Russian Federation (for grey and bowhead whales), St Vincent and the Grenadines (for humpback), and in the USA (for bowhead and grey whales). Any whale taken for subsistence purposes must be exclusively used for local consumption in meeting nutritional, subsistence and cultural needs. Scientific advice on catch limits is supplied by the IWC's Scientific Committee, which is also engaged in the development of a new procedure for the management of aboriginal whaling to form part of a comprehensive Aboriginal Subsistence Whaling Management Procedure.

The taking of whales by aboriginals has at times proved controversial. For example, the Makah tribe of Washington State was given permission in 1997 by the IWC to hunt up to five grey whales per year in the period from 1997 to 2002. In accordance with the 1855 US–Makah Treaty of Neah Bay, the Makah tribe was granted the 'right of taking fish and of whaling'.[94] Accordingly, the US government controversially supported the Makah's request for an aboriginal quota. The Makah have long underlined the importance of whaling in their culture. Although the Makah landed a grey whale in May 1999 more than seventy years after their last whale hunt, their plans to hunt on a regular basis have been halted by litigation in US courts brought by environmental groups.[95]

e) *Sanctuaries*

By virtue of Article V(1)c of the Convention,[96] the Commission can designate sanctuary areas. In 1979, prior to the amendment of the Schedule introducing the ban on commercial whaling, the IWC established the Indian Ocean Sanctuary following a proposal by the Republic of Seychelles. The southern boundary of the sanctuary is at fifty-five degrees southern latitude. All commercial whaling in this area is prohibited as long as the sanctuary remains in place. This will be the case even if the global ban on commercial whaling is lifted at some time in the future. In 1994, the Southern Ocean Sanctuary was also established, which similarly bans commercial whaling in the area south of forty degrees southern latitude apart from in the Indian Ocean (where the

94 Article 4.

95 See, for example, *Metcalf v Daley* (9th Cir. 2000) 214 F.3d 1135 in which it was declared that there was a need for a new environmental impact assessment in relation to the proposed Makah activities.

96 Whaling Convention, Article V(1)c.

sanctuary meets up with the Indian Ocean Sanctuary at fifty-five degrees southern latitude), and the waters around South America and part of the South Pacific (where the limits of the sanctuary follow the line of sixty degrees southern latitude, the outer limit of the Antarctic convergence). Japan lodged an objection to this sanctuary, and so any Japanese Antarctic commercial whaling operations would not be bound by the amendment to the Schedule introducing this sanctuary if the global ban on commercial whaling is lifted in the future. Debate concerning the status of these sanctuaries reflects the general polarisation of the views within the IWC. It will be recalled that any amendment to the Schedule 'shall be based on scientific findings'.[97] Japan takes the view that the amendments to the Schedule which established these sanctuaries were not so based, while other countries, such as New Zealand, strongly refute such a suggestion.[98]

In successive IWC meetings held between 2000 and 2004, proposals to establish a sanctuary in the South Pacific have been put forward by Australia with support from New Zealand. In addition, Brazil has in particular sponsored moves to establish a South Atlantic sanctuary, and proposals were submitted to IWC meetings held between 2001 and 2007. On each occasion there has been insufficient support to reach the three-quarters majority required. Whilst countries such as Australia and New Zealand point to the scientific evidence that a large number of whale stocks remain depleted, pro-whaling countries reject any move towards the setting up of new sanctuaries. Japan in particular takes the view that calls for these new areas of sanctuary lack a scientific basis, and run contrary to the principle of sustainable utilisation in relation to those whale stocks which have recovered sufficiently since the ban on commercial whaling was introduced.

f) Small cetaceans

Despite the lack of agreement as to competence, the IWC has accepted that international co-operation is required to conserve small cetaceans. The forty-fourth IWC meeting established a working group to consider a mechanism to address small cetaceans in the Commission. The deliberations of this working group were presented to the IWC in May 1994, and the IWC subsequently passed a resolution which established a basic

[97] Ibid., Article V(2)b.
[98] Annual Report of the International Whaling Commission 2001, p. 16.

structure within which problems relating to small cetaceans could be considered within the Commission.[99] This resolution underlines the importance of engaging relevant coastal and range states in the process of selecting particular stocks for review, as well as the need to co-operate with those same states both in the examination of scientific data relating to stocks, and in the assessment of the status of those stocks. A voluntary fund was also established to facilitate the participation of developing countries in work relating to small cetaceans.

The Scientific Committee has established a Small Cetaceans subcommittee which has reviewed the status and exploitation of numerous populations of small cetaceans. It has paid special attention to those small cetaceans in particular danger (such as vaquita, which are often caught incidentally in gillnets, and the boto). In the light of the subcommittee's deliberations, the Scientific Committee itself has provided information and advice to the Commission in relation to a variety of small cetaceans, such as the humpback dolphin, the Yangtze River baiji, the harbour and Dall's porpoises and the Indus River dolphin.[100] The work of the Scientific Committee is ongoing and has served to highlight to members of the Commission that co-operation is needed to prevent the overexploitation as well as the incidental by-catch of certain small cetaceans. Efforts to raise awareness of the particular plight of the Yangtze River baiji appear to have been in vain. In 2007 the IWC voiced concern in the light of Scientific Committee deliberations that agreed with the conclusions of a survey pointing to the extinction of this species.[101] The apparent fate of this baiji is thought to be the first time a cetacean species has become extinct in the modern era and is likely to have been brought about by high levels of incidental by-catch and degradation of habitat.[102]

To enable the Scientific Committee effectively to review small-cetacean stock status, state parties have been encouraged to pass on information as to direct and incidental takes, population estimates and known threats to stocks of small cetaceans.[103] Whilst some countries

[99] IWC Resolution 1994–2; *Rep. Int. Whal. Commn* 45:41–2, 1995.

[100] See *Rep. Int. Whal. Commn* 41:38, 1991; *Rep. Int. Whal. Commn* 42:36–7, 1992; and Chairman's summary report for the Fifty-Seventh Annual IWC Meeting, Ulsan, Republic of Korea, June 2005, p. 2.

[101] IWC Resolution 2007–5; see the first paragraph of the preamble. [102] Ibid.

[103] See, for example, IWC Resolution 2001–12, Annual Report of the International Whaling Commission 2001, p. 59.

have seen fit to provide this information in their annual reports, it is clear that other state parties appear reluctant to supply this data.[104]

g) *Pirate whaling*

In 1979, alarmed by the amount of pirate whaling outside its jurisdiction, the IWC recommended each party to 'cease immediately any importation of whale meat and products from, and the export of whaling vessels and equipment to, non-member countries and operations' and to consider prohibiting 'whaling by non-member countries within their fishery conservation zones'.[105] Taking the case against pirate whaling one step further in 1980, the IWC recommended each party to

> prevent the transfer of whaling vessels and equipment and, as far as possible, the dissemination of whaling information and expertise, or the provision of any other type of assistance specifically designed for and likely to be used for whaling, to any nation or entity under the jurisdiction of such a nation which is not a member of the IWC

and to take

> all practicable steps within their competence to prohibit their nationals from offering services or expertise directly relevant to whaling to any vessel belonging to any nation, or entity under the jurisdiction of any nation, which is not a member of the IWC.[106]

These recommendations seem to have had a significant practical impact, although credit in this respect is also due to non-governmental organisations, such as Greenpeace, for their work in highlighting the pirate whaling problem. There is little doubt that pirate whaling is no longer practised on the scale it once was in the 1970s. Nonetheless, whale blubber washed ashore in 1991 on West Falkland raised fears that pirate whalers were again at work,[107] and an Australian government report indicated in 1997 that some pirate whaling continued to occur in the Philippines.[108]

[104] Ibid. [105] *Rep. Int. Whal. Commn* 30:38, 1990 (Appendix 9).
[106] *Rep. Int. Whal. Commn* 31:30–1, 1981 (Appendix 1).
[107] See *Rep. Int. Whal.Commn* 43:18–9, 1993.
[108] 'Recent information indicates that some whaling occurs in the Philippines . . . with catches in the range of forty to sixty per year, possibly Bryde's whale'. Australian National Task Force on Whaling, *A Universal Metaphor: Australia's Opposition to Commercial Whaling* (Environment Australia, 1997).

h) Whalewatching

The whalewatching issue provides a further example of the tensions within the IWC between those that advocate a return to commercial whaling and those countries that oppose a lifting of the moratorium. Whilst pro-whaling states regard the issue as a low priority and outside the IWC's competence, other countries see whalewatching as a real alternative to commercial whaling. The IWC first took action on this issue at the forty-fifth IWC meeting in May 1993. A resolution was adopted by consensus which noted that approximately 4 million people went on whalewatching trips in 1991, creating about US$300 million.[109] More recently it is estimated that whalewatching raises as much as US$1,000 million per annum.[110]

The potential risks of unregulated whalewatching activities have, however, been acknowledged. In June 1996 the IWC passed a resolution which noted that it considered 'that the IWC has a continuing part to play in monitoring and providing guidance on the sustainable development of whalewatching',[111] and adopted the General Principles for the Managing of Whalewatching which had been put forward by the Scientific Committee. These recommendations (as subsequently amended) offer guidance to coastal states in the formulation of national rules, and endeavour to ensure that whalewatching does not significantly increase the risks to the survival of affected whale populations. The recommendations are not regarded as legally binding, with coastal states retaining competence to regulate their own whalewatching activities.

i) Welfare issues

The issue of humane killing has been a controversial one within the Commission. The IWC has recently noted its concern that the current methods of killing whales 'do not guarantee death without pain, stress or distress',[112] and some anti-whaling countries have sought to link the

[109] IWC Resolution on Whalewatching, *Rep. Int. Whal. Commn* 44:33–4, 1994.

[110] IWC Resolution 2003-1 (annex); Annual Report of the International Whaling Commission 2003, p. 58–9.

[111] IWC Resolution 1996-2, *Rep. Int. Whal. Commn* 47:48, 1997. Furthermore, the IWC has recently recognised the 'valuable benefits that can be derived from the non-lethal uses of cetaceans as a resource, both in socio-economic and scientific development'. IWC Resolution 2007-3.

[112] IWC Resolution 2004-3, Annual Report of the International Whaling Commission 2004, pp. 67–8.

issue of humane killing to any possible lifting of the moratorium. This issue is further addressed in the chapter on welfare.[113]

6. Special permits for scientific research

Notwithstanding any of its other provisions, including the Schedule, the Whaling Convention allows party governments to grant special permits authorising their nationals to kill whales for the purposes of scientific research.[114] Whilst each party authorising such takes is obliged to report to the IWC as to the permits it has granted,[115] the issuing of scientific permits remains the responsibility of each concerned party exercising its sovereign rights in areas within its jurisdiction and over its vessels on the high seas. The IWC has no authority to withdraw the authorisation of a special permit or to ban the granting of such a permit.[116] Nonetheless, the Schedule provides that 'proposed permits shall be reviewed and commented on by the scientific committee when possible',[117] and the IWC has adopted guidelines for the scientific committee to enable it to carry out such reviews.[118]

Since the introduction of the moratorium, a number of countries have embarked on scientific research programmes. For example, before leaving the IWC Iceland began a four-year programme in 1986 in which 292 fin whales and seventy sei whales were caught.[119] Having rejoined the IWC, Iceland in August 2003 indicated its intention to resume the issuing of special permits by authorising the taking of thirty-eight minke whales in order to evaluate the impact of minke on fish stocks around Iceland.[120] In 2004 Iceland issued permits for the taking of

[113] Chapter 20 below.

[114] Whaling Convention, Article 8(1). On the ethics of such research, see A. Gillespie, 'Whaling under a Scientific Auspice: The Ethics of Scientific Whaling Operations' (2000) 3(1) *JIWLP* 1.

[115] Whaling Convention, Article 8(1).

[116] See also Gambell, *supra* n. 81, p. 59.

[117] Schedule, para. 30.

[118] See guidelines adopted in 1986 and 1987 (*Rep. Int. Whal. Commn* 37:25, 1987; and *Rep. Int. Whal. Commn* 38:27, 1988), now replaced by Resolution 1995–9 on whaling under special permit (*Rep. Int. Whal. Commn* 46:46–7, 1996). In 2007 the IWC adopted a new procedure for reviewing new permit proposals; this procedure importantly includes the establishment of a specialist workshop to review proposals and comment on results of whaling under scientific permits.

[119] Gambell, *supra* n. 81, p. 59.

[120] Iceland had unveiled plans to take up to 500 whales over a two-year period – just the taking of thirty-nine minke were in fact authorised by special permit in 2003. Final Press Release, IWC's Fifty-Sixth Meeting, 2004.

twenty-five minke. Between 1988 and 1994 Norway issued scientific permits for the taking of minke whales in the North East Atlantic, enabling the carrying out of research into feeding and food, age determination and the role of minke in the ecosystem. Just under 300 whales were taken under the Norwegian programme.[121]

Japan has carried out a scientific research programme in the Antarctic in relation to southern hemisphere minke whale stocks (the Japanese Whale Research Program under Special Permit in the Antarctic, known as JARPA). This was an eighteen-year programme which commenced in 1987 and in which approximately 300 to 400 whales were caught each year.[122] It is noteworthy that Japan issued special permits for the taking of minke in the Antarctic region despite the introduction of the Southern Ocean Sanctuary. JARPA's objectives included gaining an appreciation of life history parameters of minke whales in the region (such as age at sexual maturity), understanding the role of whales in the Antarctic ecosystem and an assessment of the impact of environmental concerns on cetaceans. JARPA also aimed to gain a greater understanding of the southern hemisphere minke whale stock structure. Japan began a new programme entitled JARPA II in 2005–6, at which time proposed annual sample sizes involved the taking of 850 Antarctic minke, fifty humpback and fifty fin whales.

In addition to research in the Antarctic, Japan began a programme of scientific research on minke in the North Pacific in 1994 (JARPN) in a bid to provide information on stock structure and mixing rates of minke in waters around Japan. The IWC noted in 2001 that over 600 whales had been taken in the North Pacific since 1994.[123] The JARPN programme was deemed necessary by Japan bearing in mind difficulties faced by the Scientific Committee in gauging stocks in this area. Under the JARPN II programme, which concentrates in particular on the feeding ecology of cetaceans, special permits have been issued by Japan since 2000 for the taking not only of minke, but also of Bryde's and sperm whales. JARPN II includes the taking of 150 minke, fifty Bryde's, fifty sei and ten sperm whales each year from the western North Pacific.

Those countries that have issued special permits for scientific research have pointed to the benefits of this research for the general management

[121] Gambell, *supra* n. 81, p. 59. [122] Ibid., p. 59.
[123] Resolution 2001–8, Annual Report of the International Whaling Commission 2001, p. 57.

of whales. Japan in particular takes the view that such research can only assist in identifying those whale stocks which can now be sustainably utilised, and in generally facilitating the effective management of stocks. On the other hand, opponents highlight that the objectives of scientific research programmes could be met by non-lethal methods. Japan has refuted such a suggestion in relation to studies on the impact of pollution, and in relation to stock management.[124] Additionally, Japan has indicated that research into issues concerning age, growth and pregnancy would be restricted if limited simply to the use of non-lethal methods.[125]

Anti-whaling countries look on the ability to issue special permits as a way in which the impact of the commercial whaling moratorium can be undermined, and a convenient way to engage whaling fleets prior to a possible resumption of commercial whaling operations. The Convention indicates that '[a]ny whales taken under these special permits shall so far as practicable be processed',[126] and meat from Japanese scientific whaling operations often finds its way to restaurants in Japan, where it is regarded as a delicacy. An IWC resolution passed in 2003 noted that 'whales caught in Japan's special permit operations provide over 3,000 tonnes of edible products per year that are sold for commercial purposes'.[127] In 2007 the IWC called on Japan 'to suspend indefinitely the lethal aspects of JARPA II conducted within the Southern Ocean Whale Sanctuary'.[128]

7. Small-type coastal whaling

Since withdrawing its objection to the moratorium in 1985, Japan has endeavoured to highlight the socioeconomic implications of the ban on four communities closely linked to whaling, namely Abashiri, Ayukawa, Wadaura and Taiji. These communities have traditionally had a high dependence on their whaling operations, typically making use of smaller vessels than larger commercial whaling operations, and taking smaller-sized whales. The IWC has recognised their 'socio-economic and cultural needs ... [and] the distress which has resulted from the cessation of

[124] See Annual Report of the International Whaling Commission 1999, p. 28. [125] Ibid.
[126] Article VIII(2); see also Gambell, *supra* n. 81, p. 60.
[127] IWC Resolution 2003–2; Annual Report of the International Whaling Commission 2003, p. 60.
[128] IWC Resolution 2007–1.

minke whaling'.[129] To relieve their plight, Japan has sought to make a distinction between 'large-type' pelagic whaling and 'small-type coastal whaling' based on differences in the overall size of the operations in terms of manpower, use of technology and financial implications. Japan argues that, although large-type whaling is clearly covered by the ban, small-type coastal whaling should be allowed. Japan regards small-type whaling as sharing many of the attributes of aboriginal subsistence whaling in relation to nutritional, subsistence and cultural needs. Why, for example, should a country like the USA back the right of the Makah tribe to resume whaling when the tribe had not engaged in whaling for over seventy years, but not support a resumption of whaling by those Japanese communities recognised internationally as being particularly affected adversely by the moratorium in an economic, social and cultural context? Japanese calls for an interim relief allocation of minke whales to be landed by these communities have not been accepted by the IWC.

8. Enforcement

The enforcement provisions of the Whaling Convention and the Schedule, together with the domestic measures which party governments have taken to implement them, are particularly interesting for three reasons. First, the Convention and the Schedule established for the first time in international wildlife law a system of national enforcement with international supervision. Second, some parties have gone to unusual lengths to ensure that their nationals neither participate in nor assist whaling operations anywhere in the world. Third, US law authorises sanctions to be taken against states whose activities diminish the effectiveness of the IWC.

a) National inspectors and the International Observer Scheme

Each state party bears the responsibility of making sure that its own whaling operations comply with IWC rules.[130] Since 1949 the Schedule has stipulated that at least two inspectors shall be maintained on each

[129] *Rep. Int. Whal. Commn* 44:31, 1994. It has, however, been claimed that these Japanese communities in fact did not cease whaling after the moratorium but instead shifted their focus from taking minke to catching more Baird's beaked whales, a species Japan would regard as a small cetacean not falling within the IWC's jurisdiction. S. Holt, 'Whale Tale' (2007) 195(2611) *New Scientist* 20.

[130] Whaling Convention, Article IX.1.

factory ship 'for the purpose of maintaining twenty-four hour inspection provided that at least one such inspector shall be maintained on each catcher functioning as a factory ship'.[131] In addition, the Schedule requires that 'adequate inspection shall be maintained at each land station'.[132] Inspectors are appointed and paid by the government with jurisdiction over the factory ship or land station concerned.[133] Inspectors are, therefore, national enforcement officers responsible to their own governments and, in addition to recording information required by the Schedule such as the size and sex of whales, they have often been required to perform additional functions by their employers.

The establishment of an international observer scheme was first considered seriously in the 1960s after evidence that infractions had sometimes gone unreported. Agreement was finally reached by the IWC in 1971. More specifically, the scheme was set up because the similarity in appearance between the products of different species of whales and the capacity of factory ships to process carcasses at sea made it relatively easy for a whaling company to cover up illegal catches by falsely representing them as legal catches of other species.[134] In the 1960s, populations of certain stocks of humpback whales in the southern hemisphere showed declines of a magnitude not readily explicable by reported catches, suggesting that humpbacks had been illegally taken and reported as other species.[135] In addition, there was some concern that nationally appointed and controlled inspectors might not be totally impartial.[136]

The Schedule currently notes that '[t]here shall be received such observers as the member countries may arrange to place on factory ships and land stations or groups of land stations of other member countries'.[137] In contrast to the nationally appointed inspectors, observers have been appointed by and are responsible to the IWC, although paid by the government which nominated them.[138] The Schedule makes no provision for the number of observers to be placed on the ships and land stations of whaling nations, and in practice they have been very few in number. The IWC's International Observer Scheme has been implemented by bilateral or trilateral arrangements between the states concerned. For example, Spain and Norway have done so in the North Atlantic. One of the tasks of the IWC's Infraction subcommittee is to review the reports of observers.

131 Whaling Convention, Schedule, para. 21(a). 132 Ibid., para. 21(b).
133 Ibid. 134 See Scarff, *supra* n. 1, p. 606. 135 *Rep. Int. Whal. Commn* 14:78, 1964.
136 See Scarff, *supra* n. 1, pp. 606–7. 137 Whaling Convention, Schedule, para. 21(c).
138 Ibid., para. 21(c).

The International Observer Scheme was not able to provide a comprehensive check on the work of the inspectors, but it did give at least some international oversight of whaling operations and some degree of confidence in the accuracy of the reports submitted by the whaling states.[139] For example, as indicated above, there is clear evidence that the Soviet Union failed to report the extent of their whaling operations in the period from 1947 to 1972.[140] This underreporting included the fabrication of records on the taking of blue, humpback and right whales. However, the standard of Soviet records improved once the observer scheme was implemented.[141]

It has already been noted that debate continues within the Commission on the nature of a revised inspector and observer scheme as part of the Revised Management System. The RMS Expert Drafting Group reached agreement that the purpose of proposed revisions to Chapter 5 of the Schedule on supervision and control was to 'set out the basic requirements for a robust supervision and control system to ensure compliance with the provisions of the Convention'.[142] There would also seem to be some agreement amongst the parties that two international observers should accompany each factory ship involved in pelagic whaling, but no agreement as to the placing of observers on catcher vessels. While some take the view that the presence of observers on catcher vessels would be of benefit, others question whether they would be cost-effective.[143] Another debated issue is the extent to which the operating expenditure should be recovered by the IWC from the state responsible for the whaling operations in question. Pro-whaling countries do not consider it appropriate that they should pay the full costs of an expensive scheme, taking the view that those other countries which have insisted upon such a scheme should also be prepared to bear some of the cost.[144]

b) *Infractions*

Each party is responsible for punishing infractions against provisions of the Whaling Convention which occur in the course of operations carried

[139] Oberthur, *supra* n. 68, p. 31. [140] Zemsky et al., *supra* n. 84.
[141] Gambell, *supra* n. 81, p. 52.
[142] Report of the Revised Management Scheme Expert Drafting Group, IWC/54/RMS1 (15/3/02), p. 3.
[143] Ibid., p. 6. [144] Ibid., p. 9.

out by persons or vessels under its jurisdiction.[145] Each party must also submit an annual report of such infractions to the IWC and of measures taken to prosecute them.[146] These reports are considered by the Infractions subcommittee, which is a permanent subcommittee of the Technical Committee. Each year, a number of infractions are reported, or potential offences discussed. For instance, the Republic of Korea reported in 2002 the illegal catch of a minke whale. The captain of the vessel concerned was fined approximately US$7,000, and the vessel owner's fishing license was permanently revoked.[147]

c) *Register of whaling vessels*

In 1979 the IWC requested its Secretary to compile a register of whaling vessels subject to IWC quotas and regulations. The intention was to make it easier for states, whether parties to the Whaling Convention or not, to detect and take measures against whaling vessels flying flags of convenience and operating outside the jurisdiction of the Convention. In 1980 the Schedule was amended to require parties to supply certain statistical information on all factory ships and catcher ships.[148] In recent years, Japan and Norway have shown reluctance to provide information on ships engaged in whaling operations for fear of those vessels being attacked by groups opposed to whaling.[149] Other parties have nonetheless underlined the importance of an accurate register to facilitate the identification of pirate whalers.[150]

d) *National control of citizens and vessels*

Article 9(1) of the Convention requires each party to take 'appropriate measures' to enforce the terms of the Convention, a loosely defined obligation which gives each party broad discretion as to the action it chooses to take. Most parties have limited the scope of their regulations to whaling by vessels, whether domestic or foreign, within their coastal waters, and to whaling by vessels flying their national flag even if outside their coastal waters. However, some have gone further. The USA's Marine Mammal Protection Act 1972 prohibits US citizens or

[145] Whaling Convention, Article 9(1). [146] Ibid., Article 9(4).
[147] Report of the Infractions Subcommittee, IWC/55/Rep 4.
[148] Whaling Convention, Schedule, para. 28.
[149] For example, see *Rep. Int. Whal. Commn* 47:33–4, 1997. [150] Ibid., p. 33.

US-registered vessels from engaging in whaling on the high seas.[151] Australia's Environment Protection and Biodiversity Conservation Act 1999 makes it a strictly liable offence for an Australian citizen to kill or injure a cetacean not only within Australian waters but also in international waters and the EEZs of other countries.[152]

e) Sanctions

Two US laws, known as the 'Pelly Amendment' to the Fisherman's Protective Act of 1967[153] and the 'Packwood-Magnuson Amendment' to the Fishery Conservation and Management Act of 1976,[154] authorise the US government to take economic sanctions against any state whose activities diminish the effectiveness of the conservation measures of the IWC.[155] Under the Pelly Amendment, if the US Secretary of Commerce determines that foreign nationals are 'conducting fishing operations in a manner or under circumstances which diminish the effectiveness of an international fishery conservation program',[156] or if either the US Secretary of Commerce or the US Secretary of the Interior determines that 'nationals of a foreign country, directly or indirectly, are engaging in trade or taking which diminishes the effectiveness of any international

151 Marine Mammal Protection Act of 1972 as amended (16 USC §§1372–102(a)1). The moratorium on the taking of marine mammals established by the Marine Mammal Protection Act does not apply to aboriginal takes of whales for subsistence purposes.

152 Environment Protection and Biodiversity Conservation Act 1999; see sections 224(2)a and 229. On the application of this statute in an action brought by an Australian NGO to restrain a Japanese-registered company from taking more whales under scientific permits in waters adjacent to Australian-claimed Antarctic territory see *Humane Society International Inc v Kyodo Senpaku Kaisha Ltd* [2008] Federal Court of Australia 3 (available at www.envlaw.com.au/whale.html). Although Kyodo Senpaku Kaisha Ltd was restrained by the Federal Court of Australia from taking further Antarctic minke, fin and humpback in such waters, the Japanese have refused to accept Australia's jurisdiction in the waters concerned and over the matter in issue.

153 22 USC §1978. 154 16 USC §1821(e)(2).

155 On the application of these laws, see D. M. Wilkinson, 'The Use of Domestic Measures to Enforce International Whaling Agreements: A Critical Perspective' (1989) 17(2) *Denv. J. Int. L. and Policy* 271; and G. S. Martin and J. W. Brennan, 'Enforcing the International Convention for the Regulation of Whaling: The Pelly and Packwood-Magnuson Amendments' (1989) 17(2) *Denv. J. Int. L. and Policy* 293.

156 22 USC §1978(a)(1). An 'international fishery conservation program' is defined to include 'any ban, restriction, regulation or other measure in effect pursuant to a bilateral or multilateral agreement which is in force with respect to the United States, the purpose of which is to conserve or protect the living resources of the sea, including marine mammals' (22 USC §1978(h)(3)). This definition clearly therefore includes measures taken by the IWC to protect whales.

program for endangered or threatened species',[157] the relevant Secretary shall certify this fact to the US President. The Pelly Amendment then authorises the US President to prohibit the import of any products from the offending state 'for any duration as the President determines appropriate and to the extent that such prohibition is sanctioned by the World Trade Organization'.[158] Under the Packwood-Magnuson Amendment, if the Secretary of Commerce determines that foreign nationals, 'directly or indirectly, are conducting fishing operations or engaging in trade or taking which diminishes the effectiveness' of the Whaling Convention, the state concerned will automatically lose 50 per cent of its allocation of fish products taken within the United State's EEZ.[159] If the state refuses to rectify its conduct, its entire allocation will be terminated and its nationals will be unable to fish at all in US coastal waters until certification is terminated.[160] In contrast to the Pelly Amendment, which gives the President discretion whether to embargo products from the offending state, there is no discretion under the Packwood-Magnuson Amendment. Sanctions must be imposed once the Secretary of Commerce has certified.

Whether to certify is a matter for the relevant Secretary. In 1984, rather than certify Japan under the Pelly and Packwood-Magnuson Amendments, the USA entered into the 1984 Baldridge-Murazumi Agreement, under which the United States agreed not to certify Japan in return for Japan's withdrawal of its objection.[161] An action was subsequently brought by environmentalists with a view to compelling the Secretary of State for Commerce to certify Japan. However, the Supreme Court ruled in *Japan Whaling Association et al. v American Cetacean Society et al.* that the Secretary of State enjoyed considerable discretion to determine what 'diminishes the effectiveness' of the Whaling Convention and that certification was therefore not mandatory in this situation.[162] The political decision to enter into the Baldridge-Murazumi Agreement rather than to pursue the certification route was regarded by the Supreme Court as a decision which the Secretary of State was entitled to make in the circumstances.

[157] 22 USC §1978(a)(2). [158] 22 USC §1978(a)(4).

[159] 16 USC §§1821(e)(2)(A)(i) and 1821(e)(2)(B). Any Packwood-Magnuson Amendment certification also automatically operates as a certification under the Pelly Amendment.

[160] 16 USC §1821(e)(2)(D).

[161] See C.L. Johnson, 'Environmental Law: Certification of Japanese Violations of International Whaling Agreements', (1988) 29 *Harvard International Law Journal* 541.

[162] *Japan Whaling Association et al. v American Cetacean Society et al.* (1986) 25 *ILM* 1587.

Although reductions in fishing quotas within the US EEZ have been made on a number of occasions, successive US administrations have been reluctant to impose general trade sanctions. For example, the Secretary of Commerce made the appropriate determination under the Pelly Amendment against Japan and the Soviet Union in 1974 after both countries had objected to IWC quotas for the harvest of minke whales in the Antarctic and had set their own higher quotas. However, President Ford refused to exercise his option to impose sanctions on the grounds that he expected Japan and the Soviet Union to abide by future quotas.[163] It seems likely, however, that the threat of sanctions at that time and on some other occasions has had an influence on behaviour. For example, shortly after Norway was certified in 1986 under the Pelly Amendment for taking minke in the North Atlantic, Norway indicated that it would end commercial whaling in 1987. No sanctions were actually imposed by President Reagan under the Pelly Amendment. However, the mere threat of trade sanctions has more recently not brought about the desired results. For example, in June 2004 Iceland, in relation to its lethal scientific research programme, was certified for conducting whaling activities that diminished the effectiveness of the IWC's conservation programme. It nonetheless persisted and in the event trade sanctions were not imposed, President George W. Bush explaining to Congress that 'use of trade sanctions is not the course of action needed to resolve our current differences with Iceland over research whaling activities'.[164]

9. Relationship with other international treaties and organisations

a) The 1982 Law of the Sea Convention

UNCLOS has implications for the IWC. While coastal states are to promote the optimum utilisation of living resources within their EEZs,[165] Article 65 makes it clear that the pursuit of optimum utilisation is not required in relation to marine mammals.[166] Indeed, the coastal

[163] See M. Bean, *The Evolution of National Wildlife Law* (Praeger Publishers, 1983), p. 266.

[164] Message to the Congress of the United States (22 June 2004) at www.whitehouse.gov/news/releases/2004/06/20040622–8.html.

[165] Article 62(1) UNCLOS.

[166] R. Churchill, 'Sustaining Small Cetaceans: A Preliminary Evaluation of the ASCOBANS and ACCOBAMS Agreements', in A. E. Boyle and D. Freestone (eds.), *International Law and Sustainable Development* (Oxford University Press, 1999), pp. 228–9.

state or competent international organisation may see fit to prohibit, limit or regulate takes of cetaceans more strictly than is provided by the rest of Part V UNCLOS. Article 65 further requires that parties shall co-operate 'with a view to the conservation of marine mammals and in case of cetaceans shall in particular work through the appropriate international organisations for their conservation, management and study'. Although some states and academics dispute this,[167] it may be argued that one implication of Article 65 is that states party to UNCLOS should become a party to the Whaling Convention as 'the appropriate international organisation', pending which they should conform to IWC regulations except where stricter domestic measures for the conservation of whales have been adopted. This is particularly significant for states which ratify the Law of the Sea Convention, but are not parties to the Whaling Convention, and have allowed their national flag to be flown by pirate whalers in order to escape IWC restrictions. Article 65 might be interpreted to require them to halt this practice.

However, Article 65 LOSC refers in the plural to the 'appropriate international organisations', without reference to a single institution. Thus the IWC is arguably not the only 'appropriate organisation' for these purposes. For example, there is also the North Atlantic Marine Mammal Commission (NAMMCO), which was established by the 1992 Agreement on Cooperation on Research, Conservation and Management of Marine Mammals in the North Atlantic.[168] This agreement was signed by the fisheries ministers of the Faroe Islands, Greenland, Iceland and Norway, and aims to 'contribute through regional consultation and co-operation to the conservation, rational management and study of marine mammals in the North Atlantic'.[169] It has endorsed the need for effective conservation and the sustainable utilisation of North Atlantic marine mammal stocks. The establishment of NAMMCO can be seen as a reflection of a desire for an alternative forum to study and exchange information against the backdrop of a

[167] See W. Burke, 'Whaling and International Law', in Petursdottir, *supra* n. 81, at pp. 115 and 118.

[168] II *MMC* 1618. See Gambell, *supra* n. 28, at p. 105. On NAMMCO see D. D. Caron, 'The International Whaling Commission and the North Atlantic Marine Mammal Commission: The Institutional Risks of Coercion in Consensual Structures' (1995) 89 *AJIL* 154; and K. Sanderson, 'The North Atlantic Marine Mammal Commission – in Principle and Practice', in Petursdottir, *supra* n. 81, pp. 67–74. NAMMCO's website is located at www.nammco.no.

[169] Article 2, NAMMCO.

growing sense of disillusionment amongst certain pro-whaling countries with the IWC regime.

b) The Convention on International Trade in Endangered Species of Wild Fauna and Flora (CITES)

CITES regulates international trade in species which are listed in one of the three Appendices to the Convention. The 'introduction from the sea' of species in the Appendices – i.e. bringing specimens taken on the high seas into a state which is a party to the Convention – is deemed to be international trade and requires a CITES permit. The introduction from the sea of species in Appendix I of the Convention is prohibited if for commercial purposes. From 1 January 1986 all cetaceans whose catch has been regulated by the IWC have been added to Appendix I (apart from the West Greenland population of minke).[170] The listing of the great whales in this way was intended to bring CITES into line with the IWC decision to halt commercial whaling from 1986. This is symptomatic of the close relationship which has built up over the years between the IWC and CITES.[171] The West Greenland minke population remains on Appendix II, but all other great whales are on Appendix I. However Iceland, Japan and Norway have all entered reservations against the listing of fin,[172] minke, sei[173] and sperm whales in Appendix I. In addition, Iceland has reservations against the listing of blue, humpback and northern bottlenose whales (*Hyperoodon ampullatus*), and Japan has entered reservations to the listing of Baird's beaked and Bryde's whales. The 'reservations' procedure under CITES is similar in effect to the objection procedure under the Whaling Convention as it exempts the reserving party from being legally bound by the specific provisions concerned.

The CITES Conference of the Parties (CoP) has recommended that CITES state parties should not issue any import or export permit, or certificate for introduction from the sea under CITES for commercial

[170] The West Greenland minke population is included in Appendix II, a listing that reflects the fact that the IWC was prepared at the time of the introduction of its commercial moratorium to allow takes from this population for aboriginal subsistence purposes by Greenlanders.

[171] Certain marine dolphins, river dolphins and porpoises also appear on Appendix I. All other cetaceans are listed on Appendix II.

[172] The Norwegian reservation relates to certain populations only.

[173] The Japanese and Norwegian reservations relate to certain populations only.

purposes for whale species or stocks protected under the IWC's moratorium.[174] In addition, CITES state parties have been urged to co-operate with the CITES secretariat on the collection of information on illegal trade in whale meat.[175] Any such information received is to be shared with the IWC.[176] In recent years both Japan and Norway have made proposals at CITES meetings to downlist certain whale populations from CITES Appendix I. For example, Norway failed in an attempt to downlist minke whales in 1994, and Japan and Norway's proposal to downlist several whale populations in 1997 also met with the same fate. These attempts to downlist can be seen as evidence of the growing frustration of pro-whaling countries with the majority view within the IWC that the moratorium should remain at present, and as an attempt to put pressure on the IWC by taking the debate to a different international forum. In 2007 the IWC called on its parties to 'respect the relationship' between the Whaling Convention and CITES and 'not to seek the transfer of cetacean species from CITES Appendix I while the moratorium remains in place'.[177]

c) Bern Convention on the Conservation of European Wildlife and Natural Habitats

Under the 1979 Bern Convention on the Conservation of European Wildlife and Natural Habitats, a range of small cetaceans found in European waters are listed on Appendix II, as are the blue, Bryde's, northern fin, North Atlantic right, humpback and bowhead whales. Additionally, the Mediterranean populations of the northern minke, sperm and northern sei are also on Appendix II. All cetaceans on Appendix II are regarded as strictly protected species. In effect, therefore, the deliberate capture and keeping, and deliberate killing, of such small cetaceans is prohibited, as is the deliberate damage to or destruction of their breeding or resting sites, and their deliberate disturbance.[178] However, doubt has been cast on the ability of the Bern Convention to

[174] CITES Resolution Conf. 11.4 (eleventh meeting of CITES CoP, April 2000). This resolution also recommended that 'parties that do not currently adhere to the [Whaling Convention] be encouraged to do so'.

[175] Ibid.

[176] During the 1990s the IWC became increasingly concerned about illegal shipments of whale products. See IWC Resolution 1994–7 (*Rep. Int. Whal. Commn* 45:44–5, 1995). See also IWC Resolution 1997–2 (*Rep. Int. Whal. Commn* 48:46, 1998).

[177] IWC Resolution 2007–4.

[178] Article 6, Bern Convention.

afford effective protection to small cetaceans in European waters, due, inter alia, to the regime's primary focus on land-based species rather than on marine species and their habitats.[179]

d) *European Union*

The European Union has adopted a number of measures restricting the ability of any of its member states to facilitate the future operation of a whaling industry, and also the ability of non-EU states to either engage in whaling operations within EU waters or to sell whale products within the EU.[180] In 1981 the then European Economic Community (EEC) adopted a regulation (the Whale Products Regulation) prohibiting the import for commercial purposes of whale products that are listed in an Annex to the measure.[181] The Whale Products Regulation also requires an import license to be issued for any non-commercial imports.

Additionally, the Habitats Directive was adopted in 1992 and implements obligations under the Bern Convention.[182] All cetaceans are placed in Annex IV, thereby affording them strict protection as animals of Community interest. As such, member states are obliged to establish a protection system for all cetaceans in which the following are prohibited:

- all forms of deliberate capture or killing;
- deliberate disturbance, particularly during periods of breeding, rearing, hibernation and migration;
- deterioration or destruction of breeding sites or resting places.[183]

In addition, the sale of whale meat is banned within the territory of a member state.[184] These prohibitions are certainly applicable in the territorial waters of European Union countries, and also apply within EU member states' EEZs.[185]

[179] Churchill, *supra* n. 166, pp. 230–1.
[180] P. Davies, 'Legality of Norwegian Commercial Whaling under the Whaling Convention and Its Compatibility with EC Law' (1994) 43(2) *ICLQ* 270.
[181] Council Regulation 348/81, Article 1; OJ 1981 L39/1.
[182] Council Directive 92/43/EEC on the conservation of natural habitats and of wild fauna and flora; OJ 1992 L206/7.
[183] Habitats Directive, Article 12(1). [184] Ibid., Article 12(2).
[185] See *R v Secretary of State for Trade and Industry ex parte Greenpeace Ltd* [2000] *Env LR* 221, in which the English High Court adopted a purposive approach in ruling that the Habitats Directive applied to the UK's continental shelf and to the superjacent waters up to a 200-mile limit from the baseline from which the territorial sea is measured. See also Case C-6/04 *European Commission v UK* [2005] *ECR* I-9017.

The European Union also implements CITES within its borders by virtue of the CITES Regulation.[186] Whales are noted in Annex A to this measure. As such, the introduction into the European Union of any whale or whale part from the high seas is prohibited without the issuance of an import permit. An import permit will not be issued if, in the view of the relevant member state's management authority, the specimen is to be used for primarily commercial purposes.[187] In relation to cetacean by-catch, the Habitats Directive calls for the establishment of a monitoring system and, in the light of information subsequently gained, the adoption of appropriate conservation measures.[188] As a consequence, the European Union has now adopted the Incidental Catches Regulation, which, inter alia, introduces an on-board independent observer scheme in relation to fishing activities carried out by vessels with an overall length of fifteen metres.[189]

e) *The Convention on the Conservation of Antarctic Marine Living Resources (CCAMLR)*

This Convention, which came into force in April 1982, has potentially significant implications for whales in that it regulates the exploitation of marine living resources, notably krill (*Euphausia superba*), in Antarctica.[190] Krill is the principal food supply of several species of baleen whale, and any diminution in its abundance could impede the recovery of Antarctic whale populations. Recognising the close link between whales and krill, the Convention requires its Commission to seek to develop a co-operative working relationship with the IWC.[191] Nothing in the Convention is intended to derogate from the rights and obligations of parties under the Whaling Convention.[192] The IWC's Scientific Committee has collaborated with CCAMLR in its research

[186] Council Regulation 338/97 on the protection of species of wild fauna and flora by regulating trade therein (CITES Regulation); OJ 1997 L61/1 (as variously amended).

[187] CITES Regulation, Article 8. The sale of any whale meat or other whale product is also prohibited. CITES Regulation, Article 4.

[188] Habitats Directive, Article 12(4).

[189] Council Regulation 812/2004 laying down measures concerning incidental catches of cetaceans in fisheries and amending Regulation 88/89; OJ 2004 L150/12 (as amended by Council Regulation (EC) 809/2007 OJ 2007 L182/1).

[190] 19 *ILM* 841; *TIAS* No. 10240; *UKTS* No. 48 (1982), Cmnd. 8714. See further discussion below in Chapter 11.

[191] The Convention on the Conservation of Antarctic Marine Living Resources, Article 24(3).

[192] Article 6.

into the impact of environmental change on whales in Antarctic waters, and in the 1999–2000 Antarctic season the IWC and CCAMLR carried out joint field research for the first time in the SOWER 2000 project (also known as the CCAMLR Krill Synoptic Survey 2000).

f) The Bonn Convention on Migratory Species

Under the Bonn Convention endangered migratory species are noted on Appendix I. Appendix I species include the sperm, sei, fin, blue, humpback, bowhead and right whales, as well as the Ganges River Dolphin, the Mediterranean short-beaked common dolphin and the La Plata Dolphin. These cetaceans must therefore be subject to a system of strict protection in which the onus is placed on range states to conserve their habitats and prevent obstacles to migration, and also to prevent, reduce or control other factors that endanger them.[193] Subject to certain defined exceptions, the taking of cetacea noted in Appendix I is forbidden.[194]

Many small cetaceans do not appear on Appendix I, but are noted in Appendix II as species which either have an unfavourable conservation status, or would benefit from a system of international conservation. Article IV of the Bonn Convention encourages range states and other states to conclude agreements to protect such Appendix II species. In recent years, the IWC has endorsed the need to co-operate with other regimes active in fields relating to small cetaceans. Most importantly, these now include agreements established under Article IV(4) of the Bonn Convention (ASCOBANS and ACCOBAMS).[195]

i) Agreement on the Conservation of Small Cetaceans of the Baltic, North East Atlantic, Irish and North Seas (ASCOBANS)

Following mounting concern over the state of small cetaceans in the North and Baltic Sea region (particularly the decrease in harbour porpoise populations), the ASCOBANS agreement was opened for signature in March 1992 and came into effect on 29 March 1994. From 1 January 2007 the UNEP/CMS Secretariat has fulfilled the role of ASCOBANS Secretariat.[196] A Meeting of the Parties (MoP) to be held not less than once every three years to review progress has been established, as well as

193 Article III(4). 194 Article III(5).
195 See generally Churchill, *supra* n. 166, Chapter 10.
196 The Internet address is www.ascobans.org.

the Advisory Committee to give expert advice to the Secretariat and state parties (particularly on conservation and management issues).

The ASCOBANS area originally included the Baltic Sea, the North Sea[197] and the English Channel,[198] but was extended with effect from 3 February 2008 to include parts of the North East Atlantic and the Irish Sea.[199] In extending the area, Ireland, Portugal and Spain became additional range states. Belgium, Denmark, Finland, France, Germany, Lithuania, the Netherlands, Poland, Sweden and the UK are parties to the original agreement. Denmark, Finland, France, Germany, the Netherlands and Poland have additionally accepted the amendment extending the agreement's area of application.

Any range state may accede to the agreement (as can a regional economic organisation),[200] and the agreement is applicable to 'all small cetaceans found within' the ASCOBANS area.[201] Species which therefore are subject to the agreement include the harbour porpoise, various dolphins (Atlantic white-sided, bottlenose, common, Risso's, striped and white-beaked), as well as the killer (*Orcinus orca*), long-finned pilot, northern bottlenosed and other beaked whales.

ASCOBANS places an obligation on state parties to 'cooperate closely in order to achieve and maintain a favourable conservation status for small cetaceans'.[202] More particularly, a state party is to 'apply within the limits of its jurisdiction and in accordance with its international obligations, the conservation, research and management measures prescribed in the Annex'.[203] In relation to habitat conservation and management, the Conservation and Management Plan noted in this Annex places a vague obligation on state parties to 'work towards the prevention of the release of dangerous or potentially dangerous substances', as well as the development of modifications to fishing gear and practices to reduce

[197] Including Skagerrak (surrounded by Norway, Sweden and Denmark) and Kattegat (which is an extension of Skagerrak into the Baltic).

[198] The ASCOBANS area is more precisely defined in para. 1.2(b) ASCOBANS and clarified in MoP 1: Resolution on Clarification of the Definition of the Area of the Agreement (1994).

[199] MoP 4: Resolution No. 4 on the extension of the ASCOBANS Agreement Area (2003). The extended area has ensured that the Agreement Areas of ASCOBANS and ACCOBAMS are contiguous.

[200] Para. 1.2(f) ASCOBANS.

[201] Para. 1.1 ASCOBANS. 'Small cetaceans' are defined as 'any species, subspecies or population of toothed whales *Odontoceti*, except the sperm whale' (para. 1.2(a) ASCOBANS). In addition to sperm whales, minke are also therefore excluded.

[202] Para. 2.1 ASCOBANS. [203] Para. 2.2 ASCOBANS.

by-catches.[204] States must also work towards the regulation of activities which seriously impact on food sources, and the prevention of other significant disturbances (especially acoustic disturbance).[205] Additional obligations include the need to co-ordinate research on relevant stocks to assess status and movement, to locate areas of special importance to such stocks and to identify threats.[206] States will also 'endeavour' to establish a system for reporting and retrieving by-catches and stranded animals and investigating cause of death.[207] Other requirements include the provision of information to the general public and fishermen, particularly in relation to the importance of reporting sightings and strandings.[208] Importantly, the plan also refers to the need to introduce protective legislation at the national level, although states must only 'endeavour' to adopt laws to prevent intentional killing of small cetaceans, and to ensure the immediate release of healthy animals which are caught alive.[209]

At the first meeting of the ASCOBANS parties, a resolution was passed introducing an action plan for the period from 1994 to 1997, adding detail to ensure the full and effective implementation of the Conservation and Management Plan.[210] This action plan established certain actions of priority in the period in relation to pollution reduction, interactions with fisheries, and also relating to disturbance. It also placed the onus on parties to research into the life history of small cetaceans and into their migratory patterns, and on the ASCOBANS Secretariat to formulate a database on strandings and by-catch from information obtained from national reports.[211] At subsequent meetings the parties have adopted further resolutions inviting parties to carry out research with a view to identifying protected areas for small cetaceans, to establish relevant management measures in these areas, and to support postmortem analysis of small cetaceans.[212] Further research has additionally been encouraged on population size, structure and life history of small

[204] Annex, Conservation and Management Plan, para. 1. States must also work towards the prevention of the discarding of fishing gear at sea.

[205] Ibid. [206] Ibid., para. 2. [207] Ibid., para. 3.

[208] Ibid., para. 5. [209] Ibid., para. 4.

[210] MoP 1: Resolution on the Implementation of the Conservation and Management Plan (1994).

[211] Para. 2.5 ASCOBANS obliges parties to submit on an annual basis a report on progress made in implementing ASCOBANS.

[212] MoP 2: Resolution on Further Implementation of ASCOBANS (1997); MoP 3: Resolution No. 7 on Further Implementation of ASCOBANS (2000); MoP 4: Resolution No. 8 on Further Implementation of ASCOBANS (2003).

cetaceans.[213] Particular attention has also been given to supporting research into the impact on small cetaceans of chemicals,[214] and of seismic activities and acoustic devices.[215]

The incidental taking of harbour porpoises has been a cause for particular concern. The ASCOBANS Working Group on By-catch estimated in late 1997 that of the 170,000 harbour porpoises in the central and south North Sea, a minimum by-catch of 4,450 took place annually.[216] Furthermore, it is believed that only 600 harbour porpoises survive in the Baltic Sea. With these estimates in mind, the fourth Meeting of the Parties to ASCOBANS importantly endorsed the recovery plan for harbour porpoises in the Baltic Sea,[217] and also supported the development of a recovery plan for harbour porpoises in the North Sea.[218] The fifth Meeting of the Parties agreed a basis for harbour porpoises in the North Sea Conservation Plan.[219]

In relation to participation, it is disappointing that neither the EU nor Norway has ratified the agreement. Additionally, the absence of participation by key range states in the Baltic Sea region (such as Estonia, Latvia and the Russian Federation) will certainly not assist in the conservation of the rare harbour porpoise population in the Baltic. It is to be hoped that Ireland, Spain and Portugal will now become parties following the extension of the agreement's area.

[213] MoP 2: Resolution on Further Implementation of ASCOBANS (1997); MoP 3: Resolution No. 7 on Further Implementation of ASCOBANS (2000); MoP 4: Resolution No. 8 on Further Implementation of ASCOBANS (2003).

[214] See, in particular, MoP 3: Resolution No. 7 on Further Implementation of ASCOBANS (2000); MoP 4: Resolution No. 8 on Further Implementation of ASCOBANS (2003); and MoP 5: Resolution No. 7 on Research on Habitat Quality, Health and Status of Small Cetaceans in the Agreement Area (2006).

[215] See in particular MoP 2: Resolution on Further Implementation of ASCOBANS (1997); MoP 3: Resolution No. 4 on Disturbance (2000); and MoP 5: Resolution No. 4 on Adverse Effects of Sound, Vessels and Other Forms of Disturbance on Small Cetaceans (2006).

[216] ASCOBANS Working Group on By-catch, 'Cetacean By-catch Issues in the ASCOBANS Area' (1997).

[217] MoP 4: Resolution No. 6 on Incidental Take of Small Cetaceans (2003). Known as the 'Jastarnia Plan', the recovery plan for harbour porpoises in the Baltic Sea seeks to implement precautionary measures to reduce by-catches to two or fewer porpoises per year in the Baltic. On the Jastarnia Plan see R. Strempel, 'The ASCOBANS Jastarnia Plan: Towards a New Lease of Life for Baltic Harbor Porpoises' (2003) 6 *JIWLP* 53.

[218] MoP 4: Resolution No. 10 on the Recovery Plan for Harbour Porpoises in the North Sea (2003).

[219] MoP 5: Resolution No. 1 on a Conservation Plan for Harbour Porpoises in the North Sea (2006). The words 'Conservation Plan' replaced 'Recovery Plan' on the advice of the ASCOBANS Advisory Committee.

ii) Agreement on the Conservation of Cetaceans of the Black Sea, Mediterranean Sea and Contiguous Atlantic Area (ACCOBAMS)

ACCOBAMS was concluded in November 1996 and came into force on 1 June 2001.[220] The agreement covers the Black Sea, the Mediterranean Sea and the contiguous area of the Atlantic Ocean west of Gibraltar. This is an area in which pollution, shipping and overfishing have had a particularly adverse impact on cetacean conservation.[221] There are twenty-three state parties at present.[222] The parties are to meet as the Meeting of the Parties (MoP) at least every three years to review progress in implementation,[223] and the ACCOBAMS Secretariat has been established in Monaco.[224] The ACCOBAMS Bureau is to 'provide general policy guidance and operational and financial direction to the Secretariat', and also to subregional co-ordination units which facilitate implementation of the agreement in the Mediterranean and Black Sea areas respectively.[225]

Any range state may accede to the agreement (as can a regional economic organisation),[226] and the agreement is applicable to 'all cetaceans' that have range which lies partly or entirely in the ACCOBAMS area, or that accidentally or occasionally visit the area.[227] 'Cetaceans' are defined as 'animals ... of those species, subspecies or populations of *Odontoceti* or *Mysticeti*'.[228] Species which are therefore covered by the agreement include the harbour porpoise, various dolphins (bottlenose, common, Risso's, rough-toothed, short-beaked, and striped), as well as the Blainville's and Cuvier's beaked (*Ziphius cavirostris*), fin, humpback, killer, false killer, long-finned pilot, minke, northern right, sei, and sperm whales. Unlike ASCOBANS, some of the large cetaceans are therefore protected under the ACCOBAMS agreement.

[220] For an early assessment of this agreement see W. Burns, 'Agreement on the Conservation of Cetaceans of the Black Sea, Mediterranean Sea and Contiguous Atlantic Area: A Regional Response to the Threats Facing Cetaceans' (1998) 1(1) *JIWLP* 113. Also see Churchill, *supra* n. 166, pp. 244–50.

[221] See www.accobams.org.

[222] Albania, Algeria, Bulgaria, Croatia, Cyprus, Egypt, France, Georgia, Greece, Italy, Lebanon, Libya, Malta, Monaco, Montenegro, Morocco, Portugal, Romania, Slovenia, Spain, Syria, Tunisia and Ukraine.

[223] Para. III(2) ACCOBAMS.

[224] ACCOBAMS Secretariat, Monaco; see www.accobams.org.

[225] Para. VI(2)a ACCOBAMS.

[226] Para. 1(3)(g) ACCOBAMS. Non-coastal states can ratify if their vessels are carrying out activities in the ACCOBAMS area that can impact upon cetaceans.

[227] Para. I.2 ACCOBAMS.

[228] Para. I(3)(a) ACCOBAMS.

ACCOBAMS places an obligation on state parties to 'take coordinated measures to achieve and maintain a favourable conservation status for cetaceans'.[229] With this in mind, a state party is to 'prohibit and take all necessary measures to eliminate ... any deliberate taking of cetaceans and shall co-operate to create and maintain a network of specially protected areas to conserve cetaceans'.[230] In addition to these measures to eliminate deliberate capture and establish protected areas, parties must apply conservation, research and management measures (more particularly indicated in the Conservation Plan in Annex 2) to address the need for the 'adoption and enforcement of national legislation', the 'assessment and management of human–cetacean interactions', 'habitat protection', 'research and monitoring', 'capacity building' and 'responses to emergency situations' (such as a major polluting events).[231] The precautionary principle should be applied in implementing these measures.[232] Parties are obliged to prepare a report on implementation of the agreement at each MoP.[233]

The first Meeting of the Parties was held in Monaco in 2002. This dealt mainly with financial and also administrative matters, such as the adoption of rules and procedures. In addition, both the Secretariat and the Scientific Committee were established.[234] In relation to conservation, certain international implementation priorities for the period from 2002 to 2006 were also adopted.[235] These priorities include, inter alia, the creation of a by-catch database and the adoption of conservation plans for all cetaceans in the Black Sea and for the short-beaked common dolphins and common bottlenose dolphins in the Mediterranean Sea. The second meeting took place in Palma de Majorca in 2004 where, inter alia, a Working Programme was adopted for the period from 2005 to 2007, as well as a Conservation Plan for the Common Dolphin in the Mediterranean Sea. The third meeting was held in Dubrovnik in October 2007 and, inter alia, adopted a new conservation plan for the Black Sea region.

[229] Para. II.1 ACCOBAMS. [230] Ibid.

[231] Para. II.3 ACCOBAMS. All these measures are more particularly prescribed in Annex II of the ACCOBAMS agreement.

[232] Para. II.4 ACCOBAMS. [233] Para. VIII(b) ACCOBAMS.

[234] The ACCOBAMS Scientific Committee comprises twelve members, including a representative from the IWC's Scientific Committee. The ACCOBAMS Scientific Committee has already begun to address issues such as whalewatching, by-catch, protected areas, conservation plans for priority species, ship collisions, strandings, anthropogenic noise and the need for tissue banks.

[235] ACCOBAMS MoP 1; Resolution 1.9.

It is still relatively early days for the ACCOBAMS agreement. Time will tell whether its conservation objectives will be met. However, it can certainly be said at this stage that ratification of the agreement by other range states (such as Bosnia, Egypt, Israel, the Russian Federation and Turkey) would enhance its future prospects.[236]

10. Concluding remarks

Prior to the introduction of the commercial whaling moratorium, it could have been stated with some significant justification that the parties to the Whaling Convention had failed to achieve its objectives. The IWC had certainly neither overseen an orderly development of the whaling industry nor effectively conserved whale stocks. On the other hand, the IWC had stimulated a substantial amount of research into whales and whaling, and the annual meetings of the Commission had ensured that problems such as pirate whaling had been rapidly brought to the attention of party governments. However, whilst the system of enforcement established by the IWC had seemed to ensure that its regulations had been complied with to a certain extent, the admission by the Russian Federation in 1994 of very substantial inaccuracies in catch data provided by the Soviet Union in the 1947–71 period underlined the fragility of progress made in ensuring effective conservation.

Belatedly, the IWC did adopt the commercial whaling moratorium to give depleted stocks the opportunity to recover. However, it might be argued that the IWC has still not ensured the effective conservation of cetaceans bearing in mind that several populations still remain highly endangered. These include the bowhead stock in the North Pacific, right whales in the northern hemisphere, grey whales in the western North Pacific and Okhotsk Sea, and a number of blue whale populations.[237] On the positive side, some progress has been made on humane killing methods, important research programmes have been facilitated and encouraged, and the development of the RMS can only improve regulation if the commercial ban is eventually lifted.

Significant challenges remain. These include a range of environmental threats to cetaceans, as well as the need to tackle the current polarisation

[236] The EU has also not ratified. For a discussion of the difficulties relating to competence involved in EU ratification of both ASCOBANS and ACCOBAMS, see Churchill, *supra* n. 166, pp. 234–5, and at p. 247.

[237] See Chair's Summary Report of the 60th Annual Meeting, Santiago, Chile, June 2008.

of views within the IWC. Certain state parties clearly wish to see an immediate reintroduction of whaling, while conservationist states have seemed unprepared to contemplate a lifting of the moratorium for a number of reasons. The IWC's 2006 meeting caused particular controversy when the Commission narrowly adopted the St Kitts and Nevis Declaration with thirty-three commissioners voting in favour, thirty-two against and one abstention. The Declaration stipulated, inter alia, that the position of those states which opposed the resumption of sustainable commercial whaling ran contrary to the Convention's object and purpose, and declared a commitment to the 'normalising' of the functions of the IWC.[238] Although the number of commissioners voting in favour of Japan's proposal would have been insufficient to alter the status of the commercial moratorium, requiring as it does a three-quarters majority of those states voting, it was acclaimed by the pro-whaling lobby as being the first time for over twenty years that a significant and predominantly pro-whaling resolution had achieved a simple majority of votes cast.

In time, either the IWC will cease to function as a viable regulator if pro-whaling countries leave to concentrate on or to form alternative organisations, or parties must eventually find a way to achieving a viable compromise. Discussions within the IWC on the 'Future of the IWC' began after the 2007 IWC meeting and are intended to address the many issues that have polarised the parties in recent times. The Small Working Group on the Future of the IWC (SWG) was established in 2008 to provide the IWC with assistance in achieving consensus on no fewer than thirty-three issues of contention (including, for example, the continuance of the moratorium, the ability to enter objections and to make reservations, and competence in relation to small cetaceans). Progress within the SWG on the adoption of a suitable package of measures to address these issues remains limited to date.

[238] IWC Resolution 2006-1; attached as Annex I to the Chair's Summary Report for the 58th Annual Meeting, St Kitts and Nevis, June 2006. The preamble of the St Kitts and Nevis Declaration more specifically noted that the 'position of some members that are opposed to the resumption of commercial whaling on a sustainable basis irrespective of the status of whale stocks is contrary to the object and purpose [of the Whaling Convention]'. Commissioners also declared, inter alia, 'our commitment to normalising the functions of the IWC based on the terms of the ICRW and other relevant international law, respect for cultural diversity and traditions of coastal peoples and the fundamental principles of sustainable use of resources, and the need for science-based policy and rulemaking that are accepted as the world standard for the management of marine resources'. See Bowman's contribution on the 'normalising' process, *supra* n. 17.

Recommended further reading

P. Birnie, *International Regulation of Whaling: From Conservation of Whaling to Conservation of Whales and Regulation of Whale Watching* (Oceana Publications, 1985) Volumes I and II

M. J. Bowman '"Normalizing" the International Convention for the Regulation of Whaling' (2008) 29(3) *Mich. J. Int'l L* 293

A. D'Amato and S. K. Chopra, 'Whales: Their Emerging Right to Life' (1995) 85 *AJIL* 21

A. Gillespie, 'Iceland's Reservation at the International Whaling Commission' 14(5) *EJIL* (2003) 977

A. Gillespie, 'Small Cetaceans, International Law and the IWC' (2000) 2(2) *Melb. JIL* 257

K. Hirata, 'Why Japan Supports Whaling' (2005) 8(2–3) *JIWLP* 129

G. Petursdottir (ed.), *Whaling in the North Atlantic* (University of Iceland Fisheries Research Institute, 1997)

Chapter 7

Birds

1. Background

Human recognition of the need to protect birds goes back many centuries, although the underlying motivations have changed significantly over time. Birds were originally valued as a food source, as controllers of insect pests and as sport hunting targets.[1] More recently, emphasis has been placed on their aesthetic and ecological qualities and their importance as 'indicator' species which reflect the wellbeing of ecosystems as a whole.[2] Since so many bird species habitually migrate across international boundaries, it is not surprising that international agreements have frequently been concluded to promote their conservation. Another key consideration is that ornithological organisations, which commonly boast a sizeable and articulate membership and command substantial resources and expertise, have played a particularly significant role in the development of international wildlife law.[3]

Although various agreements have been concluded for the benefit of birds specifically, some of these are no longer of much practical importance, greater progress having often been achieved by treaties with a wider operational focus. This chapter begins by examining the instruments which have been adopted within the continent of Europe, followed by those concluded in other regions. It then briefly explains the significance in this context of certain more broadly based conservation agreements, detailed discussion of which can be found elsewhere in this work, before concluding with an analysis of the arrangements adopted

[1] O. Herman, *The International Convention for the Protection of Birds and Hungary* (1907; Bibliolife ed., 2009), p. 32.

[2] See, e.g., C. Imboden, 'Threatened Species: Birds as Indicators of Unsustainability', in G. Bennett (ed.), *Conserving Europe's Natural Heritage* (Springer, 1994); A. W. Diamond et al. (eds.), *Save the Birds* (ICBP, 1987), pp. 298–303.

[3] M. J. Bowman, 'International Treaties and the Global Protection of Birds' (1999) 11 *JEL* 88 (Part I), 281 (Part II), at pp. 89–90.

specifically for the protection of birds within the framework of the Bonn Migratory Species Convention.

2. Arrangements within the European region

It is within Europe that the longest tradition of international action for avian conservation is apparent.[4] The earliest initiative emerged from a congress of agriculturists and foresters held in Vienna in 1868, as a result of which the Foreign Ministry of Austria–Hungary undertook to pursue agreements with other countries for the protection of birds useful to agriculture. A bilateral arrangement with Italy was established shortly afterwards.[5]

a) 1902 Convention for the Protection of Birds Useful to Agriculture

The conclusion of a multilateral treaty took considerably longer, but in 1902 twelve European countries finally signed the Convention for the Protection of Birds Useful to Agriculture,[6] which entered into force on 6 December 1905. As its title implies, the Convention was strictly utilitarian in approach, offering protection to some 150 species which were designated in an Annex as 'useful to agriculture'. They were predominantly passerines,[7] owls and other birds of obvious value to farmers. Pelicans, cormorants, herons and most corvids and birds of prey were deemed 'noxious' (*nuisibles*) and unworthy of protection.[8]

The Convention established various obligations designed to secure the unconditional protection from exploitation of listed species.[9] Article 5 outlawed the killing, capture or sale of all specimens of such species between 1 March and 15 September,[10] while Article 2 prohibited the

[4] See generally R. Boardman, *International Organization and the Conservation of Nature* (Macmillan, 1981), Chapter 9.

[5] 1875 Declaration for the Protection of Birds Useful to Agriculture, 4 *IPE* 1561.

[6] 102 *BFSP* 969. Austria–Hungary itself, Belgium, France, Germany, Greece, Liechtenstein, Luxembourg, Monaco, Portugal, Spain, Sweden and Switzerland were the original signatories (though Greece never ratified). Czechoslovakia, the Netherlands and Poland became parties subsequently.

[7] The order Passeriformes comprises globally over 5,000 species of mainly small perching birds such as sparrows, finches and warblers, but also certain larger birds such as crows.

[8] See Article 9(2), and Annex II.

[9] Article 1.

[10] Northern European countries were permitted to modify this period, presumably because migratory patterns might otherwise allow them almost no open season at all.

taking, destruction, import, transport or sale of their nests, eggs and young at any time, although the owners or occupiers of buildings were allowed to destroy nests constructed on them. Article 3 prohibited the use of all methods designed to capture or destroy birds en masse.[11]

In reality, however, even 'useful' birds received little practical benefit from the 1902 Convention. In order to be successful, any initiative to protect migratory birds requires the co-operation of all the major staging posts along their flyways, and in this case a number of states in the region, including Denmark, Italy, Norway, Russia and the UK, failed to participate. Italy's absence was especially significant because its territory acts as a funnel along the migration route of many European species, and the hunting of migratory birds has long been a popular pastime there.[12] In addition, the Convention contained various loosely drafted exceptions which greatly undermined the protection it afforded.[13] The inclusion of these clauses may originally have been necessary to secure governmental support for the Convention, but was later acknowledged by French ornithologists to have deprived it of almost all practical significance in their country.[14] Indeed, the 1902 Convention appears to have had little real influence anywhere.[15] In the decades following its adoption, the UK, which did not participate, and Germany, which did, were both notable for relatively strong national conservation legislation, while Spain and Portugal, which were parties to the Convention, had virtually none.

b) 1950 International Convention for the Protection of Birds

Dissatisfaction with the shortcomings of the 1902 Convention and concern at the increasing vulnerability of bird populations in Europe led to a series of conferences culminating in the adoption of a replacement agreement, the 1950 International Convention for the Protection of Birds.[16] This Convention represents a considerable advance in terms of the values given to birds and the obligations imposed on parties to protect them, but its practical impact has again been very limited.

[11] See S. S. Hayden, *The International Protection of Wildlife* (1942; Kolthoff ed., 2007), pp. 90–1.

[12] Ibid. [13] See Articles 4, 6, 7, 9. [14] Hayden, *supra* n. 11, pp. 100–1.

[15] During the 1930s, it was invoked by the Dutch Supreme Court, but only to justify the less rigorous of the possible interpretations of relevant national legislation: *Birds Protection Act 1936* case (1939) 11 *AD* 222, Case No. 118.

[16] 638 *UNTS* 186.

The idea that certain birds are 'noxious' gave way to the notion that *all* birds should in principle be protected,[17] particularly endangered and migratory species. With those objectives in mind, Article 2 requires the parties to protect all birds at least during the breeding season; migratory birds during the period of return to their nesting areas, especially between March and July;[18] and species threatened with extinction throughout the year. Other provisions require regulation of the trade and transport of birds and prohibition both of interference with nests, eggs or broods during protected seasons and of methods of capture judged to be indiscriminate.[19] Exceptions may be made to these obligations for specified reasons,[20] but these powers are qualified by requirements either that their exercise must not lead to the total destruction in any given country of the species targeted or that 'all necessary precautions are taken to prevent abuses'. The 1950 Convention also introduced certain novel obligations not found in its predecessor,[21] encouraging the establishment of protected areas and the promotion of conservation education, and requiring the regulation of known causes of avian mortality, such as lighthouses, electric cables, insecticides, poisons, water pollution or waste.

Once again, however, lack of widespread participation destroyed the Convention's prospects of becoming a dynamic conservation instrument.[22] In addition, its provisions proved too vague. For example, while requiring year-round protection for species which are 'in danger of extinction', it omitted to identify such species definitively.[23] Finally, the Convention failed to demand regular meetings of the parties, provide for monitoring of implementation or otherwise ensure (as more modern conservation treaties tend to do) that it remained in the forefront of the

[17] Preamble, 2nd recital, which offers as justifications 'the interests of science, the protection of nature and the economy of each nation'.

[18] The intention was to protect migratory birds from spring shooting, a traditional practice in southern Europe.

[19] Articles 3–5.

[20] I.e. preventing agricultural or ecological damage, and the advancement of science, education, game-bird rearing or falconry: Articles 6, 7. Several countries also secured the insertion of specific exemptions reflecting their individual concerns.

[21] See Articles 10, 11.

[22] Only Belgium, Iceland, Italy, Luxembourg, the Netherlands, Spain, Sweden, Switzerland, Turkey and Yugoslavia became parties to the Convention, which did not even enter into force until 1963. Austria, Bulgaria, France, Greece, Monaco and Portugal all signed but never ratified.

[23] Rather, Articles 8 and 9 envisage the preparation of *national* lists of species the exploitation of which is *permitted*.

parties' attention. As a result, it is impossible to assert with any confidence that it has made a positive contribution to the conservation of any particular species, or of birds generally.

An attempt to breathe some life into the Convention through the utilisation of domestic legal procedures occurred in 1964, shortly after its entry into force, in the Belgian case of *Count Lippens v Etat Belge, Ministre de l'Agriculture.*[24] It was argued that national hunting regulations which allowed the shooting of certain game birds to continue throughout the month of March were invalidated by the requirements of Article 2 of the Convention.[25] The challenge was ultimately unsuccessful, however, because the Conseil d'Etat took the view that Article 2 was not intended to be 'self-executing': it merely created an undertaking by the parties to adopt the legislation necessary to give effect to its objectives. It could therefore not be relied upon to annul Acts or regulations of the Belgian legislature.[26] The failure of this attempt to mitigate the absence of international supervisory machinery only reaffirms the Convention's lack of practical influence on the policies of contracting governments. Indeed, an analytical survey of conservation treaties undertaken for the Rio Earth Summit declared it effectively 'moribund'.[27]

c) *1970 Benelux Convention on the Hunting and Protection of Birds*

Shortly after the *Lippens* case, the Benelux countries decided to adopt their own Convention on the Hunting and Protection of Birds.[28] Signed on 10 June 1970 and brought into force on 1 July 1972, this agreement harmonises the rules of the three countries with respect to the hunting of game birds,[29] and regulates the exploitation of such other wild birds as

[24] 47 *ILR* 336. Belgium had been the first state to ratify the Convention. The petitioner was the administrator of that country's nature reserves, and a prominent ornithologist.

[25] On the internal legal significance in Belgium of treaties to which it is party, see further Chapter 2, Section 2(d), above, and the works there cited.

[26] The possibility that other provisions of the Convention might have self-executing effect was left open, however.

[27] P. H. Sand (ed.), *The Effectiveness of International Environmental Agreements* (Cambridge, 1992), p. 63.

[28] 847 *UNTS* 255.

[29] See Article 1. Despite the Convention's title, Part I is actually applicable to numerous game species, including deer, boar, fox, wildcat, badgers, otters and seals. Part II, however, focuses exclusively upon birds.

are determined by the Committee of Ministers of the Benelux Economic Union.[30] On 30 August 1972, this Committee authorised the unlimited exploitation of three species, while granting limited protection to sixteen, and total protection from killing, selling and transport to all other non-game species.[31] A 1977 Amending Protocol amplified the regulation of certain methods of hunting.[32]

The Benelux Convention is exclusively concerned with direct exploitation, and makes no provision for the protection of habitat, the prevention of pollution or the control of pesticides, or for counteracting other known threats to wild birds. By the mid-1970s, however, the growing appreciation of the urgency of these problems throughout the continent provided the stimulus for a series of legal developments at the regional level. Within the European Community, these ultimately emerged as the 1979 Wild Birds Directive, whilst in the Council of Europe they became subsumed in wider negotiations concerning conservation of the region's wildlife generally, culminating in the adoption that same year of the Bern Convention on the Conservation of European Wildlife and Natural Habitats.

d) 1979 Bern Convention

Detailed consideration of the Bern Convention appears below in Chapter 10, and at this juncture it is necessary only to draw attention to certain aspects which are of particular relevance to birds. The Council of Europe had displayed concern for this topic as early as 1967, when its Committee of Ministers underlined the importance of reversing the downward trend in avian populations.[33] In the Convention itself, this problem is initially addressed in the general obligation under Article 2 to regulate wildlife populations so as to bring them into line with ecological, scientific and cultural requirements, 'while taking account of economic

[30] Articles 7–9.

[31] Décision de l'Union Économique Benelux relative à la Protection des Oiseaux (Décision M (72)), 30 August 1972.

[32] 1317 *UNTS* 320, in force 1 February 1983.

[33] Resolution (67) 24; see further Resolution (73) 31 and Recommendation No. R (82) 10, all entitled 'Birds in Need of Special Protection in Europe' and published in *Texts Adopted by the Council of Europe in the Field of the Conservation of European Wildlife and Natural Habitats* (Council of Europe Nature and Environment Series No. 40, Strasbourg, 1989).

and recreational requirements and the needs of sub-species, varieties or forms at risk locally'.

This protection is then reinforced through the establishment of specific measures for listed species. The comprehensiveness of the coverage of avifauna is a striking feature here, with virtually all the region's birdlife afforded either the strict protection of Appendix II listing or the less rigorous regulation offered by inclusion in Appendix III. Indeed, the only species actually excluded from these lists are the house sparrow (*Passer domesticus*), starling (*Sturnus vulgaris*) and wood pigeon (*Columba palumbus*), together with several of the more common gulls and crows, which are widely considered pests.

The regulation of direct exploitation remains a crucial element in this regime,[34] and one of the first recommendations of the Standing Committee established under the Convention concerned the prosecution of persons illegally catching, killing or trading in protected birds, emphasising the need for more effective implementation of existing legislation.[35] Some fifteen years later, while applauding the decisive measures that many parties had taken in response, the Committee noted that enforcement of local legislation was still particularly poor in Cyprus, including the UK Sovereign Base Areas, and called for immediate efforts to improve the situation.[36]

The Convention also addresses a range of other threats, however, including the loss or degradation of habitat and the introduction of exotic species.[37] An important development in this more holistic approach to conservation has been the elaboration of a series of action plans for individual avian species following a seminar held in Strasbourg during 1995.[38] Initially, plans were prepared for twenty-three globally threatened European species, including the Dalmatian pelican (*Pelecanus crispus*), lesser white-fronted goose (*Anser erythropus*), imperial eagle (*Aquila heliaca*), corncrake (*Crex crex*), great bustard (*Otis tarda*) and Scottish crossbill (*Loxia scotica*).[39] Standing Committee Recommendation No. 48 (1996) called for the adoption of national action plans for the species listed, with specific reference to the proposals

[34] See Articles 6–8, 10. [35] Recommendation No. 5 (1986).

[36] Recommendation No. 90 (2001). At the time of writing, the situation remains unresolved; see the report of BirdLife International, Council of Europe Doc. T-PVS/Files (2009) 23.

[37] Articles 4, 10, 11(2)(b). [38] See Council of Europe Doc. T-PVS (95) 33.

[39] See B. Heredia, L. Rose and M. Painter (eds.), *Globally Threatened Birds in Europe: Action Plans* (Council of Europe, 1996).

formulated by BirdLife International.[40] Subsequently, the Standing Committee established a Group of Experts on Bird Conservation to monitor implementation of these plans in collaboration with the EC's ORNIS Committee,[41] demonstrating the close, ongoing interrelationship between EU and Council of Europe conservation activities in this field.[42] The Experts Group first convened in May 1997 and has greatly assisted in maintaining momentum on this issue. Later recommendations have endorsed action plans for numerous additional species and/or drawn attention to further measures needed for effective conservation.[43]

e) 1979 EU Directive on the Conservation of Wild Birds

The regional protective regime had already been significantly enhanced by the adoption of a European Economic Community (now the EU) directive on the conservation of wild birds.[44] Although the detailed examination of EU environmental law lies beyond the purview of a work concerned with wildlife conservation under international law, a brief overview is appropriate here, for several reasons. First, the two systems are so closely interrelated in this area as to make rigid separation unrealistic: as noted above, the Birds Directive was negotiated in parallel to the Bern Convention, and addresses many of the same concerns, whilst a key objective of the later Habitats Directive[45] was to ensure implementation of the Convention by the EEC, which had become a party in 1982. Second, the mechanisms for ensuring compliance with EU law are considerably stronger than anything

[40] In fact, this whole project had largely been initiated by BirdLife International, supported by technical input from Wetlands International and funding from the RSPB, highlighting the vital contribution of NGOs to the Bern Convention system.

[41] For its terms of reference, see Report of the 17th Meeting of the Standing Committee, Doc. T-PVS (97) 63, Appendix 14.

[42] The EC had itself also provided funding for the project to develop the action plans.

[43] See, e.g., Recommendations Nos. 60–2 (1997), 75 (1999), 88, 90 (2001), 92–3, 96–7 (2002), 103 (2003), 110 (2004). For six new plans proposed in 2006, see Council of Europe Doc. T-PVS (2006) 21 rev.

[44] Council Directive 79/409 on the conservation of wild birds; OJ 1979 L103/1. This directive, together with subsequent amendments, was recently consolidated as European Parliament and Council Directive 2009/147/EC on the conservation of wild birds, OJ 2010 L20/7. See generally W. P. J. Wils, 'The Birds Directive: 15 Years Later' (1994) 6 *JEL* 219; J. Verschuuren, 'Effectiveness of Nature Protection Legislation in the EU and the US: The Birds and Habitats Directives and the Endangered Species Act' (2003) 3 *Yearbook of European Environmental Law* 305; P. G. G. Davies, *European Union Environmental Law: An Introduction to Key Selected Issues* (Ashgate, 2004), Chapter 4.

[45] Council Directive 92/43 on the conservation of natural habitats and of wild fauna and flora, OJ 1992 L206/7.

encountered in the international legal system, entailing ultimately the possibility of substantial fines being levied upon states which fail to fulfil their obligations.[46] Birds have frequently been the beneficiaries of enforcement action, with the European Commission having been generally assiduous in pursuing compliance with conservation duties and the European Court of Justice (ECJ) noticeably rigorous in its interpretation of the provisions in question. In view of these considerations, EU law serves almost as a form of surrogate mechanism for the implementation of the conservation principles contained in international treaties.[47]

The Birds Directive applies to all species of naturally occurring wild birds in the European territories of EU member states,[48] except Greenland.[49] Article 2 imposes duties regarding the maintenance of avian populations that are expressed in very similar terms to their counterparts in the Bern Convention. It also accords the same priority to ecological, scientific and cultural requirements over economic and recreational needs. At a minimum, therefore, member states must use their best endeavours to ensure that no species of bird becomes extinct, foster the recovery of threatened species and ensure that presently healthy populations do not become unduly depleted.

This general duty is supported by more specific obligations, particularly regarding direct exploitation. Member states must prohibit the deliberate killing or capture of wild birds naturally occurring on their territories, the deliberate damaging of nests or eggs, the taking of eggs from the wild and keeping them (even if empty), the keeping of protected species, and the deliberate disturbance of birds, especially during the breeding season.[50] Inevitably, however, there are exceptions to these requirements, designed in particular to cater for the interests of the hunting lobby, which represents an extremely powerful political force in many parts of Europe.

Thus Article 7 of the Directive authorises the hunting of certain birds in accordance with national legislation. Species in Annex II/1 may be hunted anywhere, while those in Annex II/2 may be hunted only in those

[46] A power first utilised in Case C-387/97, *Commission v Greece* [2000] *ECR* 1–5047, in respect of violations of EU waste legislation.

[47] Note especially the case concerning marine turtles at Laganas Bay, Zakynthos, discussed below in Chapter 10.

[48] Including, it seems, in the case of the provisions regulating sale, their *non-European sub-species*: see Case C-202/94, *Criminal Prosecution of Godefridus van der Feesten* [1996] *ECR* I-355.

[49] Birds Directive, Articles 1(1) and 1(3). Greenland was excluded because conditions of life for birds there are so fundamentally different from those in Europe generally.

[50] Article 5.

states that are specifically indicated.[51] The former category includes various common species of duck[52] and geese,[53] and certain game birds,[54] while the latter embraces additional species in those categories,[55] along with various common waders and corvids.[56] Hunting must not, however, be allowed to jeopardise conservation efforts anywhere within a species' range, and must comply both with the principles of 'wise use and ecologically balanced control' and with the requirements of Article 2 regarding population levels. Furthermore, it must be prohibited during the breeding season and, in the case of migratory species, during their return to their rearing grounds. Finally, all indiscriminate methods of taking, including a number which are specified, must be banned.[57] In support of these restrictions, Article 6 prohibits the sale, keeping, transport or offering for sale of live or dead birds and of any readily recognisable parts or derivatives. Provision is, however, made for exceptions in the case of certain game birds and other species listed in Annex III.

The Directive also allows member states to make exceptions to these controls on exploitation for the protection of certain specified interests,[58] which mirror those in the Bern Convention. The last of these, allowing 'the capture, keeping or other judicious use of certain birds in small numbers',[59] albeit only 'under strictly supervised conditions and on a selective basis', has been interpreted quite widely, permitting the capture and sale of birds for use as live decoys or for recreational use in fairs and markets, or to enable bird fanciers to stock their aviaries, and the

51 The various annexes have been periodically amended in accordance with Articles 15–17.

52 Including the mallard (*Anas platyrhynchos*), wigeon (*A. penelope*) and tufted duck (*Aythya fuligula*).

53 I.e. the bean goose (*Anser fabalis*), greylag (*A. anser*) and Canada goose (*Branta canadensis*).

54 Including the red grouse (*Lagopus lagopus*), partridge (*Perdix perdix*), pheasant (*Phasianus colchicus*), snipe (*Gallinago gallinago*) and wood pigeon (*Columba palumbus*).

55 E.g. the pink-footed and white-fronted geese (*Anser brachyrhynchus*, *A. albifrons*), scaup (*Aythya marila*), goldeneye (*Bucephala clangula*), black grouse (*Tetrao tetrix*) and capercaillie (*Tetrao urogallus*).

56 E.g. the curlew (*Numenius arquata*), redshank (*Tringa totanus*), jay (*Garrulus glandarius*) and magpie (*Pica pica*).

57 Article 8(1).

58 Significantly, this power of derogation is restricted to the provisions regarding direct exploitation, and therefore inapplicable either to those concerning habitat protection or to the maintenance of avian populations generally.

59 Naturally, this phrase must be interpreted with regard to the overall population of the species in question. See Case 252/85, *Commission v France* [1988] *ECR* 2243.

traditional use in France of generally prohibited devices such as horizontal nets to trap skylarks.[60] The power of derogation must be specifically justified in accordance with the stated criteria,[61] however, and may be exercised only where there is 'no other satisfactory solution' – a requirement which has been held to apply even to the 'judicious use' exception, despite the fact that it does not presuppose action in response to any particular problem.[62]

It is, however, in relation to habitat protection that the Birds Directive has arguably made its most distinctive contribution. Article 3(1) requires member states to take measures to maintain or re-establish a sufficient diversity and area of habitats for all species of wild birds naturally occurring in their European territories. Article 3(2) states that these measures shall include

(a) creation of protected areas,
(b) upkeep and management in accordance with the ecological needs of habitats inside and outside the protected zones,
(c) re-establishment of destroyed biotopes and
(d) creation of biotopes.

The Irish government was recently held to be in breach of this provision by failing to protect the heathland breeding habitat of the red grouse against overgrazing by sheep.[63]

These general habitat provisions are supplemented by those of Article 4, which deals with listed and migratory species. Article 4(1) requires the adoption of 'special conservation measures' for species listed in Annex I, which seeks to cater for

(a) species in danger of extinction,
(b) species vulnerable to specific changes in their habitat,
(c) species considered rare because of small populations or restricted local distribution and
(d) other species requiring particular attention for reasons of the specific nature of their habitat.

[60] See, e.g., ibid.; Case 262/85, *Commission v Italy* [1987] *ECR* 3073; Case C-10/96, *Ligue Royale pour la Protection des Oiseaux ASBL v Région Wallonne* [1996] *ECR* I-6775.

[61] See Article 9(2). General assertions that a species is harmful will not suffice: *Commission v Italy* [1987] *ECR* 3073. Article 9(3) requires the submission to the Commission of annual reports on use of this power.

[62] See, e.g., Case 247/85, *Commission v Belgium* [1987] *ECR* 3029; Case C-135/04, *Commission v Spain* [2005] *ECR* I-5261.

[63] Case C-117/00, *Commission v Ireland* [2002] *ECR* I-4221.

These criteria are such that listings currently range from species which are known to be critically endangered – the slender-billed curlew (*Numenius tenuirostris*),[64] for example – to some which are still relatively abundant, such as the common tern (*Sterna hirundo*). The measures envisaged involve the designation of suitable territories as 'special protection areas' (SPAs), taking into account the requirements of the species concerned. Article 4(2) adds that member states should adopt similar measures for regularly occurring migratory species not listed in Annex I. Particular attention is to be paid to the protection of wetlands, especially those of international importance.

The interpretation of these provisions by the ECJ has been characterised by a determination to deny significant discretion to governments in the matter of site designation, requiring them instead to classify as SPAs *all* those sites which, applying ornithological criteria, appear to be the most suitable for conserving listed species.[65] Thus governments which fail to designate sites of obvious importance to birds, such as Spain regarding the Santona Marshes, will be held to have violated their obligations under the Directive.[66] Equally, a breach may be found where the number and total area of sites designated is 'manifestly less' than the specified standard requires:[67] in *Commission v Netherlands*, for example, the twenty-three Dutch SPAs were judged to represent less than half of the total number of sites, and only around 40 per cent of the aggregated area, suitable for designation.[68] Furthermore, decisions must be made on ornithological grounds alone, the Court having repeatedly affirmed that the economic or recreational interests referred to in Article 2 do not even enter into consideration in the application of Article 4.[69] In the field of transnational conservation arrangements generally, the EU regime is extremely unusual in asserting a power to *require* states to

[64] See further Section 3(b)(iii) below.

[65] Case C-3/96, *Commission v Netherlands* [1998] *ECR* I-3031.

[66] Case C-355/90 *Commission v Spain* [1993] *ECR* I-4221. The marshes, regularly visited by nineteen Annex I species and fourteen additional migratory species, constitute one of the most important sites for aquatic birds in the Iberian peninsula.

[67] Para. 63 of the judgment.

[68] See further Case C-334/04, *Commission v Greece* [2008] *Env LR* 293, to similar effect. Interestingly, both determinations were reached exclusively by reference to the current version of the ICBP/BirdLife International Inventory of Important Bird Areas in Europe (IBA), no other documentary evidence having been presented.

[69] See also Case C-44/95, *R v Secretary of State for the Environment, ex p. RSPB* (the '*Lappel Bank*' case) [1996] *ECR* I-3843.

designate particular sites as protected areas – traditionally, much greater deference is shown to considerations of national sovereignty.

Nevertheless, the mere designation of protected areas will plainly not of itself guarantee the survival of protected species, which requires in addition the effective implementation of conservation measures at those sites. Article 4(4)[70] therefore requires member states to take appropriate steps to avoid any significant deterioration of habitats or any disturbance of protected species in the areas designated.[71] In *Commission v Ireland*, discussed above, the Irish government was held to be in breach of this provision also, in particular through permitting the degradation of the Owenduff-Nephin Beg Complex in County Mayo, which was important to listed species such as the golden plover (*Pluvialis apricarius*) and the Greenland white-fronted goose (*Anser albifrons flavirostris*).

The most controversial issue here, however, has concerned deliberate policy decisions by governments to reduce the size of protected areas or the scale of protection previously afforded. Once again, the ECJ itself had been disposed to insist upon rigorous respect for conservation,[72] severely restricting the discretion of member states to modify SPAs and denying in particular the relevance of economic or recreational considerations for this purpose.[73] This approach went beyond what governments were prepared to accept, however, and the opportunity was taken in the Habitats Directive to amend Article 4(4) in such a way as to redress the balance in favour of non-environmental interests. Specifically, a uniform regime was established,[74] applicable to all special areas of conservation, whereby plans or projects likely to affect them significantly may generally only be pursued if an environmental impact assessment discloses that the integrity of the site will not be impaired. Where, however, the plan or project 'must nevertheless' be carried out 'for imperative reasons of overriding public interest, including those of an economic or social nature', the obligation of the state concerned is only to take compensatory measures to ensure that

[70] This provision was amended by Article 7 of the Habitats Directive. In this context, the changes are relatively minor, an express reference to pollution having been omitted. See further, however, the discussion in the following paragraph.

[71] They must also strive to avoid deterioration of habitats outside protected areas.

[72] Case C-57/89, *Commission v Germany* (the '*Leybucht Dykes*' case) [1991] *ECR* I-883. The Leybucht forms part of a coastal wetland complex frequented by various Appendix I birds, including the avocet (*Recurvirostra avosetta*).

[73] Only general interests deemed superior to ecological objectives, such as the protection of human life, could be invoked, and then solely to justify absolutely necessary modifications.

[74] Article 6(2)–(4), Habitats Directive.

the overall coherence of Natura 2000, the network of sites established by the Directive (and of which the SPAs designated under the Birds Directive form part), is protected. By way of exception, if the site concerned hosts a priority habitat type and/or a priority species,[75] the only considerations which may be raised are those relating to human health or public safety, to beneficial consequences of primary importance for the environment or (further to an opinion from the European Commission) to other imperative reasons of overriding public interest.[76]

Despite this reassertion of ultimate governmental authority, there can be little doubt of the significance of these directives, particularly in terms of their impact upon the attitudes of planning authorities and developers, who are now forced to display much greater awareness of conservation considerations, at least where endangered species and critical habitats are concerned.[77] Thus the obligation to protect the heathland habitat of the woodlark (*Lullula arborea*), nightjar (*Caprimulgus europaeus*) and Dartford warbler (*Sylvia undata*) in the UK led to the establishment of the Thames Basin Heaths Special Protection Area in 2006, and to the effective imposition of a complete moratorium on house-building over 300 square miles of southern England, pending the determination of a long-term strategy for the area.[78]

3. Arrangements in other regions

Beyond the European region, numerous bilateral conventions for the conservation of birds have been adopted, the United States having pioneered this practice through agreements with its immediate neighbours, viz. the 1916 Convention for the Protection of Migratory Birds (Canada),[79] and the 1936 Convention for the Protection of Migratory

[75] 'Priority' habitats and species, as identified in Annexes I and II to the Directive, are determined by reference to the risk of their disappearance or extinction, coupled with a consideration of the proportion of their range which falls within the territory covered.

[76] Article 6(4), Habitats Directive. It seems clear from the practice of the Commission that these 'other . . . reasons' may include general social or economic interests. See Davies, *supra* n. 44, pp. 147–9; L. Kramer, 'The European Commission's Opinions under Article 6(4) of the Habitats Directive' (2009) 21(1) *JEL* 59.

[77] Verschuuren, *supra* n. 44, pp. 327–8.

[78] For the advice recently issued in this regard by the UK Planning Inspectorate, see its website at www.planning-inspectorate.gov.uk/pins/appeals/thames_basin/advice_inspectors_sept%2009.pdf.

[79] 39 Stat 1702; *USTS* 628. The treaty was originally concluded by Great Britain on behalf of Canada.

Birds and Game Mammals (Mexico).[80] From the early 1970s, a series of further agreements has been concluded, principally amongst the countries of the Pacific Rim. The US, Japan, Russia and Australia are key players here,[81] though various other countries have also been drawn into the process.[82] These agreements have much in common,[83] and, given constraints of space, it will be appropriate to focus primarily on the US and Australian agreements, which collectively span the entire historical period.

a) Values placed on birds

The motivations underlying these treaties, at least initially, were essentially anthropocentric, the preamble to the 1916 Convention expressly acknowledging the importance of birds both as a food source and as destroyers of injurious insects.[84] The latter consideration mirrors contemporary European concerns for agriculture and forestry, while the former reflects the strong North American 'pot-hunting' tradition, sustained by the enormous numbers of waterfowl which migrate between Canada and the US. By the 1970s, however, the values attributed to birds had expanded considerably. The 1972 Convention refers to the 'aesthetic'

[80] 178 *LNTS* 309.

[81] See, e.g., the 1972 Convention for the Protection of Migratory Birds and Birds in Danger of Extinction and Their Environment, 25 *UST* 3329, *TIAS* No. 7990 (Japan/US), hereafter the 1972 Convention; 1973 Convention for the Protection of Migratory Birds and Birds under Threat of Extinction and on the Means of Protecting Them, 5 *IPE* 2216 (Annex only) (Japan/Russia); 1974 Agreement for the Protection of Migratory Birds and Birds in Danger of Extinction and Their Environment (JAMBA), *ATS* 6 (1981) (Japan/Australia); 1976 Convention concerning the Conservation of Migratory Birds and Their Environment, 29 *UST* 4647, *TIAS* No. 9073 (US/Russia), hereafter the 1976 Convention.

[82] Examples include the 1981 Agreement for the Protection of Migratory Birds and Their Habitats (Japan/China); 1984 Convention on the Protection of Migratory Birds (India/Russia); 1986 Agreement for the Protection of Migratory Birds and Their Environment (CAMBA) (Australia/China), *ATS* 22 (1988); 2006 Agreement on the Conservation of Migratory Birds (ROKAMBA) (Australia/Republic of Korea), *ATS* 24 (2007). Korea also concluded an agreement with Russia (1994). Latin American examples reported include Brazil/Colombia (1973), Brazil/Peru (1975) and Argentina/Bolivia (1976). For further details, see C. de Klemm, Migratory Species in International Instruments: An Overview (IUCN Environmental Policy and Law Occasional Paper No. 2, 1986), pp. 18–19, 119–67; Wild Bird Society of Japan, Study Report on the Framework for Multilateral Co-operation for the Conservation of Migratory Birds (2000); G. C. Boere et al. (eds.), *Waterbirds around the World* (TSO, 2007).

[83] See C. de Klemm, 'The Problem of Migratory Species in International Law' (1994) *Green Globe Year Book* 67, at p. 69.

[84] It also referred more generally to species which were 'either useful to man or harmless'. See, to similar effect, the preamble to the 1936 Convention.

and 'scientific' qualities of birds as well as to their economic and recreational importance,[85] while the 1976 Convention recognises also their cultural, educational and ecological values. The Australian Agreements describe birds as 'an important element of the natural environment', while JAMBA and ROKAMBA refer additionally to their 'essential role in enriching' it. These preambular recitals are, moreover, potentially significant to the interpretation of the substantive obligations contained in the treaty in question.[86] The 1972 Convention, for example, states that the hunting of migratory birds shall be regulated so as 'to maintain their populations in optimum numbers',[87] but neither the Convention itself nor the *travaux préparatoires* clarify the meaning of this phrase. The correct interpretation of such expressions could plainly turn upon whether the treaty was motivated primarily by commercial, subsistence, recreational or ecological considerations.[88]

b) *Species covered*

These conventions adopt a variety of techniques, which have tended to become more sophisticated over time, for indicating the species which they cover. The 1916 Convention applies to specified groups (e.g. 'cranes', 'rails', 'chickadees', 'auks') of migratory birds listed in three broad categories ('game birds', 'insectivorous birds' and 'other nongame birds').[89] Some groups (viz. 'all other perching birds which feed entirely or chiefly on insects') are extremely imprecise, however. The 1936 Convention more helpfully defines coverage in terms of universally intelligible biological families,[90] such as Anatidae, Columbidae and Sylviidae, while the later conventions tend to employ the familiar modern technique of listing species in an annex capable of periodic amendment. Provision for the amendment of coverage first appeared in the 1936 Convention,[91] a power utilised in a 1972 supplementary agreement which doubled the number of taxa receiving the benefit of protection.[92] A

[85] Preamble, 1st recital.
[86] See the 1969 Vienna Convention on the Law of Treaties, Articles 31, 32.
[87] Article 3(2).
[88] For a parallel issue in US domestic law, see *Fund for Animals, Inc. v Frizzell* (DC Cir, 1975) 530 F.2d 982; A. Taylor, 'Rethinking the Irreparable Harm Factor in Wildlife Mortality Cases' (2009) 2 *Stanford Journal of Animal Law & Policy* 113.
[89] See Article 1. [90] See Article 4. [91] Ibid.
[92] 23 *UST* 260, *TIAS* No. 7302. Further amendments were adopted in 1999.

noticeable feature of the early conventions is that, in keeping with the prevailing attitudes of the day,[93] no falcons, hawks or eagles were listed despite the fact that many of their migration routes traverse national boundaries. Several raptor families – including the Accipitridae (eagles, hawks etc.), Falconidae (falcons, caracara) and Pandionidae (ospreys) – were, however, incorporated into the 1936 Convention by virtue of the 1972 amendments. The later conventions vary in terms of their coverage of birds of prey, though naturally much depends upon the extent to which such species do in fact migrate between the two countries concerned.

That said, it should be noted that migratory species represent the principal, rather than the exclusive, preoccupation of these treaties. The 1916 Convention omits to clarify whether it applies to every species within the groups mentioned, or only to those that are migratory, whereas that of 1936 stipulates that all birds in the families listed shall be deemed to be migratory for its purposes, regardless, it would seem, of whether this is actually the case.[94] Later conventions sometimes include species that are simply common to both countries or share flyways or breeding/feeding grounds,[95] though the Australian agreements require reliable evidence of migration as a defining criterion of a migratory species. At the same time, it seems that some of these instruments are designed also to embrace taxa that are *endangered*, without regard to whether they are migratory.[96]

A final point on species coverage is that the US Fish and Wildlife Service has recently confirmed that it has always interpreted the US conventions to *exclude* species which are non-native to the countries concerned, and have only been introduced as a consequence of human activities. This assumes particular importance where protected birds are listed by family, rather than as individual species.[97] A non-exhaustive list

[93] Cf. the 1902 Convention on Birds Useful to Agriculture, discussed above, and the 1900 Convention for the Preservation of Wild Animals, Birds and Fish in Africa, discussed below in Chapter 9.

[94] See Article 4.

[95] See the 1976 US/USSR Convention, Article 1(1)(b); 1972 Japan/US Convention, Article 2(1)(b).

[96] This would seem to be implicit in the very title to several of the agreements listed at n. 81 *supra*. As regards the 1972 Convention, note the list of endangered species established by the Amending Agreement of 19 September 1974, 5 *IPE* 2206.

[97] See the US *Federal Register*, 70(49), 15 March 2005.

of some 125 exotic species known to occur in the US has recently been promulgated in that connection.[98]

c) *Regulation of exploitation*

The regulation of exploitation represents the primary focus of this group of treaties, particularly the earlier examples.

i) Taking

The 1916 Convention requires the parties to prohibit the 'taking' of nests or eggs of protected birds at all times and to prohibit hunting during close seasons. The close season is year-round for migrating insectivorous and other non-game birds, while the maximum allowable hunting season for game birds is three and a half months. The 1936 Convention demands prohibition of the 'taking' both of nests or eggs of listed species during close seasons and of the birds themselves off-season or in refuges. It sets the maximum permissible hunting season at four months, forbids the hunting of wild ducks between 10 March and 1 September, and outlaws hunting from aircraft. The later conventions also prohibit the taking of listed birds or their eggs, subject to limited exceptions, which commonly include regulated hunting. The precise specification of hunting seasons is usually left to unilateral determination, but often enhanced protection, and sometimes a moratorium or complete prohibition on exploitation, is mandated in respect of particular species or those categorised as 'endangered'.[99]

Although all of these treaties regulate the 'taking' of birds or their nests or eggs, this word is invariably left undefined, leaving considerable uncertainty as to the range of activities to be regulated. If taking is deemed to cover only shooting, trapping and the like, the obligations entailed are relatively limited, whereas if it were understood to include any kind of killing – mortalities resulting from pollution, for example, or from collisions with buildings, wind turbines or vehicles – the commitment would obviously be very much more onerous. The correct

[98] Ibid. The list was published pursuant to the 2004 Migratory Bird Treaty Reform Act and identifies species to which domestic legislation (see n. 105 *infra*) is understood not to apply.

[99] Articles III and IV of the 1916 Convention, for example, provide for a close season of ten years for certain species and a possible five years for others. The later treaties commonly provide for the 'special protection' of species identified as being in danger of extinction, which may entail the complete prohibition of 'taking'. See Article 4(2), 1972 Convention.

interpretation may well differ from treaty to treaty, since they are not expressed in identical terms. Whereas the 1916 Convention establishes controls on 'hunting',[100] and only refers specifically to 'taking' in relation to nests or eggs,[101] the 1936 Convention primarily regulates the 'taking' of migratory birds but additionally prohibits the 'killing' of insectivorous birds.[102] The later conventions tend to focus upon the 'taking' of birds, eggs or nests, though some make separate provision, in diluted terms, for preserving the environment of protected species, which may include a duty to '*seek means* to prevent damage' to the birds themselves.[103] The 1976 Convention, however, also requires that 'the disturbance of nesting colonies' be prohibited.[104]

It is noteworthy that, for the purposes of US domestic law, the 1918 Migratory Bird Treaty Act (MBTA)[105] prohibits both hunting and killing migratory birds and that the latter term has on occasion been given an extensive interpretation by the American courts.[106] In *United States v FMC*,[107] for example, the operator of a pesticide manufacturing plant was found guilty of an offence when migratory birds died after using a pond which he had unwittingly contaminated. Similarly, in *United States v Corbin Farm Service*,[108] pesticide manufacturers were found guilty when their product was sprayed onto a field and caused the death of 1,100 American wigeon (*Mareca americana*). In neither case was the

[100] Article II.

[101] See Article V. The term is, however, used in Article II(1) in relation to the permitted activities of Indians.

[102] See Article II, paras. (A) and (E) respectively.

[103] See, e.g., the 1972 Convention, Article 6 (which goes on to specify particularly 'damage resulting from pollution of the seas'); 1974 Agreement, Article 6; CAMBA, Article 4(b)(i) – emphasis added.

[104] Article II(1).

[105] 16 USC 703–12. Note that all four US Conventions are implemented domestically by this single piece of legislation, as amended. In the landmark case of *Missouri v Holland* (1920) 252 US 416, the US Supreme Court confirmed that the 1916 treaty provided a valid basis for federal regulation. For the species currently covered by the MBTA, see the US Fish and Wildlife Service website at www.fws.gov/migratorybirds/RegulationsPolicies/mbta/mbtintro.html.

[106] For discussion, see S. Margolin, 'Liability under the Migratory Bird Treaty Act' (1979) 7 *Ecology Law Qly.* 989; B. Means, 'Prohibiting Conduct, Not Consequences: The Limited Reach of the Migratory Bird Treaty Act' (1998) 97 *Michigan Law Review* 823; P. Baldwin, The Endangered Species Act (ESA), the Migratory Bird Treaty Act (MBTA) and Department of Defense Readiness Activities (Congressional Research Services Report RL 31415, updated 9 August 2004).

[107] (1978) 572 F. 2d. 902.

[108] (1978) 444 F.Supp. 510. For discussion of these cases, see Margolin, *supra* n. 106.

defendant's lack of intent to kill considered relevant. Plainly, this opens up the prospect of criminal liability of an extremely extensive kind, but both courts suggested that deaths caused by collisions with motor vehicles and so on should not give rise to prosecution under the Act. Dealing with pesticides, however, was an ultra-hazardous activity to which the concept of strict liability was applicable. The absence of any need to prove fault is a significant advantage, and the threat of criminal prosecution has sometimes been used, it seems, to encourage polluters to reach settlements: following the *Exxon Valdez* incident, for example, Exxon pleaded guilty to charges of violating the MBTA.[109] The extent, if any, to which the Act applies to 'indirect' taking in the course of lawful activities – such as bird mortalities resulting incidentally from habitat modification or timber harvesting – has proved controversial, especially where the activities of government agencies are concerned,[110] though a recent report to Congress suggests that, whatever the position under other statutes,[111] such activities fall outside the scope of the MBTA.[112]

The controls on taking which these conventions establish are naturally subject to specified exceptions. Aside from lawful hunting, provision is usually made for the taking of birds with a view to species propagation, or for other scientific or educational purposes consistent with the objectives of the treaty. The earlier agreements make specific provision for controlling the populations of insectivorous birds should their proliferation become injurious to agriculture or other interests,[113] while the later ones

109 See Means, *supra* n. 106, p. 825; S. Raucher, 'Raising the Stakes for Environmental Polluters: The *Exxon Valdez* Criminal Prosecution' (1991) 19 *Ecology Law Qly*. 147, pp. 170–3.

110 In *Robertson v Seattle Audubon Society* (1992) 503 US 429, at 437–8, the US Supreme Court assumed without discussion that the Act applied even to logging-planning decisions by government agencies, but later circuit-court cases proved inconsistent on this point: see Means, *supra* n. 106; Baldwin, *supra* n. 106; Birdnet, 'The Migratory Bird Treaty Act: How It Applies to the Federal Government' at www.nmnh.si.edu/BIRDNET/OC/experthelp/MBTA_fed.html.

111 In *Babbitt v Sweet Home Chapter of Communities for a Great Oregon* (1995) 115 S Ct 2407; 515 US 687; 132 L.Ed 2d 597, the Supreme Court confirmed that 'take' in the 1973 Endangered Species Act includes 'significant habitat modification or degradation where it actually kills or injures wildlife', though in that statute, unlike the MBTA, the term is expressly defined to include 'harming' or 'harassing'. See Means, *supra* n. 106; M. Herz, 'Endangered Species: Stretching the Law to Protect Their Habitats' (1996) 8 *JEL* 158.

112 K. Alexander, What Happens to the Bald Eagle Now That It Is Not Protected under the Endangered Species Act? (Congressional Research Services Report RL34174, updated 9 October 2008).

113 1916 Convention, Article VII; 1936 Convention, Article II(e).

commonly allow more generally for the taking of birds to protect persons or property.[114] Some exceptions reflect more idiosyncratic concerns – the US conventions with Mexico and Japan, for example, both permit the exemption of hunting on private game farms,[115] while the former also authorises the live capture and use of insectivorous birds in conformity with national law, a provision designed to cater for the long-established Mexican trade in live caged birds.[116]

Of the commonly incorporated exceptions, however, perhaps the most significant relate to the activities of indigenous communities. Spring hunting is an established tradition in parts of Alaska, Canada and the former USSR, and large numbers of birds are shot every year as they return to their nesting sites. The precise scope of these exemptions varies considerably; thus the beneficiaries are variously described as 'Eskimos and Indians',[117] 'indigenous peoples'[118] or 'indigenous inhabitants',[119] sometimes of specified localities.[120] The Australian agreements all refer somewhat imprecisely to the 'inhabitants of certain regions who have traditionally carried on [hunting and gathering] activities for their own food, clothing or cultural purposes'.[121] In some cases the exception is substantively restricted to the satisfaction of such needs,[122] while in others it is limited to certain seasons[123] or must be conducted so as not to threaten the survival of target species.[124] Also, while the exception sometimes relates to migratory birds generally, the Australian agreements restrict it to 'specified birds'[125] and the 1916 Convention actually identified the species in question in the text.[126] Curiously, the species indicated did not include those which were most commonly taken (ducks and geese), rendering much of the spring hunting by indigenous

[114] See, e.g., the 1972 Convention, Article 3(1)(b); 1976 Convention, Article II(1)(d); JAMBA/CAMBA/ROKAMBA, Article 2(1)(b).

[115] 1936 Convention, Article II(e); 1972 Convention, Article 3(1)(d).

[116] Hayden, *supra* n. 11, p. 87.

[117] 1916 Convention, Article II(3); 1972 Convention, Article 3(2)(e). Article II(1) of the former also allows 'Indians' to take scoters for food (but not sale) at any time. A 1979 Amending Protocol replaces the term 'Eskimo' with 'Inuit'.

[118] 1972 Convention, Article 3(2)(e). [119] 1976 Convention, Article II(1)(c).

[120] E.g. the Trust Territory of the Pacific Islands (US/Japan); the Chukchi and Koryaksk national regions, the Commander Islands and the State of Alaska (US/Russia).

[121] Article 2(1)(d), in each case.

[122] 1972 Convention, Article 3(1)(e); 1976 Convention, Article 2(1)(c). See also 1916 Convention, Article II(3).

[123] 1972 Convention, Article 3(2); 1976 Convention, Article 2(2).

[124] JAMBA/CAMBA/ROKAMBA, Article 2(1)(d). [125] Ibid.

[126] Viz. 'auks, auklets, guillemots, murres and puffins': Article II(3).

communities technically illegal, though neither government had ever seriously attempted to enforce the law. Eventually, the relevant provision was amended to authorise the taking of any species for nutritional and other essential needs, thereby bringing the US treaty with Canada broadly into line with that with Russia.[127]

ii) Trade

The 1916 Convention prohibits international or inter-state trade in migratory birds falling within its scope, or in their eggs, during the close season.[128] The later agreements likewise mandate strict regulation of trade in protected species. International trade in wildlife is, of course, governed primarily by CITES,[129] and many of the species covered by these agreements will also be listed in the Annexes to that convention. That will not necessarily be the case, however, and the bilateral agreements also have a wider scope insofar as they regulate *internal* trade. Under the MBTA, the range of activities regulated is even more extensive than in relation to taking, creating numerous offences concerning possession, shipment or carriage of listed birds or their parts or products. It is reported that, pursuant to these provisions, a citizen of Illinois was prosecuted in 1995 for giving Hillary Clinton a 'dream catcher' made of eagle feathers.[130]

d) Other conservation measures

In the early twentieth century, excessive shooting and egg collection represented the principal threats to birds, and those were accordingly the main focus of the 1916 and 1936 treaties. Habitat conservation was essentially an ancillary consideration, though both treaties contemplate the establishment of refuges for certain purposes.[131]

More recently, habitat degradation has been recognised as by far the greatest threat to migratory species, and is therefore addressed more squarely in the later conventions, though the provisions in question are

[127] See 'Conservation and Aboriginal Treaties', US Fish and Wildlife Service Press Release, October 1999, viewable at www.gaiabooks.co.uk/environment/migratorytreaty.html.

[128] Article VI. [129] See Chapter 15 below.

[130] Anon., 'They Swooped', *The Economist*, 19 August 1995, p. 27; Means, *supra* n. 106, p. 835.

[131] See the 1916 Treaty, Article IV (which envisages them as one form of 'special protection' for wood ducks and eider ducks); 1936 Treaty, Article II(B).

usually rather bland.[132] A notable exception is the 1976 Convention, Article VII of which calls for the establishment of protected areas and facilities for the conservation of migratory birds, and for their management in such a way as to preserve and restore the natural ecosystem. Action promptly followed, with the USSR (as it then was) establishing nature reserves totalling almost 2.5 million hectares on Wrangel Island (a nesting area for the snow goose), in southern Chitin Oblast and around Lake Taimyr (a massive waterfowl nesting area), while in 1980 almost 22 million hectares were added to the US National Wildlife Refuge System in Alaska alone.[133]

In addition, Article IV(2)(c) of this Convention requires each party to identify sites within its jurisdiction which are of importance to the conservation of migratory birds, for listing in the Appendix. To the maximum extent possible, these sites are to be protected against 'pollution, detrimental alteration and other environmental degradation'. Interestingly, the following paragraph calls for the creation of a second list designating any such areas *outside* the parties' own territories, and for action to ensure that persons under their jurisdiction respect the principles of the Convention in relation to such areas. These stipulations occur within the context of a general provision requiring that, to the extent possible, the parties 'undertake measures necessary to protect and enhance the environment of migratory birds and to prevent and abate the pollution or detrimental alteration of that environment'.[134] Similar, albeit less rigorous, provisions occur in other modern agreements, but there is no equivalent in the earlier treaties – oil spills, pesticides and other forms of environmental pollution being a minimal threat to birds at the time of their adoption. The 1972 Convention is additionally noteworthy for its establishment of an early warning system between US and Japanese national authorities in the event of substantial harm, actual or

[132] Commonly, parties are required merely to *endeavour* to provide sanctuaries and other facilities for the management of migratory birds. 1972 Convention, Article 3(3); CAMBA/ROKAMBA, Article 4; JAMBA, Article 5.

[133] Collaboration is now pursued within the wider framework of the 1994 bilateral Agreement on Co-operation in the Field of Protection of the Environment and Natural Resources, *TIAS* No. 12589. For a report on recent activities, see US–Russia Co-operative Efforts for the Conservation of Wildlife and Wildlife Habitat: Activities for 2007–8, at www.fws.gov/international/dic/regional%20prgrams/russia/pdf/Area%205%20Work%20Plan%202007-2008%20ENG.pdf.

[134] Article IV(1).

anticipated, to migratory birds or their environment, backed by an agreement to co-operate in taking remedial action.[135]

Finally, the later instruments also address the problems posed by exotic species, now recognised as a major threat. The introduction, for example, of predators such as rats or cats to islands that are important nesting colonies for seabirds can cause severe ecological disruption.[136] Recognising this, these treaties require their respective parties to control both the importation of animals and plants which might prove detrimental to the preservation of migratory or endangered birds[137] and the introduction of species which might disturb the ecological balance of natural environments.[138] Early actions undertaken pursuant to these obligations included attempts by Japan to eradicate introduced species from coastal islands with important nesting colonies, and the prohibition by the US of further introductions of grass carp (*Ctenopharyngodon idella*) on account of its adverse impact on the food resources of migratory birds.[139]

e) Research and co-operation

The later conventions tend to make specific provision for co-operation in research,[140] and information from bird-banding programmes has duly been exchanged between the countries concerned and a number of joint research projects have been established. There are, however, severe limitations to what can be achieved on a purely bilateral basis. Fortunately, the Bonn and Ramsar Conventions have served as catalysts for the recent advancement of multilateral collaboration.[141]

Although the 1916 and 1936 Conventions make no mention of research or co-operation, Canada, the US and Mexico have in fact co-operated

[135] Article IV(2)(a).

[136] As in the case of the endangered short-tailed albatross (*Diomeda albatrus*) on Torishima Island in Japan.

[137] See, e.g., the 1972 Convention, Article 6(b); 1976 Convention, Article IV(2)(b); JAMBA, Article 6(b); CAMBA, Article 4(b)(ii); ROKAMBA, Article 5(b).

[138] 1976 Convention, Article 4(2)(b); 1972 Convention, Article 6(c); JAMBA, Article 6(c) – 'unique island environments' are sometimes specified.

[139] See United States Statement on Implementation of the US–USSR Convention Concerning the Conservation of Migratory Birds and Their Environment for the Year 1980 (US Fish and Wildlife Service, Washington, DC).

[140] See, e.g., the 1972 Convention, Article 5; JAMBA, Article 4; CAMBA/ROKAMBA, Article 3.

[141] See Section 3 below.

extensively in the field of avian conservation. Valuable information regarding the movements of birds has been obtained from their joint participation in the North American Bird Banding Programme, which commenced in the 1920s, and other collaborative research has involved waterfowl surveys, the identification of suitable habitats for wildlife management areas and assessment of the effects of pesticides. Collaboration has, moreover, extended beyond research into actual management, embracing government agencies at both the federal and state levels, along with NGOs, academic institutions and the business sector. Initially, this was achieved through the operation of the North American Waterfowl Management Plan (NAWMP), adopted by Canada and the US in the mid-1980s and extended to Mexico shortly afterwards.[142] This arrangement established a framework for joint long-term planning, based on a tripartite committee, to re-establish depleted waterfowl populations and secure protection for their habitat.[143]

Subsequently, collaboration has been expanded through the North American Bird Conservation Initiative (NABCI),[144] a CEC-facilitated[145] project which seeks to extend protection to all birds in all habitats through the integration of NAWMP with other regional conservation plans and strategies. One significant limitation of the arrangements adopted by these three countries, however, is that bird migration routes are not confined to the areas covered by their jurisdictions, but commonly extend into Latin America as well. Bearing that in mind, an important development was the launching in 1986 of the Western Hemisphere Shorebird Reserve Network, which brings together organisations and individuals from both North and South America that share an interest in the conservation of shorebirds with a view to promoting the establishment of reserves. The network currently embraces seventy-seven key sites, extending over 12 million hectares, in twelve countries.[146]

[142] For discussion, see de Klemm, *supra* n. 83, pp. 71–2. For fuller details, see the NAWMP website at www.nawmp.ca. Previously, management plans had been adopted for individual (sub)species, such as the Pacific coast brant goose (*Branta bernicla nigricans*) and greater snow goose (*Anser caerulescens atlanticus*).

[143] On the funding of these arrangements through the Federal 'Duck Stamp' programme, and under the 1989 North American Wetlands Conservation Act, see de Klemm, *supra* n. 83.

[144] NABCI/ICAAN/ICOAN was launched in 1998; see generally www.nabci.net.

[145] For discussion of CEC, see section 2(f) below.

[146] Delaware Bay was the first. For further information, see www.whsrn.org.

f) Implementation

The most glaring deficiency exhibited by these treaties as a group lies in the weakness of their provision for formal institutional arrangements. This factor, when coupled with the purely bilateral character of the instruments themselves, undoubtedly restricts their potential for generating a coherent and comprehensive approach to the conservation of the species and flyways they seek to protect.[147] On the other hand, this problem has to some extent been mitigated by the emergence, often independently of any specific treaty foundations, of informal arrangements, such as those already described in respect of North America.

It is also in North America, of course, that opportunities are most likely to arise for the utilisation of domestic legal proceedings for the enforcement of international conservation commitments. An additional, supra-national, forum for this purpose has, moreover, recently emerged in the form of the Commission for Environmental Co-operation (CEC),[148] created by Article 8 of the 1993 North American Agreement on Environmental Co-operation,[149] a 'side agreement' to the NAFTA accords.[150] Articles 14 and 15 establish a procedure whereby private citizens may refer to the Secretariat any case of alleged failure by a party to effectively enforce its own environmental laws.[151] The Secretariat cannot make 'rulings', but may, in appropriate cases, prepare a 'factual record' relating to this alleged non-enforcement. Under this procedure, cases concerning the destruction of migratory bird nests in the course of logging operations were submitted by various organisations in 1999 against the US, and in 2002 and 2004 against Canada. The nature of the record produced is not guaranteed to produce any immediate, decisive response, however, and it remains to be seen how effective these procedures will prove in the longer term.[152] The Agreement also envisages a second category of proceeding under Article 13. Here, the CEC Secretariat may, on its own initiative, prepare a report on any matter

[147] See de Klemm, *supra* n. 83. [148] For general information, see www.cec.org.
[149] (1993) 4 *YBIEL* 831.
[150] For discussion of the relevant procedures, see D. Hunter, J. Salzman and D. Zaelke, *International Environmental Law and Policy* (Foundation Press, 3rd ed., 2007), pp. 1318 ff.
[151] For a guide to the revised procedure, see CEC, *Bringing the Facts to Light* (2007).
[152] For details of these cases (SEM-99-002, SEM-02-001, SEM-04-006), see the CEC website at www.cec.org/citizen/index.cfm?varlan=english. For appraisal, see J. Wilson, 'The Commission for Environmental Co-operation and North American Migratory Bird Conservation: The Potential of the Citizen Submission Procedure' (2003) 6 *JIWLP* 205.

falling within the annual programme of the CEC Council. An early example, prompted by complaints from NGOs in both the US and Mexico, resulted from an investigation into the deaths of some 40,000 migratory birds at Silva Reservoir in Guanjuato, Mexico. It was determined that the overriding cause of mortality was botulism, though there was also evidence of exposure to contamination from heavy metals. One key recommendation was that Mexico develop a national programme for wildlife health surveillance, along the lines of existing schemes in its NAFTA partners.[153]

The more recent of the bilateral migratory bird treaties do tend to provide for 'consultations' to be held if any party requests them,[154] and such proceedings are in fact now convened on a reasonably regular basis,[155] both to amend the lists of protected species and to discuss substantive aspects of implementation.[156] A further advance has seen the consolidation of some of these meetings,[157] whilst more overarching arrangements for the Asia–Pacific region have been developed under the Bonn and Ramsar Conventions. Subsequently, the Western Hemisphere Migratory Species Initiative (WHMSI) established a similar framework for co-operation in the Americas.[158] These developments have undoubtedly helped to offset the problems of fragmentation posed by the bilateral nature of the treaties themselves, though the consolidation of all of these into a single, multilateral regime remains a desirable objective.

[153] CEC Secretariat Report on the Death of Migratory Birds at the Silva Reservoir (1995), viewable via www.cec.org/files/pdf/silvae_EN.pdf. For a later example, see *Ribbon of Life* (1999), which concerned the preservation of avian habitat on the Upper San Pedro River.

[154] 1976 Convention, Article X; JAMBA, Article 8; CAMBA, Article 5; ROKAMBA, Article 7.

[155] Information regarding consultations under the Japanese treaties, for example, can be found in the News Archive of the Japanese Environment Ministry, viewable via www.env.go.jp.

[156] For the 2006 Amendments to the Australian Agreements with Japan and China, for example, see www.aph.gov.au/house/committee/jsct/5_6_september2006/report/chapter5.pdf.

[157] This is true of the Australian treaties in particular. Furthermore, bilateral consultations under the treaties between Japan, Russia and the US were held contemporaneously in Honolulu in February 2009 to permit informal trilateral talks.

[158] See www.fws.gov/international/WHMSI/whmsi_Eng.htm. Note also in this context the funding arrangements established by the US Neotropical Migratory Bird Conservation Act, 2000. See further Chapter 8 below.

4. Global conservation conventions

Mention of the Bonn and Ramsar Conventions provides a timely reminder of the significance in this context of treaties with a wider substantive focus. In fact, birds are likely to derive some benefit from almost *any* treaty concerned with conservation generally, or indeed with pollution control or other forms of environmental regulation.[159] Obviously, however, those devoted specifically to the protection of migratory species and of wetland habitat are likely to have most to offer. A fuller analysis of these conventions can be found in other chapters, and for present purposes it is necessary only to draw attention to certain features of particular significance to birds.

a) 1971 Convention on Wetlands of International Importance

The Ramsar Convention calls for the wise use of wetlands generally, and in particular those sites designated for the List of Wetlands of International Importance. Significantly, the criteria governing eligibility for listing include several that relate specifically to avian species; for example, a site should be considered internationally important if it regularly supports 20,000 waterfowl in total, substantial numbers of individuals from particular groups of waterfowl (e.g. loons/divers, cormorants, pelicans, cranes, terns etc.) or 1 per cent of the individuals in a population of any particular species. Although there are other criteria which are not focused upon birds, it was those related to waterfowl which played the key role in the early development of the Convention, partly on account of their ready applicability. This stems from the combination of their relatively precise, quantitative nature and the unusually extensive information available on waterfowl populations worldwide. Thus it was calculated in 1993 that the percentage of Ramsar sites designated by reference to the waterfowl criteria ranged from 73 per cent in Oceania to 97 per cent in North America.[160]

The very wide definition of wetlands adopted for Ramsar purposes embraces an enormous variety of habitat types of importance to birds, including water meadows, bogs and fens, lakes and marshes, man-made reservoirs, coastal beaches, mudflats and mountain streams. Indeed, as its full title indicates, the protection of the breeding and resting places of waterfowl was the primary motivation for the Convention's adoption. Although recent policy has been to increase the emphasis placed upon

[159] See Bowman, *supra* n. 3, pp. 294–7. [160] See further Chapter 13 below.

the broader functions and values of wetlands, the interests of waterfowl conservation nonetheless remain central to the entire Ramsar operation.

Given the fact that so many waterbirds undertake lengthy migrations, a key aspect of Ramsar activity has been the enhancement not merely of national management practices but of international co-operation in that regard.[161] One important development of this kind was the adoption in 1996 of the Asia–Pacific Migratory Waterbird Conservation Strategy,[162] along with its Shorebird Site Network. This was designed to foster mutual support and co-operation amongst governmental and non-governmental agencies, wetland managers and local communities with regard to site management and conservation. A Migratory Waterbird Conservation Committee, incorporating representation from all these sectors, was established to oversee its implementation. More recently, however, the focus for co-operation has shifted to individual flyways, of which there are several within the Asia–Pacific region. The East Asian/Australasian flyway, for example, extends from the Arctic to New Zealand, embracing around 700 major sites in twenty countries, and effective conservation action would ideally involve the participation of all of them. It is therefore encouraging to note the launching in November 2006 of an informal international partnership for this flyway – currently embracing ten governments,[163] three inter-governmental agencies and seven international NGOs – dedicated to co-operation in the conservation of migratory waterbirds and their habitats.[164] A significant tangible benefit from this process was the recent announcement by the Republic of Korea of its abandonment of authorisation of further large-scale reclamation projects regarding intertidal mudflats along its coasts.[165]

b) 1979 Bonn Convention on the Conservation of Migratory Species of Wild Animals

The Bonn Convention (CMS) establishes a potentially comprehensive regime for the conservation of migratory species, including strict

[161] See Article 5 of the Convention.

[162] On the so-called 'Brisbane Initiative', see Ramsar REC 6(4).

[163] Australia, Cambodia, China, Indonesia, Japan, Republic of Korea, the Philippines, Russia, Singapore and the US. As noted in the previous section, these governments already have a significant network of bilateral treaty arrangements amongst themselves.

[164] For further details, see www.eaaflyway.net. Similar partnerships are evolving for other flyways.

[165] See Ramsar Resolution X.22, Annex II.

protection for those which are currently endangered.[166] These are listed in Appendix I, which at present incorporates over fifty avian species, including the Dalmatian pelican (*Pelecanus crispus*), bald ibis (*Geronticus eremita*), Steller's sea eagle (*Haliaeetus pelagicus*), black-necked crane (*Grus nigricollis*), Eskimo curlew (*Numenius borealis*), Japanese murrelet (*Synthliboranthus wumizusume*) and white-eyed gull (*Larus leucophthalmus*). In addition, any species which might significantly benefit from international co-operation may be listed in Appendix II, which contains a much wider array of birds, including several entire families, such as the Phoenicopteridae (flamingos), Cathartidae (New World vultures), Falconidae (falcons and caracaras) and Charadriidae (plovers and lapwings). In this case, however, the protective measures are not set out in the Convention itself, but are, in accordance with Article IV(3), reserved for elaboration in ancillary AGREEMENTS[167] to be negotiated amongst range states within the framework provided by Article V.[168] Disappointingly, only four Article IV(3) AGREEMENTS have actually been concluded to date, but two of these – the 1995 Agreement on the Conservation of African–Eurasian Migratory Waterbirds (AEWA)[169] and the 2001 Agreement on the Conservation of Albatrosses and Petrels (ACAP)[170] – relate to birds and are potentially of great importance.

i) AEWA

This ambitious treaty originated from a proposal at the very first meeting of the CMS CoP to develop an AGREEMENT for the conservation of Western palaearctic Anatidae (ducks, geese and swans), but its scope was later progressively widened to embrace over 250 species of waterbirds spanning twenty-eight biological families.[171] The migration routes of these species collectively cover an enormous range, and the geographical scope of AEWA accordingly extends to the whole of Africa and Europe, adjacent parts of Asia and the Middle East and, at the other extreme, Greenland and the outlying islands of Canada.[172] Its eastern ranges

[166] See in particular Article III.
[167] All references to such instruments in the Convention appear in upper-case lettering.
[168] For discussion of this provision, see Chapter 16 below.
[169] (1995) 6 *YIEL* 306. For discussion, see B. Lenten, 'A Flying Start for the Agreement on the Conservation of African–Eurasian Waterbirds (AEWA)' (2001) 4 *JIWLP* 159.
[170] *ATS* 5 (2004).
[171] See Annex 2, as amended. Conservation measures are actually targeted at individual *populations*, of which well over 500 are identified.
[172] See the map and definition of the Agreement area in Annex 1.

overlap considerably with those of the Central Asian flyway, for which an action plan was recently approved by the CMS,[173] so some mechanism for co-ordination, if not actual amalgamation, of the two schemes is certain to be required.[174] AEWA, which came into force in November 1999, establishes its own financial and institutional arrangements, with provision for a Secretariat, Standing Committee, Technical Committee and regular Meetings of the Parties (MoPs),[175] of which there have been four to date.

Under Article 2, the parties must take co-ordinated measures to maintain waterbird species in a favourable conservation status or to restore them to such a condition, paying due regard to the precautionary principle in their implementation. More detailed conservation commitments are spelled out in Article 3, and relate, inter alia, to the identification, protection and rehabilitation of appropriate habitats on a co-ordinated basis; the investigation and remediation of problems posed by human activities; control of the introduction of non-native waterbird species; co-operation in emergency situations; the initiation and harmonisation of research; and the provision of appropriate training programmes. Amongst the substantive questions to which the MoP has already turned its attention are the phasing out of lead shot for hunting in wetlands,[176] the development of general conservation guidelines and of best practice for re-establishment projects,[177] and the problems posed by climate change and the implication of migratory waterbirds in the spread of avian influenza.[178]

Central to the implementation of AEWA is the Action Plan appended to the Agreement,[179] which is reviewed at each ordinary session of the MoP,[180] and elaborates more fully the various measures established under the Agreement itself.[181] For this purpose, it divides waterbird

173 CMS Resolution IX.2, para. 5(i).

174 See Report of the 4th Session of the MoP, Agenda Item 31(b): reports of all AEWA meetings can be found on the AEWA website at www.unep-aewa.org.

175 See Articles 6–8, and Resolution 2.6 (which established the Standing Committee). For current committee arrangements, see Resolutions 4.17, 4.18.

176 See currently Resolution 4.1 and Action Plan, para. 4.1.4, which aim to phase out the use of lead shot 'as soon as possible', an original target year of 2000 having proved grossly overambitious. For the limited progress achieved to date, see AEWA/MOP4.7 Rev.1.

177 See Resolutions 2.3, 4.13 and 4.4.

178 See Resolutions 4.14 and 4.15 respectively.

179 See Article 4 and Annex 3.

180 The current Plan, which incorporates the amendments effected by Resolution 4.11, covers the period 2009–12.

181 Conservation and restoration of habitat, for example, is dealt with in paragraph 3.

populations into six categories reflecting current conservation status;[182] these are distinguished primarily by reference to population size, moderated by other factors indicative of vulnerability (including concentration within a small number of sites, dependence on threatened habitat, evidence of long-term decline, etc.). They range from Column A, Category 1 populations (embracing all species included in CMS Appendix I or listed as threatened in the IUCN Red List, together with any populations numbering less than 10,000 individuals) to Column C, Category 1 populations (i.e. those exceeding 100,000 individuals which could significantly benefit from international co-operation, even though unaffected by the threats which characterise the higher categories).[183]

Paragraph 2(1) of the Action Plan then establishes a graduated system of controls on the taking or disturbance of birds where this would have an unfavourable impact on their conservation status.[184] Whereas the parties must generally prohibit the taking of birds or their eggs from all populations listed in Column A, the sustainable hunting of certain Category 2 or 3 populations may be permitted where this is a long-established cultural practice, and provided it is conducted pursuant to a species action plan. For Column B populations, such taking must be regulated with a view to achieving a favourable conservation status. Exemptions may, however, be granted in respect of *any* population for specified purposes, including the prevention of serious damage to crops, water and fisheries; protection of air safety or other overriding public interests; or the selective, limited and supervised taking or judicious use of certain birds in small numbers. It is noticeable that these exceptions have been drafted – quite deliberately, it seems[185] – to reflect those permitted under the Bern Convention and the EU Directive rather than those of the Bonn Convention itself.[186] While this may help to achieve consistency on one level, any incongruity of obligations between AEWA and its parent instrument could conceivably generate problems of a legal character. The utilisation of any such exemptions is, however,

[182] I.e. Column A, Categories 1–3, Column B, Categories 1–2 and Column C, Category 1.

[183] Guidelines for applying the criteria used to distinguish these categories were established by Resolutions 3.3 and 4.12 (see further Doc. AEWA/MOP 4.25).

[184] See further para. 4, concerning the regulation of hunting and other human activities.

[185] Ibid., para. 2.1.3.

[186] Specifically, AEWA omits the CMS reference to traditional subsistence use, addressing this issue instead by the qualified exception concerning long-established cultural practices, discussed above. More seriously, AEWA *includes* an exception not recognised in the parent Convention – i.e. the judicious use of small numbers of birds.

subject to similar overarching constraints as are applicable under the CMS,[187] and in particular cannot be allowed to operate to the detriment of the population concerned. The Plan also envisages yet a further tier of conservation norms through the progressive elaboration of single-species action plans for populations most at risk, a number of which are now in place.[188]

AEWA should ultimately prove an extremely important mechanism for avian conservation, though the scale of its task is daunting, especially in Asia, where the overall trend of declining populations is most marked.[189] Inevitably, much will depend upon the level of participation it is ultimately able to secure: while it has done reasonably well to attract sixty-three parties (including the EU) so far,[190] there are actually 118 range states in all within the current Agreement area. No less vital will be the attraction of increased funding for capacity building and, indeed, for the maintenance of basic operations, a matter emphasised in the current Strategic Plan for 2009–2017.[191] Financial constraints have already impeded institutional activities and the activation of a long-standing plan for small conservation grants.[192] External support has been obtained from the GEF for a major capacity-building initiative for critical sites along AEWA flyways,[193] though this project, too, faces significant shortfalls.[194]

ii) ACAP

The origins of ACAP are more recent, being traceable to decisions of the fifth and sixth meetings of the CMS CoP to list various petrel species and all southern hemisphere albatrosses in one or other of the Convention's Appendices.[195] Resolutions 6.2 and 6.3 noted their particular susceptibility to depletion through fisheries by-catch, while the latter accepted

[187] Action Plan, para. 2.1.3.

[188] Early examples concern the sociable plover (*Chettusia gregaria*), black-winged pratincole (*Glariola nordmanni*) and ferruginous duck (*Aythya nyroca*) (Resolutions 2.13, 3.12), while seven further plans were adopted by Resolution 4.16.

[189] For current trends, see Report on the Conservation Status of Migratory Waterbirds in the Agreement Area (3rd ed., 2007), compiled by Wetlands International and available via the AEWA website.

[190] In addition, Greece and Morocco are signatories.

[191] See Resolution 4.7.

[192] On the creation of such a fund, see Resolution 2.9.

[193] The Wings over Wetlands project (WOW), on which see www.wingsoverwetlands.org.

[194] For a sense of the financial situation generally, see the Report of the 4th Session of the MoP, Agenda Items 14–21.

[195] See Proceedings of the 5th and 6th Meetings of the Parties to CMS.

Australia's offer to pursue discussions amongst range states regarding the development of a conservation instrument. The Agreement was expeditiously concluded, in Canberra on 19 June 2001, and entered into force on 1 February 2004. It currently has thirteen parties.[196]

ACAP's objective is to achieve and maintain a favourable conservation status for albatrosses and petrels,[197] and the parties pledge to take measures individually and collectively to that end, in accordance with the precautionary approach.[198] They must prohibit the deliberate taking of, or harmful interference with, these birds, their eggs or breeding sites, and 'taking' is given the same expansive definition as in the CMS itself.[199] Article 3(5), however, excludes from this prohibition cases of humane killing by authorised persons, designed to end the suffering of seriously injured or moribund specimens. In addition, where there is no satisfactory alternative, Article 3(3) permits the recognition of specified exemptions, which (unlike AEWA) closely reflect those indicated in the parent convention, though with some additional safeguards. For example, the residual power to grant exemptions 'in other exceptional circumstances' is constrained by a requirement, other than in cases of emergency, to perform and publish a prior environmental impact assessment.[200] As under the CMS, all exemptions must be precise and limited in space and time, and not operate to the detriment of the conservation status of the species covered. Full details must be submitted to the ACAP Secretariat.[201]

In addition to this prohibition on taking, Article 3(1) establishes a series of more general protective measures, requiring the parties, inter alia, to conserve and, where feasible, restore key habitats; eliminate and control harmful non-native species; implement measures to prevent, remove or mitigate the effects of activities that may adversely affect

[196] Argentina, Australia, Brazil, Chile, Ecuador, France, New Zealand, Norway, Peru, South Africa, Spain, the UK and Uruguay. For information on ACAP generally, see its website at www.acap.aq.

[197] ACAP focused initially on southern hemisphere populations but has recently been extended, as envisaged by the preamble, to certain of their northern counterparts. The species covered (currently twenty-nine) are listed in Annex 1 to the Agreement, as amended by MoP Resolution 3.1.

[198] Article 2(1)–(3).

[199] I.e. to mean 'taking, hunting, fishing, capturing, harassing, deliberate killing or attempting to engage in any such conduct'. Article 1(q).

[200] The Action Plan appended to the Agreement spells out the modalities in slightly more detail.

[201] Article 3(4).

conservation; foster research, information exchange, public awareness and conservation training; and support the implementation of those aspects of FAO's Plan of Action for Reducing Incidental Catch of Seabirds in Longline Fisheries which complement ACAP's own objectives.

These obligations are complemented by the Action Plan set out in Annex 2 to the Agreement, which elaborates 'the actions that the parties shall progressively undertake . . . consistent with the general conservation measures specified' in Article 3.[202] One advantage of this approach is that the Plan is significantly easier to amend than the provisions of the Agreement itself.[203] As noted above, one of the principal threats to ACAP species is incidental mortality in the course of fishing operations, and paragraph 3.2 of the Plan requires the parties to take appropriate measures to reduce or eliminate this risk, following best current practice where possible. Where fishing activities are conducted under the auspices of a regional fisheries organisation or similar body (e.g. the CCAMLR Commission), the parties must consider information and evaluations from that body and adopt any measures it agrees, but remain free to adopt stricter measures if they choose.[204]

As regards institutional arrangements, the parties must designate a national authority, together with a specified contact point, to undertake, monitor and control all activities pursued in application of the Agreement.[205] At the international level, ACAP, like other CMS agreements, is furnished with a suite of institutions of its own, namely a Meeting of the Parties,[206] Advisory Committee and Secretariat.[207] The functions and activities of these institutions are specified in particular detail:[208] one interesting responsibility of the Advisory Committee is to request the Secretariat to convene a meeting of relevant parties in the event of an emergency situation requiring immediate measures to avoid a deterioration in the conservation status of any ACAP species, whereupon

[202] Article 6(1). See also Article 3(6).

[203] Amendments to an annex automatically become effective ninety days after adoption for all parties except those which enter a reservation. Article 12.

[204] Resolution 3.7 authorises the Secretariat to enter into formal arrangements with certain such bodies.

[205] Article 7.

[206] Three have been held to date: Hobart, 2004; Christchurch, 2006; and Bergen, 2009.

[207] The Secretariat is based in Hobart, Tasmania. For its staff regulations, see Resolution 3.3.

[208] See Articles 8–10. For the current Work Programmes of the latter bodies, see Resolutions 3.2, 3.4.

those concerned must meet as soon as possible, and subsequently report back on implementation of any recommendations adopted.[209]

Although of much more limited substantive scope than AEWA, ACAP is an agreement with a number of interesting features which give it genuine potential to address the problems within its compass. Only time will tell to what extent this potential is fulfilled.

iii) Article IV(4) agreements

In addition, Article IV(4) of the CMS encourages the parties

> to take action with a view to concluding agreements for any population or any geographically separate part of the population of any species or lower taxon of wild animals, members of which *periodically* cross one or more national jurisdictional boundaries.[210]

As explained in Chapter 16 below, this provision establishes a foundation for the development of subsidiary instruments which is in several respects more flexible than that created by Article IV(3). It permits action through a variety of legal mechanisms, including formally binding treaties, informal memoranda of understanding, administrative arrangements and conference resolutions. While several formal treaties have been concluded pursuant to this provision, none to date has related to birds,[211] in respect of which the non-binding memorandum of understanding has become the more widely utilised mechanism.[212]

The earlier instruments concluded in this category relate to single species, namely the Siberian crane (*Grus leucogeranus*) (1993, revised 1998), slender-billed curlew (*Numenius tenuirostris*) (1995),[213] great bustard (*Otis tarda*) (2000), aquatic warbler (*Acrocephalus paludicola*) (2003) and ruddy-headed goose (*Chloephaga rubidiceps*) (2006):[214] some of these, indeed, focus upon particular populations, rather than on the

[209] Article 9(7). As prescribed by Article 8(11)(e), Resolution 1.4 established criteria for the definition of emergency situations and the assignment of responsibilities for action.

[210] Emphasis added. Use of the word 'periodically' is just one of the factors which give this provision a potentially wider scope than that of the rest of the Convention.

[211] Protracted negotiations for an agreement concerning the Asian houbara bustard (*Chlamydotis undulata macqueenii*) – on which see CMS Resolution 7.7 – seem not to have come to fruition at the time of writing.

[212] The texts of these instruments, along with current status information, are published on the CMS website at www.cms.int, accessible via the 'Species Activities' link.

[213] For fuller discussion of these pioneering instruments, see Bowman, *supra* n. 3, pp. 290–2.

[214] Work has been undertaken on MoUs covering other species, such as the sand grouse (see CMS Resolution 7.7), though the current focus is more upon the 'operationalisation' of existing instruments. Resolution 9.2.

species as a whole.[215] More recently, however, MoUs have been adopted in relation to more broadly drawn categories, specifically grassland birds of southern South America (2007), High Andean flamingos and African–Eurasian raptors (both 2008).

Each instrument incorporates an action plan prescribing specific conservation measures for the species in question. In the case of the slender-billed curlew, the main emphasis is on controlling hunting and more effective conservation of wetland areas, while the great bustard MoU requires the creation of protected grasslands, together with the modification of agricultural practices to increase the availability of suitable habitat. Some instruments provide for the augmentation of wild populations with specimens bred in captivity, while a particularly fascinating aspect of the Siberian crane programme concerns the use of microlight aircraft to teach captive-bred juveniles the traditional migration routes of their species.[216] The action plans also customarily address the need for better information on population size, distribution, behaviour and/or migration patterns. Until recently, for example, little was known about the African wintering sites of the aquatic warbler; encouragingly, following the discovery that the vast majority of them are located in its territory, Senegal agreed to participate in what was originally a European-based project.[217] In the case of the Siberian crane, the MoU provides for the fitting of birds with platform terminal transmitters in order that their precise migration movements may be monitored.

As noted in Chapter 16 below, the 'soft-law' status of these instruments facilitates the undertaking of very specific, and sometimes potentially onerous, commitments by particular countries. Belarus, for example, whose wetlands contain the breeding grounds of over half the world's population of aquatic warblers, has undertaken to restore some 720,000 hectares of drained peatlands. The MoU format also facilitates the active participation of non-state actors; thus BirdLife International often plays a crucial role, not least in having drawn up many of the action plans, while vital technical expertise and practical commitment in

[215] Viz. great bustard – middle European population; ruddy-headed goose – migrants between Chile and Argentina (sedentary Falkland Islands population excluded). The Siberian crane MoU was originally limited to the near-extinct western and central populations, but later extended to embrace the much larger eastern population as well.

[216] See International Crane Foundation, 'Hang Glider-Assisted Migration Takes Off', *CMS Bulletin* No. 16 (2002), pp. 16–17.

[217] See Heredia, Rose and Painter, *supra* n. 39, p. 327. The UK sponsored the project to identify these sites.

relation to cranes are provided by the International Crane Foundation and the Wild Bird Society of Japan. The former also serves as the executing agency for a project to develop a network of wetland sites for conservation of the Siberian crane and other Asian waterbirds, which has attracted a GEF Full Project Grant of US$10 million, matched by over US$12 million from other sources.[218] The sharp, iconic focus of these single-species instruments may prove advantageous when it comes to attracting funding of this kind.

The flamingos MoU is only marginally more inclusive, embracing just two species occurring in four Andean states,[219] but the raptors agreement is on an altogether different scale, aiming to secure a favourable conservation status for *all* birds of prey (including owls) occurring in some 130 range states in the Africa–Eurasia region, of which twenty-nine are signatories so far.[220] A seven-year action plan, focusing particularly on unlawful persecution, loss and degradation of habitat, land use policy and industrial practice, and intensified research and consciousness-raising, is already in place. The grassland birds MoU is noteworthy for its application to, inter alia, several CMS Appendix I-listed species, including two which are critically endangered. It primarily emphasises the threats posed by hunting, as well as fragmentation and loss of habitat, though a detailed action plan has yet to be formulated.

Finally, the East Asian/Australasian Flyway Partnership, discussed in section 4(a) above, was recognised at the ninth meeting of the CMS CoP as fulfilling the criteria for consideration as an Article IV(4) Agreement, thereby providing further testimony to the flexibility of this category.

iv) Other measures

In addition to these instruments, various other mechanisms have evolved for addressing the needs of particular CMS species. First, the 'concerted actions' procedure agreed in 1991 involves a formal review at each CoP of the conservation status of selected Appendix I species on the basis of information provided by range states.[221] Numerous avian species have benefited from this procedure,[222] the objective of which is to recommend appropriate conservation initiatives. In the case of the ruddy-headed

[218] See C. Mirande, 'Siberian Crane Wetland Project', *CMS Bulletin* No. 18 (2003), p. 16.

[219] Argentina, Bolivia, Chile and Peru, though Argentina has yet to sign.

[220] Annex I contains a list of some seventy-six species, distributed into three categories in accordance with current conservation status.

[221] See Resolution 3.2, adopted in implementation of Article VII(5) of the Convention.

[222] For a complete list, see Resolution 7.1.

goose, these sought primarily to mitigate the damage caused by the Patagonian fox (*Duscycion griseus*), a predator originally introduced to control rabbits,[223] while the prescription for High Andean flamingos involved a more integrated approach to management of their wetland habitat.[224] In both cases these measures subsequently ripened into an Article IV(4) MoU. The parallel 'co-operative actions' procedure, designed for Appendix II species which require urgent conservation measures, has also been applied to various birds, including the corncrake and quail (*Coturnix coturnix*).[225] This process has also on occasion prompted more formal action, as when its application to albatrosses and petrels in 1999 led to the negotiation of ACAP shortly afterwards.

The CoP's general power to make recommendations has also been extensively utilised for the benefit of birds, and is of particular value in view of its applicability to any migratory species, whether listed or not.[226] Recommendation 4.3, for example, urged the promotion of agricultural practices sympathetic to the corncrake even prior to its inclusion in Appendix II. The flexibility of such measures is evident from the 1994 recommendation concerning birds of the cormorant family (Phalacrocoracidae),[227] for which population trends were markedly divergent in the Africa–Eurasia region. On the one hand, the conservation status of the pygmy cormorant (*Phalacrocorax pygmaeus*) and the Socotra cormorant (*P. nigrogularis*) – both at the time proposed for Appendix II listing – was respectively characterised as 'globally threatened and decreasing' and 'unknown'. On the other hand, the great cormorant (*P. carbo*) was evidently proliferating – so much so, indeed, that it had become the victim of persecution as a result of perceived conflicts with human fishing and fish-farming activities. Since cormorant species often share breeding and wintering sites, there was an obvious risk of this retaliatory action having indiscriminate effects. Accordingly, range states were urged to protect and improve the conservation status of the former two species, while maintaining a favourable status for the great cormorant, through the comprehensive monitoring of population levels, the commissioning and dissemination of research, and the enhancement of public awareness of conservation requirements (for

223 See, e.g., *CMS Bulletin* No. 10 (2000), p. 13, and No. 13 (2001), p. 4.

224 See, e.g., *CMS Bulletin* No. 13 (2001) at p. 3, and No. 14 (2001), at p. 6.

225 See Recommendation 5.2 and, for the most recent application, Recommendation 7.1.

226 See Article 7(5)(e)–(g).

227 Recommendation 4(1). See further Recommendation 5.3, on the adoption of a formal action plan.

which purposes a working group was established). In addition, parties were to ensure that cormorants could only be killed under controlled conditions.

5. Conclusions

This survey of international measures for the conservation of birds not only reflects the considerable complexity of the issue, but confirms its centrality to the evolution of international wildlife law as a whole. Birds were amongst the first creatures to attract the attention of treaty-makers over one hundred years ago, and have scarcely been off the international legislative agenda since. Growing awareness of the threats to their conservation posed by human activities has developed alongside the evolution of a finer appreciation of their many values, both for humans and in their own right. The non-governmental sector has played a particularly vital role in both aspects of this process, as well as in the crafting of the legal response. Currently, the measures in place for the conservation and management of avian species run the entire gamut from the most complex and sophisticated of legally binding instruments to the most simple and informal co-operative arrangements and action plans. Just as birds themselves are treated as indicators of the biological health of ecosystems, so the success or failure of this network of instruments may serve as a barometer of the vigour and vitality of international environmental law as a whole. At present, however, the situation gives cause for cautious optimism at best.

Recommended further reading

R. Boardman, *The International Politics of Bird Conservation* (Edward Elgar, 2006)

G. C. Boere, C. A. Galbraith and D. A. Stroud (eds.), *Waterbirds around the World* (TSO, 2007)

M. J. Bowman, 'International Treaties and the Global Protection of Birds, Parts I and II' (1999) 11 *JEL* 87, 281

P. G. G. Davies, *European Union Environmental Law: An Introduction to Key Selected Issues* (Ashgate, 2004), Chapter 4

J. Verschuuren, 'Effectiveness of Nature Protection Legislation in the EU and the US: The Birds and Habitats Directives and the Endangered Species Act' (2003) 3 *Yearbook of European Environmental Law* 305

PART III

Regional wildlife regulation

Chapter 8

The Convention on Nature Protection and Wildlife Preservation in the Western Hemisphere

1. Background

In December 1938 the Eighth International Conference of American States met in Lima and recommended that the Pan American Union establish a committee of experts to study problems relating to nature and wildlife in the American republics and prepare a draft convention for their protection.[1] Pursuant to this recommendation, the Convention on Nature Protection and Wildlife Preservation in the Western Hemisphere (the Western Hemisphere Convention)[2] was concluded and opened for signature to member states of the Pan American Union (now the Organization of American States, and hereinafter referred to as the OAS) on 12 October 1940. It entered into force on 30 April 1942.[3] It has been signed by twenty-two member states of the OAS and ratified by nineteen of them, the last ratification being that by Suriname in 1985.[4]

The Western Hemisphere Convention was a visionary instrument, well ahead of its time in terms of the concepts it espouses. The protection of species from human-induced extinction, the establishment of protected areas, the regulation of international trade in wildlife, special measures for migratory birds and stressing the need for co-operation

[1] Resolution 38: Protection of Nature and Wildlife, Eighth International Conference of American States.

[2] 161 *UNTS* 193, *UTS* 981, 56 *Stat* 1374.

[3] As required by Article XI(3) of the Western Hemisphere Convention, this was three months after the fifth instrument of ratification had been deposited with the Pan American Union.

[4] The following are parties (dates of ratification in brackets): Argentina (1946), Brazil (1965), Chile (1967), Costa Rica (1966), Dominican Republic (1942), Ecuador (1943), El Salvador (1941), Guatemala (1941), Haiti (1941), Mexico (1942), Nicaragua (1946), Panama (1972), Paraguay (1980), Peru (1946), Suriname (1985), Trinidad and Tobago (1969), USA (1941), Uruguay (1969) and Venezuela (1941). Bolivia, Colombia and Cuba signed the Convention but have not yet deposited instruments of ratification with the OAS.

in scientific research and other fields are all elements of wildlife conservation which are covered by the Convention – many of them for the first time by an international treaty – and which have reappeared time and again in other conventions concluded since 1940.

The greatest weakness of the Convention, which plagues it still, was its failure to set up an administrative structure to review and promote enforcement of its terms. In consequence, although the Convention has stimulated the establishment of some protected areas and the enactment of some national conservation legislation, it has become a 'sleeping convention' which, with a few notable exceptions, is now of limited practical value in most party countries. Calls were made in both the 1970s and the 1990s to revise the treaty with a view to establishing an effective regional forum to promote hemispheric conservation issues, but proved unsuccessful. Nevertheless, it should not be forgotten that it remains a binding legal treaty on its parties. Furthermore, as will be noted later in the chapter, there are a number of regional co-operative programmes and agreements in place which do to an extent provide alternative platforms for conservation efforts in the region.

2. Objectives

The parties had two main objectives in concluding the Western Hemisphere Convention. The first was to protect all native animals and plants from extinction through means within man's control. The Western Hemisphere Convention was the first international agreement to have such a clear and all-embracing objective. The preamble to the Convention proclaimed the Parties' desire to

> protect and preserve in their natural habitat representatives of all species and genera of native flora and fauna, including migratory birds, in sufficient numbers and over areas extensive enough to assure them from becoming extinct through any agency within man's control.

A second objective expressed in the preamble is to

> protect and preserve scenery of extraordinary beauty, unusual and striking geologic formations, regions and natural objects of aesthetic, historic or scientific value, and areas characterized by primitive conditions in those cases covered by this Convention.[5]

[5] To this end, Article V(2) places states under an obligation 'to adopt or to recommend that their respective legislatures adopt laws which will assure the protection and preservation of the natural scenery, striking geological formations, and regions and natural objects of aesthetic interest or historic or scientific value'.

Thus features displaying, for example, historic or scientific value are not the only aspects of the environment to be protected: the inherent value of 'scenery of extraordinary beauty' and also 'regions and natural objects of aesthetic . . . value' are also recognised.[6]

The objectives noted in the preamble are especially significant when one bears in mind the richness in biodiversity of the combined territories of the parties, particularly the hemisphere's tropical region. The parties have committed themselves to the ambitious goal of conserving the natural diversity of the largest and one of the most threatened 'reservoirs' of species in the world.

3. Conservation of habitat

The Western Hemisphere Convention was one of the first international agreements to emphasise the need to conserve habitats as a means of protecting species. Its primary focus is on the establishment of 'national parks, national reserves, nature monuments and strict wilderness reserves'.

a) Definitions

Article I of the Western Hemisphere Convention defines 'national parks' as

> areas established for the protection and preservation of superlative scenery, flora and fauna of national significance which the general public may enjoy and from which it may benefit when placed under public control;[7]

'national reserves' as

> regions established for conservation and utilization of natural resources under government control, on which protection of animal and plant life will be afforded in so far as this may be consistent with the primary purpose of such reserves;[8]

'nature monuments' as

> regions, objects or living species of flora or fauna of aesthetic, historic or scientific interests to which strict protection is given. The purpose of nature monuments is the protection of a specific object, or a species of flora or fauna, by setting aside an area, an object or a single species, as an inviolate nature monument, except for duly authorised scientific investigations or government inspection;[9]

[6] See further Chapter 3 above. [7] Western Hemisphere Convention, Article I(1).
[8] Ibid., Article I(2). [9] Ibid., Article I(3).

a 'strict wilderness reserve' as

> a region under public control characterized by primitive conditions of flora, fauna, transportation and habitation wherein there is no provision for the passage of motorised transportation and all commercial developments are excluded.[10]

b) *Establishment of protected areas*

Article II of the Convention requires its parties to

> explore at once the possibility of establishing in their territories national parks, national reserves, nature monuments and strict wilderness reserves as defined in the preceding article. In all cases where such establishment is feasible, the creation thereof shall be begun as soon as possible.[11]

Where such establishment is impractical it shall be done 'as soon as . . . circumstances will permit'.[12] Parties are required to notify the OAS of any national parks, national reserves, nature monuments and strict wilderness reserves which they have established, and of the legislation and methods of administrative control adopted in connection therewith.[13] For example, when Suriname ratified the treaty in 1985 it provided information relating to the location of the Coppename Rivermouth Nature Reserve situated on the Atlantic Ocean and east of the Coppename Rivermouth. It also highlighted the national legislation that related to this reserve.

Each of the four categories of protected area described by the Western Hemisphere Convention has been established by one or more parties.[14] National parks are the most widespread. All but one of the parties have at least one and many have considerably more – Chile, for example, has over thirty national parks covering over 8 million hectares, and Costa Rica has more than twenty such parks covering over 700,000 hectares (more than 14 per cent of its land mass).[15] The Dominican Republic fares even better in this latter respect with over 25 per cent declared as national park.[16] The state party hosting the largest

[10] Ibid., Article I(4). [11] Ibid., Article II(1).
[12] Ibid., Article II(2). [13] Ibid., Article II(3).
[14] For details of the current state and classification of the world's protected areas, see the *United Nations List of Protected Areas* (prepared by the IUCN and UNEP-WCMC, and published by IUCN, Gland, Switzerland and Cambridge, UK, and UNEP-World Conservation Monitoring Centre, Cambridge, UK). See also the World Database on Protected Areas at www.wdpa.org.
[15] See www.wdpa.org. [16] Ibid.

area protected as national park is the USA, with territory covering more than 25 million hectares in this category.[17] Suriname is the only state party not to have designated any areas as national parks as such, but its one 'nature park' at Brownsberg can be regarded as a national park in all but name.

'National reserves' are less common, with under half of the state parties declaring such areas.[18] Where the term 'national reserve' has been used it has not always had the same meaning. However, the practice of setting aside areas for the purpose of rational use of their natural resources, which is the basic concept behind the Convention's definition of national reserves, is widespread even if the terminology varies. The 'national forests' of Argentina, Brazil and the USA, and the 'forest reserves' of Venezuela, all have this kind of management objective.[19]

In relation to 'nature monuments', Argentina, Brazil, Chile, Mexico, Panama, Paraguay, the USA and Venezuela all use the term 'nature monument' or 'natural monument' to describe an object or area which is strictly protected in much the same sense as is intended by the Western Hemisphere Convention. They are generally smaller than national parks, although the US government's designation of 22.7 million hectares in Alaska as a 'national monument' in 1978 is a major exception to this rule. Panama's Barro Colorado Island provides a good example of a natural monument established under the Convention. The island was formed when the Chagres River was dammed to facilitate the building of the Panama Canal, leaving what was previously a hill in the river valley exposed above water. The island is a tropical forest rich in biodiversity – for example, the Smithsonian Institute has noted that 'more species of plants are found in the fifteen square km of forests on Barro Colorado Island than in all of Europe'.[20] It is of interest to highlight that in addition

[17] Ibid.

[18] The term 'national reserve' is used by Argentina, Chile, Nicaragua, Paraquay, Peru, Suriname and the USA; see www.wdpa.org.

[19] See G. Wetterberg and M. T. J. Padua, 'Vocabulary of the Western Hemisphere Convention', Final Report of Technical Meeting on Legal Aspects Related to the Convention on Nature Protection and Wildlife Preservation in the Western Hemisphere (March 1980), OAS Doc. OEA/Ser.J/XI,CICYT/Doc.199, p. 44 (hereinafter Final Report of Technical Meeting on Legal Aspects).

[20] See www.hrw.com/science/si-science/biology/ecology/barro/bci.html. The Smithsonian Tropical Research Institute is responsible for the administration of the island. The Barro Colorado Nature Monument comprises Barro Colorado Island as well as five nearby mainland peninsulas.

to an area or object, 'specific living species of flora or fauna' can also be regarded as 'nature monuments' in their own right.[21]

The term 'strict wilderness reserve' is not used by any party per se, although the scientific zones of national parks that are closed to the public and many of the scientific and biological reserves of Brazil, Chile and Ecuador are all designed to protect remote and primitive land, which is the basic objective of a strict wilderness reserve.[22] The USA comes closest to using the terminology of the Western Hemisphere Convention. The Wilderness Act of 1964 established the National Wilderness Preservation System in the USA 'to secure for the American people of present and future generations the benefits of an enduring resource of wilderness'.[23] The Act defines wilderness as 'an area where the earth and its community of life are untrammelled by man, where man is himself a visitor who does not remain'.[24] To qualify as a wilderness area in the US, an area must, among other things, be at least five thousand acres in size and be 'undeveloped Federal land retaining its primeval character and influence ... which generally appears to have been affected primarily by the forces of nature, with the imprint of man's work substantially unnoticeable'.[25] Unless exceptionally approved, no commercial enterprises or permanent roads are allowed in a wilderness area.[26] Forty years on from the enactment of the Wilderness Act, the National Wilderness Preservation System in 2004 comprised 106 million acres of wilderness across forty-four US states.[27] Areas designated as national parks or forests can form part of the National Wilderness Preservation System, and will be given greater protection as a consequence. Around half of the land declared as wilderness areas is located in Alaska.

There are, of course, many factors which may have influenced the decisions of party governments to establish national parks, national reserves, nature monuments or strict wilderness reserves, and a desire

[21] For example, Chile in 2008 established a natural monument concerning certain specified cetaceans (information supplied by Claudia de Windt, senior legal specialist, Department of Sustainable Development, OAS, in a communication dated 4 January 2010). In relation to this natural monument see faolex.fao.org/docs/pdf/chi81512.pdf.

[22] See Wetterberg and Padua, *supra* n. 19, p. 45.

[23] Wilderness Act of 1964, 16 *USC* 1131–6, section 2(a). For further information on the national Wilderness Preservation System, see www.wilderness.net.

[24] Wilderness Act of 1964, 16 *USC* 1131–6, section 2(c).

[25] Ibid. [26] Ibid., section 4(c).

[27] US Senate Resolution 387, 'Commemorating the 40th Anniversary of the Wilderness Act', 22 June 2004.

to implement the Western Hemisphere Convention may or may not have been of practical significance. It is impossible to be certain how important the Convention has been to the establishment of protected areas in party countries because parties have never submitted reports to the OAS on measures they have taken to implement the Convention, and only a few of the domestic legislative or administrative instruments used by parties to create protected areas refer back to the Convention as a source of legal authority or inspiration. Nevertheless, correspondence with bureaucrats in national parks departments in party countries indicates that the Convention has been of considerable value both in the conceptual development of habitat protection since 1940 and as a leverage to support their efforts to establish protected areas.[28]

c) *Management*

The Western Hemisphere Convention has specific requirements regarding the management of national parks and strict wilderness reserves (but not of national reserves or nature monuments).

i) National Parks

Article III stipulates that boundaries of national parks 'shall not be altered, or any portion thereof be capable of alienation except by the competent legislative authority' and their resources 'shall not be subject to exploitation for commercial profit'. It also prohibits the 'hunting, killing and capturing of members of the fauna and destruction or collection of representatives of the flora in national parks except by or under the direction or control of the park authorities or for duly authorised scientific investigations'. The latter is particularly important because grazing by domestic animals and felling of trees for domestic use both pose problems in a number of national parks. Unless these activities are directed or controlled by the park authorities, they appear to be prohibited by Article III since they destroy vegetation. The Western Hemisphere Convention does not, however, intend national parks to be wilderness areas devoid of human presence. Recognising that they should be used for educational and recreational purposes provided that this does not conflict with conservation needs, Article III requires each party 'to provide facilities for public recreation and education in national parks consistent with the purposes of this Convention'.

[28] In the first edition of this book Simon Lyster formed this view based on correspondence with government officials in North, Central and South America during the course of research for this chapter.

ii) Strict wilderness reserves

Article IV of the Western Hemisphere Convention stipulates that strict wilderness reserves shall be maintained 'inviolate, as far as practicable, except for duly authorized scientific investigations or government inspection, or such uses as are consistent with the purposes for which the area was established'. In contrast to its designs for national parks, the Convention clearly intends that strict wilderness reserves shall remain primitive areas to which humans can gain access only with some difficulty.

4. Conservation of species

The Western Hemisphere Convention selects three categories of species for special attention: species found outside the protected areas it recognises, migratory birds and species listed in a special Annex to the Convention.

a) Species found outside national parks, national reserves, nature monuments or strict wilderness reserves

Article V(1) states:

> The Contracting Governments agree to adopt, or to propose such adoption to their respective appropriate law-making bodies, suitable laws and regulations for the protection and preservation of flora and fauna within their national boundaries, but not included in the national parks, national reserves, nature monuments, or strict wilderness reserves referred to in Article II hereof. Such regulations shall contain proper provisions for the taking of specimens of flora and fauna for scientific study and investigation by properly accredited individuals and agencies.

In normative terms, Article V(1) is weakly drafted. It does not establish a clear absolute duty to adopt laws and regulations to protect wildlife outside parks and reserves, as states need only 'propose such adoption'. Neither does it set any standards which should apply in relation to exploitation of wildlife, modifications of natural habitats, use of toxic chemicals and the many other threats to wildlife populations. It requires only that the laws and regulations should be 'suitable' and that provisions governing the taking of specimens for scientific research by accredited individuals and agencies should be 'proper'. Accordingly, every party which has any sort of legislation to protect wildlife outside parks and reserves can justifiably claim to have fulfilled its obligations under Article V(1), however weak that legislation may be. However, as with much of the Convention, the value of Article V(1) lies not so much in its specific legal requirements as in its general recognition of the need to protect wildlife outside parks and reserves and in the authority it provides for parties to do so. The USA's Endangered Species Act, for example, protects endangered species from harmful activities even if they are carried out in an area which is not a national park or a specially protected zone, and the original preamble to the Act specifically made reference to the Western Hemisphere Convention as an influence on its enactment.[29]

b) *Migratory birds*

Article VII states:

> The Contracting Governments shall adopt appropriate measures for the protection of migratory birds of economic or aesthetic value or to prevent the threatened extinction of any given species. Adequate measures shall be adopted which will permit, in so far as the respective governments may see fit, a rational utilization of migratory birds for the purpose of sports as well as for food, commerce and industry, and for scientific study and investigation.

Although Article VII allows parties to choose the methods ('appropriate measures') by which they implement their obligations, it nevertheless imposes on them a legal duty to protect economically or aesthetically valuable migratory birds and to prevent the extinction 'of any species'. However, the exact scope of Article VII is unclear because the terms 'economic' and 'aesthetic' are undefined, and there is no list of economically and aesthetically valuable migratory birds attached to the Convention. Neither is 'any given species' defined and could refer to migratory birds in general or only to those which are economically or aesthetically valuable. It is striking that Article VII is limited to migratory birds. Migratory fish, sea turtles and marine mammals might also benefit from inclusion within its scope.

Some parties, notably the USA, have enacted strong domestic measures to protect migratory birds,[30] as well as measures to facilitate the financing of habitat protection programmes and capacity building.[31] There are now several examples of international agreements for the protection of migratory

[29] See Endangered Species Act of 1973, 16 *USC* 1531–44.

[30] See Migratory Bird Treaty Act of 1918, 16 *USC* 703–11 as amended. See further discussion in Chapter 7.

[31] See Neotropical Migratory Bird Conservation Act of 2000, *PL* 106–247. This Act provides finance for projects in the Caribbean, Latin America and the US to protect neotropical birds which spend the winter in the Caribbean and in Latin America and then migrate in the summer months to the USA.

birds in the region and, more generally, growing indications of broader co-operation.[32] For example, the Western Hemisphere Shorebird Reserve Network was established in 1985 to preserve critical migratory stopover and wintering sites, and now comprises around eighty sites in twelve countries.[33] The North American Waterfowl Management Plan is another example of international co-operation; Canada, Mexico and the USA have worked together under this plan with a view to returning waterfowl populations to their 1970s levels.[34] More than US$2 million has been invested since 1986 to afford key habitat protection.

c) *Species included in the Annex*

Article VIII states that

> the protection of the species mentioned in the Annex to the present Convention is declared to be of special urgency and importance. Species included therein shall be protected as completely as possible, and their hunting, killing, capturing or taking, shall be allowed only with the permission of the appropriate government authorities in the country. Such permission shall be granted only under special circumstances, in order to further scientific purposes, or when essential for the administration of the area in which the animal or plant is found.

The Annex is particularly confusing. It is not a single comprehensive list of species agreed by the parties (the normal system adopted by wildlife treaties), but is a compilation of national lists submitted separately by individual parties. Some of the lists are long, others are short,[35] and some species appear on more than one list. Neither the Convention nor the Annex itself establishes criteria for the inclusion of a species, although most parties have limited their selections to species occurring within their territories which they deem to be threatened or potentially threatened with extinction. There are no procedures for amending the Annex

[32] See Chapter 7 above.

[33] See www.manomet.org/WHSRN/strategic.htm. Note also the US Shorebird Conservation Plan at www.shorebirdplan.fws.gov, the North American Bird Conservation Initiative at www.nabci.net, and the work of Taking Wing at www.fs.fed.us/biology/wildlife/takingwing.

[34] See www.nawmp.ca and the work of Partners in Flight at www.partnersinflight.org.

[35] Sheinin notes that 'Pan American Union member countries designated hundreds of species of plants and animals as protected by the terms of the convention – though the United States listed a scant ten species, including the Manatee, the Whooping Crane, and the Puerto Rican Parrot'. D. Sheinin, 'Wilderness and Pan American Preservation, 1910–1948' a paper presented at the Latin American Studies Association, XXI International Congress, Chicago, Illinois, 24–6 September 1998, p. 5 (available at http://168.96.200.17/ar/libros/lasa98/Sheinin.pdf).

although, since parties may submit their own lists, there is no apparent reason why they should not amend them unilaterally. The US government has adopted this attitude, stating,

> It is understood by this Government that such lists are to be considered as flexible rather than permanent in character and may from time to time be altered by the respective Governments by the addition or removal of such species from their several lists as changes and conditions may seem to them to warrant.[36]

Finally, it is not clear whether parties must apply the provisions of Article VIII to all species in the Annex or only to those included in their own national lists. De Klemm favours the latter interpretation, noting that the Annex does not 'list species that must be protected by all parties . . . but only species that each party has unilaterally agreed to protect'.[37] In practice, the Annex has had very limited conservation value. Parties have naturally tended to include in the Annex species which are already protected under their national legislation, with the result that it has tended to reflect the status quo rather than stimulate additional protection. In addition, there is no provision for the circulation of lists to parties, with the result that even if a party wishes to help protect species listed by other parties it may not know what those species are. However, the OAS in late 2009 confirmed that it was then 'requesting updated information from member states' in relation to the Annex and 'working on a portal that will consolidate the information housed by the OAS, including on protected areas'.[38]

5. International trade

The provisions of Article IX, which regulate international trade in wildlife, have been largely superseded by the 1973 Convention on International Trade in Endangered Species of Wild Fauna and Flora (CITES).[39] Only one state party to the Western Hemisphere Convention, Haiti, has not in fact yet acceded to CITES. Article IX nevertheless merits brief consideration.

[36] See *Treaties and other International Agreements on Fisheries, Oceanographic Resources and Wildlife Involving the United States* (US Government Printing Office, 1977) p. 150, n. 1.

[37] C. De Klemm, 'Migratory Species in International Law' (1989) 29 *Natl Resources J.* 935, at n. 64.

[38] Communication received dated 30 December 2009 from Claudia de Windt, senior legal specialist, Department of Sustainable Development, OAS (cited with permission).

[39] See Chapter 15 below.

Article IX requires each party to regulate the export or transit of 'protected fauna and flora' or parts thereof by issuing export or transit certificates as appropriate. The Convention is more restrictive than the text of CITES with respect to transit since CITES exempts certain specimens in transit from permit requirements.[40] Article IX also obliges each party to prohibit the import of species or parts thereof which are 'protected by the country of origin' unless they are accompanied by a lawful export certificate. 'Protected species' are not defined but apparently refer to species listed in the Annex, again raising the problem as to how an importing country can discover which species are currently protected in the country of origin.

Even if this information can be obtained, Article IX causes other difficulties. In contrast to CITES it does not require a standard form for an export certificate in order to help enforcement officers in an importing country recognise counterfeit certificates immediately. Neither does it require parties to designate specific government agencies with responsibility for the issue of export permits. Without such designation it will be difficult for parties to assist each other in the interception of illegal trade because an enforcement officer in an importing country needs to know the identity of the agency responsible for issuing permits in the exporting country in order to be able to check the legality of documents accompanying a shipment.

6. Co-operation

Article VI requires parties 'to cooperate among themselves in promoting the objectives of the present Convention' and, in particular, to assist each other with scientific research and field study, to 'enter into agreement with one another . . . in order to increase the effectiveness of this collaboration' and to 'make available to all the American Republics equally through publication or otherwise the scientific knowledge resulting from such co-operative effort'. These provisions are some of the most important of the Western Hemisphere Convention. So many of the species found in the Western Hemisphere are either migratory or are found in more than one country that mutual co-operation between parties is essential if efforts to protect them are to succeed. In addition, the financial resources and technical expertise in wildlife management are so heavily weighted in favour of a few countries in the region that

40 CITES, Article VII(1).

assistance to the poorer countries is vital if the latter are to be able to carry out sound scientific conservation policies.

In 1976, after many years of relative inactivity in the field of co-operation, the General Assembly of the OAS unanimously agreed

> to urge the implementation of the Convention by the member states through mutual cooperation in activities such as scientific research and technical cooperation and assistance relating to wild flora and fauna, the creation, planning and training in the management of parks and reserves, the adoption of measures to conserve wild flora and fauna, and to protect species which are in danger of extinction.[41]

Whether as a result of the OAS resolution or not, there has unquestionably been an expansion in co-operative activities under the aegis of the Western Hemisphere Convention since the mid-1970s.[42] Early examples of co-operation are numerous. Pursuant to an Executive Order issued by the president in relation to the Convention in 1976,[43] the USA substantially increased its co-operative activities in the area of technical assistance and training through its National Park Service and Fish and Wildlife Service. A US government lawyer assisted El Salvador in drafting its first national wildlife law, and US biologists visited Ecuador to help initiate a population survey of the American crocodile (*Crocodylus acutus*) and Chile to assist in a study of the pudu (*Pudu pudu*).[44] In 1981, trainees from Guatemala, Costa Rica, Panama, the Dominican Republic, Ecuador and Brazil visited ten national wildlife refuges in the USA as part of a one-month course in wildlife management.[45] Using the Convention to authorise its actions, the US National Park Service provided instructors for two 'Central American Mobile Seminars on Wildland Planning and Management', an urban park planner for a month in Caracas, guidance on management and interpretation of

[41] See C. Freese and G. Wetterberg, 'Cooperative Action under the Aegis of the Western Hemisphere Convention', Final Report of Technical Meeting on Legal Aspects Related to the Convention on Nature Protection and Wildlife Preservation in the Western Hemisphere (1980), OAS document OEA/Ser.J/XI, CICYT/Doc.199, p. 69.

[42] Note, however, that Argentina, Bolivia, Chile, Ecuador and Peru agreed as early as the late 1960s to co-operate in the conservation of vicuña in the form of the 1969 Convention for the Conservation of Vicuña.

[43] Executive Order 11911 of 1976. For further details of the Order and subsequent action taken by the US government, see Freese and Wetterberg, *supra* n. 41, pp. 68–9.

[44] See Freese and Wetterberg, *supra* n. 41, p. 73.

[45] See C. Freese, 'The Western Hemisphere Convention: International Framework for Wildlife Conservation' (January 1982) 7(1) *Endangered Species Technical Bulletin* (Department of the Interior, Washington DC), pp. 4–5.

limestone cave formations to the Parks Directorate of the Dominican Republic, and a landscape architect to assist with development plans in Trinidad and Tobago's Caroni Swamp National Park.[46]

This type of co-operation has continued since 1983 within the US Fish and Wildlife Service's Western Hemisphere Program (Wildlife Without Borders – Latin America and the Caribbean). This programme was specifically established by the US Congress to facilitate implementation of the Western Hemisphere Convention. Its aims include local capacity building (through activities such as manager training initiatives and environmental education programmes), information exchange, and the support of projects which conserve both species and habitats. In the period from 1983 to 2000 more than 200 people graduated from wildlife and ecosystem management programmes established in Argentina, Brazil, Costa Rica, Mexico and Venezuela, and around 300 received reserve manager training.[47] Other supported projects included funding the teaching of a mapping and resource inventory system to analyse biological data,[48] projects seeking to conserve Mexican wild cats and sea turtles in Guatemala,[49] and initiatives established to assist wetland conservation.[50] In the period from 1995 to 2007 projects in the Western Hemisphere Program received funding to the amount of US$9.6 million; a further US$36 million was raised for these projects in matching funds.[51] The United States has also entered into a number of co-operative agreements with South American countries in relation to protected areas and environmental protection.[52]

Numerous co-operative programmes outside the Western Hemisphere Program have also been activated. Costa Rica and Panama have, for instance, initiated the establishment of contiguous national parks on either

[46] See Freese and Wetterberg, *supra* n. 41, p. 74.
[47] US Fisheries and Wildlife Service, *Wildlife without Borders – Latin America and the Caribbean* (US Fisheries and Wildlife Service, 2001), p. 11.
[48] Ibid., p. 23. [49] Ibid., p. 25.
[50] Ibid., p. 29. On wetland protection see Chapter 13 below.
[51] US Fisheries and Wildlife Service, *Wildlife without Borders: Latin America and the Caribbean* (US Fisheries and Wildlife Service, 2008).
[52] See, for example, Memorandum of Understanding between USA and Mexico (*TIAS* No. 11599; entered into force on 24 January 1989), and Memorandum of Understanding between USA and Costa Rica (*TIAS* No. 11793; entered into force on 8 October 1991). See also the 1994 Central American–US Joint Accord on Biodiversity, Energy, Environmental Legislation and Trade and Investment (CONCAUSA) under which the USA became the first extra-regional partner to the Central American Alliance for Sustainable Development (ALIDES); www.state.gov/g/oes/rls/fs/2002/13233.htm.

side of their borders. Andean states (Bolivia, Colombia, Ecuador, Peru and Venezuela) have adopted a Regional Biodiversity Strategy for the Tropical Andean Countries.[53] Additionally, the adjacent national parks of Pico da Neblina in Brazil and Serrania de la Neblina in Venezuela enhance the mutual objective of protecting the important ecosystems of that region,[54] and the Centro Agronomico Tropical de Investigación y Ensenanza (in Costa Rica)[55] and the Instituto Nacional de Pesquisas da Amazonia (in Brazil)[56] are academic and research institutions which play an important role in international training in various aspects of sustainable wildland management.[57] Moreover, the MesoAmerican Biological Corridor project has evolved in the 1990s out of the Path of the Panther initiative. It is a regional initiative involving the southern states of Mexico and also the Central American countries of Guatemala, Belize, El Salvador, Honduras, Nicaragua, Costa Rica and Panama. The project's objective is to conserve biological and ecological diversity whilst allowing for sustainable development,[58] and was an initiative proposed by the Central American Commission of Environment and Development (CCAD).[59] Additionally, the Latin American Cooperation Network of National Parks (REDPARQUES) and the IUCN organised the first Latin American Congress of National Parks and Other Protected Areas in 1997 (Santa Marta, Colombia) and a second such meeting in 2007 (Bariloche, Argentina).

Legally binding agreements adopted in the region since the entry into force of the Western Hemisphere Convention which seek to protect wildlife include the 1978 Treaty for Amazonian Co-operation,[60] the 1979 Convention for the Conservation and Management of the Vicuña,[61] the 1981 Convention for the Protection of the Marine Environment and Coastal Area of the South East Pacific,[62] the 1990 Kingston Protocol Concerning

[53] See www.comunidadandina.org. Also see (2004) 13 *Yb. Int'l Env. L 2000* 463–4.

[54] On other such arrangements and co-operative programmes, see K. Rogers and J. A. Moore, 'Revitalizing the Convention on Nature Protection and Wildlife Preservation in the Western Hemisphere: Might Awakening a Visionary but "Sleeping" Treaty Be the Key to Preserving Biodiversity and Threatened Natural Areas in the Americas?' (1995) 36 *Harv. IL* 465, at pp. 477–8.

[55] See www.catie.ac.cr. [56] See www.inpa.gov.br.

[57] See Freese and Wetterberg, *supra* n. 41, p. 74.

[58] See K. Miller, E. Chang and L. Johnson, *Defining Common Ground for the MesoAmerican Biological Corridor* (World Resources Institute, 2001).

[59] The CCAD was established in 1989. On its remit and work, see www.ccad.ws.

[60] 17 *ILM* 1045; see P. Sands, *Principles of International Environmental Law* (Cambridge University Press, 2nd ed., 2003), pp. 529–31.

[61] *IELMT* 979:94. [62] See eelink.net/~asilwildlife/SoutheastPac.html.

Specially Protected Areas and Wildlife (SPAW),[63] the 1992 Convention for the Conservation of the Biodiversity and the Protection of Priority Wilderness Areas in Central America,[64] and the 1996 Inter-American Convention on the Protection and Conservation of Sea Turtles.[65] One of the objectives of the 1993 North American Agreement on Environmental Cooperation is also to protect wildlife.[66]

Co-operation in relation to the exchange of biodiversity information (scientific and technical) has improved in recent years. Heads of state at the Summit of the Americas on Sustainable Development held in Bolivia in December 1996 called for the establishment of the Inter-American Biodiversity Information Network (IABIN). Officially endorsed by resolution of the OAS Inter-American Committee on Sustainable Development in October 1999,[67] IABIN has established an Internet-based information database to facilitate and improve decision-making in relation to biodiversity conservation.[68] It provides decision- and policy-makers in the hemisphere with access to biodiversity information, data and knowledge which previously would have been unavailable to them or difficult to locate. All OAS states have established an IABIN Focal Point. IABIN is financially supported in the main by the OAS, the US Agency for International Development, the Brazilian government and the World Bank.

The Western Hemisphere Migratory Species Initiative (WHMSI) is potentially the most important example of hemispheric co-operative

[63] 1990 Protocol Concerning Specially Protected Areas and Wildlife in the Wider Caribbean to the 1983 Convention for the Protection and Development of the Marine Environment in the Wider Caribbean Region (1989) 19 *EPL* 224. See further discussion in Chapter 12 below.

[64] See (1993) 3 *Yb. Int'l Env. L 1992* p. 373.

[65] Reproduced in (2002) 5 *JIWLP* 167–78; also available at http://seaturtle.org/iac/convention.shtml. See also E. Naro-Maciel, 'The Inter-American Convention for the Protection and Conservation of Sea Turtles: An Historical Overview' (1998) 1 *JIWLP* 169.

[66] 32 *ILM* 1480. Article 1(c) notes that an objective of the agreement is to 'increase co-operation between Parties to better conserve, protect, and enhance the environment including wild flora and fauna'. The agreement supplements the North American Free Trade Agreement (NAFTA), and established the Commission for Environmental Co-operation; see further www.cec.org. On the application of this side agreement to NAFTA, see J. Wilson, 'The Commission for Environmental Cooperation and North American Migratory Bird Conservation: The Potential of the NAAEC Citizen Submission Procedure' (2003) 6(3) *JIWLP* 205.

[67] OAS Committee on Sustainable Development, CIDI/CIDS/RES.2 (II-0/99).

[68] See www.iabin.net.

effort,[69] and has been described as 'an overarching initiative which helps . . . states [to] deliver on various international commitments pertinent to the conservation of migratory species'.[70] The Quebec Summit of the Americas in 2001 had declared a need to 'advance hemispheric conservation of plants, animals and ecosystems through . . . the development of a hemispheric strategy to support the conservation of migratory wildlife throughout the Americas'.[71] In response to this call, the First Western Hemisphere Migratory Species Conference was held in Termas de Puyehue, Chile in October 2003 to develop co-operative strategies for migratory species conservation, and to facilitate regional collaboration in wildlife conservation.[72] Twenty-five countries attended, together with over forty observers (including a variety of wildlife conservation groups). An Interim Steering Committee was established to maintain momentum in this co-operative initiative. An important task of the Interim Steering Committee was to report on conservation priorities highlighted at the first meeting, as well as on tools that could be utilised for conservation purposes. The first of the Interim Steering Committee's meetings took place in August 2004 in Costa Rica with country representatives from Colombia, Costa Rica, St Lucia, Uruguay and the US in attendance. They were joined by representatives from the American Bird Conservancy, BirdLife International, the Bonn Convention Secretariat, the Inter-American Convention on the Protection and Conservation of Sea Turtles Secretariat, the Ramsar Wetlands Bureau, the Western Hemisphere Reserve Shorebird Network and WWF-Centroamerica, as well as the SPAW Caribbean Regional Co-ordinating Unit.

The Second Western Hemisphere Migratory Species Conference took place in San José, Costa Rica in January 2006. It was attended by thirty countries and over sixty NGOs and representatives of conventions. It

[69] Note also the adoption of the 'Inter-American Program of Action for Environmental Protection' in the OAS Resolution AG/RES. 1114 (XXI-O/91). An element of this programme was consideration of the need to revise the Convention. Due consideration was given but ultimately failed to attract the consent of enough states; see OAS General Assembly Resolution AG/RES. 1357 (XXV-O/95), and *infra* nn. 74–84 and accompanying text. See also the Plan of Action of the Summit of the Americas on Sustainable Development approved in December 1996 and the work of the Summit of the Americas Inter-agency Task Force (IATF) established to assist in implementation of the plan. Note also the related work of the OAS Office for Sustainable Development and Environment at www.oas.org/usde.

[70] WHMSI, Migratory Species: Biological, Cultural, and Economic Assets of the Americas (2009) p. 10.

[71] Summit of the Americas, Plan of Action (Quebec, 2001), section 9.

[72] See international.fws.gov/whc/AboutWHMSC.htm.

deliberated on capacity-building needs and effective training for wildlife personnel. Underlining a degree of momentum in the process, the Third Conference took place in June 2008 in Asunción, Paraguay and was attended by twenty-two country delegates and over twenty NGO representatives. Issues under discussion included the sharing of information on migratory species, capacity-building initiatives for migratory species conservation, and the impact of climate change on migratory species and their habitats.

Such developments provide clear testimony to the extent to which hemispheric co-operation has improved in relation to the protection of wildlife since the 1970s. It is, however, uncertain how far the Western Hemisphere Convention itself has actually served as a real source of influence upon these arrangements.

7. Administration

One of the themes appearing consistently throughout this book is that conventions with an administrative mechanism to promote their enforcement are generally far more effective than those without one. Unfortunately, the Western Hemisphere Convention still falls into the latter category. It neither requires its parties to meet regularly in order to review implementation of the Convention (with the result that they have never formally done so since the Convention was concluded), nor requires them to submit regular reports on the domestic measures that they have taken to enforce its provisions. In comparison with the wide-ranging responsibilities of the permanent Secretariats or Commissions established by other treaties, the role of the OAS within the Convention is very limited. It acts as a depositary for the original text of the Convention, for instruments of ratification and for denunciations, and is responsible for receiving notification of protected areas which have been established and of species which have been listed in the Annex. Its only other function is to inform the parties of any relevant information communicated to it by national museums or other interested organisations.[73]

8. Efforts to revise the Convention

In response to the resolution on co-operation passed at its General Assembly in 1976, the OAS sponsored five technical meetings specifically

[73] Western Hemisphere Convention, Article X(2).

on implementation of the Convention in co-operation with the national park and wildlife agencies of several parties between 1977 and 1979. These meetings covered marine mammals, terrestrial ecosystems, migratory animals, education and training in relation to the administration of protected areas, and legal aspects of the Convention. However, much as they may have achieved by way of an exchange of information and an analysis of what needs to be done to implement the Convention, many of the recommendations made by these meetings have not been acted upon.[74] The meeting on legal aspects, for example, recommended that the OAS should perform the functions of a Secretariat and, in particular, submit an annual report on enforcement of the Convention. It also suggested that representatives of party governments should meet every two years to review enforcement of the Convention and to make appropriate recommendations on how to improve it.[75]

Advocates of change renewed efforts in the 1990s to revise the treaty.[76] Canada, Guatemala, Mexico and the US all argued that it should be updated.[77] The OAS General Assembly mandated its Committee on the Environment to form a Working Group to study the Convention and draw conclusions on the need to update it.[78] This Working Group noted the 'extraordinary pioneering value which the inter-American juridical community places on the 1940 Convention . . . and how practical and useful it has been in establishing many national parks and protected areas in our Hemisphere in the decades since it entered into force'.[79] Nevertheless, it further indicated that 'updating the 1940 American Convention is neither necessary nor advisable . . . as the current international and regional instruments, particularly the United Nations Convention on Biological Diversity, are considered to be adequate in serving the common purpose of protecting the biological wealth of our Hemisphere'.[80] The Working Group's conclusions ran

[74] Though see *supra* n. 38 regarding recent OAS requests of the state parties to provide updated information.

[75] See Final Report of Technical Meeting on Legal Aspects, *supra* n. 19, pp. 6–8.

[76] See, for example, Rogers and Moore, *supra* n. 54.

[77] Permanent Council of the Organization of American States (Committee on the Environment), Report of the Chairman of the Working Group Charged with Studying the American Convention on Nature Protection and Wildlife Preservation in the Western Hemisphere (document OEA/Ser.G, CP/CMA-146/95 dated 31 March 1995), p. 1.

[78] AG/RES. 1241 (XXIII-O/93).

[79] Permanent Council of the Organization of American States (Committee on the Environment), *supra* n. 77.

[80] Ibid.

contrary to the view held by the US that the Western Hemisphere Convention provided 'an existing forum which could be further developed to more effectively address hemispheric conservation needs; and that this regional agenda would become fragmented and diluted within the much broader global and issue context of the CBD'.[81] The US additionally took the stance that 'Latin American viewpoints and interests may not be wholly recognized or understood within a global forum',[82] and that the Western Hemisphere Convention could 'help establish a common regional conservation position vis-à-vis extra-regional and global issues, and ... provide a valuable forum to develop a regional position preparatory to participation in the more complex global arena'.[83] The position held by the USA that the Western Hemisphere Convention 'should complement, not be replaced by the CBD'[84] failed to attract the support of enough OAS members.

9. Conclusion

The Western Hemisphere Convention is seventy years old in late 2010, but most of the concepts which it espouses are sufficiently relevant for it still to be a legal instrument of considerable potential value to wildlife in the Americas. Some of its potential has already been fulfilled, one commentator noting that the treaty 'helped entrench preservation policy in many countries, served as a starting point for the international classification of endangered species in the Americas, and contributed to the exchange of scientific information on wildlife and parks'.[85] Additionally, the US Fish and Wildlife Service has taken the view that the Convention 'has been used by the legislative bodies of its contracting parties to write national conservation legislation and wildlife regulations, and to justify establishing numerous protected areas and national monuments'.[86] Undoubtedly protected areas have indeed been established, several parties have given special attention to migratory birds and a growing number of co-operative programmes either are being or have

[81] Communication received from the Division of International Conservation, US Fish and Wildlife Service (dated 1 December 2004) summarising the view of the USA in the mid-1990s (cited with permission).
[82] Ibid. [83] Ibid. [84] Ibid. [85] Sheinin, *supra* n. 35, p. 20.
[86] US Fisheries and Wildlife Service, *supra* n. 47, p. 38. Furthermore, 'legal instruments in signatory states continue to use the convention as a basis for conservation'; communication received dated 30 December 2009 from Claudia de Windt, senior legal specialist, Department of Sustainable Development, OAS (cited with permission).

been successfully carried out. However, the degree to which the Convention stimulated or provided the legal impetus for these activities remains difficult to judge. The Western Hemisphere Migratory Species Initiative mentioned above may develop in such a manner as to provide the best opportunity for effective regional action, but it must also be considered whether this much-needed attempt to develop a hemispheric initiative would have been required if the Convention had been allowed to fulfil its true potential. In many respects the Convention most certainly remains a 'sleeping treaty'; commenting in 1996 the OAS itself acknowledged that the Convention 'has remained relatively inactive'.[87]

Recommended further reading

K. Rogers and J. A. Moore, 'Revitalizing the Convention on Nature Protection and Wildlife Preservation in the Western Hemisphere: Might Awakening a Visionary but "Sleeping" Treaty Be the Key to Preserving Biodiversity and Threatened Natural Areas in the Americas?' (1995) 36 *Harv. IL* 465

D. Sheinin, 'Wilderness and Pan American Preservation, 1910–1948', paper presented at the Latin American Studies Association, XXI International Congress, Chicago, Illinois, 24–6 September 1998 (available at http://168.96.200.17/ar/libros/lasa98/Sheinin.pdf)

[87] OAS, Program for the Development of Law on Environment and Sustainable Development in the Americas, 13 September 1996, section 3.2 (technical document prepared for the 1996 Summit of the Americas Conference on Sustainable Development, Santa Cruz, Bolivia).

Chapter 9

The African Convention on the Conservation of Nature and Natural Resources

1. Background

The first international agreement to conserve African wildlife was signed in London on 19 May 1900 and was called the Convention for the Preservation of Wild Animals, Birds and Fish in Africa.[1] It was signed by the colonial powers then governing much of Africa – France, Germany, Great Britain, Italy, Portugal and Spain – and its objective was 'to prevent the uncontrolled massacre and to ensure the conservation of diverse wild animal species in their African possessions which are useful to man or inoffensive'.[2] The teeming herds of African wild animals were already starting to diminish, and the primary goal of the Convention was to preserve a good supply of game for trophy hunters, ivory traders and skin dealers.

The 1900 Convention prohibited the killing of all specimens of species listed in Schedule 1 of the Convention and 'any other animals whose protection, owing to their usefulness or to their rarity and threatened extermination, may be considered necessary by each Local Government'.[3] Schedule 1 was divided into Series A ('useful animals') and Series B ('animals that are rare and in danger of disappearance'). Series A contained the secretary bird and all vultures, owls and oxpeckers. Series B consisted of 'giraffe, gorillas, chimpanzee, mountain zebra, wild asses, white tailed gnu, elands and pygmy hippopotamus'. The Convention also prohibited the killing of non-adults[4] and females 'when accompanied by their young'[5] of 'elephant, rhinoceros, hippopotamus, zebra other than mountain zebra, buffalo, antelope and gazelles, ibex and mouse deer'. Certain methods of killing, including the use of

[1] 94 *BFSP* 715. [2] Preamble to the 1900 Convention.
[3] 1900 Convention, Article II(1). [4] Article II(2). [5] Article II(3).

explosives for fishing, were also outlawed.[6] The 1900 Convention was the first treaty to encourage the establishment of nature reserves, and it prohibited the hunting, killing or capture of any bird or animal 'except those specifically exempted from protection by the local authorities' in nature reserves.[7] However, it also considered numerous species unworthy of protection, and urged signatory governments to destroy the eggs of crocodiles, poisonous snakes and pythons,[8] and to 'reduce' certain other species including lions, leopards, hyaenas, wild dogs and birds of prey except owls and vultures.[9]

The 1900 Convention never actually entered into force, and was superseded in 1933 by the Convention Relative to the Preservation of Fauna and Flora in their Natural State,[10] which was also signed in London and became known as the London Convention. Like its predecessor, the London Convention was a treaty between African colonial governments, and Belgium, France (without formally ratifying), Egypt, Italy, Portugal, South Africa, Sudan, Tanzania and the UK became parties to it.[11] The London Convention expanded on the requirements of the 1900 Convention, but its principal objective – to preserve supplies of species which were economically valuable or popular with trophy hunters – was much the same except that it ended the concept of nuisance species.

The main emphasis of the London Convention was on the creation of protected areas. It required its parties to explore the possibility of establishing 'national parks' and 'strict natural reserves' forthwith.[12] In cases where such establishment was possible, the Convention stipulated that work should begin within two years of its entry into force.[13] Where it was 'impracticable at present, suitable areas shall be selected as early as possible . . . and transformed into national parks or strict nature reserves as soon as . . . circumstances will permit'.[14] The Convention prohibited the hunting, killing or capture of fauna and the collection or destruction of flora in national parks and national reserves,[15] and it required parties

6 Article II(9). Article II(8) states that the use of nets and traps for animal capture shall be 'restricted'.

7 Article II(5). 8 Article II(15).

9 Article II(13). The full list of species to be 'reduced' is contained in Table V of the Convention.

10 172 *LNTS* 241; *UKTS* No. 27 (1930), Cmd. 5280. The London Convention was signed on 8 November 1933 and came into force on 14 January 1936.

11 In addition, India acceded to the London Convention on 9 May 1939 (in relation to the import of trophies only).

12 London Convention, Article 3(1). 13 Ibid.

14 Article 3(2). 15 Article 2(1) and (2).

to establish 'intermediate zones' around the borders of parks and reserves in which the killing or capture of animals was to be controlled by the park or reserve authorities and in which no person 'shall have any claim in respect of depredations caused by animals'.[16] The intention of this latter provision was to create buffer zones around the parks where farmers farmed at their own risk and where any animal migrating out of the park would not immediately be shot. These provisions are very similar to the habitat provisions of the Western Hemisphere Convention which was signed seven years later and which was probably heavily influenced by its African counterpart.[17]

Like its predecessor, the London Convention highlighted certain species for special protection. They were listed in an Annex to the Convention and consisted of one plant and forty animals (mostly ungulates), plus all lemurs and pangolins. The Convention prohibited the hunting, killing and capture of these species except with a special licence.[18] It also regulated internal and international trade in their trophies,[19] which were defined to include parts and products.[20] The Convention banned certain methods of hunting, killing and capture including the use of poison, nets and dazzling lights.[21]

As more and more African states gained independence, the need for a new treaty, more relevant to modern Africa, became increasingly evident. In 1968 the London Convention was superseded by the African Convention on the Conservation of Nature and Natural Resources (the 1968 Algiers Convention).[22] The Algiers Convention was signed on 15 September 1968 in Algiers on the recommendation of the Organization of African Unity (OAU) and entered into force on 7 May 1969.[23]

Primarily concerned with wildlife, the 1968 Algiers Convention placed parties under obligations to maintain, extend and assess the need for new conservation areas, and to introduce conservation measures for species already threatened or which might become threatened with extinction, as well as their habitats.[24] However, it also embraced the conservation of

[16] Article 4(2). [17] See Chapter 8 above.

[18] London Convention, Article 8(1). [19] Article 9(2).

[20] Article 9(8). However, a trophy which 'by process of *bona fide* manufacture ... has lost its original identity' is not covered by the Convention.

[21] Article 10.

[22] 1001 *UNTS* 3. On the 1968 Algiers Convention see the first edition of this book; S. Lyster, *International Wildlife Law* (1985), Chapter 7; and P. H. Sand (ed.), *The Effectiveness of International Environmental Agreements* (Grotius, 1992) pp. 69–72.

[23] By January 2010 a total of thirty African countries had ratified the 1968 Algiers Convention.

[24] Articles VI–VIII and Article X.

other natural resources such as soil and water,[25] and placed an obligation on states to 'ensure that conservation and management of natural resources are treated as an integral part of . . . development plans'.[26] In addition, the Convention addressed other topics such as trade in endangered species,[27] the protection of customary rights,[28] the need for conservation education,[29] and the need for research 'in the conservation, utilisation and management of natural resources'.[30] Overall, these features made it the most comprehensive and innovative multilateral treaty for the conservation of nature then negotiated. However, and very unfortunately, the 1968 Algiers Convention made the same mistake as both the London and Western Hemisphere Conventions in not establishing an administrative structure to facilitate implementation or oversee its enforcement. It had no permanent secretariat responsible for overseeing its implementation. Nor was there any requirement for regular meetings of the parties. As a result, little was done to encourage parties to implement its provisions. Despite these deficiencies, it is certainly arguable that it did stimulate useful conservation measures in some countries.[31] Many parties established new protected areas after 1969 and tightened up on hunting and trading regulations. However, it would be impossible to state categorically that the Convention, rather than other factors, had been directly responsible for this progress. Undoubtedly the 1968 Algiers Convention provided the framework on which a substantial body of national legislation was based but its practical value for African wildlife would have been considerably greater if it had established a central body with responsibility for overseeing and promoting its implementation and enforcement.

The 1968 Algiers Convention was soon seen to require updating to take account of the very considerable progress made in the field of international environmental law since its conclusion. In particular, there was an obvious need to establish permanent institutions, and also to embrace the latest developments. Efforts to revise the treaty

[25] Articles IV and V.

[26] Article XIV(1). The integration of conservation and development was a key theme of the World Conservation Strategy launched by the IUCN in 1980 as a blueprint of modern conservation philosophy; see further discussion in Chapter 2 above.

[27] Article IX. [28] Article XI. [29] Article XIII. [30] Article XII.

[31] Correspondence with officials in party countries indicated that the Convention was a useful stimulant. In a letter to Simon Lyster dated 21 March 1983, the chief administrator of Ghana's Forestry Commission stated, 'it is also relevant to note the tremendous increase in conservation areas in Africa since 1968. I would attribute this to the Convention as one of the major factors.'

began in 1983 when Algeria, Cameroon and Nigeria called for modification, but then stalled in 1986.[32] In 1996 Burkina Faso gave renewed momentum to the process by calling for the updating of the 1968 Algiers Convention in the light of major developments in international environmental law since 1968. Consequently, the OAU (now the African Union) in 1999 asked the IUCN and UNEP to assist in producing a revision.[33] A revised draft was put forward in 2001 and then modified following a process of consultation with African governments.[34] A revised convention (hereinafter the 2003 African Convention) was finally opened for signature by any member state of the African Union (AU) having been adopted by the Assembly of the AU on 11 July 2003 at Maputo, Mozambique.[35] At the time of writing, the 2003 African Convention has not yet come into force. It will do so only on the thirtieth day following the date of deposit of the fifteenth instrument of ratification, acceptance, approval or accession.[36] The 1968 Algiers Convention therefore remains of importance until the 2003 African Convention comes into force, and will to an extent still retain some significance even when the 2003 African Convention becomes fully functional.[37]

In line with the drafters' mandate, the 2003 African Convention underlines that it represents a revision of the 1968 Algiers Convention rather than a completely new instrument.[38] Radical change was thought to be undesirable as it might have led to greater opposition from those countries that wanted only limited reform.[39] Although the structure

[32] IUCN, *An Introduction to the African Convention on the Conservation of Nature and Natural Resources* (IUCN, 2004), p. 5.

[33] Ibid. [34] Ibid.

[35] It can be ratified, accepted or approved by any AU member state (Article XXXVI), and the Chairman of the African Union acts as the depositary (Article XLII). By January 2010 thirty-six of the fifty-three AU states had signed. The text of the treaty is available at www.africa-union.org (documents section).

[36] Article XXXVIII(1). By January 2010 eight countries had ratified the treaty; Burundi, Comoros, Ghana, Lesotho, Libya, Mali, Niger and Rwanda.

[37] Once in force, Article XXXIV of the 2003 African Convention provides that, as between parties to the 2003 African Convention, only the 2003 African Convention will apply (Article XXXIV(1)). However, the 1968 Algiers Convention will continue to govern relationships between a party to the 2003 African Convention and a state which is bound only by the 1968 Algiers Convention (Article XXXIV(2)).

[38] 'Convinced that the above objectives would be better achieved by amending the 1968 Algiers Convention on Nature and Natural Resources by expanding elements relating to sustainable development' (preamble).

[39] Mohamed Ali Mekouar, 'La Convention africaine: petite histoire d'une grande renovation' (2004) 34(1) *Environmental Policy and Law* 43, p. 45.

remains the same as the 1968 Algiers Convention, there is no doubt that its content has been very considerably amended and updated in line with developments since 1968.[40] The influence of the Biodiversity Convention and the Rio Declaration is particularly apparent, although the inspiration of Agenda 21 is also evident in encouraging activities with a view to facilitating sustainable development. To ensure uniformity of approach, no reservations are permitted to the Convention, thus avoiding from the outset any risk of the Convention's objectives being unduly detracted from.[41]

The preamble of the 2003 African Convention acknowledges that 'the natural environment of Africa and the natural resources with which Africa is endowed are an irreplaceable part of the African heritage and constitute a capital of vital importance to the continent and humankind as a whole'. In relation to the continent's natural resources, their 'ever-growing importance ... from economic, social, cultural and environmental points of view' is underlined, as is the responsibility of states 'for protecting and conserving their environment and natural resources and for using them in a sustainable manner with the aim to satisfy human needs according to the carrying capacity of the environment'. With this in mind, a clear desire is expressed to undertake 'individual and joint action for the conservation, utilization and development of these assets by establishing and maintaining their sustainable use'.

The principle of sustainable utilisation is therefore keenly endorsed in the preamble and is an important feature of the text. It is also of interest to note that parties in the preamble acknowledge that 'the conservation of the global environment is a common concern of human kind as a whole' before affirming 'the conservation of the African environment' to be 'a primary concern of all Africans'. The significance of the 1982 World Charter for Nature is also expressly recognised.[42]

2. Fundamental elements of the 2003 African Convention

a) Objectives

The objectives of the treaty, 'with a view to achieving ecologically rational, economically sound and socially acceptable development policies and programmes', are to 'enhance environmental protection', 'foster

[40] IUCN, *supra* n. 32, p. 5. [41] Article XXXIX.

[42] On the World Charter for Nature, see discussion in Chapters 1 and 2 above.

the conservation and sustainable use of natural resources', and 'harmonize and coordinate policies in these fields'.[43] Environmental protection is therefore a key element of the treaty's objectives, but so is the promotion of sustainable use of the region's resources. The Convention's goals are therefore closely linked with the furthering of sustainable development, a path and vision endorsed by Africa's leaders in the New Partnership for Africa's Development (NEPAD).[44] The objectives certainly do not exclusively relate to wildlife protection, but 'natural resources' are defined as 'renewable resources, tangible and non tangible, including soil, water, flora and fauna and non renewable resources'.[45] As such, the importance of conserving flora and fauna is endorsed, as is the need to foster their sustainable use. In addition, the Convention in Article IX specifically stipulates in relation to wildlife conservation that parties shall 'maintain and enhance species and genetic diversity of plants and animals whether terrestrial, fresh-water or marine'.[46] Promoting the conservation and sustainable use of wildlife is therefore undoubtedly a key component of the treaty regime. The treaty applies to 'all areas' within parties' national jurisdiction, and to 'activities carried out under the jurisdiction or control of any party within the area of its national jurisdiction or beyond the limits of its national jurisdiction'.[47]

b) Fundamental Obligation

Article IV (entitled the 'Fundamental Obligation') notes that the aforementioned treaty objectives are to be achieved by the adoption and implementation of 'all measures necessary ... in particular through preventive measures and the application of the precautionary principle, and with due regard to ethical and traditional values as well as scientific knowledge in the interest of present and future generations'.[48] This is a very modern recognition not only of the preventive principle, but also of the precautionary principle, the important role of science, and the interests of present and future generations. The obligation to give 'due regard' to ethical and cultural/traditional values in the implementation of the Convention further underscores the modern flavour of these provisions.

[43] Article II.
[44] NEPAD was adopted at the OAU summit in July 2001 (specifically in relation to the environment; see paras. 135–9 of NEPAD). See the NEPAD website at www.nepad.org.
[45] Article V(1). [46] Article IX(1). [47] Article I(1).
[48] Article IV. For general discussion of these concepts and principles, see Chapter 2 above.

The process of incorporating modern environmental principles in national-framework environmental laws has in fact already taken place in certain African states.[49] However, the 2003 African Convention may provide the catalyst to continue this process throughout the continent. It also has the potential to establish an international legal regime within which the practical endorsement of modern environmental principles within systems of national regulation can be assessed.[50] A key role in this regard is to be played by the institutions to be established by the parties.

3. Institutional arrangements

a) Conference of the Parties

It has been noted that the lack of institutional arrangements to ensure implementation and enforcement severely undermined the effectiveness of the 1968 Algiers Convention. This lesson was heeded by the drafters of the 2003 African Convention. Article XXVI establishes a Conference of the Parties as the key decision-making body.[51] The first meeting is to be held within a year of the entry into force of the Convention.[52] Thereafter, meetings will be held at least once every two years.[53] The Conference of the Parties will adopt the budget,[54] and review and promote implementation of the Convention. More particularly, it will make recommendations, give consideration to information and reports from the Secretariat or by any party, and promote the exchange of information on national implementing measures.[55] It also has the power to set up appropriate subsidiary bodies (especially of a scientific and technical nature), review the reports of any such body and offer them guidance.[56] Moreover, it can consider and take any additional action deemed necessary to achieve the Convention's aims, and strengthen any links with other relevant conventions as well as seek the co-operation of other competent bodies.[57]

[49] D. Dzidzornu, 'Environmental Protection in Africa: A Panorama of the Law and Practice' (2004) 22(2) *JERL* 148, at pp. 156–8. See generally, on national approaches, P. Kameri-Mbote and P. Cullet, 'Biological Diversity Management in Africa: Legal and Policy Perspectives in the Run-up to WSSD' (2002) 11(1) *RECIEL* 38–52.

[50] Practical implementation and enforcement of environmental legislation is too often conspicuous by its absence; Dzidzornu, *supra* n. 49, pp. 158–65.

[51] Article XXVI(1). [52] Ibid. [53] Article XXVI(1).

[54] Article XXVI(4). [55] See XXVI(5). [56] Ibid. [57] Ibid.

The Conference of the Parties will additionally consider the need for amendments to the Convention and adopt such amendments accordingly.[58] Amendments can be proposed by any party.[59] The parties will endeavour to reach agreement by consensus on the proposed amendment but, if all efforts fail, the proposed amendment can be adopted by a two-thirds majority vote of the parties present and voting.[60] Annexes to the Convention or amendments to existing Annexes can also be adopted.[61] This will add flexibility to the legal regime established. Annexes form an integral part of the Convention and will be limited to scientific, technical, financial and administrative issues.

b) Secretariat

Article XXVII establishes the Secretariat. This article further notes that the first meeting of the Conference of the Parties will either determine an organisation to carry out secretariat functions or establish its own Secretariat. In the interim, secretariat functions will be carried out by the chairperson of the African Union.[62] The Secretariat is, inter alia, responsible for arranging meetings of the Conference of the Parties and any subsidiary bodies, carrying out any decision of the Conference of the Parties addressed to it, collecting and disseminating national reports on implementation, administering the Convention's budget, and carrying out any other functions as determined by the Conference of the Parties.[63]

c) National authorities

The drafters of the Convention were wise to recognise that action must also be taken at the national level to establish an authority with the responsibility to 'deal with all matters covered by this Convention' and/or 'a co-ordinating machinery between existing national institutions'.[64] The establishment of a single efficient national body or co-ordinating machinery of this kind will facilitate effective implementation. Parties must inform the Secretariat of the names of agencies or

[58] Ibid. [59] Article XXXI(1). [60] Article XXXI(3).

[61] Article XXXII. Any state may propose the adoption of an additional annex. Efforts will be made to reach a consensus on any such proposal but it will 'as a last resort be adopted by a two-third majority vote of the Parties present and voting'. Those states which find the additional annex unacceptable must notify the depositary within six months of communication of the adoption; the annex will not bind such objecting States.

[62] Article XLI. [63] Article XXVII(3). [64] Article XXI.

co-ordinating institutions designated as national focal points for the purposes of the Convention.[65]

4. Conservation measures

a) *Guiding principles*

In implementing their obligations, Article III establishes that the following principles, all closely and importantly linked to the concept of sustainable development, shall guide the parties:

1. the right of all peoples to a satisfactory environment favourable to their development;
2. the duty of States, individually and collectively, to ensure the enjoyment of the right to development;
3. the duty of States to ensure that developmental and environmental needs are met in a sustainable, fair and equitable manner.

These guiding principles therefore endorse a number of evolving principles, concepts and rights in international environmental law: the link between the adequacy of human beings' environment and the enjoyment of human rights as endorsed in the 1981 African Charter on Human and Peoples' Rights,[66] the right to development,[67] the principle of sustainable use of natural resources,[68] and the principle of equitable use of natural resources.

The 'integration principle', closely linked to the concept of sustainable development, should also be mentioned at this point. Although not specifically noted in Article III as a guiding principle, the need to integrate environmental factors into the planning process is an important element of the obligations imposed on state parties and is expressly endorsed in Article XIV(1) (entitled 'Sustainable Development and Natural Resources'):

[65] Article XXIX(2)(c).

[66] 'All Peoples shall have the right to a general satisfactory environment favourable to their development'; African Charter, Article 24 (1982) 21 *ILM* 58.

[67] Endorsed in the Rio Declaration, Principle 3: '[t]he right to development must be fulfilled so as to equitably meet developmental and environmental needs of present and future generations'.

[68] The 1982 World Charter for Nature stipulates that '[e]cosystems and organisms, as well as the land, marine and atmospheric resources that are utilised by man, shall be managed to achieve and maintain optimum sustainable productivity'.

The Parties shall ensure that

a) conservation and management of natural resources are treated as an integral part of national and/or local development plans;
b) in the formulation of all development plans, full consideration is given to ecological, as well as to economic, cultural and social factors

in order to promote sustainable development.

With this in mind, parties must 'to the maximum extent possible' ensure 'that development activities and projects are based on sound environmental policies and do not have adverse effects on natural resources and the environment in general',[69] and that activities (including projects, policies, plans, programmes and strategies) which are 'likely to affect natural resources, ecosystems and the environment in general' are made subject to environmental impact assessment (EIA), regular monitoring and auditing.[70] Parties should also ensure that the state of their natural resources is the subject of monitoring.[71] These obligations seek to ensure progress towards the important goal of sustainable development. They also complement the need under the Biodiversity Convention to 'integrate . . . the conservation and sustainable use of biodiversity into relevant sectoral or cross-sectoral plans, programmes and policies',[72] and to 'integrate consideration of the conservation and sustainable use of biological resources into national decision-making'.[73]

b) Species and genetic diversity: the promotion of conservation and sustainable use in management

The Africa Environment Outlook published in July 2002 produced a welcome if disheartening insight into the state of the African environment prior to the adoption of the Convention.[74] A total of 126 animal species are estimated to have become extinct in Africa and 2,018 animal species are under threat.[75] In addition, 123 plant species are extinct and 1,771 are threatened with the same fate.[76] No doubt bearing such species depletion in mind, parties must facilitate the conservation and sustainable use of natural resources. To maintain and enhance

[69] Article XIV(2)(a). [70] Article XIV(2)(b). [71] Article XIV(2)(c).
[72] Article 6(b) of the Biodiversity Convention.
[73] Article 10(a) of the Biodiversity Convention.
[74] UNEP/African Ministerial Conference on the Environment (AMCEN), *Africa Environment Outlook* (UNEP, 2002); for an overview, see (2002) 32(6) *EPL* 261.
[75] Ibid., Chapter 2. [76] Ibid.

'species'[77] and the genetic diversity of plants and animals (terrestrial, freshwater or marine), parties are obliged to

> establish and implement policies for the conservation and sustainable use of such resources; particular attention shall be paid to socially, economically and ecologically valuable species, which are threatened and species which are only represented in areas under the jurisdiction of one party.[78]

They must also

> ensure the conservation of species and their habitats within the framework of land-use planning and of sustainable development. Management of species and their habitats shall be based on the results of continued scientific research.[79]

With this in mind, parties are obliged to 'manage plant and animal populations inside conservation areas according to the objectives of such areas'.[80] We will note later that a system of conservation areas is indeed to be maintained, and that these conservation areas have differing management objectives according to how they are classified. Outside these conservation areas, 'harvestable populations' should be managed in a 'sustainable manner'.[81]

Approaches to species management in the 2003 African Convention have clearly been inspired by relevant provisions of the 1992 Biodiversity Convention.[82] Parties are obliged to facilitate *ex situ* conservation measures,[83] protect aquatic environments from adverse impacts,[84] establish inventories of species and maps of their location and conduct reviews to monitor the status of both species and their habitats.[85] The inventories, maps and reviews are designed to provide the necessary scientific knowledge required to conserve and use plants and animals, and to identify those that are threatened, migratory or congregatory in nature so as to facilitate effective protection.[86] Other management measures must 'identify areas of critical importance for the survival of species' of threatened fauna and flora,[87] and 'preserve as many varieties as possible of domestic or cultivated species and their wild relatives,

[77] Defined as 'any species, sub species, or geographically separate population thereof'. Article V(4).

[78] Article IX(1). [79] Article IX(2). [80] Article IX(2)(a). [81] Article IX(2)(b).

[82] In particular by Articles 6 (measures for conservation and sustainable use), 7 (identification and monitoring), 8 (*in situ* conservation), and 9 (*ex situ* conservation) of the Biodiversity Convention. IUCN, *supra* n. 32, p. 9.

[83] Article IX(2)(c). [84] Article IX(2)(d). [85] Article IX(2)(e).

[86] Article IX(2)(e)(i)–(iii). [87] Article IX(2)(f).

as well as of other economically valuable species, including forest trees and micro-organisms'.[88] Controls should be adopted in relation to the introduction of non-native species, including genetically modified organisms,[89] and efforts made to try to eradicate existing non-native species detrimental to native species or to the general environment.[90] Pests must additionally be controlled and animal and plant diseases eradicated.[91]

In relation to the sharing of benefits arising out of biotechnologies and again clearly influenced by the Biodiversity Convention,[92] the 2003 African Convention provides for the 'fair and equitable sharing of benefits arising out of biotechnologies based upon genetic resources and related traditional knowledge with the providers of such resources'.[93] '[F]air and equitable access' to genetic resources must be ensured 'on terms mutually agreed between the providers and users of such resources'.[94] This fleshes out to a modest degree the manner and type of access to genetic resources provided for in the Biodiversity Convention.[95]

The taking of fauna and flora must be regulated by legislation.[96] 'Taking' includes, but is not limited to, hunting, capture and fishing and the collection of plants. Legislation must ensure that an appropriate system of regulation involving the issuing of permits is in place in relation to the taking of such species.[97] Regulation must ensure that the use of a population is sustainable.[98] Legislation will accordingly be needed introducing closed seasons,[99] and also providing for temporary bans on taking where appropriate.[100] Indiscriminate means of taking (such as the use of gas, automatic weapons, aircraft and explosives) must also be prohibited.[101] The products of hunting and fishing and

[88] Article IX(2)(g).
[89] On biosafety issues on the African continent see generally P. Kameri-Mbote, 'The Development of Biosafety Regulation in Africa in the Context of the Cartagena Protocol' (2002) 11(1) *RECIEL* 62–73.
[90] Article IX(2)h. It is documented that the introduction of the Nile perch (*lates nilotica*) into Lake Victoria has led to the loss of 'more than 200 endemic species'; UNEP/AMCEN, *supra* n. 74, Chapter 2.
[91] Article IX(2)(i). [92] See Article 19(2) of the Biodiversity Convention.
[93] Article IX(2)(k). [94] Article IX(2)(j).
[95] Article 15 of the Biodiversity Convention; see IUCN, *supra* n. 32, p. 9.
[96] Article IX(3). [97] Article IX(3)(a). [98] Article IX(3)(b).
[99] Article IX(3)(b)(i). [100] Article IX(3)(b)(ii).
[101] Article IX(3)(b)(iii). Annex III notes the 'prohibited means of taking' in full.

plant collection must additionally be regulated 'with a view to as rational use as possible'.[102] Excluded by Article IX(3)(d) from such restrictions, however, are 'operations carried out by, or under the control of, the competent authority for management purposes', an exception which could be applied to a range of activities including relocations, research, and culls of wildlife having detrimental impact on the human environment.

c) *Protected species*

A special system of protection is established for species under threat or which may become so, and also for the habitats of these species. By virtue of Article X(1), parties

> undertake to identify the factors that are causing the depletion of animal and plant species which are threatened or which may become so, with a view to their elimination, and to accord a special protection to such species, whether terrestrial, freshwater or marine, and to the habitat necessary for their survival. Where a species is represented only in areas under the jurisdiction of one Party, that Party has a particular responsibility for its protection.

Article V(5) defines 'threatened species' as

> any species of fauna or flora which is considered critically endangered, endangered, or vulnerable, for which definitions are contained in Annex 1 to this Convention, and for which criteria may be adopted and from time to time reviewed by the Conference of the Parties, taking into consideration the work of competent international organisations in this field.

'Threatened Species' are therefore classified as either critically endangered, endangered or vulnerable. Annex I defines these classifications in the following manner:

> a) Critically Endangered:
> A taxon is 'critically endangered' when the best available evidence indicates that it is considered to be facing an extremely high risk of extinction in the wild.
> b) Endangered:
> A taxon is 'endangered' when the available evidence indicates that it is considered to be facing a very high risk of extinction in the wild.

[102] Article IX(3)(c).

c) Vulnerable:
A taxon is 'vulnerable' when the best available evidence indicates that it is considered to be facing a high risk of extinction in the wild.

The influence of the IUCN in the drafting process is apparent as these categorisations are identical to those used by the IUCN in its 'Red List' of threatened species.[103] It is important to stress that the system of special protection is extended not only to threatened species, but also to those which may become threatened. However, there is very little guidance on the system of protection which should be introduced. Instead, parties are obliged to adopt legislation 'taking into particular account the need to develop or maintain throughout the African continent concerted protection measures for such species'.[104] The Convention perhaps acknowledges that there may be a need for further guidance to states in the exercise of their discretion in this regard, as Article X(2) further stipulates that '[o]ne or several Annexes to this Convention may be adopted by the Conference of the Parties to that effect'. Proposed Annexes should include amendable lists of species that fall within the three classifications noted above.

d) Conservation areas

Loss of natural habitat due to land clearance and overharvesting is a critical problem on the continent. The 2002 Africa Environment Outlook report has indicated that 'over 211 million hectares of African forest have been lost since 1970, amounting to almost 30 per cent of the original extent. In the same period, the land area under cultivation has increased by 36 million hectares, or 21 per cent.'[105] The establishment of conservation areas is one way to halt this trend. States are obliged to maintain and extend conservation areas,[106] and to establish new conservation areas where necessary.[107] Article XII(1)a and (1)b indicates that new conservation areas are particularly intended to

[103] IUCN, *supra* n. 32, p. 9. See IUCN, *IUCN Red List Categories and Criteria: Version 3.1* (IUCN, 2001), p. 14. For the latest Red List, see www.redlist.org.
[104] Article X(2).
[105] UNEP/African Ministerial Conference on the Environment (AMCEN), *supra* n. 74, Chapter 2.
[106] Article XII(1). Parties are also placed under an obligation to, 'where necessary, and if possible, control activities outside conservation areas which are detrimental to the achievement of the purpose for which the conservation areas were created, and establish for that purpose buffer zones around their borders'. Article 12(4).
[107] Ibid.

> a) conserve those ecosystems which are most representative of and peculiar to areas under their jurisdiction, or are characterized by a high degree of biological diversity;
> b) ensure the conservation of all species and particularly of those which are:
>   i) only represented in areas under their jurisdiction;
>   ii) threatened, or of special scientific or aesthetic value;
>
> and of the habitats that are critical for the survival of such species.

In relation to the obligations placed on states to identify new sites for conservation areas in accordance with these articles, parties importantly must

> seek to identify areas critically important to the goals referred to in sub paragraph 1(a) and 1(b) above which are not yet included in conservation areas, taking into consideration the work of competent international organisations in this field.[108]

This interesting provision is closely related to the fact that Article IV specifies that measures taken to achieve the Convention's objectives must be adopted and implemented with due regard to scientific knowledge.[109] States likely to become parties to this Convention will often lack accurate scientific data and the means to acquire such information. In this regard, relevant bodies may well be able to offer assistance.[110]

The area classifications and their respective management objectives are outlined in Annex 2 of the Convention.[111] The various types of 'conservation area' (strict nature/wilderness areas, national park, national monuments, habitat/species management area, protected landscape/seascape, and managed resource protected area) reflect the revised categorisation of protected areas endorsed by the IUCN in 1994.[112] Reference in the following discussion will be made to IUCN general guidelines for selection of protected areas which, though not noted in the text of the Convention, are clearly relevant given the Convention's open endorsement of the IUCN's approach to

[108] Article XII(2). [109] IUCN, *supra* n. 32, p. 11. [110] Ibid.

[111] See Article V(6)(a) and Annex 2. Also falling under the definition of a 'conservation area' are 'other areas designated and/or managed primarily for the conservation and sustainable use of natural resources, for which criteria may be adopted and from time to time reviewed by the Conference of the Parties'. Article V(6)(b).

[112] See IUCN, *Guidelines for Protected Areas Management Categories* (IUCN, 1994).

classification of such areas. The parties could, of course, decide not to adopt these guidelines in their entirety or at all, but, given that the IUCN was asked to assist with drafting the treaty, there is every reason to suppose that the IUCN will be actively involved once the treaty enters into force.[113]

i) Strict nature reserve: protected area managed mainly for science

A 'strict nature reserve' is defined as an

> [a]rea of land and/or sea possessing some outstanding or representative ecosystems, geological or physiological features and/or species, available primarily for scientific research and/or environmental monitoring.

Such an area has the following management objectives:

- to preserve habitats, ecosystems and species in as undisturbed a state as possible;
- to maintain genetic resources in a dynamic and evolutionary state;
- to maintain established ecological processes;
- to safeguard structural landscape features or rock exposures;
- to secure examples of the natural environment for scientific studies, environmental monitoring and education, including baseline areas from which all avoidable access is excluded;
- to minimise disturbance by careful planning and execution of research and other approved activities; and
- to limit public access.

A Ramsar Wetland of International Importance, the De Hoop Marine Protected Area, provides a good example of this type of conservation area. Located in the Western Cape, it is one of Africa's largest marine protected areas. Extending approximately five kilometres from the shore into the marine environment, it possesses a rich intertidal ecosystem and is a breeding ground for the southern right whale. According to IUCN guidance, biodiversity in nature reserves of this type 'should be achievable through protection and not require substantial active management or habitat manipulation'.[114]

[113] On classification of protected areas and the extent to which the IUCN's categorisation has been utilised in practice, see A. Gillespie, 'Defining Internationally Protected Areas' (2009) 12(4) *JIWLP* 229.

[114] IUCN, *supra* n. 112, p. 17.

ii) Wilderness area: protected area managed mainly for wilderness protection

A 'wilderness area' is defined as a

> [l]arge area of unmodified or slightly modified land and/or sea, retaining its natural character and influence, without permanent or significant habitation, which is protected and managed so as to preserve its natural condition.

Such an area has the following management objectives:

- to ensure that future generations have the opportunity to experience understanding and enjoyment of areas that have been largely undisturbed by human action over a long period of time;
- to maintain the essential natural attributes and qualities of the environment over the long term;
- to provide for public access at levels and of a type which will serve best the physical and spiritual wellbeing of visitors and maintain the wilderness qualities of the area for present and future generations; and
- to enable local communities living at low density and in balance with the available resources to maintain their life style.

IUCN guidance for selection of such areas notes, inter alia, that the area in question should 'contain significant ecological, geological, physiogeographic, or other features of scientific, educational, scenic or historic value', and also 'possess high natural quality, be governed primarily by the forces of nature, with human disturbance substantially absent, and be likely to continue to display those attributes if managed as proposed'.[115] The Groot Winterhoek wilderness area in South Africa provides an example. Located 120 kilometres north of Cape Town, it is an area of significance for the conservation of klipspringers, leopards, mongooses, black eagles, southern rock lizards and mountain fynbos, and possesses a rocky, rugged mountainous landscape.

iii) National park: protected area managed mainly for ecosystem protection and recreation

A 'national park' is defined as a

> [n]atural area of land and/or sea, designated to (a) protect the ecological integrity of one or more ecosystems for present and future generations, (b) exclude exploitation or occupation inimical to the purposes of designation of the area and (c) provide a foundation for spiritual, scientific,

[115] Ibid., p. 18.

educational, recreational and visitor opportunities, all of which must be environmentally and culturally compatible.

These following management objectives are to be pursued:

- to protect natural and scenic areas of national and international significance for spiritual, scientific, educational, recreational or tourist purposes;
- to perpetuate, in as natural a state as possible, representative examples of physiographic regions, biotic communities, genetic resources and species, to provide ecological stability and diversity;
- to manage visitor use for inspirational, educational, cultural and recreational purposes at a level which will maintain the area in a natural or near natural state;
- to eliminate and thereafter prevent exploitation or occupation inimical to the purposes of designation;
- to maintain respect for the ecological, geomorphologic, sacred or aesthetic attributes which warranted designation; and
- to take into account the needs of local communities, including subsistence resource use, in so far as these will not adversely affect the other objectives of management.

IUCN guidelines for selecting national parks stipulate that the area in question 'should contain representative sample of major natural regions, features or scenery, where plant and animal species, habitats and geomorphological sites are of special spiritual, scientific, educational, recreational and tourist significance'.[116] Kenya's Masai Mara National Reserve (bordering Tanzania's Serengeti National Park) and South Africa's Kruger National Park are typical examples of this type of protected area, as is Algeria's Tassili N'Ajjer National Park. Located in the Sahara with a boundary which extends to the Libya and Niger borders, Tassili is a mountainous area which is home to a variety of rare flora, such as wild olive and myrtle. It is also well known for prehistoric cave paintings, contains numerous threatened fauna including Barbary sheep and cheetah, and is an important resting site for migratory birds.

iv) Natural monument: protected area managed mainly for conservation of specific natural features

A 'natural monument' is defined as an

> [a]rea containing one, or more, specific natural or natural/cultural feature which is of outstanding or unique value because of its inherent rarity, representative or aesthetic qualities or cultural significance.

[116] Ibid., p. 19.

The Convention stipulates the following management objectives for such a site:

- to protect or preserve in perpetuity specific outstanding natural features because of their natural significance, unique or representational quality, and/or spiritual connotations;
- to an extent consistent with the foregoing objective, to provide opportunities for research, education, interpretation and public appreciation;
- to eliminate and thereafter prevent exploitation or occupation inimical to the purpose of designation; and
- to deliver to any resident population such benefits as are consistent with the other objectives of management.

IUCN guidance indicates, inter alia, that 'the area should contain one or more features of outstanding significance (appropriate natural features include spectacular waterfalls, caves, craters, fossil beds, sand dunes and marine features, along with unique or representative fauna and flora)'.[117] Zimbabwe's renowned Victoria Falls, listed in UNESCO's World Heritage List, is a national monument and provides a good example of this type of conservation area. The delicate riverine ecosystem below the Falls is also noteworthy for rare flora.

v) Habitat/species management area: protected area managed mainly for conservation through management intervention

This is defined as an

> [a]rea of land and/or sea subject to active intervention for management purposes so as to ensure the maintenance of habitats and/or to meet the requirements of specific species.

These management objectives should be followed in a habitat/species management area:

- to secure and maintain the habitat conditions necessary to protect significant species, groups of species, biotic communities or physical features of the environment where these require specific human manipulation for optimum management;
- to facilitate scientific research and environmental monitoring as primary activities associated with sustainable resource management;
- to develop limited areas for public education and appreciation of the characteristics of the habitats concerned and of the work of wildlife management;

[117] Ibid., p. 20.

- to eliminate and thereafter prevent exploitation or occupation inimical to the purposes of designation; and
- to deliver such benefits to people living within the designated area as are consistent with the other objectives of management.

Unlike the strict nature reserves addressed earlier, these areas therefore require significant active management and even habitat manipulation.[118] IUCN guidelines on selection note that such an area should 'play an important role in the protection of nature and the survival of species' and 'be one where the protection of the habitat is essential to the well-being of nationally or locally-important flora, or to resident or migratory fauna'.[119] This type of area would include the Ruvubu National Park in Burundi (providing important habitat for, inter alia, the lion, waterbuck, buffalo, impala, warthog and a variety of waterbirds), and the Selous Game Reserve in Tanzania (particularly noteworthy for its miombo woodland, and populations of crocodile, elephant and hippopotamus). Protection of the miombo woodland in the Selous Game Reserve provides a good example of the sort of active management that may be necessary as the woodland 'can only be maintained under a particular burning regime, and its preservation requires an active fire-management programme'.[120]

vi) Protected landscape/seascape: protected area managed mainly for landscape/seascape conservation and recreation

A 'protected landscape/seascape' is defined as an

> [a]rea of land, with coast and sea as appropriate, where the interaction of people and nature over time has produced an area of distinct character with significant aesthetic, ecological and/or cultural value, and often with high biological diversity. Safeguarding the integrity of this traditional interaction is vital to the protection, maintenance and evolution of such an area.

In these areas the following management objectives are to be pursued:

- to maintain the harmonious interaction of nature and culture through the protection of landscape and/or seascape and the continuation of traditional land uses, building practices and social and cultural manifestations;

[118] Ibid., p. 21. [119] Ibid. [120] Ibid., p. 65.

- to support lifestyles and economic activities which are in harmony with nature and the preservation of the social and cultural fabric of the communities concerned;
- to maintain the diversity of landscape and habitat, and of associated species and ecosystems;
- to eliminate where necessary, and thereafter prevent, land uses and activities which are inappropriate in scale and/or character;
- to provide opportunities for public enjoyment through recreation and tourism appropriate in type and scale to the essential qualities of the areas;
- to encourage scientific and educational activities which will contribute to the long term well-being of resident populations and to the development of public support for the environmental protection of such areas; and
- to bring benefits to, and to contribute to the welfare of, the local community through the provision of natural products (such as forest and fisheries products) and services (such as clean water or income derived from sustainable forms of tourism).

The IUCN suggests that protected landscape or seascape conservation areas 'should possess a landscape and/or coastal and island seascape of high scenic quality, with diverse associated habitats, flora and fauna along with manifestations of unique or traditional land-use patterns and social organisations as evidenced in human settlements and local customs, livelihoods, and beliefs'.[121] Lake Burullus, for example, a lagoon some 65 kilometres in length situated on Egypt's Mediterranean coastline, affords an important site for wintering waterfowl, and, as a lake fishery, is also of significant social and cultural value.

vii) Managed resource protected area: protected area managed mainly for the sustainable use of natural ecosystems

Defined as an

> [a]rea containing predominantly unmodified natural systems, managed to ensure long term protection and maintenance of biological diversity, while providing at the same time a sustainable flow of natural products and services to meet community needs.

[121] Ibid., p. 22.

Stated management objectives include:

- to protect and maintain the biological diversity and other natural values of the area in the long term;
- to promote sound management practices for sustainable production purposes;
- to protect the natural resource base from being alienated for other land-use purposes that would be detrimental to the area's biological diversity; and
- to contribute to regional and national development.

The establishment of this type of conservation area is in line with the general obligation stipulated in Article XII(2) which obliges parties to 'promote the establishment by local communities of areas managed by them primarily for the conservation and sustainable use of natural resources'.[122] Although managed resource protected areas could be owned by central or regional government, there is nothing to stop them being managed by the local community in partnership with or with appropriate support from the government.

IUCN guidance on selection notes that a managed resource protected area 'should be at least two-thirds in a natural condition, although it may also contain limited areas of modified ecosystems; large commercial plantations would not be appropriate for inclusion'.[123] In addition, the area 'should be large enough to absorb sustainable resource uses without detriment to its overall long-term natural values'.[124] The Kiunga Marine National Reserve in Kenya is typical of a managed resource protected area.[125] The area embraces a small piece of mainland, numerous offshore islands and adjacent waters. An abundance of nesting seabirds inhabit the approximately fifty offshore islands in the reserve, and the whole area is managed with a view to preserving its coastal habitats and promoting the sustainable use of natural resources; the local community in particular utilises the region's fishing resources.[126]

e) Land and water resources

The need to ensure effective conservation and protection of wildlife is a highly important focus of the Convention but, as with the 1968 Algiers

[122] Article XII(3). [123] IUCN, *supra* n. 112, p. 23. [124] Ibid.
[125] Ibid., p. 83. [126] Ibid.

Convention, the 2003 African Convention should certainly not be seen only as a treaty which protects fauna and flora. With a view to furthering the pursuit of sustainable development and affording general environmental protection, the Convention's provisions also embrace the conservation of other natural resources such as soil and water.[127] For example, parties 'shall take effective measures to prevent land degradation' (including its erosion, misuse and general deterioration), and 'shall develop long-term integrated strategies for the conservation and sustainable management of land resources, including soil, vegetation and related hydrological processes'.[128] More particularly, parties should, inter alia, 'establish land-use plans based on scientific investigations as well as local knowledge and experience', implement agricultural practices and agrarian reforms to improve soil conservation, establish sustainable farming and forestry practices, and also control pollution caused by agriculture.[129] Any such measures promoting the conservation of a natural resource other than fauna and flora may well, of course, beneficially impact upon the status of wildlife and their habitats.

In relation to the aquatic environment, parties must 'manage their water resources so as to maintain them at the highest possible quantitative and qualitative levels'.[130] With this in mind, parties must take measures to 'maintain water-based essential ecological processes as well as to protect human health against pollutants and water-borne diseases', and avoid water abstraction levels which are excessive.[131] Particularly relevant in relation to fauna and flora, parties must take measures to ensure that damage is prevented to water resources 'that could affect human health *or natural resource* in another State by the discharge of pollutants'.[132] 'Natural resources' are of course defined in Article V(I) to include fauna and flora. In addition, in relation to transboundary water resources and related ecosystems, including wetlands which play host to a range of wildlife, affected parties must act in consultation, and may, 'if the need arises', establish inter-state Commissions to manage such sites.[133]

The Convention further stipulates that parties 'shall take all necessary measures for the protection, conservation, sustainable use and rehabilitation of vegetation cover',[134] which also, of course, offers valuable habitat for many wildlife species. With this in mind, they must

[127] Article VI (soil) and Article VII (water). [128] Article VI(1). [129] Article VI(3).
[130] Article VII(1). [131] Ibid. [132] Article VII(1)(b) (emphasis added).
[133] Article VII(3). [134] Article VIII (vegetation cover).

> adopt scientifically-based and sound traditional conservation, utilization and management plans for forests, woodlands, rangelands, wetlands and other areas with vegetation cover, taking into account the social and economic needs of the peoples concerned, the importance of the vegetation cover for the maintenance of the water balance of an area, the productivity of soils and the habitat requirements of species.[135]

In this regard, it is of interest to note the conclusion of the Central African Forest Treaty in February 2005.[136] Burundi, Cameroon, Central African Republic, Chad, Democratic Republic of Congo, Equatorial Guinea, Gabon, the Republic of Congo, Rwanda and São Tomé and Príncipe are signatories.[137] The agreement seeks to protect forests in the Congo basin, which is home to the second-largest rainforest in the world.[138] These forests are the natural habitat of 'half of Africa's wild animals . . . as well as more than 10,000 plant species'.[139] It is hoped that the Central African Forest Treaty will foster greater co-operation in the area to reduce poaching, unlawful logging and the illegal trade in bushmeat.[140] In relation to bushmeat, a recent report has indicated that trade in bushmeat in Central and Western Africa 'is contributing significantly to the decline in populations of gorillas, chimpanzees, elephants, bush pigs and forest antelopes'.[141]

f) Environmental damage

To complement action to protect wildlife, the Convention also provides for the introduction of 'all appropriate measures to prevent, mitigate and eliminate to the maximum extent possible, detrimental effects on the environment, in particular from radioactive, toxic, and other hazardous substances and wastes'.[142] Such measures include, inter alia, implementation of national standards for ambient environmental quality, emission limits, process and production methods and product quality, the introduction of economic incentives and disincentives, and regulations ensuring reuse and recycling of resources.[143]

135 Article VIII(a).
136 See 2005 Treaty on the Conservation and Sustainable Management of Forest Ecosystems in Central Africa and to establish the Central African Forests Commission, reproduced at www.lead-journal.org/content/06145.pdf.
137 (2005) 35(2) *EPL*, p. 15. 138 Ibid.; the largest is located in the Amazon region.
139 Ibid. 140 Ibid. 141 UNEP/AMCEN, *supra* n. 74, Chapter 2.
142 Article XIII(1). 143 Article XIII(2)(a)–(c).

5. Participation arrangements

a) *Indigenous and local communities*

The importance of promoting the role of local communities in environmental management was underlined by Principle 22 of the Rio Declaration:

> Indigenous people and their communities and other local communities have a vital role in environmental management and development because of their knowledge and traditional practices. States should recognize and duly support their identity, culture and interests and enable their effective participation in the achievement of sustainable development.

With regard to natural resources (including wildlife) upon which local communities have a dependence, parties to the 2003 African Convention must ensure that such communities are given the opportunity to play an active part in the planning and management process.[144] In this way 'local incentives for the conservation and sustainable use of such resources' may be fashioned.[145] Species management projects, such as CAMPFIRE in Zimbabwe, have seen a degree of success in giving local people a real and tangible interest in local conservation activities.[146]

By virtue of Article XVII, parties shall also take action to protect traditional rights and intellectual property rights of local communities.[147] Action must be taken that ensures that access to indigenous knowledge, as well as the use of such knowledge, is made subject to the prior informed consent of the relevant communities, and to regulation which recognises both their rights to this knowledge and its economic value.[148] Indigenous knowledge is crucial both to the development of new traditional and/or commercial medicines and to the cultivation of plant varieties utilised in the production of high-yield crops.[149]

b) *Empowering the individual*

Promotion of public participation rights in the 2003 African Convention is reflective of the growing consensus that the individual can play a key role in

144 Article XVII(3). 145 Ibid.

146 For a critical analysis of communal approaches, see M. Murphree, 'Communal Approaches to Natural Resource Management in Africa: From Whence to Where?' (2004) 7 *JIWLP* 203.

147 Article XVII(1). 148 Article XVII(2).

149 See A. Meyer, 'International Environmental Law and Human Rights: Towards the Explicit Recognition of Traditional Knowledge' (2001) 10(1) *RECIEL* 37, pp. 38–9.

encouraging practical implementation and enforcement of environmental law.[150] Article XVI places the onus on parties to ensure 'timely and appropriate' access to and dissemination of environmental information, and public participation in decision-making which may have a significant environmental impact. Providing greater access to information allows the individual to participate in an informed and meaningful way in decision-making. The fostering of greater public participation in decision-making is of vital importance as there is evidence that some protected areas have been established in Africa without consultation with local people and without their approval.[151] This has led to a lack of respect for the boundaries of these areas from the local population.[152] The process of empowering the individual is further facilitated by Article XVI, which provides that parties must ensure 'access to justice in matters related to protection of the environment and natural resources'. Like the 1998 UN/Economic Commission for Europe's Aarhus Convention on Access to Information, Public Participation in Decision-Making and Access to Justice in Environmental Matters,[153] Article XVI thus represents regional reinforcement of the three 'pillars' of Rio Principle 10.

6. Ancillary measures

a) Trade

Trade in endangered species is a real threat to African biological diversity. Designed to complement the international regulation of trade in endangered species under CITES, Article XI(1) provides that parties shall

> a) regulate the domestic trade in, as well as the transport and possession of, specimens[154] and products[155] to ensure that such specimens and products have been taken or obtained in conformity with domestic law and international obligations related to trade in species;

[150] See generally M. Lee and C. A. Abbot, 'The Usual Suspects? Public Participation under the Aarhus Convention' (2006) 66(1) *MLR* 80; P. Davies in Don Zillman, Al Lucas and Rock Pring, *Human Rights in Natural Resource Management: Public Participation in the Sustainable Development of Mining and Energy Resources* (Oxford University Press, 2001), Chapter 4; and Principle 10 of the Rio Declaration. On public participation in decision-making and the enforcement of environmental rights, see discussion in Chapter 4 above.

[151] UNEP/AMCEN, *supra* n. 74, Chapter 2. [152] Ibid. [153] (1999) 38 *ILM* 517.

[154] Article V(2) notes that 'specimen' means 'any animal or plant or micro organism, alive or dead'.

[155] Article V(3) notes that 'product' means 'any part or derivative of a specimen'.

b) in the measures referred to under a) above, provide for appropriate penal sanctions, including confiscation measures.

These provisions are intended to ensure that African state parties improve efforts taken at the national level to implement and enforce CITES.[156] In this regard, parties shall, 'where appropriate, cooperate through bilateral or sub-regional agreements with a view to reducing and ultimately eliminating illegal trade in wild fauna and flora or their specimens or products'.[157] The onus is thus placed on parties to co-operate in a manner similar to action taken under the 1994 Lusaka Agreement on Cooperative Enforcement Operations Directed at Illegal Trade in Wild Fauna and Flora.[158]

b) Protection in time of armed conflict

The impact of armed conflicts on wildlife is a highly topical issue. It has, for example, been noted that mountain gorillas living in Rwanda's Volcans National Park, the adjacent Democratic Republic of Congo's Virunga National Park, and the Bwindi and Mgahinga National Park in Uganda 'have all been affected by poaching, facilitated by the collapse of law enforcement and the emergence of armed militias during the civil wars there'.[159] Article XV(1) of the Convention seeks to minimise these detrimental affects by obliging parties to:

a) take every practical measure, during periods of armed conflict, to protect the environment against harm;
b) refrain from employing or threatening to employ methods or means of combat which are intended or may be expected to cause widespread, long-term, or severe harm to the environment and ensure that such means and methods of warfare are not developed, produced, tested or transferred;
c) refrain from using the destruction or modification of the environment as a means of combat or reprisal;
d) undertake to restore and rehabilitate areas damaged in the course of armed conflicts.

156 IUCN, *supra* n. 32, p. 10. 157 Article XI(2).

158 IUCN, *supra* n. 32, p. 10. See 1994 Lusaka Agreement on Co-operative Enforcement Operations Directed at Illegal Trade in Wild Fauna and Flora (1998) 1 *JIWLP* 155. Also E. Mrema, 'Lusaka Agreement: Fighting Wild Fauna and Flora Crime' (2006) 36/1 *EPL* 35.

159 D.S. Wilkie, E. Hakizumwami, N. Gami and B. Difara, *Beyond Boundaries: Regional Overview of Transboundary Natural Resources Management in Central Africa* (Biodiversity Support Program, 2001), Chapter 2 (available at www.worldwildlife.org/bsp/publications/Africa/125/125/titlepage.HTML).

The aims behind these obligations are laudable but those actively involved in conflicts may well in practice be unlikely to regard protection of wildlife and of the wider environment as immediate and pressing concerns in times of war. Nonetheless, the obligation to 'undertake to restore and rehabilitate areas damaged in the course of armed conflicts' may well present an opportunity to seek review at the national level in the absence of such action.

c) *Scientific and technological research*

The Convention places the onus on parties to strengthen their research capacities in relation to conservation, sustainable utilisation and management of natural resources.[160] In doing so, attention must particularly be given to ecological and socioeconomic factors and the integration of these factors.[161] Parties must also apply research results in their respective national conservation policies.[162] These obligations in relation to research must be seen as being of great potential importance if the legal regime established by the Convention is to keep abreast of new developments, insights and practices. Since some parties may lack the expertise and financial ability to carry out such research, it is helpful that the Convention further requires parties to promote co-operation in this field both with other parties and with other entities in the area of environmental conservation and sustainable use of natural resources by means of the co-ordination of research programmes, the exchange of results and the promotion of joint research activities.[163] In this way expertise can be shared and costs reduced.

d) *Technology*

Linked to their obligations in relation to research, parties must also

> encourage and strengthen cooperation for the development and use, as well as access to and transfer of, environmentally sound technologies on mutually agreed terms, with a view to accelerating the transition to sustainable development, in particular by establishing joint research programmes and ventures.[164]

[160] Article XVIII(1). [161] Ibid. [162] Ibid.
[163] Article XVIII(2). [164] Article XIX(1).

Particular attention must be given to technologies which can be locally utilised.[165] In this regard, parties must take legislative and regulatory action providing economic incentives to develop, import, transfer and use environmentally sound technologies in the private and public sectors.[166] Economic incentives could include tax reductions, subsidies and/or the development or respect of intellectual property rights.[167]

e) *Capacity building, education and training*

The treaty acknowledges that steps must be taken to ensure that the public is aware of human interdependence with wildlife and other natural resources, and of their concomitant responsibilities towards conservation and sustainable use. In this regard, Article XX(1)(a) indicates that parties shall promote 'environmental education, training and awareness creation'. Environmental issues must be a part of educational and training programmes, and of information campaigns 'capable of acquainting the public with, and winning it over to, the concepts of conservation and sustainable use of natural resources'.[168] Conservation areas and the experience of local communities are to be utilised for their importance in relation to education and training.[169] Parties are also obliged to develop their education and training capacities concerning the conservation and use of the environment and natural resources.[170] To assist in the promotion of education, training and awareness, and in the ability of parties to deliver in this regard, parties must co-operate among themselves by, for example, setting up regional or subregional training institutions, joint training programmes, and giving support to libraries.[171]

7. Mechanisms for implementation

a) *Co-operation*

The parties are placed under a general obligation to 'co-operate between themselves and, where appropriate and possible, with other states' to

[165] Article XIX(2). [166] Ibid. [167] IUCN, *supra* n. 32, p. 15.
[168] Article XX(1)(b)(ii). The promotion of public education and awareness is also a feature of the Biodiversity Convention; see Article 13.
[169] Article XX(1)(c). [170] Article XX(2). [171] Article XX(3).

ensure implementation of the Convention.[172] In addition, and more specifically, states should co-operate when a national measure is likely to impact on a neighbouring state.[173] Collaboration between parties is also to take place in an effort to enhance the effectiveness of their respective policies, and also of decisions taken under the Convention's legal regime and under other international environmental conventions.[174] The type of co-operation envisaged includes working together in the conservation and management of fauna where the range of the animal in question covers the territory of two or more parties.[175] For example, parties may well need to co-operate in the designation of conservation areas to ensure these protected areas cover those places throughout the species' natural range so as to ensure adequate management of their habitats. Similar co-operative obligations already exist under Ramsar and the Bonn Convention. In addition, if a proposed project (such as a new dam) in State A is to impact on the habitat of a threatened species in State B, it is submitted that information should be given to State B by State A, and an opportunity given for State B to consult with State A.[176] If State B objects to the development, the two countries should begin negotiations with a view to resolving the issue to their mutual satisfaction.[177]

b) Liability

Article XXIV indicates that 'Parties shall, as soon as possible, adopt rules and procedures concerning liability and compensation of damage related to matters covered by this Convention.' States too often seem to regard the important issue of Liability as one which they simply do not wish to address, perhaps because there is little chance of reaching a consensus.[178] The inclusion of a clause addressing liability is not particularly common in species and habitat protection treaties and, arguably, its inclusion in the revised 2003 African Convention reflects the latter's wider remit beyond the protection of fauna and flora.

The adoption of rules concerning liability and compensation would act as a significant deterrent to those uninterested in conserving and

[172] Article XXII(1)(a). This is in line with the obligation stipulated in Article 5 of the Biodiversity Convention.
[173] Article XXII(1)(b). [174] Article XXII(1)(c). [175] See Article XXII(2)(e).
[176] See Article XXII(2)(b). [177] See Article XXII(2)(c).
[178] On the shift of emphasis from liability to regulation, see discussion in Chapter 2 above.

utilising biodiversity on a sustainable basis. Attributing financial liability to operators of activities and/or state parties would have a castigating effect and could also be preventive in nature in that future practices may well be modified as a result. Once the Convention is in force, the Conference of the Parties should establish at an early stage a working group with legal expertise to provide guidance to the parties with a view to producing draft rules. Whether this materialises remains to be seen.

c) Compliance and enforcement

An important enforcement tool is provided by the need for parties to report to the Conference of the Parties on measures taken to implement their obligations.[179] The Conference of the Parties will have to determine how often these reports must be submitted.[180] The Secretariat is obliged to comment on any failure to report, as well as on the suitability of reports and national action noted in them.[181]

In relation to compliance, the Conference of the Parties is obliged 'as soon as possible' to 'develop and adopt rules, procedures and institutional mechanisms to promote and enhance compliance'.[182] The fact that the need for 'institutional mechanisms' is mentioned in this regard is particularly to be welcomed. The Conference of the Parties itself will need to take an active role in relation to compliance, and should be assisted by an additional body established to assess compliance. Such a body should be able to make recommendations to the Conference of the Parties on the manner in which a party in non-compliance could be assisted in remedying the situation. An important source of information in any compliance procedure will be provided by the above-mentioned national reports as part of the compliance continuum.[183]

d) Financial resources

Article XXVIII recognises the 'central importance of financing to the achievement of the purposes of this Convention', and calls on each state party 'taking into account its capability' to 'make every effort to ensure that adequate financial resources are available for the

[179] Article XXIX. [180] Ibid. [181] Ibid. [182] Article XXIII.
[183] See further Chapter 4 above.

implementation of this Convention'. Parties will make assessed contributions and the African Union itself will also contribute annually.[184] However, the drafters of the text appear correctly to have acknowledged that such contributions alone will be insufficient to fund an effective regime. Contributions from other institutions are envisaged,[185] and the onus is placed on parties to 'mobilize further financial resources'.[186] The establishment of a conservation fund may also be established 'constituted from voluntary contributions of parties or from any other source accepted by the Conference for the purpose of financing projects and activities relating to the conservation of the environment and natural resources'.[187] Any such fund will be accountable to the Conference of the Parties. It is to be emphasised that this fund will not contribute to the running of the institutional structure established by the Convention.[188] Only conservation projects and activities are to be given assistance.

8. Conclusion

There is no doubt that once in force the 2003 African Convention will establish a legal regime better equipped to achieve its objectives than the 1968 Algiers Convention which it will revise. The IUCN indeed takes the view that it 'consolidates 30 years of learning and experience in international environmental law and policy'.[189] Like the 1968 Algiers Convention, the 2003 African Convention presents a vision for the future in which conservation needs and developmental aims are effectively integrated. Additionally, tools and techniques to assist in facilitating sustainable development (such as EIAs, access to information and to justice) are openly embraced. Very importantly, the revised Convention also establishes a Conference of the Parties and a Secretariat. These institutions can take meaningful steps to ensure that the Convention will not become the sleeping treaty which many would say that the 1968 Algiers Convention has become. They must seek to ensure that state parties do more than merely ratify this treaty: practical implementation of and compliance with the Convention's provisions must be kept under constant and effective review.

In the past, the conservation of natural resources has not been seen as a priority for many African countries, crippled as they are by debt and the

[184] Article XXVIII(2). [185] Ibid. [186] Article XXVIII(4).
[187] Article XXVIII(3). [188] IUCN, *supra* n. 32, p. 20. [189] Ibid., p. 5.

need to eradicate poverty amongst their growing populations. For the future, however, the 2003 African Convention will target continued economic development, but in a way which is sustainable. It is vital that this important opportunity is not undermined by political inertia, either at the national or the regional level. Lack of political will is not the only potential danger. State parties and the African Union are unlikely to be able to provide adequate funding to ensure effective implementation. It is therefore essential that development agencies outside Africa assist in funding, and that the private sector is given incentives to fund conservation activities in Africa.[190] If the 2003 African Convention is to achieve its aims, so much will depend on the extent to which non-African countries and development agencies contribute financially to support the Convention's institutions and relevant education programmes, as well as the applicable conservation, capacity-building, research and technical activities. The Convention should be seen as a new beginning which offers the foundation for real progress in the future. However, without adequate funding and the political will to implement its obligations, any prospect of progress under the 2003 African Convention will undoubtedly be lost.

Recommended further reading

D. M. Dzidzornu, 'Environmental Protection in Africa: A Panorama of the Law and Practice' (2004) 22(2) *JERL* 148

IUCN, *An Introduction to the African Convention on the Conservation of Nature and Natural Resources* (IUCN, 2004)

P. Kameri-Mbote, 'The Development of Biosafety Regulation in Africa in the Context of the Cartagena Protocol' (2002) 11(1) *RECIEL* 62

P. Kameri-Mbote and P. Cullet, 'Biological Diversity Management in Africa: Legal and Policy Perspectives in the Run-up to WSSD' (2002) 11(1) *RECIEL* 38

M. A. Mekouar, 'La Convention africaine: petite histoire d'une grande renovation' (2004) 34(1) *EPL* 43.

A. Meyer, 'International Environmental Law and Human Rights: Towards the Explicit Recognition of Traditional Knowledge' (2001) 10(1) *RECIEL* 37

E. Mrema, 'Lusaka Agreement: Fighting Wild Fauna and Flora Crime' (2006) 36 (1) *EPL* 35

[190] See also IUCN, *supra* n. 32, p. 20.

M. Murphree, 'Communal Approaches to Natural Resource Management in Africa: From Whence to Where?' (2004) 7 *JIWLP* 203

D. S. Wilkie, E. Hakizumwami, N. Gami and B. Difara, *Beyond Boundaries: Regional Overview of Transboundary Natural Resources Management in Central Africa* (Biodiversity Support Program, 2001), Chapter 2 (available at www.worldwildlife.org/bsp/publications/Africa/125/125/titlepage.HTML)

Chapter 10

The Convention on the Conservation of European Wildlife and Natural Habitats

1. Background

In view of mounting political concern during the 1970s regarding the poor implementation of existing wildlife conventions in the region,[1] the Committee of Ministers of the Council of Europe established a committee of experts to prepare a draft of a new treaty.[2] The resulting Convention on the Conservation of European Wildlife and Natural Habitats[3] was formally approved by the Committee of Ministers in June 1979 and opened for signature on 19 September in Bern. The Bern Convention came into force on 1 June 1982.[4] By January 2010, there were fifty contracting parties in total, including the EU, four African countries,[5] and all but two member states of the Council of Europe itself.[6]

The aims of the Convention are to conserve wild flora and fauna and their natural habitats, to promote co-operation between countries in their conservation efforts and to give special attention to endangered and vulnerable species, including those that are migratory.[7] Detailed provision is accordingly made for the conservation of wildlife and habitat

[1] See, e.g., Resolution No. 2, 2nd European Ministerial Conference on the Environment, Conclusions (Brussels, 23–4 March 1976).

[2] The Council of Europe, established in 1949, is a regional consultative organisation with a current membership of 47 European countries. The Committee of Ministers of Foreign Affairs acts as its executive body.

[3] *ETS* 104. For a useful, albeit not conclusive, guide to the treaty and its interpretation, see the official *Explanatory Report Concerning the Convention on the Conservation of European Wildlife and Natural Habitats* (Council of Europe, 1979), revised versions of which have been published to take account of amendments to the Appendices etc.

[4] I.e. three months after the deposit of the fifth instrument of ratification. Article 19(2).

[5] EU participation is specifically authorised, while that of non-member states of the Council of Europe depends upon invitation by its Committee of Ministers. See Articles 19(1), 20(1).

[6] I.e. Russia and San Marino. [7] Article 1.

generally and for the specific protection of species listed in Appendices I (strictly protected plants), II (strictly protected animals) and III (protected animals). Alongside the aesthetic, scientific, cultural, recreational and economic values of the wildlife heritage, the preamble recognises also its *intrinsic* value – the first such affirmation in a major wildlife treaty.

This is not the only feature that demonstrates the importance of the Bern Convention in the conservation field. Others include the imposition of clear and unequivocal obligations on the parties (i) to protect all important breeding and resting sites of the hundreds of animal species in Appendix II and (ii) to prohibit the collection or uprooting of the many plant species in Appendix I. They are also required to take the measures necessary to maintain populations of *all* species of flora and fauna at levels that correspond to ecological, cultural and social requirements – even if this means overriding economic interests. The Convention permits parties to exclude these obligations in specified circumstances, but in no event may they exercise this power so as to threaten the survival of a species or of a population thereof.

Two aspects of the Convention are especially noteworthy. The first is that almost every one of its provisions is mandatory, as opposed to being couched in the hortatory language favoured by many conservation treaties. The second is the system of administration it has created to promote and oversee its implementation, which represents a major advance from earlier regional wildlife conventions. Its Standing Committee not only meets regularly to review implementation of the Convention,[8] but also conducts detailed investigations of problems identified at specific locations. As a result, the parties are only too aware that they risk public criticism if they do not comply with their obligations.

This chapter looks initially at the general conservation provisions of the Convention, before discussing the listing of species in the Appendices and the special provisions in the text for their protection. It goes on to consider various supplementary clauses which cover, amongst other things, migratory and exotic species, and then explores the complex question of the geographical area to which the Convention applies.

[8] Unless otherwise indicated, all references in this chapter to recommendations, resolutions and declarations, or to meetings, relate to the Bern Convention's Standing Committee. The texts of these measures, and reports of meetings, can be found via the 'Documentation' links on the Council of Europe website at www.coe.int/t/dg4/culture-heritage/nature/bern/default_fn.asp.

Next, it examines the institutions and administrative arrangements set up to promote implementation of the Convention, and, finally, its relationship with other agreements.

2. General conservation provisions

Although the Convention is primarily concerned with the protection of the species listed in its Appendices, Articles 2 and 3 establish certain obligations with respect to *all* wildlife species, whether listed or not.

a) Maintenance of population levels

Article 2 states:

> The Contracting Parties shall take requisite measures to maintain the population of wild flora and fauna at, or adapt it to, a level which corresponds in particular to ecological, scientific and cultural requirements, while taking account of economic and recreational requirements and the needs of sub-species, varieties or forms at risk locally.[9]

This provision, the wording of which closely resembles that of Article 2 of the 1979 EU Wild Birds Directive,[10] is significant for two reasons. First, it sets a standard at which populations of wildlife must be maintained, or to which depleted or excessive populations must be adjusted. Second, although it permits the parties to cater for economic and recreational needs in fulfilling these obligations, it is clear that their primary duty is to maintain wildlife populations at levels corresponding to ecological, scientific and cultural requirements. In the event of an irreconcilable conflict between economic and ecological requirements, therefore, the parties would seem to have undertaken to give priority to the latter.

The reference to 'cultural' requirements is interesting in that, although the cultural values of wildlife are often mentioned in the preambles to wildlife treaties,[11] it is much less common to find such reference in the substantive provisions. As noted in Chapter 3 above, animals and plants

[9] The reference to flora is currently interpreted to extend to fungi, despite the fact that they are now known to represent an entirely separate biological kingdom from plants and animals. See the Report of the 27th Meeting, para. 4.2, and Recommendation 132 (2007).

[10] For references and discussion, see Chapter 7 above.

[11] For discussion, see A. Gillespie, *International Environmental Law, Policy and Ethics* (Clarendon Press, 1997), Chapter 5.

may be culturally important for many reasons, ranging from their religious or totemic significance for particular communities to their importance in children's stories. Standing Committee recommendations have drawn specific attention to the 'symbolic' and 'cultural' value of species such as the badger, the hamster and the lynx.[12]

The Convention does not define a population level which corresponds to 'ecological, scientific or cultural requirements' (and it would certainly be difficult to do so by reference to cultural considerations), but it can safely be assumed to be well above that at which a species is in danger of extinction.[13] At a minimum, therefore, the parties must ensure that species do not become extinct through agencies within their control, help endangered species recover to a point where their numbers are sufficient for performance of their ecological functions, and maintain presently healthy populations at or above that level. To that end, action plans and recovery plans for the conservation of particular species have been extensively employed.[14] In addition, the Convention's Standing Committee regularly calls upon particular parties to take appropriate conservation measures. For example, recent recommendations addressed primarily to Belgium, France, Germany and the Netherlands have pressed for urgent action to prevent the extinction of the common hamster (*Cricetus cricetus*), which, despite its name, is now seriously endangered throughout Western Europe and in unprecedented decline in many other areas.[15]

Given the many factors which are adversely affecting wildlife populations, the obligations established by Article 2 will not be easy to discharge. In the case of the hamster, for example, the principal reasons for its decline include the fragmentation of its range and the loss of suitable habitat in agricultural areas. The measures proposed accordingly include the drawing up of conservation plans to ensure the species' long-term

[12] See Recommendations 68 and 69 (1998), 79 (1999) and 94 (2002).

[13] Note that Article 7(2) of the Convention expressly requires that the permitted exploitation of Appendix III species be regulated 'in order to keep the populations out of danger, taking into account the requirements of Article 2'.

[14] Note in this context the Guidelines on the Drafting and Implementation of Action Plans of Wild Fauna Species, annexed to Recommendation 59 (1997). For examples of recent measures concerning action plans, see Recommendations 122 (2006) (birds); 115 (2005) and 137 (2008) (large carnivores); 119 (2006) (amphibians and reptiles); and 136 (2008) (hamsters); regarding recovery plans, see Recommendations 104 (2003) and 118 (2005) (tortoises).

[15] See Recommendations 59 (1997), 68 (1998), 79 (1999) and 136 (2008). The common hamster is listed in Appendix II.

viability; the enforcement of domestic legislation for its protection, and the strict control of exemptions (especially significant in view of the hamster's propensity to damage crops);[16] the establishment of a network of reserves and the reintroduction of the species over its former range; the implementation of necessary agricultural and environmental measures within the framework of the common agricultural policy; and the promotion of awareness campaigns targeting farmers, local authorities and the general public.[17]

A final point to note is that Article 2 may occasionally require the regulation of overabundant populations which are having adverse effects on other wildlife species. For instance, the action plan for the Audouin's gull (*Larus audonii*),[18] endorsed by Recommendation 60 (1996), called for the humane culling of yellow-legged gulls (*L. michahellis*) where there was evidence of harmful competition and predation between the species.

b) National policies, development and education

Article 3(1) obliges parties to 'promote national policies for the conservation of wild flora, wild fauna and natural habitats', with particular attention to 'endangered and vulnerable species, especially endemic ones, and endangered habitats'. Pursuing this theme, Recommendation 87 (2001), which endorsed the recently devised European Plant Conservation Strategy,[19] urged all Bern Convention parties to formulate and implement national strategies regarding plants and to integrate them within their national biodiversity conservation strategies.[20] This was seen as representing Europe's contribution to the Biodiversity Convention's Global Strategy on Plant Conservation.[21]

Article 3(3) requires parties to promote education and disseminate general information on the need to conserve species and their habitats,

[16] See Article 9, discussed in section 4(c)(ii) below.

[17] See generally the revised Draft European Action Plan for the Conservation of the Common Hamster, Doc.T-PVS/Inf (2008) 9.

[18] See B. Heredia, L. Rose and M. Painter (eds.), *Globally Threatened Birds in Europe: Action Plans* (Council of Europe, 1996). This species is currently classified as 'near threatened'.

[19] For the current version for the years 2008–14, see Recommendation 138 (2008). In similar vein, note Recommendation 120 (2006), concerning the European Strategy for the Conservation of Invertebrates.

[20] For an early example of such a strategy document, see Biodiversity: The UK Action Plan, Cm 2428 (1994).

[21] See the Report of the 21st Meeting, para. 4.3.

while Article 3(2) obliges them to have regard to wildlife conservation in their planning and development policies and in their measures against pollution – a functional reflection of the principle of integration, which is now regarded as a key element of sustainable development.[22] The Convention gives no further details, however, as to how this obligation should be implemented, and progress to date remains sketchy. In recognition of this fact, a formal declaration adopted by the Standing Committee at its most recent meeting strongly reiterated the need for greater effort regarding the integration of biodiversity concerns into sectoral policies, and the urgency of securing engagement with all economic sectors to that end.[23]

3. Species included in the Appendices

This section examines the process of listing species in the three Appendices.[24]

a) Species listed

Appendix I is reserved exclusively for plants[25] and now contains over 700 species. The Convention's concern with flora as well as fauna is a major step forward because plants have historically suffered as the poor relation of animals in terms of conservation priorities. Appendix I was originally based upon a list drawn up by the Threatened Plants Committee of the IUCN, and displayed a distinct bias towards southern European species. It has subsequently been considerably expanded, however, and, at the 16th Meeting alone, well over 100 central and eastern European species were added to reflect the growing participation in the Convention of the former Soviet bloc states.[26]

Appendix II relates to animals, incorporating several hundred species. Originally, it contained only mammals, birds, reptiles and

[22] See, e.g., the Biodiversity Convention, Article 6(b). For discussion of the principle, see Chapter 2 above.

[23] 2009 Bern Declaration on the Conservation and Sustainable Use of Biodiversity: 2010 and Beyond.

[24] There are actually four Appendices in all, but the last is concerned not with species designation but with the specification of proscribed methods of capture and killing of exploitable animals. See further section 4(b)(iii) below.

[25] But see n. 9 *supra*: on the possibility of listing fungi species, see the Report of the 23rd Meeting, para. 3.1.

[26] See the Report of the 16th Meeting, para. 4.1 and Appendix 4.

amphibians, but it has subsequently been extended to embrace certain fish and invertebrate species, including insects, crustaceans, molluscs, echinoderms, cnidarians and sponges.[27] A number of listings are of biological taxa higher than the species; usually these are families, such as bears (Ursidae), pelicans (Pelecanidae) or flamingos (Phoenicopteridae), but a few entire orders, such as Falconiformes (diurnal raptors), or suborders, such as Microchiroptera (smaller bats),[28] are included. Unlike Appendix I, which contains species that are mostly endemic to Europe, Appendix II includes many animals which are migratory and spend only a portion of their life cycle in the region, including the humpback whale (*Megaptera novaengliae*), Kemp's ridley turtle (*Lepidochelys kempii*) and numerous bird species. Appendix III is something of a 'catch all' list for animals not included in Appendix II. It incorporates a handful of additional invertebrate species together with a large number of mammals, including some which are relatively common, and *all* birds, reptiles and amphibians not in Appendix II, with the exception of eleven very common avian species.

In contrast to certain other wildlife treaties, the Bern Convention does not specifically provide for the designation in their own right of subspecies, varieties or geographically separate populations, and the tendency has been to avoid such listings.[29] Guidelines agreed in 1997 stipulate that the parties should, as a general rule, confine their listing proposals to the species level, 'except in cases with very good conservation reasons that must be clearly stated'.[30] A proposal by Moldova at the 20th Meeting to list two subspecies of carabid beetles in Appendix II was accordingly defeated,[31] whereas a revised proposal the following year to list the two species to which they belonged, *Carabus bessarabicus* and *C. hungaricus*, was unanimously accepted.[32] One unusual development during the mid-1990s involved the addition to Appendices I and II, at the instigation of Monaco and France, of various species accompanied by the designation 'for the Mediterranean'.[33] This is not a taxonomic notation at all, but is associated with the creation by those states of a geographical sanctuary for marine mammals. Given the

[27] The echinoderms include the starfish, sea urchins and sea cucumbers, while the cnidarians (the 'c' is silent) embrace the corals, jellyfish and sea anemones.

[28] The pipistrelle (*Pipistrellus pipistrellus*) is, however, excluded and consigned to Appendix III.

[29] The original listings incorporated just one subspecies (*Rupicapra rupicapra ornata*, a chamois), in Appendix II; see para. 78, *Explanatory Report*. There are now over twenty in Appendices I and II, but such listings are still regarded as exceptional.

[30] See section 3(b) below. [31] See the Report of the 20th Meeting, para. 4.1.

[32] See the Report of the 21st Meeting, para. 3.4.

[33] See the Reports of the 16th Meeting, para. 4.1(d), and 17th Meeting, para. 4.1(b), (c).

inclusion of certain cetaceans in this list, Iceland and Norway were anxious to place on record their understanding that this listing had no legal consequences whatever outside the Mediterranean area.[34]

b) Listing criteria

A conspicuous feature of the Convention is that no criteria are specified to govern the listing process and, in particular, the threat of extinction is not stipulated as a precondition. The plant species originally included in Appendix I were for the most part either endangered or vulnerable,[35] but this was certainly not the case for listed animals: indeed, Appendices II and III between them cover *all* species of birds found in Europe with the exception of only a few that were regarded as overabundant or even as 'pests'.[36] The fact that Appendix II species receive a significantly stricter form of protection than those in Appendix III implies that the former category is designed for those that are at greater risk, but even here the standards applied do not seem to have been at all rigorous: the wren (*Troglodytes troglodytes*), for example, is included in Appendix II even though it is common throughout much of Europe. Furthermore, where listings are of higher biological taxa, it is plain that the conservation status of the various species within them may differ significantly.

The *Explanatory Report* makes clear that the original listings did not represent any sort of definitive determination, but simply reflected what could be achieved by consensus at the time. It was therefore envisaged from the outset that changes would be needed, and Article 17 duly provides for the periodic amendment of the Appendices by the Standing Committee. In view of the controversy generated by certain proposals, it was decided that approved criteria were required for this purpose, and these were ultimately adopted in 1997.[37] Despite the Convention's explicit concern for cultural considerations, the Guidelines focus exclusively upon ecological factors, since it was unanimously agreed that these represented the highest priority.[38] The

[34] As defined for the purposes of the 1976 Convention for the Protection of the Mediterranean Sea against Pollution (1976) 15 *ILM* 290.

[35] Recommendation 30 (1991) on the Conservation of Species in Appendix I expressly confirms this point. For further discussion, see the Report of the 16th Meeting, para. 4.1.

[36] E.g. the more common species of gulls and crows. [37] Recommendation 56 (1997).

[38] See the Report of the 17th Meeting, para. 4.1. A working group proved unable to resolve a dispute as to whether cultural and symbolic values should play any part in this process, and the Recommendation ultimately adopted excluded any reference to such considerations.

Guidelines are not at all prescriptive, however, merely recommending that the parties 'take into account' the twin factors of the ecological role of the species and the nature and degree of the threat it faces. As to the latter, regard should be paid to population levels and trends in the light of the vulnerability of the species to unsustainable utilisation or to loss or deterioration of its habitat. Another relevant factor is whether any observed decline is occurring at the heart of the species' range, or only at the margins. As regards ecology, account should be taken of the species' position in the food chain, its structural role in ecosystems and the possibility that endangered species or ecosystems may be highly dependent upon it, or risk becoming threatened by its exploitation. This relatively relaxed approach to conservation status for listing purposes was underlined by the Secretariat's reminder at the 25th Meeting that Appendix II represents a list not of *threatened* species as such but of *protected* species,[39] which suggests a slightly different philosophical emphasis from that of some other conservation treaties. Possibly cultural factors may sometimes justify a stricter form of protection than would be required by ecological considerations alone.

Amendment may, of course, involve not only the addition of species to the Appendices but also their removal, though it is likely that a precautionary approach will be taken here. Thus a recent Swiss proposal, prompted by the concerns of livestock owners, to transfer the wolf (*Canis lupus*) from Appendix II to Appendix III was ultimately rejected.[40] It was noted that, while protection and reintroduction programmes had undoubtedly succeeded in increasing overall wolf numbers, populations were still critical in many areas. Furthermore, the Convention contained other mechanisms for addressing the problem of livestock predation.[41]

4. Conservation of listed species

Articles 4–9 of the Convention establish the regime for the protection of listed species, which encompasses both habitat conservation and regulation of direct exploitation.

[39] Report of the 25th Meeting, para. 3.1.

[40] See ibid., and Report of the 26th Meeting, para. 3.1.

[41] Specifically, the powers to formulate reservations and exceptions, discussed in section 4 (c) below.

a) *Habitat conservation*

The question of habitat conservation is addressed primarily, though not exclusively, in Article 4, the effect of which extends beyond the habitats of listed species.

i) General provisions

Article 4(1) requires each party to 'take appropriate measures to ensure the conservation of the habitats of the wild flora and fauna species, especially those specified in Appendices I and II, and the conservation of endangered natural habitats'. Under Article 4(2) they must have regard in their planning and development policies to the conservation requirements of the areas so protected in order to guard against their deterioration. If the key ecological characteristics of important sites are to be maintained, these provisions may entail the adoption of appropriate supporting measures, such as the establishment of 'buffer zones' or migration corridors. Interpreted widely, they may require a new commitment to a more environmentally sensitive approach to land use generally.[42]

The Convention has sometimes been criticised, even from within, for the imprecision of these habitat conservation provisions,[43] and, as early as 1989, the Standing Committee highlighted three further prerequisites to the effective realisation of its habitat objectives.[44] These were (i) the identification of species requiring specific habitat conservation measures, (ii) the identification of endangered natural habitats requiring specific conservation measures and (iii) the designation of areas of special conservation interest. Encouragingly, major developments on all three fronts can be reported.

First, following the endorsement of the Pan-European Biological and Landscape Diversity Strategy at a ministerial conference held in Sofia, Bulgaria, during 1995, the Standing Committee adopted Resolution No. 3. By this measure, it resolved to create a network of conservation areas (to be known as the Emerald Network) and to encourage both Bern Convention parties and observer states to designate sites for inclusion. Three years later, following work by a Group of Experts convened to

[42] See, e.g., Recommendations 25 (1991) on the conservation of habitat outside protected areas, and 71 (1998) on habitat management through private or voluntary systems.

[43] E. Fernandez-Galiano, 'A Personal View' (1995) 77 *Naturopa* 5.

[44] For the determinations in question, see Resolution No. 1 (1989) and Recommendations 14, 15 and 16 (1989).

advance the project, principles to govern the detailed operation of the Emerald Network scheme were agreed through Resolution No. 5. Essentially, any area of land or sea may be designated an Area of Special Conservation Interest (ASCI) if it supports significant numbers of species; if it contributes substantially to the survival of threatened, endemic or listed species; if it is important for migratory species; if it contains outstanding examples of particular habitat types or important and/or representative samples of endangered habitat types; or if it otherwise contributes substantially to the achievement of the Convention's objectives.[45] Proposals for designation are made initially by the relevant government, though the Standing Committee has the ultimate power to reject such proposals and may also offer advice on suitable sites for inclusion. Governments are to monitor the species and habitats contained in ASCIs, and alert the Secretariat to any significant threat of adverse ecological change, whereupon the Standing Committee may advise on the need for remedial measures. The Committee also assumes responsibility for supervising the overall operation of the scheme.

The Emerald project closely parallels the European Union's Natura 2000 Network, and the preamble to Resolution No. 5 states that for EU members the sites for the two networks will be the same and will be governed exclusively by EU rules and procedures. Consequently, the main practical significance of the Emerald Network will lie in the extent to which it attracts participation from the non-EU parties to the Bern Convention, or even observer states.[46] Despite numerous difficulties and delays, most of the parties, including certain African countries, have now at least implemented a pilot project to launch the process of site designation.[47] Later phases entail the charting of up to 80 per cent of suitable sites, and ultimately all of them.[48]

General guidance has also been forthcoming on the other two prerequisites to effective habitat conservation indicated above, and should prove of considerable assistance in the designation of sites for the Network. First, Standing Committee Resolution No. 4, of December 1996, enumerated the various habitat types which were considered to

[45] These criteria were originally stipulated by Recommendation 16 (1989).

[46] Note that the CoE/EU joint programme supporting CBD endeavours regarding protected areas in Eastern Europe embraces both Belarus and the Russian Federation, and that the former has already expressed interest in joining the Emerald Network.

[47] See generally Doc. T-PVS (2006) 22.

[48] For recent developments, see the Reports of the 28th and 29th Meetings, paras. 4.8 and 5.5 respectively.

be endangered and consequently in need of special conservation measures. These were grouped into seven main categories,[49] and then subdivided so as to specify, for example, sublittoral rocky seabeds and kelp communities, estuaries, Mediterranean salt meadows, dunes, salt lake islands, dry and wet heaths, blanket bogs, continental steppes, and mixed ravine and slope forests.

Finally, in 1998, species that were in need of specific habitat conservation measures were identified in Resolution No. 6. This list was compiled following extensive consultations with the European Commission,[50] and incorporates many species not yet included in the Bern Convention Appendices. There are in fact over 1,000 entries in all, though some are of subspecies or groups of species. It was accepted, however, that some of these taxa were abundant in certain parts of Europe, and might not require habitat conservation measures everywhere.

The Convention's remit, moreover, extends far beyond mere policy guidance, and involves active oversight of compliance with conservation commitments, as illustrated by the attention paid over many years to such endangered habitat as heathland.[51] Lowland heaths provide vital habitat for such species as the nightjar (*Caprimulgus europaeus*), Dartford warbler (*Sylvia undata*) and sand lizard (*Lacerta agilis*), but are often under heavy threat from development, not least because of their proximity to built-up areas in certain countries. Following intense pressure at the 1989 Meeting of the Standing Committee,[52] the United Kingdom decided ultimately to revoke planning permission for housing development on one such area, Canford Heath in Dorset,[53] and the EC subsequently provided some £421,000 to assist conservation work.[54] Development pressures upon such areas seldom disappear entirely, however, and are commonly exacerbated by other problems, in this case degradation caused by the uncontrolled spread of fires. It was such

[49] Viz. coastal and halophytic communities; non-marine waters; scrub and grassland; forests; bogs and marshes; inland rocks, screes and sands; and wooded grassland and scrub.

[50] See the Report of the 18th Meeting, para. 5.4.

[51] Heathland is a 'semi-natural' landscape type with its own distinctive vegetation, which would revert to woodland if not mown, grazed or burnt. Unlike moorland, it is not characterised by the presence of peat. The ecological importance of both was recognised in Recommendation 3 (1984), which called for national inventories of peatlands, heathlands and dry grasslands.

[52] See C. de Klemm, 'Bern Convention' (1990) 20(1/2) *EPL* 25, p. 28.

[53] See 'Current Topics' [1991] *JPL* 505; *Birds* (Summer 1991), p. 12.

[54] *Birds* (Autumn 1992), p. 20.

considerations which brought the Dorset heathlands back to the Standing Committee's agenda in the late 1990s.[55] Following an on-the-spot investigation, the UK was urged to devise a general policy for their conservation, concentrating upon the protection and restoration of fire-damaged areas and the prevention of further loss or degradation. Particular recommendations included the avoidance of further housing development or road construction close to heathland,[56] the prohibition of mineral extraction, the improvement of firefighting capacities and the regulation of public access.[57]

ii) Transboundary issues

These general habitat conservation commitments are supplemented by further provisions which specifically address issues of a transboundary nature. Under Article 4(3), the parties 'undertake to give special attention to the protection of areas that are of importance for the migratory species specified in Appendices II and III and which are appropriately situated in relation to migration routes as wintering, staging, feeding, breeding or moulting areas', while Article 4(4) requires them to co-ordinate their efforts to protect habitats situated in frontier areas.

Obviously, Article 4(3) relates primarily to the protection of sites within the parties' own territories, and might entail, for example, conservation of wetland sites or prohibition of development projects in sensitive areas. Many sites of importance to listed migratory species will, however, lie outside their territories entirely – perhaps as far afield as Africa and Asia – but the wording of Article 4(3) is seemingly wide enough to require the parties to do what they can to protect these sites as well. In particular, they can encourage the establishment of nature reserves in the countries concerned and support conservation efforts through the provision of financial and technical assistance. It was accordingly suggested at the very first meeting of the Standing Committee that parties should give attention to this issue in the context of their development aid programmes.[58]

As regards collaboration in frontier areas, the joint arrangements involving Denmark, Germany and the Netherlands to conserve the

[55] See, e.g., the Report of the 17th Meeting, para. 6.2.

[56] This led to the adoption of a policy establishing 400-metre building exclusion zones around protected heathlands, though it was recently suggested that this be extended in some cases to five kilometres.

[57] Recommendation 67 (1998).

[58] See the Report of the 1st Meeting, para. 8.1.4.

natural values of the Wadden Sea are now particularly well established.[59] By contrast, a worrying instance of failure to ensure proper consultation and advance consideration of transboundary effects is evident in the Ukrainian government's plan to construct a navigable waterway through the Bystroe estuary, which is thought to threaten the ecological dynamics of the entire Danube Delta.[60] In 2004, the Standing Committee called for the suspension of Phase 2 of this project until a full EIA and public consultation had occurred.[61] Although an initial assessment, published in April 2006, favoured continuation of the project, the Ukrainian Court of Auditors later ruled it unsatisfactory. Following further intense international pressure, and an on-the-spot appraisal by a Bern Convention expert in 2008, the Ukrainian government informed the Secretariat in March 2009 that further work on Phase 2 was suspended pending the completion of appropriate procedures. Yet only a month later, the government of neighbouring Romania asserted that substantial work had in fact been undertaken.[62] A consortium of international treaty bodies promptly formulated a joint statement indicating their concern regarding possible breaches of Ukraine's international obligations,[63] and the case remains under review by the Bern Convention Standing Committee.[64]

iii) Appendix II species

The strong links between the conservation of habitat and of wild fauna are underlined by the terms of Article 6(b), which prohibit 'the deliberate damage to or destruction of breeding or resting sites' of Appendix II species. By comparison with Article 4, this provision is stated in very precise terms and its implications are extremely far-reaching. Appendix II lists hundreds of species, and their breeding and resting sites occur in countless different locations across Europe: the hedge sparrow (*Prunella modularis*), for example, might be found in almost any European hedgerow. Potentially, therefore, the restrictions imposed by

[59] For further discussion, see Chapters 13 and 16 below.
[60] The case has, of course, attracted the attention of numerous treaty institutions; see further Chapter 13 below.
[61] Resolution 111 (2004).
[62] For statements by the governments in question, see Docs. T-PVS/Files (2009) 3 and 30.
[63] For their current position, see Doc. T-PVS/Files (2009) 20.
[64] See the Report of the 29th Meeting, para. 6.1. For discussion of the review process itself, see section 8(b)(iv) below.

Article 6(b) upon agricultural, industrial, residential or recreational development are very severe indeed.

There are, however, two factors which prevent this provision from producing absurd consequences. The first is that Article 9 allows the parties to make exceptions from the provisions of Article 6 for the protection of certain specified interests.[65] More importantly, ordinary principles of treaty interpretation are designed to avoid such extreme results as the imposition of an obligation to preserve every hedgerow in Europe in pristine condition. In the light of the overall object and purpose of the treaty, Article 6(b) is best interpreted so as to require the maintenance of a sufficient network of hedges to sustain the wildlife species which are dependent upon them,[66] together with the strict protection of any particular sites which are vital to the conservation of species especially at risk.[67]

Even so, a breach of Article 6(b) may plainly occur where the site at risk *is* vital to a particular listed species. Thus, in 2002, a proposal for a major tourist development in the Souss Massa National Park, Morocco, was judged to be contrary to the Convention on the grounds that the area in question constituted the last stronghold of the critically endangered northern bald ibis (*Geronticus eremita*).[68] This species represents a particularly potent symbol for the Convention, as it is one of the very few birds actually to have become extinct in Europe during historical times, clinging on only in North Africa and the Middle East.[69] The Standing Committee recommended[70] that the government reacquire the land in question, strengthen the existing conservation measures and confine any development to nature-based tourism built around the ecological importance of the site, if necessary seeking international funding to facilitate this approach. The Moroccan government appeared willing to show flexibility over this issue, acknowledging in particular the need for better communications between

65 For discussion of this provision, see section 4(c)(ii) below.

66 In fact, this has been Council of Europe policy since the mid-1970s: see Resolution 76 (33) of the Committee of Ministers on the Evolution and Conservation of Hedgerow Landscapes (Bocages) in Europe, *Texts Adopted by the Council of Europe in the Field of the Conservation of European Wildlife and Natural Habitats*, Nature and Environment Series, No. 40 (1989).

67 Para. 29 of the *Explanatory Report* indicates that the aim is to protect 'important fauna sites'.

68 Also known as the hermit ibis, or waldrapp.

69 A colony in Turkey is maintained only by the most intensive management, while a tiny, genetically distinct population has recently been discovered in Syria.

70 Recommendation 97 (2002).

its own government departments regarding conservation commitments.[71] It seems that major development has been suspended for the time being, and a management plan adopted for the park, built around the rehabilitation and sustainable utilisation of natural ecosystems. Emphasis is placed on the recruitment of local people to act as wardens for ecotourism, which is already well established. Concern has persisted, however, over the creeping expansion of summer chalets in unprotected areas around the park. Nevertheless, the ibis population remains more or less stable at present.[72]

In such critical cases, Article 6(b) is understood to require the *in situ* protection of listed species in the locations where they naturally occur, so that 'translocation of specimens to other habitats can only be considered as a partially compensatory measure'.[73] Thus a decision of the UK authorities to relocate an entire colony of 25,000 great crested newts (*Triturus cristatus*) from the Orton Brick Pits site in Peterborough,[74] in order to permit housing development, was regarded by the Standing Committee as 'contrary to the spirit and letter of Article 6'. Consequently, the grant of planning permission could be justified only as an instance of the power to make exceptions under Article 9: the UK was accordingly obliged to satisfy the requirements of that procedure, including keeping the Standing Committee informed of future developments.[75] It was later reported that the newts had bred successfully in twenty-six of the thirty ponds to which they had been relocated, but the NGO Societas Europaea Herpetologica nevertheless questioned the adequacy of long-term funding and planning for the project.[76] For many species, relocation is in any event impossible, and consequently there may be no alternative to the suspension of development unless it can be justified in accordance with Article 9.

It is therefore clear on any view that the obligations imposed by Article 6(b) are extremely far-reaching and demanding,[77] and the determination

71 See the Reports of the 21st Meeting, para. 5.2; 23rd Meeting, para. 5.4; and 24th Meeting, para. 5.4.

72 For further information, see Birdlife IBA Factsheet MAO38, viewable via www.birdlife.org, and C. G. R. Bowden et al., 'Contribution of Research to Conservation Action for the Northern Bald Ibis in Morocco' (2008) 18 *Bird Conservation International* S74.

73 Recommendation 70 (1998).

74 This represented the largest known population in Europe.

75 For ongoing monitoring of the situation by the Committee, see, e.g., the Report of the 21st Meeting, para. 5.3.

76 Ibid.

77 Further noteworthy illustrations concern the conservation of marine turtle nesting sites in Cyprus, Greece and Turkey. See, e.g., Recommendations 54 (1996), 63 and 64 (1997), 66 (1998) and 95 (2002).

to ensure compliance has in fact provided the Bern Convention system with its most serious challenge to date.[78]

b) Regulation of exploitation

The Bern Convention also regulates the taking, killing and exploitation of species listed in its Appendices. As well as imposing general duties on the parties to take the legislative and administrative measures necessary to ensure the 'protection' of species in Appendix III and the 'special protection' of those in Appendices I and II,[79] it creates a number of more specific obligations.

i) Appendix I

First, Article 5 requires the prohibition of 'deliberate picking, collecting, cutting or uprooting' of Appendix I plants, and, where appropriate, of 'the possession or sale of these species'. According to the *Explanatory Report*, 'sale' is intended to include exchange and barter, but regulation should be limited to internal trade[80] on the basis that international transactions fall within the remit of CITES.[81]

Although difficult questions of interpretation undoubtedly arise regarding the precise scope of Article 5 – does 'uprooting', for example, include the bulldozing of a site for development or the ploughing up of fields for agricultural purposes? – there is little indication of such questions having being explored in concrete cases. Whereas problem situations referred to the Standing Committee have commonly stemmed from concern for individual *animal* species, this has seldom been the case with regard to plants.[82] It may be that issues arising in connection with development activities of the kind referred to above are more likely to be dealt with by reference to the Convention's habitat conservation provisions.

[78] Concerning turtle nesting sites at Laganas Bay, Zakynthos: see section 8(b)(iv) below.

[79] Articles 5, 6 and 7(1).

[80] This formulation is expressly employed in relation to the protection of animal species in Article 6(e).

[81] See Chapter 15 below.

[82] It is, however, not uncommon for large-scale development projects to be challenged on the basis that a combination of plant and animal species will be adversely affected. See, e.g., the debate regarding the Akamas peninsula, Cyprus, Report of the 29th Meeting, para. 6.1.

ii) Appendix II

In order to give Appendix II species appropriate protection from exploitation, Article 6 of the Convention requires prohibition of the following activities:[83]

(a) all forms of deliberate capture and keeping and deliberate killing; . . .
(c) the deliberate disturbance of wild fauna particularly during the period of breeding, rearing and hibernation, insofar as disturbance would be significant in relation to the objectives of this Convention;
(d) the deliberate taking or destruction of eggs from the wild or keeping these eggs even if empty;
(e) the possession of and internal trade[84] in these animals, alive or dead, including stuffed animals and any readily recognisable part or derivative thereof, where this would contribute to the effectiveness of the provisions of this Article.

These provisions again raise several problems of interpretation: what is the precise scope of the obligation in paragraph (a), for example? At first sight, it might appear to require the prohibition of three activities (deliberate capture, keeping and deliberate killing), but this interpretation is weakened by the precise wording of the phrase (deliberate capture *and* keeping *and* deliberate killing). In addition, paragraph (e) does not seem to envisage that possession and trade, which necessarily involve some form of keeping, must be prohibited in all cases. It is therefore more likely that the activities to be proscribed are (i) deliberate capture followed by retention of the specimen and (ii) deliberate killing: thus deliberate capture followed by *release* is not precluded per se, but only if it falls foul of some other prohibition, such as that upon deliberate disturbance during the period of breeding, rearing or hibernation in accordance with paragraph (c). It is important to note, however, that the text is merely specifying *examples* of activities to be prohibited in pursuance of the Convention's objectives,[85] and that Article 12 in any event allows the parties to enforce stricter national standards of protection if they choose.

[83] Para. (b) is omitted here, having already been considered in relation to habitat protection.
[84] See the discussion in the previous subsection. For ongoing monitoring of problems concerning the illegal catching, killing and trading of protected birds in Cyprus, and the Mediterranean area generally, see the Report of the 29th Meeting, para. 6.5.
[85] 'The following will *in particular* be prohibited . . .' (emphasis added).

iii) Appendix III

The Bern Convention does not prohibit the killing, capture or trade of species in Appendix III, but Article 7(2) stipulates that exploitation must be regulated 'in order to keep the populations out of danger, taking into account the requirements of Article 2'. Article 7(3) envisages that these measures may include the establishment of closed seasons, the temporary or local prohibition of exploitation where necessary to restore satisfactory population levels and the 'regulation as appropriate of sale, keeping for sale, transport for sale or offering for sale of live and dead wild animals'. Paragraph 36 of the *Explanatory Report* states that the parties must also, in accordance with Article 2 of the Convention, have regard for subspecies and varieties at risk locally when implementing this provision.

In addition, Article 8 strictly controls methods of exploitation, requiring prohibition of 'the use of all indiscriminate means of capture and killing and the use of all means capable of causing local disappearance of, or serious disturbance to, populations of species, and, in particular, the means specified in Appendix IV'. This Appendix makes separate provision for mammals, birds, freshwater fish and crayfish, the use of explosives and poisons being prohibited in all cases. Other prohibited devices include artificial light sources (mammals, birds, fish); electricity with alternating current (fish) or electrical devices capable of killing and stunning (mammals, birds); aircraft and vehicles in motion, certain (semi-)automatic weapons, snares, nets and traps, dazzling devices and blind or mutilated specimens used as decoys (mammals, birds); birdlime and hooks (birds); and gassing or smoking out (mammals). The ban upon the use of such methods applies not only to Appendix III species but also to those in Appendix II whenever taking is exceptionally authorised under Article 9.

Plainly, the regime of protection for Appendix III species is much less strict than that for Appendix II, but parties must nevertheless ensure that they have adequate regulatory mechanisms at their disposal to control exploitation of the former where necessary.

iv) Unlisted plant species

The discussion above highlights an important distinction between the Convention's treatment of flora and fauna species, in that plants are dealt with at only the strict-protection level. Accordingly, there was originally no specific mechanism for maintaining the conservation status of plants not (yet) deemed to be in need of such protection. In response to concerns regarding the excessive collection of certain unlisted plants from the wild for commercial exploitation, Recommendation 49 (1996) identified species specially affected in an Appendix, urging the parties to monitor their exploitation, and, wherever necessary, ensure that their currently favourable conservation status was not prejudiced. Measures might include temporary or local prohibitions on taking; the regulation of times and methods of taking and of related activities such as sale, keeping, transport and so on; and the promotion of artificial propagation programmes. This was not intended to prohibit exploitation of the species in question entirely – indeed it was recognised that controlled exploitation might represent a legitimate source of income for many people – but to contain it within limits so that the conservation status of the species in question is not put at risk. This regime effectively parallels that applicable to Appendix III animal specimens under Article 7 of the Convention.

c) *Exclusion of the protective regime*

In common with other conservation treaties, the Bern Convention permits parties to exclude the operation of the protective regime it establishes in certain circumstances. Two principal mechanisms of this sort are established.

i) Reservations

Although general reservations are not permitted, Article 22 allows the parties to exempt particular species listed in Appendices I–III from the scope of their acceptance. In addition, they may reserve the power to employ, in relation to any species they specify, techniques of killing, capture or exploitation which would normally be prohibited under Appendix IV.[86] These powers may only be exercised at the time of signature, ratification, accession and so on,[87] or, in respect of any species

[86] This power may also be exercised with respect to any overseas territory to which the Convention has been extended. Article 22(2).

[87] Article 22(1), reflecting the provisions of Article 19 of the 1969 Vienna Convention on the Law of Treaties. Thus, when in 1996 Estonia sought to formulate reservations which had not been specified upon its accession in 1992, it was advised that the proper course of action was for it to denounce the Convention and then tender a new instrument incorporating the reservations in question. Report of the Meeting of the Bureau (20 May 1996), Doc T-PVS (96) 32.

or methods subsequently added to the Appendices, within three months of the adoption of the relevant amendment.[88]

To date, around half of the parties have registered reservations of one sort or another.[89] In the main, these apply to only a handful of species – usually those regarded as plentiful within the country concerned or thought to pose a particular risk to humans, livestock or fisheries, such as the grey wolf (*Canis lupus*), brown bear (*Ursus arctos*) or great cormorant (*Phalacrocorax carbo*). Some are not explicable on this basis, however, such as the French reservation regarding the green turtle (*Chelonia mydas*). Occasionally, the effect of the reservation in question is not to exclude the operation of the Convention entirely but to 'downgrade' Appendix II species to Appendix III status.[90] A few countries have formulated extensive reservations: Hungary, for example, has specified over forty species and Turkey around a hundred (predominantly reptiles, amphibians and invertebrates). A number of statements relate to prohibited devices or methods of capture: the UK, for example, permits a surprising array of relatively indiscriminate techniques for taking hares, stoats, weasels, deer and seals.

Plainly, achievement of the Convention's objectives could be significantly jeopardised by excessive resort to these powers, and one of the Standing Committee's earliest actions was to urge the parties to re-examine the need for any reservations they might have formulated.[91] Happily, states have responded to this call in some instances: Norway, for example, has withdrawn objections originally formulated with respect to certain plant species, as well as some of those relating to cetacean species added to Appendix II in 1987, while Malta has withdrawn reservations made upon ratification with regard to several species of birds and methods of capture.

ii) Authorised exceptions

In addition, even where parties do not wish to exclude particular species from the operation of the Convention entirely, it is recognised that, in the defence of certain interests, they may from time to time wish to authorise activities that would normally be prohibited. Accordingly, Article 9 permits them to create specific exceptions from the provisions of Articles 4–8:

88 Article 17(3).
89 Details of all such statements may be found on the Council of Europe's Treaty Office website at http://conventions.coe.int.
90 Note, for example, the reservations of Croatia and Cyprus.
91 Recommendation 4 (1986). Under Article 22(4), reservations may be withdrawn wholly or in part at any time.

(i) for the protection of flora and fauna;
(ii) to prevent serious damage to crops, livestock, forests, fisheries, water and other forms of property;
(iii) in the interests of public health and safety, air safety or other overriding public interests;
(iv) for the purposes of research and education, of repopulation, of reintroduction and for the necessary breeding; and
(v) to permit, under strictly supervised conditions, on a selective basis and to a limited extent, the taking, keeping or other judicious exploitation of certain wild animals and plants in small numbers.

These exceptions closely reflect those contained in the EU Birds Directive.[92] Plainly, some of them, especially the first and fourth, are designed to advance the interests of conservation, and might be relied upon to justify the taking of specimens from the wild to carry out research on species in decline, to provide breeding stock for reintroduction projects,[93] or to regulate populations of species that have become locally overabundant at the expense of others.[94] Most, however, are not of that character, and have the potential significantly to undermine the protection which the Convention would otherwise establish. The needs of air safety, for instance, could be used to justify the eradication of wildfowl in the vicinity of airports, 'bird strike' being a relatively common cause of aeronautical accidents.[95] More generally, the phrase 'other overriding public interests' appears to give the parties a disturbingly wide margin of discretion.[96]

Reassuringly, however, various controls have been established on the use of such exceptions to minimise their potentially deleterious effects. The issue was explored by a working party of jurists in a commentary appended to Standing Committee Resolution No. 2 (1993) on the Scope of Articles 8 and 9. It noted, first, that certain exceptions are qualified by explicit limitations;[97] thus measures to protect crops or livestock may only be taken to prevent 'serious' damage (though this was not

[92] For discussion, see Chapter 7 above.
[93] On this point, see the discussion of Article 11(2), section 5(b) below.
[94] Note, e.g., the discussion regarding the yellow-legged gull in section 2(a) above.
[95] Apparently there are up to 2,000 incidents every year of aircraft hitting birds in the US alone, a Boeing 747 averaging one such incident for every 1,000 hours of flying time. N. Faith, *The Black Box* (Channel 4 Books, 1996).
[96] This was presumably the justification invoked by the UK in the Orton Brick Pits case, discussed in section 4(a)(iii) above.
[97] See in particular paras. 9–12 of the Appendix.

interpreted to require that the damage be widespread). As regards the final exception, where such limitations are most numerous, the requirement that exploitation be 'judicious' was understood to mean that it must be reasonable and not excessive, while the phrase 'under strictly supervised conditions' entailed either individual authorisation in advance or 'effective on-the-spot supervision', or possibly both. The expression 'on a selective basis' was considered particularly problematic, not least because it might be invoked specifically in order to circumvent the Article 8 prohibition on non-selective methods of capture. To avoid any contradiction here, it must be taken to mean that non-selective means of taking might be authorised, but only where non-target specimens could subsequently be released unharmed; that is, it was the *keeping* that must be selective in that context.

The second safeguard lies in the stipulation in Article 9 itself that none of these exceptions may be invoked unless 'there is no other satisfactory solution' to the problem in question, which entails that alternative approaches must at least have been considered and found to be ineffective or impracticable. The working party judged it to entail a requirement of proportionality; thus justifiable action to prevent damage to crops and so on 'must be evaluated in terms of the intensity and duration of the prejudicial action, the direct or indirect links between that action and the results, and the scale of the destruction or deterioration committed'.[98] One problem identified with regard to the final exception is that since, uniquely, it is not expressed in terms of advancing any particular goal, it may be invoked by a party 'for any reason which to it seems valid . . . and without any reason having to be given'.[99] Consequently, unless the party in question spontaneously indicates those reasons, it will be impossible to check the correlation of use of the exception with such purpose, or the viability of alternative solutions. Monitoring will therefore be limited to ensuring that the formal conditions governing its exercise have been complied with.

The final overriding requirement specified in Article 9 is that action authorised by way of exception to the usual principles of conservation must 'not be detrimental to the survival of the population concerned'. This vital safeguard means that, however important the interests which the government in question is seeking to defend, they cannot be pursued

[98] Para. 16 of the Appendix.

[99] Ibid., para. 11(a). Cf. the approach taken under the EU Birds Directive, discussed in Chapter 7 above.

to the extent of precipitating the extinction of the population to which they relate. This appears consistent with the general principle in Article 2, which accords ultimate priority to ecological requirements over economic or recreational considerations.[100]

Essential as these substantive restrictions upon the use of exceptions undoubtedly are, they are unlikely in themselves to be sufficient to prevent abuses. The additional, procedural, safeguard which is established by Article 9(2), involving an element of international supervision of the entire process, is accordingly likely to prove crucial. The details of this supervisory regime are more fully discussed below.[101]

5. Supplementary conservation provisions

Articles 10 and 11 of the Convention contain provisions designed to supplement and reinforce the obligations discussed above. These concern the conservation of migratory species, the reintroduction of native species and the eradication of exotic ones.

a) Migratory species

It has already been mentioned that the Bern Convention requires that special attention be given to protecting areas of importance for listed migratory species. In addition, Article 10(1) requires parties to co-ordinate their efforts for the protection of such species whose range extends into their territories, while Article 10(2) obliges them to ensure that closed seasons and other measures regulating the exploitation of Appendix III species adequately reflect the needs of any that are migratory. One key objective is to ensure that shooting and trapping seasons are set at times which will not be unduly damaging to migrating birds. More detailed provision for such matters is, of course, to be found in other treaties, most notably the Bonn Convention and its various 'daughter' agreements.

Various measures have addressed the need for enhanced international co-operation to conserve species likely to inhabit border areas; thus Recommendation 82 (2000) calls for the implementation of action plans amongst various combinations of parties for the conservation of

[100] It is to be noted here that Article 9 authorises the creation of exceptions to the provisions of Articles 4–8, but not to Articles 2 or 3.

[101] See section 8(a)(ii) below.

bear, lynx and wolf in the Alps, Carpathians and Pyrenees, southern Fennoscandia and the Baltic region. Objectives highlighted include the conservation and restoration of suitable habitat, the creation of migration corridors and the removal of incentives which reduce the suitability of the landscape for these particular species.[102]

b) *Introductions and reintroductions*

Article 11(2) deals with the related questions of the introduction of exotic species and the reintroduction of native ones, issues judged to be of sufficient complexity and importance to have required the establishment of another Group of Experts. The disruption of ecological processes by exotic species, whether through direct predation upon indigenous species, competition for food or space, hybridisation, habitat degradation or the transmission of diseases and parasites, is now universally recognised as a major threat to conservation.[103] Article 11(2)(b) accordingly obliges the parties 'to strictly control the introduction of non-native species'. In contrast to other treaties, this provision does not refer expressly to the eradication of species *already introduced*,[104] but it has certainly been interpreted to cover that situation. One example concerns the call for eradication of the ruddy duck (*Oxyura jamaicensis*), a North American species which escaped from various wildfowl collections during the 1950s and has thereby put at risk (through competition and hybridisation) its close European relative, the white-headed duck (*Oxyura leucocephala*), which is already of globally threatened status.[105]

Following the promulgation in 1997 of detailed guidance concerning the problems posed by non-native species,[106] it was decided to retune the regional approach to accord with that adopted globally under the CBD; Recommendation 99 (2003) therefore called for the development of national strategies on this matter based upon the European Strategy on Invasive Alien Species, which was approved at the 23rd Meeting.[107] The Strategy mirrors its global counterpart in its approach to tackling the

[102] See further, e.g., Recommendations 100 and 101 (2003), 115 (2005).

[103] See, e.g., IUCN, World Conservation Strategy (1980), section 3; J. A. McNeeley et al., *Conserving the World's Biological Diversity* (IUCN, 1990), Chapter 3, esp. at p. 38.

[104] Cf. Articles 3(4)(c) and 5(5)(e), CMS; Article 8(h), CBD.

[105] See Recommendations 61 (1997) and 124 (2007), and, for a report on implementation by the UK, Doc. T-PVS/Inf (2005) 19.

[106] See Recommendation 57 (1997).

[107] See Doc. T-PVS (2003) 7 rev.

major implications of the introduction[108] (accidental or deliberate) of invasive alien species;[109] these include the enhancement of awareness, early detection and response, prevention and mitigation strategies and capacity building. The Standing Committee also called for enhanced international co-operation in tackling the problem, and regular reports from the parties on the process of implementation.[110]

Subsequently, Recommendation 125 (2007) called for increased research and enhanced regulation with regard to trade-related pathways for the introduction of exotics.

This guidance on general policy is complemented by various measures which address specific problem cases. Recommendation 77 (1999), for example,[111] calls for the eradication, wherever feasible, of eleven non-native terrestrial vertebrates, including the American mink (*Mustela vison*), Canadian beaver (*Castor canadensis*), grey squirrel (*Sciurus carolinensis*),[112] sika deer (*Cervus nippon*), bullfrog (*Rana catesbeiana*) and red-eared terrapin (*Trachemys scripta*). The mink, for example, was originally imported into Europe for fur-farming purposes, but many have escaped (or been deliberately released by animal rights activists) into the wild, sometimes with devastating effect upon the indigenous wildlife, especially the water vole (*Arvicola terrestris*).[113] It is recognised that awareness-raising campaigns may be required to overcome public antipathy to eradication programmes and, with that in mind, the preamble to the Recommendation recognises that the methods used should be as 'selective, ethical and without cruelty as possible, consistent with the aim of permanently eliminating the invasive species'.

[108] 'Introduction' is 'the movement by human agency, indirect or direct, of an alien species outside of its natural range (past or present)', whether within countries or between countries/areas beyond national jurisdiction.

[109] An 'alien species' is one 'introduced outside its natural past or present distribution'; it includes lower taxa, as well as parts, gametes, seeds, eggs or propagules that might survive and reproduce, but excludes genetically modified organisms. Such species are considered 'invasive' if their 'introduction and/or spread threaten biological diversity'. Recommendation 142 (2009) indicates, however, that native species extending their range in response to climate change should not be considered 'alien'.

[110] See further Recommendation 125 (2007) on the impact of trade upon the spread of invasive species.

[111] See most recently Recommendations 139 and 140 (2009), concerning the racoon dog and small Indian mongoose.

[112] See further section 8(b)(iv) below.

[113] The water vole is widespread across Europe and not listed under the Bern Convention, but its rate of decline in the UK is such as to raise issues under Article 2.

The threat posed by alien species is not, of course confined to animals, and Recommendation 126 (2007) called for the eradication or containment of certain invasive alien plants which are not yet well established. Other recommendations have sought to tackle the problems known or suspected to be associated with the spread of particular species, such as the water hyacinth (*Eichhornia crassipes*),[114] imported extensively for ornamental use in ponds and aquaria, and the tropical seaweed *Caulerpa taxifolia*, which has proliferated in the Mediterranean.[115] Finally, the Standing Committee has adopted measures to address the invasive potential of plants imported for use in horticulture or as biofuel crops.[116]

The Convention also provides for the reintroduction of native species that have disappeared from their former habitat. Such projects are, however, by no means straightforward – in particular, there is little point in seeking to reintroduce a species if the factors which caused its original disappearance are still operative. They are therefore envisaged by Article 11(2) only where they will contribute to the conservation of the species in question and on condition that 'a study is first made in the light of the experience of other Contracting Parties to establish that such an introduction would be effective and acceptable'. The issue of acceptability is fundamental because the reintroduction of predators, such as the wolf, is often of great concern to farmers and other constituencies.[117] Such matters are addressed by Recommendation 58 (1997), which provides for detailed regulation of the entire process of reintroduction, including the holding of widespread consultations beforehand and provision for compensation with respect to resulting damage.

6. The geographical and taxonomic scope of the Convention

Although the Bern Convention, by virtue of its very title, presents itself as a European regional arrangement, there is in fact no substantive provision which specifically determines its geographical sphere of application. The *Explanatory Report* makes clear that this omission was quite deliberate,[118] and that the intention was

[114] Recommendation 133 (2008).

[115] Recommendation 45 (1995), which is interesting both as an early invocation of the precautionary principle and in its call for collaboration with other (i.e. regional seas) treaty institutions.

[116] See respectively Recommendations 134 (2008) and 141 (2009).

[117] This species has nevertheless been reintroduced into various European countries.

[118] See para. 17.

(i) not to restrict the geographical coverage of the convention to the European continent, with a view to the fact that many species of flora and fauna of Europe are found outside Europe; and
(ii) to include visiting migratory animals that are not confined to Europe.

This observation confirms that the overall substantive scope of the Convention is a complex question, and depends upon the interrelationships amongst various factors, including (i) the incidence of participation, (ii) the territorial ambit of the obligations undertaken by each party and (iii) the species to which the Convention applies.

a) *The incidence of participation*

Since jurisdiction in international law is primarily territorial, the sphere of application of the conservation obligations which the Bern Convention imposes will in the first instance be determined by the combined physical extent of the parties' national territories. Initially, that represented a relatively limited area, since by 1984 the Convention had attracted only fourteen contracting parties. It must be remembered that the Council of Europe was in origin essentially a Western European organisation, and even in that region many governments did not regard wildlife as an urgent priority. From the early 1990s, however, an increased political commitment to nature conservation globally, bolstered by a sudden influx into the Council of former Soviet-bloc countries, precipitated a substantial expansion of its territorial coverage. The involvement of geographically peripheral states such as Iceland in the north-west and Cyprus, Malta, Turkey, Armenia and Azerbaijan in the south-east has now effectively extended its ambit all the way from the Arctic to Africa and the Middle East.[119] Thus the Bern conservation regime has been gradually transformed into one of genuinely pan-Continental application.[120]

[119] Russia remains the one territorially significant absentee.

[120] Note that Council members with overseas or outlying territories have tended, through declarations under Article 21, to limit their application of the Convention to Europe: viz. Denmark – excludes Greenland, Faroe Islands; Netherlands – Kingdom in Europe only; Norway – continental territory of the Kingdom (though with a statement concerning conservation policy in Svalbard and Jan Mayen); UK – extended only to Isle of Man (from August 1992), Sovereign Base Areas in Cyprus (from October 2001); Jersey (from October 2002).

Furthermore, since many species of 'European wildlife' spend at least part of their life cycle beyond the confines of the continent, it was never intended that participation be limited to Council members,[121] and from a relatively early stage the involvement of other countries, particularly in Africa, was actively encouraged. Senegal and Burkina Faso became the first to accede and they were followed by Tunisia and Morocco, extending the total geographical area covered by the Convention still further. The application of its provisions in such countries raises some uncertainties, however. Undoubtedly, their obligations extend to the protection of *listed* species, the controversy surrounding the bald ibis in Morocco having already been noted as an example.[122] At the same time, it would seem that the broader conservation obligations which those countries have undertaken – under Articles 2 and 3, for example – must be applied for the benefit of *their own* national wildlife populations generally, *without regard to any connection with Europe*, since there is nothing in the Convention to restrict the scope of those duties in that way. Thus discussions regarding the conservation of large carnivores have on occasion addressed the precarious situation of the lion (*Panthera leo*) and the African hunting dog (*Lycaon pictus*),[123] even though these are neither listed under the Convention nor found anywhere in Europe. While one would not expect such species to form a primary focus of concern for the Bern regime, they do seem legitimately to fall within its purview as determined by the territorial jurisdiction of its non-European parties.

It should not be assumed, however, that the Convention's sphere of application is exclusively territorial, since there is ample practice to support the view that the parties' commitments may extend to certain activities beyond national frontiers.[124]

b) Extraterritorial application of commitments undertaken

Thus, at the very first meeting of the Standing Committee, the observer from the Federal Republic of Germany stated that, since the provisions of the Convention apply to acts 'performed on the high seas on vessels navigating under the flag of the Contracting Parties or in no-man's land', his government would not ratify until its domestic legislation had been

[121] See Articles 19(1), 20(1). [122] For discussion, see section 4(a)(iii) above.

[123] See, e.g., the Report of the 21st Meeting, para. 4.5.

[124] See the discussion of Article 4(3) in section 4(a)(ii) above.

modified to cover those points.[125] Such amendments were duly made,[126] prompting the further question of whether the Convention requires the exercise of extraterritorial jurisdiction beyond the situations specified: does the obligation under Article 6(a) to take appropriate measures to prohibit the deliberate killing of Appendix II specimens, for instance, require regulation of the activities of a party's nationals overseas, such as the shooting of migratory birds in Africa?

Where activities of the state itself are concerned, there is certainly reason to believe that the Convention does envisage extraterritorial effect, so that, for example, the duty under Article 6(b) concerning deliberate damage to important nesting sites of listed species might be understood to require abstention from the funding of development projects, such as the building of dams, in other countries where this would involve the destruction or degradation of such sites.[127] Indeed, in 1983 the UK's Nature Conservancy Council wrote to the Department of the Environment,[128] the government agency then responsible for implementing the Convention, specifically to confirm this point.

There must, however, be some limits to this approach. It seems unlikely, for example, that the general obligation under Article 2 regarding the maintenance of wildlife populations at appropriate levels can be interpreted in such a way as to have extraterritorial effect, since that would effectively constitute the parties as guardians of all wildlife everywhere, regardless of any connection with Europe. While such an interpretation would seem to go far beyond the Convention's object and purpose, some difficult problems of applicability do arise from the way in which the listing process has been implemented.

[125] Report of the 1st Meeting, para. 8.1.5.3. States are, of course, customarily invested with jurisdiction over events occurring on ships flying their flag, and certain duties are also thereby entailed (note, e.g., the CMS definition of the term 'range states', discussed in Chapter 16 below), but the reference to 'no-man's-land' is arguably more significant in terms of its potential for expanding the scope of Bern Convention commitments through the exercise of purely *personal* jurisdiction.

[126] Section 3(1) of the Bill Relating to the Convention on the Conservation of European Wildlife and Natural Habitats, passed by the German Bundestag in 1983, prohibited, 'in areas which do not form part of the territory of any sovereign State', the taking from the wild of any specimen of Appendix I or II-listed species, especially from German-registered ships or aircraft.

[127] Unless the project could be justified as an exception under Article 9.

[128] This letter, dated 21 September 1983, was written by Dr Peter Gay (head, NCC Scientific Services Division), to Keith Dow (Wildlife Division, DoE).

c) *Species covered by the Appendices*

Naturally, the species which are listed individually under the Convention's Appendices are those which spend at least some part of their life cycle in Europe, and the Amendment Guidelines now state specifically that parties should exclude species not native to Europe from their proposals.[129] Some of the apparently incongruous original Appendix II listings – notably the leopard (*Panthera pardus*) and the tiger (*P. tigris*) – are probably explained by the fact that the range of the leopard, though primarily non-European, does skirt Asia Minor, while a few Caspian tigers (*P. tigris virgata*) may also have been thought to survive in Turkey. Listing of the leopard may, moreover, now assume real practical significance for African parties,[130] while the extraterritorial aspect of every party's obligations will be applicable to these species wherever they are found.

Given this extraterritorial dimension, however, additional problems of interpretation arise from the inclusion within the Appendices of certain higher taxonomic categories, such as the family Ursidae (bears) or the order Falconiformes, which embraces five distinct families of raptors. Is it the case that the parties' obligations extend to *all* bear and raptor species, including those, such as the South American spectacled bear (*Tremarctos ornatus*) or the Mauritius kestrel (*Falco punctatus*), that have no connection with Europe whatsoever? Although this might seem to follow literally from the wording of the text, it does appear to be an absurd result in the light of (i) the title of the Convention, (ii) its objectives as illuminated by the *Explanatory Report* and (iii) the policy evident in the Amendment Guidelines. It is one thing to extend the Convention's protection to species within those higher categories that migrate through Europe, or even to the non-European populations of sedentary species also found in that continent, but quite another to interpret it as applying to species *none* of whose members naturally occur in the parties' territories at *any* stage of their life cycle. These are better regarded as being beyond the scope of the Convention entirely.[131]

[129] See Recommendation 56 (1997).

[130] See, e.g., Doc T-PVS (96) 60 and the Report of the 16th Meeting, para. 5.5 (regarding Burkina Faso).

[131] This conclusion is not undermined by the attention paid to the fate of the bald ibis (brought within the Appendices through the listing of the family Threskiornithidae) since, although this species no longer occurs naturally in Europe, it certainly did so historically and, moreover, reintroduction programmes are already under way. See section 4(a)(iii) above.

7. Institutional arrangements

Other chapters have shown that the relative ineffectiveness of earlier regional conventions was partly attributable to the absence of suitable institutional arrangements for their implementation. This is a lesson which had clearly been learned by the time the Bern Convention was concluded, and the arrangements established have avoided any risk of it becoming a 'sleeping treaty'. They differ from those adopted under most other modern conservation treaties in drawing to some extent upon existing institutions – those of the Council of Europe – but also involve the creation of certain new bodies specifically for the purposes of the Convention. In that particular respect, the Bern Convention most closely resembles the World Heritage Convention.[132]

a) The Standing Committee

The key treaty body is the Standing Committee, established under Article 13(1). Each party has the right to be represented on this Committee,[133] which must meet at least every two years and whenever a majority of the parties so request.[134] In practice it has tended to meet annually, towards the end of the year, at Council of Europe headquarters in Strasbourg. The attendance of a majority of contracting parties is required to constitute a quorum for Standing Committee meetings,[135] which are conducted in accordance with Rules of Procedure adopted pursuant to Article 13(6).[136] Only parties are entitled to vote,[137] but various entities may be represented by observers.[138] These include any Council of Europe member state which is not party to the Convention, while non-member states may be invited to attend by unanimous decision of the Committee itself. Provision is also made for the participation of certain bodies or agencies qualified in the protection, conservation or management of wild fauna and flora and their habitats; these may be national or international, governmental or non-governmental, though national NGOs must first be approved for this purpose by the state in which they are located. Any

[132] See Chapter 14 below. [133] Article 13(2). [134] Article 13(4). [135] Article 13(5).

[136] For the current (recently amended) version, see the Report of the 29th Meeting, Appendix 10.

[137] Article 13(2), which also permits the EU, within its areas of competence, to vote in place of its member states with a number of votes equal to those which are parties to the Convention.

[138] Article 13(3).

such entity wishing to attend must inform the Secretary-General of the Council of Europe at least three months before the meeting, and will be admitted unless one-third of the parties have registered objections within a period of two months. The most recent meeting, held during November 2009 in Bern to celebrate the Convention's thirtieth anniversary,[139] was attended by thirty-six state parties, the European Commission, the Holy See, Secretariat representatives from seven other conservation agreements and around a dozen NGOs.[140]

Article 14(1) confers upon the Standing Committee a general responsibility for monitoring the application of the Convention, which entails consideration of the need for amendments, especially of the Appendices, and making any other proposal for improving its effectiveness, including the conclusion of agreements with non-party states aimed at enhancing species conservation. In addition, it may formulate recommendations to the parties concerning measures to be taken for the purposes of the Convention, to the Committee of Ministers concerning invitations to accede and, generally, for keeping the public informed of activities undertaken within the framework of the Convention. In practice, its agenda is currently organised around four principal areas of business. These are (i) the monitoring and implementation of legal aspects (including the adoption of amendments, the consideration of party reports, and the adoption of substantive recommendations involving legal issues); (ii) the scientific segment, concerning monitoring of species and habitats generally, the adoption of action plans for particular taxa, the establishment of ecological networks, and the consideration of expert recommendations on technical aspects; (iii) the monitoring of specific sites and populations, which centres around application of the Convention's innovative 'files' procedure; and (iv) strategic development, involving relationships with other organisations, the need for major institutional changes and the programming of activities under the Convention.

The broad powers given to the Standing Committee, and the central role accorded to it with regard to implementation, inevitably mean that much of the Convention's substantive potential rests in its hands, and it is encouraging to report that it has from the outset adopted an extremely active and generally progressive approach towards its responsibilities.

139 Note in that regard the celebratory statements appended to the Report of the 29th Meeting.

140 Ibid., Appendix 1.

The compliance procedures it has devised, which are considered below,[141] are of particular interest.

b) The Bureau

The Bureau is not mentioned in the text of the Convention, but was established in 1990 in order to enhance continuity between meetings of the Standing Committee, convening twice a year to organise its business.[142] It therefore serves a similar function to the Standing Committees established under treaties such as the Ramsar and Bonn Conventions, where the plenary body is known as the Conference of the Parties. The Bureau's membership has recently been expanded to comprise the chair, vice-chair and previous chair of the Standing Committee,[143] and two additional members.[144] The Secretariat is also in attendance.

c) The Secretary-General of the Council of Europe

The Bern Convention makes no express provision for a Secretariat, but the Secretary-General of the Council of Europe has been authorised by the Council's Committee of Ministers to perform all conventional secretariat functions,[145] with any expenditure incurred to be met out of the general funds of the organisation. While this element of relief from institutional expense might seem advantageous to the Convention's functioning, obviously everything depends upon the generosity with which the Council views this particular aspect of its operations in the light of its numerous other commitments. In the event, repeated restructuring within the Council's administration in recent years has produced significant ebbs and flows in the budgetary allocation for Secretariat activities, with one substantial augmentation of funding later offset by further cutbacks,[146] and budgetary growth set at zero for 2009.[147] Bern Convention activities have accordingly remained heavily reliant upon

[141] See section 8(b)(iii), (iv) below.
[142] For reports of recent meetings, see Docs. T-PVS (2009) 7, 12.
[143] See Doc. T-PVS (2009) 5 rev.
[144] Or a third additional member where the previous chair is unavailable.
[145] These services are provided by the Council's Directorate of Culture and of Cultural and Natural Heritage.
[146] See, e.g., the Reports of the 20th Meeting, para. 3.1; 25th Meeting, para. 6.1; 26th Meeting, para. 2.
[147] Report of the 28th Meeting, para. 2.

voluntary contributions from the parties, though fortunately the record here has been reasonably encouraging.[148]

d) The Committee of Ministers

The Committee of Ministers of the Council of Europe, which played an important role in the conclusion of the Bern Convention, retains unusual authority in two respects. First, the power to invite non-member states to accede is reserved to it (albeit after consultation with the parties), and second – in view of the political and financial implications – amendment of the Convention's institutional provisions or final clauses (i.e. Articles 12–24) require its approval in addition to acceptance by the parties themselves.[149] Furthermore, the Committee maintains an overall supervisory role through its receipt of reports from the Standing Committee regarding the operation of the Convention.[150] In February 1993, the Committee of Ministers took note of a formal Declaration from the Standing Committee – the first of its kind – that a violation of the Convention had occurred, specifically through the Greek government's failure to secure adequate protection for the breeding sites of marine turtles at Laganas Bay, Zakynthos, and decided to draw this problem to the attention of all Council of Europe governments.[151]

e) Groups of experts

Article 14(2) provides that the Standing Committee may, on its own initiative, arrange for meetings of groups of experts to assist it in the performance of its functions – a power which it has utilised extensively. Thus specialist groups have been established to address conservation issues concerning various plant and animal plant taxa, as well as the legal aspects of the introduction and reintroduction of wildlife species, and the creation of the Emerald Network. Groups whose work is currently at the forefront of attention include those concerned with invasive alien species, island biodiversity and climate-change implications. These entities operate on the basis of terms of reference established by the Standing Committee.[152] They have been instrumental in the organisation of

[148] Details are included as Appendices to the reports of Standing Committee meetings.
[149] See respectively Articles 19(1) and 20(1), and 16, especially para. 2(b).
[150] See Article 15. [151] See section 8(b)(iv) below.
[152] For an example, see the terms of reference of the Group of Experts on Bird Conservation, Report of the 17th Meeting, Appendix 14.

numerous seminars on topics within their respective spheres of interest and in the preparation of various recommendations and action plans which have subsequently been adopted by the Committee. In addition, individual consultants have frequently been engaged either to assist in the work of the expert groups, or to perform additional functions arising out of the conservation activities generated under the Convention.

In the light of recurrent concerns over financing, institutional arrangements and relationships with other treaties and programmes, it was decided at the 19th Meeting to establish a Select Group on Strategic Development of the Convention in order to identify priorities and review its operations and procedures generally.[153] One significant proposal to emerge from this review, envisaging the creation of a single Scientific Committee to advise the Standing Committee on technical matters on its agenda, was ultimately not pursued, however.[154] This decision reflected general satisfaction with the contribution of expert groups, and it was decided to maintain their activities, albeit with a keener eye to the outsourcing of technical activities where appropriate, increased collaboration with other programmes and agencies and any other adaptations that might prove necessary.

f) Non-governmental organisations

As noted above, provision is made in Article 13(3) for the participation of NGOs at Standing Committee meetings, and typically between ten and twenty such organisations are likely to be in attendance. These customarily include not only the major global players, such as IUCN, WWF and BirdLife International, but a variety of national nature conservation organisations[155] and national or international special-interest groups.[156] The reference to bodies 'qualified in the protection, conservation or management' of wildlife is deemed sufficiently wide to embrace those whose principal focus is not upon conservation per se, but on the hunting or other exploitation of animals[157] or, conversely, animal welfare.[158] It is therefore not to be

[153] See Report, Agenda Item 7. [154] See the Report of the 21st Meeting, para. 6.1.

[155] The Cyprus Conservation Foundation, the French National Society for Nature Protection (SNPN) and Pro Natura (Switzerland) are amongst the most regular participants in this category.

[156] Regular attenders include Planta Europa, the Societas Europaea Herpetologica (SEH) and the Mediterranean Association to Save the Sea Turtles (MEDASSET).

[157] The Federation of Associations for Hunting and Conservation of the EU (FACE) and the International Association for Falconry and Conservation of Birds of Prey are notable examples.

[158] Eurogroup for Animal Welfare has been the most regular participant of this description.

expected that these groups will necessarily speak with one voice on issues arising under the Convention. Equally, their interest in Standing Committee discussions may well be restricted to particular agenda items.

NGOs have unquestionably made a substantial contribution to the implementation of the Convention, with respect to both the development of policy and the monitoring of compliance. As to the former, BirdLife International was primarily responsible for the elaboration of various action plans for avian species,[159] many of which have subsequently been endorsed by the Standing Committee, while Planta Europa has taken a leading role in the formulation of the European Plant Conservation Strategy, the Bern Convention's own Group of Experts having met on occasions within the framework of its conferences.[160] As to compliance, there are numerous applications of the 'files' procedure which have been initiated by communications from NGOs, with groups such as MEDASSET predictably prominent in pursuing cases involving the breeding sites of marine turtles.[161]

8. Implementation

The Bern Convention has developed a number of mechanisms for implementation of its commitments, including some which display novel and interesting features. As expected, these involve a range of activities at both national and international levels.[162]

a) Implementation at the national level

Inevitably, much of the detailed, practical work of implementation is achieved through national institutions, procedures and measures. These are complemented by reporting obligations, which provide the link to international mechanisms of supervision.

i) Legislative and administrative measures

As noted above,[163] Article 3 calls for the adoption of national conservation policies, and the integration of conservation into planning and

[159] See Heredia, Rose and Painter, *supra* n. 18.

[160] See, e.g., the Report of the 21st Meeting, Agenda Item 4.3.

[161] See, e.g., Docs. T-PVS (98) 43; T-PVS (99) 69, 70 and n. 203 *infra*.

[162] On implementation generally, see S. Jen, 'The Convention on the Conservation of European Wildlife and Natural Habitats (Bern, 1979): Procedures of Application in Practice' (1999) 2 *JIWLP* 224.

[163] See section 2(b).

development programmes. Furthermore, the parties are to promote education and disseminate information on the importance of conservation. In addition, the key substantive provisions of the Convention, Articles 4–7, all require that parties take 'appropriate and necessary legislative and administrative measures' for their implementation, while Article 2 refers to the adoption of 'requisite measures' for the maintenance of wildlife populations. Article 12 confirms that these measures may be stricter than the Convention itself requires. The importance of national implementation was underlined in Recommendation 76 (1999), which commended ratification of the 1998 Aarhus Convention on Access to Information, Public Participation in Decision-Making and Access to Justice in Environmental Matters,[164] as well as stressing the importance of the courts in the enforcement of conservation laws, and the role of NGOs and the public generally in the initiation of legal proceedings.[165] This followed the convening of a workshop on the significance of national case law in 1999.[166]

Naturally, the parties to this Convention are likely to have achieved a relatively high degree of harmonisation of their approaches to wildlife protection through the common membership of many of them in the European Union, and the close integration of the two regimes. Greater divergence is likely to be apparent in non-EU states, however, with the long list of reservations formulated by Turkey, for example, indicating the much narrower ambit of species protection in that country.

ii) National reports

It has become the norm in modern conservation treaties to arrange for the regular submission of reports by the parties on the steps they have taken to fulfil their commitments. The only specific requirement of this kind under the Bern Convention, however, relates to the exceptions procedure under Article 9. By virtue of paragraph 2 of that article, parties must report to the Standing Committee every two years on their use of this power. The reports in question must incorporate specific details, including the populations which have been the subject of exceptions and,

164 (1999) 38 *ILM* 517.

165 Disappointingly, neither of the two major Council of Europe conventions in this field, the 1993 Convention on Civil Liability for Damage resulting from Activities Dangerous to the Environment, *ETS* 150, and the 1998 Convention on the Protection of the Environment through Criminal Law, *ETS* 172, has actually entered into force.

166 See the Report of the 19th Meeting, para. 4.2. For the report of the workshop itself, see Doc. T-PVS (99) 34.

where possible, the numbers of specimens involved, the means authorised for killing or capture, the circumstances of time and place, the national authority with responsibility for overseeing these activities and any controls imposed. A model form for the presentation of such data has been devised.[167] If utilised appropriately, this system offers the opportunity for an extremely rigorous form of monitoring, but in the early years it proved rather too demanding for the parties' taste, and reports frequently failed to materialise on time or, indeed, at all. The Standing Committee therefore resolved in 1993 to lessen the burden by agreeing that reports need cover only general exceptions,[168] and individual exceptions if they (i) were so numerous as to result in a generalised practice, (ii) involved more than ten individuals of a species or (iii) concerned endangered or vulnerable populations. Problems in securing the timely submission of these reports have, nevertheless, persisted, and the chair of the Standing Committee has on occasion felt the need to remind the parties that this represents a formal legal requirement of participation in the Convention.[169]

Although the Convention itself imposes no other reporting requirements, the evolving practice of the Standing Committee has generated various expectations in that regard. The UK, for example, was requested to report back in relation to its programme of badger culling to control bovine tuberculosis,[170] while Recommendation 79 (1999) urged parties with declining hamster populations to submit annual reports for a period of five years on the results of their conservation efforts. There have been numerous other instances of this kind.[171] More generally, the Standing Committee is required by Article 15 to forward a report on *its* work to the Committee of Ministers of the Council of Europe after each meeting, and in 1992 it was agreed that this process would be facilitated by the preparation of general reports by the parties themselves on steps they have taken to implement the Convention. It is accordingly expected that they will submit such reports on a four-yearly basis,[172] though,

167 For the current version, see Doc. T-PVS/Inf (2005) 8.

168 Resolution No. 2 (1993).

169 See, e.g., the Reports of the 16th and 19th Meetings, paras. 4.2 and 4.3 respectively. It seems that, for the most part, they are now submitted eventually: for the recent record, see Doc. T-PVS/Inf (2009) 18.

170 See Recommendation 69 (1998) and, for the latest response, Doc. T-PVS/Inf (2008) 10.

171 See, e.g., the various reports concerning implementation of recommendations regarding invasive alien species in Doc. T-PVS/Inf (2009) 5. A further sixteen reports on ongoing, country-specific issues were prepared by governments for this meeting.

172 Guidelines for their presentation were adopted in 1993. See Report of the 13th Meeting, Appendix 12. For the current version, see Doc. T-PVS/Inf (2005) 9.

predictably, submission rates for these reports have been even worse than for those required under Article 9(2).[173] Given the current lack of Secretariat resources to process and analyse this material, it is now customary for it simply to note that it has received certain reports 'prepared on a voluntary basis'.[174] Their significance, however, has in any event arguably been diminished by the establishment of alternative mechanisms, such as the demand for comprehensive introductory reports from new parties,[175] the occasional commissioning of expert reports on national implementation, prepared in collaboration with national authorities,[176] and the institution of highly innovative, 'inquisitorial' procedures at the international level. It is to this question that we should now turn.

b) Implementation at the international level

Implementation of the Convention at the international level is manifest in a variety of different forms.

i) International co-operation

The necessity of addressing the transboundary aspects of environmental problems is now well understood, while the elaboration of conservation policy generally is sure to benefit from the sharing of experience and the development of awareness regarding best practice. Article 11(1)(a) accordingly requires the parties to co-operate, whenever appropriate, in implementing the Convention, particularly where this would enhance the effectiveness of measures adopted.[177] In some cases, such co-operation has been cemented by formal agreements, as in the case of the Wadden Sea. A more recent example is the arrangement establishing a cross-border protected area in the Danube Delta, concluded in 2000 by Moldova, Romania and Ukraine as a consequence of the Bystroe estuary crisis.[178] In addition, Article 11(1)(b) requires the encouragement and

[173] For the recent record, see Doc. T-PVS/Inf (2009) 19.
[174] See, e.g., the Report of the 29th Meeting, para. 3.3.
[175] For a recent example, see Doc. T-PVS/Inf (2009) 23 (Bosnia and Herzegovina).
[176] Note, e.g., the recent reports on implementation of the Convention in Spain, Doc. T-PVS (2006) 7; Morocco, Doc. T-PVS/Inf (2007) 8; and Slovenia, Doc. T-PVS/Inf (2009) 14.
[177] For examples, see section 4(a)(ii) above.
[178] A Declaration on Co-operation for the Creation of a Lower Danube Green Corridor, involving Bulgaria also, was signed on the same day. Unfortunately, the tripartite agreement did not enter into force until 2006, and then only subject to a controversial declaration by Ukraine regarding procedures for modifying the boundaries of the

co-ordination of research related to the purposes of the Convention. In fact, such research has been generated through various mechanisms, including the activities of expert groups and specialist NGOs, as well as by the dissemination of research findings by individual governments.

ii) Dispute settlement

Article 18(1) requires the Standing Committee to use its best endeavours to facilitate a friendly settlement of any difficulty to which the execution of the Convention may give rise. If an amicable solution is not forthcoming, Article 18(2) provides that any party to the dispute may request that it be submitted to arbitration. Each party is then to designate an arbitrator, who jointly select a third.[179] The decision of the tribunal is taken by majority vote and is final and binding.[180]

Of course, such provisions are commonly encountered in treaties generally, but rarely relied on in practice. In this instance, the possibility of collective institution of such proceedings against Greece over its failure to protect turtle breeding sites was actively canvassed in 1998, though ultimately a different solution was adopted.[181] It is clear that, of the various means available for securing the Convention's implementation, litigation will only ever be contemplated as absolutely the last resort.

iii) Monitoring through the Standing Committee

The role of the Standing Committee is accordingly critical, its powers with regard to implementation having already been noted. Its schedule of annual meetings has helped to maintain considerable momentum in this respect, with the thirteenth, held in December 1993, arguably being pivotal in terms of noteworthy developments.[182] Apart from periodic amendment of the Appendices, the Committee has adopted several key resolutions and declarations, together with almost 150 recommendations on particular aspects of implementation. These have variously concerned

protected area. For information on agreements affecting the Danube Delta generally, see www.ddbra.ro/en/international-relations.php.

179 Interestingly, the President of the European Court of Human Rights is accorded a role in resolving any impasse that may arise in this process (Article 18(2)). Article 18(3) makes special provision for the situation where one of the parties is an EU member.

180 Article 18(4).

181 See subsection (iv) below.

182 These included several significant amendments to the Appendices, various measures concerning recovery plans for particular species, elaboration of the 'files' procedure, guidelines for the contents of general reports on implementation of the Convention, and principles governing the interpretation of Articles 8 and 9.

the interpretation of key provisions of the Convention, the formulation of guidance on the scientific and practical aspects of conservation policy, the encouragement of individual parties to address particular conservation problems and the means by which they might do so. Specific instances of such measures are highlighted throughout this chapter. The Committee also provides the forum for reporting arrangements under the Convention, though, as indicated above, these have been marginalised somewhat through the elaboration of other mechanisms, most notably the 'files' procedure.

iv) The 'files' procedure

A striking feature of the Bern Convention is that, from the earliest stages, attention has been devoted not merely to the formulation of general policy guidance, but to concrete conservation problems at particular sites or localities. Indeed, even before the Convention was formally in force, an Interim Committee established to pave the way for the permanent institutions was urging Austria to take action to protect *Artemisia laciniata* (an endangered plant of the wormwood family) at its last remaining natural western European habitat near Lake Neusiedl. This encouragement bore fruit when the Committee was informed that 'the competent authorities have undertaken to ensure its strict protection in an integrated nature reserve'.[183] The Standing Committee itself has viewed its responsibilities in a similar light, its two very first recommendations in 1982 being requests to Italy to take measures to safeguard the Gran Sasso, home to numerous listed species, and to ensure respect for its obligations under the Convention in the light of a proposal to reopen hunting in the Valle Furlana.[184]

Over time, pressure grew for formalisation of the procedures in accordance with which problems at particular sites were considered, with NGOs especially anxious to ensure provision for follow-up action with respect to Committee recommendations. Following extensive discussions,[185] a procedure for the *Opening and Closing of Files and Follow-up to Recommendations* was agreed at the 13th Meeting,[186] though on a provisional basis only at the request of the EC Commission, which foresaw problems regarding its application to EC member states. The convening of a group of experts in 1995 failed to resolve these difficulties,

[183] Report of the Fourth Meeting of the Interim Committee of the Convention on the Conservation of European Wildlife and Natural Habitats, Doc. T-VS (81) 9, paras. 35–8.
[184] Recommendations 1 and 2 (1982). [185] See the Report of the 13th Meeting, para. 4.4.
[186] Ibid., Appendix 4. For discussion, see Jen, *supra* n. 162.

but it was nevertheless decided at the 15th Meeting simply to continue applying the procedure on a provisional basis.[187] It was essentially confirmed in 2008, and supplemented by a new form for online submission of complaints.[188]

The procedure may be initiated by the submission of a complaint to the Standing Committee, its chair or the Secretariat alleging failure by any party to comply with its obligations under the Convention. Such complaints may emanate either from another contracting party or from an individual, group of private persons or non-governmental organisation, though anonymous applications will not be entertained. The Secretariat, having acquired additional information if necessary, informs both the Bureau and the party in question of the complaint and decides whether it is sufficiently serious to merit international attention, taking account of any other procedures that may already be pending at the national or international level. If it is so satisfied, it formally transmits the complaint to the party concerned for its response, which is expected 'within a period of about four months'.

In the light of the reply, the Secretariat decides in consultation with the Bureau whether there are grounds for referring the matter to the Standing Committee. In cases of urgency, the Bureau may arrange an onsite assessment to expedite a solution, though this, of course, requires the consent of the party in question. Once on the Committee's agenda, the complaint will be presented by the Secretariat, or even – with the consent of the chair or of a party – by an observer, along with proposals for the acquisition of further information, the holding of an on-the-spot enquiry,[189] or the immediate adoption of a specific recommendation. Proposals by observers may, however, only be voted upon if sponsored by one of the parties. The Standing Committee then decides whether it is appropriate to open a file and, if so, what precise course of action is to be followed.[190] Any recommendations made are communicated to the parties and are considered public documents. Thereafter, files remain open until the Committee is satisfied that the problem has been resolved. This is decided on the basis of a report prepared either by an expert after an on-the-spot enquiry, or by the party itself as part of the follow-up to a specific recommendation.

[187] See the Report of the 15th Meeting, para. 4.1.

[188] See the Report of the 28th Meeting, para. 5.5, and Doc. T-PVS (2008) 7.

[189] For the rules applicable to such enquiries, see the Appendix to the Rules of Procedure.

[190] All decisions under this procedure are taken by consensus or, failing that, by a two-thirds majority of votes cast.

This procedure represents an unusually direct, focused and transparent form of response to allegations of failure by states to comply with international conservation obligations. About a hundred cases have been thought sufficiently substantial to merit Standing Committee attention to date, with files definitively opened in over thirty.[191] Long-running examples[192] concern the Akamas peninsula in Cyprus, where a tourist development is planned in an area supporting many rare plant and animal species, including marine turtles; Kresna Gorge in Bulgaria, where it is proposed to expand a motorway crossing an area of high biological diversity; and the Bystroe estuary project, discussed above.[193] In all three instances, NGOs have expressed scepticism regarding the professed willingness of the governments in question to modify their projects so as to comply with previous Standing Committee recommendations:[194] significantly, while the adoption of measures to address the problems has in each case been noted, the file has nonetheless been kept open. Other files currently open include those concerning conservation of the common hamster in Alsace, eradication of the grey squirrel in Italy and the planned construction of wind farms on the Bulgarian Black Sea coast, on one of Europe's principal bird migration routes.[195] All three cases have already been addressed by Standing Committee recommendations, both general and specific.[196]

The most notorious application of the 'files' procedure to date, however, has concerned the failure of the Greek government to afford adequate protection to the nesting sites of marine turtles on beaches at Laganas Bay, Zakynthos.[197] This site, with its well-preserved dune system and seagrass formations, was once considered the most important breeding area for the

[191] See generally Doc. T-PVS (2008) 7, Annex II. Some situations are maintained on the agenda as 'possible files' pending a definitive determination (e.g., in 2009, the development of windfarms in the Smola archipelago, Norway) or in 'stand-by' mode, pending the outcome of national response measures (e.g. conservation of tortoises and toads in various regions of France and Sweden).

[192] Many files have eventually been closed. For a summary of current cases, see Doc. T-PVS (2009) 6 rev .

[193] See sections 4(a)(ii) and 8(b)(ii).

[194] See respectively Recommendations 63 (1997), 98 (2002) and 111 (2004).

[195] For the latest developments in all the cases discussed above, see the Report of the 29th Meeting, para. 6.1. It seems that the Kresna Gorge file is to be closed following a decision to reroute the road, though a further report has been requested.

[196] See respectively Recommendations 68 (1998), 79 (1999) and 136 (2008); 78 (1999), 114 (2005) and 123 (2007); 117 (2005) and 130 (2007).

[197] For detailed information regarding this case, see the Memorandum prepared by the Secretariat for the 18th Meeting of the Standing Committee, and the Report by the organisation MEDASSET, Docs T-PVS (98) 43 and 48 respectively.

loggerhead turtle (*Caretta caretta*) in the entire Mediterranean, but the rapid development of tourism during the 1960s and 1970s triggered a significant deterioration in its beaches as suitable habitat for egg-laying. The issue first appeared on the Committee's agenda in 1986, following which an on-the-spot visit prompted a number of urgent recommendations at the 6th Meeting,[198] including the closure of vehicular access to beaches; removal of prefabricated buildings; prohibition of deck-chairs, sunshades and pedalos; reorientation of existing lighting; demarcation and public acquisition of currently undeveloped areas of land; reassessment of the potential impact of further development; and appraisal of the Bay's suitability for strict protection as a marine or nature park.

Repeated efforts over the next few years to cajole Greece into fulfilling these responsibilities were largely unsuccessful, and in 1992 the Standing Committee formally notified the Committee of Ministers that a violation of the Convention had occurred[199] – the first occasion on which such a step had been taken. A change of government in Greece produced indications of a more amenable attitude, but little sign of real improvements on the ground. Considering that the credibility of the Convention was at stake, the Standing Committee adopted a formal decision in 1995 urging full implementation of the provisions of Recommendation 9 (1987), with specific attention to the demolition of illegal buildings and the creation, within three years, of a marine national park. Furthermore, it declared that any failure by Greece to comply with the specified conditions would be considered 'a grave and continuing breach of its obligations under the Convention' and an encouragement to activate the Article 18(2) arbitration procedure.[200] Although plans were adopted, and EU funding obtained, for the establishment of a marine park and designation of the site for the Natura 2000 network, the reality remained that local people were effectively frustrating the enforcement of the relevant legislation. Finally, in 1999, the Committee concluded that it could do no more, and the file was closed, with a declaration that Greece had failed to comply with the conditions set in 1995.[201]

[198] See Recommendations 7 (1987), on the protection of marine turtles generally, and 9 (1987), concerning specifically *Caretta caretta* in Laganas Bay, Zakynthos.

[199] Declaration of 4 December 1992 concerning Laganas Bay, Zakynthos.

[200] See the Report of the 14th Meeting, Appendix 9.

[201] For the text of the decision, and the debate which led to it, see the Report of the 19th Meeting, Appendix 11 and para. 6.1 respectively. For an earlier draft decision to institute arbitration proceedings, see the Report of the 18th Meeting, Appendix 3, and for the ultimate decision not to proceed with it, ibid., para. 6.1.

Although this may seem tantamount to capitulation, it was at that stage actually more akin to a change of tactics and forum. Thus in March 2000 the EC Commission instituted proceedings before the European Court of Justice complaining of the Greek government's failure, contrary to the EC Treaty and Article 12 of the 1992 Habitats Directive, to establish an effective system of strict protection for the sea turtle *Caretta caretta*. In a brief judgment in January 2002, the Court's 6th Chamber duly found Greece to be in violation of its obligations and ordered it to pay the costs of the hearing.[202] In 2007, however, in the light of measures taken by the Greek government in the interim to implement properly a 1999 Presidential Decree establishing a National Marine Park, the Commission decided not to pursue the case further, despite press and NGO reports suggesting that considerable problems remain to be resolved at the site.[203]

9. Relationship with other agreements

The Bern Convention contains no formal provision governing its relationship with other agreements. It has, however, inevitably come to be seen in part as a mechanism for regional implementation of the Biodiversity Convention, as evidenced by the 1994 Monaco Declaration on the Role of the Bern Convention in the Implementation of Worldwide International Instruments for the Protection of Biodiversity.[204] This instrument called in particular for the formulation of a strategy for long-term development of the Convention in the light of global conservation trends and requirements. The Declaration was endorsed, though not entirely without misgivings, at the 14th Meeting of the Standing Committee in March 1995.[205] Subsequently, Resolution No. 7 (2000) emphasised the importance of co-ordination with other conservation regimes, leading to the establishment of Strategic Development as a key element of the regular agenda.[206] A Memorandum of Co-operation with the CBD was formally signed in 2001,[207] ushering in an era of more intensive co-ordination of activities:

[202] *Commission v Hellenic Republic* (2002) *ECR* I-01147.

[203] See, e.g., the regular reports compiled by MEDASSET, the latest of which (dated December 2009 and viewable via its website at www.medasset.org), suggests that the number of nests recorded in 2009 (829) was the lowest in twenty-five years.

[204] For the text, see the Report of the 14th Meeting, Appendix 4.

[205] Ibid., para. 3.1.

[206] See the Report of the 21st Meeting, Agenda, Part V.

[207] Ibid., para. 6.1. A revised partnership agreement was signed in May 2008.

the role of CBD strategies on plant conservation and exotic species in shaping the Bern Convention's own approach represent conspicuous examples.[208] Later declarations have reaffirmed the Standing Committee's commitment to the policies laid down in the global instruments.[209] Noting that the Johannesburg Summit's goal of achieving significant reductions in the rate of biodiversity loss by the year 2010 is now unlikely to be achieved, the recent Bern Declaration identifies climate change and invasive alien species as pre-eminent threats, and reiterates the urgent need to secure the more effective integration of biodiversity considerations into decision-making processes generally.

As regards other major conservation treaties, the intention of the drafters of the Bern Convention not to trespass into the realm regulated by CITES has already been noted.[210] A degree of overlap with the activities of other agreements is inevitable, however, and numerous instances of interaction with the Ramsar Wetlands Convention, UNEP Regional Seas Agreements, the Bonn Migratory Species Convention (CMS) and its ancillary arrangements – especially AEWA, EUROBATS, ACCOBAMS, ASCOBANS – can be found in the records of Standing Committee meetings.[211] In 2004, for example, recommendations adopted in relation to wind turbines and power lines specifically endorsed the measures already approved within the CMS system.[212] The secretariats of these various agreements regularly attend each other's meetings in order to ensure more effective co-ordination of their activities, and a formal Memorandum of Co-operation with the CMS Secretariat was signed in 2009.[213]

Most recently, Recommendation 143 (2009) underlines the need for co-operation with the UN Framework Convention on Climate Change, especially with regard to its programmes on impacts, vulnerability and adaptation.[214]

Although the Bern Convention is not a 'framework' agreement as such, it includes various provisions calling for co-operation between its

[208] See sections 2(b), 5(b) above.

[209] See the 2004 Strasbourg Declaration on the Role of the Bern Convention in the Preservation of Biological Diversity, Report of the 24th Meeting, Appendix 8; 2009 Bern Declaration, *supra* n. 23.

[210] See section 4(b)(i) above.

[211] For examples noted in this chapter, see sections 4(a)(ii), 5(b), 8(b)(i) and 8(b)(iv).

[212] Recommendations 109, 110 (2004). [213] Doc. T-PVS (2009) 3.

[214] For earlier Standing Committee measures regarding climate change, see Recommendations 122 (2006) and 135 (2008). See further Chapter 21 below.

parties in the conservation field,[215] and these arrangements have sometimes been enshrined in treaty form, whether concluded under the aegis of the Council of Europe or independently. Agreements relating to the Wadden Sea and the Danube Delta have already been noted, while other examples include the mountain range conventions covering the Alps and the Carpathians.[216] Other treaties concluded within the Council of Europe system may also impinge upon matters covered by the Bern Convention. Foremost amongst these is the 2000 European Landscape Convention,[217] which requires the parties to recognise landscapes (including both natural and man-made elements) as an essential component of people's surroundings and a foundation of their identity, and to establish policies aimed at their protection, management and planned development through a series of specified measures.[218] Treaties of potential relevance in a procedural sense include the 1980 Outline Convention on Transfrontier Co-operation between Territorial Communities or Authorities,[219] and those concerning the legal aspects of environmental protection.[220] Finally, the pervasive relevance of and interaction with European Union law must be noted, examples of which have been encountered throughout this chapter.

10. Conclusions

The Bern Convention has undeniably proved to be of considerable value. It imposes strictly worded conservation obligations upon its contracting governments for the benefit of hundreds of species of both plants and animals, while also giving due emphasis to the protection of habitat – the paramount factor in wildlife conservation. Its Standing Committee has generated a vast quantity of policy guidance, fostered the development and dissemination of technical expertise and helped to halt or mitigate environmentally damaging projects in numerous places. To that end, it

215 See Articles 1, 4(4), 10(1). Note also Article 14(1), which authorises the Standing Committee to propose the conclusion of agreements with non-party states concerning species conservation.

216 For discussion, see Chapter 18 below and, more generally, T. Treves, L. Pineschi and A. Fodella (eds.), *Sustainable Development of Mountain Areas* (Giuffre, 2004).

217 *CETS* 176, in force 1 March 2004; thirty parties to date, plus six signatories.

218 The notion of landscape protection was foreshadowed, and its link with conservation confirmed, by the 1982 Benelux Convention on Nature Conservation and Landscape Protection, 2 *SMTE* 163.

219 *ETS* 106, in force 22 December 1981; thirty-six parties to date, plus three signatories.

220 But see n. 165 *supra*.

has established an array of mechanisms which have already contributed greatly to the process of implementation, and promise more for the future. In particular, they offer the opportunity for specialist NGOs or ordinary members of the public to call governments to account in respect of conservation problems arising all the way from the Arctic Circle to North West Africa and the shores of the Caspian Sea.

On the other hand, there is little cause for complacency. The Laganas Bay case demonstrates that there is ample scope for governments to procrastinate, and ultimately even defy the full weight of European opinion on critical conservation questions, whether through lack of genuine commitment to the cause or for fear of incurring the wrath of vociferous local communities. There is still insufficient indication of modern conservation thinking having penetrated the further reaches of European governmental decision-making processes, with the result that damaging and ill-considered projects are frequently well under way before environmental considerations begin to intrude. Although impact-assessment procedures are now reasonably well established, they are all too commonly token affairs. And all this in a region where wildlife has already suffered the devastation wrought by decades of urban and industrial expansion. The Bern Convention accordingly still has much work to do.

Recommended further reading

Council of Europe, 'The 25 Years of the Bern Convention' (2004) 101 *Naturopa*

Explanatory Report Concerning the Convention on the Conservation of European Wildlife and Natural Habitats (Council of Europe, 1979)

S. Jen, 'The Convention on the Conservation of European Wildlife and Natural Habitats (Bern, 1979): Procedures of Application in Practice' (1999) 2 *JIWLP* 224

C. Lasén Diaz, 'The Bern Convention: A Tool for Implementing International Biodiversity Obligations in Europe' *MEA Bulletin Guest Article 43 (IISD,* 2008)

Chapter 11

Polar regions

1. Introduction

Both the Arctic and Antarctic polar regions are subject to regional rules for, inter alia, the protection of species and of habitat.[1] While special rules exist for other regions, as for example explored in the other chapters in Part III of this book, the polar regions are different by virtue of 'their size compared to other regions, the unique problems they face, the interest of the whole international community in their management and resource potential, and the means that have been adopted to deal with management problems'.[2] Additionally, while other areas may be more severely affected by climate change,[3] its impact on polar bear habitat, and the consequences for sea-level rise of the melting of 'permanent' Antarctic ice shelves, have had catalytic effect upon perceptions of this global problem. The polar regions are considered key to our general understanding of climate change.[4] In 2009, the first ever (largely symbolic) Joint Ministerial Meeting of the Antarctic Treaty/Arctic Council took place in Washington on 6 April 2009 on the occasion of the conclusion of the fourth International Polar Year (2007–8) and the fiftieth anniversary of the Antarctic Treaty.[5]

Yet there are also significant differences between them. Geographically, the Arctic comprises an ocean surrounded by

[1] The focus of this chapter is regional regulation of the Arctic and Antarctic, though it is recognised that a number of the multilateral agreements considered elsewhere in this volume are also applicable and references will be made as appropriate.

[2] D. Rothwell, *The Polar Regions and the Development of International Law* (Cambridge University Press, 1996), p. xiii.

[3] See general discussion of climate change impacts on wildlife in Chapter 21 below.

[4] See O. Anisimov et al., 'Polar Regions (Arctic and Antarctic)', in M. Parry et al. (eds.), *Climate Change 2007: Impacts, Adaptation and Vulnerability. Contribution of Working Group II to the Fourth Assessment Report of the Intergovernmental Panel on Climate Change* (Cambridge University Press, 2000).

[5] For text of the Washington Ministerial Declaration on the International Polar Year and Polar Science see www.state.gov/g/oes/rls/other/2009/121340.htm.

continental land masses, while the Antarctic is a continent surrounded by ocean. Arctic peoples have inhabited the northern polar region for thousands of years, while Antarctica has no permanent population save for scientists. Regulation of the Antarctic has emerged against a backdrop of contested claims to the Antarctic continent, which, by virtue of Article IV of the 1959 Antarctic Treaty, are 'frozen' to permit scientific co-operation and other activities to take place in the Antarctic. There is now in place a complex structure of interlinking treaty instruments and measures for Antarctic governance, including for species and habitat conservation. In addition to the 1959 Antarctic Treaty (AT), the Antarctic Treaty System (ATS) comprises the 1972 Convention on the Conservation of Antarctic Seals (CCAS), the 1980 Convention for the Conservation of Antarctic Marine Living Resources (CCAMLR), the 1991 Environmental Protocol to the Antarctic Treaty (EP), and the measures in effect under these instruments.[6] In addition, and subject to the 'freezing' effect of Article IV AT noted above, a wide range of other international agreements are of application within the Antarctic region, including the 1982 LOSC, a number of IMO and fisheries agreements, and biodiversity conservation instruments such as the CBD.

In contrast, the Arctic indisputably falls within the jurisdiction of certain states,[7] and protection of wildlife and habitat is principally through their national laws. Increasingly, however, there is regional co-operation amongst Arctic states, though thus far only through non-binding instruments. However, while no binding Arctic treaty exists, this is not to say that the region exists in an international legal vacuum. There are treaties which apply to particular species found wholly or partly in the Arctic region, most notably polar bears[8] and fur seals.[9] Certain highly migratory species spend part of their life cycle in the

[6] A further potential element of the ATS, the 1988 Convention for the Regulation of Antarctic Mineral Resource Activities, is not likely to enter into force, and a fifty-year moratorium on mining activities is contained in the 1991 EP.

[7] Canada, Denmark, Norway, the United States, Russia (the five Arctic Ocean littoral states) and Finland, Iceland, and Sweden. Though of limited relevance in the living-resources context, it should be noted that the geographic limits of this jurisdiction are still undefined to the extent that submissions regarding the outer limits of the continental shelf are under consideration by LOSC's Commission on the Outer Limits of the Continental Shelf.

[8] The 1973 Agreement on the Conservation of Polar Bears, considered further below.

[9] The 1957 Interim Convention on the Conservation of North Pacific Fur Seals (now lapsed, and considered only briefly below).

Arctic, requiring the extension of their conservatory agreements to this region.[10] Additionally, a number of maritime conventions apply to the Arctic Ocean, including the 1982 LOSC to which all Arctic states save the United States are party, and a number of fisheries agreements.[11] A flavour of the scope and extent of the general international treaties of application to the Arctic region is found in the national presentations made at the 2009 meeting of the Arctic Council.[12]

The purpose of this chapter is to consider the regulation of wildlife in the Arctic and Antarctic regions.[13] Each regional section below briefly sets out the wildlife and ecosystem significance of the region, followed by examination of the key instruments, binding and non-binding, of pertinence for wildlife regulation there.

2. The Arctic region

a) Background

There is no single geographic definition of the Arctic area, which comprises the northern territory of the Arctic states and the Arctic Ocean. In consequence, the inter-governmental Arctic Council relies on national definitions by the eight Arctic states.[14] Moreover, whilst capable of precise definition in astronomical and latitudinal terms, 'in biological terms, the Arctic circle is merely an abstraction', with the Arctic 'intimately linked with the rest of the world' through circulation of ocean water and air masses, and through the life cycle of migratory species (such as the Arctic tern, *Terna paradisaea*, which makes the largest-known seasonal migration, from pole to pole).[15]

[10] For example, the 1995 Agreement on the Conservation of Eurasian-Migratory Water Birds covers part of the Arctic, in addition to the whole of Europe, Africa and Arabia. See further Chapter 7 above.

[11] See further Chapter 5 above.

[12] Available at arctic-council.org. See also Part 4 of 1991 Arctic Environmental Protection Strategy, 'International Mechanisms for the Protection of the Arctic Environment', also available at arctic-council.org.

[13] In so doing it subsumes under the polar regions umbrella the separate discussion of polar bears and seals, and of Antarctic marine living resources, contained in Chapters 3 and 9 of the first edition of this work.

[14] Thus, for example, Iceland includes the entire island within its definition of Arctic, while Norway has no standard definition. See Annex A, 'Definition of Arctic', of the 2009 Arctic Oil and Gas Guidelines prepared by the Arctic Council's Working Group on Protection of the Arctic Marine Environment, available at arctic-council.org.

[15] CAFF et al., *Arctic Flora and Fauna: Status and Conservation* (Edita, 2001), pp. 11 and 14; see also L. J. Murray, 'Physical/Geographic Characteristics of the Arctic', in *AMAP Assessment Report: Arctic Pollution Issues* (AMAP, 1998).

The Arctic region also comprises a wide range of major biomes including middle boreal forest; forest, mountain and lowland tundra; arctic desert; and glaciers. The dominant feature of the Arctic Ocean is sea ice, with permanent pack ice in the Arctic Basin and seasonal fluctuations on the periphery. The ice edge is a critical habitat of many species, while for marine mammals sea ice provides vital protection from predators and resting or breeding areas. Although not as species-diverse as other regions – it has, for example, a high of 12 per cent of global lichen species but only 0.3 per cent of insect species and >0.1 per cent of reptile species[16] – the Arctic 'contains many species not found elsewhere, and many habitats and ecological processes and adaptations that are unique'.[17] Threats to Arctic biodiversity are various, including species introduction (e.g. the Nootka lupine in Iceland), overexploitation (e.g. of capelin in the Barents Sea, leading in the 1980s to collapse of predatory populations of seals and seabirds), pollution (e.g. high levels of PCBs have been found in polar bears), physical disturbance (e.g. oil and gas installations and their accompanying infrastructure such as roads affecting the tundra habitat of large mammals in Alaska and Siberia) and, increasingly, tourism. The impacts of global environmental issues such as ozone depletion and climate change are significant for the Arctic region, with the latter considered the greatest threat to the Arctic environment as it exists today. There are 'observed changes in species abundance and distribution, and to permafrost and to sea ice' impacting on species and habitat already precariously situated in a difficult environment.[18] The pressures on Arctic wildlife and habitat are such that forty-three mammal species and subspecies, sixteen bird species, twelve fish species and seventy-three plant species are found on the IUCN's Red List of Threatened Species 2009. Of these, a number are listed as critically endangered (bowhead whale stocks in Russia, Greenland and Norway, and the snow crane and Vinogradov's lemming in Russia) or endangered (Siberian sturgeon in Russia, shortspine thornyhead in Russia and Canada, and *Polystichum aleuticum* in the US).

[16] *Arctic Flora and Fauna, supra* n. 15, p. 48.

[17] And willows, sawflies and sandpipers are found in greater diversity in the Arctic region than anywhere else. *Arctic Flora and Fauna, supra* n. 15, p. 45.

[18] Ibid. p. 255; see also the 2004 Arctic Climate Impact Assessment; and Global Resource Information Database (GRID-Arendal), *Global Outlook for Ice & Snow* 9 (UNEP, 2007).

b) *Species-specific regulation in the Arctic*

There is only one agreement which relates exclusively to a species in the Arctic region, the 1973 Agreement on the Conservation of Polar Bears. For convenience, however, North Pacific fur seals are also addressed here since their range includes Arctic waters, and historically the states most concerned with their regulation include polar states.

i) Seals

Sealing is one of the oldest forms of commercial exploitation of wildlife,[19] dating back to at least the late eighteenth century and reaching its peak around 1890. In 1891, Great Britain (on behalf of Canada) and the United States concluded the first bilateral sealing treaty, designed to limit exploitation of overharvested North Pacific fur seals. It lasted less than a year and was followed by a number of other bilateral arrangements. Multilateral regulation occurred only later, and as a direct result of the outcome in the 1893 *Behring Sea Fur Seal* arbitration between the United States and Great Britain (on behalf of Canada).[20] This resource dispute arose in consequence of the depletion of Alaskan seal stocks and the United States' attempt to protect its investment (an exclusive license to harvest seals had been awarded to an Alaskan company) against unrestrained high-seas harvesting by Canadian sealers. While the Tribunal rejected the United States' innovative claim to be acting as trustees 'for the benefit of mankind' in the management of seal stocks and upheld the high-seas freedom to fish,[21] the regulations adopted in the award anticipated techniques for the conservation of shared natural resources used in later instruments – and their frailties. Thus, for example, though sealing was banned in a sixty-mile zone created around the Pribilov Islands and seasonally in a further buffer zone, this applied only to British and American sealing vessels (some of which reflagged under foreign flags to avoid the ban) and sealers were in any event able to pursue the seals on the high seas beyond the zone.[22]

[19] For in-depth analysis see Chapter 3 of the first edition of this work.

[20] (1893) 1 *Moore's International Arbitration Awards* 755. For discussion see P. Sands, *Principles of International Environmental Law* (Cambridge University Press, 2nd ed., 2003), pp. 561–5; and V. Lowe, *International Law* (Oxford University Press, 2007), pp. 235–9.

[21] *Behring Sea Fur Seal* arbitration, *supra* n. 20.

[22] Lowe, *supra* n. 20, p. 236.

The response to these problems of enforcement is also familiar in the contemporary context, namely to seek agreement with all states whose nationals are engaged in harvesting in the area, and to employ mechanisms such as import restrictions and certification requirements to compel compliance. This was the approach of the 1911 Convention for the Prevention and Protection of Fur Seals,[23] one of the first multilateral agreements addressed to the regulation of a living resource. The four states with nationals active in sealing – the US, Great Britain (for Canada), Japan and Russia – became parties to the Convention which, inter alia, permitted the import by contracting states of only certified seal skins, with certification dependent on 'taking' in accordance with the Convention. As Lowe has observed, the peculiarity of the seal trade, with virtually all commercial processing of seal skins then taking place in London, gave this provision a potent edge.[24]

The 1911 Convention lapsed after 1940 with the withdrawal of Japan but was subsequently replaced by the 1957 Interim Convention on North Pacific Fur Seals.[25] This established a North Pacific Fur Seals Commission for the regulation of harvesting and co-ordination of scientific research. Article VI contained innovative enforcement provisions which permitted the seizure of a vessel of another state party where there was reasonable cause to believe that prohibited pelagic sealing was taking place on the high seas of the North Pacific region, though only the flag state had jurisdiction to bring proceedings and to impose any penalties in connection with breach of the Convention. The Interim Convention was amended several times and remained in force until 1984 when, owing to US opposition to sealing which prevented ratification of a protocol renewing the Convention, it lapsed and has not been replaced. Today, seals in the polar region are protected by a combination of national laws and multilateral treaty instruments such as CITES.[26] In the Antarctic region, in contrast, the 1972 Convention on the Conservation of Antarctic Seals (CCAS) considered below remains in force (though no commercial sealing is taking place).

ii) Polar bears

In 1965 the five circumpolar states[27] in which polar bears (*Ursus maritimus*) are found met to discuss the future of the species, whose

[23] 104 *BFSP* 175. By 1940 the Pribilov seal stock had grown to over 2 million animals from a low of around 125,000 in 1911. Lowe, *supra* n. 20, p. 237.

[24] Lowe, *supra* n. 20, p. 238. [25] 314 *UNTS* 105.

[26] Conservation of seals is also found in other regional seas agreements considered in Chapter 5 above.

[27] Canada, Denmark (including Greenland), Norway, the USA and the USSR. The USSR has been succeeded by Russia as one of five polar bear range states party to the ACPB.

numbers (to the extent then known) were dwindling owing to increased harvesting, warming of the Arctic and the expansion of human activities.[28] A draft text was prepared by the IUCN and adopted by the five states in 1973 as the Agreement on the Conservation of Polar Bears (ACPB).[29] The three key objectives of the ACPB are to encourage co-operative research programmes,[30] to restrict the killing and capture of polar bears[31] and prohibit certain hunting methods,[32] and to protect the ecosystem of which polar bears are a part. In this last respect the provisions of Article II are quite progressive for the time, albeit qualified by the reference merely to 'appropriate action':

> Each Contracting Party shall take appropriate action to protect the ecosystems of which polar bears are a part, with special attention to habitat components such as denning and feeding sites and migration patterns, and shall manage polar bear populations in accordance with sound conservation practices based on the best available scientific data.

Trade in polar bears or any part or product thereof taken in violation of the ACPB is prohibited.[33] In any event, apart from the trade and certain commercial restrictions contained in the ACPB itself, all five polar bear range States are also party to CITES, which lists polar bear on Appendix II (export of bears or their parts and products must be limited to a level which is not detrimental to the survival of the species).[34]

Until 2009 the contracting states had met only once, at a 'Consultative Meeting' in Oslo in 1981, where it was decided, inter alia, that the ACPB would be of indefinite duration.[35] The impetus for the 2009 meeting

[28] See the statement of the USSR quoted in the first edition of this work, p. 55.

[29] 13 *ILM* 13, in force 26 May 1976, although it took until 25 January 1978 before all five polar bear range states had ratified. For background see T. S. Larsen and I. Stirling, *The Agreement on the Conservation of Polar Bears: Its History and Future* (Norsk Polarinstitutt rapportserie, No. 127, 2009).

[30] Article VII.

[31] Article I(1) prohibits the 'taking' of polar bears except in accordance with Article III, and defines 'taking' to include hunting, killing and capturing (Article I(2)). Article III permits 'taking' where carried out, inter alia, for bona fide scientific research and/or conservation purposes, the prevention of serious disturbance of the management of other living resources, or by local people using traditional methods and exercising legally recognised traditional rights. Use of skins for commercial purposes in certain such instances is restricted (Article III(2)).

[32] Unless inconsistent with domestic law, the taking of polar bears using aircraft and 'large motorized vehicles' is prohibited (Article IV).

[33] Article V. [34] See further Chapter 15 below.

[35] Proposals by Norway to expand the scope of the ACPB to Arctic marine mammals and birds, and wider Arctic conservation, were resisted. Larsen and Stirling, *supra* n. 29.

came from a 2007 polar bear range state conference which, conscious of the acute threat posed to polar bear habitat by, inter alia, increased global warming, resolved upon biennial meetings.[36] By this time several of the twenty or so discrete polar bear populations of the Arctic were known to be declining, while for others population trends are simply not known.[37] The purpose of the 2009 meeting was to provide an update on the conservation status of the polar bears, review implementation of the ACPB, identify useful polar bear conservation strategies, and discuss mechanisms for enhanced implementation of the ACPB.[38] In particular, it was recognised that 'adaptive management in response to climate change' is needed, with the 'primary adaptation strategy' of reducing other stresses on polar bears and their ecosystems caused by habitat destruction, harvesting, pollution and anthropogenic disturbance.[39]

In 2000, a US/Russia Bilateral Agreement for Conservation and Management of the Alaska/Chukotka Polar Bear Population was concluded, which is linked with the ACPB through its enforcement provisions. Designed to facilitate long-term conservation of the Chukchi/Bering polar bear population through the development of a conservation programme to be implemented and enforced by both states, the agreement permits sustainable indigenous subsistence hunting so long as programmes for monitoring harvesting and for enforcement are in place and consistent with the ACPB. Advance harvest quota systems based on sustainable yield are to be established. A striking feature of the Agreement is the prominent role of the key indigenous groups concerned in its conclusion, implementation and enforcement. It has been suggested that it might form the basis for co-operative management of other shared stocks in the Arctic, such as the Pacific walrus.[40]

[36] See the (non-binding) 'Outcome of Meeting', Meeting of the 1973 Agreement on the Conservation of Polar Bears, 17–19 March 2009, Tromsø, Norway, p. 1, available at www.polarbearmeeting.org. The next meetings are provisionally scheduled for 2011 (Canada) and 2013 (Russia).

[37] Larsen and Stirling, *supra* n. 29, p. 5. They also note potential conflict between traditional ecological knowledge (TEK) and scientific assessments of polar bear populations, with Nunavut unilaterally raising harvesting yield in response to the former (ibid., p. 16). The Tromsø Declaration on the occasion of the Sixth Ministerial Meeting of the Arctic Council, 29 April 2009, available at arctic-council.org, merely acknowledges the role both science and TEK play in the conservation of Arctic flora and fauna.

[38] For text of the ACPB and Final Act, and records of the 1981 and 2009 meetings, see www.polarbearmeeting.org. The site also includes 'reports' from five range states: Canada, Norway, Denmark (Greenland), Russia and the US. The 2009 'outcome of meeting' document is expressly stated to be non-binding.

[39] Ibid., Final Act, p. 2. [40] *Arctic Flora and Fauna*, *supra* n. 15, p. 108.

c) *Arctic environmental co-operation*

Since 1989, at the initiative of Finland, the eight Arctic states have increased co-operation to combat threats to the Arctic ecosystem which cannot effectively be addressed individually. The 1991 Arctic Environmental Protection Strategy (AEPS) is a non-binding instrument designed 'to ensure the protection of the Arctic environment and its sustainable and equitable development, while protecting the cultures of indigenous peoples'.[41] The objectives of the AEPS pertinent to wildlife include protection of the Arctic ecosystem; protection, enhancement and restoration of environmental quality and sustainable utilisation of natural resources; reviewing the state of the Arctic environment; and eliminating pollution.[42] It addresses, inter alia, the protection of the marine environment and the conservation of flora and fauna.

The institutional mechanism for co-ordinating AEPS activities and programmes is the Arctic Council,[43] a high-level inter-governmental forum established in 1996. In addition to Arctic states, there are on the Council six permanent participants representing indigenous peoples (including the Inuit Circumpolar Conference and the Saami Conference), and there is observer participation by non-Arctic states (France, Germany, Poland, Spain, the Netherlands and the UK), international organisations (such as the IUCN, NAMMCO, UNEP, the UNDP and the UNECE) and international and regional NGOs (such as WWF and the Circumpolar Conservation Union). To date there have been six Ministerial Meetings of the Arctic Council, most recently in April 2009 in Norway.[44]

There are now six working groups of the Arctic Council, on Protection of the Arctic Marine Environment (PAME); Arctic Monitoring and Assessment (AMAP); Conservation of Arctic Flora and Fauna (CAFF); Emergency Prevention, Preparedness and Response (EPPR); Sustainable

41 Arctic Environmental Protection Strategy, Declaration on the Protection of the Arctic Environment (Rovaniemi, Finland, June 1991), available at arctic-council.org. See generally D. Rothwell, 'The Arctic Environmental Protection Strategy and International Environmental Co-operation in the Far North' (1995) 6 *YBIEL* 65, and Rothwell, 'International Law and the Protection of the Arctic Environment' (1995) 44 *ICLQ* 280.

42 Para. 2.1.

43 Declaration on the Establishment of the Arctic Council (Ottawa, 19 September 1996), available at (1996) 35 *ILM* 1382. See arctic-council.org.

44 The seventh Ministerial meeting is scheduled for 2011 in Denmark. Each meeting has produced a Declaration; see arctic-council.org for texts. Norway, in co-operation with Denmark and Sweden, is hosting an Arctic Council Secretariat from 2007 to 2013.

Development (SDWG); and the Arctic Contaminants Action Program (ACAP). Each group has a work plan[45] and a number of working groups.[46] Of particular relevance is the work of CAFF for the conservation of Arctic biodiversity. Research and monitoring are key activities, reflected in the Circumpolar Biodiversity Monitoring Program, and it has expert groups on Arctic Flora and Seabirds, respectively, with the former also serving as the IUCN Plant Specialist Group.

Key techniques for Arctic biodiversity conservation are the protection of species[47] and habitat. With respect to the latter, in 1996 a Circumpolar Protected Areas Network (CPAN) under CAFF's Strategy and Action Plan for a Circumpolar Protected Areas Network was established to promote habitat conservation in protected areas and to represent the full range of Arctic biodiversity. The network component is particularly important for conservation of migratory species.Over 405 sites, including Ramsar sites, exist across the polar region, though progress across ecosystems and habitat has been patchy.[48] A 2001 report found 27 per cent of Arctic desert and glacier protected, but only 1.7 per cent of the marine environment.[49] Further measures are planned in concert with the International Biodiversity Year 2010: an Arctic biodiversity assessment, the Arctic Highlights Report 2010, as the Arctic Council's immediate contribution, and a full Biodiversity Assessment to follow in 2013.[50]

d) Conclusion

Significant co-operation has taken place for environmental protection in the Arctic. While initially there was a heavy emphasis on combating pollution, including its deleterious effects on habitat, there has been increasing emphasis on species and habitat conservation as reflected in the protected areas network and the work of CAFF. Yet to date only one binding instrument addressed exclusively to Arctic wildlife exists, the 1973 ACPB, with

45 For example, CAFF is presently functioning within its 2009–11 work plan, available at arctic-council.org.

46 For an overview of their work and future work plans, see Senior Arctic Official (SAO) Report to Ministers, Tromsø, Norway, April 2009, available at arctic-council.org.

47 For example, the International Murre (Guillemot) Conservation Strategy and Action Plan.

48 There are presently forty-four Ramsar sites, six MAB sites, and three world heritage sites designated within the Arctic.

49 *Arctic Flora and Fauna*, *supra* n. 15, p. 78.

50 See the 2009 Tromsø Declaration of the Arctic Council, *supra* n. 37; and SAO Report 2009, *supra* n. 46, p. 31.

Norwegian attempts in the 1980s to expand this instrument for wider Arctic conservation unsuccessful. Indeed, while an 'Arctic Treaty' modelled in part on the Antarctic Treaty has been discussed in the literature,[51] there appears little political appetite for such amongst Arctic states today – not even on the part of Norway.[52] The 2009 Tromsø Arctic Council Ministerial Declaration merely decides 'to further consider how the Arctic Council should best be structured to fulfil its objectives'. In any event, as the Declaration also acknowledges, the solution to the most pressing problem for Arctic wildlife and habitat – climate change – is beyond the polar states alone to address.

3. The Antarctic Treaty System

a) Background

Geographically Antarctica comprises the land continent, its ice shelves, a number of sub-Antarctic islands and the ocean up to the 'Antarctic Convergence'. Situated at approximately fifty degrees south latitude, the Convergence is a biological boundary that marks the change in temperature and salinity of the surface waters of the Southern Ocean where warmer northern waters meet colder southern waters, producing a zone of high biological productivity. Krill, a key component of the Antarctic ecosystem, is only present within the Antarctic convergence. This biologically determined boundary comprises the area of application of the 1980 Convention on the Conservation of Antarctic Marine Living Resources (CCAMLR), while the AT applies to the more rigid geographic boundary south of sixty degrees south latitude.[53]

The Antarctic environment and its associated and dependent ecosystems form a distinctive component of biodiversity.[54] Although there is some dispute as to the number of plant and animal species endemic to the Antarctic region, hundreds of native species of flora and fauna have been identified.[55] But there is a stark contrast between land and

[51] See, for example, M. Watson, 'An Arctic Treaty: A Solution to the International Dispute over the Polar Region' (2008–9) 14 *Ocean & Coastal LJ* 307.

[52] See, for example, the opening remarks of the Norwegian minister for foreign affairs at the (first) joint meeting of the Antarctic Treaty/Arctic Council, *supra* n. 5.

[53] R. Baird, 'Fishing and the Southern Ocean: The Development of Fisheries and the Role of CCAMLR in their Management' (1997) 16(2) *UTLR* 160, p. 168.

[54] See, generally, C. Redgwell, 'The Protection of the Antarctic Environment and the Ecosystem Approach', in M. Bowman and C. Redgwell (eds.), *International Law and the Conservation of Biological Diversity* (Kluwer, 1995), Chapter 6.

[55] See IUCN, *A Strategy for Antarctic Conservation* (IUCN, 1991), pp. 13–14, Tables 2 and 3.

sea, with a relative paucity of terrestrial life compared with the richness of the Antarctic marine ecosystem: there are no trees on the Antarctic continent, no indigenous land vertebrates, and only two flowering plant species.[56] On the other hand, the apparent richness of the marine environment is deceptive since this relates to high individual species populations rather than to species diversity, which is relatively low when compared with low and mid-latitude areas.[57] With only three trophic levels, the Antarctic food chain is very short – for example plant plankton, krill and baleen whales – and has particular consequences for the implementation of an ecosystem approach to conservation, discussed below. Antarctica's natural environment and dependent ecosystems also afford 'unique opportunities as a reference against which to assess the impacts of pollutants on global ecosystems and processes in the atmosphere, on land and at sea elsewhere in the world'.[58]

There are two sources of law within the Antarctic Treaty System of relevance for wildlife conservation and environmental protection. First, there is the umbrella 1957 Antarctic Treaty (AT). Article IX of the AT provides for measures to be recommended for adoption by governments by the Antarctic Treaty Consultative Parties (ATCPs) at Consultative Meetings.[59] Consultative parties are entitled to participate at the biennial (which, from 1991, became annual) Antarctic Treaty Consultative Meetings (ATCMs), at which, since 1983, non-Consultative Parties (NCPs) are observers. Since 2001 these meetings have been supported by a permanent secretariat based in Buenos Aires. ATCPs comprise the original signatories to the Antarctic Treaty and those parties to the AT which have demonstrated their 'interest in Antarctica by conducting substantial research activity there, such as the establishment of a scientific station or the despatch of a scientific expedition'.[60] One of the most significant early measures under the AT was the 1964 Agreed Measures

[56] C. Joyner, *Antarctica and the Law of the Sea* (Martinus Nijhoff, 1992), pp. 13–14.

[57] See R. Tucker Scully, 'The Marine Living Resources of the Southern Ocean' (1978) 33 *UMLRev* 341, p. 344; G. Billen and C. Lancelot, 'The Functioning of the Antarctic Marine Ecosystem: A Fragile Equilibrium', in J. Verhoeven, P. Sands and M. Bruce (eds.), *The Antarctic Environment and International Law* (Martinus Nijhoff, 1992), p. 49; and Joyner, *supra* n. 56, Chapters 1 and 5.

[58] IUCN, *supra* n. 55, p. 21, para. 55.

[59] On the legal status of these measures see A. Watts, *International Law and the Antarctic Treaty System* (Grotius Publications, 1992), p. 24.

[60] Article IX.2 AT. With the entry into force of the 1991 Environmental Protocol, an additional requirement for consultative status is ratification, acceptance approval or accession to the Protocol (Article 22 EP).

for the Conservation of Antarctic Fauna and Flora (Recommendations III–VIII). Their purpose was 'to promote, and achieve, the objectives of protection, scientific study, and rational use of [Antarctic] fauna and flora'. Although no reference is made to 'ecosystem' as such, the 1964 Agreed Measures refer to maintenance of the balance of ecological systems and the variety of species in designated specially protected areas (SPAs). The concept of a specially protected area was introduced in the 1964 Agreed Measures in order to preserve the unique natural ecological system of areas of outstanding scientific interest.[61]

The second source of law within the ATS, as indicated above, is the separate conventions interlinked with the AT, namely 1972 CCAS (in force since 1978), 1980 CCAMLR (in force since 1985) and the 1991 EP (in force since 1998).[62] These last two are of particular importance, CCAMLR because of its ecosystem approach and the relative abundance of Antarctic marine flora and fauna, and the EP because of its comprehensive approach to protection of the Antarctic environment. Together, CCAMLR and the EP comprehensively cover the marine and terrestrial ecosystems of Antarctica, including its dependent and associated ecosystems.[63]

b) CCAS

Of the six species of seal found in the Antarctic, only two have been commercially exploited. Indeed, CCAS was concluded before a sealing industry emerged in Antarctica but in the awareness that Antarctic seals then represented 'by far the world's largest unexploited mammal stock'.[64] It applies to the same geographic area as the AT, though parties must also report on seal catches made on ice floes north of the ATS by ships flying their flag.[65] The Convention adopts a traditional approach to

61 See further discussion in Redgwell, *supra* n. 54, pp. 114–16.

62 CCAS and CCAMLR are also open to non-AT parties. Thus the EC is a party to CCAMLR, though not the AT (which does not provide for participation by regional economic-integration organisations).

63 See C. Redgwell, 'Protection of Ecosystems under International Law: Lessons from Antarctica', in A. E. Boyle and D. Freestone (eds.), *International Law and Sustainable Development: Past Achievements and Future Challenges* (Oxford University Press, 1999), pp. 208–9.

64 J. Heap, 'Has CCAMLR Worked? Management Policies and Ecological Needs', in A. Jorgensen-Dahl and W. Ostreng (eds.), *The Antarctic Treaty System in World Politics* (Macmillan, 1991), p. 46.

65 Article 5(7).

jurisdiction, with each party required to adopt for its nationals and vessels 'such laws, regulations and other measures, including a permit system as appropriate, as may be necessary to implement the Convention'.[66] Conservative harvesting quotas, even for relatively abundant species, are set forth in the Annex to CCAS.[67]

Unlike CCAMLR, CCAS does not adopt an ecosystem approach, though the preamble refers to the parties' desire 'to promote and achieve the objectives of protection, scientific study and rational use of Antarctic seals and to maintaining a satisfactory balance within the ecological system'. Instead, CCAS adopts what Heap refers to as a 'traffic lights' approach.[68] The green light constitutes harvesting in accordance with quotas set pursuant to the Annex. The amber light is triggered by any party requesting a meeting where the Scientific Committee for Antarctic Research (SCAR)[69] has reported that harvesting is having a significant harmful effect on total stocks or on the ecological system of any particular locality.[70] The red light is signalled where permissible catches are likely to be exceeded, with harvesting to cease until the parties decide otherwise.[71] In essence this places the burden on the harvesting state(s) to demonstrate that sealing may be resumed. In practice, however, commercial sealing has not taken place and the precautionary stoplights approach of CCAS has not been tested, nor have the institutions provided for (a Commission and a Scientific Advisory Committee) been established. The chief importance of CCAS is its inherently precautionary approach, and the backdrop it afforded for the negotiation of CCAMLR.

c) CCAMLR

i) Background

Negotiations to conclude the Convention began in the 1970s as a response to Japanese and Soviet fishing for krill, which is the foundation

[66] Article 2(2).

[67] See D. Overholt, 'Environmental Protection in Antarctica: Past, Present and Future' (1990) 28 *CYIL* 227, p. 238.

[68] Heap, *supra* n. 64.

[69] SCAR is a non-governmental organisation that provides independent scientific advice.

[70] Article 6(3); there is also provision in Article 6 for a meeting of the parties to consider, inter alia, 'further regulatory measures, including moratoria'. See further Heap, *supra* n. 64.

[71] Redgwell, *supra* n. 54, p. 116–17.

of the Antarctic ecosystem.[72] The dependence on krill of other marine species in the Southern Ocean dictated from the outset a multiple- rather than the single-species approach to resource management characteristic of other living-resource management regimes.[73] Increased fishing activity in the Southern Ocean was a response to the exclusion of many distant-water fishing nations from traditional fishing grounds in consequence of the extension of fisheries jurisdiction to 200 nautical miles as the new concept of the EEZ emerged from LOSC and passed rapidly into customary law. International agreement on Antarctic marine resources governance was necessary because the proclamation of an EEZ, and the assertion of national measures of protection in it, would potentially conflict with both Article IV (freezing of territorial claims) and Article IV AT (preserving existing high-seas freedoms in the Southern Ocean).[74] The swiftness of the legislative response ensured that CCAMLR was concluded before a major Antarctic fishery had emerged; thus CCAMLR (like CCAS) is one of the few international treaties concerned with wildlife conservation to be concluded prior to heavy commercial pressure on the species it was designed to protect. Both the circumstances of its conclusion and the substantive principles adopted ensure that CCAMLR evidences a general precautionary approach to the conservation of marine living resources. It has also influenced other developments, such as the precautionary methodology of the CBD[75] and the ecosystem approach more fully developed in the FAO's 1998 Code of Conduct for Responsible Fisheries and 2003 Ecosystem Approach to Fisheries.[76]

ii) Substantive and geographic scope

The Convention applies to 'Antarctic marine living resources', which are defined in Article I(2) as 'populations of fin fish, molluscs, crustaceans and all other species of living organisms, including birds, found south of the Antarctic convergence'. This encompasses all marine living resources except

[72] See D. L. Alverson, 'Tug-of-War for the Antarctic Krill' (1980) 8 *ODIL* 171; R. F. Frank, 'The Convention on the Conservation of Antarctic Marine Living Resources' (1983–4) 13 *ODIL* 316; and M. Howard, 'The Convention on the Conservation of Antarctic Marine Living Resources: A Five-Year Review' (1989) 38 *ICLQ* 104, p. 111.

[73] L. Cordonnery, 'Environmental Protection in Antarctica: Drawing Lessons from the CCAMLR for the Implementation of the Madrid Protocol' (1998) 29 *ODIL* 125, p. 126.

[74] See further Joyner, *supra* n. 56.

[75] Report of the Executive Secretary, Conservation and Sustainable Use of Marine and Coastal Biological Diversity, UNEP/CBD/SBSTTA/3/4, 12 May 1997, para. 39.

[76] *Report of the CCAMLR Performance Review Panel* (CCAMLR, 2008), p. 32.

seals and whales, which are covered separately by CCAS and the Whaling Convention. The rights and obligations of CCAMLR contracting parties under these other Conventions are expressly preserved by Article VI.

In some cases the CCAMLR area is superimposed over areas where undisputed sovereignty over islands has been claimed and where an EEZ (or EFZ) may be proclaimed, such as for France's Kerguelen and Crozet Islands and the Antarctic and sub-Antarctic islands of Australia, the UK and South Africa.[77] A chairman's statement is annexed to the Final Act of the Conference exempting the waters adjacent to these islands from the Convention and all other 'waters adjacent to the islands within the area to which this Convention applies over which the existence of State sovereignty is recognized by all the Contracting Parties'.[78] It is further provided that these marine areas will be subject to the conservation measures to be established by the CCAMLR Commission by consensus, including the agreement of the sovereign state concerned – in essence, national management subject to an overlay of international management. Thus, for example, the Australian Fisheries Management Authority observes CCAMLR conservation measures in developing fisheries policy for the EEZs of Heard, McDonald and Macquarie Islands located within the Convergence.[79] The efficacy of CCAMLR conservation measures may be enhanced within these zones where national powers of enforcement can be utilised to enforce CCAMLR conservation measures. Indeed, it was recently observed that maritime enforcement action in the CCAMLR area is largely a product of French and Australian enforcement action in the EEZs surrounding their Antarctic island territories[80] – but with the consequence that this may simply be displacing IUU fishing to adjacent CCAMLR waters.[81]

[77] Joyner, *supra* n. 56, p. 88.

[78] On the legal effect of this statement, see D. Vignes, 'Protection of the Antarctic Marine Fauna and Flora: The Canberra Convention of 20 May 1980 and the Commission Set up by It', in F. Francioni and T. Scovazzi (eds.), *International Law for Antarctica* (Giuffre, 2nd ed., 1996), p. 162; and N. Bankes, 'Environmental Protection in Antarctica: A Comment on the Convention on the Conservation of Antarctic Marine Living Resources' (1981) 19 *CYIL* 303, pp. 316–17.

[79] See S. Kaye and D. Rothwell, 'Australia's Antarctic Maritime Claims and Boundaries' (1995) 26(3) *ODIL* 195, pp. 208–9.

[80] See also the 2003 Treaty between the Government of Australia and the Government of the French Republic on Cooperation in the Maritime Areas Adjacent to the French Southern and Antarctic Territories [2005] *ATS* 6.

[81] D. Guilfoyle, *Shipping Interdiction and the Law of the Sea* (Cambridge University Press, 2009), pp. 141–2.

Nonetheless, this is potentially an important strengthening of the CCAMLR system, which, as discussed further below, operates a vessel observation and inspection system in the CCAMLR area[82] but enjoys no independent powers of enforcement. In addition, upward derogation from CCAMLR's measures is permissible within national zones which, when exercised, strengthens consensus-driven CCAMLR conservation measures.

iii) The CCAMLR management regime

At present the largest catch in Antarctic waters is krill, with Patagonian toothfish and Mackerel icefish significantly lower.[83] These are only some of the components of the Antarctic marine ecosystem, which CCAMLR defines as 'the complex of relationships of Antarctic marine living resources with each other and with their physical environment'.[84] The purpose of CCAMLR is the conservation of Antarctic marine living resources, with conservation defined in Article II(2) to include 'rational use' as a nod towards harvesting states and avoiding 'reference to the criticized criteria of MSY, MEY, OP etc'.[85] Any harvesting must take place in accordance with the principles of conservation set forth in Article II(3), which have been applied by the CCAMLR Commission as an integrated whole. These conservation principles represent a compromise between the maximum-sustainable-yield approach sought by harvesting states and the conservation standard sought by non-harvesting states, with the result embodied in Article II, for which 'there is no unambiguous interpretation'.[86] Nonetheless, what is clear is that with its broader ecosystem approach, Article II adopts a more advanced conservation strategy than the maximum sustainable yield of earlier living-resource agreements. These conservation principles are to:

> (a) prevent decrease in size of any harvested population to levels below those which ensure stable recruitment; for this purpose, its size

[82] But within national maritime zones only with the consent of the state exercising sovereignty; see, for example, statements by South Africa and France, Report of the Fourteenth Meeting of the CCAMLR Commission 1995, p. 25.

[83] For the most recent report of annual catch statistics in the CCAMLR Conservation Area, see CCAMLR (2009) 21 *Statistical Bulletin*, produced by the CCAMLR Secretariat in Hobart, Tasmania, and available at www.ccamlr.org (covering the period 1999–2008).

[84] Article I.

[85] P. W. Birnie, A. E. Boyle and C. J. Redgwell, *International Law and the Environment* (Oxford University Press, 3rd ed., 2009), p. 592.

[86] M. Basson and J. R. Beddington, 'CCAMLR: The Practical Implications of an Eco-system Approach', in Jorgensen-Dahl and Ostreng, *supra* n. 64; Scully, *supra* n. 57, pp. 341–2.

should not be allowed to fall below a level close to that which ensures the greatest net annual increment;

(b) maintain the ecological relationship between harvested, dependent and related populations of Antarctic marine living resources and the restoration of depleted populations to the levels defined in (a) above; [(a) and (b) to be given equal priority] and

(c) prevent, or minimize risk of, changes in the marine ecosystem which are not potentially reversible over 2–3 decades, taking into account:
   (i) the state of available knowledge of the direct and indirect impact of harvesting;
   (ii) the effect of the introduction of alien species;
   (iii) the effects of associated activities on the marine ecosystem and of the effects of environmental changes with the aim of making possible the sustained conservation of Antarctic marine living resources.[87]

Over a hundred conservation measures adopted by the Commission are presently in effect.[88] This was a slow process initially, with no measures adopted until the third meeting of the CCAMLR Commission, when standard fisheries measures not dependent on an ecosystem approach were adopted.[89] It took eleven years from the entry into force of CCAMLR for precautionary catch limits for krill to be adopted.[90] Today, however, a significant number and range of conservation measures are in effect, and may be classified in four broad categories.[91] First, total allowable catch limits have been set for targeted species – namely

87 Article II(3).

88 The CCAMLR Secretariat regularly produces a summary of conservation measures in force, most recently for the 2008–9 season, available in the annual report at www.ccamlr.org. This also includes Commission resolutions, of which seventeen are presently in force on a variety of subjects ranging from climate change (30/XXVIII) and best science (31/XXVIII), to drift net fishing (7/IX) and flags of non-compliance (19/XXI).

89 This is not to say that a multispecies approach is necessary in respect of all Antarctic marine living resources; finfish management, for example, has adopted more traditional methodologies (e.g. mesh size and catch limits).

90 See further Howard, *supra* n. 72.

91 The CCAMLR summary of conservation measures similarly groups these under four headings: compliance (e.g. catch documentation scheme, notification of transhipments, and the vessel monitoring system), general fishery matters (e.g. gear regulations, data reporting, minimisation of incidental mortality and environmental protection), fishery regulations (e.g. fishing seasons, closed areas, fishing prohibitions, by-catch limits and species-specific measures) and protected areas (e.g. procedures for protecting CEMP sites, protection of the South Orkney Islands southern shelf).

toothfish, icefish, krill (precautionary catch limits) and crab – with additional controls over general fishery matters such as the timing and methods of harvesting with the use of, for example, open and close seasons and/or areas and regulation of mesh size, as provided for in Article IX(2) CCAMLR. Notice of the intention to initiate a new, or exploratory, fishery anywhere in the CCAMLR area and in any season must be given to the Commission. Second, limits have been set on by-catch of non-target species (e.g. 300 tonnes for *Notothenia rossii* in subarea 48.3 during all seasons, set in 1995). Such measures are envisaged by Article IX(2)(i), which states that the Commission may take 'measures concerning the effects of harvesting and associated activities on components of the marine ecosystem other than the harvested populations'.

A third group of measures has been adopted to reduce incidental mortality of seabirds and of marine mammals through trawl fishing, and of seabirds from longline fishing. The latter was in response to the establishment of the longline fishery for Patagonian toothfish in the Antarctic Conservation Area, which led to significant loss of albatross and petrel species.[92] Finally, there are a number of measures on inspection and compliance. A catch data reporting system has been implemented (now electronic) as well as a vessel monitoring system to improve compliance with conservation measures through more effective monitoring of harvesting activities. Port inspections of vessels carrying toothfish, and notification of transhipments within the CCAMLR area, are further examples of compliance measures designed particularly to reduce IUU fishing. The various regulatory methods noted here may, of course, be used in conjunction to achieve ecosystem protection objectives, as the range of measures in place for the conservation of toothfish stocks attests.

iv) Institutions

Implementation of Article II is the task of the twenty-three-member Commission for the Conservation of Antarctic Marine Living Resources, which is charged with giving effect to the general principles and objectives of CCAMLR. Based in Hobart, Tasmania, the Commission was the first permanent body to be established within the ATS. It meets annually and, like the Scientific Committee also

[92] For discussion of the Agreement on the Conservation of Albatrosses and Petrels (ACAP), see Chapter 7 above.

established under CCAMLR, adopts decisions by consensus.[93] The Commission's functions include identification of conservation needs and the efficacy of conservation measures, formulating and adopting such measures on the basis of the best scientific evidence available, and implementing the system of observation and inspection established under CCAMLR.[94] Conservation measures are subject to an objection or opt-out procedure,[95] a common and unfortunate feature of fishery agreements.[96] The Commission is also charged with drawing the attention of non-CCAMLR states to activity affecting the implementation of CCAMLR.[97]

In adopting conservation measures, the Commission is to take full account of the recommendations and advice of the Scientific Committee.[98] A recent study concluded that CCAMLR is one of only three RFMOs 'where the Contracting Parties appear to comply consistently with both scientific advice and corresponding management measures'.[99] Further work is carried out in three standing committees under CCAMLR (on finance and administration, observation and inspection, and implementation and compliance)[100] and through a number of working groups. These include an Ad Hoc Working Group on Incidental Mortality Arising from Longline Fishing, and Permanent Working Groups on Fish

[93] Annual reports of its meetings are published by the Secretariat, most recently the Report of the 28th Meeting (2009), available at www.ccamlr.org. CCAMLR also reports to the ATCM.

[94] The Commission's structure and powers are set out in detail in Articles VII–XIII. It reports annually to the ATCM.

[95] Article IX(6)(b). In addition, other members of the Commission having accepted a measure may nonetheless opt out within thirty days of the Commission's reconsidering a measure objected to by another member and which has been duly notified to the Commission (Article IX(6)(d)).

[96] See further Chapter 5 above. [97] Article XI.

[98] See, generally, K.-H. Kock (ed.), *Understanding CCAMLR's Approach to Management* (CCAMLR, 2000). Article XV further defines the functions of the Committee as, inter alia, 'a forum for consultation and co-operation'. The early days of CCAMLR were marked by an uneasy relationship between the two bodies; see further Howard, *supra* n. 72; and F. Orrego Vicuna, 'The Effectiveness of the Decision-Making Machinery of CCAMLR: An Assessment', in Jorgensen-Dahl and Ostreng, *supra* n. 64, p. 129.

[99] IPHC and IATTC being the other RFMOs. M. L. Mooney-Seus and A. Rosenberg, *Regional Fisheries Management Organizations: Progress in Adopting the Precautionary Approach and Ecosystem-Based Management*, Recommended Best Practices for Regional Fisheries Management Organizations Technical Study No. 1 (Chatham House, 2007), p. xiii.

[100] A Standing Committee on Implementation (SOI) was established in 1987, and replaced in 2002 by the Standing Committee on Implementation and Compliance (SCIC) in recognition of the importance of compliance for the effectiveness of CCAMLR.

Stock Assessment and on Ecosystem Monitoring and Management. The last is of particular relevance, for in 1996 it established the first strategy for an ecosystem assessment model for Antarctica which allows information collected from established monitoring programmes to be integrated into management advice. Understanding the linkages between harvested species, dependent species, the environment and fisheries is a key objective of such information gathering.[101]

v) Implementation

The system of inspection envisaged in Article XXIV was established from the 1989–90 season, and the system of observation from the 1992–3 season. The function of observers is to collect information on fishing activities, particularly biological data on the catch and rates of incidental mortality. They are nominated by contracting parties and appointed on a bilateral basis, thus falling short of an independent scheme of scientific observers operated by the Commission itself.[102] Inspectors have authority to inspect fishing gear, the catch and general fishing activities, and are appointed by national authorities. Given the logistics involved, inspectors are frequently of the same nationality as the fishing vessel being inspected, and may spend little time on the vessel.[103] Violations must be reported to the Commission, as must the steps taken by the flag state to sanction such violations. There is some evidence of such offences going unreported and unpunished.[104] A further weakness of the CCAMLR system, identified in the 2008 Report of the CCAMLR Performance Review Panel, is the absence of compulsory dispute settlement.[105]

However, by far the most urgent issue facing the CCAMLR regime, threatening the efficacy of its ecosystem approach, is the problem of illegal, unreported and unregulated (IUU) fishing.[106] The Commission has adopted a number of measures on compliance in an attempt to address the problem, drawing on the experience of other RFMOs such

[101] See the Comprehensive Ecosystem Monitoring Programme (CEMP) Standard Methods at www.ccamlr.org.

[102] K.-H. Kock, 'Fishing and Conservation in Southern Waters' (1994) 30(172) *Polar Record* 3, p. 15; for text of the present scheme of international scientific observation, see www.ccamlr.org.

[103] See, for example, Kock, *supra* n. 102, p. 14. [104] Ibid. [105] *Supra* n. 76.

[106] See, generally, R. Baird, *Aspects of Illegal, Unreported and Unregulated Fishing in the Southern Ocean* (Springer, 2006).

as NAFO[107] and, to a lesser extent, ICCAT.[108] Contracting parties are required to prohibit fishing in the CCAMLR area by their flag vessels except in accordance with a licence or permit issued by the flag state; such permits are to extend beyond the CCAMLR area since stocks extend across borders. Flag states are further required now to report annually to the Commission on enforcement action taken, and to ensure that sanctions are sufficiently severe to ensure compliance with CCAMLR conservation measures (CM 10–02). CCAMLR members must report to the Commission sightings of vessels of non-contracting parties engaged in illegal fishing, with the landing or transhipment of any fish from such vessels to be prohibited until an inspection determines that the fish were not caught in contravention of CCAMLR Conservation Measures.[109] Further measures relating to port-state control over, inter alia, illegal landing, and a catch documentation scheme for toothfish, have also been implemented. The latter allows fish product to be tracked from landing, but has been criticised because it is not triggered at point of capture, nor is it integrated properly with catch reporting.[110] Finally, a 'blacklist' of non-complying vessels of members and non-members is now maintained (CM 10/6 and CM 10/7), but there is evidence that CCAMLR members are blocking the consensus required for listing of their vessels and that, even where detected and pursued, penalties for non-compliance are inadequate.[111] The 2008 *Report of the CCAMLR Performance Review Panel* found that IUU fishing 'continues to provide significant threats to achieving the Ecosystem Approach to Fisheries and there remain gaps in relation to transhipment'.[112]

vi) Relationship with other agreements

There is close co-operation between CCAMLR and the International Whaling Convention in particular. Most notable, perhaps, is the

[107] See M.H. Carr, 'Recent Developments in Compliance and Enforcement for International Fisheries' (1997) 24(4) *ELQ* 857–60, and Guilfoyle, *supra* n. 81, p. 143.

[108] Proposals to introduce trade restrictions on non-parties such as those adopted under ICCAT have repeatedly failed. See, for example, Commission Report 2009, *supra* n. 93.

[109] See CCAMLR, 'Part 9: System of Inspection', *Basic Documents* (CCAMLR, 2005), pp. 104–12, available at www.ccamlr.org.

[110] See the evaluation in 2008 *Report, supra* n. 76, Chapter 4, para. 67 et seq.

[111] Ibid., pp. 33 and 77. The Antarctic and Southern Ocean Coalition (ASOC) maintains its own 'Red List' of illegal vessels (www.asoc.org); see also the Southern Ocean listing at www.illegal-fishing.org (managed by Chatham House under its Energy, Environment and Development programme).

[112] 2008 *Report, supra* n. 76, p. 33.

designation of the Southern Ocean as a Sanctuary under the Whaling Convention.[113] Collaborative research is also carried out. For example, the Scientific Committee under the Whaling Convention developed a major co-operative research programme into the effects of environmental change on whales in the Sanctuary with Southern Ocean GLOBEC and CCAMLR for the years 2000 and 2001.[114] The IWC has observer status in the meetings of the CCAMLR Commission.[115]

As indicated above, there are three potentially overlapping areas of regulation: national maritime zones, the CCAMLR area, and the high seas. The high seas are presently regulated by the 1982 LOSC, read in the light of the 1995 SSA discussed in Chapter 5 above. The CCAMLR Commission has urged states to become party to the 1995 Straddling Stocks Agreement.[116] Where a vessel's flag state is a party to the SSA and it engages in IUU fishing in the CCAMLR area and then later passes into the coastal state's EEZ,[117] that coastal state may assert jurisdiction over both high-seas and EEZ offences.[118] Indeed, some of the longest hot pursuits of recent times have occurred in the Southern Ocean, commenced from the EEZ of Antarctic islands of Australia in particular.[119]

d) *The 1991 Environmental Protocol to the Antarctic Treaty*

The EP was negotiated to provide for comprehensive environmental protection in Antarctica, and to serve as a complement to the existing

113 See further P. W. Birnie, 'Are Twentieth-Century Marine Conservation Conventions Adaptable to Twenty-First Century Goals and Principles? Part II' (1997) 12(4) *IJMCL* 488, pp. 510–14, and Chapter 6 above.

114 Final Press Release, 50th Annual General Meeting of the International Whaling Commission, Oman, 20 May 1998. This builds on existing collaborative research, such as a baleen whale habitat and prey study.

115 A number of other international and inter-governmental organisations with whom CCAMLR co-operates also have observer status at meetings of the CCAMLR Commission (ACAP, ASOC (Antarctic Southern Ocean Coalition), CCSBT, and COLTO (Coalition of Legal Toothfish Operators)).

116 Indeed, Article XI CCAMLR addresses 'relations with adjacent areas', urging contracting parties exercising jurisdiction in such areas to co-operate in respect of conservation of straddling stocks, including associated species, with a view to harmonising conservation measures adopted in respect of such stocks within and beyond CCAMLR's area of application.

117 Specifically in the Antarctic context, the EEZ of an island over which sovereignty is undisputed; see discussion at n. 74 above.

118 Article 21(14); see Guilfoyle, *supra* n. 81, p. 154.

119 Such as the *South Tomi* (fifteen days, 3,300 nautical miles) and the *Viarsa* (twenty-one days, 3,900 nautical miles). Guilfoyle, *supra* n. 81, p. 147.

ATS.[120] It constitutes a significant consolidation of existing measures within the ATS, for example elevating the 1964 Agreed Measures to treaty status in Annex II. Unsurprisingly, as a protocol to the AT, the EP is governed by the general provisions of the AT, which it neither modifies nor amends, thus preserving the 'integrity and continuing efficacy' of the ATS.[121] The Protocol has a framework character, setting out general obligations and institutions in the main text supplemented by five annexes covering environmental impact assessment (Annex I), conservation of Antarctic flora and fauna (Annex II), waste disposal and waste management (Annex III), prevention of marine pollution (Annex IV) and area protection and management (Annex V). A sixth annex, on liability arising from environmental emergencies, was added in 2005 but has not yet entered into force.[122] The focus here will be upon the general framework provisions and the provisions of the Annexes most pertinent for the conservation of wildlife, Annexes II and V.

General provisions For the first time in the ATS, the EP extends on a treaty basis environmental protection measures to the whole of the Antarctic Treaty area (but not the Convergence) and elevates to treaty status the conservation of the Antarctic environment. Pursuant to Article 2 the parties 'commit themselves to the comprehensive protection of the Antarctic environment and dependent and associated ecosystems and hereby designate Antarctica as a nature reserve, devoted to peace and science'. Thus the Protocol adopts an explicitly ecosystem approach. In the planning and conduct of all activities in the Antarctic Treaty area, Article 3(1) elaborates a set of environmental principles which are to govern such activities, and requires that:

> The protection of the Antarctic environment and dependent and associated ecosystems and the intrinsic value of Antarctica, including its wilderness and aesthetic values and its value as an area for the conduct

[120] For detailed analysis see C. Redgwell, 'Environmental Protection in Antarctica: The 1991 Protocol' (1994) 43 *ICLQ* 599; and www.ats.aq.

[121] F. Francioni, 'The Madrid Protocol on the Protection of the Antarctic Environment' (1993) 28(1) *Texas JIL* 47, p. 55. Furthermore, the EP applies to the same geographical area as the AT, decision-making is governed by Article IX AT and inspections under the Protocol are to be performed in accordance with the observer system established under Article VII AT.

[122] The annexes contain a common provision for expedited amendment or modification to ensure the speedy implementation of modifications to the annexes which may be of a largely technical nature and to ensure also that the standards set keep pace with technological and other developments.

of scientific research, in particular research essential to understanding the global environment, shall be fundamental considerations . . .

This is followed by a list of consequences of activities in the Antarctic Treaty area which are to be avoided, including (i) detrimental changes in the distribution, abundance or productivity of species or populations of species of fauna and flora; (ii) further jeopardy to endangered or threatened species or populations of such species; and (iii) degradation of, or substantial risk to, areas of biological, scientific, historic, aesthetic or wilderness significance.[123] It is notable that, while the EP contains compulsory dispute settlement provisions, these are not applicable to Article 3, regarding which parties have merely the obligation peacefully to settle any disputes.[124]

Prior assessment of the impact of activities upon the Antarctic environment and dependent and associated ecosystems is a general environmental principle set forth in Article 8 and further elaborated in Annex I. One of the factors to be taken into account in making such assessments is

> whether there exists the capacity to monitor the key environmental parameters and ecosystem components so as to identify and provide early warning of any adverse effects of the activity and to provide for such modification of operating procedures as may be necessary in the light of the results of monitoring or increased knowledge of the Antarctic environment and dependent and associated ecosystems.[125]

Regular and effective monitoring are required to be carried out to detect, inter alia, unforeseen effects of activities carried on both within and outside the Antarctic Treaty area on the Antarctic environment.

Institutions One of the deficiencies of the ATS had been the absence of one body with Antarctica-wide interests and responsibilities in respect of Antarctic conservation.[126] This deficiency is addressed with the establishment under the EP of a new permanent body, the Committee for Environmental Protection (CEP), of which each party is a member, with

[123] Article 3(2).

[124] Articles 18–20, with disputes with respect to Article 3 subject only to the general obligation in Article 18 to resolve disputes by peaceful means.

[125] Article 3(2)(c)(v).

[126] See, for example, IUCN, *A Strategy for Antarctic Conservation* (IUCN, 1991), p. 28, para. 77.

observer status for CCAMLR's Scientific Committee and SCAR.[127] However, the CEP lacks legislative and enforcement functions and falls short of the 'Antarctic Environmental Protection Agency' called for by some.[128] Thus, for example, there is no independent power of review such as that contained in the original draft submitted by Australia, Belgium, France and Italy during the negotiation of the EP.[129] It is thus an advisory body only, and may formulate recommendations to the parties on matters such as the functioning of the Protocol, its effectiveness, inspection procedures, the need for scientific research (including environmental monitoring), and the state of the Antarctic environment.[130] The CEP must submit to the ATCM an annual report of its sessions, which must reflect all the views expressed – the latter a requirement reflecting a battle fought by CCAMLR's Scientific Committee to ensure that the range of views expressed is reflected in the final report. The public availability of these reports after consideration by the ATCPs, coupled with the steps already taken towards increased availability of documentation regarding the functioning of the ATS, is a positive development in the provision of environmental information regarding Antarctica.[131] Access to environmental information is one hallmark of an effectively functioning environmental regulatory system. Much will depend, of course, upon what information is related in the reports and upon the capacity of parties within the ATS and outside to respond to them. Non-governmental organisations have played a significant role in stimulating environmental concern for Antarctica and in drawing attention to parties' breaches of existing environmental measures, a role of continuing importance given the purely advisory character of the CEP. The continued efficacy of such efforts will to a large part depend upon the

[127] There have been twelve meetings of the CEP, most recently in Baltimore in 2009. With the approval of the ATCM, other relevant scientific environmental and technical organisations may be invited to participate as observers (Article 11).

[128] E.g. Barnes, in C. Joyner and S. K. Chopra (eds.), *The Antarctic Legal Regime* (Giuffre, 1988), pp. 245–9.

[129] Reproduced in W. Bush, *Antarctica and International Law: A Collection of Inter-state and National Documents*, Part AT917C (November 1992), p. 42, n. 6 (d. AT04101991A.1). A New Zealand draft would have permitted the Committee to review and comment upon draft Comprehensive Environmental Evaluations (discussed below). Ibid. p. 87, n. 19 (d.AT25101990).

[130] Article 12. As Scully observes, the CEP attempts to chart a middle course between duplicating the efforts of SCAR and other bodies, and creating a costly and extensive new institutional machinery. R. Tucker Scully, 'Protecting Antarctica: Progress in Chile' (1991) 26(1) *Antarctica J. of the U.S.* 4, p. 8.

[131] And available on the ATS website at www.ats.aq.

continuing ability of such organisations to access relevant information and to bring breaches and potential gaps in the system to public attention.

Inspection and enforcement The inspection system established in the AT is carried forward into the Protocol,[132] with explicit recognition of collective inspections, a practice well established under the Antarctic Treaty. Enforcement is left to the contracting parties, who are obliged to take 'appropriate measures' to ensure compliance with the Protocol[133] and to publish annually a report of the measures taken which are made publicly available following circulation to other parties and the CEP and consideration at the next ATCM.[134]

Annex II: conservation of flora and fauna Annex II of the Protocol reproduces to a significant degree the provisions of the 1964 Agreed Measures for the Conservation of Antarctic Fauna and Flora, which it strengthens and updates. There is more emphasis than formerly upon the protection of the diversity of flora and invertebrates in the Antarctic Treaty area and upon humane methods of taking. Annex II also banned the introduction of dogs onto land or ice shelves in the Antarctic Treaty area from 1 April 1994. In general, however, the scope of the Agreed Measures is retained.

The Agreed Measures introduced into the ATS the concepts of specially protected species and specially protected areas (SPAs), both found in Annexes to the 1991 Protocol, as well as prohibiting within the Treaty Area the 'killing, wounding, capturing, or molesting of any native mammal or native bird' without a permit. Annex II contains a similar prohibition, with the addition of a prohibition in respect of native plants. Thus Article 1(g) EP defines 'take' or 'taking' to include removing or damaging such quantities of native plants that their local distribution or abundance would be significantly affected.

The Agreed Measures attached certain general conditions to the issuing of permits, a pattern also carried through to Annex II. Thus, for example, the Annex sets forth a permit condition ensuring that 'the diversity of species, as well as the habitats essential to their existence, and the balance of the ecological systems existing within the Antarctic Treaty area are maintained'. The standard for activities with the Treaty area is to minimise, not eliminate, harmful interference with the normal

[132] Article 14. [133] Article 13. [134] Article 17.

living conditions of any native mammal, bird or plant. Article 1(h) of Annex II defines 'harmful interference' to include, inter alia, 'any activity that results in the significant adverse modification of habitats of any species or populations of native mammal, bird, plant or invertebrate'.

Annex V: area protection Annex V consolidates measures taken over the years with respect to SPAs, redesignating them Antarctic Specially Protected Areas (ASPAs) with entry prohibited except by permit and their management regulated by an adopted plan. Proposals for designation as an ASPA may be made by any party, the CEP, SCAR or the CCAMLR Commission (from whom prior approval is needed before designation of a marine ASPA),[135] by submitting a proposed management plan to the ATCM. Included within a series of ASPAs are, inter alia,

> (a) areas kept free from human interference for future comparisons;
> (b) representative examples of major terrestrial, including glacial and aquatic, ecosystems and marine ecosystems;
> (c) areas with important or unusual assemblages of species . . .;
> (d) the type of locality of only known habitat of any species;
> (e) areas of outstanding aesthetic and wilderness value.[136]

The area is to be of sufficient size to protect the values for which the special protection or management is required – an important shift in focus from the 'minimum disruption to other Antarctic activities' requirement under the Agreed Measures. Designation is for an indefinite period, but subject to a management plan which is reviewed every five years. SCAR has produced an 'ecosystem classification matrix' to assist with designation and management of new protected and managed areas, and guidelines for inspection.[137]

Similar procedures, including for designation, apply to the second category of protected area in Annex V, Antarctic Specially Managed Areas (ASMAs), where activities pose risks of mutual interference or cumulative environmental impacts (or the area contains sites or

[135] The 2008 report of the CCAMLR Performance Review Panel noted that none of the existing marine protected areas is an IUCN Category I MPA. It concludes that '[t]aking a proactive approach towards the design and establishment of new MPAs would be consistent with CCAMLR's "unique" position as a conservation-based organisation and provide CCAMLR with the opportunity to provide leadership amongst RFMOs'. 2008 *Report*, *supra* n. 76, p. 14.

[136] Article 3, Annex V. [137] Final Report of the 17th ATCM, p. 25, paras. 110–11.

monuments of recognised historic value). Here a permit is not required for entry, but the area is subject to a management plan.

4. Conclusions

The Protocol is part of a continuing and evolving process of ensuring the conservation of Antarctic flora, fauna and habitat which started with the 1964 Agreed Measures. Protected-area status, and the requirement of prior environmental assessment, has been strengthened by the EP. Yet gaps remain, most notably in the effective institutional oversight of SPA designation and compliance. With respect to living marine resources, CCAMLR plays a crucial role in the conservation of marine species and habitat. However, there are many practical problems in the application of an ecosystem approach to resources management which have only been gradually surmounted, and IUU fishing continues to be a major problem in the Southern Ocean, as elsewhere in the oceans. Indeed, the fate of the Patagonian toothfish imparts an important lesson: the frailties of traditional mono-species management are not addressed if only an ecosystem approach to management is adopted. Other problems, such as non-parties' participation, flags of convenience, and implementation and enforcement, remain. Last but not least, as was also observed in the Arctic context, the long-term health of the Antarctic ecosystem is threatened by global warming, with impacts on deep ocean circulation potentially leading to reduced upwelling in the Antarctic Convergence and anoxic conditions, with the 'total collapse of the Antarctic ecosystem' one possible outcome.[138]

Recommended further reading

C. Redgwell, 'The Protection of the Antarctic Environment and the Ecosystem Approach', in M. Bowman and C. Redgwell (eds.), *International Law and the Conservation of Biological Diversity* (Kluwer, 1995)

C. Redgwell, 'Protection of Ecosystems under International Law: Lessons from Antarctica', in A. Boyle and D. Freestone (eds.), *International Law and Sustainable Development: Past Achievements and Future Challenges* (Oxford University Press, 1999)

[138] See Redgwell, *supra* n. 54, p. 222; and CCAMLR Resolution 12/10 (2009) on Climate Change.

D. Rothwell, *The Polar Regions and the Development of International Law* (Cambridge University Press, 1996)

D. Rothwell, 'The Arctic Environmental Protection Strategy and International Environmental Co-operation in the Far North' (1995) 6 *YBIEL* 65

D. Rothwell, 'International Law and the Protection of the Arctic Environment' (1995) 44 *ICLQ* 280

Chapter 12

Other regional and subregional arrangements

1. Introduction

Efforts to establish international legal regimes for wildlife conservation in the Asian and the South Pacific regions, together with the adoption of four Specially Protected Area (SPA) protocols relating to the Caribbean, Eastern African, Mediterranean, and South East Pacific regions under the UN Regional Seas Programme, provide the focus for discussion in this chapter. These regional and subregional activities have met with varying degrees of success. In Asia, the 1985 Agreement on the Conservation of Nature and Natural Resources (the ASEAN Agreement)[1] has still to enter into force, and in the South Pacific the operation of the 1976 Convention on Conservation of Nature in the South Pacific[2] (the Apia Convention) has effectively been suspended since 2006. They nevertheless merit brief attention both as historical instances of law-making initiatives, and as practical indications of matters of concern within the regions in question. Furthermore, it is not completely inconceivable that they might be activated, or reactivated, in the future. On a more positive note, some encouraging progress has been made particularly in the Mediterranean and Caribbean in facilitating the establishment of protected areas under the Regional Seas Programme. The SPA protocols offer the prospect of contributing significantly to the management and conservation of wildlife within their own sphere of application.

2. The 1985 ASEAN Agreement

The Association of South East Asian Nations (ASEAN) was established in 1967 and has ten members.[3] The founding ASEAN Declaration (the

[1] (1985) 15 *EPL* 64. [2] [1990] *Australian Treaty Series* 41.

[3] Brunei Darussalam, Cambodia, Indonesia, Lao PDR, Malaysia, Myanmar, Singapore, Thailand, the Philippines and Vietnam.

Bangkok Declaration) notes that the organisation's aims include the acceleration of 'economic growth, social progress and cultural development in the region', as well as the promotion of 'regional peace and stability' and of 'active collaboration and mutual assistance on matters of common interest'.[4] On 9 July 1985 the six states then party to the organisation – namely Brunei Darussalam, Indonesia, Malaysia, Singapore, Thailand and the Philippines – signed the ASEAN Agreement. This agreement must receive six ratifications before it can enter into force. Only Indonesia, Thailand and the Philippines have ratified to date and disappointingly, therefore, the treaty has not entered into force.

a) Conservation and development

At the time of its adoption the ASEAN agreement endorsed the most modern principles and approaches in international environmental law. The 'fundamental principle' noted in Article 1(1) stipulates that state parties agree to adopt measures

> necessary to maintain essential ecological processes and life-support systems, to preserve genetic diversity, and to ensure the sustainable utilization of harvested natural resources under their jurisdiction in accordance with scientific principles and with a view to attaining the goal of sustainable development.

The concept of sustainable use and the pursuit of sustainable development are thereby endorsed. This was certainly enlightened at the time; the Brundtland Report was not published until 1987 yet the ASEAN Agreement makes the pursuit of sustainable development one of its key goals.[5] The important role of science is also emphasised, as is the need to maintain essential habitats, ecological processes and genetic diversity. Additionally, the treaty acknowledged the relationship between conservation and development in the application of the integration principle, ensuring that 'conservation and management of natural

4 The ASEAN Declaration is available at www.aseansec.org/1212.htm.

5 See K. L. Koh, 'ASEAN Agreement on the Conservation of Nature and Natural Resources, 1985: A Study in Environmental Governance', paper given to the World Parks Congress 2003 (Durban, 8–17 September 2003), p. 4, available at law.nus.edu.sg/apcel/publications/pub/kohkhenglian/aseanagreement.doc.

resources are treated as an integral part of development planning at all stages and at all levels'.[6]

b) *Species protection*

A detailed regime of species protection is to be established to 'maintain maximum genetic diversity';[7] indeed, action must be taken with the aim of ensuring the survival of *all* species in the jurisdiction of state parties.[8] To this end, measures must be adopted which, inter alia, 'conserve natural, terrestrial, freshwater and coastal or marine habitats',[9] and which also ensure 'the sustainable use of harvested species'.[10] Special attention is to be paid to harvested species to ensure their sustainable use,[11] and also to the protection of endangered and the conservation of endemic species.[12]

With respect to endangered species, parties are to take 'all measures in their power' to prevent species extinction,[13] and, more particularly, an appendix lists such species which are of 'prime importance to the region and deserving special attention'.[14] Parties are to take action 'wherever possible' to prohibit the taking of and trade in these endangered species and to protect their habitat 'by ensuring that sufficient portions are included in protected areas'.[15] Measures must also be taken to ensure that 'the highest possible level' of population of endemic species is maintained, although this obligation is again softened by the words 'where possible'.[16] Since the treaty has not entered into force, the opportunity to clarify the undoubted imprecision of these provisions has not presented itself.[17]

c) *Vegetation, soil, water and air*

Bearing in mind their importance to the existence of natural ecosystems, parties shall take 'all necessary measures' to conserve vegetation cover (particularly forest cover).[18] In particular, parties should

[6] Article 2(1). [7] Article 3. [8] Article 3(1). [9] Article 3(2)(a).
[10] Article 3(2)(b). [11] Article 4. [12] Article 5. [13] Article 3(2)(e). [14] Article 5(1).
[15] Ibid. [16] Article 5(3).
[17] Koh, *supra* n. 5, p. 4, notes that use of such qualifying words takes 'into consideration the level of development of a member state to fulfill its obligations – thus it embodies the notion of "common but differentiated responsibilities"'.
[18] Article 6(1).

'endeavour' to prevent overgrazing, to establish forest reserves and to prevent bush and forest fires.[19] This obligation has real potential to reduce the widespread incidence of illegal logging in the ASEAN area as well as the starting of fires by farmers in the clearance of land and/or forests.

Soil, water and air are, of course, equally important to the functioning of natural ecosystems. Parties shall adopt measures 'wherever possible towards soil conservation, improvement and rehabilitation',[20] take 'all appropriate measures towards the conservation of their underground and surface water resources',[21] and 'endeavour to take all appropriate measures towards air quality management compatible with sustainable development'.[22] These are all laudable proposals but the obligations they entail are clearly heavily diluted by the use of qualifying words such as 'wherever possible' and 'endeavour'. No doubt these words were included to facilitate the ratification of the agreement by developing ASEAN countries which lack the technical and financial ability, and perhaps political will, to implement more rigorous obligations.

d) Protection of ecological processes – combating pollution

The ASEAN Agreement acknowledges that measures to combat pollution must be introduced to accompany those designed to conserve biodiversity. Parties therefore undertake 'wherever possible' to prevent, reduce and control environmental degradation in order to protect essential ecological processes.[23] More specifically, they 'shall endeavour to undertake' the promotion of agricultural practices that are environmentally sound,[24] and the promotion both of pollution control and of the development of environmentally sound industrial processes.[25] Furthermore, parties are to 'endeavour' to prevent, reduce and control the emission of pollutants by taking into account their cumulative impact on natural ecosystems, and should establish national monitoring programmes to establish the impact of pollutants on the environment.[26] Interestingly, the agreement also seeks to implement the polluter-pays principle in that parties must 'as far as possible ... consider the originator of the activity which may lead to environmental degradation responsible for its prevention, reduction and control as well as, wherever

[19] Article 6(2). [20] Article 7(1). [21] Article 8(1). [22] Article 9(1).
[23] Article 10. [24] Article 10(a). [25] Article 10(b). [26] Article 11(a) and (c).

possible, for rehabilitation and remedial measures required'.[27] The use of the qualifying words 'as far as possible' is endemic throughout the treaty.

e) Land-use planning and protected areas

A number of provisions relate to land-use planning. Parties must 'endeavour' to introduce measures to ensure the 'integration of natural resource conservation' into the planning process, and 'give as full consideration as possible to ecological factors as to economic and social ones' both in the preparation of land-use plans and in their implementation.[28] Protected areas are also to be established including both 'national parks' and 'reserves'.[29] Management plans must be established for all protected areas, along with surrounding buffer zones. National parks are to be of a size that allows for 'ecological self-regulation of one or several ecosystems',[30] and are to be areas which have not been substantially altered by human activity. These areas are to be placed under public control and their borders left unchanged. National parks are to be 'dedicated to conservation and to scientific, educational and recreational uses and the common welfare of the people'.[31] 'Reserves', on the other hand, are to be established for specific purposes: the preservation of a specific ecosystem; the habitat of specific species; a water catchment area; or for any other reason relating to the conservation of natural resources or 'objects or areas of scientific, aesthetic, cultural, educational or recreational interest'.[32] Reserves will be 'dedicated to the purposes for which they have been created',[33] and their boundaries must not be altered.

The agreement importantly calls for co-operation between parties to establish a 'co-ordinated network of protected areas'. It also provides for adoption, by a meeting of the parties, of an appendix establishing appropriate 'principles, objectives, criteria and guidelines' to govern the 'selection, establishment and management of protected areas' within this network.[34]

f) Environmental impact assessment

In line with the objective of promoting sustainable development, the environmental impact assessment (EIA) procedure is to be applied 'as far

[27] Article 10(d). [28] Article 12(1). [29] Article 13. [30] Article 13(3)(a)(i).
[31] Article 13(3)(a)(iii). [32] Article 13(3)(b)(i). [33] Article 13(3)(b)(iii).
[34] Article 13(6).

as possible' in relation to any 'proposals for any activity which may significantly affect the natural environment'.[35] Results of any EIA must be taken into account in decision-making, and, if the project proceeds, steps must be taken to overcome or reduce adverse effects. A system of post-project monitoring is also to be established to enable appropriate remedial action to be taken where appropriate.[36] The fact that the text of the agreement so fully endorses EIA as an applicable procedure in such a way was a novel feature at the time of the agreement's adoption.

g) *Research, education and the promotion of public participation*

Further obligations address the promotion of scientific research, education and public participation. States are, for example, obliged to promote and 'wherever possible' support relevant scientific and technical programmes (such as monitoring and research programmes),[37] to 'endeavour' to promote knowledge of natural-resource management and conservation,[38] and 'as far as possible' to facilitate public participation in planning and implementation of conservation measures.[39] At the international level, states are obliged to co-operate with other parties with a view to co-ordinating conservation and management activities (such as monitoring activities, research and exchange of information).[40]

Where natural resources are shared, co-operation is expected between relevant parties concerning their conservation and use.[41] States 'shall endeavour' not only to undertake impact assessments before initiating operations that may lead to a significant risk of affecting the environment or natural resources of another state, but also to notify other concerned parties in advance of plans to so initiate operations, consult with such parties on these plans upon their request, and inform other state parties of emergency situations which may have transboundary effects.[42]

h) *Institutions*

The drafters of the ASEAN agreement, assisted in their task by the IUCN, were determined to ensure that the text established an adequate institutional infrastructure to oversee the evolution of a legal regime capable of responding to conservation needs. A meeting of the parties would be held at least every three years to review implementation and consider national

[35] Article 14(1). [36] Article 14(2). [37] Article 15. [38] Article 16(1).
[39] Article 16(2). [40] Article 18. [41] Article 19. [42] Article 20(3).

reports,[43] a Secretariat was to have been established to convene meetings and generally facilitate co-ordination,[44] and each state party would designate a particular institution as a national focal point.[45] Of course, none of these institutions has been established bearing in mind the treaty's failure to enter into force.

i) Co-operation within ASEAN

It may well be that the ASEAN Agreement will never enter into force. Nevertheless, it is acknowledged that co-operation between ASEAN countries has in practice taken place over the years in relation to environmental protection; ASEAN environment ministers have, for example, met regularly, either formally or informally, since the 1980s. ASEAN as an organisation has adopted various resolutions, action plans and declarations relating to environmental protection during that time,[46] and the 2002 Agreement on Transboundary Haze Pollution became the first legally binding instrument adopted by ASEAN countries when it entered into force on 25 November 2003.[47] Specifically in relation to the conservation of biodiversity, the intergovernmental ASEAN Centre for Biodiversity (ACB) was launched at the ninth Informal ASEAN Ministerial Meeting in September 2005 to act as a regional centre of excellence with a view to facilitating networking and greater co-ordination in the region on biodiversity matters.[48] Additionally, the non-binding ASEAN Declaration on Heritage Parks was agreed in December 2003,[49] listing twenty-seven nationally protected areas as ASEAN heritage parks. All ten ASEAN countries have agreed that common co-operation is required to conserve and manage these ASEAN heritage parks, which include the Kinabalu and Mulu National Parks in Malaysia, the Lorentz and Leuser National Parks in Indonesia, the Kor Tarutao and Khao Yai National Parks in Thailand, and the Ba Be and Chu Mom Ray National Parks in Vietnam.

j) Some reflections

The ASEAN Agreement has arguably fallen victim to its sophisticated and innovative nature. It would undoubtedly have placed significant

[43] Article 21. [44] Article 22. [45] Article 23.
[46] Further information of these initiatives can be obtained from ASEAN's website at www.aseansec.org.
[47] Reproduced at www.aseansec.org/6086.htm.
[48] See the ACB's website at www.aseanbiodiversity.org.
[49] Reproduced at www.aseansec.org/15524.htm.

technical, administrative and financial burdens on its parties, and this perhaps has deterred further ratification despite the extensive use of language which diluted the obligations it imposed. Although co-operative programmes have been introduced and political declarations signed over the years, the region's terrestrial and marine environments have continued to deteriorate. As a result, important habitats, such as forests, coral reefs and mangrove swamps, are in decline. The region's deforestation rate, for example, was estimated to be more than four times the global average in the period from 1990 to 2000.[50]

All of ASEAN's ten members are party to the Biodiversity Convention. The 2002 Strategic Plan for the CBD fully endorses collaboration between parties 'at the regional and subregional levels to implement the Convention'.[51] Accordingly, a given state's participation in legal regimes at both the international and at the regional/subregional level should certainly not be seen as inappropriate. Indeed, regional activities can complement action under the CBD regime.[52] Of course, some action has taken place within ASEAN to protect wildlife and habitats and it is not suggested that, had it entered into force, the ASEAN Agreement would have alleviated all pressures that today face the region's biodiversity. However, it would most certainly have introduced an advanced, legally binding regime which would have provided a real regional focus and could only have been of benefit to the preservation of the region's rich biodiversity.

3. The 1976 Apia Convention

The Apia Convention was adopted on 12 June 1976 but did not enter into force until 28 June 1990. There are currently only five parties; Australia, Cook Islands, Fiji, France and Samoa.[53] It is certainly less progressive in nature than the ASEAN Agreement but seeks nonetheless to protect endangered species and encourage the establishment of protected areas.

a) Protected areas

The text places an obligation on its parties to 'encourage the creation of protected areas' which, together with existing areas under protection,

[50] ASEAN Secretariat, Our Heritage, Our Future, Second ASEAN State of the Environment Report 2000 (2001).
[51] Strategic Plan for the CBD, Goal 1.6; CBD CoP Decision VI/26 (7–19 April 2002).
[52] Koh, *supra* n. 5, p. 9.
[53] Papua New Guinea signed in June 1976 but has not ratified.

will 'safeguard representative samples of the natural ecosystems' in the region with 'particular attention being given to endangered species'.[54] Such areas will additionally protect 'superlative scenery, striking geological formations, and regions and objects of aesthetic interest or historic, cultural or scientific value'.[55] A system of protected areas is to be established, as well as a system of species protection, though parties may nonetheless make 'appropriate provision for customary use of areas and species in accordance with traditional cultural practices'.[56] The establishment of protected areas under the Apia Convention is complemented by an obligation under the 1986 SPREP (Noumea) Convention designed to establish marine protected areas in the South Pacific.[57]

Having been drafted in the 1970s, the Apia Convention unsurprisingly fails to reflect contemporary conceptions of protected areas, as reflected, for example, in the revised 2003 African Convention.[58] It refers instead to 'national parks', by which is meant

> an area established for the protection and conservation of ecosystems, containing animal and plant species, geomorphological sites and habitats of special scientific, educative and recreational interest or a natural landscape of great beauty, which is under the control of the appropriate public authority and open to visits by the public . . .[59]

and also 'national reserves', which is

> an area recognised and controlled by the appropriate public authority and established for protection and conservation of nature, and includes strict nature reserve, managed nature reserve, wilderness reserve, fauna or flora reserve, game reserve, bird sanctuary, geological or forest reserve, archaeological reserve and historic reserve, these being reserves affording various degrees of protection to the natural and cultural heritage according to the purposes for which they are established.

Boundaries of national parks must not be changed 'except after the fullest examination',[60] nor can resources in such areas be used for commercial gain without comparable considerations.[61] A ban is to be imposed on hunting, killing, capture or collection of fauna and the

[54] Article II(1). [55] Ibid. [56] Article VI.

[57] Article 14 of the 1986 Convention for the Protection of the Natural Resources and Environment of the South Pacific Region (1987) 26 *ILM* 38; known commonly as the SPREP or Noumea Convention.

[58] See Chapter 9 above and Articles V(6) and XII and Annex 2 of the 2003 African Convention.

[59] Article I(1)b. [60] Article III(1). [61] Article III(2).

destruction or collection of fauna unless duly authorised by appropriate authorities.[62] Visitors can enter national parks but only for 'inspirational, educative, cultural and recreative purposes'.[63] National reserves, on the other hand, must remain 'inviolate', although permission can be given for scientific research and for 'such uses as are consistent with the purposes for which a national reserve was established'.[64]

b) Species protection

In addition to protection inside protected areas, parties are to 'use their best endeavours' to protect indigenous fauna and flora by safeguarding them against 'unwise use and other threats that may lead to their extinction'.[65] Special attention is to be given to fauna and flora threatened with extinction. All hunting, killing, capture or collection is generally prohibited.[66] In an attempt to reduce the introduction of alien species which may have a harmful impact on ecosystems, parties are to 'carefully consider the consequences of the deliberate introduction . . . of species which have not previously occurred therein'.[67]

c) Co-operation

The Apia Agreement also encourages co-operation between the parties especially in relation to training of personnel, exchange of information and research on conservation issues.[68]

d) Institutions

Despite the fact that no provision is made in the Agreement for meetings of the parties, there have in fact been eight such meetings since 1991. The South Pacific Regional Environment Programme (SPREP), an inter-governmental organisation representing twenty-five countries (including twenty-one Pacific island countries), has become firmly established as the key entity in the region promoting regional

[62] Article III(3). [63] Article III(4). [64] Article IV. [65] Article V(1).
[66] Article V(3). [67] Article V(4). [68] Article VII.

co-operation to protect the environment, and has acted as secretariat to the Apia Convention.[69]

e) *Some reflections*

The Apia Convention has recently been described by Australia as having played 'a valuable role in the creation of protected areas, protection of indigenous fauna and flora, and promotion of research and public awareness of conservation of nature in the South Pacific'.[70] However, many recent activities designed to protect wildlife and habitats in the region have actually been co-ordinated by SPREP, and it is by no means clear to what extent such activity can be attributed to the Apia Convention.[71] The Apia Convention has undoubtedly failed to attract the majority of Pacific island countries as parties. One reason may be that it requires updating to take account of the more recent developments in relation to conservation and development, including the need for scientific knowledge to drive the decision-making process.[72] Another may well be that island states have preferred to concentrate on action within the CBD regime, bearing in mind the funding opportunities available within that system.

In 2004, the parties decided that a new agreement should be adopted to supersede the Apia Convention. However, insufficient funds were made

[69] See, for example, SPREP's 'Island Ecosystem' programme, sprep.org/programme/island_eco.htm, and its Action Strategy for Nature Conservation in the Pacific Island Region 2003–2007 at sprep.org/legal/documents/PACIFIC-Action Strategy for Nature Conservation2003-2007-full.doc. On the role of SPREP, see R. Herr, 'Environmental Protection in the South Pacific: The Effectiveness of SPREP and its Conventions', in O. S. Stokke and O. B. Thommessen (eds.), Yearbook of International Cooperation on Environment and Development 2002/2003 (2002), pp. 41–9.

[70] 'Australia's Concept Paper on the Future of the Apia Convention', SPREP Report on the Joint Eighth Conference of the Parties to the APIA and Noumea Conventions (2006), Annex 5.

[71] See, for example, SPREP's report to the 8th Joint Meeting of the Apia and Noumea Conventions on the Apia Convention (Doc. 8AC/8SC/WP.4). The report makes reference to a range of activities, most of which would have been very likely to have taken place even if the Apia Convention had not actually been in force: the CBD's IBPOW, co-operation between SPREP and RAMSAR, and the Coral Reef Initiative (a project which has attracted interest from fifteen Pacific island countries and three French territories; see www.crisponline.net).

[72] See SPREP, 'Concept Paper on the Relationship between the Apia Convention and Other Relevant Conventions' (2006) (Document 8AC/8SC/WP.6.1.1/Att.1), p. 1 (this paper was prepared at the behest of the Joint 7th Conference of the Parties to the APIA and Noumea Conventions held in 2004).

available to set up a suitable working group. The revision process now looks to have come to a halt following the decision of the CBD's eighth CoP to adopt the Island Biodiversity Programme of Work (IBPOW) to reduce island biodiversity loss.[73] Bearing in mind the considerable functional overlap between the Apia Convention and the CBD,[74] and the fact that all parties to the former are also parties to the latter, the Apia Convention states decided in 2006 to suspend its operation. This move was proposed by Australia, which noted that, especially after the adoption of the IBPOW,[75] the CBD 'provides a much more comprehensive basis for nature conservation at a global, regional and national level, and importantly allows for financial assistance through the Global Environment Facility'.[76] The Apia Convention is therefore now effectively suspended, but not terminated.[77]

4. Protected Area Protocols under the Regional Seas Programme

The Regional Seas Programme was established by UNEP in 1974 to promote the sustainable use and management of the marine and coastal environment. Thirteen regions have now adopted regional programmes specifically under the guidance of UNEP,[78] and each of these regions has adopted an Action Plan. Many have additionally adopted a legal framework in the form of treaties and additional protocols. Discussion will focus on those programmes that have adopted legally binding protocols in relation to Specially Protected Areas (SPAs).

The Jakarta Mandate on Marine and Coastal Biological Diversity adopted by CBD parties in 1995 underlines the importance of establishing coastal and marine protected areas, and the CBD parties have subsequently agreed that 'marine and coastal protected areas are one of the

[73] On IBPOW see Decision VIII/1 'Island Biodiversity' adopted by the CBD CoP 8 2006.

[74] SPREP report, *supra* n. 71. [75] Ibid.

[76] 'Australia's Concept Paper on the Future of the Apia Convention', *supra* n. 70.

[77] The Australian proposal notes, inter alia, that the CBD covers the same subject matter as the Apia Convention and that the parties to the latter intended that the CBD 'should govern the subject-matter and so regard the Apia Convention as suspended in operation until further notice'. Australia, the Cook Islands and Fiji have agreed to the wording; confirmation is still awaited from France and Samoa. No meetings of the parties are now held.

[78] UNEP is directly responsible for the administration of six of these schemes. In addition to the thirteen programmes, a further five regions have adopted independent programmes. See generally www.unep.org/regionalseas/Programmes/default.asp.

essential tools and approaches in the conservation and sustainable use of marine and coastal biodiversity'.[79] The Regional Seas Programme acts as an important means by which such objectives can be achieved. Four SPA Protocols have entered into force at the time of writing;[80] while most activity relating to protected areas has taken place under the protocols relating to the Caribbean and Mediterranean regions, two other Regional Seas programmes (the South East Pacific and the Eastern African) have operational protocols promoting the establishment of protected areas.

a) *The Barcelona SPA Protocol (Mediterranean)*

The 1995 Protocol concerning Specially Protected Areas and Biological Diversity in the Mediterranean was adopted in Barcelona,[81] and came into force on 12 December 1999 (the Barcelona SPA Protocol).[82] It is a key facilitator of CBD implementation in the Mediterranean area. Under the instrument, parties are obliged to take action to 'protect, preserve and manage in a sustainable and environmentally sound way areas of particular natural or cultural value, notably by the establishment of specially protected areas',[83] and to 'protect, preserve and manage threatened or endangered species of flora and fauna'.[84] Additionally, parties are to co-operate in the conservation and sustainable use of biological diversity,[85] and adopt 'strategies, plans and programmes for the conservation of biological diversity and the sustainable use of marine and coastal

[79] CBD CoP Decision VII/5.

[80] Note also the 2005 Protocol Concerning the Conservation of Biological Diversity and the Establishment of Protected Areas in the Red Sea and Gulf of Aden, which has not as yet entered into force; see *infra* n. 179 and accompanying text.

[81] See generally www.unep.org/regionalseas/programmes/unpro/mediterranean/default.asp. Also A. Vallega, 'Towards the Sustainable Management of the Mediterranean Sea' (1995) 19(1) *Marine Policy* 47; T. Scovazzi, *Marine Specially Protected Areas: The General Aspects and the Mediterranean Regional System* (Kluwer, 1999); and T. Scovazzi, 'New International Instruments for Marine Protected Areas in the Mediterranean Sea', in M. Gavouneli, N. Skourtos and A. Strati (eds.), *Unresolved Issues and New Challenges to the Law of the Sea: Time before and Time after* (Martinus Nijhoff, 2006), Chapter 5.

[82] Reproduced at www.unep.org/regionalseas/Programmes/unpro/mediterranean/instruments/default.asp, it replaces the 1982 Protocol Concerning Mediterranean Specially Protected Areas and has seventeen parties. The Barcelona SPA Protocol was negotiated within the remit of the 1995 Convention for the Protection of the Marine Environment and the Coastal Region of the Mediterranean (Barcelona Convention), reproduced at www.unepmap.org/index.php?module=content2&catid=001001004.

[83] Article 3(1)a. [84] Article 3(1)b. [85] Article 3(2).

biological resources and ... integrate them into their relevant sectoral and intersectoral policies'.[86]

The establishment of Specially Protected Areas is designed to safeguard representative ecosystems; disappearing habitats; habitats of importance to the survival of endangered, threatened or endemic species; and areas of particular scientific, aesthetic, cultural or educational importance.[87] A range of protection measures must be introduced in every protected area,[88] as well as a variety of planning, supervision and monitoring measures.[89] The instrument obliges parties to establish a List of Specially Protected Areas of Mediterranean Importance (the SPAMI List).[90] Common criteria have been established for the listing of protected marine and coastal areas on this list.[91] The criteria stipulate that to be eligible a site must have at least two of the attributes noted in Article 8(2) of the Protocol,[92] and that any such areas 'must have a protected status guaranteeing their effective long-term protection'.[93]

A SPAMI can be established in an area which is partly or wholly in international waters, and in this respect the Barcelona SPA Protocol differs from its counterparts in the Eastern African, South East Pacific and Caribbean regions, which apply only to areas within which parties exercise either sovereignty or sovereign rights.[94] The ability to include the relatively small areas of high seas within protected areas is designed to ensure full protection of migratory species through their natural range in the Mediterranean.[95] The first SPAMI sites were officially listed at the 12th Meeting of the Parties to the Barcelona Convention and its protocols in 2001. Of these sites, the Monegasque Sanctuary for the protection of marine mammals is a transboundary site nominated by three countries (France, Italy and Monaco) and covers 87,000 square kilometres. All species of marine mammal are afforded protection within the sanctuary.[96]

[86] Article 3(4). [87] Article 4. [88] Article 6. [89] Article 7. [90] Article 8.

[91] Annex I to the Barcelona SPA Protocol adopted on 24 November 1996.

[92] Article 8(2) indicates that the SPAMI list 'may include sites which: are of importance for conserving the components of biological diversity in the Mediterranean; contain ecosystems specific to the Mediterranean area or the habitats of endangered species; are of special interest at the scientific, aesthetic, cultural or educational levels'.

[93] Annex I, part C(1).

[94] T. Scovazzi, 'Marine Protected Areas on the High Seas: Some Legal and Policy Considerations', paper delivered at the World Parks Congress (Durban, South Africa, 11 September 2003), pp. 12–13, available at https://69.90.183.227/doc/articles/2004/A-00150.pdf.

[95] Ibid., p. 13. [96] On the sanctuary see further at ibid., p. 15.

In addition to promoting the establishment of protected areas, the Barcelona SPA Protocol places obligations on state parties to 'manage species of flora and fauna with the aim of maintaining them in a favourable state of conservation'.[97] Parties must draw up lists of threatened species and give them protected status,[98] and conservation efforts are to be co-ordinated if needs be.[99] Certain flora and fauna, such as the green turtle (*Chelonia mydas*), Eleonora's falcon (*Falco eleonorae*) and the harbour porpoise (*Phocoena phocoena*), have been noted by all parties in the 'List of Endangered or Threatened Species' in Annex II. All parties must introduce at the national level measures to protect these Annex II species and their habitats. Parties must also ensure the conservation of 'species whose exploitation is regulated' and which are listed in Annex III.

The Protocol additionally imposes obligations concerning impact assessment,[100] and with regard to the provision of publicity on the establishment of protected sites and the designation of protected species.[101] The pursuit of scientific and technical research is encouraged.[102] Parties are also obliged to report on implementation of the protocol to the regular meetings of the parties,[103] and to designate national focal points to liaise with the UNEP Mediterranean Action Plan Regional Activity Centre for Specially Protected Areas.[104] The latter is located in Tunis and supports a variety of activities, including efforts of the parties to establish and manage protected areas, the preparation of management plans, and the facilitation of scientific and technical studies.

A key feature of the work initiated under the Protocol is the range of action plans adopted to guide national activities in relation to specific species. Plans have been adopted regarding, inter alia, the management of the highly endangered monk seal and also the conservation of cetaceans, marine turtles, marine vegetation, cartilaginous fish and marine bird species. SPAs in the Mediterranean now cover 144,000 square kilometres and total 800 in number.[105] Nonetheless, '63% of the fish and 60% of the mammals listed in the [Barcelona SPA Protocol] have endangered status, from increasing pressures (construction/disappearance of such

[97] Article 11(1). [98] Article 11(2). [99] Article 11(4). [100] Article 17.
[101] Article 19. [102] Article 20. [103] Article 23. [104] Article 24.
[105] UNEP/MAP-Plan Bleu, *State of the Environment and Development in the Mediterranean* (UNEP/MAP-Plan Bleu, 2009), p. 11.

ecosystems as lagoons, grassbeds), coastal erosion, over-exploited marine resources and expansion of invasive species'.[106]

b) The Kingston SPAW Protocol (Caribbean)[107]

The Caribbean Action Plan was enacted in 1981 and was followed by the adoption of the 1983 Convention for the Protection and Development of the Marine Environment of the Wider Caribbean Region (Cartagena Convention).[108] In 1990 the Protocol Concerning Specially Protected Areas and Wildlife in the Wider Caribbean Region was also opened for signature (the Kingston SPAW Protocol).[109] It came into force on 18 June 2000 and currently has thirteen parties.[110] The 'marine seascape of the Caribbean supports a complex interaction of three distinct ecosystems: coral reefs, mangrove stands, and seagrass beds',[111] and the Protocol acts as a regional vehicle for implementation of the CBD, CITES, CMS and Ramsar, and the Western Hemisphere Convention.[112] The Kingston SPAW Protocol obliges parties to introduce measures 'to protect, preserve and manage in a sustainable way' not only areas that 'require protection to safeguard their special value', but also 'threatened or endangered species of flora and fauna'.[113] Activities having adverse effects in protected areas must be regulated and parties are to co-operate in the enforcement of regulatory measures.[114] Fauna and flora are to be managed in a way which prevents species becoming endangered or threatened.[115]

Protected areas are to be established not only to conserve and maintain, but importantly also to restore representative types of both marine and coastal ecosystems; habitats of importance to the survival of endangered, threatened and endemic species; and areas of special importance 'whose ecological and biological processes are essential to the

[106] Ibid.

[107] See generally http://www.unep.org/regionalseas/programmes/unpro/caribbean/default.asp.

[108] (1983) 22 *ILM* 221.

[109] (1990) 1 *Yearbook of International Environmental Law* 441.

[110] Barbados, Belize, Colombia, Cuba, Dominican Republic, France, the Netherlands, Panama, St Lucia, Saint Vincent and the Grenadines, Trinidad and Tobago, the USA and Venezuela.

[111] www.unep.org/regionalseas/programmes/unpro/caribbean/instruments/r_profile_car.pdf, p. 7.

[112] See www.cep.unep.org/welcome/about-cep/spaw/objectives.

[113] Article 3(1).

[114] Article 3(2).

[115] Article 3(3).

functioning of the wider Caribbean ecosystems'.[116] Additionally, areas are to be set up to conserve, maintain and restore 'the productivity of ecosystems and natural resources that provide economic or social benefits and upon which the welfare of local inhabitants is dependent'.[117] To protect these areas, various measures should be enacted 'as appropriate', including the regulation or prohibition of certain activities such as the dumping of waste and the hunting of endangered or threatened species.[118] Planning, management and enforcement measures must be introduced,[119] and buffer zones around protected areas may be put into place 'as necessary'.[120] Where protected or buffer zones run adjacent to the borders of another party, the two states shall consult each other on measures and discuss the possibility of a contiguous protected and/or buffer zone being introduced.[121]

A system of species protection is introduced for endangered and threatened flora and fauna. In relation to migratory species, parties are to co-ordinate their efforts to protect such species.[122] The level of protection afforded to endangered and threatened species depends on whether they are placed in Annex I, II or III. All forms of destruction or disturbance of flora in Annex I, such as Chapman's rhododendron (*Rhododendron chapmanii*), is prohibited (including commercial trade).[123] The taking, possession, killing and commercial trade of protected fauna in Annex II, such as the American crocodile (*Crocodylus acutus*), is also prohibited.[124] 'To the extent possible' the disturbance of Annex II protected fauna is banned.[125] As regards flora and fauna noted in Annex III, while their use is not prohibited, it may be regulated 'to ensure and maintain their populations at the highest possible levels'.[126] Examples of Annex III species include the common iguana (*Iguana iguana*) and the tayra (*Eira barbara*). The Protocol also seeks to regulate or prohibit the introduction of harmful non-indigenous or genetically altered species.[127] Projects that would have a 'negative environmental impact and significantly affect' either protected areas or species shall be subject to a system of environmental impact assessment.[128]

In establishing the system of protection and management at national level, parties can grant exemptions to meet traditional subsistence and cultural needs. However, no exemption is to endanger the maintenance

[116] Article 4. [117] Ibid. [118] Articles 5(2)(a) and 5(2)(d). [119] Article 6.
[120] Article 7. [121] Article 9. [122] Article 10(5). [123] Article 11(1)(a).
[124] Article 11(2)(i). [125] Article 11(2)(2). [126] Article 11(3). [127] Article 12.
[128] Article 13.

of protected areas, or cause the extinction of, substantial risk to or substantial reduction in the populations of fauna and flora in those protected areas.[129] Public awareness and education is to be encouraged, with publicity being given to the protected areas and species, and the reasons for their importance and protection underlined.[130] Parties must additionally endeavour to ensure public participation in decisions relating to the protected areas and species.[131]

Scientific and technical research regarding protected areas and species and their management is to be encouraged.[132] The results of such research are to be exchanged between the parties,[133] and research and monitoring activities co-ordinated.[134] The Scientific and Technical Advisory Committee (STAC) has met on four occasions since the Protocol entered into force and provides advice on a range of issues including the listing of protected areas and species, impact assessments and technical assistance for training, education, management and research.[135] Parties have committed themselves to providing assistance to each other in developing and financing programmes related to the protection of areas and species; these programmes are to include provision for such matters as the training of personnel, scientific research and public education.[136]

In relation to implementation, each party must report periodically and these reports are to be analysed by the meeting of the parties (MoP), which has general responsibility for reviewing the Protocol and directing implementation.[137] The MoP meets once every two years in conjunction with meetings of parties of the Cartagena Convention. The parties are obliged to adopt and update common guidelines and criteria for the identification of protected areas and species, as well as the establishment and management of protected areas.[138] UNEP's regional office based in Kingston, Jamaica, fulfils Secretariat functions, and each party to the Protocol has designated a Focal Point to liaise with UNEP in this respect.

The Kingston Protocol's current SPAW Programme is an active one and has six elements: programme co-ordination, the strengthening of protected areas, the development of guidelines for protected areas and species management, the conservation of threatened and endangered species, the conservation and sustainable use of coastal

[129] Article 14. [130] Article 16. [131] Ibid. [132] Article 17(1). [133] Article 17(3). [134] Article 17(4). [135] Article 20. [136] Article 18. [137] Articles 19 and 23(8). [138] Article 21.

and marine ecosystems, and sustainable tourism.[139] The Secretariat already has memoranda of co-operation with the CBD and Ramsar, and has collaborated with the CMS, CITES, the Inter-American Convention for the Protection and Conservation of Marine Turtles, and also the World Heritage Convention. In this way, the duplication of work is avoided and resources most effectively utilised at the regional level.

Initiatives within the régime include support for the protection of marine mammals (including the manatee), hawksbill sea turtles, and threatened birds such as the West Indian whistling duck (*Dendrocygna arborea*). A SPAW species database has also been introduced, and assistance provided in protected areas management by means of, inter alia, the Caribbean Marine Protected Areas Managers network. In addition, the Secretariat has been designated as the regional contact point under the International Coral Reef Initiative (ICRI), and manages the International Coral Reef Action Network (ICRAN) regional project known as the Mesoamerican Reef Alliance (MAR). Designed to reduce coral reef destruction, MAR is in part funded by USAID. It seeks to promote the sustainable management of the Mesoamerican reef, which spans more than 600 miles of the coastline of Mexico, Belize, Guatemala and Honduras.

c) Nairobi SPAW Protocol (Eastern Africa)

The drafting of the East African Action Plan commenced in September 1982 and was finalised in Kenya in June 1985.[140] At the same meeting the 1985 Convention for the Protection, Management and Development of the Marine and Coastal Environment of the Eastern African Region (Nairobi Convention) was adopted.[141] In addition, the Protocol Concerning Protected Areas and Wild Fauna and Flora in the Eastern African Region (Nairobi SPAW Protocol) was opened for signature.[142] However, it took until the end of May 1996 for the Nairobi SPAW Protocol to enter into force. There is no doubt that a lack of funding and capacity hindered the effectiveness of the Protocol in its early years,

[139] Workplan and Budget for the SPAW Regional Programme for the 2008–2009 Biennium, doc. UNEP(DEPI)/CAR WG.31/5.Rev.1.

[140] See generally www.unep.org/regionalseas/programmes/unpro/easternafrica/default.asp.

[141] *IELMT* 985:46. In force 30 May 1996.

[142] Available at eelink.net/~asilwildlife/EastAfrPro.html. There are ten parties.

though activity has increased more recently. In particular, funding has been forthcoming from a number of countries, including Belgium, Finland, France, Ireland, the Netherlands, Norway, Sweden and the USA. UNEP offices in Nairobi act as the Secretariat for the Nairobi Convention and associated protocols.

Recognising that the Protocol was outdated, the parties have initiated moves to amend it in the light of subsequent developments and practice, such as Agenda 21 and the CBD. Nevertheless, the agreement does oblige parties to 'take all appropriate measures to maintain essential ecological processes and life support systems, to preserve genetic diversity, and to ensure the sustainable utilization of harvested natural resources under their jurisdiction'.[143] Annex I lists protected species of wild flora such as endangered African violets (*Saintpaulia rupicola*). Activities 'having adverse effects on the habitats of these species' shall be prohibited, as must the 'uncontrolled picking, collecting, cutting or uprooting' of such species.[144] Fauna noted in Annex II must be made subject to a system of special protection due to their endangered status.[145] Annex II fauna include the dugong (*Dugong dugon* – a marine mammal which grazes on seagrass), the aye-aye (*Daubentonia madagascariensis* – an endangered lemur from Madagascar), and a variety of threatened birds such as the Grand Comoro drongo (*Dicrurus fuscipennis*). Annex III species, including the African buffalo (*Syncerus caffer*), can be harvested but their exploitation must be made subject to a system of regulation 'to restore and maintain the populations at optimum levels'.[146] Certain migratory species are noted in Annex IV and include the humpback whale (*Megaptera novaeangliae*). Efforts by parties to protect Annex IV migratory species are to be co-ordinated.[147] Additionally, the introduction of harmful alien species is to be prohibited.[148]

It is important to note that many of the species protected under the Protocol are not in fact marine species, the parties being obliged to, 'where necessary, establish protected areas in areas under their jurisdiction with a view to safeguarding the natural resources of the Eastern African region'.[149] Buffer zones may be set up around these areas.[150] Measures which may be introduced in protected areas include a planning and management system; a ban on waste discharge; prohibition of plant destruction; the regulation of recreational, archaeological, fishing and hunting activities and any other activity

[143] Article 2(1). [144] Article 3. [145] Article 4. [146] Article 5. [147] Article 6.
[148] Article 7. [149] Article 8(1). [150] Article 11.

'likely to harm or disturb the fauna or flora'.[151] Protected areas in the region include the Cousin Island Marine Protected Area (Seychelles), known for its coral reefs and as a highly important breeding site for hawksbill turtles. Others include the Malindi and Watamu Marine National Park and Reserve (Kenya), the Nosy Atafana Marine Park (Madagascar), and the Dar es Salaam Marine Reserve (Tanzania), where the bleaching of coral reefs has been a particular issue in recent times. Also of particular importance under the Nairobi SPAW Protocol is ensuring the effective protection of mangroves and seagrass beds. These important habitats and the species that inhabit them are under threat from various activities, including overfishing and the discharge of waste.

The Nairobi SPAW Protocol additionally includes provisions which seek to promote exchange of information,[152] publicity on the establishment of protected areas,[153] public education on the importance of protected species and areas,[154] scientific and technical research,[155] and the adoption of a regional programme to co-ordinate the selection and management of protected areas and the protection of protected species.[156] Meetings of the parties are held in conjunction with meetings under the Nairobi Convention.[157] In collaboration with organisations such as the IUCN, the IMO, WWF, the Western Indian Ocean Marine Science Association and the International Coral Reef Initiative, activities in the region have included efforts to prevent the destruction of coral reefs, to protect marine mammals and to facilitate the effective management of protected sites.

d) The Paipa SPA Protocol (South East Pacific)

The 1981 Lima Convention for the Protection of the Marine Environment and Coastal Areas of the South East Pacific[158] (Lima Convention) came into force on 19 May 1986.[159] At the first meeting of the parties, held in Paipa, Colombia, in September 1989, Chile, Colombia, Ecuador, Panama and Peru signed the Protocol for the Conservation and Management of Protected Marine and Coastal Areas

151 Article 10. 152 Article 18. 153 Article 14. 154 Article 15. 155 Article 17.
156 Article 16. 157 Article 21.
158 See generally www.unep.org/regionalseas/programmes/nonunep/sepacific/default.asp.
159 *IELMT* 981:85.

of the South East Pacific (the Paipa SPA Protocol),[160] which entered into force in 1994.

The South East Pacific is a region affected by natural phenomena such as the cold Humboldt Current and El Niño, both of which impact upon the abundance of regional biodiversity.[161] The uniqueness of the region necessitates a regional approach to conservation and management.[162] Although concluded within the Regional Seas programme, the Paipa SPA Protocol is administered by the Permanent Commission for the South Pacific (CPPS) rather than by UNEP. The CPPS acts as the Protocol's Executive Secretariat.[163] Regular meetings of the parties are to be held at least every two years to discuss implementation.[164]

The Protocol endorses the promotion of scientific as well as technical research, and also seeks to promote education on the environment and increased public participation in the conservation and management of protected areas.[165] Co-operation between the parties is additionally endorsed on such matters as the exchange of information on experiences in management and research.[166] Moreover, parties are to promote 'programmes of scientific, technical, legal, educational and other assistance', to include training of personnel and the supply of experts and equipment.[167]

An obligation is placed on parties to establish protected areas to 'protect and preserve those ecosystems which are fragile, vulnerable or of unique natural or cultural value, with particular emphasis on flora and fauna threatened by depletion or extinction'.[168] Common criteria for the establishment of these areas are to be adopted,[169] and each party is to put in place a system of 'integrated environmental management' to include the management of flora and fauna and the specific prohibition of mining activities. Regulation of scientific, archaeological and tourism activities is to be introduced, in addition to the regulation of trade affecting fauna and flora and their habitats.[170] Any activity 'liable to have adverse effects on species, ecosystems or biological processes protecting such areas' is to be prohibited.[171]

A Regional Network of Coastal and Marine Protected Areas has been established. Protected coastal and marine areas in the region include La

[160] *IELMT* 989:71.
[161] Permanent Commission for the South Pacific, Regional Network of Coastal and Marine Protected Areas of the South East Pacific (available at www.cpps-int.org/spanish/planaccion/sep_fng.pdf), p. 2.
[162] Ibid. [163] Article XV. [164] Article IX. [165] Articles IX and XI. [166] Article X.
[167] Ibid. [168] Article II. [169] Article IV. [170] Article V. [171] Ibid.

Barqueta Agricola Wildlife Reserve (Panama), known for its beaches and nesting sea turtles, as well as the biodiversity-rich Tumbers Mangroves National Sanctuary (Peru), Pan de Azucar National Park (Chile), Parque Natural Ensenada de Utria (Colombia) and Churute-Mangrove Ecological Reserve (Ecuador). The Paipa SPA Protocol envisages the establishment of buffer zones around protected areas,[172] and the use of the environmental impact assessment procedure where activities are liable to bring about adverse effects.[173] Measures must be taken to prevent harm to the environment in protected areas.[174]

5. Conclusion

The CBD's 2002 Strategic Plan notes that the

> need to mainstream the conservation and sustainable use of biological resources across all sectors of the national economy, the society and the policy-making framework is a complex challenge at the heart of the Convention. This will mean cooperation with many different actors, such as regional bodies and organizations.[175]

In the South Pacific, SPREP activities now provide the key focus for such regional co-operation and the CBD's IBPOW will add renewed momentum in this regard. In Asia, whilst some ASEAN initiatives have been taken to protect wildlife at the regional level, an important opportunity has so far been missed to establish a legally binding regime which would have encouraged regional co-operation and capacity building. The ASEAN Agreement would also have introduced a means by which to gauge regional implementation of and compliance with international obligations not only under the CBD but also under other multilateral environmental agreements.

The adoption and implementation of SPA Protocols, particularly within the Caribbean and Mediterranean regional seas programmes, has undoubtedly facilitated regional activities which seek to implement CBD objectives.[176] Underlining the internationally acknowledged

[172] Article VI. [173] Article VIII. [174] Article VII.

[175] Strategic Plan for the CBD, *supra* n. 50, A.8.

[176] Additionally, and instead of facilitating the establishment of protected areas by means of a SPA protocol, the governing organisations of two independent regional seas programmes have adopted a series of recommendations relating to the promotion of such areas (Helcom in the Baltic area, and OSPAR in relation to the North East Atlantic). In the Baltic area, see the Helsinki Commission (Helcom) Recommendation 15/5 (1994) and associated guidance in Helcom HOD 11/2003 and Helcom Habitat 7/2005 (available at http://bspa.helcom.fi); in

importance of creating protected areas, relevant legal instruments relating to the Black Sea[177] and the North East Pacific[178] regions have also recently been adopted, partly at least with a view to the establishment of such areas. However, neither instrument is in force at the time of writing. A SPA Protocol to the 1982 Regional Convention for the Conservation of the Red Sea and Gulf of Aden (the Jeddah Convention)[179] has also been adopted within PERSGA (the Regional Organization for the Conservation of the Environment of the Red Sea and Gulf of Aden), but also has yet to enter into force.[180]

Recommended further reading

D. Freestone, 'Specially Protected Areas and Wildlife in the Caribbean: The 1990 Kingston Protocol to the Cartegena Convention' (1990) 5 *IJECL* 362

R. Herr, 'Environmental Protection in the South Pacific: The Effectiveness of SPREP and Its Conventions', in O. S. Stokke and O. B. Thommessen (eds.), Yearbook of International Cooperation on Environment and Development 2002/2003 (2002), pp. 41–9

K. L. Koh, 'ASEAN Agreement on the Conservation of Nature and Natural Resources, 1985: A Study in Environmental Governance', paper given to the World Parks Congress 2003 (Durban, 8–17 September 2003) available at law.nus.edu.sg/apcel/publications/pub/kohkhenglian/aseanagreement.doc

T. Scovazzi, *Marine Specially Protected Areas: The General Aspects and the Mediterranean Regional System* (Kluwer, 1999)

UNEP-WCMC, *National and Regional Networks of Marine Protected Areas: A Review of Progress* (UNEP-WCMC, 2008)

relation to the North East Atlantic, see OSPAR Commission Recommendation 2003/3 (available at www.ospar.org).

177 See Articles 4(1)(a) and Annex 1 of the 2003 Black Sea Biodiversity and Landscape Conservation Protocol to the 1992 Convention on the Protection of the Black Sea against Pollution. This instrument is available at http://blacksea-commission.org.

178 See Articles 6(2)(c) and 10(2)(h) of the 2002 Convention for Cooperation in the Protection and Sustainable Development of the Marine and Coastal Environment of the Northeast Pacific (the 'Antigua Convention'). This instrument is available at http://unep.org/regionalseas/Publications/neo.doc.

179 Reproduced at www.persga.org/inner.php?id=62.

180 The 2005 Protocol Concerning the Conservation of Biological Diversity and the Establishment of Protected Areas in the Red Sea and Gulf of Aden is reproduced at www.persga.org/inner.php?id=62. Additionally it is understood at the time of writing that a SPA protocol is being negotiated in the Kuwait region under the auspices of ROPME (the Regional Organization for the Protection of the Marine Environment – Kuwait).

PART IV

Global wildlife regulation

Chapter 13

The Ramsar Convention on Wetlands

1. Background

Wetlands are estimated to cover approximately 9 per cent of the earth's land surface,[1] and they are amongst the most productive of all ecosystems, a subtropical saltmarsh having the capacity to produce organic material at more than twice the rate of the most fertile hayfield. Similarly, coral reefs, despite covering less than 1 per cent of the world's ocean area, are home to one-third of all marine fish species, their associated fisheries yielding a catch of some 6 million metric tons annually.[2] Apart from fish, wetlands provide essential habitat for countless species of waterfowl, amphibians, reptiles, mammals and plants. In addition, they act as natural sponges which control floods and droughts, and can absorb sediments, nutrients and toxicants, many of which are put to productive use within the wetland ecosystem. They are also an important source of water supply, with up to three billion people globally being dependent upon groundwater for drinking purposes. The total value of the services delivered by wetlands has been speculatively valued at US$14 trillion annually,[3] and their conservation is accordingly essential.[4] Yet in spite of these vital functions, wetlands in many parts of the world have been destroyed at an alarming rate in recent decades by excessive extraction, drainage, land reclamation and pollution. It has recently been

[1] I.e. around 1,280 million hectares, on one estimate.

[2] Ramsar Resolution IX.4, preamble.

[3] See Annexes II and III to the Report of the 9th Meeting of the Conference of the Parties to the Ramsar Convention. All such reports, together with the text of CoP resolutions, recommendations and other key documents, can be found via the 'Documents' link on the Ramsar website at www.ramsar.org. Documents not available on the site may be obtainable in hard copy from the Ramsar Convention Secretariat, rue Mauverney 28, CH-1196 Gland, Switzerland.

[4] See generally E. Maltby, *Waterlogged Wealth* (Earthscan, 2nd ed., 2007); P. J. Dugan (ed.), *Wetland Conservation: A Review of Current Issues and Required Action* (IUCN, 1990); M. Finlayson and M. Moser (eds.), *Wetlands* (IWRB/Facts on File, 1991).

noted that in the United States, for example, 'over half of the 230 million hectares of wetlands that the first settlers found upon arrival has been lost'.[5]

In an effort to stem this tide of destruction, a series of international conferences and technical meetings were held during the 1960s,[6] mainly under the auspices of the International Waterfowl Research Bureau (IWRB),[7] whose primary concern was to protect the numerous species of bird that were dependent upon wetland habitats. As a result, the Convention on Wetlands of International Importance, Especially as Waterfowl Habitat[8] was concluded on 2 February 1971 in the Iranian town of Ramsar (hence the name 'Ramsar' by which the Convention is commonly known). It came into force on 21 December 1975 and currently has 160 parties in total. Ramsar's administrative centre is located at IUCN headquarters in Gland, Switzerland.[9] A significant, innovative feature of the Convention was the provision for the convening of periodic conferences to review its implementation.[10]

This chapter first considers the objectives and general nature of the Convention before examining one of its key features, the Ramsar List of Wetlands of International Importance ('the List'), which currently contains almost 1,900 wetlands globally. It then analyses the substantive obligations relating to these and other wetland sites, before describing the Convention's administrative structure, arrangements for implementation and relationships with other instruments.

2. Objectives

The preamble to the Convention states that its objective is 'to stem the progressive encroachment on and loss of wetlands now and in the future', recognising them as 'a resource of great economic, cultural, scientific and recreational value'. Article 1(1) defines wetlands as 'areas of marsh, fen, peatland or water, whether natural or artificial, permanent or temporary, with water that is static or flowing, fresh, brackish

5 C. Di Leva, The Ramsar Convention on Wetlands: The Role of 'Urgent National Interests' and 'Compensation' in Wetland Protection (IUCN Consultation Paper, 2000), p. 11.

6 See G. V. T. Matthews, *The Ramsar Convention on Wetlands: Its History and Development* (Ramsar Bureau, 1993).

7 IWRB, an NGO based in Slimbridge, Gloucestershire, UK, subsequently changed its name to the International Waterfowl and Wetlands Research Bureau, and later joined with the Asian Wetland Bureau and Wetlands for the Americas to form Wetlands International.

8 996 *UNTS* 245. See further Ramsar Convention Secretariat, The Ramsar Convention Manual: A Guide to the Convention on Wetlands (4th ed., 2006).

9 See section 5(b) below. 10 See further section 5(a) below.

or salt, including areas of marine water the depth of which at low tide does not exceed six metres'. This is an exceptionally broad definition,[11] and Ramsar accordingly aims to protect habitats as diverse as peat bogs, floodplains, coastal waters and beaches, mangrove swamps, coral reefs, tidal flats, mountain lakes, tropical rivers, rice paddies, flooded gravel pits and even subterranean karst systems.[12] Specifically, it seeks to promote the 'wise use' of all wetlands and special protection for those included in the List. It also encourages research into wetland ecosystems, seeks to promote training in the fields of wetland research and management and requires the parties to co-operate in implementing their obligations under the Convention. There is no doubt that it has had a considerable positive impact on wetland conservation in many states,[13] particularly through the promulgation of guidance regarding best practice.[14]

Nevertheless, Ramsar was initially the subject of considerable criticism,[15] not least from within,[16] on the basis that the conservation obligations it imposed were insufficiently rigorous, that there were too few non-European parties and that its administrative and financial arrangements were woefully inadequate by comparison with comparable treaties. Considerable efforts have been made to tackle these problems, however, and the prospects for the Convention are consequently much improved. At recent meetings of the CoP, it has been decided to streamline implementation of the Convention's Strategic Plan around five key goals.[17] These are, essentially, to work towards achieving the wise use of all wetlands, and in particular to maintain an international network of sites that are important for the conservation of global biological diversity; to promote effective international co-operation and to ensure that the

[11] It has been suggested that of over fifty definitions of wetlands currently in use this is the broadest: P. J. Dugan, *Wetlands in Danger* (Oxford University Press, 1993), p. 12.

[12] See the Ramsar Classification System for Wetland Type, Resolution VII.11, Appendix A.

[13] See G. Castro et al., *The Ramsar Convention: Measuring its Effectiveness for Conserving Wetlands of International Importance* (World Bank/WWF, 2002); M. J. Bowman, 'The Ramsar Convention on Wetlands: Has It Made a Difference?' (2002–3) *YBICED* 61; R. C. Gardner and K. D. Connolly, 'The Ramsar Convention on Wetlands: Assessment of International Designations within the United States' (2007) 37 *Environmental Law Reporter* 10089; and R. C. Gardner, K. D. Connolly and A. Bamba, 'African Wetlands of International Importance' (2009) 21 *Georgetown IELR* 257.

[14] Note especially the Ramsar *Handbooks for Wise Use*, discussed in section 4(a) below.

[15] See, e.g., the World Conservation Strategy (1980), section 15, para. 5.

[16] Key deficiencies identified at the first CoP are listed in Recommendation 1.8.

[17] See currently Resolution X.1, which sets out the Strategic Plan for 2009–15.

Convention itself possesses the appropriate mechanisms, resources and capacity to achieve its mission; and to progress towards universal Ramsar membership.

3. The List of Wetlands of International Importance

A central feature of the Ramsar Convention is the List of Wetlands of International Importance which has been established pursuant to Article 2.

a) Designation of sites for the List

In contrast to the World Heritage Convention,[18] which has a screening procedure for the inclusion of sites in the World Heritage List, Ramsar allows the unilateral designation of sites for the List of Wetlands of International Importance. Indeed, each party is obliged to designate 'suitable wetlands within its territory' for inclusion in the List,[19] including at least one at the time it signs, ratifies or accedes to the Convention.[20] It is expressly provided that the inclusion of a wetland in the List does not prejudice the exclusive sovereign rights of the party in whose territory it is situated.[21] The boundaries of each listed site must be 'precisely described and also delimited on a map', and may include adjacent riparian and coastal zones, as well as 'islands and bodies of marine water deeper than six metres at low tide lying within the wetlands' in question,[22] thereby effectively extending the wide definition of wetlands still further for this particular purpose. A pro forma Ramsar Information Sheet (RIS), to be completed upon designation and periodically updated,[23] calls for the provision of data concerning the site, its legal status and ecological characteristics.[24] The parties may extend

[18] See Chapter 14 below.

[19] Article 2(1). A controversial Swiss proposal to extend Ramsar coverage to Antarctica was recently withdrawn 'in a spirit of compromise'. See Report of the 9th Meeting of the CoP, paras. 178–80.

[20] Article 2(4). [21] Article 2(3). [22] Article 2(1).

[23] Resolution VI.13 calls for the submission of revised data 'at least every six years'. The current version of the Information Sheet was established by Resolution VIII.13, as amended by Resolution IX.1, Annex B. Resolution X.15 provides guidance on the provision of complementary information regarding the ecological character of wetlands.

[24] See Resolutions VI.13, VIII.13 and VIII.21. Resolution X.13 lists over 120 parties that were in default of this obligation in some respect. Such failures are not regarded as invalidating the designation, however: see *Minister for the Environment and Heritage v Greentree (No.2)* 2004 FCA 741 (Australia).

the boundaries of listed sites or add further wetlands to the List at any time.[25] The List is maintained by IUCN in its capacity as 'Bureau' (i.e. Secretariat) under the Convention.[26]

Designated wetlands vary greatly in size, from tiny sites occupying no more than one hectare, such as Ile Alcatraz in Guinea and Hosnie's Spring on Christmas Island,[27] to the vast expanses of Queen Maud Gulf in Canada and the Okavango Delta in Botswana, each extending to around 6 million hectares. Recognising that achievement of the Convention's aims requires the designation of as many, widely varied, wetlands of international importance as possible, the CoP has frequently exhorted the parties to increase the global total of listed sites, as well as calling for particular sites to be added, or for the listing of wetlands of particular types.[28]

At the time of completion of the first edition of this work in 1985, the List contained some 294 wetlands covering around 20 million hectares; now, twenty-five years on, the total has increased to 1,898 sites occupying 186 million hectares.[29] Various parties which initially designated only the legal minimum of one site have subsequently added many others: thus Australia, the first country to ratify the Convention, currently has sixty-five listed sites in all, while Mexico, which did not ratify until 1986, now has 114. Algeria, which for many years had only two Ramsar sites, has added a further forty-five since 1999, while the UK, which originally listed thirteen sites, now boasts a total of 168. Even states which have only designated one site[30] may still have made a potentially substantial contribution to the cause of wetland conservation: Botswana's Okavango Delta, for example, is vastly larger than the aggregated area of all the UK sites. Azraq Oasis, listed by Jordan, is reckoned to be that country's only wetland of importance to waterfowl, while the Banc d'Arguin, which for a number of years was the only site designated by Mauritania,[31] is a crucial wintering ground and resting point for millions of migratory waterfowl, emphasising the ecological

[25] Article 2(5). [26] See below, section 5(b). [27] Listed by Australia.

[28] See generally the Strategic Framework and Guidelines for the Future Development of the List, Resolution VII.11, as supplemented and revised by Resolutions VIII.10, IX.1, Annex B, and X.20.

[29] The List is viewable via the link indicated *supra* n. 3.

[30] This is currently true of around thirty parties, though most are either small island states or developing countries that have only recently acceded.

[31] Mauritania currently has four listed sites.

links between sites in different continents and the vital need for international co-operation in the conservation of major flyways.

Despite these noteworthy developments, progress regarding site designation has tended to fall behind the ambitious targets set by successive Strategic Plans, and the current goal of expanding the Ramsar List to at least 2,500 sites covering 250 million hectares has been deferred to 2015 from its original target date of 2010.[32]

b) *Criteria for inclusion*

Article 2(2) of Ramsar states,

> Wetlands should be selected for the List on account of their international significance in terms of ecology, botany, zoology, limnology or hydrology. In the first instance, wetlands of international importance to waterfowl at any season should be included.[33]

Recognising the need for more specific guidance on eligibility, the parties have formulated a set of criteria for that purpose,[34] which have been revised on several occasions.[35] The current version incorporates nine criteria in all, including Criterion 1, for assessing the value of representative, rare or unique wetlands; Criteria 2–4, concerning species and ecological communities generally; and Criteria 5–9, which focus specifically upon waterfowl, fish or other species to identify wetlands of international importance. Under this scheme, a site may be listed if, for instance, it contains a representative example of a (near-)natural wetland type found within the appropriate biogeographical region; if it supports vulnerable or endangered species or threatened ecological communities, or helps to sustain plant or animal species at a critical stage in their life cycles, or provides refuge during adverse conditions; if it regularly supports 20,000 or more waterbirds, or 1 per cent of the population of any (sub)species of waterfowl, or of other wetland fauna; or if it is an important source of food for fish, or a spawning ground, nursery and/or migration path on which fish stocks, either within the wetland or

[32] See Resolutions IX.1, Annex B, and X.1, Strategy 2.1.

[33] Limnology is the study of lakes and other freshwater bodies.

[34] The initial version was adopted at a conference organised by IWRB in Heiligenhafen, Germany, in December 1974, even before the Convention had entered into force; see Matthews, *supra* n. 6, p. 48. The official report is viewable on the website, via the 'Documents' and 'Conferences of the Parties' links.

[35] See generally the Strategic Framework for Development of the List, *supra* n. 28.

elsewhere, depend. These criteria are all supported by guidelines concerning their detailed application.[36]

Under these criteria, nesting beaches for endangered sea turtles, rivers containing rare endemic crustaceans, estuaries which serve as breeding areas for commercial fisheries or other wetlands with comparable qualities are just as worthy of inclusion in the List as habitat for waterfowl.[37] Indeed, there has been a deliberate attempt over the years to de-emphasise the waterfowl criteria to some extent, not least for the reason that the conservation of birds is unlikely to be the highest priority of developing countries, whose participation in the Convention is rightly considered essential.[38] Recently, particular efforts have been made to enhance recognition of the cultural values of wetlands, and to strengthen the role of local communities and indigenous peoples in their management.[39] The socioeconomic importance of wetlands has also been stressed, whether in respect of water supply, agriculture or fishery resources;[40] human health;[41] or the reduction of poverty.[42] It nevertheless remains the case that a substantial proportion of listed sites have been designated, particularly during the earlier period of the Convention's history, on account of their importance to waterfowl.[43] This is partly due to the continuous involvement of ornithological organisations in Ramsar's implementation, coupled with the consideration that the waterfowl criteria have generally proved the easiest to apply: while IWRB's extended network of

[36] Ibid.

[37] Waterfowl are defined by Article 1(2) as 'birds ecologically dependent on wetlands'.

[38] The Honduran environment minister observed at the Brisbane CoP, 'It is hard to convince people to conserve wetlands because of animals when they are living on the border of misery. Poverty is the root cause of wetland loss.' Report of the 6th Meeting of the CoP, para. 83.

[39] See especially Resolutions VIII.19 and IX.21, and Strategy 4.1.iii of the current Strategic Plan for 2009–15. Although these measures recognise various socioeconomic principles and criteria indicative of the international importance of wetlands, these are to be applied in conjunction with the key ecological criteria, rather than independently. See further *Culture and Wetlands: A Ramsar Guidance Document* (Ramsar Secretariat, 2008).

[40] For recent examples, see Resolutions VIII.34, VIII.40, IX.4.

[41] See Resolution X.23.

[42] See Resolutions IX.14 and X.28, and Strategic Plan, Strategy 1.4.i.

[43] In 1993, it was estimated that of all listed sites the percentage designated by reference to the waterfowl criteria was: Africa 85 per cent, Asia 78 per cent, Eastern Europe 84 per cent, North America 97 per cent, Oceania 73 per cent, Neotropics 93 per cent, Western Europe 83 per cent. See generally M. E. Moser, P. M. Rose and D. A. Scott, 'Waterfowl Estimates and the Ramsar Convention' WG C.5.4, Annex 15 (Report of the 5th Meeting of the CoP, Volume II, hard-copy format).

observers has amassed an immense amount of data on waterfowl all over the world,[44] information on other wetland species has often been deficient.

Although the Convention is silent on the point, the CoP has expressly confirmed that Ramsar designation 'does not require that the wetland in question must enjoy any type of previously conferred protected area status or must necessarily acquire this after designation'.[45] Some parties have, nevertheless, chosen to restrict their designations to sites which already enjoy national legal protection, reasoning that designation under Ramsar raises this commitment to an international level and provides a valuable extra safeguard for their conservation. There is no doubt that this additional element of protection may be needed – the UK report to the 1980 Cagliari Conference indicated that eleven of its thirteen original listed sites were either actually or potentially threatened, despite all being theoretically protected by national legislation.[46] Ramsar designation may, moreover, prove significant in unexpected ways: in 1978 it was proposed to blow up a stricken oil tanker just off the coast of Minsmere in Suffolk but, following protestations that this might damage a Ramsar site, the hulk was towed twenty miles out to sea before detonation.[47]

Plainly, however, designation is a matter of national discretion, and at the same Conference the Italian delegation strongly commended the listing of biologically suitable, but legally unprotected, wetlands as a means of enhancing their status in the eyes of the public. He cited Lake Burano and Valle Cavanata as examples of privately owned wetlands which were saved from development because the acquisition of Ramsar status provided the necessary political stimulus to secure their protection under Italian law.[48] In the same way, several listed sites in Australia have also subsequently received statutory protection at the national level.[49] In some cases, furthermore, designation may trigger automatic consequences for domestic law. At Montreux, it was reported that in New Zealand any land containing listed wetlands was assumed to have national

44 Note that this is collated in Wetlands International's *International Waterfowl Population Estimates*, the periodic publication of which is synchronised with the timetable for the Ramsar CoP; see further Resolution VIII.38.

45 Resolution VII.11, Annex, para. 41. See further the Guidelines for completing the current Information Sheet (*supra* n. 23), para. 27.

46 See the UK national report to the Cagliari Conference, p. 2.

47 See Cagliari Conference Doc. CONF/4, para. 57.

48 See the Report of the 1st Meeting of the CoP, paras. 25–6.

49 See generally D. Farrier and L. Tucker, 'Wise Use of Wetlands under the Ramsar Convention' (2000) 12 *JEL* 21.

conservation value and was therefore allocated to the Department of Conservation rather than local government, and that the international status of Lake Rotoehu had formed the basis of an objection to a proposed development on the lake shore.[50] Of course, designation under Ramsar is by no means guaranteed to result in effective protection at the national level: Greece is another example of a country which has included unprotected wetlands in the List, but its failure to secure the effective conservation of these sites has been a major focus of concern for many years.[51]

c) Deletion and restriction of listed sites

In cases of 'urgent national interests', Ramsar permits the deletion of listed sites, or restriction of their boundaries, subject to an obligation to inform the Secretariat of such changes at the earliest possible time.[52] Since contracting governments are recognised to be the sole judge of their own interests,[53] this represents a potentially serious loophole in the Convention's protective regime. The process is not entirely devoid of safeguards, however. First, Article 2(6) requires each party, when exercising its right to change entries in the List, to 'consider its international responsibilities for the conservation, management and wise use of migratory stocks of waterfowl', though this duty is perhaps too narrowly and weakly drafted to be of much value. More significantly, Resolution IX.20 proposes a checklist of twelve factors for consideration, including the particular values of the site in question, the significance of the national interest involved, the urgency of the threat, and the possibility of alternative solutions. An environmental impact assessment is suggested as an appropriate preliminary, and the importance of the precautionary principle is stressed in that context. Finally, the Secretariat is required to notify all contracting parties of any such changes, and arrange for the matter to be discussed at the next CoP, where recommendations may be made to the party in question.[54] Although this is not the same as requiring advance warning of deletions,[55] it does at least

[50] DOC.C.4.18.

[51] Although Resolution VII.12.1 acknowledged some progress in that regard, the problems are evidently ongoing. See Resolution X.23, para. 27(iii).

[52] Article 2(5). See also Article 8(2)(b).

[53] Resolution VIII.20, Annex, para. 1.

[54] See Article 8(2)(d) and (e).

[55] See M. J. Bowman, 'The Ramsar Convention Comes of Age' (1995) 42 *Neths ILR* 1, pp. 24–5.

create an opportunity to persuade the government in question to think again.

Assuming that a decision to delete or restrict a site has been taken, Article 4(2) requires parties 'as far as possible [to] compensate for any loss of wetland resources' resulting from such action. In particular, they should 'create additional nature reserves for waterfowl and for the protection, either in the same area or elsewhere, of an adequate portion of the original habitat'. This is a curious formulation,[56] in that the appropriate compensation for loss of listed habitat is envisaged to be the creation of a nature reserve, which does not appear to correlate very closely with other provisions. As seen above, there is no specific duty to ensure that listed sites are accorded the status of nature reserves, while, at the same time, a general obligation to promote wetland conservation through the creation of such reserves applies by virtue of Article 4(1) regardless of whether such sites are listed or not. Nevertheless, that is what the Convention provides, and Resolution VIII.20 duly identifies the key considerations which should be borne in mind in that context, including maintenance of the total area of listed sites within a party's territory, the availability of replacement areas, their relevance to the values of the original site, and possible adverse effects of the compensatory measures themselves. Resolution VII.24 had already called for the general question of compensation for wetland loss to be integrated into national planning policies, and expressed a preference for compensation with wetlands of a similar type and in the same local water catchment.

In point of fact there has been no case of outright deletion from the List on account of urgent national interests to date,[57] though numerous boundary reductions have been reported. The diminution has often been relatively small,[58] however, and sometimes outweighed by expansion elsewhere. At the 1990 CoP, for example, Belgium confirmed a thirty-hectare reduction in its Galgenschoor site on the Lower Scheldt river, but proposed compensation in the form of 2,000 hectares of wet

[56] For fuller discussion, see ibid., at 25–6; C. de Klemm, 'International Law Requirements', DOC. C.4.7, section ii.

[57] Note that several sites (principally in Belize, Mali and the UK) which once appeared in the List but no longer do so have in fact been rationalised into larger sites. See further the discussion immediately following concerning deletion of sites on other grounds.

[58] In 1990, for example, the Netherlands reported the removal of just two hectares from its 250,000-hectare Wadden Sea site for the purpose of constructing a car park. Report of the 4th Meeting of the CoP, DOC. C.4.18, paras. 105–19.

grassland habitat in the Yzer valley,[59] whilst the UK reported the deletion of a 274-hectare section of its North Norfolk coastal site, but increased its overall area from 5,559 to 7,700 hectares.[60] A more controversial, ongoing case concerns Germany's reduction of its Muhlenberger Loch site in Hamburg in order to extend a factory engaged in the building of the European Airbus. Although the EC Commission recognised a compelling public interest in this development for EC purposes back in 2001, concern has persisted within Ramsar circles over the long delay in compensating for the loss of some 420 acres of tidal freshwater mudflats, and associated habitat of waterfowl and rare endemic plants.[61] Resolution X.13 therefore reiterates the request from earlier CoPs for a consolidated report on the implementation and effectiveness of the measures adopted under Article 4(2).[62]

The deletion or reduction of listed sites may, however, occasionally come about for other reasons. In the case of reduction, the typical scenario involves simply the more accurate demarcation or measurement of the site; thus the Okavango recently 'shrank' by a massive 1.3 million hectares when a purely indicative rectangle drawn around the Delta was replaced by a formal delineation of the site.[63] Deletion is more likely to occur where sites no longer satisfy the criteria for listing. Although failure to preserve the ecological characteristics of a listed site may sometimes amount to a breach of the Convention, that will not be the case where the deterioration is an unavoidable consequence of purely natural considerations.[64] Furthermore, designated wetlands might conceivably fail to meet current criteria even though no adverse changes have occurred at all: at Kushiro, for example, several small sites designated by Pakistan in 1976 were identified as probably never having met the criteria for listing.[65] Here the approved solution[66] entails

[59] Ibid. [60] Ibid.

[61] See the Secretary-General's Report pursuant to Article 8(2) for 2008, COP10 DOC.7, para. 13, and Ramsar Advisory Mission No. 46.

[62] For a similar request to Georgia with regard to the construction of an oil terminal within the Kolkheti Ramsar site, see Resolution IX.15, para. 27(iii), and the Secretary-General's Report, *supra* n. 61, para. 14.

[63] Secretary-General's Report, *supra* n. 61, para. 12.

[64] Note, however, Resolutions VIII.35 and IX.9, the latter of which urges parties to maintain or restore wetland ecosystems so as to reduce their vulnerability to natural disasters.

[65] See the Report of the 5th Meeting of the CoP, 2nd Plenary Session, Agenda Item 10. The sites were Kandar Dam, Kheshki Reservoir, Khabbaki Lake and Malugul Dhand.

[66] See, e.g., Resolutions 5.3, IX.6. Another possible scenario is where changes in the criteria themselves effectively disqualify a site which previously qualified.

consultations with the Secretariat in order to explore whether the ecological characteristics of the site can be restored or enhanced so as to meet the standards demanded. If not, the site is to be removed from the List, but, interestingly, the party in question is still expected to identify alternative reserves in accordance with Article 4(2). This is the solution which appears to have been adopted in relation to the Pakistani sites.[67]

4. Substantive conservation obligations regarding wetlands

The key provision in this context is Article 3(1), which provides,

> The Contracting Parties shall formulate and implement their planning so as to promote the conservation of the wetlands included in the List, and as far as possible the wise use of wetlands in their territory.

Plainly, therefore, the obligations undertaken by the parties are not restricted to listed sites, but extend to wetlands in their territory generally. An important question, however, concerns the precise nature and scope of the obligations applicable to these two categories.

a) Conservation and wise use

The clear impression created by this wording upon first reading is of the establishment of a dual standard, based upon the 'conservation' of listed sites and the 'wise use' of others.[68] This may conceivably have been the intention of those who originally drafted the Convention, though it should not be overlooked that Article 4(1), which requires the parties to 'promote the *conservation* of wetlands and waterfowl by establishing nature reserves on wetlands, *whether they are included in the List or not*',[69] seems to undermine the idea that 'conservation' connotes a more rigorous form of protection reserved exclusively for listed sites. More importantly, consistent practice under the Convention appears to reject any sharp distinction between the concepts of conservation and

67 Several new sites were listed in 1996, with Khabbaki Lake, for example, incorporated in the larger Uchhali Complex.

68 For such an interpretation, see A. S. Timoshenko, 'Protection of Wetlands in International Law', in *Legal Aspects of the Conservation of Wetlands* (IUCN Environmental Policy & Law Paper No. 25, 1991), p. 69. The presumption that different terms juxtaposed within the same provision bear different meanings follows from application of the so-called principle of effectiveness, as to which see Chapter 2, section 3(iv), above.

69 Emphasis added.

wise use. Thus early interpretations of 'wise use' adopted within the Ramsar system were founded upon the notion of sustainable utilisation,[70] which was itself defined in terms almost identical to the definition of 'conservation' espoused by the World Conservation Strategy,[71] leaving little room for distinction between the concepts of conservation and wise use. Nor does it seem that the term 'conservation' has been accorded some special, strict meaning for Ramsar purposes – connoting, perhaps, complete protection from human interference, in contrast to the regulated exploitation envisaged by 'wise use'. To the contrary, the entire scheme of activity under the Convention flatly contradicts any presumption of a 'hands-off' approach to listed wetlands: descriptions of many Ramsar sites indicate substantial human exploitation,[72] and the clear recent trend has been to emphasise the practical benefits of wetland conservation[73] in connection with water supply, fisheries and so on. The adoption of a 'preservationist' stance would, indeed, make very little sense in this context, since the key ecological characteristics of many wetlands (such as the blanket peat bogs of upland Britain, which are the product of prehistoric forest clearance) have in fact been significantly moulded by human activities over the centuries, while others, such as rice paddies and reservoirs, have been specifically created for human purposes.[74]

It is perhaps for these reasons that the principal emphasis of Ramsar deliberations has been upon 'wise use', even in relation to listed sites. In that vein, it is particularly significant that Section III of the current Strategic Framework and Guidelines for the Future Development of the List of Wetlands of International Importance[75] is headed 'Wetlands of International Importance and the Ramsar Principle of Wise Use' and

[70] 'The wise use of wetlands is their sustainable utilization for the benefit of humankind in a way compatible with the maintenance of the natural properties of the ecosystem.' See Recommendation 3.3 and Annex to the 1987 Regina Recommendations. For the current definition of 'wise use', see the subsection following.

[71] For elaboration, see Bowman, *supra* n. 55, pp. 12–15.

[72] See the *Ramsar Sites Information Service* at www.wetlands.org/RSIS/_COP9Directory/Default.htm. Note also that the Ramsar Information Sheet for sites to be listed (*supra* n. 23) includes questions concerning current land use, social and cultural values, leisure and tourism activities etc.

[73] Indeed, this point has been repeatedly highlighted in the keynote themes for recent CoPs – e.g. 'Healthy Wetlands, Healthy People' at Changwon, 2008.

[74] See E. Maltby, 'Wetlands and Their Values', in Finlayson and Moser, *supra* n. 4.

[75] Resolution VII.11, Annex. Subsequent revisions to the Framework leave this point unaffected.

contains a statement that the designation of a wetland as internationally important is 'an appropriate first step along a conservation and sustainable use pathway, the endpoint of which is achieving the long-term wise (sustainable) use of the site'. Recent resolutions confirm the absence of any clear distinction between conservation and wise use by treating them as a sort of composite concept,[76] while the current Strategic Plan for the Convention proclaims its basic mission to be 'the conservation and wise use of all wetlands'.[77] Any distinction between the protective regimes envisaged for listed and unlisted sites must consequently derive from sources other than this terminological dichotomy. Before considering this question, however, it is desirable to examine the concept of wise use in more detail.

b) The concept of wise use

Although the basic obligation upon the parties to 'formulate and implement their planning so as to promote . . . the wise use of wetlands in their territory' is undeniably open to criticism as being both vague and weakly drafted, there are two points which should not be overlooked in this context. The first concerns the pioneering nature of the Convention in seeking to establish an international regime which would impinge upon governmental freedom of action in respect of an extraordinarily wide range of natural habitats. Obligations regarding habitat protection are inevitably perceived as being more intrusive than those regulating the exploitation of species, which had been the primary focus of earlier wildlife treaties. There would therefore have been little chance of states signing up to a convention which appeared to encroach too dramatically upon their sovereign rights.[78] At the same time, an important countervailing factor lies in the incorporation within the Convention of an institutional mechanism for ongoing review of its implementation, which has provided an opportunity for clarifying the vaguer aspects of the text and adapting them to the evolving requirements of global environmental policies. The concept of wise use has, indeed, been the

[76] For a good example, see Resolution VIII.14. [77] See Resolution X.1, p. 7.

[78] See on this point Matthews, *supra* n. 6, Chapter 3; R. Boardman, *International Organizations and the Conservation of Nature* (Macmillan, 1981), pp. 164–8. Even now, the matter is highly sensitive; thus the Indian delegation recently emphasised the need to ensure that Ramsar guidance did not become 'overly intrusive, restrictive or prescriptive'. Report of the 9th Meeting of the CoP, para. 220.

focus of particularly extensive deliberation, so much so that it has become the central theme of the Convention as a whole. Following consideration of this issue at earlier meetings,[79] the 2005 Kampala Conference established a revised Conceptual Framework for the Wise Use of Wetlands and the Maintenance of Their Ecological Character, which incorporated the following definition:[80]

> Wise use of wetlands is the maintenance of their ecological character, achieved through the implementation of ecosystem approaches, within the context of sustainable development.

This revised definition is intended to bring the wise-use obligation more clearly into line with the principles elaborated in other key environmental documents. Thus the slightly delphic allusion to 'ecosystem approaches' is an invocation of practice under the Biodiversity Convention, which requires the adaptive, integrated management of land, water and living resources based upon scientific methodologies encompassing all aspects of the essential interactions amongst organisms and their environment.[81] Equally, the phrase 'within the context of sustainable development' is intended to recognise, following the Brundtland Report, that while some development is both inevitable and beneficial, it must be achieved in a sustainable fashion.

It is certainly not intended to imply, however, that development is an objective for every wetland.[82] Rather, since wise use demands *maintenance of the ecological character* of the wetland in question, each case must be treated on its merits with a view to achieving that goal. Thus small or large-scale exploitation may be permissible (or, indeed, necessary) in appropriate cases, whereas in others strict protection may be required, or even active intervention aimed at restoration.[83] This new formulation of the concept of wise use also removes the uncertainties entailed in previous definitions,[84] particularly by achieving greater coherence with Article 3(2), by virtue of which ecological deterioration in listed sites must be reported. To avoid any doubt, the Conceptual Framework goes on to specify that 'ecological character' should be understood to mean

79 See the discussion of this issue in the previous subsection.

80 Resolution IX.1, Annex A.

81 Ibid., n. 2. See especially CBD Decision V/6, which elaborates twelve key principles entailed in the ecosystem approach, together with operational guidance on their application.

82 Ibid., n. 3. The Ramsar Convention Manual, at para. 4.2, has always been at pains to distance itself from the North American 'wise-use movement', whose philosophy it does not necessarily share.

83 See the Manual, Section 4.2.3(b).

84 See on this point Bowman, *supra* n. 55, pp. 19–20.

> the combination of the ecosystem components, processes and benefits/services that characterise the wetland at any given point in time.

The final phrase underlines the need for continuous monitoring of sites in order to determine whether their essential characteristics have been maintained.

It is important to note, moreover, that the CoP has gone far beyond the mere definition of wise use, establishing valuable guidelines for its practical application at the Regina Conference in 1987.[85] These were elaborated much more fully at the 1990 Montreux Conference[86] and supplemented by detailed additional guidance three years later at Kushiro.[87] Briefly, the guidelines envisaged the establishment of national wetland policies, together with the implementation of priority measures both at the national level and in relation to individual wetland sites. Issues to be addressed include the improvement of institutional arrangements, the review of existing policy and legislation and the development of awareness of wetland values. More specifically, states should undertake the preparation of national inventories of wetlands, identifying the values of individual sites, the specification of conservation and management priorities for each site in accordance with national needs, the conduct of environmental impact assessments in connection with development projects, the use of development funds for conservation purposes and the regulated utilisation of the natural elements of wetland systems so as to avoid overexploitation. Action should also be taken regarding the international exchange of experience and information, the training of staff, the review of traditional techniques of wetland utilisation and the elaboration of pilot projects to demonstrate wise use. In the light of these developments, the observer from UNEP remarked approvingly at Kushiro that the 'Ramsar concept of "wise use" coincided perfectly with the aims and objectives of Agenda 21'.[88]

Virtually all the elements of this guidance have since been supplemented[89] (or, indeed, superseded)[90] by more fully elaborated guidelines adopted by later meetings of the CoP and now consolidated in the

[85] See Recommendation 3.3 and Annex to the Regina Recommendations.
[86] Recommendation 4.10. [87] Resolution 5.6, Annex.
[88] Report of the 5th Meeting of the CoP, 4th Plenary Session, Agenda Item 11.
[89] According to Resolution IX.1, Annex A, the only elements of the original guidance not to have been expanded concern research, training and technical issues relating to sustainable technologies.
[90] Even the very definition of 'wise use', as noted above.

Ramsar 'toolkit' of *Wise Use Handbooks*.[91] The first of these sets out the original basic principles with cross-reference to the volumes which contain relevant supplementary material: thus *Handbook 2* and *Handbook 3* address respectively the questions of national wetland policies and the development of national laws and institutions, while other volumes focus upon such matters as wetland inventory, impact assessment, international co-operation and the wetland management process.[92] Specific management issues, such as water allocation or community participation,[93] or the principles applicable to specific wetland types, such as river basins or coastal zones,[94] are also the subject of extended treatment. It therefore can no longer be argued that the parties lack sufficient guidance as to what the wise-use obligation entails. These principles are, furthermore, kept under continual review, and modified where necessary. In this vein, the ninth CoP established integrated frameworks for the Convention's water-related guidance and for wetland inventory, assessment and monitoring,[95] while the tenth did likewise for river basin management,[96] and updated existing guidance on EIA/SEA and addressing ecological change.[97] Consequently, although the duty generated by Article 3(1) still cannot be regarded as particularly precise or rigorous in purely legal terms, it has at least provided the foundation for an extremely comprehensive and sophisticated policy framework for the management of wetland areas generally.[98]

c) Enhanced protection for listed wetlands

Even though the practice of the parties has tended to treat the wise-use criterion as applicable to all wetlands, whether designated or not, it is

[91] 3rd ed., 2007, hereafter *Handbooks*, of which there are seventeen in all, viewable on the Ramsar website, via the 'Publications' link.

[92] See respectively *Handbook 11*, *Handbook 12*, *Handbook 13*, *Handbook 17* and *Handbook 16*.

[93] See respectively *Handbook 8* and *Handbook 5*.

[94] See respectively *Handbook 7* and *Handbook 10*.

[95] See Resolution IX.1, Annexes C and E. [96] Resolution X.19.

[97] See Resolutions X.15–X.17.

[98] Note that Article 3, as amplified by CoP resolutions, has been held to be enforceable at the national level by the Dutch Council of State in the *Bonaire* case, 11 September 2007. See J. Verschuuren, 'Ramsar Soft Law is Not Soft at All' (2008) 35 *Milieu en Recht* 28. Here, a local planning decision to allow construction of a holiday resort partly within the buffer zone surrounding Het Lac Ramsar site was annulled by the governor of Netherlands Antilles, as no EIA had been conducted. An appeal to the Dutch Crown was unsuccessful, as the planning decision was judged to violate Article 3.

only to be expected, unless the significance of designation is to be purely symbolic, that a more rigorous regime of protection would be applicable to sites included in the List of Wetlands of International Importance. This is indeed the case, as both the text of the Convention and subsequent developments amply confirm. The essence of the distinction lies in two key aspects of Article 3.

i) Nature and scope of the substantive obligation

First, while the obligation imposed on the parties by Article 3(1) is to promote the conservation or wise use of wetlands 'included in the List', that applicable to other wetlands is restricted to those 'within their territory', and obtains only 'as far as possible'. The absence of any *territorial* limitation in relation to designated wetlands strongly implies the assumption of some form of collective responsibility for such sites,[99] while the responsibility for unlisted sites remains purely individual. This can doubtless be rationalised on the basis that the international importance which all designated sites *ex hypothesi* possess is sufficient (without prejudice to the sovereignty of the state in whose territory they are situated) to enable them to be regarded as resources of 'common concern' to the international community as a whole. The implications of this conclusion are of sufficient practical significance to merit further consideration below.[100]

Furthermore, the absence of any *substantive* restriction on the duty applicable to sites in the List confirms that their conservation is seen to be a matter of higher priority than that of other wetlands, where protection is qualified by the phrase 'as far as possible'. Of course, even the obligation relating to listed sites – to formulate and implement national planning so as to 'promote' (not *ensure* or *guarantee*) their conservation – is not particularly rigorous, but the requirement to provide detailed information about such sites upon designation at least creates the rudiments of a mechanism for ensuring that this duty is capable of international supervision. This point is reinforced by the fact that an additional, and potentially very significant, obligation in relation to listed sites arises under Article 3(2).

[99] This inference is reinforced by the wording of Article 3(2), which creates certain obligations for each party with regard to any site 'in its territory and included in the List', a form of words which could have been, but was not, utilised in Article 3(1).

[100] See section 4(c)(iv).

ii) Notification of adverse ecological changes

Article 3(2) provides:

> Each Contracting Party shall arrange to be informed at the earliest possible time if the ecological character of any wetland in its territory and included in the List has changed, is changing or is likely to change as the result of technological developments, pollution or other human interference. Information on such changes shall be passed without delay to the organization or government responsible for the continuing bureau duties specified in Article 8.

This procedure is linked to the power of the Conference to consider such information and make appropriate recommendations.[101] Despite its potential importance, the early years of the Convention saw very little information submitted by the parties pursuant to this provision,[102] even though data from other sources suggested that deterioration in the ecological character of listed wetlands was relatively widespread. A number of factors are likely to have contributed to this reticence. Many parties will have lacked the technical capacity to acquire, collate or interpret such information, while some may have been uncertain about the precise implications of the obligation. Most of all, states are likely to have resisted drawing attention to possible problems regarding compliance with their conservation obligations in a new and unfamiliar public forum. The Ramsar institutions have accordingly devoted strenuous efforts towards overcoming these difficulties.

First, action has been taken to elaborate the meaning of the terms used in Article 3(2). Following earlier attempts at clarification,[103] it is now understood that

> change in ecological character is the human-induced adverse alteration of any ecosystem component, process and/or ecosystem benefit/service.[104]

Though not the most elegant of definitions, this formulation has the merit of harmonising with CBD perspectives regarding the concept of 'ecological character',[105] and confirms that the focus of the reporting obligation in this context is upon anthropogenic forms of degradation.[106]

101 See Article 6(2)(c) and (d).

102 A few instances can be found in national reports to early meetings of the CoP, but, by 1984, only two such notifications had ever been made between meetings. See Report of the 2nd Meeting of the CoP, 3rd Plenary Session, Agenda Item 9.

103 See Recommendation 5.2 and Resolutions VI.1 and VII.10.

104 See Resolution IX.1, Annex A, esp. paras. 15–21.

105 See the discussion in section 4(b) above.

106 For other purposes, however, information may be required regarding all types of change. See, e.g., CoP8 DOC.20 and Resolution VIII.8. Also, Resolution VIII.35 notes

Resolution X.15 then provides comprehensive guidance on the content and presentation of the information required for an appropriate and reliable description of wetland ecological character.

Second, the CoP has repeatedly reaffirmed the importance of the Article 3(2) obligation, and has very recently approved an advisory procedural framework, comprising a series of flowcharts, to govern the entire process of detecting, reporting and responding to ecological change.[107] It has also reminded the parties of the financial and technical support facilities that may be available for those purposes,[108] and of the guidance available on a range of key issues, including wetland monitoring and impact assessment.[109] One important element is the Wetland Risk Assessment Framework,[110] which establishes a six-stage process for detecting biological, chemical or physical changes in wetland ecosystems resulting from alterations in the water regime, pollution, physical modification, the exploitation of biological resources or the introduction of exotic species. It also offers guidance on the use of early-warning indicators for that purpose. Although there will doubtless be scope for the further refinement of these principles, they should significantly ease the task of any party which was previously uncertain how to comply with the obligation under Article 3(2).

These developments have no doubt already produced some improvements in the record of implementation of Article 3(2), but there is plainly little room for complacency. While it was noted at Changwon that, since the previous CoP, eighteen governments had made timely notification of adverse changes at twenty-two listed wetlands, and that twenty-six had disclosed such problems regarding a further forty-seven sites in their national reports, these figures were still exceeded by reports of adverse change received from third parties, including local communities, scientific bodies and NGOS.[111] Although the receipt of such reports may in itself provide testimony to the value of the Ramsar system – not least

that *human responses* to natural disasters may cause ecological changes which have to be reported under Article 3(2).

107 Resolution X.16.

108 Including advice from the Ramsar STRP or national wetland institutions, or emergency funding from the Ramsar SGF or other sources.

109 See especially *Handbook 11*, *Handbook 14*, *Handbook 15*, *Handbook 16*. Note in particular the Integrated Framework for Wetland Inventory, Assessment, Monitoring (IF-WIAM), Resolution IX.1, Annex E.

110 *Handbook 16*, Section E.

111 See on this point Resolution X.13, and the Secretary-General's Report, *supra* n. 61, paras. 17–22 and Annex 3.

because the practice of the Secretariat is to follow them up with the state in question – the record suggests that many parties still lack either the technical capacity or the political will to implement their obligations in full. A further consequence has been the undermining of the Montreux Record, the mechanism devised by the CoP for addressing the more serious problems of adverse ecological change on a co-ordinated basis.[112]

iii) Remedial action

Although the Convention itself does not expressly demand remedial action in relation to sites undergoing adverse ecological change, there would be little purpose in requiring information about such deterioration unless the intention was to address it in some way. In any event, the obligation regarding wise use might be thought to imply a commitment to tackle such problems as they arise, and Recommendation 4.8 accordingly called upon parties with sites at risk 'to take swift and effective action' to prevent or remedy changes in ecological character. This responsibility has been frequently reaffirmed,[113] and is also implicit in the Montreux Record procedure. Furthermore, a key element of the current Strategic Plan is to 'maintain the ecological character of all designated Ramsar sites'.[114] At each meeting of the CoP, particular parties are accordingly congratulated for action they have taken to address ecological problems, called upon to provide further information in that regard, or, on occasion, pointedly urged to adopt appropriate remedial measures. Thus, at Kampala,[115] the government of Cyprus, for example, was commended for resolving the problem of lead poisoning of flamingos at its Lamaca Salt Lake site through the removal of contaminated sediments, and that of Bulgaria for seeking to improve the ecological character of the Belene Islands Complex with the assistance of GEF funding. Australia was congratulated on its restoration of the damage suffered by the Gwydir Wetlands and requested to offer its advice on lessons learned from the application of national legislation in this case.[116] Both there and at Changwon,[117] several states were asked to provide details of industrial activities or legal developments thought to pose a risk to listed

[112] For discussion, see section 6(b)(iii).

[113] See, e.g., Resolutions VIII.8, para. 20, IX.15, para. 20.

[114] Resolution X.1, Strategy 2.4.

[115] See Resolution IX.15, paras. 25–7.

[116] See *Minister for the Environment and Heritage v Greentree (Nos. 2 and 3)* 2004 FCA 741, 1317, which concerned a prosecution in respect of unlawful agricultural activities on the site. The Federal Court imposed a fine of AUS$450,000, prohibited further agricultural activity for several years and ordered the defendants to rehabilitate the site.

[117] See Resolutions IX.15, X.13.

sites, or commended for having done so, while the government of Ukraine remained the focus of intense concern regarding developments in the Danube Delta.[118]

In addition, the general principles governing restoration of degraded wetlands have been explored in some detail,[119] especially in Resolution VIII.16, which establishes a flowchart-based procedure to govern the decision-making process, based upon recognition of the need for long-term stewardship, adaptable management, stakeholder involvement, incorporation (where appropriate) of traditional knowledge, attention to the wider ecological context and avoidance of undesirable side effects. The current Strategic Plan calls for *all* parties to have identified priority sites for restoration (with at least half having actual restoration projects under way or completed) by 2015.[120]

iv) Extraterritorial aspects

It was noted above that the obligations which the parties undertake regarding conservation of listed sites is not restricted to those within their own territory. The precise nature and extent of their responsibility towards sites designated by other states is uncertain, but should at least involve an obligation to avoid causing them significant harm. Allegations of such damage have occasionally been made: at Groningen, for example, Sweden complained of the acidification of its lakes as a consequence of transboundary pollution,[121] while at Changwon Iraq alleged that dams constructed in neighbouring states were restricting water flows into the Hawizeh Marsh.[122] The infliction of harm beyond national frontiers is, of course, already regulated by general customary rules and under various treaty-based regimes,[123] but Ramsar may nonetheless offer a valuable forum for discussion of the ecological effects of such conduct specifically. In fact, there is an increasing tendency for such matters to be addressed by a range of treaty regimes, sometimes in close collaboration. Thus the Ukrainian government's controversial project to construct a deep-water navigation canal through its section of the Danube Delta – thereby risking significant transboundary harm to this internationally renowned

[118] For details of this last case, see the following section.
[119] See generally *Handbook 15*, Sections F, G. [120] Resolution X.1, Strategy 1.8.
[121] See the Report of the 2nd Meeting of the CoP, 4th Plenary Session, Agenda Item 9.
[122] Secretary-General's Report, *supra* n. 61, para. 20. In response, Iran and Turkey attributed the problems to the deliberate draining of the marshes by Saddam Hussein: Report of the 10th Meeting of the CoP, paras. 91–2.
[123] See generally Chapter 21 below.

wetland – prompted a joint mission of delegates from the EC and several treaty-based institutions to conduct an on-site investigation in October 2004.[124] An earlier Ramsar/UNESCO-MAB report had concluded that the route proposed would represent the worst possible solution,[125] and Ramsar Resolution IX.15 called for the suspension of further works pending a full EIA; notification of its findings to stakeholders, especially the government of Romania; implementation of compensatory provision in respect of any ecological damage to Ramsar sites or other wetlands; and the establishment of co-operative monitoring arrangements.[126] Concerns regarding this project have persisted notwithstanding the apparent review by Ukraine of its decision to proceed with phase II of the project, and Resolution X.13 called for prompt and comprehensive information on recent developments.

Aside from the direct, physical infliction of transboundary harm, Ramsar parties may be obliged to refrain from other kinds of activity which endanger designated wetlands in other states. An obvious instance concerns the funding of development projects, such as dams and irrigation schemes, which might prove damaging to their ecology. Indeed, development assistance was identified at Kushiro as the 'single most important source of wetland loss in the developing world'.[127] Recommendation 3.4 had already urged development agencies[128] to pursue coherent policies directed at sustainable utilisation, wise management and conservation of wetlands, ensuring the integration of environmental aspects into all phases of the project cycle, especially prior impact assessment. The parties themselves were exhorted to require national agencies to adhere to this strategy and, by a subsequent recommendation,[129] to ensure that their representatives to the Multilateral Development Banks adopted voting standards which supported wetland conservation. The issue has remained a recurrent feature on the Ramsar agenda,[130] and the current Plan seeks to ensure that environmental safeguards and assessments are incorporated as an integral component of all development projects.[131]

[124] For the report of the team of experts that undertook the mission, dated 17 November 2004, see http://ec.europa.eu./environment/enlarg/bystroe_project_fn.htm.

[125] See Ramsar Advisory Mission Report No. 53, concerning Kyliiske Mouth (Danube Delta), October 2003, and follow-ups, April 2005 and July 2008.

[126] See para. 27(e).

[127] Report of the 5th Meeting of the CoP, Summary Report of Workshop D, Section (a).

[128] I.e. 'all banks, government institutions and international governmental agencies ... with a significant role in providing funds to countries for their development'.

[129] Recommendation 4.13. [130] See, e.g., Recommendations 5.5, 6.12, 6.16.

[131] Resolution X.1, Strategy 3.3.

A further question is whether this element of collective responsibility for listed sites goes beyond the mere avoidance of harm and embraces also a duty to take positive action for their conservation. The main difficulty here lies in determining the precise scope and content of any such duty, though the notion of 'common but differentiated responsibility' would doubtless demand more of developed states in that regard. Whatever the strict legal position may be, it is noteworthy that the parties have, as a matter of fact, been prepared to undertake various initiatives for the protection of listed sites outside their own territories. These have commonly involved the provision of funding, training or technical assistance to enhance their conservation, and such action can be linked both to the various ancillary obligations which arise under Article 4[132] and to the duty of international co-operation under Article 5.[133]

d) Ancillary obligations

The basic duties regarding wise use are reinforced by a number of ancillary obligations.[134] Article 4(1) requires the parties to promote the conservation of wetlands and waterfowl by establishing nature reserves on wetland sites, whether listed or not, and to provide adequately for their wardening. While designated sites often enjoy protected status under domestic law, the Convention also seeks to encourage the creation of reserves on sites which, while not satisfying the exacting criteria for Ramsar designation, nonetheless perform an important role in local ecology. At the very first CoP, Finland, Hungary, Iceland, Norway, Pakistan, Poland and the UK all gave details of such reserves,[135] and there can be little doubt that the Convention has subsequently provided the stimulus for a substantial increase in their numbers.[136] In 1990, Recommendation 4.4 urged all parties to compile national inventories detailing the location and values of their wetlands and to establish networks of reserves covering both listed and non-listed sites.[137] A related

[132] For discussion, see the subsection immediately following. [133] See section 6(b).

[134] Note that, in addition to their independent existence under Article 4, a number of these obligations have effectively been woven into the duty of wise use by virtue of the guidelines on the meaning and application of that concept. See section 4(b) above.

[135] See Cagliari Conference Doc, CONF/4, paras. 39–50.

[136] At Groningen, for example, Norway noted that it currently had 346 wetland reserves, by comparison with only twenty ten years earlier. Report of the 2nd Meeting of the CoP, 3rd Plenary Session, Agenda Item 9.

[137] On the question of inventory generally, see *Handbook 11*, *Handbook 12*.

obligation arises under Article 4(4), whereby the parties undertake to endeavour through management to increase waterfowl populations on appropriate wetlands. Obviously the creation of nature reserves or other forms of protected status for wetlands may be one means of achieving this goal.

The raising of awareness of wetland values amongst the general public is also considered vital,[138] and Recommendation 4.5 accordingly called for the development of comprehensive strategies both through the formal educational system and informally, stressing the use of nature reserves for instructional purposes.[139] In the UK, the expanding network of reserves operated by the Wildfowl and Wetlands Trust provides an interesting example of this approach. The seventh CoP pursued the issue of public awareness still further through the adoption of a formal Outreach Programme,[140] and this has developed into a more comprehensive, ongoing Communications, Education and Public Awareness (CEPA) Programme.[141]

In addition, Article 4(3) requires the parties to 'encourage research and the exchange of data and publications regarding wetlands and their flora and fauna', while Article 4(5) requires them to 'promote the training of personnel competent in the fields of wetland research, management and wardening'. Despite repeated exhortations to parties to develop training courses,[142] progress here was initially slow, since, as pointed out by Senegal and Tunisia at the very first CoP, it is in such areas that developing countries are certain to require support. Recommendation 1.2 accordingly urged the parties themselves, and appropriate international aid organisations, to assist in the establishment of suitable programmes. Following early ad hoc developments,[143] several major initiatives may be noted. Since 1994, for example, the United States has contributed around US$250,000 per annum to sustain the Wetlands for the Future Initiative, which, a decade after its formal absorption into the Ramsar system,[144] had funded 225 capacity-building projects, involving the training of over 8,000 individuals, in twenty-one different countries in the western hemisphere.[145] In addition, training has

[138] As to which, see Bowman, *supra* n. 13. [139] See also Recommendation 4.4.

[140] See Resolution VII.9.

[141] For the programme for 2009–15, see Resolution X.8, which retains the CEPA Oversight Panel established by Resolution IX.18.

[142] See, e.g., Recommendations 4.5, 6.5. [143] See, e.g., Groningen Doc. C2.6.

[144] It has been operated jointly with the Secretariat since 1997.

[145] Current information regarding the Fund is available from the Ramsar website, via the 'Activities' and 'Grants Programmes' links. Other prominent contributors to training in various regions include Australia, Canada, Japan, the Netherlands, Sweden, the UK and the Ramsar Partner Organisations.

always been one of the functions for which funding from the Ramsar Small Grants Fund (SGF) may be sought,[146] with Kenya and Niger numbering amongst the early beneficiaries.[147]

During the early 1990s, moreover, the Dutch Water Management Agency (RIZA) began to provide courses for wetland managers and administrators at its training centre in Lelystad, and later assisted in the establishment of the East African Wetland Management Course, run by the Kenyan Wildlife Service. The growing Ramsar emphasis on regionalisation almost inevitably served to stimulate a series of training events at that level,[148] and this in turn led to the formal establishment of further regional centres for training and research in wetland conservation.[149] The need to co-ordinate these arrangements ultimately prompted the inauguration of a 'Training of Trainers' programme by the Wageningen Institute, assisted by RIZA, and in 2004 the RIZA Advisory Board (which was always chaired by the Ramsar secretary-general) became the Ramsar Capacity Building Advisory Board, assuming a general advisory role regarding this area of Ramsar activity under the aegis of the Standing Committee.[150]

The current Strategic Plan calls for the assessment, by 2015, of national and local training needs regarding conservation/wise use by at least half of the parties, and of those regarding the implementation of policy, legislative and institutional mechanisms by a 'significant proportion'. The Advisory Board is to provide practical guidance to facilitate the achievement of these objectives.[151]

5. Institutional arrangements

The provision made in the original text of the Convention with regard to its administration was decidedly modest, but institutional arrangements have been developed significantly over the course of its history. In 2005, moreover, a Management Working Group was established to maintain a continuous review of the effectiveness of Ramsar's organisational

146 See Resolution 4.3, para. (e)(i), and, for further discussion, section 6(b)(iii) below.
147 See DOC. C.5.5, pp. 8–9. 148 See section 6(b)(ii) below.
149 Specifically, for the western hemisphere (at the City of Knowledge in Panama, see Resolution VII.26), and for Western and Central Asia (at Ramsar itself, Resolution VIII.41). An East Asian centre is planned by Korea (Resolution X.32).
150 Information on its activities is available from the Ramsar website.
151 Resolution X.1, Strategy 4.1.

structures and systems, and to report regularly to the Standing Committee.[152]

a) Conference of the Parties

In its current, amended form, Ramsar makes provision for both ordinary and extraordinary meetings of the Conference of the Parties. Since the Convention came into force there have been ten ordinary and two extraordinary meetings.[153]

i) Extraordinary meetings

The purpose of extraordinary meetings is to consider amendments to the Convention, and they may now be convened at the written request of at least one-third of the contracting parties.[154] Following a review of the original text of Ramsar at the first ordinary meeting, it was decided that it would indeed require amendment in certain respects, and, ironically, the most glaring deficiency identified was the absence of any procedure to enable such changes to be made. An extraordinary meeting of the parties was therefore convened in Paris in 1982 to adopt a Protocol of Amendment to the Convention,[155] the primary purpose of which was to establish such a procedure.[156] Article 1 of the Protocol duly inserted a new provision, Article 10*bis*,[157] paragraph 1 of which provides that the Convention may be amended at a meeting of the contracting parties *convened for that purpose*, which confirms the extraordinary status of such meetings. The Paris Protocol entered into force in 1986 and the new procedure was utilised the following year to amend Articles 6 and 7,[158] though on that occasion the extraordinary meeting was actually

152 Resolution IX.24, as amended by Resolution X.4.

153 Ordinary meetings were held in Cagliari, Italy (1980), Groningen, the Netherlands (1984); Regina, Canada (1987); Montreux, Switzerland (1990); Kushiro, Japan (1993); Brisbane, Australia (1996); San José, Costa Rica (1999); Valencia, Spain (2002); Kampala, Uganda (2005); and Changwon, Republic of Korea (2008). Note also the 1974 Heiligenhafen meeting, referred to in section 3(b) above. Extraordinary meetings were held in Paris (1982) and Regina (1987).

154 Article 6(1), as amended in 1987. 155 22 *ILM* 698.

156 In addition, the Protocol amended the Convention's testimonium clause so as to accord equal status to its various authentic language texts – see further above, Chapter 2, section 3(iv).

157 The provision was modelled upon Article 10 of the Migratory Species Convention, as to which see Chapter 16 below.

158 For the effect of these amendments, see the following subsection.

convened in Regina in parallel with the third ordinary meeting of the Conference.[159]

ii) Ordinary meetings

The original wording of Article 6(1) referred to 'Conferences on the Conservation of Wetlands and Waterfowl', which were to 'have an advisory character' and to be convened only 'as the necessity arises'. It was rapidly decided, however, that it would be more appropriate to convene formal meetings of a 'Conference of the Contracting Parties' on a regular basis, and the necessary changes were effected by the 1987 amendments discussed above. The Conference has in fact met on a regular, three-yearly cycle since 1984.[160]

The functions of the Conference are to review implementation of the Convention; to discuss modifications to the List; to consider information on ecological changes at listed sites; to make general or specific recommendations to the parties regarding the conservation, management and wise use of wetlands and their flora and fauna; and to procure the preparation of reports and statistics on wetland matters.[161] The 1987 amendments established a more general power to adopt recommendations or resolutions to promote the functioning of the Convention and the responsibility to adopt rules of procedure and financial regulations.[162] It is noteworthy that measures adopted by the CoP are now generally couched in the form of resolutions rather than recommendations,[163] though the precise significance of this change is unclear. With the exception of those concerning budgetary contributions,[164] there is little to suggest that resolutions are formally binding,[165] though some may qualify as authoritative interpretations of the Convention for the

[159] For analysis of the considerable problems involved in amending Ramsar, see M. J. Bowman, 'The Multilateral Treaty Amendment Process: A Case Study' (1995) 44 *ICLQ* 540.

[160] A proposal to move to a four-yearly cycle was rejected at Changwon. See COP10DOC.14 and Report of the 10th Meeting, paras. 131–4.

[161] Article 6(2)(a)–(e). [162] Article 6(2)(f), (4), (5).

[163] The first resolutions were adopted at Regina in 1987, while the last recommendations emanated from San José in 1999. Subsequently, *all* measures adopted have been resolutions.

[164] See Article 6(6), inserted by the 1987 amendments.

[165] Though parties themselves sometimes appear to assume the contrary: at San José, Turkey, supported by India, sought to exclude itself from the binding effect of certain measures concerning international river basin management (which were, in fact, expressed only as guidelines). Report of the 7th Meeting of the CoP, para. 135.

purposes of treaty law.[166] The body of material deriving from these measures is now very substantial, and Resolution IX.17 instructed the Secretariat to organise a review of the entire canon in order to identify areas of redundancy, ambiguity or contradiction, so that superseded material might be withdrawn and currently valid guidance repackaged into more manageable form.[167]

A crucial feature of the Conference, and indeed of the Ramsar system generally, is the central involvement of non-governmental organisations. Interestingly, the Colombian delegate remarked at Brisbane that in this Convention, unlike many others, NGO and governmental representatives seemed like members of the same family.[168] Participation levels are generally high: the Kampala meeting, for example, was attended by over a hundred delegates from twenty-six international NGOs and an even larger number from national organisations.[169] Attendance has also diversified beyond traditional ornithological and conservation organisations to embrace such groups as Livelihood Development International, the Indigenous Peoples Alliance and the World Association of Zoos and Aquariums. In recognition of their pre-eminent contribution to Ramsar's ongoing implementation and development, four organisations – BirdLife International, IUCN, Wetlands International and WWF – were formally confirmed as International Organization Partners to the Convention in 1999,[170] and subsequently the International Water Management Institute was also accorded this status.[171] Partnership entails the right to participate as observers and advisers in all Ramsar institutions and activities.

b) Bureau (Secretariat)

Article 8 of the Convention provides for the performance of secretariat functions in broadly similar fashion to other conservation treaties, but with one or two notable distinctions. First, the tasks specifically identified in the text are relatively limited: they include convening and organising conferences on wetland conservation, maintaining the List, receiving information concerning ecological changes at designated sites and

166 See above, Chapter 2, section 3(iv).
167 The *Ramsar Handbooks* already perform a valuable service in that respect.
168 Report of the 6th Meeting, para. 89.
169 Complete lists of CoP participants are available from the Ramsar website.
170 Resolution VII.3. 171 Resolution IX.16.

transmitting such details to the parties, along with any recommendations adopted in response. In reality, however, administrative activities are now considerably more extensive, and are specified in detail in periodically approved Work Plans.[172] Second, the Convention actually makes no express reference to a Secretariat at all, but only to 'continuing bureau duties':[173] for that reason, the institution in question has traditionally been known as the Ramsar Bureau. At Kampala, however, concerns were expressed by the Bureau itself, supported by a formal legal opinion,[174] that this title was unsatisfactory for purposes of external relations. It was therefore resolved that, without any alteration of functions, the term 'Ramsar Secretariat' might henceforth be used whenever it was judged more appropriate,[175] and this terminology seems already to have become the norm.

Another distinctive, and closely related, feature is that the functions in question are actually performed by IUCN, a non-governmental organisation. While this is certainly unusual in a treaty-based regime, it can be attributed to Ramsar's pioneering nature, and the initial uncertainty surrounding its financial situation. Indeed, without the willingness of IUCN to fulfil this role, the negotiations to establish the Convention would probably not have come to fruition.[176] In the difficult early years, the operation was sustained by voluntary contributions from NGOs and governments favourably disposed towards Ramsar's objectives,[177] but the adoption of a formal budget pursuant to the 1987 amendments, sustained by regular financial contributions from the parties, did much to consolidate the Bureau's position. It has subsequently operated as a discrete unit within IUCN, under the direction of the Ramsar CoP.[178] In 1992, the Swiss government provided new premises for IUCN in Gland, near Geneva,[179] where the Bureau/Secretariat has continued to be

[172] The Secretariat's Work Plan for 2009 was approved by the Standing Committee in Decision SC40-23.

[173] See Article 8(1), (2); also Articles 2(5), 3(2). Article 2(1) refers to 'the bureau established under Article 8', which became 'the Bureau' in the amendments effected by the 1982 Protocol.

[174] CoP9 DOC.19. [175] Resolution IX.10.

[176] Matthews, *supra* n. 6, Chapter 7, where the crucial role of IWRB is also stressed.

[177] See Recommendation 2.4 and DOC. C.2.6, 'Voluntary Contributions towards Interim Secretariat Costs'.

[178] Direct involvement by IUCN itself is now rare, but the relationship is in any event now under review; see text accompanying n. 183 *infra*.

[179] See Recommendation 5.11.

housed,[180] despite occasional expressions of concern regarding high living costs.[181] It is clear from the Convention, however, that IUCN's role was originally envisaged to be temporary,[182] and the Secretariat's future is currently under review.[183] Options include maintenance of the status quo, reconstitution as an independent international organisation, and transfer of responsibility for secretariat services to UNEP.[184]

c) *Standing Committee*

The Convention itself made no provision for institutional arrangements beyond the Bureau and Conference of the Parties. The experience of environmental treaties generally, however, has been that some form of bridge is usually required between the day-to-day functioning of the Secretariat and the relatively infrequent meetings of the CoP, if only to ensure that the activities of the former remain consistent with the policy mandates of the latter. The creation of a Standing Committee to fulfil that role within the Ramsar system was accordingly one of the key recommendations of a task force established at Groningen to address the Convention's institutional deficiencies.[185] The Committee was formally established at Regina,[186] and its activities are now governed by Resolution VII.1. It operates on the basis of proportional representation, with each Ramsar region allocated between one and five members depending upon the number of contracting parties it contains.[187] Representatives are elected by the CoP on the basis of nominations from the region, and serve from the end of one Conference to the end of the next, with any single party limited to a maximum of two consecutive terms. In addition, the host countries of the previous and forthcoming meetings of the CoP are also members.

180 On the short-lived division of Bureau functions between IUCN in Gland and IWRB in Slimbridge, UK, see Bowman, *supra* n. 55, pp. 35–7.

181 Especially at the Brisbane CoP. See Resolution VI.22.

182 See Article 8(1).

183 See Resolutions IX.10, X.5 and Report of the 10th Meeting of the CoP, paras. 94–101.

184 See COP10 DOC.35.

185 The idea had originally been surprisingly controversial. See the Report of the 2nd Meeting of the CoP, 7th Plenary Session, Agenda Item 13.

186 See Resolution 3.3.

187 Specifically, one member per one to twelve parties, resulting in the following representation for 2009–12: Africa – 4; Asia – 3; Europe – 4; Neotropics – 3; North America – 1; Oceania – 1. Note that, in view of ongoing controversies, Israel participates (without voting rights) in European, rather than Asian, regional activities.

The Committee meets at least once a year,[188] normally at Ramsar headquarters, and has a wide range of functions, including the implementation of CoP policies between meetings, supervision of the Secretariat and the Scientific and Technical Review Panel, organisation of CoP meetings and the allocation of funds under the Ramsar SGF. This last function, together with other budgetary issues, is handled by a Subgroup on Finance comprising one member per region. All non-member Ramsar parties may attend Standing Committee meetings as observers, together with other states which have expressed an interest in joining the Convention, the chair of the STRP (along with other experts invited ad hoc) and the Partner Organisations. The host countries of the Ramsar Bureau and of the International Office of Wetlands International have the status of Permanent Observers.

d) Scientific and Technical Review Panel

Conservation treaties have also generally felt the need for input of a specifically scientific nature, and the creation in 1993 of the Scientific and Technical Review Panel (STRP) accordingly represented the final major piece of the Ramsar institutional jigsaw.[189] Its composition and modus operandi are currently governed by Resolutions X.9 and X.10. One panel member is appointed from each Ramsar region, with special reference to the strength of their contacts with other wetland experts at local, regional or international levels. Additional members are appointed on the basis of their expertise in key thematic areas,[190] including one specifically with CEPA expertise.[191] Each Partner Organisation may also nominate a representative, while other scientific and technical organisations may be invited to participate as observers.[192] In order to ensure continuity, at least one-third of the appointed members should be reappointed to a second term. Fluency in English and access to the Internet, through

[188] More frequently in CoP years: there have been forty meetings to date.

[189] See Recommendation 4.7 and Resolution 5.5.

[190] Resolution X.9 currently specifies seven: wetland inventory and assessment; site designation; restoration and management; and wetland relationships to water resources, agriculture, human health and climate change respectively. Regional and gender balance are also to be considered.

[191] See section 4(d) above.

[192] For current invitees (which include the Society of Wetland Scientists, the Society for Ecological Restoration and the International Association for Impact Assessment, together with the secretariats and scientific organs of the CBD, CMS and Desertification and Climate Change Conventions) see Resolution X.9, para. 18.

which intersessional work is conducted, are also specified attributes. The overall aim is to develop as wide a network of expertise as possible, and each Ramsar party is invited to designate its own National Focal Point to liaise with the STRP. The Partners are also expected to tap into their own expert networks and specialist groups.

The work programme and priorities of the STRP are determined ultimately by the CoP and Standing Committee, to whom it reports. One significant recent development involved the creation at Kampala of an STRP Oversight Committee to give a sharper focus to the Panel's activities.[193] This group, comprising the chairs and vice-chairs of both the Standing Committee and the STRP itself, together with the Ramsar secretary-general and deputy, is now responsible for appointing the full Panel, providing it with intersessional guidance and support and maintaining liaison between the various institutions. Current tasks include the provision of advice (proactive and reactive) on strategic scientific and technical matters; review of draft CoP resolutions; enhancement of the contribution of national focal points; responding to requests for guidance concerning site designation, ecological change and other technical issues; and the integration of CEPA expertise in all these areas of activity.[194] The Panel may operate through working groups and task forces as appropriate, with assistance from the Secretariat when required.

Lack of adequate funding has proved a recurrent problem, however, leaving the STRP all too often dependent on voluntary, unpaid activity by its members, in-kind support from Partner Organisations and financial subsidies from governments, most notably Sweden.[195] The annual budgetary allocation for 2006–8 was almost doubled from the previous triennium,[196] but (in common with non-salary budget lines generally) shows zero increase for 2009–12.[197]

6. Implementation arrangements

Like all conservation treaties, Ramsar depends for the achievement of its objectives upon securing an appropriate balance between national implementation of its provisions and international supervision of compliance. The text of the Convention says relatively little about this issue, but from the outset Ramsar institutions have devoted considerable attention to

[193] Resolution IX.11. [194] See Resolution IX.2, Annex 1.
[195] See Resolution X.9, para. 4, and successive STRP reports.
[196] I.e. from SFr 110,000 to SFr 206,000. [197] See Resolution X.2, Annex I.

developing structures and procedures aimed at enhancing implementation of the commitments it imposes.[198] It is fair to say, however, that, in pursuing this goal, they have tended to rely primarily on the carrot rather than the stick.

a) National implementation

Plainly, the principal focus for all forms of conservation activity lies at the national level, and Ramsar's role is accordingly to shape and develop the policies, practices and procedures of its parties with regard to wetlands specifically. For each CoP meeting, the secretary-general prepares a report indicating progress towards the achievement of key objectives, based on information submitted in the parties' own reports, in order that the Strategic Plan may be formulated or fine-tuned.[199] The San José Conference in 1999 represented a high-water mark in terms of setting precise, quantitative targets for that purpose, but these commonly proved both overoptimistic and of limited practical utility,[200] and have since been de-emphasised.[201]

i) Domestic policy, institutions and legislation

As indicated above, Ramsar institutions have developed a substantial body of guidance in this field, principally by elaborating the wise-use principle in such a way as to elucidate issues of domestic implementation. Clearly, effective performance of the commitments undertaken by the parties depends significantly upon their possession of full and reliable information regarding wetland resources and their current status, but ostensibly impressive governmental claims in that regard have sometimes proved misleading, in the sense that the data collected did not embrace the entire national territory, or covered only the more important sites.[202] Resolution VII.20 consequently urged the parties to give the highest priority to the compilation of comprehensive inventories,

[198] Note that Resolution VIII.24 commended implementation of the 2002 UNEP Guidelines on Compliance and National Enforcement.

[199] This is conventionally entitled Report of the Secretary-General on the Implementation of the Convention at the Global Level (hereafter the Implementation Report, identified by the year of the CoP in question). For national reports, see subsection (ii) below.

[200] See Bowman, *supra* n. 13, pp. 64–7.

[201] See the 2005 Implementation Report, COP9 DOC.5, paras. 8–13; Resolution IX.8, preamble.

[202] See Resolution VII.27, Annex, Operational Objective 6.1.

recording the relevant information in accessible databases wherever possible. At Changwon, it was reported that 37 per cent of respondents had developed such inventories or were in the process of doing so, up from 25 per cent at the previous CoP.[203] Further progress on this front therefore remains a key objective of the current Plan, with all parties expected to have completed, and as far as possible disseminated, suitable inventories by 2015, as well as having Strategic Environmental Assessment systems in place regarding the impact on wetlands of their individual development programmes.[204]

Another important task, already undertaken by a number of parties, is the review of national laws and institutions to ensure compatibility with Ramsar requirements: guidelines were approved in 1999 to facilitate this process also.[205] The adoption and implementation of national wetland policies, for which detailed guidance has also been provided,[206] is considered a particularly high priority.[207] In 1993, it was noted that only two parties (Canada and Uganda) had formally adopted such policies,[208] but by 2008 around sixty had done so or were in the process of doing so.[209] The current Plan calls for such action to be initiated by *all* parties by 2015.[210]

Finally, on the institutional front, the value of national wetland committees has been emphasised as means of sharpening the focus for implementation of the Convention at that level,[211] and by 2008 almost half of all parties had such institutions in place.[212] The extent to which such entities exert significant influence over government policy is another question, however. A further vital, if mundane, function is the designation of Ramsar national focal points, which all parties are expected to have accomplished (for both CEPA and STRP purposes) by 2015.[213]

ii) National reports

Although the importance of regular reporting on treaty implementation is now widely appreciated, the text of Ramsar provides only for the duty

[203] 2008 Implementation Report, COP10 DOC.6, para. 28.
[204] Resolution X.1, Strategy 1.1. Resolution X.17 provides elaborate, updated guidance on both SEA and EIA.
[205] See Resolution VII.7 and *Handbook 3*. [206] See Resolution VII.6.
[207] See, e.g., Recommendations 4.10, Annex, and 6.9, and *Handbook 2*.
[208] See the Report of the 5th Meeting of the CoP, Summary Report of Workshop B.
[209] 2008 Implementation Report, para. 34.
[210] See Resolution VIII.25, Annex, section II, Operational Objective 2.1.
[211] Recommendation 5.6. [212] 2008 Implementation Report, para. 79.
[213] Strategic Plan, Strategy 4.3.i.

to notify the Secretariat of adverse ecological changes at listed sites. The reluctance of states to volunteer information even of that kind strongly underlines the need for a routine reporting system whereby this, along with all other aspects of implementation, may be addressed. This point was recognised at an early stage, with twenty-five of the then twenty-eight parties responding to a request to submit such reports to the very first Conference at Cagliari.[214] This has since become an established feature of the system and an outline format for such reports has accordingly been agreed and repeatedly modified.[215] Submission rates have fluctuated considerably over the years, peaking at San José, when 107 of the 113 parties produced reports prior to the meeting – an extremely impressive proportion by the standards of environmental treaties generally.[216] Unfortunately, performance declined sharply at Kampala,[217] where a widespread complaint was that the current format for reports was far too complex and burdensome.[218] Further streamlining by the Standing Committee, however, who had been urged in particular to enhance harmonisation with the reporting procedures of other conventions,[219] rendered it more 'user-friendly', and 129 parties submitted timely reports for Changwon.[220]

b) Implementation at the international level

Article 5 requires the parties to consult with each other regarding the implementation of their obligations, especially in the case of transboundary wetlands and shared water systems. They are also to endeavour to co-ordinate and support present and future policies and regulations concerning the conservation of wetlands and their flora and fauna. Such co-operation manifests itself at various levels and in numerous forms.

i) Bilateral and local co-operation

Duties of consultation and co-operation in relation to shared freshwater resources are already well established in customary international

[214] For a record of submission rates for all the early CoPs, see DOC. C.4.18, National Reports.
[215] See, e.g., Recommendation 2.1, Resolution VII.27.
[216] Particularly as new parties are not expected to submit a report on the occasion of their first CoP.
[217] To 110 of 146. See 2005 Implementation Report, paras. 4–8.
[218] Ibid., para. 9.
[219] Resolution IX.8, para. 9.
[220] 2008 Implementation Report, para. 24.

law,[221] while various multilateral conventions have recently been concluded to codify and develop those principles.[222] A considerable number of individual watercourses,[223] and coastal wetlands, have also been the subject of specific treaty regimes, which may provide an appropriate framework for collaboration.[224] The parallel obligation under Article 5 of Ramsar has itself been amplified through the adoption at San José of Guidelines for International Co-operation under the Convention,[225] which reiterate and consolidate many of these traditional principles and illustrate their application in the particular context of wetland management. They also emphasise the importance of dedicated international institutions to address such matters. In addition, Resolution X.19 provides consolidated technical guidance on Wetlands and River Basin Management generally,[226] integrating the principles of international co-operation into this broader context.

Despite the well-established nature of these principles, it is clear that they raise issues of considerable sensitivity, and at Kampala a draft resolution,[227] endorsing a step-by-step process leading to the formal joint administration of transnational wetlands, was deferred for further consideration in the light of serious reservations expressed by Brazil, Chile, El Salvador and Russia, and doubtless shared by other parties. The current Plan accordingly calls only for parties with shared basins and coastal systems to 'consider' participation in joint management bodies.[228]

Nonetheless, transnational co-operation in relation to listed sites is becoming much more firmly established, particularly within the European region.[229] One relatively sophisticated model is the tripartite arrangement between Denmark, Germany and the Netherlands for the

221 *Lac Lanoux Arbitration* (1957) 24 *ILR* 101; P. W. Birnie, A. E. Boyle and C. J. Redgwell, *International Law and the Environment* (Oxford University Press, 3rd ed., 2009), Chapter 10.

222 See in particular the 1992 UNECE Convention on the Protection and Use of Transboundary Watercourses and International Lakes, 31 *ILM* 1312, and the 1997 UN Convention on the Non-navigational Uses of International Watercourses, 36 *ILM* 703.

223 For examples, see S. C. McCaffrey, *The Law of International Watercourses* (Oxford University Press, 2001).

224 See Resolution VII.19, Annex, para. 13.

225 See Resolution VII.19; *Handbook 17.*

226 The integration of principles of wise use into basin management is demonstrated diagrammatically through a 'Critical Path', embracing ten sequential steps over five organisational phases.

227 Ramsar CoP 9, Draft Resolution 6.

228 Strategy 3.5.ii.

229 See especially the Report of the 5th European pre-CoP Regional Meeting (Yerevan, 2004), Workshop D, prepared for the 9th CoP.

protection of the Wadden Sea, a vast expanse of tidal flats, salt marshes, sandbanks and islands in respect of which joint institutional arrangements have been in existence since 1982. These are aimed at harmonising conservation measures and moving progressively towards an integrated management plan for the entire area.[230] Other regions are not without their own examples, however, including those concerning Lake Victoria (Kenya, Uganda and Tanzania) and the Lake Chad Basin (Chad, Nigeria, Niger, Cameroon and the Central African Republic) in Africa.[231] Instances of multilateral co-operation with regard to international rivers can, of course, be found in all parts of the globe.[232] In addition, an emerging development, inspired by the long-standing co-operative management arrangements between Austria and Hungary over Neusiedlersee/Lake Ferto, involves the designation of appropriate wetlands as Transboundary Ramsar Sites, with these two states and Slovakia standing out as pioneers in this respect.[233]

The scope for bilateral co-operation extends far beyond neighbouring states, however, since there are many situations where parties may profit from the sharing of experience concerning aspects of wetland conservation, particularly where they have sites with similar characteristics. With that in mind, the Bureau emphasised the potential of the 'twinning' of wetlands in different countries in its report to the Kushiro Conference, a notable example being the arrangement involving the Camargue Ramsar site in France and the Danube Delta in Romania. Although similar links have been established elsewhere, including a trilateral networking of the Kakadu National Park (Australia), the Wasur National Park (Indonesia) and the Tonda Wildlife Management Area, these have been relatively few in total and the idea is not pressed in the Plan for 2009–15. A further, increasingly common, form of bilateral co-operation involves arrangements between developed and developing countries, such as the joint project between Mauretania and the Netherlands to secure the sustainable use of the Banc d'Arguin site

230 See C. Dettmann and J. A. Enemark, 'The Trilateral Wadden Sea: Common Management of a Shared Wetland', in ibid.

231 See 'Overview of the Convention in the African Region', Section D, appended to the Report of the 6th Meeting of the CoP.

232 At San José, the existence was noted of over 200 agreements of this kind. See Resolution VII.19, Annex, p. 8.

233 For the evolution of this initiative (which expresses a commitment to co-operation without creating any distinct legal status for the site), and for current examples, see COP10 DOC.32.

by maintaining the traditional fishing methods of the local Imraguen people.[234]

Finally, it is to be noted that the obligation under Article 5 to endeavour to co-ordinate and support policies and regulations extends not merely to the conservation of wetlands but to their flora and fauna. There are accordingly a number of arrangements of this kind, including the Greenland White-Fronted Goose Conservation Plan, developed by Denmark, Iceland, Ireland and the UK. Some have been enshrined in treaty form, including certain bilateral agreements concerning migratory birds and subregional arrangements concerning marine mammals adopted under the 1979 Bonn Migratory Species Convention.[235] A further significant initiative in this category, equally relevant to the CMS, is the promotion of international co-operation for the conservation of waterbird flyways. This was the focus of detailed proposals at a major conference in Edinburgh in 2004, which secured Ramsar endorsement at Changwon.[236]

ii) Regional activities

The Convention itself makes no mention of regional issues at all, but the decision to establish a Standing Committee proved the catalyst for the creation of this new, intermediate tier of activity, since Committee membership is constituted primarily on a regional basis.[237] The Ramsar regions are, unsurprisingly, Africa, Asia, Europe, the Neotropics, North America and Oceania.[238]

It was inevitable that Ramsar parties within each region would feel the need for consultations with their representatives, and from the early 1990s this process has mushroomed into a more elaborate programme of meetings, seminars and workshops. This trend has arguably been most marked in the Asian region,[239] where periodic Asian Wetland Symposia involving all sectors and stakeholders have been convened under the leadership of a specialist NGO – Ramsar Center Japan. These were commended at Kampala as an excellent forum for the exploration of

[234] See Report of the 5th Meeting of the CoP, Summary Report of Workshop D. [235] Ibid.

[236] See Resolution X.22 and Annex. For further discussion of the arrangements discussed in this paragraph, see Chapters 6 and 7 above and 16 below.

[237] See section 5(c) above.

[238] Initially (largely for political reasons) there were two European regions, East and West, but these were amalgamated by virtue of Resolution VII.1.

[239] Note, for example, the impressive series of regional events reported to the Brisbane CoP in Document INFO.6.8.

scientific and technical aspects, thereby complementing the regional meetings of the parties themselves, which tend to focus more upon political and administrative issues. Other regions were encouraged to adopt a similar approach, if they had not already done so.[240] In some cases, deliberations at the regional level have resulted in the adoption of substantive conservation initiatives for the protection of wetlands or their flora and fauna,[241] such as the rapidly expanding MedWet programme concerning wetlands in the Mediterranean,[242] and the Strategy for the Conservation and Wise Use of High Andean Wetlands.[243] Finally, the application of certain of the criteria for site designation (regarding, for example, wetland types that are 'underrepresented' in the List) requires the accumulation and pooling of knowledge at the regional level, and the STRP has recently provided technical guidance regarding this process.[244]

iii) Implementation at the global level

Although Ramsar deserves credit for being one of the first wildlife treaties to incorporate supervisory machinery, in the form of periodic meetings of the parties, to monitor the implementation of the obligations it imposes, it has subsequently proved necessary to expand considerably upon the rather modest provisions in the original text.

These are found in Article 6(2), which empowers the Conference to discuss implementation of the Convention generally and, more particularly, to comment upon changes to the List, consider information regarding ecological change in listed sites and make recommendations regarding the wise use of wetlands and their flora and fauna. As noted above,[245] these powers have been utilised not merely for the adoption of general guidelines on the performance of Ramsar obligations, but also to urge specific action by individual parties, such as the listing of particular sites or the adoption of remedial measures at wetlands undergoing adverse ecological change. It is apparent that, while some states have responded promptly to concerns expressed by the CoP, others have been more dilatory or have failed to address problems at all, particularly where the threat to wetland sites derives from major development projects.

[240] Resolution IX.19.
[241] For information on recent initiatives, see Resolution IX.7, Annex I; and, for Operational Guidelines to govern future endeavours, Resolution X.6.
[242] See, e.g., Resolutions VII.22; IX.7, Annex II. For an overview, see *Handbook 17*, pp. 22–3.
[243] Resolution VIII.39. [244] Resolution X.20. [245] See especially section 4(c)(iii), (iv).

Thus high-profile schemes such as the proposed construction of the Danube–Elbe–Oder canal,[246] which is thought to threaten several listed sites in Austria and the Czech and Slovak Republics, have been the subject of repeated attention.[247] Even so, Ramsar has had its successes, and the decision by the newly elected South African government in 1996 to abandon plans to mine for heavy metals at its St Lucia site was hailed as a particular triumph.[248] The ability to influence events in this way has, however, required the constant development and refinement of supervisory procedures far beyond the slender foundations of Article 6.

Montreux Record First, it was decided at a relatively early stage that it would be appropriate to formalise the process by which information concerning ecological change was collated. In 1987, the Bureau was instructed by Recommendation 4.8 to maintain a record, later known as the Montreux Record, of all such changes. Initially, this was to comprise a list of some forty-four sites compiled on the basis of national reports submitted to the Montreux meeting.[249] A formal procedure for maintaining this Record was established at Kushiro, and subsequently revised.[250] The current version gives the parties themselves the primary responsibility for initiating the procedure as a means of drawing attention to the need for action or support, but also allows the Secretariat to raise potential problems identified by other sources, thereby harnessing the energy and expertise of NGOs and the scientific community in a 'watchdog' capacity.[251] It is important to note, however, that in deference to national sovereignty the site may not formally be added to the Record without the consent of the party concerned. In some cases, states have been insistent upon this power of veto: at Kushiro, for example, while the US indicated that it had no objection to the incorporation of the Everglades within the Record, Japan appeared determined to resist pressure to include Lake Utonai, insisting that there was no evidence of

[246] For information on the scheme, see .www.daphne.sk/docs/DOL_handout_03-05-15.pdf.
[247] See most recently Resolution X.13, para. 10.
[248] See, e.g., A. Zaloumis et al., 'Greater St Lucia Wetland Park World Heritage Site' *World Heritage Review* No. 40, July 2005.
[249] See DOC. INF. C.4.18. [250] See Resolutions V.4 and VI.1, Annex.
[251] At Changwon, the Secretariat noted that third parties had reported adverse changes concerning seventy-four sites in twenty-six countries since the previous CoP. See Secretary-General's Report, *supra* n. 61, paras. 19–21, and text accompanying n. 111.

ecological change at the site.[252] The fact that Japan was hosting the Conference, and may have felt that local NGOs were seeking to exploit the attendant glare of publicity, may have been a significant factor here, however.

Governmental sensitivities of this kind represent one key reason why the number of sites included in the Record is well below that at which adverse changes are known or suspected to be occurring.[253] By the time of the tenth CoP, the number of sites listed stood at fifty-six,[254] though it has since been reduced to fifty. They include Srebarna (Bulgaria), Laguna del Tigre (Guatemala), Keolodeo National Park (India), Azraq Oasis (Jordan), Donana (Spain), Ichkeul (Tunisia), Lake George (Uganda) and the Ouse Washes (UK). Ironically, Iran, which hosted the diplomatic conference which adopted the Convention, and Greece, whose ratification brought it into force, together account for over one-quarter of the sites within the Record.[255] Parties are obliged, in their triennial national reports, to report on the conservation status of such sites, which may be removed from the Record upon receipt of information indicating the successful remediation of ecological problems. Significantly, however, the final decision is again that of the contracting party concerned. Thirty-two sites in total have been removed from the Record in accordance with this procedure, including Lac Tonga (Algeria), Laguna Colorada (Bolivia), Lake Miki Prespa and the Evros Delta (Greece), Chilaka Lake (India), St Lucia (South Africa), Nariva Swamp (Trinidad and Tobago) and Tendrivska Bay and Yagorlytska Bay (Ukraine).[256] Some environmental problems are of a recurrent nature, however, and in 1999 Belgium informed the Secretariat that the De Ijzerbroeken te Diksmuide en Lo-Reninge site, which had previously been removed from the Record, should once again be included on account of difficulties in maintaining

[252] This issue was a recurrent focus of discussion. See Report of the 5th Meeting of the CoP, 3rd, 4th and 8th Plenary Sessions, Agenda Item X; Summary Report of Workshop A.

[253] Another reason may be that listing would serve little purpose, as the changes at particular sites are judged to be temporary or trivial, or because anticipated harm fails to materialise.

[254] This figure should be compared to that for sites reported at recent Conferences as being under threat (100–150), which is itself likely to be affected by significant underreporting. At the Kushiro CoP, Friends of the Earth estimated that some 38 per cent of all listed sites were undergoing changes in ecological character, substantially more than the forty-four sites then included in the Record. Report of the 5th Meeting of the CoP, Summary Report of Workshop A.

[255] Full details are available via the 'Documents' link on the Ramsar website.

[256] See the 'Documents' link on the Ramsar website.

adequate water quantity and quality.[257] Furthermore, novel threats may sometimes emerge; thus, although problems associated with management of the Donau-March-Auen wetland in Austria seemed to have been overcome by the mid-1990s, and a plan to build a hydro-electric power station within its boundaries abandoned, successive Austrian national reports have suggested that the site must be maintained in the Record for as long as the uncertainties posed by the Danube–Oder–Elbe Canal project remain unresolved.

Compliance mechanisms which result *only* in the subjection of governments to criticism are unlikely to deliver long-term benefits, however, and it has accordingly been recognised that, to ensure their ongoing co-operation, this should at least be balanced by the prospect of material support, albeit on a relatively modest scale, for their attempts at remediation.[258] A highly significant development here was the establishment of the procedure now known as the Ramsar Advisory Mission.

Ramsar Advisory Mission This procedure, devised originally by the Standing Committee pursuant to Recommendation 3.9, is designed to identify solutions to the problems posed by ecological changes at listed wetlands. Following a number of relatively informal inspections by Bureau staff dating from 1988,[259] it was formally adopted by the CoP in 1990,[260] and now generally involves a site visit by a team of experts, who produce a detailed analysis of the situation and recommendations for remedial action. In some instances, including Ichkeul (Tunisia), Srebarna (Bulgaria), Djoudj/Diawling (Senegal/Mauritania) and Kyliiske Mouth (Ukraine), these missions have been conducted jointly with other bodies, such as IUCN, the World Heritage Committee or UNESCO's Man and the Biosphere Programme. Sites do not have to be included in the Montreux Record in order to be eligible, though the resulting report may propose such listing, as in the case of the Bluefields

257 See Resolution VII.12.

258 Note also the proposal approved in Resolution VIII.15, to be implemented when resources permit, to establish a *San José Record* comprising sites which exemplify good practice in the application of principles of wise use.

259 The first applications were in respect of Schorren van de Beneden-Schelde (Belgium), Las Tablas de Daimiel (Spain) and Ichkeul (Tunisia), all conducted by Michael Smart.

260 See Recommendation 4.7 and Annex 1. It was originally known as the Monitoring Procedure and then, briefly, as the Management Guidance Procedure. For details of Advisory Missions to date, see the Ramsar website.

Bay site in Nicaragua,[261] at risk from construction of an all-weather road. Other recent missions include Bahia de Panama (Panama), Kopacki Rit (Croatia), Muhlenberger Loch (Germany), Lake Natron (Tanzania) and the Ouse Washes (UK). As will be apparent, it is not only developing countries who stand to benefit from the technical guidance which such visits may provide. Although it would be foolish to claim that Advisory Missions invariably result in the solution of the ecological problems at the sites in question,[262] they have certainly enjoyed some success. In particular, a number of instances of removal from the Montreux Record – including Chilaka Lake, Nariva Swamp, St Lucia, Lac Oubeira (Algeria) and Ria Lagartos (Mexico) – have followed the implementation of measures proposed by an Advisory Mission. Occasionally, moreover, the Mission has concluded that remedial work already undertaken at the site justifies its immediate removal from the Record.[263]

Financial support While technical advice is likely to be of great value, many governments will lack the resources to ensure its implementation, and another important development was therefore the decision in 1990 to establish a fund, now known as the Ramsar Small Grants Fund for Wetlands Conservation and Wise Use (Ramsar SGF), to support wetland conservation efforts in developing countries and transitional economies.[264] Under the current Operational Guidelines,[265] funding of up to SFr 40,000 may be sought for emergency measures at listed sites, or other activities that clearly contribute towards achievement of the Strategic Plan. Even non-parties may apply for 'preparatory assistance' of up to SFr 25,000, to facilitate accession to the Convention. Decisions are made by the Standing Committee on the basis of recommendations from the Subgroup on Finance, following input from the Secretariat and relevant regional representatives. Successful applicants initially receive 60 per cent (formerly 80 per cent) of the sum awarded, and the remainder following submission of final project reports.

[261] RAM No. 57, November 2005. Other recommendations included the conduct of a full EIA, investigation of wetland hydrodynamics and preparation of a site management plan.

[262] Several sites, including Ichkeul, Srebarna, Banados del Este (Uruguay), the Dee Estuary (UK) and the Greek Ramsar sites have been visited more than once.

[263] See, e.g., RAM No. 60 (Alagol, Iran, 2009).

[264] See Resolution IV.3, which created the 'Wetland Conservation Fund'. For later developments, see Resolutions V.8, VI.6, VII.5.

[265] See the Ramsar website via 'Activities > Grants Programmes'.

By 2008, the Fund had disbursed more than SFr 7.5 million to support over 200 projects in numerous countries, including the development of wetland inventories and site management plans, the study of wetland species, the training of personnel, the convening of regional meetings, the improvement of visitor facilities at nature reserves, the elaboration of public education programmes, the mapping of sites and the restoration of particular wetlands. In addition, several emergency projects have been granted small awards outside the normal project cycle. In 2008, sums close to the maximum available were awarded, for example, to Albania for capacity building and enhancement of public awareness regarding key wetlands, to Cameroon for the development of management plans and ecotourism for its listed sites, to Cape Verde for wetland survey and designation of a new site on Maio Island, and to Chile for conservation and participative management at the Bahia Lomas site. Total disbursements exceeded SFr 285,000.[266]

Plainly, the sums involved are extremely small, but they are nonetheless much sought-after: in 2007, for instance, only five awards could be made in response to forty-seven completed applications in all. Shortage of money has always been a problem, as the SGF has never remotely achieved the annual income of US$1 million dollars which has long been its target.[267] It is sustained largely by voluntary contributions from sympathetic governments, of which Austria, the Czech Republic, Japan, Sweden and the UK have been especially prominent in recent years. Following the reluctant abandonment of an earlier plan to establish a multisourced Ramsar Endowment Fund,[268] the CoP resolved instead to advertise Secretariat-approved but ultimately unsuccessful SGF applications in a Small Projects Portfolio with a view to attracting earmarked funding from potential new donors.[269]

The SGF is not the only available source of finance, however, and governments from the Neotropical region may qualify for training grants from the Wetlands for the Future Initiative, discussed above.[270] In addition, the Swiss government has for some years provided funding of around SFr 150,000 p.a. to finance emergency action or other conservation measures for African wetlands, from which a number of parties have benefited.[271] Much larger sums may be available from external sources,

[266] Ibid. [267] See Resolutions 5.8, preamble and X.7, para. 9.

[268] See Resolutions VIII.29, IX.13.

[269] See the Report of the 34th Meeting of the Standing Committee, Agenda Item 12.4.

[270] Section 4(d).

[271] In 2008, grants went to Côte d'Ivoire, Equatorial Guinea, Gabon, Mozambique, Niger and Seychelles to support projects concerning wetland conservation and inventory, awareness raising or institutional/policy development.

such as the EC, development banks or the GEF, where the international status of Ramsar sites may prove a stimulant for support.[272] The Bureau has, for example, assisted the government of Jordan in obtaining GEF funding to help tackle the ongoing ecological problems at Azraq Oasis.[273] Wetland management and conservation in fact cuts across several GEF focal areas, and it was noted in 2004 that the Facility had already supported some twenty-eight projects on lakes alone.[274] Such funding is often substantial, with two early awards (relating to wetland conservation in Iran and enhancing the network of migration sites on the African–Eurasian flyway) together amounting to US$1 million in total, while a major MedWet programme to manage coastal wetlands in six Mediterranean countries was co-funded with other donors to the tune of US$15.5 million.[275]

7. Relationship with other institutions and agreements

Given that Ramsar activities will inevitably impinge upon those of other international agreements and institutions on a regular basis, the need for collaboration has been recognised from an early stage.[276] It is also strongly endorsed in the current Strategic Plan,[277] which refers to links with the Climate Change and Desertification Conventions, the New Partnership for Africa's Development (NEPAD), and a host of other institutions and initiatives. Arguably the most vital links are with the other major biodiversity-related agreements, and are pursued at a general level through participation in the Biodiversity Liaison Group (BLG) established under the aegis of the CBD.[278] Formal links with the CBD are consolidated through a Memorandum of Co-operation, now in its second incarnation,[279] and an associated Joint Work Plan identifying

[272] Note in that context the regional Signature Initiatives scheme endorsed by Resolution X.7.
[273] See Recommendation 5.1. On the relationship with GEF and its implementing agencies generally, see Recommendation 5.4 and Resolution VI.10.
[274] S. S. Guitart, 'Towards a Lake Basin Management Initiative', Ramsar Bulletin Board, April 2004. See generally ILEC, *Managing Lakes and Their Basins for Sustainable Use* (ILEC, 2005), Chapter 9.
[275] See generally 'Reservoirs of Biodiversity', in *Wetland Values and Functions* (Ramsar Information Pack, 2000).
[276] Recommendation 4.11, on Co-operation with International Organisations, is perhaps the earliest measure of this kind. See currently Resolution X.11.
[277] See Resolution X.1, Strategy 3.1.
[278] See Resolution IX.5.
[279] Of 10 May 2005, superseding that of 19 January 1996. The texts of all Ramsar memoranda of co-operation are available on the Ramsar website, via the 'Documents' link.

numerous mechanisms through which the respective sets of parties, Secretariats and other Convention bodies may work towards harmonisation of the two regimes.[280] Of the other BLG participants, links are strongest with the Migratory Species and World Heritage Conventions,[281] and instances have already been cited of co-operation concerning both the establishment of conservation initiatives and monitoring at particular sites.[282] One issue which has especially exercised the Ramsar CoP in recent times is the need for increased harmonisation of reporting procedures in order to reduce the cumulative burden upon the parties to these various treaties.[283]

8. Conclusions

Ramsar was the first conservation treaty to aim for truly worldwide participation and the first to concern itself exclusively with habitat: while earlier regional treaties certainly contained provisions addressing that issue, they tended to concentrate primarily on species protection. In any event, Ramsar's approach to habitat conservation is rather different from that of these earlier treaties. Rather than emphasising the establishment of specified categories of protected areas, with progressively stricter regulation of exploitation, Ramsar advocates and elaborates a general policy of 'wise use'. Although it acknowledges the need for nature reserves, it does not specifically regulate hunting, trapping or fishing on wetlands in its List, and the only real restriction on agricultural or other usage is that it should not harm the 'ecological character' of the wetland. Ramsar is therefore very much in line with the sustainable-development theme which has become the centrepiece of international environmental regulation.

There is no doubt that, as originally conceived, Ramsar contained numerous deficiencies of a structural and institutional character, certainly by comparison with other major conservation conventions which were concluded only shortly afterwards. This was partly attributable to its pioneering nature, however, and considerable time and effort has subsequently been devoted towards correcting these deficiencies, the

[280] Fourth Joint Work Plan (2007–10), available on the Ramsar website, via the 'Documents' link.

[281] See the 1997 MoU with CMS, backed by a CMS/AEWA/Ramsar Work Plan, and the 1999 MoU with the WHC. Note also the 2002 Joint Programme of Work with UNESCO-MAB. All viewable ibid.

[282] See section 6(b)(iii), *supra*.

[283] See Resolution IX.5, and section 6(a)(ii), *supra*.

Ramsar organs having borrowed liberally from the cumulative experience of these other instruments. Participation has grown to a level more in keeping with the aspirations of a treaty aiming for global applicability and the number and variety of sites in the List of Wetlands of International Importance has increased substantially. An invaluable framework of policy for the conservation of wetland areas has been devised. In terms of its involvement and integration of the non-governmental sector, Ramsar has a record from which other treaty operations could learn a great deal. It may well be the case that the pressures upon wetland conservation are intensifying at a rate which will ultimately defy human remediation, but the Ramsar Convention can at least make a plausible claim to have established itself as a viable mechanism for tackling the task.

Recommended further reading

M. J. Bowman, 'The Ramsar Convention Comes of Age' (1995) 42 *Neths ILR* 1

M. Finlayson and M. Moser (eds.), *Wetlands* (IWRB/Facts on File, 1991)

E. Maltby, *Waterlogged Wealth* (Earthscan, 2nd ed., 2007)

G. V. T. Matthews, *The Ramsar Convention on Wetlands: Its History and Development* (Ramsar Bureau, 1993)

Ramsar Convention Secretariat, The Ramsar Convention Manual: A Guide to the Convention on Wetlands (4th ed., 2006)

Further useful materials can be found in the Ramsar Wise Use Resource Library, accessible on the Ramsar website, via the 'Documents' link.

Chapter 14

The World Heritage Convention

1. Background

The UNESCO Convention Concerning the Protection of the World Cultural and Natural Heritage (WHC)[1] was adopted on 16 November 1972 and came into force on 17 December 1975.[2] Its origins can be traced to three separate but related factors.[3] The first is that by 1972 the international community was becoming increasingly receptive to the concept of a 'common heritage'. In the context of the Convention, this is reflected in the idea that there are certain outstanding natural or man-made features, such as the Serengeti or the Pyramids, the Galapagos Islands or the Taj Mahal, which should be seen as the heritage of more than just one state. They constitute part of the heritage of all people, and humankind as a whole accordingly has certain rights and duties with respect to their conservation. In this respect, the Convention tapped into the emergence in the 1960s and 1970s of the concept of the common heritage of mankind, which was to feature prominently in the negotiation of the 1982 Law of the Sea Convention.[4] It also reflects the concepts of 'universal heritage' and 'the common heritage of humanity' found in other UNESCO

[1] 11 *ILM* 1358, *TIAS* no. 8226, 27 *UST* 37.

[2] Pursuant to Article 33, the Convention entered into force three months after the twentieth state (Switzerland) deposited an instrument of ratification, acceptance or accession.

[3] An abbreviated history of the origins of the Convention is provided by the 'father of the world heritage' concept, R. E. Train, in *World Heritage 2002: Shared Legacy, Common Responsibility* (UNESCO World Heritage Centre, 2003), pp. 36–7; see also 'Genesis of International Protection of Cultural and Natural Heritage', in *World Heritage: Challenges for the Millennium* (UNESCO, 2007), pp. 26–9; R. L. Meyer, 'Travaux Préparatoires for the UNESCO World Heritage Convention' (1976) 2 *Earth Law Journal* 45; and M. Batisse and G. Bolla, *The Invention of 'World Heritage'*, History Papers: UNESCO Action as Seen by Protagonists and Witnesses, Paper 2 (Association of Former UNESCO Staff Members, 2003).

[4] See Article 136 LOSC, which declares the resources of the deep seabed to be the common heritage of mankind.

instruments.[5] In the particular context of wildlife protection, the Convention has maintained this distinctive perspective in protecting the natural heritage both within UNESCO and, more widely, as part of a web of biodiversity-related treaties under the umbrella of the 1992 CBD.[6]

The second factor is that by 1972 the international community had shown itself willing to take positive action to help protect these sites. When the Nubian monuments of the Upper Nile, including the thirty-foot-high statue of Ramses II at Abu Simbel, were threatened by flooding in 1960 as a result of the newly constructed Aswan High Dam, the international response was prompt, with international campaigns organised by UNESCO and others to save the famous monuments from destruction.[7] On the natural side, the IUCN was active in the 1950s and 1960s in securing protection for important natural habitats, aided by the financial support of a variety of governments, companies and individuals. As the threats grew, however, it became increasingly evident that a permanent legal, administrative and financial framework for the identification and conservation of areas of outstanding cultural and natural importance would greatly assist the ad hoc efforts of UNESCO, the IUCN and others.[8]

Third, international efforts were stimulated by preparations for the United Nations-sponsored 1972 Stockholm Conference on the Human Environment. UNESCO had completed a draft text for the International Protection of Monuments, Groups of Buildings and Sites of Universal Value in 1971, while the IUCN prepared a draft Convention for the Conservation of the World's Heritage. These parallel developments became entwined with preparations for Stockholm but, cognisant of these developments within UNESCO, state delegates at Stockholm refrained from direct mention of 'world heritage' in the formal Conference Declaration. 'Heritage' is only fleetingly mentioned, in

[5] For a recent example see Article 1 of the UNESCO 2001 Universal Declaration on Cultural Diversity, which provides that 'cultural diversity is as necessary for humankind as biodiversity is for nature. In this sense, it is the common heritage of humanity and should be recognized and affirmed for the benefit of present and future generations.'

[6] See C. Redgwell, 'The World Heritage Convention and Other Conventions Relating to the Protection of the Natural Heritage', in F. Francioni (ed.), *The 1972 World Heritage Convention: A Commentary* (Oxford University Press, 2008), and Part 6 below.

[7] See *Protection of Mankind's Cultural Heritage, Sites and Monuments* (UNESCO, 1970), pp. 39–60.

[8] See, generally, Meyer, *supra* n. 3.

Principle 4, which refers to the special responsibility of humankind 'to safeguard and wisely manage the heritage of wildlife and its habitat'.[9]

The adoption of a text designed to preserve both natural and cultural heritage of outstanding interest as 'world heritage of mankind as a whole' duly took place at the next General Conference of UNESCO in November 1972. It introduced a novel dimension to the protection of natural property under international law – the concept of 'natural heritage'.[10] Hitherto international law had addressed the conservation of 'nature' or specific flora and fauna, but without reference to the notion of patrimony or heritage. Indeed, the reasons for conservation were frequently both anthropocentric and limited temporally to the present generation.[11] The innovation of the Convention was to embrace the natural environment within a wider category of 'world heritage' and to make express the inter-generational obligation of conservation and transmission.[12] This was at a time when 'it was widely accepted that general international law placed hardly any obligations upon states in the management of their natural resources'.[13]

The United States was the first state to ratify the Convention, which entered into force on 17 December 1975 and today has 186 state parties, including all the EU member states.[14] Such widespread participation embraces countries with important wildlife habitats (e.g. Botswana, Indonesia, Kenya and Papua New Guinea), those best able to contribute to funding the Convention (e.g. the US, France and Germany) and countries with large areas under their control (e.g. China, Brazil and Russia). However, the value of the WHC for wildlife – the chief focus of this chapter – will always be limited because the objective of the Convention is to protect only the world's most select cultural and natural

[9] The accompanying Recommendations for Action call on governments to note 'that the draft convention prepared by [UNESCO] concerning the protection of the world natural and cultural heritage marks a significant step towards the protection, on an international scale, of the environment, [and to] examine this draft convention with a view to its adoption at the next General Conference of UNESCO'. Recommendations 98 and 99, UN Doc. A/CONF.48/14/REV.1.(1972); see also www.unep.org.

[10] See F. Francioni, 'The Preamble', in Francioni, *supra* n. 6.

[11] While 'world heritage' retained a strongly anthropocentric flavour, underscored in the preamble to the Convention, this has been mitigated over time, particularly through the development of the criteria for listing natural heritage under the Convention which are discussed further below.

[12] Article 4, discussed further below.

[13] Francioni, *supra* n. 10, at p. 1. Exceptions cited concern the use of international watercourses and liability for transboundary harm.

[14] But not the EC itself since Article 32 does not provide for its participation.

areas.[15] Natural habitats which contain animals and plants not of exceptional significance will not benefit, at least not directly, from the Convention. However, within these limitations, the Convention has the potential to be of great importance to wildlife. The World Heritage List provides a mechanism for giving international recognition to some of the most outstanding natural habitats in the world, and the World Heritage Fund offers developing state parties the prospect of receiving financial and technical assistance to help protect such areas within their territory. Indeed, the World Heritage Convention was the first amongst the 'big four' treaties of the time (along with CITES and the Ramsar and Bonn Conventions) to offer developing countries a material incentive to protect outstanding wildlife habitats, though the other Conventions, in particular Ramsar, have now followed suit.

2. Key elements of the Convention

a) The duty to identify, protect, present and transmit

In accordance with Article 4, each state party recognises that the duty of ensuring the identification, protection, conservation, presentation and transmission to future generations of the cultural and natural heritage of outstanding universal value situated on its territory belongs primarily to that state.[16] This treaty obligation extends to *all* cultural and natural heritage of outstanding universal value and not only to that inscribed on the World Heritage List.[17] It is doubtful, however, whether this obligation exists at customary international law.[18] The Convention further

[15] See the discussion of 'outstanding universal value' and representativity, below.

[16] Article 4 and Operational Guidelines 2008, para. 7 (discussed further below, section 2(c)). Article 4 further provides that each state party 'will do all it can to this end, to the utmost of its own resources and, where appropriate, with any international assistance and co-operation, in particular, financial, ... scientific and technical which it may be able to obtain'. The assistance provisions of the Convention are considered further in Part 5 below.

[17] Articles 6(1) and 6(3) refer to world heritage as 'the cultural and natural heritage mentioned in Articles 1 and 2', i.e. all heritage protected by the Convention and not just properties listed under Article 11. This is reinforced by Article 12, which states that the fact that a cultural or natural heritage property has not been added to the Article 11 Lists 'shall in no way be construed to mean that it does not have outstanding universal value for purposes other than those resulting from inclusion in these lists'. For further discussion see G. Carducci (Article 6) and F. Lenzerini (Article 12), in Francioni, *supra* n. 6.

[18] See R. O'Keefe, 'World Cultural Heritage: Obligations to the International Community as a Whole?' (2004) 53 *ICLQ* 189, p. 205.

recognises 'the duty of the international community as a whole to co-operate' in the protection of such heritage, and each party 'undertakes not to take any deliberate measures which might damage directly or indirectly' world heritage located on the territory of other state parties.[19]

It is for each state party to identify and delineate the cultural and natural heritage properties on its territory,[20] an obligation which has been interpreted by the Australian High Court as resting exclusively with the state party in whose territory the heritage is situated.[21] The High Court has had several opportunities to consider the Convention and Australia remains the only state party to have developed a significant 'world heritage jurisprudence',[22] starting with the well-known *Tasmanian Dam* case explored in detail in the first edition of this work.[23] There the question arose whether the Convention imposed a legal duty on state parties to protect listed property within their territory. Article 5 in particular conditions the obligation to take 'effective and active measures' for the protection, conservation and presentation of cultural and natural heritage within the state party's territory 'in so far as possible, and as appropriate for each country'.[24] The Court considered that Articles 4 and 5 of the Convention impose a legal duty on each party to protect World Heritage sites situated in its territory 'to the utmost of its own resources'.[25]

[19] Article 6(1) and (3).

[20] Article 3. Article 11(3) requires the consent of the state in whose territory the property is situated to the listing and the additional safeguard that listing of 'a property situated in a territory, sovereignty or jurisdiction over which is claimed by more than one state', is 'without prejudice to the rights of the other party to the dispute'.

[21] *Richardson v Forestry Commission* [1988] HCA 10; (1988) 164 *CLR* 261 – challenge by the Tasmanian Forestry Commission of the Commonwealth of Australia's suspension of its logging operations while the Commonwealth established a Commission of Inquiry to determine whether certain forest areas in south-west Tasmania were suitable for nomination as world heritage properties.

[22] Discussed further in B. Boer and G. Wiffen, *Heritage Law in Australia* (Oxford University Press, 2006), Chapter 3.

[23] *The Commonwealth of Australia v Tasmania* [1983] HCA 21; (1983) 68 *ILR* 266 – Tasmania's challenge to legal measures taken by the (federal) Commonwealth of Australia to halt the construction of a dam on the Franklin River in the Western Tasmanian Wilderness National Parks which the Commonwealth had successfully nominated for inscription on the World Heritage List.

[24] In Magraw's typology of norms (differential, contextual and absolute), this is a contextual norm, the application of which will vary according to the particular circumstances of each party, within the scope of the obligations set forth in the Convention. D. B. Magraw, 'Legal Treatment of Developing Countries: Differential, Contextual and Absolute Norms' (1989) 1 *Colo. J. Int'l. Envt'l. L & Pol'y* 69.

[25] *Per* Brennan J., citing Article 4, ibid.

Revealing is the strongly worded dissent of the Chief Justice, who considered it 'impossible to conclude' that Articles 4 and 5 impose binding obligations because these 'would extend to any property which might reasonably be regarded as cultural or natural heritage within the meaning of Arts. 1 and 2 of the Convention, whether or not included on the World Heritage List'.[26]

In addition to obligations of state parties arising with respect to world heritage property identified and delineated within their territory, whether or not on the World Heritage List, the Convention in Article 6 imposes two further obligations with respect to listed sites situated outside their territory. The first is a modest positive obligation of assistance, if requested, to help other parties on whose territory a property in the World Heritage List or the List of World Heritage in Danger is situated with its identification, protection, conservation and preservation.[27] The second obligation is a negative one: to refrain from taking any deliberate measures which might damage directly or indirectly the heritage situated on the territory of other parties.[28] Here the obligation is not linked to listed sites, but rather to the wider category of heritage as defined in Articles 1 and 2. It is broad in its reference to both direct and indirect damage, but narrow in the restriction to 'deliberate measures'. In 2005 the World Heritage Committee relied on this obligation in requesting the co-operation of Sudan to do 'its best to prevent transborder poaching activities' in the Democratic Republic of Congo 'and that no action will be taken that threatens the value or integrity of a property located on the territory of another State Party to the Convention'.[29]

b) The notion of world heritage

While 'world heritage' is not defined in the Convention, Articles 1 and 2 contain definitions of cultural and natural heritage respectively. Of particular relevance here is the definition of the 'natural heritage' to be protected, conserved and transmitted to future generations. Article 2 provides that:

[26] Ibid., *per* Gibbs CJ.

[27] Article 6(2). See further G. Carducci, 'Articles 4–7', in Francioni, *supra* n. 6, pp. 124–6.

[28] Article 6(3), discussed further in ibid., pp. 126–8. See also the 2003 UNESCO Declaration concerning the Intentional Destruction of Cultural Heritage, a response to the destruction of the Bamiyan Buddhas in Afghanistan, discussed in ibid., pp. 128–31.

[29] Decision 29 COM 7A.4, adopted at the twenty-ninth session of the Committee (Durban, 2005), para. 11.

> For the purposes of this Convention, the following shall be considered as 'natural heritage':
>
> natural features consisting of physical and biological formations or groups of such formations, which are of outstanding universal value from the aesthetic or scientific point of view;
>
> geological and physiographical formations and precisely delineated areas which constitute the habitat of threatened species of animals and plants of outstanding universal value from the point of view of science or conservation;
>
> natural sites or precisely delineated areas of outstanding universal value from the point of view of science, conservation, or natural beauty.

The Convention emphasises *physical* areas, features, formations or sites, of outstanding universal value, rather than specific flora or fauna, thus further distinguishing the Convention from other habitat and species conservation treaties. One might argue, for example, that the blue whale (*Baleanoptera musculus*) should be considered part of the world's natural heritage because it is the largest creature ever to have inhabited the planet, but it does not qualify under Article 2 because it is a mobile animal and not immovable property.[30]

Indeed, while clearly innovative in its recognition of natural heritage, the language of Article 2 does not refer to modern ecological concepts such as ecosystems or biological diversity, nor have these been introduced subsequently to the treaty text. In fact, Article 2 has remained unchanged since 1972. Also omitted are provisions setting out good practice in the management of such sites – e.g. protected-area designation, buffer zones, and an appropriate management regime for the site buttressed by legal and administrative controls – such as that found in Article 8 of the 1992 CBD. Nor are marine areas expressly mentioned, in part owing to concerns about a number of unsettled issues in the law of the sea about to be addressed by the Third United Nations Conference on the Law of the Sea (1973–1982).[31] However, all of these elements have emerged in the subsequent practice of the parties, and in the implementation of the Convention through its Operational Guidelines.[32] Within the general jurisdictional framework provided by the 1982 Law of the Sea

[30] But see the notion of a 'nature monument' under the Western Hemisphere Convention, discussed in Chapter 8 above.

[31] Meyer, *supra* n. 3, p. 50.

[32] The most recent revision being in 2008. See Operational Guidelines for the Implementation of the World Heritage Convention, UNESCO World Heritage Centre, Paris, January 2008. For this and previous versions see whc.unesco.org.

Convention, and customary law, coastal and marine ecosystems and flora and fauna are clearly encompassed within the criteria for inscription of natural heritage on the World Heritage List,[33] under the Operational Guidelines.[34]

c) The World Heritage List

Protection of designated natural and cultural heritage is conferred by inscription on the World Heritage List. In the thirty-five years since the entry into force of the Convention, 890 properties in 148 of the 186 state parties have been added to this List, of which 176 constitute natural heritage and twenty-five are mixed natural and cultural heritage properties.[35] This numerical discrepancy between state parties and protected-site locations is explained by the fact that, unlike under the Ramsar Convention, for example, it is not necessary to have a site listed in order to become a party to the World Heritage Convention. It is also a reflection of the interest of the global community in the protection under the Convention of world heritage of outstanding universal value, regardless of its location. There is, however, no independent list of protected sites (unlike, say, the approach of CITES in listing endangered species in appendices), nor do the bodies established under the Convention have the authority to list a site absent nomination by the state(s) within which it is located. Rather, the World Heritage List is compiled 'from sites nominated by the Party in whose territory they are situated';[36] however much a site might be considered worthy of inclusion in the List, it only becomes eligible for selection after the party in whose territory it is situated has made an appropriate nomination.

The Convention requires the World Heritage Committee[37] to 'establish, keep up to date and publish' the List and to distribute an updated version at least every two years.[38] In practice, an updated version is

33 See generally A. Hillary, M. Kokkonen, L. Max (eds.), *Proceedings of the World Heritage Marine Biodiversity Workshop: Recommendations for Establishing and/or Extending Coastal World Heritage Sites* (UNESCO, 2003).

34 Operational Guidelines, *supra* n. 32, para. 77. These criteria are discussed further below.

35 As of the thirty-third session of the World Heritage Committee in June 2009. A full list with descriptions of the inscribed properties is available from whc.unesco.org/en/list.

36 Article 11(2). On the role of tentative lists see further section 3(b)(i) below.

37 This comprises twenty-one members appointed for a six-year term, meeting annually, and selected equitably to represent the different regions and cultures of the world (Article 8). See further commentary by T. Scovazzi, 'Articles 8–11', in Francioni, *supra* n. 6, and section 4 below.

38 Article 11(2).

published after each of the Committee's annual meetings. For example, after its thirty-first meeting in Christchurch, New Zealand, in 2007, the Committee added eighteen cultural, five natural and one mixed property to the List.[39] It is the responsibility of the Committee to stipulate the criteria for listing, published since 1977 in the regularly revised Operational Guidelines.[40] These are non-binding guidance prepared by the Committee for the operation and implementation of the Convention, which perform a valuable policy function in guiding the implementation of the Convention by the key stakeholders such as state parties, members of the Committee, the Secretariat, Convention advisory bodies and site managers.

While it is for states to nominate sites for protection,[41] such nomination is subject to a screening procedure in the light of these listing criteria. Independent evaluation of proposed sites is carried out by two main advisory bodies, the International Council on Monuments and Sites (ICOMOS) in respect of cultural properties,[42] and the IUCN in respect of natural properties. Thus listing under the WHC may be contrasted with the essentially unilateral character of designation under Ramsar. This procedure of 'nomination subject to scrutiny' reflects the balance established under the Convention between the recognition of state sovereignty on the one hand, and of the common interest on the other.[43] Indeed, although this recognition of state sovereignty has been described as a product of its time,[44] more recent environmental treaty instruments continue to assert, albeit in less robust terms, the sovereign rights of states over their natural resources,

[39] At its most recent meeting, in 2009, the Committee added eleven cultural and two natural properties (the Dolomites and the Wadden Sea) to the List, bringing the overall total to 890 properties. For listing criteria see further discussion in section 3 below.

[40] Operational Guidelines, *supra* n. 32.

[41] State parties are required to indicate a tentative list of properties from which such nominations are made, a procedure introduced to enhance the representativity of the List and to ensure an appropriate balance between natural and cultural site nominations. See further section 3(b)(i) below.

[42] See www.icomos.org. The International Centre for the Study of Preservation and Restoration of Cultural Property (ICCROM) also provides expert advice.

[43] For further analysis, including whether the Convention gives rise to enforceable *erga omnes partes* obligations, see G. Garducci, 'Articles 4–7', in Francioni, *supra* n. 6, pp. 132–43.

[44] Francioni (*supra* n. 6) refers to the dated character of the Convention in its recognition of full state sovereignty and of private property rights 'as provided by national legislation' over the sites and objects to be protected by the Convention (Article 6(1)).

while at the same time acknowledging these resources as the common concern of humankind.[45]

Listing applications must include details of how the site will be managed and protected under national legislation. Subsequent protection is thus a task for national law, subject to the general treaty obligation in Article 4 to protect and preserve the natural and cultural heritage. The Convention makes clear that international protection of world natural and cultural heritage is limited to 'the establishment of a system of international co-operation and assistance designed to support state parties to the Convention in their efforts to conserve and identify that heritage'.[46] It is the World Heritage Committee which monitors the state of preservation of properties on the List through, inter alia, the data supplied by state parties in the reports required under Articles 11 (national inventories) and 29 (implementation reports). Where property is in danger, it may provide international assistance through recourse to the World Heritage Fund established pursuant to Article 15 et seq. (see below).

d) World heritage at risk

i) The List of World Heritage in Danger

The Committee is also responsible for establishing the List of World Heritage in Danger ('Danger List'), a designation which signals that major operations are necessary to conserve the site and for which assistance may be sought under Article 11 of the Convention.[47] An estimate of the cost of such operations must also be included in a request for assistance. Requests for assistance may be made with respect to properties under Article 11(2) (the List) and Article 11(4) (the Danger List) 'in order to secure the protection, conservation, presentation or rehabilitation of such property'.[48] In cases of urgent need, the Committee is authorised to make a new entry in the Danger List and to publicise such entry immediately. Of the 890 listed properties, thirty-one are presently on the Danger List, fifteen of which have outstanding natural heritage value.[49] The most recent (2009) natural heritage additions

[45] See, for example, CBD, recitals 3 and 4 of the Preamble, and Article 3. [46] Article 7.

[47] For further discussion of the List of World Heritage in Danger, see G. P. Buzzini and L. Condorelli, 'Article 11', in Francioni, *supra* n. 6.

[48] Article 13(1).

[49] For the complete list see whc.unesco.org/en/danger. The oldest entry is the Old City of Jerusalem and its Walls (1982).

are the Belize Barrier Reef System and Los Katios National Park in Colombia. Other examples are the Galapagos Islands (since 2007), all five natural heritage sites in the Democratic Republic of Congo (since, variously, between 1994 and 1999) and, since 1992, the transboundary Mount Nimba Strict Nature Reserve between Guinea and Côte d'Ivoire. Djoudj National Bird Sanctuary in Senegal, a vulnerable wetland area particularly important as a wintering area for migratory waterfowl, has been on the List twice: first, from 1984 to 1988, owing to the adverse impact of proposed dam works, and again from 2000 to 2006 owing to the threat to the wetland posed by an invasive water plant, *Salvinia molesta*.

A controversial question which arose concerning Australia's Kakadu National Park, a mixed site with both natural and cultural heritage values, is whether state consent is required under Article 11(4) for the inscription of a property on the Danger List.[50] While Article 11(3) explicitly requires such consent for Listing, such a condition is not laid down for inscription on the Danger List. In the event, this property was not placed on the Danger List,[51] but Australia maintained that its consent would have been required to do so.[52] While neither the Convention nor the Operational Guidelines require a prior request from, or the consent of, the state party in whose territory the property is located for inscription on the Danger List,[53] the preparatory work of the Convention appears to support consent.[54] However, this preparatory work is not without its own interpretative difficulties, and it is far from clear that an interpretation that a prior request or state consent is not required renders the meaning of Article 11(4) 'ambiguous or obscure' or leads to a

[50] The Report of the WHC Mission recommended such listing: Rapporteur, Bureau of the WHC 23rd session, WHC-99/CONF.204/15, 16 September 1999. See further discussion in C. Redgwell, 'The International Law of Public Participation: Protected Areas, Endangered Species and Biological Diversity', and G. Triggs, 'The Rights of Indigenous Peoples to Participate in Resource Development: An International Legal Perspective', in D. Zillman et al. (eds.), *Human Rights in Natural Resource Development* (Oxford University Press, 2002), at pp. 191–201 and pp. 145–54 respectively.

[51] For emphasis of its 'vigilant role' in this case, see Report of the World Heritage Committee, 22nd session (Kyoto, 1998), VII.28.

[52] Solicitor-General of Australia, Opinion in the matter of the 'List of World Heritage in Danger' under the World Heritage Convention, 20 May 1999, p. 10.

[53] Buzzini and Condorelli, *supra* n. 47, pp. 185–6.

[54] Report of the Intergovernmental Committee of Experts submitted to the UNESCO General Conference, June 1972, para. 29.

'manifestly absurd or unreasonable' result.[55] Recent analysis of the practice in the implementation of this provision concludes that,

> in the absence of any request from the State Party, [the Committee] has only included properties in the List of World Heritage in Danger in cases where the property in question had been the subject of one or more requests for assistance or in situations of 'urgent need' (a case of 'urgent need' either generated or aggravated, as the case may be, by a lesser degree of cooperation on the part of the States concerned).[56]

ii) Deletion from the World Heritage List

While the Convention does not expressly provide for deletion from the World Heritage List, this possibility was considered by the Committee at an early stage and has been included in the Operational Guidelines since their first (1977) edition. These stipulate that the Committee shall delete properties from the List in the following circumstances:

> **a)** Where the property has deteriorated to the extent that it has lost those characteristics which determined its inclusion in the World Heritage List; and
> **b)** where the intrinsic qualities of a world heritage site were already threatened at the time of its nomination by action of man and where the necessary corrective measures as outlined by the State Party at the time have not been taken within the time proposed.[57]

When either of these circumstances arises, the party on whose territory the property is situated should inform the Secretariat. If the information comes from a source other than the party concerned, the Secretariat will verify the source and the contents of the information received in consultation with the state party concerned. In either case the relevant advisory body will be requested to comment. A decision to delete a property from the List is taken in consultation with – but does not require the consent of – the state party concerned.[58] The Operational

[55] The trigger in Article 32 of the 1969 Vienna Convention on the Law of Treaties, generally considered reflective of customary international law, for recourse to preparatory work as a 'supplementary means of interpretation'. See further detailed discussion in Buzzini and Condorelli, *supra* n. 47, pp. 187–95 (analysis of preparatory work and subsequent practice).

[56] Ibid., p. 195.

[57] Operational Guidelines 2008, para. 192.

[58] Buzzini and Condorelli, *supra* n. 47, pp. 198–9, conclude that, while the consent of the state is needed for inscription, it is the Committee which has ultimate authority to add – and, by way of legal parallelism, to delete – properties from the List. Nor is it necessary first for the property to have been included in the List of World Heritage in Danger, e.g. where there has been permanent and irrevocable loss of the outstanding universal value which led to inscription.

Guidelines emphasise that 'all possible measures should be taken to prevent the deletion of any property from the List' and that the Committee is 'ready to offer technical cooperation as far as possible to States Parties in this connection'. Though highly likely, the procedures for eventual deletion of properties from the List set forth in the Operational Guidelines do not require a property to be on the List of World Heritage in Danger before delisting by the Committee may be considered.

Removal of a property from the List occurred for the first time in 2007 when the Arabian Oryx Sanctuary in Oman, a natural heritage site, was removed from the List, and for a second time in 2009 when Dresden Elbe Valley in Germany, a cultural landscape site, was delisted. In each case the property was on the List of World Heritage in Danger and, as part of the annual review of the state of conservation of properties on this List, the Committee considered whether it had deteriorated to the extent that the characteristics which determined its inscription on the World Heritage List were lost.[59] In the case of Dresden, the Committee signalled that in future Germany could present a new nomination (under different criteria and boundaries) as parts of the site might still be considered to be of outstanding universal value. In the case of the Arabian Oryx, however, poaching and habitat destruction had caused numbers to dwindle from 450 to sixty-five, with only four breeding pairs, rendering uncertain the future viability of this rare antelope. The immediate spur for delisting was Oman's decision to reduce the size of the sanctuary by 90 per cent. In consequence,

> [a]fter extensive consultation with the State Party, the Committee felt that the unilateral reduction in the size of the Sanctuary and plans to proceed with hydrocarbon prospection would destroy the value and integrity of the property, which is also home to other endangered species, including the Arabian Gazelle and houbara bustard.[60]

[59] See, for example, Committee Decision 30COM 7B.77 'State of Conservation (Dresden Elbe Valley)' inscribing the property on the World Heritage in Danger List 'with a view to considering delisting the property from the World Heritage List at its 31st session in 2007, if the plans [to construct a four-lane bridge] are carried out'.

[60] 'Oman's Arabian Oryx Sanctuary: First Site Ever to Be Deleted from UNESCO's World Heritage List', 28 June 2007, available at whc.unesco.org. The description of the site further notes that the Sanctuary is where 'the only wild breeding sites in Arabia of the endangered houbara bustard, a species of wader, are also to be found, as well as Nubian ibex, Arabian wolves, honey badgers, caracals and the largest wild population of Arabian gazelle'. Ibid.

3. The concept of natural heritage

a) *Definition of 'natural heritage'*

As indicated above, the natural heritage to be protected, conserved and transmitted to future generations must be of 'outstanding universal value'. Little guidance is given in Article 2 for the identification of properties of such value,[61] save for the linkage with science (all three paragraphs), conservation (second and third paragraphs) and aesthetics (first and third paragraphs). The emphasis on science introduces an objective element to the identification of outstanding universal value, a necessary counterbalance in the design of the Convention to the reliance on state parties to identify and to delineate properties for inclusion on the World Heritage List.[62] In the absence of definition in the Convention, it is the Operational Guidelines which amplify the definition of the keystone concept of outstanding universal value. The current (2008) version reflects significant changes introduced in 1992 and first reflected in the 1994 Guidelines.[63] The timing is significant when compared against the backdrop of the Convention, and of general developments in international environmental law. Not only was 1992 the twentieth anniversary of the Convention, an event which prompted review of its implementation, but it was also the year of the twenty-year follow up to the Stockholm Conference, the 1992 Rio Conference on Environment and Development. The 1992 revision of the natural heritage criteria is clearly influenced by contemporary developments and in particular by new environmental concepts such as the conservation of biological diversity and sustainable development.

As paragraph 49 of the Operational Guidelines underscores, the concept of outstanding universal value is intrinsically linked with the transnational dimension to the concept of heritage and with its intergenerational transmission. It sets forth the following definition:

> Outstanding universal value means cultural and/or natural significance which is so exceptional as to transcend national boundaries and to be of common importance for present and future generations of all humanity.

[61] Reproduced above, p. 457.

[62] Identification of cultural and natural properties is addressed in Article 3. See the commentary by B. Boer, 'Article 3', in Francioni, *supra* n. 6.

[63] These revisions were agreed at the sixteenth session of the Committee at Santa Fe in 1992, based on discussions from 1988–91 and the recommendation of the World Heritage Bureau at its fifteenth session in 1991.

> As such, the permanent protection of this heritage is of the highest importance to the international community as a whole. The Committee defines the criteria for inscription of properties on the World Heritage List.[64]

There are three key requirements which the Committee currently applies to decide whether a natural heritage property is of outstanding natural value. The property must: (i) meet one or more of the criteria for outstanding universal value set forth in the Guidelines, (ii) meet the conditions of integrity and (iii) have an adequate protection and management system in place.[65] Each will be considered briefly in turn.

i) Criteria for outstanding universal value

The criteria are set forth in paragraph 77 of the Guidelines, which state that nominated natural heritage properties must:

> **(vii)** contain superlative natural phenomena or areas of exceptional natural beauty and aesthetic importance;[66]
> **(viii)** be outstanding examples representing major stages of earth's history, including the record of life, significant ongoing geological processes in the development of landforms, or significant geomorphic or physiographic features;[67]
> **(ix)** be outstanding examples representing significant ongoing ecological and biological processes in the evolution and development of terrestrial, fresh water, coastal and marine ecosystems and communities of plants and animals;[68]
> **(x)** contain the most important and significant natural habitats for in-situ conservation of biological diversity, including those containing threatened species of outstanding universal value from the point of view of science or conservation.[69]

All of these criteria are related to *in situ* conservation, implicitly or explicitly. The Operational Guidelines also emphasise sustainable use

64 For recent consideration see IUCN, The World Heritage List: Guidance and Future Priorities for Identifying Natural Heritage of Potential Outstanding Universal Value (draft paper of 15 May 2006), available at www.iucn.org.

65 As set forth in paras. 77, 78 and 87–95 of the Guidelines.

66 Such as the Belovezhskaya Pushcha/Bialowieza Forest (Belarus/Poland 1979, 1992).

67 For example, the Triassic fossils in Ischigualastol/Talampaya Natural Park (Argentina, 2000) and the meteorite impact structure of Vredefort Dome (South Africa, 2005).

68 Such as the island biogeography of East Rennell (Solomon Islands, 1998) and the beech forest of Shirakami-Sanchi (Japan, 1993).

69 For example, the Peninsula Valdes (Argentina, 1999), a site of global significance for the conservation of marine mammals, as is the Whale Sanctuary of El Vizcaino (Mexico, 1993).

(paragraph 119), in harmony with the approach of other nature protection treaties such as wise use under the Ramsar Convention and sustainable use under the CBD.[70] Indeed, the World Heritage Convention criteria for designating natural heritage sites are considered consistent with the ecosystem approach developed under the CBD, with the added benefit of integration of the approach into the management plan for the site.[71]

Criterion (x) is especially interesting from a wildlife perspective because it means that an area is eligible for inclusion in the World Heritage List if it is an important habitat for a threatened species of outstanding universal value even if it has no other notable features. It also presents an interesting problem. By referring to species 'of outstanding universal value from the point of view of science or conservation', it implies that some species are of outstanding universal value whilst others are not. Yet who is to say that well-known charismatic species such as the mountain gorilla (*Gorilla beringei beringei*) or giant panda (*Ailuropoda melanoleuca*) are more important for science and conservation than the tiny snail darter (*Percina tanasi*) in the Tennessee river or an undiscovered species of mouse? One might argue that a species such as the aye-aye (*Daubentonia madagascariensis*) is particularly important since it is the only species in an endangered family of mammals (Daubentonidae), whereas the mountain gorilla is a subspecies and mice and snail darters belong to prolific genera which speciate readily.[72] Or one could claim that the mountain gorilla is especially valuable because tourists will pay to come and see it and their money pays for the protection of a habitat which is also important for other less glamorous species.

The Operational Guidelines do not address the problem and, in practice, the Committee appears to have adopted the line that all species are of outstanding universal value. For example, Virunga National Park and Kahuzi-Biega National Park in the Democratic Republic of the Congo (DRC) were included in the World Heritage List at least in part

[70] 'Wise use' was defined by the 3rd Conference of the Ramsar Parties in 1987 to be synonymous with 'sustainable use'. See further Ramsar Convention Secretariat, *Ramsar Handbooks for Wise Use* (3rd ed., 2007).

[71] 'Cooperation with Other Conventions, Organizations and Initiatives, and Engagement of Stakeholders in the Implementation of the Convention', Addendum, Options for Enhanced Cooperation among the Biodiversity-Related Conventions, UNEP/CBD/WG-RI/1/7/Add.2, 14 July 2005, para. 40.

[72] Until recently there was considered to be only one gorilla species, with three subspecies. It is now thought that there are two species of *Gorilla* with two subspecies each, with the mountain gorilla a subspecies of the eastern Gorilla (*Gorilla beringei*). The Bwindi population of mountain gorilla may be a third subspecies of *Gorilla beringei*.

because they contain important habitat for mountain gorillas.[73] The World Heritage List entry for Virunga notes, under criterion (x), that '[t]he park is home to 22 species of primates, including three great ape species (mountain gorilla *Gorilla beringei beringei*, eastern lowland gorilla *Gorilla beringei graueri* and eastern chimpanzee *Pan troglodytes schweinfurthi)*, with one third of the remaining mountain gorilla population in the world'.[74] However, Mount Nimba Strict Nature Reserve in Guinea was listed under what are now criteria (ix) and (x) partly because of its importance to less well-known endemic species such as the viviparous toad and dwarf African otter shrew.[75] Darien National Park in Panama, 'the best available example of Central American rainforest ecosystems', was listed at least in part because 'scientific opinion is that thousands of species remain to be discovered, and that many of these will prove to be endemic to Darien'.[76] Most of these undiscovered endemics are certain to be 'unglamorous' insects and plants.

ii) Conditions of integrity

In addition to meeting one or more of criteria (vii)–(x) set out above, to be considered of outstanding universal value a natural property must also meet the conditions of integrity, which have featured in the Guidelines since 1977. In the 2008 Operational Guidelines the conditions of integrity apply to all properties nominated for inscription, natural and/or cultural. Integrity is defined as 'a measure of wholeness and intactness of the natural and/or cultural heritage and its attributes' and its assessment involves considering the extent to which a nominated property 'a) includes all elements necessary to its outstanding universal value; b) is of adequate size to ensure the complete representation of the features and processes which convey the property's significance; c) suffers from adverse effects of development and/or neglect'.[77] With respect to natural properties, the conditions of

[73] See (1979) 15(4) *Nature and Resources* 22.

[74] See www.unesco.whc/llist/63. The entry for Kahuzi-Biega notes that '[o]ne of the last groups of eastern lowland (*graueri*) gorillas (consisting of only some 250 individuals) lives at between 2,100 and 2,400 m above sea-level'. See www.unesco.whc/list/137.

[75] See IUCN Technical Review for 1981, No. 155, para. 5.

[76] Ibid., paras. 5 and 8. It also contains endangered species such as the bush dog, ocelot, jaguar, Baird's tapir, spider monkey, harpy eagle, Central American caiman and American crocodile. Ibid.

[77] Ibid., para. 88.

integrity require that 'bio-physical processes and landform features should be relatively intact'.[78]

iii) Protection and management

Outstanding universal value and the conditions of integrity are linked to the protection and management of properties and with the requirement of adequate long-term legislative, regulatory, institutional and/or traditional protection and management to ensure their safeguarding.[79] The explicitly intra- and inter-generational purpose of management systems is highlighted in the Operational Guidelines, which state that '[t]he purpose of management is to ensure the effective protection of the nominated property for present and future generations'.[80] For natural sites, effective boundaries, buffer zones and reactive and periodic monitoring are key management features. In this regard the 2008 Operational Guidelines set out what might be viewed as a 'code of good practice' for the effective implementation of the Convention for natural heritage protection.

Neither the Convention nor the Operational Guidelines insist that a site need be a protected area such as a national park or a nature reserve in order to qualify for inclusion in the World Heritage List; in practice, however, over half the listed natural heritage sites are protected areas. Indeed, as under Ramsar, some parties have apparently decided only to nominate sites which are already protected at the time of their nomination. Most of the twenty US sites in the List,[81] for example, are national parks which are strictly protected by the US National Park Service Act.[82] Furthermore, every one of the thirty-four natural properties submitted to the World Heritage Committee by the US in May 1982 as part of its inventory of properties which may qualify for future nominations to the

[78] Ibid., para. 90.

[79] Ibid., paras. 108 and 97 respectively. This is within the broad framework of Article 5 which requires each party, inter alia, 'to take the appropriate legal, scientific, technical, administrative and financial measures necessary for the identification' etc. of heritage located on its territory.

[80] Ibid., para. 109.

[81] Two natural heritage sites are jointly administered with Canada: Waterton-Glacier, and Wrangell-St. Elias/Glacier Bay/Tatshenshini/Alsek/Kluane.

[82] James Charleton (Office of International Affairs, US National Parks Service), 'The United States and the World Heritage Convention', paper presented at US/ICOMOS symposium U.S. Preservation in the Global Context, April 2000, available at www.icomos.org/usicomos/Symposium/SYMP00/charleton.htm. As a matter of domestic law, all US nominations for World Heritage listing must have been formally designated as nationally significant, such as being a National Historic Landmark, National Natural Landmark, National Monument, National Park or National Wildlife Refuge.

List – the first state to make such a submission – was either a national park, a national monument, a national seashore, a coast reserve or a national wildlife refuge, all of which are protected by US law.[83]

There are advantages to including an already protected area in the List. The party concerned may be entitled to apply for assistance from the World Heritage Fund (discussed below), and the added status given by the Convention may help bolster protection for an area which is protected in name but is threatened in fact. Darien National Park in Panama is a case in point. Although national parks are protected by Panamanian law, the IUCN advised the Committee prior to the inclusion of Darien in the List that

> the area is under powerful pressures from north and south for a wide range of purposes, many of them inimical to the national park's interests (and the interests of Panama as a whole) . . . *Awarding World Heritage status to this unique and particularly important area will provide additional leverage for long-term protection of the area.* Panama is very concerned to establish political control over the area. The early awarding of support to the newly established national park will help ensure its proper management and development, with particular reference to boundary demarcation and to integration of the area into overall regional development plans.[84]

Other parties have nominated unprotected sites for inclusion in the List. Australia nominated almost the entire Great Barrier Reef in 1981, and the World Heritage Committee accepted the nomination notwithstanding that about half of the area was outside the scope of Australia's Great Barrier Reef Marine Park Act of 1975. It is shown in Chapter 13 above how the designation of unprotected sites in the Ramsar List of Wetlands of International Importance has helped to secure their protection, and the same may also be true with respect to the inclusion of sites in the

[83] See 'Indicative Inventory of Potential Future U.S. Nominations to the World Heritage List', US *Federal Register*, 47(88), 6 May 1982, pp. 19648–55. A new US World Heritage Tentative List was transmitted to the World Heritage Committee on 24 January 2008 containing fourteen properties, with a further eleven under consideration. Of the fourteen, four are natural properties: Fagatele Bay National Marine Sanctuary, American Samoa; Okefenokee Swamp National Wildlife Refuge, Georgia; Petrified Forest National Park, Arizona; and White Sands National Monument, New Mexico. See www.nps.gov/oia/topics/worldheritage/TL_List.doc.

[84] See IUCN Technical Review for 1981, No. 159, para. 6 (emphasis added). Following inscription on the List, Panama received financial assistance under the Convention on five occasions, amounting to over US$120,000 in total. See whc.unesco.org/en/list/159/assistance.

World Heritage List. Noting that large areas of the Great Barrier Reef were not yet protected under national law, the Committee followed their acceptance of the nomination with a request to the Australian government 'to take steps to ensure that the whole area is proclaimed under relevant legislation as soon as possible and that the necessary environmental protection measures are taken'.[85] Today, 99.3 per cent of this world heritage property – the largest on the List at 348,000 square kilometres – enjoys marine protected-area status within the (federal) Great Barrier Reef Marine Park.[86]

b) *Identification of world heritage*

i) Tentative lists

The Convention is dependent upon state identification and nomination of properties for inclusion on the List. As Francioni has observed, the notion of an ideal inventory, though initially attractive, was abandoned as unrealistic and unworkable.[87] However, pursuant to Article 11(1),[88] state parties are required to submit tentative lists – essentially an inventory of property forming part of the cultural and natural heritage situated in their territory and suitable for inclusion on the World Heritage List.[89] This forms a benchmark against which to judge the inclusiveness of the World Heritage List, particularly since a nomination to the List will not be considered unless the property is included on the state party's tentative list. Such lists are not static but will evolve over time, as will the criteria for inclusion of natural properties, reflecting the evolutionary character of scientific knowledge as it impacts upon law, such as in the emergence of the concept of biological diversity. Their efficacy is, of course, dependent on state compliance with the

[85] Report of the Rapporteur, World Heritage Committee, Fifth Session (1981), Conf. Doc. CC-81/CONF.003/6, para. 15.

[86] The remainder lies in Queensland waters and islands where zoning mirrors the provisions of the federal park area.

[87] Francioni, *supra* n. 10. The CBD does not employ inventories or lists, which led France initially to refuse to sign the Nairobi Final Act of the Conference for the Adoption of an Agreed Text on the Convention on Biological Diversity in protest against the omission of a global list of protected areas and species emulating the mechanism employed by the World Heritage Convention.

[88] See further T. Scovazzi 'Articles 8–11', in Francioni, *supra* n. 6.

[89] State parties are encouraged to review and resubmit their tentative list every ten years. Operational Guidelines 2008, para. 65.

obligation to prepare and submit the lists (and ultimately to nominate properties from it).[90]

In addition to tentative lists compiled by state parties, independent lists have been prepared for example by the IUCN, with regional and biome studies to enhance knowledge of natural heritage of outstanding universal value particularly in underrepresented regions of the world. For example, a 1997 overview of wetland and marine protected areas on the World Heritage list analysed seventy-seven sites, 'cross-referenced with their relations with other international programmes and conventions (e.g. Ramsar, Biosphere Reserves and WWF Global 200 Ecoregions)', and concluded that the World Heritage Convention protects sites with a broader range of biome values than under the Ramsar Convention because of the role of the World Heritage Committee in approving sites. That said, at the time of the report six of the seventy-seven sites were on the World Heritage Sites in Danger List, 'indicating that inscription on the World Heritage List does not necessarily guarantee effective stewardship'.[91]

ii) Representativity

The desire for wider distribution of listed sites (the preponderance are in developed states) and an improved balance between cultural and natural sites (the preponderance are cultural sites) led the World Heritage Committee to adopt the Global Strategy for a Representative, Balanced and Credible World Heritage List in 1994.[92] From 2006, on an experimental basis, the Committee has examined up to two nominations per state party, provided at least one nomination concerns a natural property.[93] The IUCN, however, has noted the potential for representativity to undermine outstanding universal value, reminding the Committee that 'it is not intended that the List should be completely representative of the earth's entire cultural and natural heritage as this would be

[90] As of the thirty-third meeting of the World Heritage Committee in 2009, 166 of the 186 states party to the Convention had submitted tentative lists in accordance with the requirements set out in the Operational Guidelines. The complete tentative lists of all state parties are available at whc.unesco.org/en/tentativelists.

[91] J. Thorsell, R. Ferster Levy and T. Sigaty, *A Global Overview of Wetland and Marine Protected Areas on the World Heritage List* (IUCN 1997), p. 1. See also J. Thorsell and L. Hamilton in *A Global Overview of Mountain Protected Areas on the World Heritage List* (IUCN, 2002), Working Paper 6.

[92] Eighteenth session, Phuket 1994. See further whc.unesco.org/en/globalstrategy.

[93] Within an overall limit of forty-five nominations. For discussion of the compatibility of this limitation with the Convention, see Scovazzi, *supra* n. 88.

contrary to the concept of *outstanding universal value*'.[94] Other conventions, and national and regional measures, have a large role to play in the protection of natural areas and in the conservation of ecosystems, landscapes, habitats and species, only a small number of which are likely also to meet one or more of the criteria of outstanding universal value.[95] Current concerns with representativity underscore the evolution which has taken place in the concept of outstanding universal value, from a conception of 'the best of the best' to 'representative of the best'.[96]

4. Institutions

The General Assembly of State Parties meets biennially, during the sessions of UNESCO's General Conference. Its main functions are to determine the uniform percentage of contributions to the World Heritage Fund applicable to all parties, and to elect members of the World Heritage Committee.[97] The Committee reports to the General Assembly and to the UNESCO General Conference on its activities. It is the 'engine' of the Convention, comprising twenty-one members who meet at least once annually. Decisions are taken by a two-thirds majority of Committee members present and voting.[98]

The Committee is assisted by three Advisory Bodies, two with respect to the cultural heritage and one, the IUCN, with respect to natural heritage. Amongst other things, the IUCN assists in the evaluation of properties nominated for inscription on the World Heritage List, monitors the state of conservation of World Heritage natural properties and reviews requests for assistance.[99] The Committee's work is also supported by a Secretariat.[100]

The main functions of the Committee, in co-operation with state parties, are: selecting, on the basis of tentative lists and nominations submitted by state parties, cultural and natural sites of outstanding universal value, and inscribing them on the World Heritage List;

[94] The World Heritage List, *supra* n. 64, p. 1, original emphasis. The paper states that it will not make use of the term '[t]o avoid any ambiguity or misunderstanding'. Ibid., p. 2.

[95] Ibid. This is represented diagrammatically by a pyramid, with World Heritage at the pinnacle and national and subnational sites forming its broad base.

[96] WHC-06/30 COM/9, para. 6, 23 June 2006.

[97] Articles 8(1), 16(1) and 29, and Operational Guidelines 2008, paras. 17–18. With respect to the latter, elections are on a rotating basis, and members are to constitute an 'equitable representation of the different regions and cultures of the world' (Article 8(2)).

[98] Article 13(8). [99] Operational Guidelines 2008, para. 37.

[100] Article 8; Operational Guidelines 2008, paras. 27–9.

examining their state of conservation through reactive and periodic monitoring; inscribing properties on, and deleting them from, the World Heritage in Danger List; deciding which properties should be deleted from the World Heritage List; defining the procedures by which requests for international assistance are to be considered; determining how the resources of the World Heritage Fund are to be utilised and seeking ways to increase its resources; reporting on its activities biennially to the UNESCO General Conference; reviewing and evaluating periodically implementation of the Convention; and revising and adopting the Operational Guidelines.[101] The Committee has also developed strategic objectives for the implementation of the Convention, described as 'the 5 Cs'. These are: strengthening the credibility of the World Heritage List; ensuring the effective conservation of World Heritage Properties; promoting the development of effective capacity building in state parties; increasing public awareness, involvement and support for World Heritage through communication; and enhancing the role of communities in the implementation of the Convention.[102] In the discharge of its various functions, the Committee 'can be considered as representing the common interest of the parties in the cultural and natural heritage of outstanding interest'.[103]

5. Implementation

a) Reporting

In common with the other major treaties considered in this work, the WHC sets forth in Article 13 a reporting obligation on state parties. Submitted biennially to the UNESCO General Conference, the report must 'give information on the legislative and administrative provisions which they have adopted and other action which they have taken for the application of this Convention, together with details of the experience acquired in this field'.[104] These reports are also submitted to the Committee,[105] in a process referred to under the Operational

[101] In co-operation with state parties and as provided for in the Convention. See Operational Guidelines 2008, para. 24(a)–(j).

[102] Revised in 2002. Budapest Declaration on World Heritage (2002), available at whc.unesco.org/en/budapestdeclaration; see also Decision 31COM 13B.

[103] Scovazzi, *supra* n. 88, p. 149. [104] Article 29(1). [105] Article 29(2).

Guidelines as 'periodic reporting'.[106] This serves four purposes: it forms an assessment of the application of the Convention by the state party, and of whether the outstanding universal value of inscribed properties is being maintained, and it provides an update on the state of conservation of properties and a mechanism for the exchange of implementation information and experiences.[107] In addition, a product of reactive monitoring of properties under threat is a State of Conservation Report produced by the state party in whose territory the threatened property is located. This is used by the Committee to evaluate, inter alia, the threat or any improvement in conservation since the last report and follow-up on any previous Committee decisions.[108] Fact-finding missions may also take place, gathering more information and reporting such to the Committee.[109] The Committee submits a report on its activities at the biennial ordinary sessions of the General Conference of UNESCO.[110] The other bodies under the Convention also have significant reporting obligations: one of the central roles of the Advisory Bodies is to produce evaluation reports to the Committee as part of the inscription process.[111]

b) The World Heritage Fund

The World Heritage Fund was one of the most distinctive features of the World Heritage Convention when established, though subsequently it has been emulated by a number of the other wildlife treaties considered here. It is widely credited with having fostered widespread participation in the Convention. It is a trust fund to which parties must contribute according to the scale of their contributions to the regular budget of UNESCO.[112] This is an important 'carrot' for states whose contributions to UNESCO are small and involves a significant commitment from the developed state parties.

106 See Part V, paras. 199–210, of the Operational Guidelines 2008 and analysis by B. Boer, 'Article 29', in Francioni, *supra* n. 6.

107 Operational Guidelines 2008, para. 201.

108 Ibid., para. 173.

109 Ibid., paras. 175–6. See the example of Kakadu National Park above, n. 54.

110 Articles 29(3).

111 The submission by state parties of national inventories of cultural and natural heritage as required by Article 11(1), and the development of tentative lists, is discussed above.

112 Article 15(2). It is governed by special regulations, the Financial Regulations for the World Heritage Fund, available at whc.unesco.org/en/financial regulations. For detailed analysis see F. Lenzerini, 'Articles 15 and 16', in Francioni, *supra* n. 6.

Parties may apply to the World Heritage Committee for assistance,[113] to be paid for out of the resources of the Fund, in order to secure the protection, conservation, presentation or rehabilitation of sites situated within their territories which have been included, or are potentially suitable for inclusion, in either the World Heritage List or the List of World Heritage in Danger.[114] They may also apply for assistance 'with identification of cultural or natural [heritage sites] ... when preliminary investigations have shown that further inquiries would be justified'.[115] The Operational Guidelines specify the types of assistance that are available and lay down an order of priorities for the granting of assistance.

In 2006 the Committee streamlined assistance into three categories: emergency assistance, preparatory assistance, and conservation and management assistance.[116] Most requests have been in this last category (1,316), followed by preparatory assistance (364) and then emergency assistance (155). The majority of requests across these categories relate to cultural property (1,018), followed by natural (652) and mixed (166) properties. The geographic distribution of such requests is relatively even, though with most requests coming from Africa (440) and the least from Europe and North America (286) and Arab states (240). Where assistance is granted, the Convention requires that, as a general rule, the international community should bear 'only part of the cost of the work necessary' and that the party benefiting from assistance should contribute 'a substantial share of the resources devoted to each programme or project unless its resources do not permit this'.[117]

c) *External financial support*

Increasingly the focus of the Convention – and of the other four biodiversity-related conventions – is on attracting external sources of financial support. The need for such support was recognised at the outset, with one of the sources of funding for the World Heritage Fund

[113] Applications are made through the Secretariat. The chairperson of the Committee is authorised to approve requests for emergency, preparatory or training and research assistance up to a fixed maximum without obtaining the approval of the whole Committee. Operational Guidelines 2008, para. 241 (summary table).

[114] Article 13(1). [115] Article 13(2).

[116] Decision 30 COM 14A, para. 5(b). Statistics are available at whc.unesco.org/en/intassistance/action=stats.

[117] Article 25.

being 'contributions, gifts or bequests made by', inter alia, 'public or private bodies or individuals', as well as income from fund-raising events.[118] It is acknowledged that the implementation of the strategic objectives of the Convention 'will require substantial additional resources to those currently available through the World Heritage Fund and extra-budgetary resources'.[119] The international congress organised to mark the thirtieth anniversary of the Convention in 2002 provided stimulus for seeking external funding through the World Heritage Partnerships Initiative.[120] One initiative to arise from the Trieste Workshop on Partnerships to Conserve Nature and Biodiversity is the Rapid Response Facility (RRF).[121] This became operational in October 2005 with its first application on 2 February 2006 from the DRC with respect to Kahuzi-Biega National Park. Another example of international co-ordination in emergency response is the Great Apes Survival Project (GRASP), a public–private partnership launched in 2001 and led by UNESCO and UNEP. It now involves twenty-three range states, several donor nations, thirty non-governmental organisations and four of the biodiversity conventions: the World Heritage Convention, the CBD, CMS and CITES.[122]

One significant source of external funding is the UN Foundation (UNF),[123] which has contributed financially to the protection of world heritage, in particular natural heritage located in areas of important biological diversity. This includes natural heritage threatened by armed conflict, as is the case with Virunga, Garamba, Kahuzi (the first application of the RRF mentioned above) and Salonga National Parks and Okapi Wildlife Reserve in the DRC, all of which are inscribed on the World

[118] Article 15(3); see also Article 15(4), Articles 17 (donor foundations) and 18 (international fund-raising).

[119] Report of the Chairperson of the World Heritage Committee on the Activities of the World Heritage Committee, available at www.whc.org.

[120] The proceedings of the Congress were published as *World Heritage 2002*, *supra* n. 3. The World Heritage Partnerships Initiative was subsequently renamed World Heritage PACT and is further discussed by L. Patchett, 'Articles 17 and 18', in Francioni, *supra* n. 6.

[121] At the end of the Trieste Workshop, 'FFI (Fauna & Flora International) pledged . . . [to] raise capital and co-operate with UNESCO, UNF and other interested partners to build a Rapid Response mechanism to respond to threats to World Natural Heritage'. *World Heritage 2002*, *supra* n. 3, p. 155.

[122] Report of the World Heritage Centre on its activities and on the implementation of Decisions of the World Heritage Committee, WHC-06/30.COM/6, Vilnius, 7 July 2006, p. 4.

[123] An independent public charity under US law founded in 1998 after Ted Turner's gift of $1 billion to the United Nations. A memorandum of understanding was concluded between the World Heritage Centre and the UNF in 2004.

Heritage in Danger List. In 2000, the UNF launched a US$4.2 million Project on Biodiversity Conservation in Regions of Armed Conflict: Protecting World Heritage in the Democratic Republic of the Congo, with the participation of the UNF, the DRC authorities, UNESCO and the United Nations Fund for International Partnerships. On the thirtieth anniversary of the Convention, a three-year US$15 million partnership between the UNF, Conservation International and the World Heritage Convention was announced to mobilise funding to establish sustainable financing mechanisms such as trust funds for selected sites of outstanding biodiversity. Another example of UN Fund partnership is the April 2004 agreement with the World Heritage Centre providing US$5 million for the conservation of biological diversity in India through the protection of its World Heritage sites, Manas and Kaziranga, which contain endangered species such as the one-horned rhinoceros and the pygmy hog.[124]

Wetlands habitat is the focus of another initiative launched in 2004, the International Corporate Wetlands Restoration Partnership, a joint initiative of the UNF in conjunction with the Nature Conservancy and the Gillette Company designed to leverage private financial contributions to match existing international mechanisms under conventions such as Ramsar and the World Heritage Convention. Large-scale projects will be implemented at natural heritage sites for which the UNF will provide matching resources to private investment; small-scale projects will be filtered through partnership arrangements under Ramsar.[125] The first large-scale project is Sian Ka'an in Mexico, a Ramsar and World Heritage site, as well as a Biosphere reserve.[126]

In 2006 the first regional funding initiative within the framework of the Convention was taken with the establishment of the African World Heritage Fund (AWHF). It is open to African Union member states party to the World Heritage Convention, and is established as a trust under South African law and administered (at least initially) by the African Development Bank. A ten-year action plan targets increasing the number of African sites on the World Heritage List and progressively removing all African sites from the List of World Heritage in Danger.[127]

[124] Further details of the UNFIP–UNESCO agreement are available at whc.unesco.org/en/initiatives/24.

[125] See www.ramsar.org/wn/w.n.icwrp_project.htm.

[126] For further details of the International Corporate Wetlands Restoration Partnership (ICWRP) see www.icwrp.org.

[127] See further www.awhf.net.

6. Relationship with other agreements

a) Co-operation

The Convention is part of a biodiversity-related web of instruments comprising the Ramsar and Bonn Conventions, CITES and the CBD.[128] The particular contribution of the World Heritage Convention to biodiversity conservation is recognised in 'concrete international support and partnership for the conservation and sustainable use of biodiversity, including ecosystems, at World Heritage sites'.[129] This is achieved through the 'simple fact' of the inscription of natural heritage sites for protection under the Convention,[130] with criteria (ix) and (x) the most significant in terms of sites most likely to contribute to biodiversity conservation.[131]

While each of these biodiversity-related conventions has its own distinctive object and purpose, there is increasing recognition of the linkages and interrelationships between them,[132] and the realisation that improved information exchange and support between biodiversity-related conventions contributes to sustainable development.[133] Such exchange and support may take place on an informal basis, or a framework for co-operation may be provided in a more formal sense through, for example, the conclusion of a memorandum of understanding. An

[128] In 2002 a Biodiversity Liaison Group (BLG) comprising the executive heads of the five biodiversity-related conventions was established to enhance co-operation. See further www.biodiv.org/cooperation/related-conventions/blg.shtml.

[129] Para. 42(f) of the Johannesburg Plan of Implementation agreed at the World Summit for Sustainable Development in 2002. There is also reference to 'heritage preservation' in para. 41 addressed to ecotourism. These are the only two references to world heritage in the Plan of Implementation. See J. Scanlon, 'The World Heritage Convention and Outcomes from the WSSD', Siena Workshop on The Legal Tools for World Heritage Conservation, 11–12 November 2002.

[130] UNEP/CBD/WG-RI/1/7/Add.2, 14 July 2005, Annex, paras. 14–15.

[131] The Durban Action Plan resulting from the 2003 IUCN World Parks Congress includes in respect of the contribution of protected areas to biodiversity conservation the target that '[a]ll sites whose biodiversity values are of outstanding universal value are inscribed on the World Heritage List by the time of the next World Parks Congress'. World Heritage at the Vth IUCN World Parks Congress, Durban (South Africa), 8–17 September 2003, World Heritage Reports 16 (UNESCO World Heritage Centre, 2005), p. 36.

[132] For comparative overview see www.biodiv.org/rioconv/websites/html.

[133] This is also expressed in the programme for the further implementation of Agenda 21 approved by the XXth Special Session of the UN General Assembly in 1997 in the five-year follow-up to the 1992 Rio Conference on Environment and Development.

example of the latter is the 1999 Memorandum of Understanding between the World Heritage Convention and the Ramsar Convention, which is an agreement between secretariats, between UNESCO, represented by the World Heritage Centre, and the Bureau of the Ramsar Convention. Co-operation and synergies among these instruments take a variety of forms, ranging from dual, and even multiple, site designations and joint site visits, to the pooling of technical and financial resources.

The Ramsar Convention in particular has much in common with the World Heritage Convention, using a site designation process, listing for protection, and employing a danger-listing mechanism.[134] There are presently thirty-three properties listed for conservation and protection under both the Ramsar and World Heritage Conventions, with four of these properties both on the World Heritage in Danger List and on Ramsar's Montreux Record of sites where changes in ecological character are threatened or occurring. These four properties (using World Heritage designation) are Bulgaria's Srebarna Nature Reserve, Senegal's Djoudj National Bird Sanctuary, Tunisia's Ichkeul National Park and the United States' Everglades National Park.[135] For sites covered by both Conventions, site visits may be requested and carried out jointly. For example, Ichkeul National Park in Tunisia was on both the Ramsar Montreux Record and the World Heritage in Danger List owing to the impact of dam projects on the river flowing into Ichkeul. In the year 2000, a visit by the Ramsar Advisory Mission was carried out at the request of the World Heritage Centre, the IUCN and the Bureau of the Ramsar Convention.[136] In general, dual listing is seen as a 'useful strategy

[134] As already noted above, a key difference is the requirement under Ramsar for a state to have a site listed in order to participate in the Convention and the absence of an advisory body comparable to the IUCN entrusted under the Convention to carry out independent review of the nomination. In practice, non-governmental organisations perform this latter function – e.g. BirdLife International. Indeed, BirdLife International and UNESCO have agreed to co-operate under Ramsar 'to develop world heritage nominations linking networks of bird migratory sites'. See the Report of the Trieste Workshop, Partnerships to Conserve Nature and Biodiversity, in *World Heritage 2002*, *supra* n. 3, p. 155.

[135] For the full list, see www.ramsar.org/world_heritage.htm. For comparison of the World Heritage and Ramsar Conventions, see Redgwell, *supra* n. 50; and D. E. Pritchard, *Review of cooperation between the Convention on Wetlands (Ramsar, Iran, 1971) and the United Nations Educational, Scientific and Cultural Organisation (UNESCO)* (IUCN, 2004).

[136] See www.ramsar.org/ram_rpt_41e.htm. The site is also a biosphere reserve under the MAB programme. It was first inscribed on the Danger List in 1996 owing to increased salinity in the freshwater lake caused by agricultural activities, and an emergency plan for safeguarding the park was agreed. With a subsequent reduction in salinity – and a

for taking advantage of the different legal, scientific, management and advocacy approaches of each'.[137] Nonetheless, a 2005 report by the biodiversity-related conventions' secretariats makes a number of suggestions for harmonisation of criteria, guidelines and definitions such as 'sustainable use' and 'migratory species', where possible. It also advocates inclusion of criteria from several conventions in deciding priorities for site-based conservation, e.g. CITES appendices listing with Ramsar and World Heritage Convention listing criteria.[138]

b) *Legal relationship*

The Convention does not explicitly address its relationship with other treaty instruments. This lacuna may be explained by the novelty of the Convention's approach to heritage in 1972, and the relative paucity of related instruments at that time. The closest acknowledgement of existing governmental and non-governmental organisations with similar remit is found in Article 13(7), which requires the Committee to co-operate with 'organizations having objectives similar to those of the Convention' and, in the implementation of its programmes and projects, makes express reference to ICCROM, ICOMOS and IUCN – the advisory bodies to the World Heritage Committee.[139] However, the proliferation of environmental treaty-making from 1972, stimulated by the Stockholm Conference and subsequent developments, has led increasingly to the need for formal and informal modes of co-operation between the Convention and other instruments with similar or overlapping objectives for the protection of the natural heritage. This is now expressly recognised in the Operational Guidelines, which call for appropriate co-ordination and information-sharing between the World Heritage Convention and other treaties, programmes and international organisations related to the conservation of cultural and natural heritage,[140] as

return of numerous migratory bird species – it was removed from the Danger List in 2006. See further whc.unesco.org/en/list/8.

137 UNEP/CBD/WG-RI/1/7/Add.2, 14 July 2005, *supra* n. 130, para. 39.

138 Ibid., para. 42. There are also trilateral meetings on protected areas between the World Heritage, Biodiversity and Ramsar Conventions.

139 See also Article 14(2) (co-operation with same bodies by UNESCO director-general in preparing documents for Committee meetings and in implementing the Committee's decisions). See further discussion by A. F. Vrdoljak, 'Article 14', in Francioni, *supra* n. 6.

140 Para. 44 provides a list of 'selected Conventions and programmes relating to the protection of the cultural and natural heritage' comprising MAB, Ramsar, CITES, Bonn, CBD, LOSC and the UNFCCC.

well as for the possibility of reciprocal observer status in meetings of the inter-governmental bodies. 'Cooperation with other Conventions' is now a regular feature of the report of its activities made by the World Heritage Centre to the World Heritage Committee.[141]

7. Conclusion

The World Heritage Convention does not have a very broad scope as far as wildlife conservation is concerned, but it does offer a tremendous opportunity to protect unique wildlife habitats and representative examples of the most important ecosystems. Although Ramsar's List of Wetlands of International Importance and the World Heritage Lists both provide international prestige for listed sites, the World Heritage Convention goes far beyond Ramsar in that it imposes stricter obligations on its parties to conserve listed sites than does Ramsar.

Key differences exist between cultural and natural properties. One is the inevitability of the number of cultural properties outstripping natural properties. Even with adjustments to the natural heritage criteria to take into account changes in technological and scientific knowledge, this category is an essentially closed one, whilst the product of human cultural endeavour continues to flourish in the more open category of cultural heritage. The 163 natural and twenty-four mixed properties presently inscribed on the List represent about 60 per cent of what might constitute a complete list of global natural heritage of outstanding universal value. The IUCN estimates that a complete list of natural and mixed properties might number between 250 and 300.[142] As the List moves closer to completion, a shift in emphasis from procedures for nomination and inscription – identified by the 2000 Expert Review[143] as

[141] See, for example, the Report of the World Heritage Centre on its Activities and on the Implementation of Decisions of the World Heritage Committee, WHC-06/30.COM/6, Vilnius, 7 July 2006, p. 6, section I.C, paras. 28–30.

[142] See the Evaluation of the Global Strategy for a Representative, Balanced and Credible World Heritage List (1994–2004), WHC-04/28.COM/13, Paris, 25 May 2004, para. 24. This evaluation by the IUCN of natural and mixed properties is based on a more detailed analysis of natural and mixed properties contained in A Review of the Global World Heritage Network: Biogeography, Habitats and Biodiversity (2000) prepared by UNEP's World Conservation Monitoring Centre in collaboration with the IUCN and the World Heritage Centre, the full text of which is available at www.unep-wcmc.org/protected_areas/world_heritage/wh_review.htm.

[143] Review of the Global World Heritage Network: Biogeography, Habitats and Biodiversity (2000).

a preoccupation of the Guidelines – to better management of existing properties, viz. their state of conservation and the maintenance of integrity, is both desirable and inevitable.[144] A second difference is that, as for any natural resource, natural heritage of outstanding universal value is not evenly distributed across the globe. In consequence, it is impossible to achieve an equal balance for all regions or countries and for the different criteria. Equal distribution is an illusory goal, as is parity with cultural properties.

Several other recent trends may be detected in the evolution of the application of Article 2. One is a rise in the number of serial property and transboundary nominations. Another is the slowing 'success rate' of nominations, signalling both the robustness of the application of the criteria for inscription and the fact that the initial nominations tended to focus on iconic natural heritage such as Mosi-oa-Tunya/Victoria Falls (1989), Grand Canyon National Park (1979) and the Galapagos Islands (1978). With an estimated 60 per cent of global natural heritage of outstanding universal value represented on the List, securing ongoing protection and integrity of inscribed sites and targeting the remaining gaps in the List remains the key challenge.

Recommended further reading

B. Boer and G. Wiffen, *Heritage Law in Australia* (Oxford University Press, 2006)

F. Francioni, with F. Lenzerini, ed., *The 1972 World Heritage Convention: A Commentary* (Oxford University Press, 2008)

E. J. Goodwin, 'The World Heritage Convention, the Environment and Compliance' (2009) 20(2) *Colo. J. Int'l Envtl. L. & Pol'y* 157

World Heritage: Challenges for the Millennium (UNESCO, 2007)

[144] See the recommendations by the IUCN in the Evaluation of the Global Strategy, *supra* n. 142, para. 25(h). See also the recent IUCN review of the World Heritage List, *supra* n. 64.

Chapter 15

The Convention on International Trade in Endangered Species of Wild Fauna and Flora

1. Background

International trade in wildlife is big business, 'estimated to be worth billions of dollars and to include hundreds of millions of plant and animal specimens'.[1] The trade goes back for centuries, but there was a dramatic increase in its volume during the 1960s and 1970s. For example, by the late 1960s a staggering 5–10 million crocodilian skins were entering international trade each year. International wildlife trade continues apace today – during 2002 and 2003 the USA alone issued 1,547 permits for imported sport-hunted leopard trophies and 250 permits for sport-hunted elephant trophies.[2] In addition, European Union member states imported 'six million live birds, 1.6 million live reptiles, around 10 million reptile skins, 21 million orchids and 579 t of sturgeon caviar' between 1996 and 2002,[3] and the legal trade in 2005 'in wildlife products in the EU had an estimated declared import value of EUR93 billion'.[4] Often involvement in wildlife trade can make the difference between a comfortable lifestyle and a basic one; for example, those involved in the collection of marine specimens in Fiji can expect to receive a monthly income of US$425 when compared to the average wage of US$50 per month.[5]

The first demand for controls on the international wildlife trade was made as early as 1911 when Paul Sarasin, a Swiss conservationist, called for restrictions on the import and export of bird feathers because of the effect of the vogue for plumed hats on bird populations. Sarasin's pleas came to nothing, but in 1963, aware of the increasing levels of trade, the General Assembly of the International Union for Conservation of Nature and Natural Resources

[1] CITES Secretariat, 'What is CITES?', at www.cites.org/eng/disc/what.shtml.
[2] US Fish and Wildlife Service, US CITES Biennial Report 2002–2003 (2004), p. 11.
[3] (2004) 20(1) *TRAFFIC Bulletin* 4.
[4] M. Engler and R. Parry-Jones, *Opportunity or Threat: The role of the EU in Global Wildlife Trade* (TRAFFIC Europe, 2007), p. 6.
[5] TRAFFIC Dispatches No. 23, February 2005, p. 4.

(IUCN) called for 'an international convention on regulations of export, transit and import of rare or threatened wildlife species or their skins and trophies'. The IUCN initiative was more successful, and ten years later, on 3 March 1973, the Convention on International Trade in Endangered Species of Wild Fauna and Flora (CITES) was finally concluded in Washington, DC.[6] CITES was originally signed by twenty-one states but it did not enter into force until 1 July 1975, being ninety days after the tenth signatory had deposited an instrument of ratification.[7] There are now 175 parties to the Convention.[8] More than 33,000 animal and plant species now fall within the remit of CITES,[9] the preamble of the treaty noting that 'international cooperation is essential for the protection of certain species of wild fauna and flora against over-exploitation through international trade'.

CITES is arguably the most successful of all international treaties concerned with the conservation of wildlife. Its success is explained primarily by its basic principles, which most states have proved willing to accept, and by the way in which it operates, which ensures that on the whole it is better enforced than many other treaties. The basic principles of CITES are quite straightforward. It regulates international trade in wild animals and plants which are listed in the three Appendices to the Convention.[10] It is a protectionist treaty in the sense that it prohibits, with a few exceptions, international commercial trade in species that are threatened with extinction (they are listed in Appendix I). It is also a trading treaty in the sense that it allows a controlled international trade in species whose survival is not yet threatened but may become so unless trade is controlled (they are listed in Appendix II). CITES limits exports of Appendix II species to a level which will not be detrimental to their survival. Appendix III provides a mechanism whereby a party which has domestic legislation regulating the export of species not in Appendix I or II can seek the support of other parties in enforcing that domestic legislation.

6 993 UNTS 243; 12 *ILM* 1085 (1973). For an excellent practical guide to the application of CITES, see W. Wijnstekers, *The Evolution of CITES* (CITES, 8th ed., 2005), published online by the CITES Secretariat. The CITES Secretariat is host to a well-maintained website at www.cites.org, where the text of the treaty can be downloaded.

7 As required by Article XXII(1) of the Convention.

8 Non-parties include Angola, the Democratic People's Republic of Korea and Iraq. The European Union is not yet a Party; see later discussion at section 11 below.

9 CITES Secretariat, *supra* n. 1.

10 On trade and wildlife generally see Chapter 19 below.

In essence, the importance of conserving wildlife is endorsed by CITES, as is the sustainable utilisation of wild fauna and flora. The current CITES vision statement notes the need to

> [c]onserve biodiversity and contribute to its sustainable use by ensuring that no species of wild fauna and flora becomes or remains subject to unsustainable exploitation through international trade, thereby contributing to the significant reduction of the rate of biodiversity loss.[11]

The Convention operates by means of a permit system. With a few exceptions it prohibits international trade in specimens of species included in any of the Appendices without the prior grant of a CITES permit. It lays down strict conditions that must be satisfied before a permit is granted, and it requires each party to establish one or more Management Authorities and Scientific Authorities which, between them, are responsible for ensuring that these conditions have been satisfied and, if they have been, for granting a permit.

It would certainly be misleading to suggest that the permit system always works perfectly, but on the whole it is arguable that it has proved to be relatively effective. This is due in large part to the administrative structure of the Convention. In addition to the Management and Scientific Authorities operating on a national level, there is a Secretariat in Switzerland whose function is to oversee the permit system on an international level, and the parties are required to meet regularly in order to review implementation of CITES and to make appropriate recommendations on how to improve it. Thus there are opportunities for the parties to take the necessary measures to solve any problems that may arise. At the time of writing there have been fourteen of these meetings known as ordinary meetings of the Conference of the Parties (CoPs): Bern, 1976; San José, 1979; New Delhi, 1981; Gaborone, Botswana, 1983; Buenos Aires, 1985; Ottawa, 1987; Lausanne, 1989; Kyoto, 1992; Fort Lauderdale, 1994; Harare, 1997; Gigiri, 2000; Santiago, Chile, 2002; Bangkok, 2004; and The Hague, 2007. The parties have also held two extraordinary meetings – one in Bonn in 1979 and the other in Gaborone in 1983 – at which proposed amendments to the Convention were discussed, and they have also held a 'special working session' in Geneva in 1977.[12]

[11] Resolution Conf. 14.2; CITES Strategic Vision 2008–2013. This establishes certain goals to be achieved to improve the implementation of CITES globally.

[12] The fifteenth ordinary meeting of the CoP is to convene in Doha in 2010. Amendments to the text of the Convention, as opposed to amendments to the Appendices, can only be considered at extraordinary meetings of the parties and are adopted if approved by a

The fact that so many states have become parties to CITES demonstrates the widespread appeal of a treaty which strictly limits international trade in species in genuine need of protection, allows a controlled trade in those able to sustain some exploitation and sets up a system of international co-operation to help it achieve its objectives. The Convention is attractive to the 'producer' nations who see controls at the place of import as well as the place of export as essential weapons in their fight to protect their valuable wildlife resources from poachers and illegal traders. The 'consumer' nations support it because without controls their legitimate dealers might have no raw material in which to trade in the generations to come.

This chapter starts by looking at the system of administration established by CITES. It then addresses the Convention's definitions of 'specimens' and 'species', and gives consideration to the criteria for adding species to or removing them from the Appendices, the procedures for amending the Appendices, the rules governing international trade in species listed in the Appendices, the exceptional circumstances where these rules do not apply, the measures taken to ensure compliance and those which parties are required to take to enforce CITES, the Convention's relationship with other treaties, and the amendment to the Convention designed to allow the European Union to become a party to CITES in its own right.

2. Administration

The administrative structure established by CITES consists of a Secretariat, the Conference of the Parties, the Standing Committee and certain other permanent committees, and the national Management and Scientific Authorities, all of which have different functions and responsibilities. In practice, this structure is imperative in facilitating implementation and enforcement of the Convention as it ensures that there are official bodies continually watching over the operation of the Convention on both a national and an international level.

a) Secretariat

Established by Article XII of CITES, the Secretariat is located in Geneva and is administered by UNEP. The Secretariat comprises the Secretary-

two-thirds majority of the parties present and voting. An amendment enters into force, for those parties which have accepted it, sixty days after two-thirds of the parties at the time of adoption of the amendment have deposited an instrument of acceptance with the Depositary government (Switzerland); see Article XVII(3) and Resolution Conf. 4.27.

General's Office and several units: Legal Affairs and Trade Policy Support; Management Authority and Conference Support; Scientific Support; Enforcement Assistance; and Capacity Building. These units are headed by their own chief of unit, who in turn reports to the secretary-general.[13]

The Secretariat performs many different functions.[14] It arranges and services meetings of the parties and prepares numerous reports and draft resolutions on items to be considered at those meetings. It prepares an annual report on its work and on the implementation of the Convention. After each meeting of the parties, it publishes and distributes reports of the proceedings to all party governments. It also issues numerous official notifications to the parties each year on matters ranging from recommendations to suspend trade with certain parties to the introduction of the CITES Customs training CD-ROM. The Secretariat additionally plays an important role in ensuring compliance, as will be discussed below.

b) Conference of the Parties

The Conference of the Parties (CoP), the official title given to a meeting of the parties, is the decision-making body on all matters related to CITES. It has met regularly every two to three years and may hold extraordinary meetings on the written request of at least one-third of the parties.[15] For the purpose of saving costs, the Bangkok Conference decided that all further Conferences of the Parties will take place in Geneva unless a candidate host state agrees to pay the difference in costs between the proposed venue and the cost of hosting the meeting in Geneva.[16]

The scope of the activities of the Conference of the Parties is wide. It must approve a budget for the Secretariat; UNEP had initially provided

[13] Parties contribute to the CITES Trust Fund, which meets the costs of the Secretariat. This fund also finances the running of the Conference of the Parties and all CITES committees. Contributions to the Trust Fund are based on the UN scale of assessment, although 'adjusted to take account of the fact that not all members of the United Nations are Parties' to CITES; see Resolution Conf. 14.1. External sources have provided finance for activities not funded by the Trust Fund. Sources of such external funding are state parties but also NGOs and business; for example, in 2004 funding was obtained from, inter alia, the All Japan Association of Reptile Skins and Leather Industry, Birds International, the Humane Society of the United States, the International Fur Trade Federation, Safari Club International, WWF International and the World Association of Zoos and Aquariums. A list of approved donors is available at www.cites.org/eng/disc/fund.shtml.

[14] Article XII(2) sets out the functions of the Secretariat in detail. [15] Article XI(2).

[16] Resolution Conf. 13.1; now repealed by Resolution Conf. 14.1, which endorses a similar provision.

the financial support for the Secretariat but, when it became evident that this would be phased out, the Conference of the Parties amended the text of the Convention in order to allow subsequent Conferences to adopt financial provisions.[17] The CoP is also responsible for making appropriate recommendations in order to improve the effectiveness of the Convention.[18] These recommendations take the form of either new or revised resolutions, and of decisions. Recommendations are not to be regarded as 'hard' law, but they have assisted in establishing the CITES legal regime and should be regarded as 'soft' law in nature.[19] Another major responsibility of the Conference of the Parties is to review the list of species included in the Appendices. Large numbers of amendments, affecting hundreds of species, have been made at all meetings.

Non-party governments, the International Atomic Energy Agency and the United Nations and its specialised agencies have a right to be represented as observers at meetings of the Conference of the Parties but may not vote.[20] International, national, governmental and non-governmental bodies or agencies which are technically qualified in the protection, conservation or management of wildlife may also attend as observers unless at least one-third of the parties present object.[21]

c) CITES Committees

To assist it in its task, the Conference of the Parties has established several committees. The Standing Committee is a permanent advisory committee and its voting members represent six major geographical regions (Africa, Asia, Europe, North America, Central and South America and the Caribbean, and Oceania). It has generally met at least

[17] The amendment entered into force on 13 April 1987. Article XI.3 now notes that '[a]t meetings . . . the Parties shall review the implementation of the present Convention and may:

(a) make such provisions as may be necessary to enable the Secretariat to carry out its duties, *and adopt financial provisions*; . . .'.

The emphasised words were added by the amendment. On this first amendment to CITES, see P. H. Sand, 'Whither CITES? The Evolution of a Treaty Regime in the Borderline of Trade and the Environment' (1997) 8 *EJIL* 29, at p. 46.

[18] Article XI(3). [19] Sand, *supra* n. 17, at p. 35. On soft law generally see Chapter 2 above.

[20] Article XI(6).

[21] Article XI(7). See also Resolution Conf. 13.8 in relation to requirements on the participation of observers.

once a year but holds two meetings in the year in which the Conference of the Parties takes place. The Standing Committee has become something of an 'inner cabinet' which performs such functions on behalf of the parties as may be necessary between ordinary meetings of the parties. In particular, as will be discussed in more depth later, the Standing Committee is responsible for monitoring and assessing compliance with obligations and taking decisions in relation to implementation and enforcement. It also oversees the execution of the Secretariat's budget, provides general policy advice on matters brought to it by the Secretariat, and is responsible for the drafting of resolutions for consideration by the Conference of the Parties. Additionally, the Standing Committee performs specific tasks given to it by the Conference of the Parties,[22] and must report to the Conference of the Parties.[23] Decisions of the Standing Committee are taken either by consensus or by a simple majority of the members voting.[24]

The Animals Committee and the Plants Committee were also established by the Conference of the Parties and must report to it and the Standing Committee. They are sources of specialised knowledge on species that are either controlled by CITES or may become so. Both committees were established in 1987 and have been assigned tasks which include the provision of scientific advice on issues relevant to trade in animal and plant species included in the Appendices, the undertaking of periodic reviews on such animal or plant species, and the handling of nomenclature issues. They have also been assigned an important role in the Review of Significant Trade procedure discussed below.

d) The Management and Scientific Authorities

CITES was the first wildlife treaty to require its parties to establish specific national authorities to administer the provisions of the Convention, thereby establishing a global network of institutions which co-operate directly with their counterparts in other states, unfettered by the constraints of formal diplomatic channels.

22 For example, see its role in relation to rhinoceros conservation (Resolution Conf. 9.14 (Rev. CoP 14)) and ivory trade controls (Resolution Conf. 10.10 (Rev. CoP 14)).

23 Resolution Conf. 11.1 (Rev. CoP 14).

24 Rules of Procedure of the Standing Committee (as amended at the fifty-eighth meeting, Geneva, July 2009).

Each party is required to designate one or more Management Authorities competent to grant permits or certificates on behalf of that party, and also to designate one or more Scientific Authorities.[25] The specific role played by each Authority with respect to the granting of CITES permits will be the focus of discussion later but it is important at this stage to note that their roles firmly underline the importance of taking into account scientific evidence when making deliberations as to whether or not trade in wildlife is sustainable. Their establishment is additionally significant for two reasons. First, the mere fact that each party has two permanent bodies responsible for implementing CITES goes a long way towards ensuring that each party makes at least some effort to enforce the Convention. Second, although their mandate under CITES is limited to international trade, some parties have given Management and Scientific Authorities additional responsibilities relating to wildlife conservation. As a result, their establishment has not only helped regulate international trade but also contributed to an organised and rational approach to the overall management of wildlife resources in those states. In order to fulfil their responsibilities, Management Authorities in importing countries frequently have to correspond with Management Authorities in exporting countries. To facilitate such communication, CITES requires each party to inform the depositary (Swiss) government of the name and address of its Management Authority and to inform the Secretariat of any changes thereto.[26] The Secretariat has compiled and regularly updates a CITES Directory containing contact details of Management and Scientific Authorities and each party is supplied with a copy.

3. Definitions

CITES applies to 'specimens of species' listed in the Appendices to the Convention.

a) 'Specimens'

Article I(b) of CITES stipulates that 'specimens' may be living or dead and include 'any readily recognisable part or derivative thereof'. The latter is important because it means that the Convention covers international trade in products such as ivory, skins and horns which form the

[25] Article IX(1). [26] Article IX(2)–(3).

bulk of the wildlife trade. The Convention itself does not define 'readily recognisable', with the result that trade in certain parts and derivatives is regulated by some parties but not by others. Because of the confusion arising from different parties adopting different practices, Switzerland, the UK and the Federal Republic of Germany proposed at the San José Conference that a 'minimum list' of readily recognisable parts and derivatives be adopted by all parties. The proposal was defeated on the grounds that a 'minimum list' would soon become a 'maximum list' and that products such as turtle soup and ground rhinoceros horn, which might be deemed readily recognisable by some parties but not by others, would be freely traded everywhere.[27] A degree of general guidance has since been provided by the Fort Lauderdale conference where the parties agreed that

> the term 'readily recognizable part or derivative', as used in the Convention, shall be interpreted to include any specimen which appears from an accompanying document, the packaging or a mark or label, or from other circumstances, to be a part or derivative of an animal or plant of a species included in the Appendices, unless such part or derivative is specifically exempted from the provisions of the Convention.[28]

Problems have still arisen in practice, particularly where there is trade between parties in disagreement as to whether a part or derivative is readily recognisable. In such circumstances, it has been recommended that an importing party should not waive its requirement that a CITES export or re-export permit accompany the importation of parts and derivatives.[29]

b) 'Species'

Article I(a) defines 'species' to include 'any species, subspecies or geographically separate population thereof'. Although the parties have recommended that '[l]isting of a species in more than one Appendix should be avoided in general in view of the enforcement problems it creates',[30] different populations of the same species have been considered independently for listing purposes. All populations of saltwater crocodile (*Crocodylus porosus*), for example, are in Appendix I, except for the

[27] See M. Hornblower, 'Noble Sentiments, Sharp Disagreements', (1979) 81(4) *Audubon*, p. 111.

[28] Resolution Conf. 9.6 (Rev.). [29] Ibid.

[30] Resolution Conf. 9.24 (Rev. CoP 14), Annex 3.

Australian, Indonesian and Papua New Guinean populations, which have Appendix II status. In addition, the African elephant (*Loxodonta africana*) enjoys Appendix I status apart from the populations of Botswana, Namibia, South Africa and Zimbabwe, which are in Appendix II. The fact that CITES allows these split listings is important because it enables a party with a non-endangered, well-managed population of a species that is endangered in other parts of its range to include its own population in Appendix II and thus allow a limited commercial trade which would be prohibited if the population was in Appendix I. Conversely, it has allowed parties to list an endangered population of a species in Appendix I and thus protect it from commercial trade in situations where the species is not endangered in other parts of its range.

4. Criteria for including species in or removing them from the Appendices

The text of CITES lays down the basic conditions for the inclusion of a species in Appendix I, II or III. However, it was agreed at the Bern Conference, held just one year after the Convention's entry into force, that more detailed guidelines on the listing of species in, and their removal from, Appendices I and II would be useful. The Bern Conference therefore adopted the 'Bern criteria' to guide proposals to list or de-list species in or from Appendices I and II.[31] The Bern criteria proved controversial because, for reasons of precaution, they made it difficult to remove a species from Appendix I or II or to transfer a species from Appendix I to II. Those in range states who supported the sustainable utilisation of wildlife pointed to the inflexibility in the Bern criteria and the consequent difficulties in the downlisting of species.[32] Too many species appeared on the Appendices even though they may not actually have been threatened by commercial trade.[33] By the early 1990s it was appreciated that the Bern criteria were outdated and needed to be replaced by a more appropriate set of criteria. At the eighth meeting of the parties in 1992 a review process was commenced,[34] as a result of which, at the ninth meeting of the parties, in Fort Lauderdale, a new set

[31] Resolution Conf. 1.1. [32] Sand, *supra* n. 17 at p. 45. [33] Resolution Conf. 8.20.
[34] Ibid.

of criteria, the 'Fort Lauderdale criteria', for amending the appendices was established.[35]

The Fort Lauderdale criteria have therefore replaced the Bern criteria and importantly recognise that 'range states of a species subject to an amendment proposal should be consulted by the proponent'. Although the CoP had previously recommended that range states be consulted in this way,[36] many proposals had been put forward for discussion at meetings without consultation with range states taking place beforehand.[37] The Fort Lauderdale criteria note that the results of any such consultation procedure should be made available in the proponent's proposal to amend.[38] The Fort Lauderdale criteria additionally expressly endorse the need for a precautionary approach.[39]

The remainder of this section analyses the listing criteria established by the Convention and the amplifications made thereto by the Fort Lauderdale criteria.

a) Inclusion of species in Appendix I

Article II(1) of CITES stipulates that Appendix I shall include

> all species threatened with extinction which are or may be affected by trade. Trade in specimens of these species must be subject to particularly strict regulation in order not to endanger further their survival and must only be authorized in exceptional circumstances.

Annex 1 of the Fort Lauderdale criteria indicate that a species 'is or may be affected by trade' if:[40]

> i) it is known to be in trade (using the definition of 'trade' in Article I of the Convention),[41] and that trade has or may have a detrimental impact on the status of the species; or

[35] Resolution Conf. 9.24 (Rev. CoP 14). This resolution contains the listing criteria established at Fort Lauderdale as amended by subsequent meetings of the parties. On the criteria see A. G. Blundell and B. D. Rodan, 'Confusing Controversy with Failure: The Fort Lauderdale Listing Criteria and CITES Appendix I and II Species Proposals' (2001) 4(1) *JIWLP* 35; and B. Dickson, 'The Precautionary Principle in CITES: A Critical Assessment' (1999) 39 *Nat. Resources J* 211.

[36] See Resolution Conf. 8.21. [37] Ibid.

[38] Resolution Conf. 9.24 (Rev. CoP 14), Annex VI(C)(10).

[39] See text accompanying n. 49. [40] Ibid., Annex V.

[41] Article 1(c) notes that 'trade' means export, re-export, import and introduction from the sea.

> ii) it is suspected to be in trade, or there is demonstrable potential international demand for the species, that may be detrimental to its survival in the wild.

In addition to satisfying one of the criteria relating to trade, a species must also satisfy biological criteria related to the words 'threatened with extinction'. One of the problems with the Bern criteria had been the lack of a definition of these words. Annex I of the Fort Lauderdale criteria rectifies this omission by setting detailed biological criteria relevant to Appendix I. The latter notes that a species is now to be treated as threatened with extinction if, for example,

> the wild population is small, and is characterized by at least one of the following: i) an observed, inferred or projected decline in the number of individuals or the area and quality of habitat; or ii) each subpopulation being very small; or iii) a majority of individuals being concentrated geographically during one or more life-history phases; or iv) large short-term fluctuations in population size; or v) a high vulnerability to either intrinsic or extrinsic factors.

What of species that look like Appendix I species? The Convention itself makes no reference to species similar in appearance to Appendix I species and which therefore could be confused with those listed in Appendix I. Reference is only made in Article II(2)(b) to the inclusion of so-called 'look-alike' species in Appendix II in relation to Appendix II species only. This apparent omission was rectified as early as the first CoP, when the parties noted that those species which looked like Appendix I species should be included in Appendix II.[42] The objective behind this provision is to control trade in species, even if they are widespread and common, which look like and could be confused with a threatened species. Without this safeguard, unscrupulous traders might deceive customs officers and other enforcement agents into believing that a specimen of a threatened species was in fact a specimen of a common one and thereby escape CITES controls. Having duly noted that Article II(2)(b) only stipulates that species are to be included in Appendix II which must be subject to regulation in order that trade in other Appendix II species may be brought under effective control, the Fort Lauderdale criteria proceed to note that this provision should also apply where there is a need to bring trade under control in species noted in Appendix I. In effect, the Fort Lauderdale criteria have continued the

[42] Resolution Conf. 1.1.

approach that species which look like Appendix I species should be included in Appendix II.

When the Convention first came into force, Appendix I contained approximately 450 species, the majority being well-known endangered animals such as the tiger (*Panthera tigris*), cheetah (*Acinonyx jubatus*), humpback whale (*Megaptera novaeangliae*) and peregrine falcon (*Falco peregrinus*). Since then, the number of Appendix I species has risen to over 800 and includes a much greater variety of wildlife, including around 300 species of endangered plants. But, as will be discussed below, the ability of states to object to listing of a species by making a reservation to it can seriously undermine the efficacy of such listing.

b) Inclusion of species in Appendix II

Article II(2) states that Appendix II shall include

> (a) all species which although not necessarily now threatened with extinction may become so unless trade in specimens of such species is subject to strict regulation in order to avoid utilization incompatible with their survival; and (b) other species which must be subject to regulation in order that trade in specimens of certain species referred to in sub-paragraph (a) of this paragraph may be brought under effective control.

The purpose behind Article II(2)(a) is to regulate international trade in species which are not sufficiently endangered to warrant inclusion in Appendix I but which may become so unless trade is controlled. Species in this category range from heavily traded species whose populations are still relatively secure to those which are not yet in trade but could be vulnerable if, as frequently happens, traders suddenly switch from one target species to another. As noted above, the purpose behind Article II(2)(b) is to control trade in species which are similar in appearance to and could be confused with those listed under Article II(2)(a) – often referred to as 'look-alike' species. Although the reasons for listing a species in Appendix II may be quite different – either because it is potentially threatened (Article II(2)(a)) or because it looks like a potentially threatened species (Article II(2)(b)) – all species are treated equally once they are in Appendix II, and the Convention regulates trade in a species listed for 2(2)(a) reasons in exactly the same way as a species listed for 2(2)(b) reasons.

Appendix II is much larger than Appendix I, containing over thirty thousand species including the hippopotamus (*Hippopotamus amphibius*), mahogany (*Swietenia humilis* and *Swietenia mahogani*), all flamingos (Phoenicopteridae), seahorses (*Hippocampus*) and Asian giant softshell turtles (*Pelochelys*). The larger size of Appendix II is a consequence of the parties' tendency to list individual species in Appendix I and whole families in Appendix II.[43] For example, there are over 30,000 species of orchids and, except for just eight in Appendix I, all of them are in Appendix II.

5. Procedures for amending Appendix I and II

Each party has the right to propose an amendment to Appendix I or II. There is a procedure which enables proposed amendments to be considered by postal vote,[44] but they are normally considered at meetings of the CoP. Parties must submit proposed amendments to the Secretariat at least 150 days prior to the meeting at which they will be considered.[45] This deadline applies in relation to a proposal where the proposing state has consulted with any relevant range state and included the latter's opinion in the proposal.[46] Where no such consultation has taken place, proposing states must submit proposals at least 330 days in advance of the next CoP to allow time for the Secretariat to circulate the proposal and obtain any comments from either range or non-range states.[47] Proposals are adopted if approved by a two-thirds majority of parties present and voting. If approved, they take effect ninety days thereafter.[48]

The text of CITES makes no mention of the kind of information needed before a species can be removed from Appendix I or II or downgraded from Appendix I to II. The Fort Lauderdale criteria, however, stipulate that

> when considering proposals to amend Appendix I or II, the Parties shall, by virtue of the precautionary approach and in case of uncertainty either as regards the status of a species or the impact of trade on the conservation of a species, act in the best interest of the conservation of the species

[43] This also assists in alleviating the 'look-alike' problem. [44] Article XV(2).

[45] Article XV(1)(a). It should be noted that parties are not limited to making proposals concerning species which are native to their own territory.

[46] Resolution Conf. 8.21.

[47] Ibid. Additionally, if a proposal relating to ranching is made for the transfer of a population from Appendix I to Appendix II it must be submitted to the Secretariat at least 330 days before the next meeting of the parties; see Resolution Conf. 11.16 (Rev. CoP 14). On ranching see text *infra* accompanying nn. 117–20.

[48] Article XV(1)(b) and (c).

> concerned and adopt measures that are proportionate to the anticipated risks to the species.[49]

In addition, it is stipulated that a species listed in Appendix I shall not be removed from the Appendices 'unless it has been first transferred to Appendix II, with monitoring of any impact of trade on the species for at least two intervals between Conferences of the Parties'.[50]

To be removed from Appendix I to Appendix II a species must no longer satisfy the relevant criteria for Appendix I status and, in addition, one of the following precautionary safeguards must be met:

> a) the species is not in demand for international trade, nor is its transfer to Appendix II likely to stimulate trade in, or cause enforcement problems for, any other species included in Appendix I; or
> b) the species is likely to be in demand for trade, but its management is such that the Conference of the Parties is satisfied with:
>   i) implementation by the range States of the requirements of the Convention, in particular Article IV;[51] and
>   ii) appropriate enforcement controls and compliance with the requirements of the Convention; or
> c) an integral part of the amendment proposal is an export quota or other special measure approved by the Conference of the Parties, based on management measures described in the supporting statement of the amendment proposal, provided that effective enforcement controls are in place; or
> d) a ranching proposal is submitted consistent with the applicable Resolutions of the Conference of the Parties and is approved.[52]

Tensions amongst parties have certainly arisen in relation to proposals for the transfer of certain species from Appendix I to Appendix II. In particular, there has been much debate in recent years between those advocating a protectionist stance and those other countries, usually range states, which promote the sustainable use of wildlife. Hepworth has succinctly characterised this divide in the following terms:

> [F]or some countries the concept of sustainable use lies at the heart of conservation and development requirements, while others are suspicious that without clearer definition the term could be used to justify an

[49] Resolution Conf. 9.24 (Rev. CoP 14), Annex 4. [50] Ibid., Annex 4.A.1.

[51] Article IV stipulates the manner in which trade of a specimen of species in Appendix II is to be carried out; see discussion below in section 6.

[52] Ibid., Annex 4.A.1. On ranching see text accompanying nn. 117–20.

increase in trade on economic grounds regardless of the impact on the conservation of species.[53]

The debate between advocates of sustainable use and those who support a more protectionist stance has been particularly prevalent in recent times in relation to the management of African elephant populations. Although all populations were placed on Appendix I in 1989, Botswana, Namibia, and Zimbabwe at the Harare meeting and South Africa at Gigiri eventually succeeded in convincing the CoP that their populations were thriving and managed effectively and that local populations and conservation programmes would benefit from the limited sale of ivory. Their respective populations are as a result now listed in Appendix II. Nevertheless, trade in ivory from these Appendix II populations has been very tightly regulated to date by means of the quotas given when appropriate by the CoP.[54] Since the downlisting there have been particular concerns that the regulated legal trade in ivory from these Appendix II populations may have led to an increased level of illegal killings and a rise in the illegal trade of ivory obtained from elephant populations still listed in Appendix I.[55]

a) Inclusion of species in Appendix III

Article II(3) stipulates that Appendix III shall include 'all species which any Party identifies as being subject to regulation within its jurisdiction

[53] R. Hepworth, 'The Independent Review of CITES' (1998) 1 *JIWLP* 412, at p. 419.

[54] In 1997 Botswana, Namibia and Zimbabwe were allowed to sell fifty tonnes of ivory to Japan. Two years later the sale took place and raised US$5 million. In 2002 the parties agreed that Botswana, Namibia and South Africa could sell a further sixty tonnes, but this sale was made conditional on the effective running of the MIKE programme (Monitoring of Illegal Killing of Elephants); the final approval of the sale was only given by the Standing Committee in June 2007. In 2007 Botswana, Namibia, Zimbabwe and South Africa were allowed to make an additional single sale of ivory. This time it related to all stocks owned by each of the governments as at the end of January 2007. No further sales are envisaged for a period of nine years following the end of these sales.

[55] See generally Resolution Conf. 10.10 (Rev. CoP 14) in relation to trade in elephant specimens. In addition to the MIKE programme, the Elephant Trade Information System (ETIS) has been established to monitor the illegal trade in ivory and is managed by TRAFFIC; the presentation of expert analysis of ETIS data to the Santiago CoP led to this meeting reaching the conclusion that Ethiopia had the 'largest unregulated ivory market in East Africa'; S. Milledge and M. Abdi, 'A Model for Africa – Ethiopia's Efforts to Close Unregulated Domestic Ivory Markets in Addis Ababa' (2005) 20(3) *TRAFFIC Bulletin* 119. Both MIKE and ETIS are supervised by the CITES Standing Committee. See Annex I of Resolution Conf. 10.10 (Rev. CoP 14) on ETIS, and Annex II on the role of MIKE.

for the purpose of preventing or restricting exploitation, and as needing the co-operation of other Parties in the control of trade'. The objective of Appendix III is to provide a mechanism whereby a party with domestic legislation regulating the export of species not listed in Appendix I or II can seek international help in enforcing its legislation. The Convention notes that any party can unilaterally amend Appendix III at any time simply by notifying the Secretariat.[56] Despite the fact that a species should only be listed in Appendix III if the party in question needs the co-operation of other parties to control trade,[57] there is evidence that some listed species have been rarely traded or perhaps even not traded at all.[58] In such cases CITES is of no practical use. In view of such inappropriate listings, the parties have made recommendations as to Appendix III listings. For example, a country seeking to add a species should, inter alia, beforehand, seek the opinion of other range states, the CITES Secretariat, known major importing countries, and the CITES Animals or Plants Committees.[59] Additions to Appendix III take effect ninety days after the Secretariat has notified all the parties, while withdrawals take effect just thirty days after such notification.[60]

6. Rules governing international trade in specimens of species listed in the Appendices

a) Appendix I species

The strictest rules apply to trade in Appendix I species. Article II(1) of CITES states that international trade in these species shall only be authorised in 'exceptional circumstances', and Article III imposes such strict conditions on the grant of trading permits that legal trade among parties is only possible if it is for non-commercial purposes.

i) Export

Article III prohibits the export of specimens of Appendix I species without the prior grant and presentation of an export permit. A permit will be granted only if a Scientific Authority of the state of export determines that the 'export will not be detrimental to the survival of that species' and if a Management Authority of the state of export is satisfied that the specimen was acquired legally and, if alive, is 'so

[56] Article XVI(1). [57] This point is reiterated in Resolution Conf. 9.25 (Rev. CoP 14).
[58] Ibid. [59] Ibid. [60] Article XVI(2) and (3).

prepared and shipped as to minimise the risk of injury, damage to health or cruel treatment'.[61] The Management Authority must also be satisfied that the state of import has already granted an import permit for the specimen.[62] In any international trading of Appendix I species, therefore, the import permit must come first.

ii) Re-export

'Re-export' is defined as the export of any specimen previously imported.[63] CITES prohibits the re-export of Appendix I species without a re-export certificate. This will only be granted after a Management Authority of the state of re-export is satisfied that the specimen was imported into that state in accordance with the provisions of CITES and, if alive, will be shipped with a minimum of risk of injury, damage to health or cruel treatment. In the case of living specimens, the Management Authority must also be satisfied that an import permit has been granted by the state of destination.[64]

iii) Import

Article III of the Convention prohibits the import of Appendix I species without the prior grant and presentation of an import permit and either an export permit or re-export certificate. Although there are strict controls on the grant of export permits, it is the tight restrictions on the grant of import permits which limit the trade so severely. An import permit may not be granted unless a Scientific Authority of the state of import has advised that the import is for purposes which are not detrimental to the survival of the species and that, if the specimen is alive, the proposed recipient is suitably equipped to house and care for it. More important still, an import permit may not be granted unless a Management Authority of the state of import is satisfied that the specimen will not be used for 'primarily commercial purposes'.[65] This latter provision effectively prohibits international commercial trade in Appendix I species and limits legal trade among the parties to specimens required for

[61] Article III(2)(a)–(c). 'Guidelines for transport and preparation for shipment of live wild animals and plants' were adopted at San José in 1979. Note also Resolution Conf. 10.21 (Rev. CoP 14). The Animals Committee carries out regular reviews of the causes of death and injury to animals during shipment. On animal welfare generally see Chapter 20 below.

[62] Article III(2)(d). [63] Article I(d). [64] Article III(4).

[65] Article III(3). For guidance as to what amounts to primarily commercial purposes see Resolution Conf. 5.10.

scientific and educational purposes and, in limited circumstances, to hunting trophies.[66]

A resolution adopted by the Gaborone Conference concerning the leopard, an Appendix I species, could be said to have set a precedent for broadening the circumstances in which Appendix I species may be traded. The Gaborone Conference rejected a proposal to transfer southern and eastern African populations of leopard from Appendix I to II on the grounds that a reopening of commercial markets for leopard skins could prejudice threatened populations of leopard in other parts of its range. But the Conference also recognised that the leopard was not endangered in Botswana, Kenya, Malawi, Mozambique, Tanzania, Zambia and Zimbabwe and agreed that these states should be allowed to utilise the skins of leopards killed each year in defence of life or property. The Conference allotted an annual quota for each of the seven states, ranging from twenty to eighty skins, and recommended that other parties should issue import permits for tagged leopard skins exported in accordance with the quotas, provided that they are satisfied that the owner of the skin will import no more than one skin in any calendar year and is importing the skin as a personal item which is not intended for resale. The leopard remains on Appendix I, and the current resolution regarding leopard trophies also sets quotas and takes into account the fact that in certain sub-Saharan countries the leopard is not endangered.[67]

iv) Introduction from the sea

Finally, CITES prohibits the introduction of Appendix I species from the sea without a permit. The Convention deems a specimen to be introduced from the sea if it is 'taken in the marine environment not under the jurisdiction of any State' and is imported into that state.[68] A permit will only be granted if a Scientific Authority of the state of introduction advises that it will not be detrimental to the survival of the species and if a Management Authority is satisfied that the other conditions for

[66] In relation to hunting trophies, see Resolution Conf. 10.14 (Rev. CoP 14) on leopard skins, Resolution Conf. 10.15 (Rev. CoP 14) on markhor trophies, and Resolution Conf. 13.5 (Rev. CoP 14) on black rhinos.

[67] Resolution Conf. 10.14 (Rev. CoP 14).

[68] Article I(e). The parties at The Hague interpreted the phrase 'the marine environment not under the jurisdiction of any State' as meaning 'those marine areas beyond the areas subject to the sovereignty or sovereign rights of a State consistent with international law'. See Resolution Conf. 14.6.

imports of Appendix I species have been met.[69] The objective of these requirements is to ensure that whales, sea turtles and other threatened marine animals are not taken on the high seas and then brought into the territory of a party for commercial purposes. It is of interest to note that all cetaceans subject to the International Whaling Commission moratorium on commercial whaling are listed in Appendix I, apart from the West Greenland population of minke, which is listed in Appendix II.[70]

b) Appendix II species

Controls imposed on the export or re-export of Appendix II species are similar to those which apply to Appendix I species, but the rules for imports are much less stringent.

i) Export

CITES prohibits the export of specimens of Appendix II species without an export permit. To obtain a permit, a Scientific Authority and Management Authority of the state of export must make determinations similar to those required for the export of Appendix I species. Article IV(2) states that an export permit shall be granted only if (a) a Management Authority of the state of export is satisfied that the specimen was acquired legally and, if alive, is 'so prepared and shipped as to minimise the risk of injury, damage to health or cruel treatment' and (b) a Scientific Authority of the state of export determines that the 'export will not be detrimental to the survival of that species'. This task of the Scientific Authority is a difficult one since '[m]any countries of origin lack the scientific data on the status of their animal and plant populations, which makes it impossible to calculate the effects thereon of different levels of exploitation'.[71]

Article IV(3) requires a Scientific Authority in each party to monitor export permits granted and actual exports made. Whenever a Scientific

[69] Article III(5).

[70] No doubt referring to the International Convention for the Regulation of Whaling, Article XIV(4) of CITES relieves parties, which are also party to any other treaty affording protection 'to marine species', of obligations imposed by CITES with respect to trade in species in Appendix II which are taken in accordance with the provisions of such other treaty. In relation to the export of a specimen taken in this way, Article XIV(5) notes that the Management Authority of the state of introduction need only issue a certificate stating the specimen was taken in accordance with the other treaty.

[71] W. Wijnstekers, *The Evolution of CITES* (CITES, 7th ed., 2003), p. 80.

Authority determines that the export of any Appendix II species should be limited 'in order to maintain that species throughout its range at a level consistent with its role in the ecosystems in which it occurs and well above the level at which that species might become eligible for inclusion in Appendix I', Article IV(3) requires it to advise the appropriate Management Authority of suitable measures to be taken to limit the grant of export permits.

ii) Re-export and introduction from the sea

CITES prohibits the re-export of specimens of Appendix II species without a re-export certificate. A re-export certificate will be granted only after a Management Authority of the state of re-export is satisfied that the specimen was imported in accordance with the provisions of CITES and that, if alive, it will be shipped with a minimum of risk of injury, damage to health or cruel treatment.[72] The Convention also prohibits the introduction of Appendix II species from the sea without a certificate, and a certificate will only be granted if a Scientific Authority of the state of introduction determines that it will not be detrimental to the survival of the species and if a Management Authority of the state of introduction is satisfied that any living specimen will be handled so as to minimise the risk of injury, damage to health or cruel treatment.[73]

iii) Import

CITES prohibits the import of specimens of Appendix II species unless they are accompanied by a valid export permit or re-export certificate.[74] However, an import permit is not required, and imports for commercial purposes are permissible. As a result, international trade in tens of thousands of specimens of a single Appendix II species for which there is a large commercial demand may be carried on quite legally each year provided that the state of export has been advised by its Scientific Authority that the export of such quantities will not be detrimental to the survival of the species and provided that the other requirements with respect to export, re-export or introduction from the sea have been met.

iv) 'No-detriment' finding

The CITES permit system undoubtedly raises an interesting question as to the amount of evidence a Scientific Authority of a state of export requires in order to determine whether or not a proposed export of a

[72] Article IV(5). [73] Article IV(6). [74] Article IV(4).

specimen of a species in Appendix I or II will be detrimental to the survival of that species. This has been the subject of litigation in the United States. In *Defenders of Wildlife, Inc. v Endangered Species Scientific Authority*, the plaintiff, a private conservation organisation, contended that the US Scientific Authority did not have adequate scientific data to support its finding that the proposed level of export of bobcat (*Felis rufus*) pelts for the 1979–80 season would not be detrimental to the survival of the species. The bobcat was and still is listed in Appendix II. The United States Court of Appeals for the District of Columbia Circuit ruled in favour of the plaintiff, holding the export quotas set by the Scientific Authority invalid, on the basis that

> the Scientific Authority cannot make a valid no-detriment finding without (1) a reliable estimate of the number of bobcats and (2) information concerning the number of animals to be killed in the particular season. If that material is not presently available, the Scientific Authority must await its development before it authorizes the export of bobcats.

The Appeals Court recognised that

> because of the secretive nature of the bobcat's life and behavior, it is difficult to obtain accurate information about the size of the bobcat population. There are indications that techniques for making more accurate population estimates can and may be developed. We do not suggest that the Scientific Authority may base a no-detriment finding only upon some kind of head count of the animals or some other method of measurement that, as a practical matter, would be virtually impossible to make. All the Scientific Authority is required to do is to have a reasonably accurate estimate of the bobcat population before it makes a no-detriment finding. The Scientific Authority has considerable discretion to determine the method by which that estimate may be made and in evaluating its reliability.

The Court went on to say that

> any doubt whether the killing of a particular number of bobcats will adversely affect the survival of the species must be resolved in favor of protecting the animals and not in favor of approving the export of their pelts . . . The approach of the Scientific Authority often seemed primarily concerned with an acceptable basis for authorizing bobcat exports despite the absence of convincing factual grounds for making no-detriment findings.[75]

[75] 659 F.2d 168 (D. C. Cir.), *cert denied*, 454 U.S. 963(1981).

The effect of the Appeals Court decision was overturned in 1982 by an amendment to the Endangered Species Act of 1973, which implements CITES in the USA. The amendment puts the duties of the US Management and Scientific Authorities into the hands of the US Secretary of the Interior, and states that

> the Secretary shall base the determinations and advice given by him under Article IV of the [CITES] Convention with respect to wildlife upon the best available biological information derived from professionally accepted wildlife management practices; but is not required to make, or require any State to make, estimates of population size in making such determinations or giving such advice.[76]

Neither the views of the US Appeals Court nor those of the US Congress on the evidence required for a 'no-detriment' finding are binding on other parties to CITES. However, it might be argued that the Appeals Court decision should carry greater weight in the eyes of other parties faced with a similar dilemma since it was a non-biased judicial interpretation of the provisions of CITES, while the amendment to the Endangered Species Act was a politically motivated action designed to bring about a resumption in the export of bobcat pelts.

The Harare CoP in 1997 encouraged the parties to facilitate the holding of workshops to 'improve the implementation of CITES by Scientific Authorities'.[77] Two workshops in the late 1990s led to the publication by the IUCN of guidance to assist in the making of non-detriment findings which has subsequently been used in a series of workshops designed to provide training for Scientific Authorities.[78] Whilst the CoP has not to date agreed on guidance as to the manner in which non-detriment findings are to be carried out, CITES Strategic Vision 2008–2013 established a goal that 'best available scientific information' should form the basis for such findings.[79]

[76] Endangered Species Act of 1973, as amended, section 8A(c)(2).

[77] Resolution Conf. 10.3.

[78] A. R. Rosser and M. J. Haywood, *Guidance for CITES Scientific Authorities: Checklist to Assist in Making Non-detriment Findings for Appendix II Exports* (IUCN, 2002). See www.cites.org/eng/prog/ndf/index.shtml, where it is also noted that Resolution Conf. 13.2 (Rev. CoP 14) urges parties to take into account the Addis Ababa Principles and Guidelines for the Sustainable Use of Biodiversity (adopted by the CoP 7 of the Biodiversity Convention) as well as recommendations of the Animals and Plants Committees noted in Resolution Conf. 13.2 (Rev. CoP 14) Annex 2.

[79] Resolution Conf. 14.2. See also www.cites.org/eng/prog/ndf/index.shtml. Also note the later discussion in this chapter on the 'review of significant trade' procedure.

v) Export of species listed under Article II(2)(b)

The USA has taken the view that if a species is listed in Appendix II for look-alike reasons only (i.e. under Article II(2)(b)), then the state of export's primary focus must be to consider whether proposed exports will be detrimental to the survival of the species that it looks like and was listed to protect rather than to determine whether proposed exports of the species will be detrimental to the survival of the look-alike species. The bobcat was once again the species most seriously affected. In August 1983, the US government announced that it considered the bobcat to be listed in Appendix II purely as a look-alike under Article II(2)(b) rather than as a potentially threatened species under Article II(2)(a). It would therefore be inappropriate, the US government stated, to consider whether proposed export levels of bobcat pelts would be detrimental to the survival of bobcats, and it would only be appropriate to consider whether proposed export levels would be detrimental to the survival of other spotted cats which the bobcat looks like and was listed to protect.[80] This primary focus appears to remain, the US Fish and Wildlife Service more recently indicating that for look-alike species 'the scientific non-detriment finding is based on the risk their export presents to the listed species they resemble', although it has acknowledged that the 'process also includes monitoring to ensure that these look-alike species are not adversely affected by trade'.[81]

In the view of other parties, Article IV(2) of CITES makes it quite clear that Scientific Authorities of exporting states must indeed be satisfied that a proposed export of a specimen of any Appendix II species will not be detrimental to the survival of *that* species before granting a permit for its export, irrespective of whether the species was listed under Article II (2)(a) or II(2)(b). Article IV(2) states that 'the export of *any* specimen of a species included in Appendix II shall require the prior grant and presentation of an export permit' and that a permit shall only be given 'if the Scientific Authority of the State of export has advised that the export will not be detrimental to the survival of *that* species' (emphasis added). Parties should not grant a permit for the export of a specimen of any Appendix II species without first being advised by their Scientific Authority that the export will not be detrimental to the survival of that particular species. Article IV(2) imposes such an obligation in clear and

80 See US *Federal Register*, 48(161), 18 August 1983, pp. 37494–8.

81 US Fish and Wildlife Service, 'CITES Appendix II Supports Sustainable Use' (2003).

unambiguous terms. This is a view which has been supported by the CITES Secretariat.[82]

c) *Appendix III species*

Restrictions on trade in Appendix III species are limited to specimens originating from the state which listed them. To export specimens from that state, Article V(2) of CITES requires the prior grant and presentation of an export permit, and to import specimens from that state the importer must present a certificate of origin and an export permit. If the import is from any other state, a certificate of origin is sufficient.[83] Re-export is permissible from any state without restriction provided a Management Authority of that state certifies that the specimen is being re-exported.[84]

d) *Permits*

CITES requires that a separate permit or certificate be obtained for each consignment of specimens and that an export permit be considered valid only for six months from the date it was granted.[85] In order to standardise permits and make them more difficult to forge, the New Delhi Conference recommended that parties should adapt their permits as closely as possible to a standard model approved at the Conference and should use security paper or serially numbered adhesive security stamps.[86] The Conference commissioned a study to evaluate the implementation and effectiveness of these recommendations.[87] In September 1982, coinciding with the entry into force of new regulations to implement CITES, the Zimbabwean Management Authority initiated the use

[82] In a letter to Simon Lyster dated 13 June 1983, the then assistant secretary-general of the CITES Secretariat stated that 'it is equally clear that when a species is listed in Appendix II, the Convention does not make any distinction as to whether the species is listed under Article II(2)(a) or II(2)(b)'. He went on to say that Article IV(2) 'should be implemented on the basis of the biological status of the species concerned in the country of export'. In a more recent communication dated 12 April 2005 to Peter Davies, the secretary-general of the CITES Secretariat reiterated this approach, noting 'the Convention does not differentiate between species listed in Appendix II and therefore the scientific and other requirements for the issue of an export permit are the same irrespective of the reason for listing in Appendix II. For species listed for look-alike reasons, a non-detriment finding is required but likely to be easier to make' (cited with permission).

[83] Article V(3). [84] Article V(4). [85] Article VI(2) and (5).

[86] Resolution Conf. 3.6 and 3.7. [87] Resolution Conf. 3.6.

of a security stamp on all CITES export documents, making Zimbabwe the first party to adopt this procedure.[88] CITES security stamps were supplied to all interested parties in June 1984. The Secretariat was given the task of reviewing the standard permit, and a resolution was passed in 1992 taking into account the Secretariat's study and recommendations.[89] At the twelfth CoP Resolution 12.3 was passed which, as amended, currently stipulates CITES permit requirements.[90] This resolution recommends, inter alia, that all parties adapt the contents and format of their permits to the standardised version, that a security stamp is fixed to each permit, and that no Management Authority issues permits retrospectively.

e) Trade with non-parties

CITES cannot prevent free trade between non-parties, but it can and does regulate trade between parties and non-parties. The text of the treaty notes that 'comparable documentation issued by the competent authorities [of a non-party] . . . which substantially conforms with the requirements of the present convention for permits and certificates may be accepted in lieu' by a party engaged in such trade.[91] At the 1994 Fort Lauderdale Conference a resolution was adopted which repealed earlier guidance, and, as amended, lays down the current requirements for trade with non-parties.[92] The preamble to the resolution notes the parties' awareness that 'illegal trade, in particular in Appendix I species, appears to avoid states that are party to the Convention and seeks trade routes to, from and through states not party to the Convention'. The tough line taken with regard to international trade with non-parties may well have contributed to the large membership of the Convention since non-parties may feel that the advantages of being a party, and therefore in a position to influence the development of the Convention, outweigh those of remaining outside where there are ever fewer states with which they can freely trade. Recommendations to suspend trade with non-parties can be made either by the CoP or the Standing Committee. At the

[88] Zimbabwe's Control of Goods (Import and Export) (Wildlife) Regulations of 1982.

[89] Resolution Conf. 8.5, which in turn was repealed by Resolution Conf. 9.3 in 1994. Resolution Conf. 9.3 was itself replaced by Resolution Conf. 10.2. The latter was replaced by Resolution Conf. 12.3 (Rev. CoP 14).

[90] Resolution Conf. 12.3 (Rev. CoP 14). [91] Article X.

[92] Resolution Conf. 9.5 (Rev. CoP 14).

beginning of 2010 such recommendations were in place in relation to trade with four non-parties (Bahrain, Haiti, Iraq and Tajikistan).

f) Non-customs zones

Each party is recognised as having sovereignty over the whole of its territory, and CITES makes no special provision for airport lounges (including duty-free shops), free ports or other non-customs zones. Aware that some parties were allowing specimens of species in the Appendices to be exported from non-customs zones without CITES permits, the Gaborone Conference urged the parties to apply the Convention to all parts of their territory including non-customs zones.[93] The Fort Lauderdale conference made a similar recommendation to parties to apply the Convention in such areas.[94]

7. Exemptions

There are a number of circumstances where the usual permit requirements are modified or excluded. These are listed below.

a) Transit

CITES permits are not required for 'the transit or transhipment of specimens through or in the territory of a party while the specimens remain in customs control'.[95] The intention behind the exemption was to avoid imposing an unreasonable burden on shipments that stop in a state on the way to their ultimate destination merely to change planes or to continue their journey by other means of transport. It was felt that stoppages for these purposes did not constitute a genuine import into the state concerned and that it would be unreasonable for that state to require valid CITES documentation before allowing the shipment to continue.

In 1980 the UK government received reports that middlemen were importing Appendix I species from non-parties without a permit and were holding them theoretically 'in transit', which meant they did not have to obtain a CITES permit, while they were in fact looking for a buyer

[93] Resolution Conf. 4.10(b).
[94] Resolution Conf. 9.5 (Rev. CoP 14), which replaced Resolution Conf. 4.10(b).
[95] Article VII(1).

in other non-parties. Once they had located a buyer, they simply sent the specimen on to him without a permit. In order to prevent traders in party countries from abusing the transit exemption in this way, the Gaborone Conference recommended that the exemption should apply to situations where a specimen was in the process of shipment to a named consignee and where the shipment was interrupted only by the necessity implicit in those arrangements.[96] The parties have since also recommended that inspections be made of specimens in transit with a view to checking that they are accompanied by relevant CITES documentation, and that 'any change in ultimate destination is investigated by the country of transit or transhipment to verify that the trade complies with the purposes of CITES'.[97] Moreover, it has been recommended that parties introduce legislation enabling them to seize and confiscate specimens in transit without valid documents.[98] Whenever an illegal shipment is found, the Secretariat should be informed as well as the country of final destination.[99]

b) Pre-Convention specimens

Permit requirements do not apply for international trade in specimens of listed species acquired before the Convention applied to them. In order to qualify for the exemption, the Management Authority of the state of export or re-export must certify that the specimen is pre-Convention.[100] The objective of this exemption was to allow traders to clear their existing stocks when the Convention first came into force and to permit them to continue to trade in items such as old leopard-skin coats. However, there has been a considerable amount of argument as to the date on which the Convention 'applies' to a specimen for the purposes of the exemption. If X species was listed in Appendix I in 2002 and Y state acceded to CITES in 2005, does the Convention apply to a specimen of X species which was acquired in Y state in 2003? It has been argued that the Convention only applies to the specimen from the date that Y state became a party and therefore that the specimen can be traded without a CITES permit by virtue of the pre-Convention exemption. However, it has also been argued that CITES applies to all specimens of a species, whether or not they are located in a state that is a party to the Convention, from the date that the species is first included in the Appendices. If this latter argument

[96] Resolution Conf. 4.10(a). This resolution has now been repealed but the same stipulation is included in current Resolution Conf. 9.7 (Rev. CoP 13).
[97] Resolution Conf. 9.7 (Rev. CoP 13). [98] Ibid. [99] Ibid. [100] Article VII(2).

is accepted, CITES does apply to the specimen acquired in 2003, which cannot therefore qualify for the pre-Convention exemption. Proponents of this argument pointed to the provisions dealing with trade with non-parties – that is, parties cannot accept a specimen of a listed species from a non-party unless the latter produces comparable documentation to that required of a party – in support of their contention because it demonstrated that CITES can apply to a specimen of a listed species before the state in which it is situated becomes a party to the Convention. Current guidance has provided clarity in noting that 'the date from which the provisions of the Convention apply to a specimen [is] the date on which the species concerned was first included in the Appendices'.[101]

There was also some argument regarding the date that a specimen is 'acquired' for purposes of the pre-Convention exemption. It has now been recommended that the date a specimen is 'acquired' be either the date it was known to have been taken from the wild, or the date it was known to have been born in captivity or artificially propagated.[102] If this date is not known, a specimen is acquired on a subsequent and provable date on which it was first possessed by an individual.[103]

c) *Personal effects*

'Personal or household effects' may also be traded without a CITES permit.[104] They are not defined by the Convention and therefore practice has differed. In acknowledging this fact the Bangkok Conference recognised a need for uniform application of this exemption in accordance with decided principles.[105] Parties have determined that 'personal and household effects' should be interpreted to mean specimens

> (a) personally owned or possessed for non-commercial purposes;
> (b) legally acquired; and
> (c) at the time of import, export or re-export either:
>   (i) worn, carried or included in personal baggage; or
>   (ii) part of a household move.[106]

[101] Resolution Conf. 13.6. [102] Ibid. [103] Ibid. [104] Article VII(3).

[105] Resolution Conf. 13.7 (Rev. CoP 14) (which replaced Resolution Conf. 10.6 and Resolution Conf. 12.9).

[106] Ibid.

There has been particular concern that Appendix I species are sold to tourists at shops in international airports, seaports and border crossings. In this regard, the parties have also agreed to take action to ban sales in places of international departure, especially in duty-free areas.[107]

The objective of the exemption is not to put an undue burden on, say, someone with a crocodile-skin wristwatch strap whose business involves a lot of international travel. However, in order to prevent the personal-effects exemption being seriously abused, the Convention specifies two circumstances where it shall not apply. The first relates to specimens of Appendix I species and applies where such specimens 'were acquired by the owner outside his state of usual residence, and are being imported into that state'.[108] It is not permissible, therefore, for an Australian who acquires the skin of a cheetah, an Appendix I species, in Africa to take it back to Australia without a CITES permit even if it is a genuine personal effect. It is interesting to note that the Convention does not prevent him from taking the skin to any other state without a CITES permit provided he can convince that state's customs officers that it is a genuine personal effect. The negotiators of CITES may have felt that the chances of someone buying a specimen of an Appendix I species outside his own state and then taking it to another state as a personal effect without then bringing it back to his own State were sufficiently small as not to jeopardise the species concerned.

The second circumstance where the personal-effects exemption does not apply relates to specimens of Appendix II species which

(i) were acquired by the owner outside his State of usual residence and in a State where removal from the wild occurred;
(ii) are being imported into the owner's State of usual residence; and
(iii) the State where removal from the wild occurred requires the prior grant of export permits before any export of such specimens.[109]

To give an example, a resident of a party will need to present a CITES export permit in order to import into his own country a Chinese cobra skin (*Naja atra*), a specimen of an Appendix II species, which he has acquired while travelling abroad in a state (such as China, Laos or Vietnam) where removal from the wild occurred if that state requires the prior grant of a permit before such skins can legally be exported.

[107] Ibid. [108] Article VII(3)(a). [109] Article VII(3)(b).

The exemption for personal or household effects is clearly open to abuse but it is difficult to make an assessment of the extent to which it has been exploited because of the lack of available information. Many parties do not keep a record of the number of personal effects that they allow to be exported or imported without a CITES permit.

d) Captive breeding and artificial propagation

CITES makes special provision for specimens that are captive-bred or artificially propagated. Article VII(4) of CITES states that specimens of Appendix I animals 'bred in captivity' for commercial purposes and specimens of Appendix I plants 'artificially propagated' for commercial purposes shall be treated as Appendix II specimens.[110] They therefore require only the issuing of an export permit or re-export certificate, and imports for commercial reasons are accordingly allowed. Furthermore, Article VII(5), as interpreted by the CoP, allows all other CITES-listed specimens which have been captive-bred or artificially propagated to be traded simply on the basis of a certificate from the Management Authority of the state of export to that effect, and without *any* of the documentation normally required by Articles III–V.[111]

The Harare Conference adopted detailed criteria which must be satisfied before an animal species may be considered to be 'bred in captivity'; importantly, the specimen in question must be 'born or otherwise produced in a controlled environment', and the parents must have either mated in a controlled environment (if reproduction is sexual) or were in a controlled environment when offspring development commenced (if asexual reproduction).[112] In addition, the breeding stock must be established 'in a manner not detrimental to the survival of the species in the wild, be maintained generally without the introduction of specimens from the wild', and either be managed in a way shown to be 'capable of reliably producing second-generation offspring in a controlled environment' or indeed have 'produced offspring of second generation or subsequent generation' in such an environment.[113] The criteria relating to animal species make good sense because they require a captive stock of Appendix I species to be

[110] Article VII(5).
[111] See Resolution Conf. 2.12 (Rev.) (now repealed by Resolution Conf. 10.16 (Rev.)). Also C. de Klemm, *Guidelines for Legislation to Implement CITES* (IUCN, 1993), p. 45.
[112] Resolution Conf. 10.16 (Rev.). [113] Ibid.

capable of sustaining itself without significant replenishment from the wild before any international trade for commercial purposes is allowed.[114]

The Gigiri Conference established criteria to be satisfied before plants can be considered 'artificially propagated'. The criteria, as amended, stipulate that plant specimens are to be regarded as artificially propagated if

> (a) grown under controlled conditions; and
> (b) grown from seeds, cuttings, divisions, callus tissues or other plant tissues, spores or other propagules that are either exempt from the provisions of the Convention or have been derived from cultivated parental stock.[115]

To be regarded as a 'cultivated parental stock' plants must inter alia be grown in controlled conditions and in a manner not detrimental to the survival of the species in the wild, and

> maintained in sufficient quantities for propagation so as to minimize or eliminate the need for augmentation from the wild, with such augmentation occurring only as an exception and limited to the amount necessary to maintain the vigour and productivity of the cultivated parental stock.[116]

e) Ranching

Although not strictly an exemption to the Convention, the question of 'ranching' Appendix I species has received special treatment from the parties and merits brief consideration here. A ranching operation is not a closed cycle like captive breeding, but involves the rearing of wildlife, usually from wild caught eggs or young, in a controlled environment.

Since they do not qualify for the captive-bred exemption, specimens of Appendix I species cannot be ranched and then traded internationally for commercial purposes without violating CITES. At the San José Conference, however, delegates from several parties argued that they

[114] A procedure to register and monitor captive-breeding operations for Appendix I species bred for commercial reasons has been established by Resolution Conf. 12.10 (Rev. CoP 14).

[115] Resolution Conf. 11.11 (Rev. CoP 14). A procedure to register nurseries exporting artificially propagated specimens of Appendix I species has been set up by Resolution Conf. 9.19 (Rev. CoP 13).

[116] Resolution Conf. 11.11 (Rev. CoP 14).

could only justify protecting habitats of endangered species from agricultural and industrial development if they could derive some economic benefit from the species. They stated that they could not realistically be expected to achieve closed-cycle captive-breeding operations, but that ranching might be a viable proposition for some species. The 'ranching criteria', which allow parties to propose a transfer of their population of an Appendix I species to Appendix II for ranching purposes in certain circumstances, were originally agreed at the Gigiri Conference.[117] The criteria stipulate that the population in question should as far as the CoP is concerned be no longer endangered and that the ranching operation will benefit the conservation of the local population. A system of marking to ensure that ranched specimens could not be confused with, and therefore lead to illegal trade in, other populations of the same species must also be introduced.

The ranching of sea turtles has proved to be a controversial issue. The parties have recognised that use of sea turtles has often not been sustainable and has led to a decline in turtle populations.[118] In addition, the Fort Lauderdale conference noted that their 'unique biology . . . makes their sustainable use difficult and imposes special restraints on their exploitation', and also recognised that 'the demand for marine turtles products in some States stimulates illegal trade both nationally and internationally'.[119] A detailed set of guidelines has therefore been adopted to evaluate any sea turtle ranching proposals.[120]

f) Science and exhibition

Article VII(6) of CITES exempts the non-commercial exchange of specimens between scientists or scientific institutions from permit requirements provided that the scientists or scientific institutions have been registered for these purposes by a Management Authority of the state in which they are situated.[121] Article VII(7) gives Management Authorities the discretion to allow specimens which are part of travelling zoos, circuses, plant exhibitions or other travelling exhibitions to move without a permit.

g) Reservations

CITES allows parties to exempt themselves from the requirements of the Convention in relation to species whose inclusion in the Appendices they

[117] Resolution Conf. 11.16 (Rev. CoP 14). [118] Resolution Conf. 9.20 (Rev.).
[119] Ibid. [120] Ibid., Annex. [121] See generally Resolution Conf. 11.15 (Rev. CoP 12).

find objectionable by taking a 'reservation'. Reservations must be specific as to the species that they cover and must be taken at the time a party deposits its instrument of ratification, acceptance, approval or accession to the Convention.[122] Parties may also reserve on any subsequent amendment to the Appendices provided that the reservation is registered with the Swiss government within ninety days of the adoption of the amendment.[123] Reservations may be withdrawn at any time.

Twenty parties had reservations (effective from September 2007) to the listing of species in Appendices I and II. Reasons for taking reservations need not be given, although they are normally made by parties objecting to increased protection for species in which they have an established trade. France and Italy, for example, in the past took reservations on species of reptiles important to their luxury leather trade,[124] and Japan has current reservations on the listing in Appendix I of certain whales, and in Appendix II of both whale sharks and basking sharks; whale meat is regarded as a luxury in Japan, as is sharkfin soup. Other pro-whaling states, Norway and Iceland, have also entered and continue to hold a number of reservations against the list of specific cetaceans in Appendix I. In addition, Kuwait, Qatar and the United Arab Emirates have entered reservations against the listing in Appendix II of certain types of agarwood (the resin from which can be distilled to form an aromatic oil).

Article XXIII(3) of CITES requires that parties be treated as non-parties in relation to trade in species on which they have taken reservations. This should mean that the effect of reservations in relation to trade between reserving and non-reserving parties is minimal because non-parties must produce documentation comparable to that required of parties. In practice, however, reservations can be very damaging. Not only can reserving parties trade freely with non-parties, but reservations sometimes encourage trade to continue, albeit illegally, with other parties. For example, Japan submitted a reservation to the Appendix I listing of green, hawksbill and olive Ridley turtles (*Chelonia mydas, Eretmochelys imbricata* and *Lepidochelys olivacea*). Under political pressure from the USA, Japan withdrew its reservation in 1994.[125] However, when the reservation was valid, Japan imported over 25,000 kilos of turtle-skin and over 10,000 kilos of turtle leather (mostly green and

[122] Article XXIII(2). [123] Articles XV(3) and XVI(2).
[124] France and Italy have now withdrawn their reservations.
[125] See Sand, *supra* n. 17, p. 39.

olive Ridley turtles) in 1981 alone. Japan also imported over 50,000 kilos of raw and worked tortoiseshell (mostly hawksbill turtles). Almost all these imports of turtle leather came from Mexico, then a non-party, but almost all imports of worked tortoiseshell came from Indonesia, which was by then a party. Ecuador, the Philippines, Kenya, Tanzania, the Seychelles, Pakistan, Nicaragua and Panama were other CITES parties which exported wild caught Appendix I sea turtles to Japan in significant quantities in 1981, notwithstanding that international commercial trade in Appendix I species was prohibited.[126]

Another damaging effect of a reservation is that parties are under no obligation to provide the Secretariat with data on trade in species on which they have made reservations because they are deemed to be non-parties with respect to those species. Valuable statistical material for the purposes of monitoring trade may therefore be lost. Recognising this, the Gaborone Conference in 1983 called on parties to maintain and report trading statistics for species on which they have reservations.[127] The Conference of the Parties has also recommended that parties which have entered reservations on the inclusion of a species in Appendix I should treat it as an Appendix II species.[128] This recommendation was made because of the Convention's provision that a party with a reservation on a species shall be treated as a non-party with respect to trade in that species.

Despite the adoption of the various recommendations at the 1983 Gaborone Conference, there is clear evidence that some parties have chosen not to implement them,[129] and it has been recognised that 'reservations made by importing countries allow loopholes through which specimens illegally acquired in the countries of origin can find legal markets without any control whatsoever'.[130] It is, however, important to note that no member state of the European Union currently has a reservation lodged against an Appendix I or II species as a result of an approach instigated by the European Commission since the adoption of regional legislation implementing CITES in late 1982. A variety of reservations by member states were withdrawn as a result of this policy and there is no doubt this has been a significant development in reducing the impact of reservations on the CITES regulatory regime bearing in mind the importance of the EU as a focal point for wildlife trade. The

[126] See *Sea Turtles in Trade* (Center for Environmental Education, 1983), pp. 1–14.
[127] Resolution Conf. 4.25 (Rev. CoP 14). [128] Ibid.
[129] Resolution Conf. 11.3 (Rev. CoP 14), preamble. [130] Ibid.

European Union's policy is designed to ensure consistency of approach at the international level amongst its member states, as well as to facilitate the functioning of the EU's internal market.

8. Ensuring compliance with treaty obligations

The Standing Committee plays a pivotal role in ensuring compliance. It effectively acts as a compliance committee in the absence of a formal committee of this nature.[131] The Conference of the Parties, the Secretariat and both the Animals and Plants Committees (particularly within the 'Review of Trade' procedure discussed below) also play important roles, and it is of particular interest that much of the compliance system of CITES has evolved over many years by means of CoP resolutions and decisions.[132]

The Standing Committee deals with issues relating to the monitoring and assessment of compliance, the verification of information, and the giving of advice to parties on compliance issues.[133] It also takes a number of measures to facilitate compliance. These ask the party concerned to produce a special report on an issue; issuing a written caution; advising as to specific capacity-building issues; offering assistance in a given state on invitation by such a state; issuing a warning that a state is not complying with its obligations in relation to, for example, reporting or the adoption of national implementing legislation; and asking for a compliance action plan to be submitted indicating those steps a given state will take to bring it back into compliance and a timescale within which it will take such action.[134] Additionally, the Standing Committee can publicly notify parties through the Secretariat that a particular compliance issue has been drawn to the attention of a state and that no satisfactory response has as yet been provided.[135] Where there is evidence of 'unresolved and persistent' non-compliance and the party has shown no intent to remedy the issue, or a non-party fails to produce documentation comparable to that required of CITES

[131] R. Reeve, 'CITES' (pp. 134–60), in G. Ulfstein (ed.) *Making Treaties Work: Human Rights, Environment and Arms Control* (Cambridge University Press, 2007), p. 136.

[132] Ibid. See in particular the 2000 Resolution Conf. 11.7 (Rev. CoP 14) re national reports, the 2002 Resolution Conf. 12.8 (Rev. CoP 13) re 'review of trade' procedure, and the 2000 Resolution Conf. 11.3 (Rev. CoP 14) re compliance and enforcement. Note also Decision 14.29 re national implementing laws.

[133] Resolution Conf. 14.3, para. 12. [134] Resolution Conf. 14.3, para. 29. [135] Ibid.

parties in relation to a CITES-listed species, the Standing Committee can recommend that commercial or all trade be suspended.[136] For example, in July 2005 the Standing Committee recommended that all parties should cease trading in CITES-listed species with Nigeria due to a lack of adequate legislation in that country and concerns as to its implementation of CITES. This recommendation remains in effect at the beginning of 2010.

As well as having the ability to delegate issues in this field to the Standing Committee, the CoP reviews Standing Committee decisions as required, gives general policy guidance on compliance, and 'directs and oversees the handling of compliance matters particularly through the identification of key obligations and procedures'.[137] The Secretariat, on the other hand, assists all other CITES Committees and the CoP in relation to their compliance roles.[138] It also collects and assesses information relating to compliance from parties; provides advice on, and makes recommendations in relation to, achieving compliance; and monitors the implementation of decisions concerning non-compliance.[139] When compliance issues come to light, parties are given time to address them 'within reasonable time limits',[140] but in the absence of effective remedial action the Secretariat brings the matter to the notice of the Standing Committee.

When the Secretariat is satisfied that a listed species is being affected adversely by trade or that the provisions of the treaty are not being effectively implemented, it is required to 'communicate such information to the authorised Management Authority of the Party or Parties concerned'.[141] The Secretariat at times issues confidential 'alerts' – for example, in 2003 two were issued on the smuggling of ivory and illegal trade from Afghanistan. Another example of the Secretariat's role in relation to compliance is provided by its technical work in Paraguay.[142] After concerns were raised regarding the implementation of CITES in Paraguay, the secretary-general and two other Secretariat personnel visited the country in September 2003. Due to the numerous changes in the Paraguayan government, it became clear that there was a lack of knowledge of CITES issues. In addition, illegal trade was apparent and

136 Ibid., para. 30. 137 Ibid., para. 10. 138 Ibid., para. 14. 139 Ibid.
140 Ibid., para. 20. 141 Article XIII(1).
142 CITES Secretariat, 'Enforcement Matters' (document prepared for the fiftieth meeting of the Standing Committee 15–19 March 2004, SC50 Doc.28).

exacerbated by the fact that national legislation was inadequate. As a consequence, Paraguay introduced a voluntary ban on wildlife trade until appropriate remedial action to the satisfaction of both the Secretariat and Paraguay itself had been introduced.

a) National legislation implementing CITES

The Secretariat identifies those parties that have failed to adopt adequate national legislation to implement CITES,[143] and can offer technical assistance to remedy the situation. In 1992 the National Legislation Project was established to review and evaluate national implementing measures. As previously noted, failure to adopt appropriate national laws can result in the Standing Committee of CITES recommending a suspension of trade in CITES-listed species with the party which has failed to comply. As of July 2009 it has been recommended that all trade with Djibouti, Mauritania, Rwanda and Somalia be suspended due to failure to adopt adequate national legislation.

b) Records and reports

Article VIII obliges each party to maintain detailed records of trade in specimens of species included in the Appendices[144] and to submit annual reports to the Secretariat summarising the trade.[145] The Secretariat is responsible for reviewing these reports[146] and, as such, plays a key role in ensuring compliance. The Secretariat has arranged for the United Nations Environment Programme–World Conservation Monitoring Centre (UNEP–WCMC) to computerise the statistics so that a detailed analysis of international trade can be produced on a species-by-species level. Once on the database, data are checked automatically and UNEP–WCMC itself notifies parties on behalf of the Secretariat if any inconsistencies are found.[147] The parties have determined that failure to submit an annual report on time 'constitutes a major problem with the implementation of the Convention which the Secretariat shall refer to the Standing Committee'.[148] The Standing Committee has been given the authority to decide which parties have failed without adequate justification to provide reports for three consecutive years,[149] and following such

[143] Resolution Conf. 8.4 (Rev. CoP 14). [144] Article VIII(6). [145] Article VIII(7)(a).
[146] Article XII(2)(d). [147] CITES Secretariat Annual Report for 2003, p. 5.
[148] Resolution Conf. 11.17 (Rev CoP 14). [149] Ibid.

a determination parties are recommended to suspend trade in CITES-listed species with any such defaulting state.[150]

The primary function of annual reports is to monitor international trade in wildlife covered by CITES, and numerous recommendations have been made with a view to making the annual reports more effective as a monitoring instrument.[151] In March 1982 the Secretariat circulated Guidelines for the Preparation of CITES Annual Reports to all parties with a view to increasing the number of reports submitted and to making these reports more uniform in nature. The guidelines have subsequently been amended over time and recommend a standardised format for reports to follow. They also provide specific instructions as to how information should be presented.[152]

In some respects, statistical material gathered from parties' annual reports has been useful. It has, for example, provided a general picture of the extent of trade in many species and of the countries involved in the trade, and it has revealed instances of illegal trade. For example, an analysis of parties' annual reports led the Secretariat to notice a marked increase of wildlife exports originating in Paraguay in 1978, and further investigation revealed that large quantities of wildlife were being smuggled into Paraguay from neighbouring countries and then exported to Europe with forged permits.[153] On the other hand, information received from annual reports has not been as useful as it should have been. Some countries fail to report at all and those that have submitted reports have often been late in so doing. Annual reports should be submitted before 31 October of the year following the year covered by the report. The Secretariat has noted that 'reporting still appears to be viewed as a burdensome obligation rather than a useful management tool',[154] and that

> [s]ince the Convention's entry into force, on-time submission levels for annual reports have waxed and waned between 60 per cent and 35 per cent. Overall submission levels can reach 80 per cent or higher about

[150] Ibid. [151] See currently Resolution Conf. 11.17 (Rev. CoP 14).

[152] CITES Secretariat, Guidelines for the Preparation and Submission of CITES Annual Reports (as amended).

[153] See Proceedings of the Third Meeting of the Conference of the Parties, Doc. 3.6, Annex 3, pp. 297–303. See also Proceedings of the Fourth Meeting of the Conference of the Parties, Doc. 4.8, para. 12.2, pp. 307–9.

[154] CITES Secretariat, 'Annual Reports' prepared for the 12th Conference of the Parties at Santiago, 3–15 November 2002 (CoP 12 Doc. 22.1).

> three years after the deadline for a particular annual report but the trade data being reported are quite old by that time.[155]

This is not a record to be proud of, and it means that the information derived from national reports reveals a limited picture of the true extent of international trade in wildlife. Too often those reports that are actually submitted are not of a high quality and can be incomplete in that only trade in certain species is covered. This is often due to the fact that various institutions at the national level have responsibilities in the area of wildlife trade but only some contribute to the national annual report.[156] As of July 2009 it has been recommended that all commercial trade with Somalia in CITES-listed species and all trade with Mauritania in CITES-listed species be suspended due to their failure to submit annual reports. The CoP has urged those parties 'experiencing problems with the regular preparation and submission of annual or biennial reports to seek assistance from the Secretariat to produce such reports'.[157]

The parties are also required to submit biennial reports on the legislative, regulatory and administrative measures they have taken to enforce the provisions of CITES.[158] Biennial reporting should be submitted by 31 October following the last year covered by the report. However, reporting obligations appear not to be taken seriously by many parties. The 2005–6 report was due by the end of October 2007 but just thirty-two parties complied with this deadline.[159] Some parties have reported late, but too often parties have failed to submit and, as a result, up-to-date information is often sparse on national implementation of CITES.

c) Review of Significant Trade procedure

Although the export of tens of thousands of specimens of an Appendix II species in one year is not necessarily illegal, the Gaborone Conference recognised that there are some heavily traded Appendix II species about which there is insufficient information on their ability to withstand such levels of trade. The Conference also acknowledged that parties are not always able to comply with the requirement of Article IV of CITES that

[155] Ibid. [156] Ibid. [157] Resolution Conf. 11.17 (Rev CoP 14).
[158] Ibid., Article VIII(7)(b).
[159] Most of these reports were submitted by developed states but a not insignificant number were submitted by developing states (Congo, Costa Rica, Cuba, Ethiopia, Mauritania, Thailand).

exports of Appendix II species shall be limited to a level which is not detrimental to their survival and which will maintain these species throughout their range at levels consistent with their roles in the ecosystems in which they occur. Worried about the possible adverse effects of excessive trade in some species, the Gaborone Conference recommended that the CITES Technical Committee should identify those Appendix II species that are subject to 'significant' international trade and for which scientific information on their capacity to withstand such levels of trade is insufficient to comply with the requirements of the Convention, as determined by the range states of the species. The Gaborone Conference also recommended that the then CITES Technical Committee should (1) at the request of the states involved, develop and negotiate measures necessary to ensure that trade in these species meets the requirements of the Convention and (2) encourage parties to develop agreements for the co-operative implementation of these measures.[160]

The work of the now defunct Technical Committee in relation to significant international trade was passed to the Animals Committee and the Plants Committee at the Ottawa CoP in 1987.[161] As a consequence of the work of these Committees, the Kyoto Conference in 1992 adopted the 'Review of Significant Trade' procedure.[162] Under this procedure the Animals or Plants Committees are obliged to co-operate with the Secretariat and experts, and consult with range states, in order to review biological, trade and other relevant information on Appendix II species subject to significant levels of trade. In this way problems and solutions can be identified in relation to the exercise of the tasks placed on Scientific Authorities to assess whether trade in such species would be detrimental to the survival of the species concerned, and to monitor exports of Appendix II species.

Under the procedure, UNEP–WCMC is to provide the Secretariat with statistics of recorded net levels of exports in Appendix II species. This and any other relevant information is taken into account in the selection of species of priority concern for review by the Animals or Plants Committees. Once a particular species is selected, the Secretariat invites comments relating to possible problems in implementation of Article IV from range states. In the light of these comments, the Animals

[160] Resolution Conf. 4.7. [161] Resolution Conf. 6.1.
[162] Resolution Conf. 8.9 (Rev.) in relation to this procedure was adopted at Kyoto and has now been replaced by Resolution Conf. 12.8 (Rev. CoP 13) entitled Review of Significant Trade in specimens of Appendix II species.

or the Plants Committee can indicate satisfaction with the way in which Article IV is implemented. However, if not satisfied, the Secretariat compiles information on the species in issue and provisionally categorises the species into one of three categories: 'species of urgent concern'; 'species of possible concern'; and 'species of least concern'. Range states are then given another chance to comment. The Animals or the Plants Committee then reviews all collected information and can amend the Secretariat's categorisation. 'Species of least concern' will then be eliminated from the review. For the other classes of species, the Animals or the Plants Committee will make appropriate recommendations directed to the range states; these can include the establishment of cautious export quotas and temporary restrictions on trade. If recommendations are heeded, the Secretariat will notify all parties that the species is no longer subject to the procedure. However, if recommendations are not implemented, the Standing Committee can decide on appropriate action which may ultimately include the suspension of trade in a species with the range state in question. As of July 2009 the Standing Committee recommended a suspension in trade with Armenia in relation to the saker falcon (*Falco cherrug*) and with Grenada regarding the Queen conch (*Strombus gigas*) due to the failure of these states to implement recommendations of the Animals or the Plants Committee. Another useful example of the Significant Trade procedure is also provided by the Animals Committee's review of the status of sturgeons and paddlefish (Acipenseriformes), which highlighted the danger to the Caspian and Black Sea populations caused in particular by illegal fishing. In June 2001 the Standing Committee made several recommendations to be implemented by Azerbaijan, Kazakhstan, the Russian Federation and Turkmenistan by specified deadlines. There is evidence that these range states had 'satisfactorily implemented' certain actions and 'substantially complied' with most other recommendations in line with these deadlines.[163] Recommendations included the establishment of a long-term survey programme which now forms the basis of sturgeon stocks management in the Caspian Sea.

Another example concerns the decision by the Animals Committee to include the Indochinese box turtle (*Cuora galbinifrons*) and the Malaysian box turtle (*Cuora amboinensis*) in the Review of Significant Trade procedure in late 2000. As a consequence of the review,

[163] See forty-seventh meeting of the Standing Committee, Santiago (Chile), 1–2 November 2002 (document SC47 Doc.11).

recommendations were made to Vietnam and Laos but were not implemented by these range countries, with the consequence that in July 2009 the Standing Committee recommended to parties that trade in the Malaysian box turtle with Vietnam and that trade in the Indochinese box turtle with both Laos and Vietnam be suspended. Such recommendations to suspend trade can be in place for a considerable length of time. Current recommendations in place include trade suspensions between parties and Tanzania with regard to Fischer's lovebirds (*Agapornis fischeri*) and pancake tortoises (*Malacochersus tornieri*). These recommendations date back to 1993.

9. National and regional enforcement

There are real practical problems with the enforcement of the Convention. Often it is very difficult to identify illegal trade, particularly bearing in mind the sheer volume of trade; in the EU alone 'over 7000 seizures involving over 3.5 million CITES-listed specimens' were made in the 2003–4 period.[164] Officials are often underresourced and inadequately trained, and effecting appropriate control mechanisms is a problem shared by all parties – especially developing states due to their socioeconomic and geographic circumstances. International and regional co-operative programmes to improve law enforcement are therefore to be welcomed. One of the most significant regional initiatives has been the 1994 Lusaka Agreement on Co-operative Enforcement Operations Directed at Illegal Trade in Wild Fauna and Flora.[165] Another example is the ASEAN Wildlife Enforcement Network (ASEAN-WEN) established in December 2005.[166]

[164] Engler and Parry-Jones, *supra* n. 4, p. 12.

[165] 1 *JIWLP* (1998) 155. The Lusaka Agreement entered into force on 10 December 1996 and the Lusaka Agreement Task Force was established in June 1999; it is located in Nairobi, Kenya. The Lusaka Agreement has been ratified by the Republic of Congo, Kenya, Uganda, Zambia, the United Republic of Tanzania and the Kingdom of Lesotho. The agreement is open to accession by any African state and is designed to reduce illegal traffic in endangered species, particularly operations carried out by traders across national boundaries. For further information on the Lusaka Agreement see its website, www.lusakaagreement.org.

[166] The ten ASEAN countries participate in this regional network (Brunei, Cambodia, Indonesia, Laos, Malaysia, Myanmar, the Philippines, Singapore, Thailand and Vietnam). It seeks to improve the capacity of and collaboration between those responsible for law enforcement in the region. See further www.asean-wen.org.

Recognising that more than two-thirds of the parties are developing countries with special difficulties in staffing, training and equipping their Management and Scientific Authorities, the New Delhi Conference urged parties to make appropriate technical assistance available to developing countries and requested the Secretariat to seek external funding for this purpose.[167] It is still, however, recognised that developing states have particular difficulties in enforcement, and the Secretariat has been directed to provide more training and technical help for such countries.[168] During 2002 and 2003, the Secretariat received external funding totalling approximately US$2.77 million, of which over US$1 million was received from the European Commission. Projects funded by external sources during this time included a survey of musk consumption in traditional Chinese medicine, a regional legislation workshop for East, South and South East Asia, a wildlife law enforcement training course for tiger range states, and the African elephant range states dialogue meeting held in October 2002.[169] During 2002 and 2003, Secretariat staff additionally undertook missions upon invitation to technical law enforcement training workshops in Anguilla, Dubai and Kenya. Moreover, the Capacity Building Unit of the Secretariat participated in a variety of workshops involving fifty-nine parties and three non-parties.[170] These included capacity-building workshops in Cambodia, Madagascar, Saint Lucia, the United Arab Emirates and Zambia.

Article VIII of the Convention requires the parties to take a number of different measures that are designed to improve the Convention's level of enforcement.[171] These include penalising trade which violates the terms of the Convention, confiscating illegally traded specimens and designating special ports of exit and entry for wildlife. The importance of prompt passing of information between governments has also been emphasised; in 2006 a significant consignment of illegal ivory was found by Hong Kong customs officials in a single container. This information was shared internationally and led to the seizure of two further containers by

[167] Resolution Conf. 3.4. [168] Resolution Conf. 11.3 (Rev. CoP 14).
[169] See *supra* n. 13 in relation to sources of external funding.
[170] CITES Secretariat Annual Report for 2003, pp. 3–4.
[171] On steps recommended to improve compliance and enforcement generally, see Resolution Conf. 11.3 (Rev. CoP 13). Also see Resolution Conf. 14.3, which established a Guide to CITES Compliance Procedures describing procedures to 'facilitate consistent and effective handling of compliance matters relating to obligations under the Convention'.

Cameroonian officials. These containers had been prepared for the transport of further quantities of illegal ivory.[172]

a) *Penalties*

Article VIII requires each party to take measures to penalise trade which violates the terms of the Convention and to penalise possession of specimens which have been so traded.[173] However, CITES gives no guidance as to the level of penalties which should be imposed on persons convicted of illegal trade or possession, with the result that there has been a considerable variation in the punishments inflicted. For example, Hong Kong made some 350 prosecutions under its Animals and Plants (Protection of Endangered Species) Ordinance between June 1978 and November 1981,[174] but a fine of approximately US$1,000 was the highest penalty levied because it was the maximum allowed under the Ordinance at that time. Thus, although a trader who had illegally imported 319 cheetah skins into Hong Kong in 1979 was fined the maximum amount, the fine bore no relation to the value of the shipment. However, in 1997 the relevant Hong Kong Ordinance was amended to allow for the imposition of a HK$5 million fine (approximately US$640,000) and a term of imprisonment of up to two years.[175] Of course, these represent maximum penalties in Hong Kong. A recent prosecution is more indicative of actual fines imposed in practice and arguably underlines that the imposition of inadequate fines remains an issue. Over three hundred live Indian star tortoises (listed on Appendix II) were found in an unclaimed bag on a flight from Malaysia, leading to the imposition on the offender of a HK$29,000 fine (approximately US$3,700) for illegal importation and a HK$1,000 fine (approximately US$130) for animal cruelty, together with a two-month suspended prison sentence.[176]

There are a growing number of cases in which offenders have been imprisoned. An individual thought to be responsible for widespread

[172] CITES Secretariat press release, 'Governments Join Forces through CITES to Catch Wildlife Criminals' 7 June 2007.

[173] Article VIII(1)(a).

[174] Comment made to Simon Lyster by C. Huxley, ex-enforcement officer, Hong Kong Management Authority.

[175] Animals and Plants (Protection of Endangered Species) Ordinance, Cap 187, §13A. This ordinance was repealed by the Protection of Endangered Species of Animals and Plants Ordinance in late 2006. The maximum fine and period of imprisonment remain the same (HK$5,000,000 and imprisonment for two years).

[176] (2005) 20(2) *Traffic Bulletin* 85.

criminal activity in wildlife in India was sentenced to five years' imprisonment in April 2004. This sentence was the harshest then imposed in India under the Wild Life (Protection) Act 1972.[177] In August 2004, following their conviction for poaching of and trading in the Sumatran tiger (*Panthera tigris*), five individuals were imprisoned for six years and also fined 70 million rupiah (approximately US$7,750).[178] It is thought that in the preceding ten-year period a minimum of sixty tigers were sold by the network to which these five people were connected.[179] Moreover, a smuggler or trader in rare birds was given the then-longest prison sentence given by a UK court for a wildlife offence of six and a half years after being arrested at Heathrow Airport in July 2000.[180] He was involved in the smuggling of twenty-three Appendix II-listed birds which had been placed in tubes fifteen centimetres in diameter for their flight from Bangkok. Around a quarter of the birds died in the flight. The offender was also found to have been keeping a large number of endangered birds at premises in Norfolk. In China, penalties can be even more severe; in March 2009 a smuggler of saker falcons was sentenced to death, and three accomplices to life imprisonment.[181]

There is certainly evidence that some parties will impose both heavy fines and prison terms on offenders; a Canadian in 2008 was sentenced in the US to five years' imprisonment and fined US$100,000 for illegally smuggling ivory from Cameroon.[182] However, the level of fines imposed by courts has at times been disappointing, a recent report noting that 'even EU Member States with legislation allowing for high penalties may find that illegal traders escape heavy fines or imprisonment because prosecutors do not understand the impact that illegal trade can have on species, ecosystems and livelihoods'.[183]

b) Confiscation

Article VIII also requires each party to provide for the confiscation of live or dead specimens which have been illegally traded or possessed.[184] Although it may be a valuable deterrent to illegal trade, confiscation

[177] Ibid. [178] Ibid., p. 86. [179] Ibid.

[180] (2002) 19(2) *Traffic Bulletin* 2. See also the jailing for two and a half years in 2000 of a smuggler of nine Lear's macaws (estimated to be worth £50,000 per breeding pair); news.bbc.co.uk/1/hi/uk/713604.stm.

[181] (2009) 22(2) *Traffic Bulletin* 76. [182] (2008) 22(1) *Traffic Bulletin* 40.

[183] Engler and Parry-Jones, *supra* n. 4, p. 14. [184] Article VIII(1)(b).

creates its own problems, particularly with respect to the disposal of confiscated stock. The problem of disposal of Appendix I specimens is particularly serious because re-entry into commercial trade is prohibited. CITES requires that confiscated live specimens are either returned to their state of export or sent to a rescue centre or other appropriate place.[185] In relation to the disposal of confiscated live specimens included in the Appendices, Conference Resolution 10.7 provides very detailed guidance. The resolution urges Management Authorities to refer to their Scientific Authority for advice on the issue of returning specimens to the wild, and that the Scientific Authority take into account certain guidelines outlined in detail in the resolution's first two annexes when giving that advice. The Harare Conference, in adopting this resolution, therefore accepted that return to the wild can indeed be a viable option if carried out with careful planning. However, it noted also that '[p]oorly planned releases of confiscated animals may doom these animals to a slow, painful death. Such release may also have strong negative conservation value by threatening existing wild populations.'[186] Potential threats to existing wild populations include the spread of diseases picked up by the returning specimen while the latter was in captivity, release of confiscated specimens in an area which is not in fact inhabited in the wild by the exact subspecies in question, and the return of specimens which have acquired 'inappropriate behavioural repertoire from individuals or other related species'[187] whilst in captivity. The resolution therefore makes the point that the decision whether or not to return a specimen to the wild is not one to be taken lightly, and that in certain cases euthanasia 'may often prove the most appropriate and most humane'.[188]

Other difficulties, notably the cost involved, inevitably make cases of return to the wild relatively rare, particularly since the Convention stipulates that the expenses involved should be met by the state of export,[189] which is normally a developing country. However, some parties, such as Australia and the UK, have enacted legislation authorising customs officials to recover from the importer any expenses incurred in returning confiscated live specimens to their country of origin. The Harare Conference approved of such a stance, noting that 'the successful recovery of the costs of confiscation and disposal from the

[185] Article VIII(4)(b). [186] Resolution Conf. 10.7, Annex I. [187] Ibid. [188] Ibid.
[189] Article VIII(4)(b).

guilty party may be a disincentive for illegal trade'.[190] Parties have been urged to adopt appropriate legislation in this regard.[191]

Despite very apparent difficulties, there have been cases of live specimens being returned to their state of export. Ten Appendix II-listed black kites (*Milvus migrans*) were, for example, returned by Belgium to Douala (Cameroon) in January 2005.[192] In December 2004 ninety parrots native to Mexico were seized by US officials. These included over twenty red-crowned Amazons (*Amazona viridigenalis*) listed in Appendix I. All of the parrots were returned to Mexico.[193]

In relation to dead specimens of Appendix I species, parties are urged to store or destroy specimens unless they can be transferred for legitimate 'scientific/educational or enforcement/identification reasons'.[194] Dead specimens of Appendix II and III species should be disposed of 'in the best manner possible to benefit enforcement and administration of the Convention'.[195]

c) Ports of exit and entry

Article VIII(3) urges each party to designate special ports of exit and entry through which all exports and imports of wildlife must pass. Recognising that identification of wildlife, especially parts and derivatives, is very difficult and that enforcement of CITES is a complex matter, Article VIII(3) was intended to encourage parties to build up expertise among their enforcement officers in a few ports and then to channel all trade through these ports. In this way delay for legal traders will be minimised and smuggling hopefully reduced because it would enable a few experts in species identification to inspect the bulk of the trade. With the designation of Houston, Louisville and Memphis with effect from January 2005, the US had at that time, for example, designated seventeen ports.[196] All member states of the European Union are legally obliged to designate ports of entry and exit for both dead and live wildlife specimens of CITES species,[197] and appropriate customs offices at these nominated ports must be 'provided with sufficient and adequately trained staff'.[198]

[190] Resolution Conf. 10.7. This might be regarded as a quasi 'polluter-pays' approach.
[191] Resolution Conf. 9.10 (Rev. CoP 14). [192] (2005) 20(2) *Traffic Bulletin* 83.
[193] Ibid., p. 88. [194] Resolution Conf. 9.10 (Rev. CoP 14). [195] Ibid.
[196] US *Federal Register*, 69(233), 6 December 2004, p. 70379.
[197] Council Regulation 338/97 on the Protection of Species of Wild Fauna and Flora by Regulating Trade therein, OJ 1997 L61/1, Article 12(1).
[198] Ibid., Article 12(2).

Evidence suggests that the designation of ports of exit and entry has helped combat illegal trade,[199] although there are concerns that other ports may be targeted by smugglers in the knowledge that customs officers at these ports would not be as educated and experienced in identifying illegal trade.[200]

10. Relationship with other international treaties

An important aim of CITES' Strategic Vision 2008–2013 is to 'contribute to significantly reducing the rate of biodiversity loss by ensuring that CITES and other multilateral instruments and processes are coherent and mutually supportive'.[201] Both the CITES and CBD treaties share a mutual goal of ensuring that use of wildlife is sustainable and there is certainly evidence of co-operation between these regimes in recent years.[202] CITES' Plants Committee has, for example, been authorised to collaborate with the CBD's Global Strategy for Plant Conservation particularly to ensure that flora is not endangered by international trade.[203] Additionally, representatives from the CBD have participated in the CITES Bushmeat Working Group. In April 2004 an expert workshop was held to discuss ways to improve co-operation between the two regimes,[204] and the CITES Conference of the Parties has urged 'the Parties who are also Parties to the CBD to take effective measures at policy and institutional level to ensure synergy between their implementation of CITES and CBD at the national level'.[205]

The CITES Secretariat is an active participant in the Liaison Group of Biodiversity-Related Conventions, together with representatives from the World Heritage Convention, the Ramsar Convention, the Bonn Convention, the International Treaty on Plant Genetic Resources for Food and Agriculture, and the CBD. This group meets regularly to enhance co-operation between these key treaty regimes.[206]

[199] See, for example, US *Federal Register*, 46(169), 1 September 1981, p. 43834.

[200] Wijnstekers, *supra* n. 71, pp. 194–5. [201] Resolution Conf. 14.2.

[202] In March 1995 a Memorandum of Cooperation was signed between the CBD and CITES Secretariats. See also Resolution Conf. 10.4 (Rev. 14) on co-operation and synergy between the two regimes.

[203] Decision 14.14.

[204] See the final report of the Expert Workshop Promoting CITES–CBD Cooperation and Synergy at www.cbd.int/cooperation/final-report-CITES%20CBD_Vilm_Workshop_Report.doc.

[205] Resolution Conf. 13.2 (Rev. CoP 14).

[206] On the Liaison Group see www.cbd.int/cooperation/related-conventions/blg.shtml.

Additionally, signed Memoranda of Understanding by the CITES Secretariat include one signed with the Bonn Convention Secretariat,[207] and another signed with the Lusaka Agreement Task Force.[208] CITES resolutions have been adopted fostering co-operation with the IWC (particularly concerning illegal trade in whale parts),[209] the International Tropical Timber Organization (in relation to, for example, bigleaf mahogany and ramin),[210] and CCAMLR regarding trade in toothfish.[211]

11. Regional economic integration organisations

The second extraordinary meeting of the Conference of the Parties, held in Gaborone immediately following the conclusion of the Gaborone Conference, agreed to amend Article XXI of CITES in order to allow 'regional economic integration organisations constituted by sovereign States which have competence in respect of the negotiation, conclusion and implementation of international agreements in matters transferred to them by their Member States and covered by this Convention' to accede to the Convention (the Gaborone Amendment). The amendment was adopted at the instigation of the then European Economic Community (now the European Union), which is anxious to become a party to CITES. The Gaborone Amendment has yet to enter into force. It requires fifty-four of the eighty states (two-thirds of the then state parties) that were party to the Convention on 30 April 1983 to deposit their instruments of acceptance. Progress on acceptance has been slow. As of the end of 2009, forty-seven of these states had accepted the amendment. Nevertheless, the European Union has implemented the provisions of CITES since the beginning of 1984.[212] Indeed, CITES Article XIV(1)a expressly states that the provisions of CITES do not affect the right of each party to introduce stricter trading measures than

207 Signed on 18 September 2002. See also Resolution Conf. 13.3 on co-operation with the Convention on the Conservation of Migratory Species of Wild Animals (CMS).

208 Signed on 11 April 2000.

209 Resolution Conf. 11.4 (Rev. CoP 12) on the relationship between CITES and the International Whaling Commission.

210 Resolution Conf. 14.4 on co-operation between CITES and ITTO regarding trade in tropical timber.

211 Resolution Conf. 12.4 on co-operation with the Commission for the Conservation of Antarctic Marine Living Resources regarding trade in toothfish.

212 Currently implemented by Council Regulation 338/97, *supra* n. 197, and Commission Regulation 1808/2001 OJ 2001 L250/1.

are required by the Convention, and several parties, especially member states of the European Union, have exercised this right. For example, as a result of regional legislation implementing CITES,[213] EU member states require import permits for the import of Appendix II species notwithstanding that CITES insists only on permits from the state of export.

12. Conclusion

Most of the major wildlife trading nations are now parties to CITES. International trade in the majority of Appendix I and II species is certainly more carefully regulated than before CITES came into force. CITES can justifiably claim much of the credit in this regard. Of all the reasons for the relative success of CITES, it is its administrative system which stands out. The existence of a permanent Secretariat and the numerous administrative obligations imposed on the parties – to set up at least two bodies to enforce the Convention, to communicate regularly with other parties, to communicate regularly with the Secretariat and to meet regularly to review implementation of the Convention – are all critical factors. In simple terms, there is no chance of CITES becoming a 'sleeping treaty' which its parties can safely ignore.

On the other hand, problems most certainly still exist. The CITES Strategic Vision 2008–2013 adopted at The Hague in 2007 underlines that 'the proper functioning of the Convention depends to a great extent on the commitment of parties to comply with and implement the Convention and its principles'.[214] However, there is much room for improvement in effecting compliance with and enforcement of CITES obligations,[215] and the illegal trade in wildlife has been recognised by the parties as continuing to be a 'major concern'.[216] The length and complexity of the Appendices makes the already difficult task of enforcement officers that much harder, and there is also very clearly insufficient implementation in some countries in relation to surveillance and the issuing of permits. The level of fines imposed on those involved in illegal traffic can be frustratingly inadequate to deter effectively. Moreover, securing sufficient financial resources to implement the Convention

[213] Council Regulation 338/97, *supra* n. 197, Article 4(2).
[214] Resolution Conf. 14.2.
[215] See J. E. Baker, 'A Substantive Theory of the Relative Efficiency of Environmental Treaty Compliance Strategies: The Case of CITES' (1999) 2(1) *JIWLP* 1. Also see Reeve, *supra* n. 131, pp. 134–60.
[216] Resolution Conf. 11.3 (Rev. CoP 14).

effectively is an ever-present problem. Additionally, despite efforts to improve capacity building, Management and Scientific Authorities are too often understaffed and their personnel inadequately trained and communication between Management Authorities could certainly be improved in many instances, as could the rate of submission of annual reports to the Secretariat.

Recommended further reading

R. Hepworth, 'The Independent Review of CITES' (1998) 1 *JIWLP* 412

R. Reeve, 'CITES' (pp. 134–60), in G. Ulfstein (ed.), *Making Treaties Work: Human Rights, Environment and Arms Control* (Cambridge University Press, 2007)

P. H. Sand, 'Japan's "Research Whaling" in the Antarctic Southern Ocean and the North Pacific Ocean in the Face of the Endangered Species Convention (CITES)' 2008 17(1) *RECIEL* 56

P. H. Sand, 'Whither CITES? The Evolution of a Treaty Regime in the Borderline of Trade and the Environment' (1997) 8 *EJIL* 29

S. Theile, A. Steiner and K. Kecse-Nagy, *Expanding Borders: New Challenges for Wildlife Trade Controls in the EU* (TRAFFIC, 2004)

W. Wijnstekers, *The Evolution of CITES* (CITES, 8th ed., 2005)

Chapter 16

The Convention on the Conservation of Migratory Species

1. Background

Amongst the measures agreed at the 1972 Stockholm Conference was Recommendation 32 of the Action Plan, which urged governments to consider the need to adopt international conventions in order to protect species which inhabit international waters or migrate from one territory to another. This was prompted by the realisation that failure to protect a migratory species throughout every stage of its migration could severely damage efforts to maintain or restore its population.[1] The endangered Siberian crane (*Grus leucogeranus*), for example, though relatively secure in its Russian breeding sites, has traditionally encountered various threats along its migration routes, including hunting in Pakistan and Afghanistan. Similarly, many species of North American breeding birds had suffered declines in population because of deforestation and the use of pesticides in their central and South American wintering habitats. Passerines breeding in Northern Europe have traditionally run a biannual gauntlet through the Mediterranean region, where they are shot and trapped in their thousands en route to and from their African wintering grounds. Although various existing treaties had accorded a degree of protection to migratory species, it was felt that these lacked uniformity or cohesion and covered only a proportion of the species that could benefit from international co-operation.[2]

[1] See generally R. Boardman, *International Organisation and the Conservation of Nature* (Macmillan, 1981), Chapters 5, 9; C. de Klemm, 'The Problem of Migratory Species in International Law' (1994) *Green Globe Yearbook* 67. For discussion of the diverse legal approaches to conservation along the migration route of a single species (the honey buzzard), see J. Ebbeson, '*Lex Pernis Apivorus*: An Experiment of Environmental Law Methodology' (2003) 15 *JEL* 153.

[2] For a survey of these instruments, see C. de Klemm, 'Migratory Species in International Instruments: An Overview', IUCN Envtl. Policy & Law Occasional Paper No. 2 (1986).

In response to these concerns, the German government undertook to initiate a draft convention for the conservation of migratory species and, after several years of negotiation, the Convention on the Conservation of Migratory Species of Wild Animals[3] (the Bonn Convention, also commonly known as the CMS) was concluded on 23 June 1979. The Convention entered into force on 1 November 1983.[4] It was initially slow to attract participation, and the total number of parties still falls well short of that appropriate for a conservation treaty of intended global scope,[5] but there are recent signs that it is at last beginning to make an appreciable contribution to the conservation of migratory species.

This chapter examines the objectives of the Bonn Convention; its definitions of key terms; the conservation regime it establishes, including the criteria for incorporating species in the Appendices and the nature of the obligations designed to protect them; the institutional structure and arrangements for implementation established under the Convention; and finally its relationship with other agreements.

2. Objectives

In common with other 'living instruments', the objectives of the Bonn Convention have been progressively clarified and refined over time, and lately harmonised with the Biodiversity Convention's mission to achieve a significant reduction in the rate of biodiversity loss by the year 2010.[6] As the current Strategic Plan for the CMS confirms, its primary goal is to ensure the favourable conservation status of migratory species, thereby contributing to global sustainability.[7] Within that overall remit, it aims to ensure that such species benefit from the best possible conservation measures based upon the best available information, by broadening

[3] 19 *ILM* 15.

[4] I.e. the first day of the third month following the deposit of the fifteenth instrument of ratification, etc. Article XVIII(1).

[5] By January 2010 there were 113 parties, plus two signatories. Notable absentees include the US, China, Russia, Japan and Canada, though the former three feature in a current tally of thirty-two non-parties that participate in at least one of the CMS ancillary agreements.

[6] Biodiversity Convention Strategic Plan, Decision VI/26, para. 11. The motif for the eighth CMS CoP was 'On the Move to 2010'.

[7] See 'Strategic Plan 2006–2011', Annex to Resolution 8.2, para. 29. Reports of meetings of the Conference of the Parties (CoP), together with the text of relevant resolutions, recommendations and documents, may be found in the Proceedings of the Meetings of the Conference of the Parties to the Bonn Convention, published in hard copy by the CMS Secretariat, United Nations Premises, Hermann-Ehlers-Str.10, 53113 Bonn, Germany, or (from the seventh CoP onwards) on the CMS website at www.cms.int.

awareness amongst key actors and enhancing their engagement in the conservation process.[8]

The Convention relies principally on two specific techniques. The first involves the establishment of a relatively high level of protection for those species listed in Appendix I, comprising migratory species endangered throughout all or a significant portion of their range. Such species are the subject of strict obligations for parties that are 'range states'.[9] The second, relating to Appendix II species, is noteworthy in that no obligations are directly imposed by the Convention itself; rather, it urges range states to conclude ancillary AGREEMENTS[10] for the conservation and management of such species and establishes guidelines as to what those instruments should contain. A key element is that it is sufficient for inclusion in Appendix II that a migratory species has a conservation status that would *significantly benefit* from international co-operation: it does not need to be (although it may be) actually or even potentially threatened with extinction in order to qualify. One consequence of this approach is that particular taxa may be listed concurrently under the Convention's two Appendices. This system is therefore quite different from that adopted by CITES, for example, where species are listed under one or other of the two major appendices depending upon their level of endangerment.

The motivations underlying the Bonn Convention are ostensibly anthropocentric in character. The preamble refers to the 'ever-growing value of wild animals from environmental, genetic, scientific, aesthetic, recreational, cultural, educational, social and economic points of view': there is no reference here to intrinsic value. It also states that wild animals represent 'an irreplaceable part of the earth's natural system which must be conserved for the good of mankind'. Yet it is doubtful that this emphasis has significantly affected the actual operation of the Convention, where species appear to be protected as much for their own sake as for any other reason. This is most clearly evident in the recently concluded ancillary AGREEMENT concerning gorillas,[11] which are afforded almost absolute protection against killing or taking; furthermore, should unavoidable conflict arise between the interests of humans and gorillas, it must be mitigated to the benefit of both.[12] Even

[8] Strategic Plan, paras. 30–5.

[9] For the definition of this and other important terms, see section 3 below.

[10] References to such instruments in the text of the Convention always appear in capital letters.

[11] 2007 Agreement on the Conservation of Gorillas and their Habitats, text available via CMS website.

[12] See Article III(2)(a), (j).

the CMS itself was never intended to focus primarily on commercially exploitable species; indeed, during the course of negotiations attempts were actually made by several countries, including Australia, Canada, Japan, New Zealand, the US and the USSR, to *exclude* many such species entirely (particularly finfish and shellfish) on the grounds that their inclusion could undermine other international arrangements.[13] Although these attempts were ultimately unsuccessful, it is significant that few fish species have actually been listed in the Convention's Appendices.[14] Furthermore, the preamble does not contain any presupposition of exploitation: although it refers to 'the *resources* of the earth' it states only that this legacy should be conserved and, '*where utilized*', used wisely.[15] The executive secretary to the CMS suggested in 2003 that its aim of conserving and managing migratory species and their habitats involves steering a middle course between 'protectionist' and overly exploitative approaches.[16]

3. Definitions

Definitions of several key terms are established by Article I(1).

a) Migratory species

Article I(1)(a) defines a 'migratory species' as:

> the entire population or any geographically separate part of the population of any species or lower taxon of wild animals, a significant proportion of whose members cyclically and predictably cross one or more national jurisdictional boundaries.

[13] See the Report of the US Delegation to the Conference to Conclude a Convention on the Conservation of Migratory Species of Wild Animals (US Department of State, Washington, DC, 17 October 1979). On the Japanese approach to such questions, see C. Mizukami, "Management of Highly Migratory Species and Fisheries Relations between Japan and South Pacific States" (1990) 24 *UBCLR* 127.

[14] Appendix I currently contains only four fish species, the Mekong catfish (*Pangasianodon gigas*), the white shark (*Carcharodon carcharias*), the basking shark (*Cetorhinus maximus*) and the Atlantic sturgeon (*Acipenser sturio*), while Appendix II contains fewer than thirty, all sturgeons or sharks, as to which see n. 272 *infra*.

[15] Second recital (emphasis added).

[16] A. Muller-Helmbrecht, 'Conservation versus Utilisation?' *CMS Bulletin* No. 17 (2003), pp. 1–2. CMS Resolution 8.1 pointedly recognises that sustainable utilisation may provide genuine incentives for conservation, and calls upon the Standing Committee to examine the value of the Biodiversity Convention's 2004 Addis Ababa Principles and Guidelines in that connection. Note, however, that Principle 10 of the latter expressly calls for intrinsic and other non-economic values to be taken into account in the formulation of policy.

Two points regarding this provision are noteworthy. They relate to the scientific concept of a 'species' and the circumstances in which animals will be considered 'migratory'.

The first is that, in common with other such treaties, the Convention does not seek formally to define the taxonomic concept of a species as such. Rather, it confines itself to indicating that the term is not being used in a strict scientific sense at all, but may be understood to embrace subspecies and even individual, geographically separate, parts of the population of a species. By following the precedent set by CITES and allowing such populations to be considered independently, the Bonn Convention creates considerable flexibility. It could, for example, allow limited exploitation of secure, well-managed populations of a species which is endangered globally, and therefore needs to be protected from exploitation everywhere else. Conversely, the parties may single out individual populations of a species for special protection where appropriate. Indeed, four of the original forty listings in Appendix I did consist of geographically separate populations of species rather than of the species as a whole,[17] and this device has been used quite extensively in later amendments to the Appendices.[18] Usually, however, the concept of a geographically separate population has been construed in an ecological rather than a geopolitical sense. Thus the 1994 Conference approved the addition of the 'Middle European' population of the great bustard (*Otis tarda*) to Appendix I and the 'Western Palaearctic' and 'West Eurasian and African' populations of various other avian species to Appendix II.[19] By contrast, a proposal at the following CoP to transfer the Chilean and Uruguayan populations of the black-necked swan (*Cygnus melanocorypha*) to Appendix I was rejected, on the ground that it would be inappropriate for the CMS to refer only to individual *national* populations of a species which was not globally at risk.[20] Practice in this regard has varied, however, and the desirability of maintaining compatibility with other treaty commitments has sometimes led to the specification of

[17] Namely the North West African populations of dorcas gazelle (*Gazella dorcas*) and houbara bustard (*Chlamydotis undulata*), Upper Amazon populations of the giant river turtle (*Podocnemis expansa*) and non-Peruvian populations of vicuña (*Vicugna vicugna*).

[18] See especially Proceedings of the Fourth Meeting of the CoP, Annex III.

[19] Ibid.

[20] In particular, a substantial population existed in neighbouring Argentina. See Proceedings of the Fifth Meeting of the CoP, Annex VI, paras. 51–6, and the list of species added to the Appendices in Annex III, ibid.

national populations in the Appendices,[21] whether for the purposes of inclusion or exclusion from protection.[22]

As regards the concept of a 'migratory' species, earlier drafts of the Convention spoke in terms of those whose members 'periodically' crossed national jurisdictional boundaries.[23] This definition could have included relatively sedentary species whose habitat was located in border areas, with the result that individuals might traverse national frontiers on a random basis. In the final version of the text, however, the word 'periodically' was replaced by the phrase 'cyclically and predictably', the report of the US delegation to the Final Conference suggesting that species were not to be considered migratory unless their movements were in response to seasonal or longer-term environmental influences.[24] Yet, here again, CMS practice does not reveal absolute consistency. On the one hand, the Final Conference decided to include the mountain gorilla (*Gorilla gorilla beringei*) in Appendix I,[25] even though it was uncertain whether its movements across the national boundaries between Rwanda, Uganda and Zaire (now DRC) were truly cyclical and predictable. On the other hand, the possibility of using CMS machinery for the protection of the Asian elephant (*Elephas maximus*) was rejected at the fourth CoP, following observations that that species was not genuinely migratory but tended merely to 'oscillate' across borders, and that the conservation of such species was better achieved through a separate mechanism.[26]

On the whole, it seems that the intention is not to adopt an unduly restrictive approach to this issue. In particular, CoP Resolution 2.2 established that the term 'cyclically' should be understood to relate to 'a cycle of any nature, such as astronomical (circadian, annual etc.), life or climatic, and of any frequency', while 'predictably' implied only 'that a phenomenon can be anticipated to recur in a given set of circumstances, though not necessarily regularly in time'. Further, the wording of Article

21 For current listings, effective from 5 March 2009, see the CMS website.

22 Thus, when the cheetah (*Acinonyx jubatus*) was recently listed in Appendix I, the populations in Botswana, Namibia and Zimbabwe were excluded on account of the trade quotas allocated to those countries for that species under CITES. See Report of the Ninth Meeting of the CoP, para. 229.

23 See, for example, the 1978 Second Revised Draft Convention, reprinted in *Convention on the Conservation of Migratory Species of Wild Animals* (Federal Ministry of Food, Agriculture and Forestry, Federal Republic of Germany, 1979).

24 1979 US Report, *supra* n. 13, pp. 2–4.

25 *Gorilla gorilla* and *Gorilla berengei* are now both listed, as separate species.

26 Proceedings of the Fourth Meeting, para. 105.

I(1)(a) itself, which defines a species as migratory if a 'significant proportion' of its members migrate, allows for the listing of relatively sedentary species. For example, adult Mediterranean monk seals (*Monachus monachus*) are not migratory, but the species is included in Appendix I because it is in danger of extinction and 'post breeding dispersal of young must regularly involve crossing of national frontiers'.[27] Finally, it is to be noted that Article IV(4) of the Convention in any event encourages the parties to conclude agreements for the protection of species whose members 'periodically' cross national boundaries, even though those species were not ultimately defined as migratory for CMS purposes.[28]

b) Questions of conservation status

The definition provision also clarifies the circumstances in which a species will be considered to be 'endangered' or to have an 'unfavourable conservation status'. 'Conservation status' signifies 'the sum of the influences acting on the migratory species that may affect its long-term distribution and abundance'.[29]

i) Endangered species

Article I(1)(e) states that a migratory species is considered 'endangered' if it 'is in danger of extinction throughout all or a significant portion of its range'. The practice of the parties has tended towards harmonising the Convention's approach to this issue with that of the IUCN wherever possible: thus, at the 2nd Meeting of the CoP, it was agreed that usage of this term for CMS purposes could be equated with that in the 1988 IUCN Red List of Threatened Animals.[30] At the 5th Meeting, the CoP decided to interpret 'endangered' to mean 'facing a very high risk of extinction in the wild in the near future' and, in determining eligibility for inclusion in Appendix I, to be guided by relevant findings of the IUCN Council, or by independent assessments undertaken by the CMS's own Scientific Council. The latter body itself had expressed the view that this would achieve maximum compatibility with the IUCN system 'whilst keeping within the definition given' in Article I(1)(e).[31]

27 See the Explanatory Notes on Second Revised Draft of the CMS in the German government publication, *supra* n. 23.

28 Note also the preambular reference to 'species that migrate across *or outside* national jurisdictional boundaries' (emphasis added).

29 Article I(1)(b). 30 Resolution 2.2. 31 Resolution 5.3.

ii) Unfavourable conservation status

Article I(1)(d) indicates that the conservation status of a migratory species will be considered 'unfavourable' if any of the following conditions set out in Article I(1)(c) is *not* met:[32]

(1) population dynamics data indicate that the migratory species is maintaining itself on a long-term basis as a viable component of its ecosystem;
(2) the range of the migratory species is neither currently being reduced, nor is likely to be reduced on a long-term basis;
(3) there is, and will be in the foreseeable future, sufficient habitat to maintain the population of the migratory species on a long-term basis; and
(4) the distribution and abundance of the migratory species approach historic coverage and levels to the extent that potentially suitable ecosystems exist and to the extent consistent with wise wildlife management.

c) Range states

Article I(1)(f) defines the 'range' of a migratory species as 'all the areas of land or water that [it] inhabits, stays in temporarily, crosses or overflies at any time on its normal migration route', while paragraph (h) provides that a 'Range State' is 'any State . . . that exercises jurisdiction over any part of the range of that migratory species, or a State, flag vessels of which are engaged outside national jurisdictional limits in taking that migratory species'. The reference to flag states represents a striking extension of what might normally be considered a range state of a migratory species,[33] particularly in view of the very wide definition of 'taking' which the Convention adopts.[34] Finally, in the case of listings of geographically separate populations, Resolution 3.1 indicates that a state may be considered a range state if a 'significant proportion' of such a population 'occasionally' occurs in its territory.

4. Conservation measures

The CMS regime is a relatively complex one, entailing provision for conservation measures at several different levels, which are considered

[32] I.e., Article I(1)(c) itself actually defines *favourable* conservation status.
[33] See, e.g., Resolution 8.22 on Adverse Human-Induced Impacts on Cetaceans.
[34] See Article I(1)(i) and, for discussion, section 4(c)(ii) below.

below. Central to all of them, however, is the role of range states, as defined above.

a) *Range states*

For obvious reasons, the substantive conservation obligations which the Bonn Convention creates are imposed, for the most part, upon the range states of particular species rather than upon the parties generally.[35] Furthermore, Article VI(3) imposes a formal requirement for range states to inform the CoP, through the Secretariat and at least six months prior to each ordinary meeting, of the measures they have taken to implement the Convention with regard to the species in question.

It is therefore crucial to ensure that the range states of any particular migratory species can be readily identified, and Article VI(2) duly requires the parties to keep the Secretariat informed as to the species listed in the Appendices in respect of which they consider themselves to be range states. This information is to include details of any taking of such species by their flag vessels outside national jurisdictional limits. Under Article VI(1) the Secretariat itself is to maintain an up-to-date list of such states, using the information it has received from the parties.[36] It is plainly not restricted to material received from that source,[37] however, since that would represent neither the most efficient nor the most effective method of data capture. Rather, Article VIII(5)(c) suggests that it is part of the function of the Scientific Council to provide an indication of the range of listed species, while appropriately qualified non-governmental organisations may also have valuable information to offer on this matter.[38] Increasingly, such information is becoming available through automated information systems, such as the Global Register of Migratory Species (GROMS).[39]

[35] See, e.g., Articles III(4)–(6), IV(3), VI(3), VII(5)(f). Note also that under Article II(1) '*The Parties* acknowledge the importance of migratory species being conserved and of *Range States* agreeing to take action to this end' (emphasis added).

[36] See the current 'List of Range States of Migratory Species Included in the CMS Appendices', UNEP/CMS/Inf.9.5.

[37] Ibid., para. 1.

[38] See on this point the Secretariat's 2005 Analysis, para. 12. For further information and references to this important document and the related 'Synthesis', along with the equivalent versions for other recent CoPs, which are referred to throughout this chapter, see n. 204 *infra*, and accompanying text.

[39] See section 6(b)(i) below.

Since conservation measures for migratory species ideally require the involvement of all range states, the relatively low levels of participation in the CMS generally must be considered problematic. Of the major non-participants, China, Russia, the two Koreas, Japan, Brazil and the US are all range states for over two dozen Appendix I species. At the 2005 CoP, indeed, the Secretariat identified nine species in Appendix I for which *none* of the range states was a CMS party, and a further fifteen in respect of which no reports on implementation had ever been received even from those which are parties. This suggested that the Convention had achieved negligible impact with regard to some 22 per cent of the species theoretically entitled to strict protection.[40] The current Strategic Plan accordingly aims to increase participation by thirty states during the quinquennium, with particular emphasis upon recruitment from Asia and the Americas.[41]

b) *Obligations regarding migratory species in general*

Article II(1) proclaims as fundamental principles the importance of conserving migratory species and of co-operative action amongst range states to that end, particularly for the benefit of species experiencing unfavourable conservation status. The parties, who are expected to promote and collaborate in research relating to migratory species, specifically recognise the need to take action to avoid any such species becoming endangered.[42] These provisions are expressed to be applicable to 'migratory species' generally – that is, whether listed under the Convention or not. In the same way, the powers of the CoP also extend beyond those species that are currently listed. Thus Article VII(5) authorises it, inter alia, to monitor the conservation status of migratory species, to review progress made in that regard and to make recommendations for further improvements.[43] Such powers, which would in any event be needed to enable new species to be listed,[44] have also frequently been used to establish interim protection for species that are

[40] 2005 Analysis, para. 9.

[41] See Resolution 8.2, Annex, Logical Framework Table, Objective 4.1. For a mid-term report on progress towards this challenging target, see UNEP/CMS/Conf.9.5, para. 17.

[42] Article II(2), 2(3)(a).

[43] Subparagraphs (a), (b), (e) respectively. The power to review progress applies 'especially' (but not exclusively) to listed species.

[44] Pursuant to Article XI.

proposed for listing or earmarked as potential subjects of an ancillary agreement.[45]

In addition, many recommendations have targeted broader categories of migratory fauna, including, most recently, raptors and owls in the African–Eurasian region, migratory sharks, grassland bird species of southern South America, central Eurasian arid-land mammals, Sahelo-Saharan megafauna and Asian big cats.[46] Such measures may ultimately benefit *any* species within these categories, whether listed or not. Resolution 8.27, moreover, sought to forestall the perceived threats to 'wild birds' arising from public concern over the spread of highly pathogenic avian influenza, emphasising that responses involving habitat destruction or culling of wild populations did not constitute wise use and might well exacerbate the problem by causing further dispersion of infected birds.[47] Other measures have focused upon the mechanisms required to tackle specific hazards to migratory fauna, such as accidental by-catch in fishing activities[48] or threats posed by climate change,[49] marine noise,[50] oil pollution, wind turbines and electricity transmission lines.[51] At the broadest level of all, the CoP is authorised to adopt any recommendation or other measure calculated to implement the objectives of the Convention or improve its effectiveness generally. In this vein, Resolution 7.2 emphasised the importance for migratory species of good-quality environmental impact assessment (EIA) and strategic environmental assessment (SEA), and urged the parties to make appropriate use of the guidelines which had been approved in that regard under the Biodiversity Convention.[52]

c) Appendix I species

Despite the existence of these general provisions, the main focus of attention under the Convention is inevitably upon the species listed

45 For a recent example, see Resolution 9.20, concerning the saker falcon (*Falco cherrug*). For an unusually elaborate suite of measures, see Recommendations 4.1 and 5.3, concerning birds of the cormorant family, discussed more fully in Chapter 7 above.

46 See Recommendations 8.12, 8.16, 8.23, 8.26 and 9.1–3.

47 It called instead for collaborative research and monitoring, and the strict application of quarantine and veterinary standards; see further Resolution 9.8.

48 Resolutions 6.2, 8.14, 9.18 and Recommendation 7.2.

49 Recommendation 5.3 and Resolutions 8.13, 9.7. 50 Resolution 9.19.

51 Resolutions 7.3, 7.4, 7.5 respectively.

52 Guidelines for Incorporating Biodiversity-Related Issues into Environmental Impact Legislation and/or Processes and in Strategic Environmental Assessment endorsed by CBD Decision VI/7.

in its Appendices, with the highest priority accorded to Appendix I species.

i) Listing process

Article III(1) requires that a species be both 'migratory' and 'endangered' as defined by the Convention in order to merit inclusion in Appendix I. Since it will suffice for this purpose that a species is in danger of extinction 'throughout . . . *a significant portion* of its range',[53] the fact that it is still relatively abundant in some areas will not of itself preclude its listing. On the other hand, even a very common species may be in danger of extinction on the fringes of its range, and it was clearly not intended that such species be eligible for Appendix I.

Given the lack of opportunity to evaluate in advance the scientific evidence regarding eligibility for inclusion in Appendix I,[54] it was decided at the Final Conference in 1979 simply to list a representative sample of forty species in order to ensure that the Convention had some practical impact as soon as it entered into force. This list comprised fifteen mammals, twenty birds, four reptiles and one freshwater fish. Since that time, the number of species listed has more than trebled.[55] Following the decision taken in 1988 to interpret the term 'endangered' consistently with IUCN practice, Resolution 3.1 resolved to apply this approach to the consideration of future proposals, 'but not necessarily retrospectively to species already listed'. It is likely, indeed, that some of the original listings may never actually have satisfied the relevant criteria.[56]

A species may be removed from Appendix I if the CoP decides that

(a) reliable evidence, including the best scientific evidence available, indicates that the species is no longer endangered, and
(b) the species is not likely to become endangered again because of loss of protection due to its removal from Appendix I.[57]

Bearing in mind this latter point, Resolution 3.1 indicates that species categorised by the IUCN as 'endangered' or 'vulnerable' or whose conservation status is unclear should be retained in Appendix I, together with any rare species breeding at a limited number of inherently vulnerable sites.

[53] Emphasis added. [54] See the 1979 US Report, *supra* n. 13, pp. 3 and 10.
[55] For the current list, see the CMS website, 'Official Documents' link.
[56] As regards the Brazilian free-tailed bat, see section 4(d)(iii) below. [57] Article III(3).

The procedure for amending the Appendices is set out in Article XI.[58] Proposals may be made by any party and must be communicated to the Secretariat, along with supporting scientific evidence, at least 150 days before the CoP meeting at which they are to be considered. The parties must be promptly notified of such proposals, and must communicate any responses no less than sixty days before the meeting, at which point the Secretariat is to circulate any comments received. Amendments are adopted by a two-thirds majority of parties present and voting, and enter into force ninety days thereafter for all parties, except those which have entered a reservation.[59] Regrettably, some reservations have been formulated, though they are few in number.[60]

ii) Regulation of taking

Article III(5) imposes a clear and unequivocal obligation on range states to prohibit the 'taking' of animals belonging to Appendix I species. Exceptions may be made to this prohibition only if the taking is (a) for scientific purposes, (b) for the purpose of enhancing the propagation or survival of the affected species, (c) to accommodate the needs of traditional subsistence users of such species or (d) if extraordinary circumstances so require.

It is noticeable that these exceptions have more in common with those allowed under the Whaling Convention than with those provided for in other treaties with which the CMS interacts, such as the Bern Convention.[61] It is likely that this reflects the influence of the United States upon the drafting process, which is ironic in view of that country's ultimate decision not to participate in the CMS. It also has the potential to create some anomalies in the overall conservation regime.[62]

Mindful of the dangers posed by uncontrolled, unilateral resort to such exemptions, the Bonn Convention seeks to restrict the powers of governments in that regard. Thus, even where exceptions are in principle permitted, Article III(5) provides that they may be invoked only if they are 'precise as to content and limited in space and time', and that any taking authorised thereunder 'should not operate to the disadvantage of

[58] Cf. Article X, concerning amendment of the Convention itself.

[59] Reservations regarding particular listed species may, of course, also be registered upon initial ratification etc. Article XIV(1).

[60] I.e. Argentina and Bolivia with regard to the vicuña, Denmark and Norway with respect to certain cetacean species and France regarding the green turtle.

[61] For fuller discussion of these provisions, see above, Chapters 6 and 10 respectively.

[62] See further section 7(a) and (b) below.

the species'. Furthermore, parties must inform the Secretariat 'as soon as possible' of every exception they allow.[63]

It was possible to incorporate such rigorous obligations in relation to the taking of Appendix I species both because such controls constitute a relatively limited incursion into state sovereignty by comparison with measures for the conservation of habitat and because many states have in any event long had in place national legislation to similar effect. Nevertheless, the strictness of the duty in question still represents a significant feature of the CMS, given especially the very broad definition of 'taking' which is established by Article I(1)(i), whereby it includes 'hunting, fishing, capturing, harassing, deliberate killing or attempting to engage in any such conduct'. It is noteworthy that, whereas 'killing' must be deliberate to constitute 'taking', capture apparently need not be. Consequently, the accidental by-catch in fishing nets of marine turtles, cetaceans and seabirds (still a major threat to certain species)[64] is an activity that must be rigorously controlled, and the measures approved by the CoP to address this problem may have considerable bearing upon the interpretation and implementation of these obligations.[65] Furthermore, the fact that 'taking' includes the actual or even attempted harassment of Appendix I animals gives this provision a very wide scope indeed.

iii) Regulation of other threats

Article III(4) provides that parties which are range states of Appendix I species shall endeavour:

> a) to conserve and, where feasible and appropriate, restore those habitats of the species which are of importance in removing the species from danger of extinction;
> b) to prevent, remove, compensate for or minimize, as appropriate, the adverse effects of activities or obstacles that seriously impede or prevent the migration of the species; and
> c) to the extent feasible and appropriate, to prevent, reduce or control factors that are endangering or are likely to further endanger the species, including strictly controlling the introduction of, or controlling or eliminating, already introduced exotic species.

[63] Article III(7).

[64] 2008 Synthesis, para. 47. At the eighth CoP, by-catch represented the most frequently reported threat to migratory species generally. 2005 Analysis, para. 5.

[65] On the measures themselves, see n. 48 *supra*. By-catch also features prominently in the 2001 ACAP Agreement, as to which see section 4(d)(iii) below and Chapter 7 above.

It is obvious that, by comparison with the obligations to control taking, these commitments are heavily diluted. In particular, the duties regarding habitat restoration and control of factors endangering the species are qualified by their limitation to whatever is 'feasible and appropriate', leaving ample room for the exercise of discretion on the part of range states. More generally, all the relevant duties are expressed in terms of a commitment to 'endeavour' to take the necessary measures. The Second Revised Draft Convention, by contrast, had provided that range states of Appendix I species 'shall' protect habitats and so on, but the United States and others campaigned successfully at the Final Conference to change the text so that it obliged them only to endeavour to do those things. The precise legal effect of this change is unclear. On the one hand, it has in the past been doubted 'whether undertakings "to use best endeavours" or "to take all possible measures" can in most cases amount to more than declarations of policy, or of goodwill towards the objects of the agreement'.[66] On the other hand, the High Court of Australia has subsequently held[67] that a justiciable legal obligation *is* established by Article 5 of the 1972 World Heritage Convention,[68] even though it is expressed in terms of a commitment to 'endeavour, in so far as possible, and as appropriate for each country' to take certain steps for the protection of World Heritage sites. The treaty-making process has, of course, changed considerably in recent years, and it may be that the organic nature of modern environmental agreements, with their comprehensive array of institutions and mechanisms for implementation, now provides the means for 'perfecting' legal obligations that initially appear inchoate or uncertain.

What cannot be denied is that any obligations that are created by Article III(4) are heavily qualified. Yet this is scarcely surprising in view of the extremely broad compass of the conservation measures specified, which, through their reference to 'obstacles' to migration and 'factors' endangering migratory species, effectively cover every possible threat. These include such ubiquitous problems as collisions with tall buildings – a constant hazard to migrating birds which can be reduced through such simple techniques as the minimisation of lighting at night and, more expensively, the installation of non-reflective glass in windows at tree level.[69] Other pervasive problems

66 J. E. S. Fawcett, 'The Legal Character of International Agreements' (1953) 30 *BYIL* 391.
67 *Commonwealth of Australia v State of Tasmania* (1983) 46 *ALR* 625; 68 *ILR* 266.
68 For discussion, see Chapter 14 above.
69 *National Geographic* magazine, September 2003 issue, pictures the neatly assembled corpses of some 2,000 birds which had fallen victim to such collisions during their

which parties have been urged to tackle with particular vigour for the benefit of Appendix I species (and with due regard, in some cases, to the precautionary principle) include the threats posed by oil pollution, wind turbines and electricity transmission cables.[70]

As regards the control of exotic species, one controversial example concerns the white-headed duck (*Oxyura leucocephala*), a globally threatened European species which has come under additional pressure from the advance across the region of a close North American relative, the ruddy duck (*O. jamaicensis*), specimens of which escaped into the wild from waterfowl collections in the UK and elsewhere during the 1950s. Not only are ruddy ducks more competitive than their European cousins, they are capable of interbreeding with them so as to produce fertile offspring, and it is feared that the indigenous species will not survive the competition generated by the exotic and hybrid forms. At the fourth CoP, it was explained that, following the listing of the white-headed duck in Appendix I, parties were obliged to participate in programmes for the control or elimination of these intruders in accordance with Article III(4)(c).[71]

iv) Recommendation of further measures

Article III(6) of the Convention expressly authorises the CoP to recommend that range states of an Appendix I species 'take further measures considered appropriate to benefit the species'. This provision reinforces the general power to make recommendations for improving the conservation status of migratory species under Article VII(5), envisaging proposals for the adoption of specific measures by particular states. A notable example is Recommendation 4.5, concerning Concerted Action for Six Appendix I Species of Sahelo-Saharan Ungulates, which encourages the parties in question to implement an action plan for the conservation of certain antelopes which are amongst the most endangered species on earth.[72]

autumn migration through a single city (Toronto). Almost as many fatalities had been counted during the previous spring migration.

[70] See section 4(b) above.

[71] See the Report of Sessional Committee I, Proceedings of the Fourth Meeting, paras. 11–14, and the List of Species Added to the Appendices, Annex IV, ibid. For the 2005 Action Plan for this species, see CMS/ScC.13/Inf.7, and, for further discussion, M. J. Bowman, 'International Treaties and the Global Protection of Birds: Part I' (1999) 11 *JEL* 87, pp. 109–10.

[72] Indeed, the scimitar-horned oryx (*Oryx dammah*) may well be extinct in the wild. For further discussion of this project, see section 6(b)(ii) below.

d) Appendix II species

A further tier of protection is provided by inclusion in Appendix II, and various factors have conspired to place a particularly heavy emphasis on this aspect of the Bonn Convention. The first is that the number of species listed in Appendix I is still relatively small, and the practical impact of the conservation obligations imposed by Article III is of correspondingly limited scope. Appendix II, by contrast, currently contains a much lengthier list of species. Second, as noted above, the value of Appendix I listing is commonly undermined by the fact that not all of the range states of listed species are actually parties to the CMS. An important feature of the Appendix II regime, however, is its ability to draw in these outsiders for particular purposes. Finally, the possibility of simultaneous listing under both Appendices is not to be forgotten: thus, even where a species is listed in Appendix I, and all the range states are CMS parties, there may be scope under Appendix II for adopting more detailed and elaborate arrangements for its conservation than are spelled out under the terms of Article III.

i) Listing process

To qualify for inclusion in Appendix II, migratory species must either 'have an unfavourable conservation status' and 'require international agreements for their conservation and management' or 'have a conservation status which would significantly benefit from the international co-operation that could be achieved by an international agreement'.[73] The latter criterion is plainly extremely comprehensive, since almost all migratory species, whether endangered or not, are likely to be capable of benefiting from international co-operation for their conservation. The phalaropes,[74] for example, were included in Appendix II because they have exceptionally long migration routes and would obviously benefit from international co-operation in their conservation, notwithstanding the fact that they have never been remotely at risk.[75] On the other hand, the Explanatory Notes to the Convention suggest that, despite its inclusion in Appendix I as an endangered species, the dark-rumped petrel (*Pterodroma phaeopygia*) will not qualify for Appendix II because its

[73] Article IV(1).

[74] I.e. waterbirds which originally featured expressly as the family Phalaropodidae, but have since been re-categorised as a subfamily (*Phalaropodinae*) within the family *Scolopacidae* (sandpipers etc.), which is listed in its entirety.

[75] The IUCN currently categorises all three species as 'least concern'.

threatened status is due to introduced predators and loss of suitable breeding habitat in the Galapagos Islands, and therefore international co-operation for its protection elsewhere along its migration route would do nothing to enhance its prospects of survival. Even in such cases, the value of a co-operative agreement cannot be ruled out entirely, however, since it might provide for international assistance to eliminate such threats, or, indeed, for the creation of suitable breeding habitat elsewhere along the route.[76]

The 1979 Final Conference agreed simply to include a representative sample of species in Appendix II. Only seven mammals, one freshwater fish and one insect were chosen, together with numerous reptiles and birds, including all sea turtles, falcons, accipiters[77] and cranes. Subsequently, this list has been considerably expanded,[78] with the number of mammal species alone having increased more than tenfold. Probably it now includes over 1,000 species.[79] The Convention provides no criteria for removing species from Appendix II, presumably because the capacity of species to benefit from international co-operation is unlikely to change even if their conservation status improves.

ii) Conclusion of AGREEMENTS

In contrast to the obligations imposed directly on CMS parties with regard to Appendix I species, Article IV(3) of the Convention merely requires the range states of Appendix II-listed species to endeavour to conclude conservation 'AGREEMENTS' amongst themselves where this would benefit the species in question, adding that priority should be given to those with an unfavourable conservation status. Although it is not specifically stated, the assumption appears to be that these instruments will be formal treaties with binding effect in international law.[80] Certainly those concluded to date have been of that character. The

[76] Note in that regard the provisions of Article V(5)(c), (f), (g).

[77] Birds of prey such as eagles, buzzards and kites.

[78] The discussion in section 4(c)(i) above concerning amendment of the Appendices applies equally in this context.

[79] See Resolution 8.2, Annex, para. 18. The uncertainty stems from the fact that, while Appendix II currently lists around 200 species/populations individually, it also includes numerous higher taxa, especially of bats, birds and marine turtles. These contain around 2,000 species in total, but, strictly, only those which are both migratory and capable of benefiting from co-operative action – 'potentially over 1000' – are eligible for Appendix II listing.

[80] See, e.g., Resolution 4.4 on Strategy for the Future Development of the Convention, Annex, para. 15.

various elements of such AGREEMENTS are regulated in considerable detail by Article V.

Content and scope Article V is fairly prescriptive in this respect. In accordance with paragraph 1, the object of each AGREEMENT 'shall be to restore the migratory species concerned to a favourable conservation status or to maintain it in such a status' and its provisions should therefore be designed accordingly. AGREEMENTS should address more than one species wherever possible,[81] and cover their entire range.[82] In addition, they should identify the species in question, describe their range and migratory routes, provide for the designation of national authorities concerned with implementation, set up (where necessary) administrative machinery to monitor and advance the effectiveness of the instrument and establish procedures for the settlement of disputes.[83] Where cetacean species are concerned, the AGREEMENT should, at the very least, prohibit any taking which is not permitted under any other multilateral agreement,[84] a provision intended primarily to ensure compatibility with the 1946 Whaling Convention.[85]

In addition to these requirements, Article V(5) suggests a wide range of matters which should be incorporated 'where appropriate and feasible'. These include periodic reviews of the conservation status of the species concerned and the identification of relevant risk factors, the adoption of co-ordinated management plans, the conservation and restoration of habitats, the elimination of obstacles to migration and the adoption of ecologically sound measures to regulate taking from the wild. Other matters mentioned include research, information exchange and the enhancement of public awareness. Plainly, those who negotiated the CMS, which in this respect operates as a parent 'framework' convention, were anxious to specify the characteristics of its offspring in some detail.

Participation Article V(2) very sensibly provides that each AGREEMENT should be open to accession by all range states of the species covered, whether or not they are parties to the Bonn Convention itself. This could prove vital to the prospects of success of the instrument in question, since states which are unwilling, for whatever reason, to participate in the CMS generally might nevertheless be prepared to commit themselves to the conservation of the species covered by a

[81] Article V(3). [82] Article V(2). [83] Article V(4)(a)–(e).
[84] Article V(4)(f). [85] See Chapter 6 above.

particular AGREEMENT. Article V(4)(f) goes even further in stipulating, in relation to AGREEMENTS concerning cetaceans, that provision should be made for the participation of states that are not actually range states at all; this, presumably, is again designed to harmonise the CMS with the Whaling Convention, to which any state (including non-whaling countries) may accede. There is no reference to the participation of non-range states in other Article IV(3) AGREEMENTS: accordingly, when the 1991 EUROBATS agreement was amended to include the European free-tailed bat (*Tadarida teniotis*), the UK accepted the amendment exclusively on behalf of Gibraltar, since the range of this species does not extend to the British Isles.

iii) Progress to date

Given the central role envisaged by the Bonn Convention for this network of ancillary AGREEMENTS, it is disappointing to record, some thirty years after the conclusion of the parent treaty, that only four have actually been adopted: the 1991 Agreement on the Conservation of Populations of European Bats (EUROBATS),[86] the 1995 African–Eurasian Waterbirds Agreement (AEWA),[87] the 2001 Agreement on the Conservation of Albatrosses and Petrels (ACAP)[88] and the 2007 Agreement on the Conservation of Gorillas and Their Habitats. Since the last of these has already been briefly mentioned, and the two instruments concerning birds are considered in Chapter 7 above, the present discussion will focus on the measures adopted for the conservation of bats. It should be noted here, however, that AEWA in particular is an extremely wide-ranging and important agreement, which in itself represents a major advance towards the achievement of the Bonn Convention's objectives.[89]

Conservation of bats Recent surveys indicate that there are over 1,000 species of bats worldwide, representing an astonishing 20 per cent of all mammal species.[90] Although very few of these occur in Europe, those that do are likely to account for an even greater percentage of that

[86] *UKTS* no. 9 (1994), Cm. 2472. For the 1995 and 2000 Amendments, see *UKTS* no. 9 (2002), Cm. 5386 and *Misc* no. 11 (2001), Cm. 5322 respectively.

[87] (1995) 6 *YBIEL* 306. [88] (2004) 7 *JIWLP* 91.

[89] See B. Lenten, 'A Flying Start for the Agreement on the Conservation of African–Eurasian Migratory Waterbirds' (2001) 4 *JIWLP* 159.

[90] See, e.g., S. P. Mickleburgh et al., 'A Review of the Global Status of Bats' (2002) 36(1) *Oryx* 18.

region's mammals, given the rather impoverished inventory of European wildlife generally.[91] Consequently, the adoption of protective measures is particularly crucial to the conservation of the region's remaining biological diversity. While no European bat species is currently endangered, several are considered vulnerable, and evidence accumulated during the 1970s and 1980s suggested that many populations were in steep decline. Following the formulation of an action plan by specialists from the IUCN's Species Survival Commission,[92] the Agreement on the Conservation of Bats in Europe was concluded in 1991 under the aegis of the CMS. The Agreement, which entered into force during 1994, is open to participation by range states and competent regional economic integration organisations: there are currently thirty-two contracting parties of an estimated forty-eight range states in total.[93] By virtue of the amendments of the year 2000,[94] its title was changed to the Agreement on the Conservation of Populations of European Bats, reflecting recognition of the need for protection of such species not only in Europe itself but across their entire range.[95]

Under Article I(b) of EUROBATS as originally drafted, its scope was limited to the European populations of the families Rhinophilidae and Vespertilionidae (twenty-nine species in total), but the 1995 Amendment extended it to incorporate the family Molossidae, thereby adding one additional species. In the year 2000, the Agreement was restructured to incorporate an Annex, which currently includes forty-five species in five families.[96] This in turn required revision of the amendment clause, Article VII, so as to create a new, streamlined procedure for future amendments of the Annex, while preserving the original arrangements for amending the body of the text.[97] Article VIII

[91] The thirty species to which EUROBATS applied as of 1995 had previously been estimated to represent some 30 per cent of the continent's native mammal fauna; see R. E. Stebbings, *The Conservation of European Bats* (Christopher Helm, 1988), p. 3. A further fifteen species have, moreover, subsequently been added.

[92] As to which, see ibid. For the EUROBATS Conservation and Management Plan 2007–2010, see EUROBATS Resolution 5.10.

[93] See the EUROBATS website at www.eurobats.org/about/parties.htm.

[94] EUROBATS Resolution 3.7.

[95] The preamble was also amended to reflect this point. As noted above, Article V(2) of the CMS requires that AGREEMENTS cover the entire range of the species to which they apply. See further EUROBATS Resolution 5.11.

[96] For the current list, see Resolution 5.3.

[97] See clauses 5 and 6 of the 2000 Amendment. With some minor adjustments, the new arrangements reflect those of the CMS itself.

allows for the formulation of reservations with regard to particular species, though general reservations are not permitted.

The principal conservation obligations of EUROBATS are set out in Article III. First, each party is to prohibit the deliberate capture, keeping or killing of bats except under permit.[98] This provision is crucial because in many countries bats were not previously protected at all, and in some they have traditionally been considered vermin: an entire colony of 5,000 Schreiber's bats (*Miniopterus schreibersii*) inhabiting a cave in Gibraltar was apparently smoked out and exterminated by local teenagers during the 1980s.[99] Incidental disturbance of roosts, caused by opening up caves for potholing or tourism, or blocking them off for safety reasons, also proved problematic in the past, and parties are accordingly required to identify sites which are important for the shelter and protection of bats and protect them from damage or disturbance, while taking into account economic and social considerations.[100] Safeguarding a relatively small number of locations in this way can produce considerable benefits, since bats commonly roost in vast numbers: indeed, individual caves in southern Europe have been found to accommodate populations of up to 100,000 individuals.[101] Apart from roosting sites, parties must also *endeavour* to protect important feeding areas, the more diluted wording of this obligation reflecting the fact that such areas are obviously much more numerous and widely distributed.

Ancillary obligations call for the encouragement and co-ordination of research programmes concerning bat conservation, and the promotion of public awareness regarding its importance.[102] Research undertaken prior to EUROBATS had been relatively limited, certainly by comparison with that regarding birds. Researchers themselves had, moreover, occasionally been guilty of creating undue disturbance or removing excessive numbers of specimens from the wild, while the 'ringing' of bats for the purpose of monitoring their movements had often resulted in injury where rings were inexpertly manufactured or fitted. Nowadays techniques have been significantly refined and modern electronic bat detection equipment can not only convert their high-frequency calls into sounds audible to humans, but enable their translation by computer into visual images which permit ready identification of species.[103] As regards public awareness, education

[98] For the current guidelines on the issue of permits, see Resolutions 4.6, 5.5.
[99] Stebbings, *supra* n. 91, p. 166. [100] See further Resolutions 2.4, 4.3, 5.7.
[101] Stebbings, *supra* n. 91, p. 5. [102] See Article III(3)–(8).
[103] See generally J. D. Altringham, *British Bats* (Collins, 2003), Chapter 7.

programmes are now under way in many countries to publicise the need for conservation, and to counteract previously unfavourable popular perceptions of bats, fuelled by fears of rabies transmission and literary associations with vampirism.

The parties are also required to address the effects of pesticides on bats, to endeavour to replace toxic timber-treatment chemicals with safer alternatives,[104] and to designate agencies to provide advice on bat conservation, particularly with regard to buildings. Finally, each party is to take such additional action as it considers necessary to safeguard populations identified as being under threat, and to report on such developments. Provision is made in Article VI for the regular presentation of national reports on implementation of the Agreement, and the precise procedures to be followed have subsequently been elaborated through the Meeting of the Parties, which is held periodically in accordance with Article V.[105] There have been five such meetings to date.[106]

Given the extent to which bats contribute to overall biological diversity, and the threatened status of many species worldwide,[107] there would seem to be a pressing need for the implementation of concerted efforts for their conservation on a global scale. Yet there is currently only one other international conservation scheme for Chiroptera – the Program for the Conservation of Migratory Bats of Mexico and the United States.[108] Until recently, moreover, the CMS Appendices themselves included only one bat species, *Tadarida brasiliensis*, additional to those covered by EUROBATS.[109] As a result, three further species were added to Appendix II at the eighth CoP, where proposals for the establishment of a Working Group to develop an instrument for the conservation of migratory bats in Africa were also initiated.[110]

104 See further Resolution 4.5. 105 See Resolutions 2.7, 3.3.

106 Details may be found on the EUROBATS website.

107 Globally, some 22 per cent of all bat species were recently judged to be threatened, with a further 25 per cent 'near threatened'. See 'Bats: Study Assesses Next CMS Steps', *CMS Bulletin* No. 16 (2002), p. 22.

108 Ibid. The study in question, authored by the co-chair of the IUCN Chiroptera Specialist Group, was presented to the 11th Meeting of the CMS Scientific Council.

109 Though listed in Appendix I, it is in fact relatively widespread in the New World, its current IUCN status being near threatened; i.e. neither endangered nor vulnerable.

110 See Resolutions 8.5 and 9.2 and, for information on African Chiroptera, UNEP/CMS/Inf.8.34 and 8.35.

e) *Action under Article IV(4)*

Despite the paucity of instruments adopted under Article IV(3), it would be a grave mistake to measure the impact of the CMS by that yardstick alone, since it is not the only mechanism by which the framework character of the Convention can be exploited. Article IV(4), it will be recalled, encourages the conclusion of agreements[111] for any population[112] of wild animals whose members 'periodically' cross one or more national jurisdictional boundaries. Though originally inserted simply to compensate for the fact that the definition of the migratory-species concept had been narrowed in the course of negotiations to those that 'cyclically and predictably' cross such boundaries, this provision has come to represent a key mechanism for the advancement of the Convention's conservation aspirations, primarily on account of its very considerable flexibility.

i) A flexible mechanism

This provision offers several potential advantages, which are to some extent interrelated, over Article IV(3): they relate to the species under consideration; the nature, contents and legal status of the protective instrument; and the entities which may participate.

Species Covered There is no requirement that a species be listed under either Appendix in order to become the beneficiary of a conservation agreement under Article IV(4).[113] Indeed, since no restriction other than 'periodic' crossing of boundaries is imposed by virtue of this provision, it is unnecessary for this purpose that it even satisfy the CMS definition of being migratory. This creates the possibility of assisting species which cross international boundaries other than 'cyclically and predictably',[114] or whose movements are not fully known or understood. In addition, it is noteworthy that the exhortation in Article V(3) that Article IV(3) AGREEMENTS should, wherever possible, cover more than one migratory species has not been thought applicable to Article IV(4)

[111] Article IV(4) agreements are referred to in lower case to distinguish them from Article IV(3) instruments.

[112] Including, once again, geographically separate parts of the population of any species or lower taxon.

[113] The bukhara deer (*Cervus elephas bactrianus*), for example, was not listed under the CMS at all when the relevant MoU was agreed; it was, however, subsequently added to both Appendices, in 2005.

[114] See the discussion in section 3(a) above concerning the interpretation of this phrase.

instruments, several of which do, in fact, relate to just a single (sub) species or population.[115]

Scope and Contents Although, as seen above, these issues are regulated very closely for Article IV(3) AGREEMENTS under the terms of Article V, this provision is inapplicable to Article IV(4) instruments. The parties are accordingly free to incorporate whatever provisions they deem appropriate. Nevertheless, there are fairly clear indications in the practice of the parties of a desire to assimilate the two categories to a considerable extent, certainly as far as implementation is concerned. Resolution 2.7, for example, established certain uniform provisions governing the administration of both types of instrument, stipulating (i) that the most efficient, economical and appropriate administrative arrangements should be adopted in every case, with the relevant tasks being handled by a party, a suitable organisation or the CMS Secretariat itself;[116] (ii) that the relevant body should in any event keep the Secretariat fully informed of progress and make regular reports to the CoP; and (iii) that all parties should be prepared to contribute to the costs of these arrangements.[117]

It was, indeed, suggested at the second CoP that an Agreement under Article IV(4) might simply be established as a first step towards the adoption of a more formal Article IV(3) instrument,[118] though it was subsequently recognised in Resolution 3.5 that this might not always be appropriate. The same resolution also reconsidered the earlier exhortation that Article V(2) (which provides that AGREEMENTS should cover the entire range of the species in question and be open to all range states) be applied also to Article IV(4) agreements, recognising that this might in certain circumstances constitute an impediment to their adoption or implementation.

Legal Status As noted above, the Convention appears to envisage that Article IV(3) AGREEMENTS will be formal treaties with legally binding effects under international law. As far as agreements under Article IV(4)

115 For examples, see section 4(e)(ii), below.

116 It was provided that the consent of the Standing Committee should be sought if the last option were chosen.

117 Resolution 3.5 also extended the provisions of Articles IV(5), VII(5)(d) and IX(4)(b) and (h) to Article IV(4) agreements. For further steps in the harmonisation process, see Resolutions 4.3 and 5.2.

118 Resolution 2.6.

are concerned, however, it was resolved in 1988 that they might take the form of administrative agreements, memoranda of understanding or even CoP resolutions.[119] The fact that they do not have to be couched in legally binding form greatly enhances the prospects of their adoption, as well as the speed and facility with which this can be achieved. In particular, cumbersome constitutional procedures attending treaty acceptance may sometimes be circumvented.

Participation Although Resolution 3.5 recognised the possible need for exceptions, it remains desirable in principle that Article IV(4) Agreements be open to all range states, and participation arrangements for these instruments have, indeed, proved noteworthy for their inclusiveness. First, they share with AGREEMENTS the feature that participation is open to states which are not CMS parties, and this has proved vital to the achievement of progress in certain cases: both Russia and China participate in the conservation arrangements for the Siberian crane, for example, though neither is party to CMS itself.[120] Since all populations of this species breed in Siberia, and by far the largest population winters in the area around Lake Poyang in China, effective conservation measures could not realistically have been established without their involvement.[121]

Second, the fact that many of these instruments are not legally binding facilitates the undertaking of commitments (albeit still, arguably, not strictly as parties) by entities which lack the formal status to assume treaty obligations as such. Accordingly, non-governmental organisations often play crucial roles in their implementation. As regards the Siberian crane, for example, one particularly vital task involves the precise identification of their migration routes, which is achieved by tracking their movements by means of transmitters. Responsibility for supplying these devices was assumed at the outset by the Wild Bird Society of Japan, while the US-based International Crane Foundation has undertaken monitoring work, as well as initiating essential conservation projects.[122] In the case of the MoU concerning the slender-billed curlew (*Numenius tenuirostris*), the International Council for Game and Wildlife

[119] Resolution 2.6.

[120] In fact, a majority of the signatory states are currently not parties to the CMS.

[121] The application of this MoU was, in fact, initially limited to the western and central migration routes of the species (i.e. towards the Caspian Sea and India), since China did not begin to participate until 1999.

[122] For discussion of these projects, see Chapter 7 above.

Conservation agreed to endeavour to educate hunters about the threats faced by the species, while BirdLife International undertook to develop a database based on local conservation measures and surveys conducted by its member organisations.

ii) Progress to date

There are currently twenty-one instruments which have been concluded under Article IV(4) – three formal agreements, seventeen memoranda of understanding and one flyway partnership.

Formal agreements To date, all formal agreements concern marine mammals,[123] namely the 1990 Agreement on the Conservation of Seals in the Wadden Sea,[124] the 1992 Agreement on the Conservation of Small Cetaceans of the Baltic and North Seas (ASCOBANS) and the 1996 Agreement on the Conservation of Cetaceans of the Black Sea, Mediterranean and Contiguous Atlantic Area (ACCOBAMS). The cetacean instruments are discussed in Chapter 6 above. The Seals Agreement focuses specifically on the common (or harbour) seal (*Phoca vitulina*) and was adopted in response to a dramatic decline in population following an outbreak of phocine distemper. It represents one facet of the wider co-operative conservation arrangements which have been implemented amongst the three Wadden Sea states (Denmark, Germany and the Netherlands) since 1978.[125] With a view to achieving a favourable conservation status for the species, the parties agree to co-ordinate research and monitoring activities and to develop a comprehensive management plan.[126] They undertake to adopt measures for the protection of habitat and the preservation of seals from undue disturbance and ecological change, including the further reduction of pollution and the investigation of its effects upon seal populations.[127] The taking of seals, other than by designated institutions engaged in scientific research or the rehabilitation of diseased individuals or abandoned sucklings, is to be prohibited.[128] The population of seals in the region recovered

[123] An agreement has long been under negotiation, however, for the conservation of an avian species, the Asian houbara bustard (*Chlamydotis undulata macqueenii*). For the latest version of the text, see CMS/HB/4 (2005).

[124] In force 1 October 1991. For the text, see www.cms.int/species/wadden_seals/sea_text.htm.

[125] The Common Wadden Sea Secretariat (CWSS), established in 1987, services the Seals Agreement. See www.waddensea-secretariat.org/index.html.

[126] Articles III–V. [127] Articles VII–VIII. [128] Article VI.

significantly during the 1990s, but was hit again by a further outbreak of distemper in 2002. Recent management plans have not only elaborated upon the matters covered by the Agreement, but extended the scope of some of them to the grey seal (*Helichoerus grypus*), notwithstanding the fact that this species is not formally covered by the Agreement.[129]

Memoranda of understanding The term 'memorandum of understanding' (MoU) carries no exact connotation in international law, and is occasionally applied to instruments with legally binding effects.[130] More commonly, it is applied to informal arrangements, which reflects the usage within the CMS system,[131] where MoUs have been described as 'political declarations of goodwill'.[132] Usually, they do not have their own institutions[133] and are managed directly under the parent Convention itself. There are currently seventeen MoUs, eight relating to birds,[134] six concerning the marine mammals[135] or turtles[136] of particular regions, and three relating to subspecies or populations of terrestrial mammals – the bukhara deer,[137] the Saiga antelope (*Saiga tatarica tatarica*)[138] and the African elephant (*Loxodonta africana*), west African population.[139]

These instruments tend to establish certain common conservation standards and principles to which the parties collectively subscribe, but also operate through the medium of action plans whereby they individually undertake specified commitments in the light of the conservation needs of the species in question within their jurisdiction. The bukhara

[129] For the 2007–10 plan, see www.waddensea-secretariat.org/management/SMP/SMP%202007-2010.pdf.

[130] See generally A. Aust, *Modern Treaty Law and Practice* (Cambridge University Press, 2nd ed., 2007), Chapters 2, 3.

[131] Here, indeed, the term 'agreement' tends to be used for all instruments that are intended to be legally binding – whether adopted under Article IV(3) or (4) – while 'MoU' is used for those which are not. For a further, very recent, example, see n. 272 infra.

[132] See, e.g., the Explanatory Note concerning the draft Agreement for the Houbara Bustard, UNEP/ CMS/HB/6 (2005), para. 10. Note further the unusually elaborate disclaimer of legal effect in clause 6 of the flamingos MoU (*infra* n. 134).

[133] Though this is not universally the case: see section 7(b) below.

[134] For details, see Chapter 7, section 3(b)(iii).

[135] I.e. cetaceans, Pacific Islands Region (2006); Mediterranean monk seal, Eastern Atlantic (2007); dugong (*Dugong dugon*), Indian Ocean (2007); small cetaceans/manatees, Western Africa (2008).

[136] I.e. the Atlantic coast of Africa (1999); and the Indian Ocean and South East Asia (2001). On the protection of marine turtles generally, see the 'Special Issue on Marine Turtle Conservation' (2002) 5(1/2) *JIWLP*.

[137] Concluded in 2002. [138] Effective September 2006.

[139] Signed by eleven range states at the eighth CoP.

deer, for example, is a subspecies of red deer found in the river valleys of central Asia. Illegal hunting and habitat destruction, especially through manipulation of the water regime, have progressively reduced its range and overall population – never large – to the point where it is now classified as 'endangered'. Following the initiation by WWF of assistance with conservation work in range states,[140] it was decided to enhance this collaboration through the creation of an informal CMS agreement.[141] The resulting MoU calls for strict protection of the deer, together with the conservation and, where feasible, restoration of its habitat. The accompanying Action Plan envisages, inter alia, the restoration of forest watering places, the development of a transnational 'econet' of protected areas, and the relocation of individuals into suitable habitat, with transitional arrangements for feeding them in enclosures and hand-rearing newborn animals. The development of deer-farming projects, allowing a sustainable trade in velvets, is also envisaged. These arrangements appear already to have contributed to an increase in the global population of bukhara to around 950, from only 350–450 a few years ago.[142]

Other measures As noted above, Resolution 2.6 provides that action under Article IV(4) may take the form of CoP Resolutions. While there have certainly been numerous resolutions and recommendations concerning particular animals, including marine and terrestrial mammals, marine turtles and birds,[143] these have not generally been treated as falling under this provision. Rather, their customary focus on the encouragement of research concerning the species in question, or the negotiation of agreements or action plans for their conservation, suggests that they represent action of the kind envisaged by Article VII(5).[144] Perhaps the most sophisticated measures adopted by recommendation to date are those concerning Sahelo-Saharan ungulates.[145] Yet although these exhibit a complexity which certainly outstrips that of certain MoUs, they have still been treated as no more than a preliminary to the adoption of

140 I.e. Kazakhstan, Tajikistan, Turkmenistan and Uzbekistan.

141 The WWF, the CMS Secretariat and the International Council for Game and Wildlife Conservation also participate.

142 See www.cms.int/species/bukhara_deer/bukhara_deer_intro.htm.

143 Examples are cited throughout this chapter.

144 Even Recommendation 4.1, on cormorants (which goes well beyond generalised exhortation and establishes specific conservation measures), asserts that it is adopted 'pursuant to Article VII(5)'.

145 See Recommendations 4.5, 6.3. For further discussion, see section 6(b)(i) below.

an Article IV(4) instrument.[146] At the 2008 CoP, however, the recently established East Asian/Australasian Flyway Partnership (EAAFP) – which builds upon a history of bilateral treaty relationships in the region – was recognised as fulfilling the conditions of a non-binding Article IV(4) agreement, and invited to submit a formal report to the next meeting.[147]

5. Institutional arrangements

The Bonn Convention is built around the four institutional pillars which have become more or less the norm for treaties of this type: Conference of the Parties, Secretariat, Standing Committee and Scientific Council. Successive Strategic Plans have envisaged an ongoing review of these institutions to ensure that they are well equipped to fulfil their respective functions effectively.[148]

a) *The Conference of the Parties*

Article VII establishes the Conference of the Parties (CoP) as the policy- and decision-making organ of the CMS and sets out its powers and functions. It is closely modelled on the corresponding provisions of CITES.[149] The Conference must convene at least every three years, and there have been nine meetings to date.[150] Eighty-six parties sent delegates to the most recent of these, held in 2008.[151]

The CoP's primary function is to review implementation of the Convention,[152] but it also has responsibility for the adoption of financial regulations and a budget for the financial period following each ordinary meeting.[153] It is empowered to determine its own Rules of Procedure.[154] Its decisions may normally be taken by a two-thirds majority of parties present and voting,[155] but those concerning financial regulations, including the scale of each party's budgetary contribution, must be unanimous.[156] The current Rules of Procedure provide for the disqualification

[146] See Resolution 8.5, para. 2(n). [147] See Resolution 9.2, para. 5(ii.i–iv).

[148] See now Resolution 8.2, Annex, Target 4.6. [149] See Chapter 15 above.

[150] Specifically, in Bonn, October 1985; Geneva, October 1988; Geneva, October 1991; Nairobi, June 1994; Geneva, April 1997; Cape Town, November 1999; Bonn, September 2002; Nairobi, November 2005; Rome, December 2008. Arrangements for future meetings are to be determined in accordance with Resolution 9.17.

[151] See Proceedings of the Ninth Meeting of the CoP, Annex XI. [152] Article VII(5).

[153] For the current financial and administrative arrangements, see Resolution 8.3.

[154] Article VII(7). For the text of the Rules, see UNEP/CMS/COP9/Report, Annex I.

[155] Article VII(7). [156] Article VII(4).

from voting of parties which are three or more years in arrears with their contributions to the CMS Trust Fund,[157] a circumstance affecting no fewer than seventeen of them at the time of the Ninth Meeting. Nine, indeed, remained ten or more years in arrears. Nevertheless, the overall collection rate for contributions still approached 95 per cent.[158]

Like CITES, the Bonn Convention allows various categories of observers to attend meetings of the CoP, and these may participate in the deliberations but not vote. The United Nations, its Specialised Agencies, the IAEA and all non-party states are automatically entitled to be represented in this capacity, as is the designated body of each individual CMS agreement.[159] Other agencies or bodies (whether national or international, governmental or non-governmental) which are 'technically qualified in protection, conservation and management of migratory species' may also be represented by observers provided that they have informed the Secretariat of their desire to attend, though such organisations may be excluded if at least one-third of the parties present at the meeting object.[160] At the Fifth Meeting of the CoP, Norway raised an objection to the admission of the International Fund for Animal Welfare (IFAW) but, given that no IFAW representative seemed actually to be present, the matter was deferred. The chairman, however, wisely saw fit to establish that there were no other objections to that organisation,[161] and IFAW has certainly attended later meetings.[162] It would be troubling if challenges to such organisations were upheld, as NGOs have played a vital role in the implementation and development of the CMS generally. Although the level of interest does not match that generated by certain other wildlife treaties,[163] it would be difficult to overstate the contribution of organisations such as IUCN and BirdLife

[157] Rule 15(2). Exceptions may be made where default is attributable to exceptional and unavoidable circumstances. Argentina succeeded with such a plea at the seventh CoP: see UNEP/CMS/Conf.8.4/Rev2. Three-year defaulters are also excluded from holding office in Convention bodies; see Resolution 8.3, para. 19.

[158] See UNEP/CMS/Conf.9.33/Rev2, Annex 3; Report of the Ninth Meeting of the CoP, paras. 267–8.

[159] Article VII(8). Twelve non-party states attended the Ninth Meeting, together with representatives from UNEP, the FAO, the Council of Europe, the UNCCD, CITES, Ramsar, the IWC and five of the CMS ancillary agreements.

[160] Article VII(9), which stipulates that national NGOs additionally require prior approval from their own state.

[161] Report of the Fifth Meeting, para. 44.

[162] Indeed, it sent eight delegates to the Eighth Meeting.

[163] Only twelve international and eleven national NGOs attended the 2005 CoP, for example, compared with fifty-one and seventy-two respectively for the CITES CoP the previous year.

International, which provided the foundations of technical expertise and other support which helped steer the Convention through its turbulent early years.[164] Formal recognition of this role was evident in Recommendation 4.6, which encouraged the participation of NGOs in the elaboration of governmental policy on migratory species conservation, as well as in the implementation and development of CMS instruments, and requested the Secretariat to organise periodic briefing meetings to consolidate their involvement.

b) The Secretariat

Article IX provides for the creation of a Secretariat, which was duly established on a permanent basis by UNEP following the Convention's entry into force.[165] Its funding arrangements and functions are very similar to those of the CITES Secretariat, and its headquarters has always been located in Bonn.[166]

Article IX(4) sets out the functions of the Secretariat, which include arranging and servicing meetings of the Conference of the Parties and of the Scientific Council, informing and liaising between the parties, publishing lists of range states of listed species, promoting the conclusion of AGREEMENTS, preparing reports for meetings of the Conference and publishing their recommendations, providing the public with information on the Convention and performing 'any other function' entrusted to it by the CoP. These responsibilities have been elaborated much more fully in the Strategic Plans adopted under the Convention.[167]

Although welcome support has been provided by UNEP and the host country, and via voluntary donations,[168] the funding required for the discharge of these functions is essentially provided by the parties themselves through their budgetary contributions. In view of their initially small numbers (and in particular the non-participation of wealthier

[164] Note, for example, the 'Assessment of the Birds Listed in Appendices I and II of the Convention', prepared by the ICBP (now BirdLife International) and included as Annex 3 to the Report of the Secretariat to the First Meeting of the Conference, CMS/Conf.1.3/ Rev.1.

[165] In accordance with Article IX(2).

[166] Since 1998, this has been at UN premises – for which a new 'campus' was provided in 2006 – alongside other UN and CMS agencies. On the juridical personality and headquarters arrangements of the Secretariat, see Resolutions 6.9 and 7.13.

[167] For an overview of its recent activities, see 'CMS – A Convention that Works', UNEP/ CMS/Conf.9.5.

[168] For details, see UNEP/CMS/Inf.9.20 and 21.

states like the US and Japan), together with the lower public profile of the CMS by comparison with certain other conventions (which may have impacted upon the level of non-budgetary contributions to its Trust Fund), the resources available to the Secretariat in the early years were sufficient really to sustain only a skeleton operation. Subsequently, however, the combination of a significant increase in the number of parties, an enhanced commitment to fund-raising,[169] and the expression of invoices in euros rather than dollars has produced some amelioration.[170] Even so, resources are constrained and the Secretariat, with a staff of under twenty, remains small in the light of the scale of its responsibilities.[171] The colocation of other Secretariats and agencies has arguably facilitated efficiency through the 'pooling' of resources, while certain functions have been discharged through a programme of internships and consultancies. Nevertheless, there has plainly been considerable behind-the-scenes controversy over organisational arrangements in recent years,[172] culminating in the controversial recent decision of UNEP to transfer the executive secretary, Robert Hepworth, back to its headquarters in Nairobi. Elizabeth Mrema was recently confirmed as his successor, while an inter-sessional review has been initiated of the entire structure and direction of CMS operations.[173]

c) The Standing Committee

The Bonn Convention itself makes no provision for a Standing Committee, but it was decided at the very first CoP to establish such a body to oversee the activities of the Secretariat and to monitor implementation of the Convention between subsequent meetings.[174] The Committee, which has held thirty-five ordinary meetings (and one extraordinary meeting)[175] to

[169] See Resolutions 6.4, 7.6 and 8.3 and UNEP/CMS/Conf.9.34.

[170] See generally the Report of the Ninth Meeting of the CoP, paras. 265–85.

[171] For further information, see 'Secretariat Manpower and Organisation', UNEP/CMS/Conf.8.17.

[172] In particular, a distinct tension between the relative informality of CMS institutional arrangements and the inevitably more bureaucratic nature of the UN system generally was exposed in an internal UN audit of the CMS Secretariat in 2004.

[173] See generally the Report of the Extraordinary Meeting of the Standing Committee of 8 June 2009, UNEP/CMS/Ex-StC/6 and, for the inter-sessional process itself, Resolution 9.13. Hepworth himself recently characterised the time and resources expended on such wrangling as 'tragic'. See www.cms.int/bodies/StC/exm09_stc/Statement_by_Executive_Secretary_of_CMS_100609.pdf.

[174] Resolution 1.1. See also Resolutions 2.5, 3.7 and 6.6.

[175] See n. 173, *supra*.

date, was recently reconstituted under the terms of Resolution 9.15. Its remit is to provide general policy and operational direction to the Secretariat, including advice on administrative matters; to oversee budgetary and financial arrangements, including the Secretariat's fund-raising activities and ensuing expenditures;[176] to represent the CoP in matters of external relations; to prepare resolutions and recommendations for the consideration of the CoP and to submit a written report on its own activities at each meeting; and finally to carry out such inter-sessional activities and other functions as may be assigned to it.

The Committee's membership is henceforth to comprise the depositary government; three parties each from Europe and Africa, two from Asia and from South/Central America/the Caribbean, and one each from North America[177] and Oceania;[178] as well as the host government of the previous and forthcoming meetings of the CoP where appropriate. Terms of office last until the close of the CoP following that of election, and regional members may not serve more than two consecutive terms. Provision is also made for the election of alternates and the participation of observers.[179] The quorum for meetings is fixed at four, and voting is normally by consensus.[180]

d) The Scientific Council

Article VIII(1) required the first meeting of the CoP to establish a Scientific Council to provide advice on scientific matters, which it accomplished through Resolution 1.4. Later meetings have engaged in fine-tuning of the regime governing the Council's activities.[181] Article VIII(2) allows each party to appoint a qualified expert to membership of the Council, while Resolution 4.5 permits them to nominate permanent alternates to cover for occasional unavailability.[182] Provision is also made for the appointment of additional experts (currently no more than eight

176 A new Finance and Budget Sub-committee was established under the terms of Resolution 9.14, para. 12.

177 Which, having no parties, currently has no representative.

178 Originally, each region had just one member. See, e.g., Resolution 3.7.

179 On the latter point, note the Committee's current Rules of Procedure, UNEP/CMS/StC35/4, Rules 10 and 11.

180 Ibid., Rules 23–5.

181 See Resolutions 3.4, 4.5, 6.7, 7.12 and 8.21. For the Council's Rules of Procedure, see UNEP/CMS/ScC15/Inf.2.

182 Resolution 8.21 urged all parties that had not already done so to appoint a Councillor; for the current list, see UNEP/CMS/Inf.9.7/Rev.1.

in total) by the CoP itself,[183] to ensure that the Council can command the full range of necessary expertise.[184] Observer status is accorded to a number of leading NGOs,[185] as well as to the appropriate agencies of certain other key conservation treaties.[186]

In accordance with Article VIII(5), the functions of the Council are determined by the CoP, and currently include the provision of scientific advice to the Secretariat, the CoP itself and certain other bodies specified by the latter;[187] initiating, co-ordinating and evaluating research on the conservation status of migratory species; reviewing the CMS Appendices; formulating guidance on specific conservation measures for listed species; developing existing and new agreements concerning migratory species; and investigating scientific problems arising out of the implementation of the Convention.[188] Since 2002, the Council has elaborated a strategy to guide its future programme of work, for subsequent endorsement by the CoP,[189] and June 2009 witnessed the first meeting dedicated specifically to the planning of future activities.

Initially, the approach to the Council's activities was rather cautious, primarily on account of concern over financial implications. Resolution 1.4, for instance, provided that for reasons of economy and efficiency it should work mainly in small groups, the full Council convening only at meetings of the CoP itself. It was subsequently agreed, however, that it should meet at least once mid-term,[190] and there have now been fifteen regular meetings in all, plus one planning meeting.[191] The current view, moreover, is that it would be advantageous to detach meetings of the Council from the CoP entirely, with the former occurring several months in advance; the Secretariat has been requested to investigate the cost

183 Article VIII(5).

184 Current appointments are G. B. Baker (Australia) – by-catch; Z. S. Hogan (US) – fish; C. Limpus (Australia) – marine turtles; T. A. Mundkur (India) – Asiatic fauna; J. O'Sullivan (UK) – birds; A. Oteng-Yeboah (Ghana) – African fauna; W. Perrin (US) – aquatic mammals; R. Schlatter (Chile) – neotropical fauna.

185 Resolution 7.12 specifies Wetlands International, BirdLife International, WCMC, IUCN and WWF.

186 These are the SBSTTA of the CBD, the Ramsar STRP, the IWC, CITES and CCAMLR. Ibid.

187 These may include any body established under the CMS itself or its 'daughter' agreements, or any party.

188 See generally Resolution 6.7.

189 Resolution 7.12. For the Strategy Implementation Plan for 2006–2011, see CMS/ScC.13/Doc.3 and, for its endorsement by the CoP, Resolution 8.21, para. 3.

190 Resolution 4.5.

191 For reports of meetings, see www.cms.int/bodies/ScC_mainpage.htm.

implications.[192] Budgetary provision is made for the funding of Council activities, particularly the cost of attendance by CoP appointees and travel undertaken by the chair on CMS business. Parties are generally expected to finance the attendance of their own nominees, though support has progressively been made available for the benefit of developing countries.[193]

6. Implementation

As in the case of all such treaties, implementation of the Bonn Convention lies in a combination of activities at the national and international levels, with the reporting system established under Article VI providing the necessary link between these two elements.

a) Implementation at the national level

Insofar as the Convention creates obligations for the parties to adopt specific conservation measures, this will normally involve the enactment and implementation of appropriate national legislation. Yet many have been slow to take even this preliminary step, with CMS-listed turtles, bats, fish and reptiles especially likely to have found themselves beyond the pale of legal protection at the domestic level.[194] Even where legislation exists, it does not always adequately address the Convention's specific concerns,[195] and there is therefore a need to ensure that it fully reflects CMS obligations.[196] The effective implementation of such legislation is a further major problem, with many parties admitting to difficulties regarding the enforcement of controls over hunting, pollution and habitat destruction.[197]

Such problems are, of course, in no way peculiar to the Bonn Convention, and fortunately there are a number of well-tried methods of addressing them. First, it is necessary that specific responsibility for

[192] Resolution 8.20.
[193] See Resolution 3.4, preamble and paragraph 2.
[194] See the '2005 Analysis', para. 6; '2008 Synthesis', para. 63.
[195] Whereas in some countries the CMS is implemented through legislation specifically dedicated to that task, in others this is not the case: the UK, for example, relies primarily on the Wildlife and the Countryside Act of 1981 (which addresses a host of conservation issues and treaty obligations) but also an array of other statutes dating back to 1934.
[196] Parties are, however, free to adopt *stricter* legislation than the Convention requires. Article XII(3).
[197] '2005 Analysis', para. 5; '2008 Synthesis', para. 64.

ensuring the implementation of domestic legislation be allocated to appropriate government agencies within each country, a requirement which seems generally to be met within the CMS system.[198] Second, protective measures adopted for the benefit of migratory species should not operate in isolation but be integrated within a broader national scheme of biodiversity conservation. The task of developing national strategies, programmes or plans for conservation is already incumbent upon all parties to the Biodiversity Convention,[199] and CMS Resolution 8.18 calls for the specific integration of migratory species into all such arrangements. Third, there is a need to monitor the consistency of the application of national laws with the obligations assumed under the Bonn Convention. At the very least, this will require clear lines of communication between the relevant institutions at the national and international levels, and all parties are accordingly requested to identify 'focal points' of contact for CMS purposes,[200] as well as involving them in the broader biodiversity planning process.[201] Ideally, however, such arrangements will also be designed so as to involve the scientific community, NGOs and other key stakeholders: the current Strategic Plan therefore aims to secure the establishment of national CMS liaison systems or committees wherever possible,[202] though 'little progress' had evidently been made on this initiative by the time of the ninth CoP.[203]

Finally, it is necessary to establish a workable system of reporting back to the relevant international bodies, so that progress may be monitored at that level. Article VI(3) duly requires the parties to inform the Secretariat, at least six months prior to each ordinary meeting of the CoP, of measures they have taken to implement the Convention with regard to listed species for which they are range states. The Secretariat itself then prepares a detailed analysis of the information and trends disclosed by these reports, which is usually now appended to a briefer overview, or 'synthesis', of that data.[204] In this way the state of progress towards implementation of CMS commitments can effectively be monitored.

[198] The National Report pro forma requires that this information be provided.

[199] CBD, Article 6(a).

[200] For the current list of national focal points, see UNEP/CMS/Inf.9.6/Rev.1.

[201] Resolution 8.18. [202] Strategic Plan, Target 4.6.

[203] UNEP/CMS/Conf.9.5, para. 24.

[204] These are the documents repeatedly referred to from n. 38 *supra* onwards. For recent examples, see the Secretariat's Analysis and Synthesis of National Reports, UNEP/CMS/Conf.8.5 and 9.10.

The process of reporting on compliance with conservation treaty commitments has become a significant burden for many states,[205] with the consequence that submission records are often extremely poor. This has certainly been true of the CMS: Resolution 4.1 noted that reports were often characterised by insufficient detail, and that many parties, indeed, had never submitted one at all.[206] Despite repeated exhortations to the parties, this issue has remained problematic. Devices employed to improve submission rates, and to enhance the utility of the information provided, have included the issue of timely reminders of submission deadlines, and the attempted harmonisation of reporting requirements with those of other biodiversity-related conventions. Standardised formats have accordingly been agreed both for the comprehensive reports submitted upon initial accession to the CMS and for the subsequent updating reports required for each meeting of the CoP. These have been repeatedly revised, so as to incorporate, for example, a 'tick box' pro forma, covering the national status of listed species, relevant national legal structures, management activities, links with other conventions and other emerging issues. Such measures have helped to nudge the submission rate upwards of late from between 50 and 55 per cent to around 65 per cent.[207] Nevertheless, there is plainly still scope for improvement, and the CoP has called for further adaptation of the format to facilitate online response and continuation of the process of harmonisation with other reporting procedures.[208]

b) Implementation at the international level

Given that the species covered by the CMS are migratory, effective conservation action will normally require a high degree of co-operation between range states, and it is therefore inevitable that a heavier emphasis will fall upon implementation at the international level. Overall responsibility for monitoring the implementation process is allocated

205 Reports received for the eighth CMS CoP were typically forty to fifty pages in length, while those of Portugal and the UK both exceeded 100 pages. Subsequently, the form has been significantly simplified.

206 Even by September 2005, this was still true of some sixteen parties; see the 2005 Synthesis, para. 9. Only nineteen parties had a 100 per cent record. Ibid.

207 See Format for Future Party Reports, UNEP/CMS/Conf.9.20/Rev.1, para. 2. Resolution 9.4 notes that, by the deadline set for the 2008 CoP, sixty reports had been submitted out of 102 that were due, a total subsequently augmented by seven late submissions.

208 See Resolutions 8.24 and 9.4.

to the CoP under Article VII(5), the terms of which allow considerable flexibility as to the exact nature of the review to be conducted. Thus it should embrace such matters as assessment of the current status of migratory species, especially those listed in the Appendices, and the progress made towards their conservation; consideration of reports from the Scientific Council, Secretariat, parties and any standing bodies established pursuant to CMS agreements; recommendation of measures for improving the conservation status of migratory species and the effectiveness of the Convention generally; and provision of guidance and support to the Scientific Council and Secretariat in the discharge of their respective functions. Many examples of such action have already been noted.

The 'framework' aspect of the Bonn Convention means that many of its concrete conservation activities are conducted through the ancillary instruments adopted under Article IV(3) and (4), and a crucial part of the CoP's role naturally involves the review of progress in that regard.[209] Since, however, these 'daughter' agreements generally establish specific monitoring processes of their own, the current trend is to concentrate more closely upon implementation of the CMS itself, with the 2008 review focusing primarily on the response to certain key resolutions and recommendations adopted at previous CoPs.[210] One pervasive impediment to progress, however, has always been the inadequacy of information regarding such crucial questions as the behaviour, migration patterns and conservation status of species of interest, the effectiveness of the measures in place to protect them in different range states and the urgency regarding further enhancement and co-ordination of such efforts. It is therefore no surprise that this has become a major preoccupation of CMS institutions generally.

i) Collection and dissemination of information

Concern over this issue originated in dissatisfaction with the poor response rates with regard to reporting,[211] and, as the practice of elaborating an overall strategy for implementation of the Convention took root, this later evolved into a broader preoccupation with the compilation of sufficient information to enable the CoP to discharge its

[209] Article VII(5)(e). For an overview of developments to date, see UNEP/CMS/Conf.9.9; it is encouraging to note, some three decades into the process, that this record does at last begin to show signs for modest satisfaction. For future action, see Resolution 9.2.

[210] See the 2008 Analysis, pp. 30–5. [211] See, e.g., Resolution 1.1.

monitoring functions effectively.[212] This is the purpose intended to be served by the reports prepared by the Secretariat for each CoP and referred to above,[213] though the utility of such documents is inevitably dependent on the information made available to the Secretariat itself. At the sixth meeting, a formal Information Management Plan (IMP) was adopted,[214] the current version of which calls for the further development of authoritative databases of listed species and range states; the establishment of a projects database to facilitate the monitoring of the contribution to conservation of CMS and its daughter agreements; the identification of 'partner organisations' for the collection, management and application of relevant information; the strengthening of linkages with other systems, such as the Biodiversity Conservation Information System (BCIS) and UNEP's Global Environmental Outlook (GEO); and the greater use of electronic media for the submission of reports and the sharing of experience generally.[215] One important milestone was the decision to improve the quality and user-friendliness of the GROMS system developed originally by the Zoological Museum Alexander Koenig in Bonn,[216] and to integrate it fully into the CMS Information Management System.[217]

Despite the importance of these developments, any appraisal of the effectiveness of the Bonn Convention must naturally focus not so much upon the mere collection of information as upon its effective deployment for practical conservation purposes, with the fate of species whose conservation status is known to be unfavourable serving as the crucial performance indicator. Not surprisingly, certain formalised procedures have also emerged for that purpose.

ii) 'Concerted Actions' for Appendix I species

As regards Appendix I, it was decided in 1991 to institute a formal review process whereby consideration would be given to selected species at each meeting of the CoP with a view to recommending initiatives for their benefit.[218] As this process envisages the pooling of information by range states and co-operation in the implementation of conservation measures,

[212] See Resolution 5.4, Annex, para. 3.3. [213] See n. 204 *supra*. [214] See Resolution 6.5.

[215] Resolution 8.10. See further Resolution 9.3 and, for a progress report on implementation of the IMP, UNEP/CMS/Conf.9.18/Rev.1.

[216] As to which, see www.cms.int/species/groms/groms.htm. GROMS is a database of migratory vertebrate species containing population data, distribution maps and bibliographical and other information. For discussion, see K. Riede, 'The Global Register of Migratory Species (GROMS)' (2000) 3 *JIWLP* 152.

[217] Resolutions 7.8, 8.9. [218] Resolution 3.2.

it has come to be known as the Concerted Actions procedure. Since its introduction, it has been applied to nearly fifty individual (sub)species,[219] as well as to certain broader categories of animals.[220] At the seventh CoP in 2002,[221] no fewer than ten species were identified for this purpose, including several of the great whales,[222] the snow leopard (*Uncia uncia*), the black-faced spoonbill (*Platalea minor*) and the Chinese crested tern (*Sterna bernsteini*). As regards the snow leopard, it was noted that, although only five of its twelve range states (India, Mongolia, Pakistan, Tajikistan and Uzbekistan) were CMS parties, the species was in fact fully protected by law right across its range. Significant uncertainty surrounded the practical implementation of such legislation, however, with only two states (Mongolia and Pakistan) having actually adopted a comprehensive management plan for the species.[223] It was agreed that Tajikistan would act as focal point in the investigation of further conservation needs, including the possible adoption of a CMS instrument to provide the framework for international action, taking into account the Snow Leopard Survival Strategy which was already being developed by a network of fifty experts from seventeen countries.[224]

Unfortunately, information regarding the effectiveness of Concerted Actions to date is both elusive and inconclusive: over a decade after its inception the chair of the Scientific Council reported that most of the species covered by it remained in rapid decline,[225] though it is fair to recognise that for many of them the procedure was still in its relatively early stages.[226] One particular concern relates to its success in prompting action which can truly be regarded as 'concerted' in circumstances where no MoU or formal agreement is in place.[227] In the case of the six antelope

219 For the complete list, see Resolution 9.1.

220 See, e.g., Resolution 7.1 (marine turtles). 221 Ibid.

222 Specifically the blue (*Balaenoptera musculus*), fin (*B. physalus*), sei (*B. borealis*), sperm (*Physeter macrocephalus*), humpback (*Megaptera novaeangliae*) and southern right (*Eubalaena australis*) whale species.

223 Though such plans were under development in two non-party states, Nepal and Russia.

224 'Living on the Edge: The Snow Leopard' *CMS Bulletin* No. 16 (2000), pp. 18–19. For further developments, see Recommendation 9.4.

225 Report of the 28th Meeting of the Standing Committee, CMS/StC29/Inf.2, para. 62.

226 As noted above, species are added periodically. For an overview of progress to date, see Major Species Projects including Concerted Actions, UNEP/CMS/Conf.9.14/Rev.1.

227 The need for joint, as opposed to several, conservation measures varies from species to species, but where it is needed it is often lacking: compare the detailed reports prepared by the WCMC for four species, CMS/ScC12/Doc.5, Attachments 2–5.

species covered by the resolution on Sahelo-Saharan ungulates, however, an impressive level of collaborative effort is certainly apparent.[228] Building upon conservation initiatives undertaken in earlier decades by FFI, WWF and IUCN, and research activities carried out in various countries, the CMS Secretariat has convened two workshops of range states,[229] attended also by official delegations from Belgium, France and Germany and various conservation experts, to develop an Action Plan for these species, based upon detailed information regarding their current conservation status.[230] This plan was devised originally by the Belgian Royal Institute of Natural Sciences and has benefited from funding provided by the French Global Environment Fund. The critical problem of illegal hunting remains to be resolved, but at least the CMS system has mobilised itself to some effect. Moves are also under way to devise an MoU to consolidate this collaboration still further.

While co-operative research and action plans for other threatened species have been initiated by NGOs such as WWF and BirdLife International, there is, unfortunately, no guarantee that, even with formal CMS endorsement,[231] such plans will actually be implemented by governments. Where, however, a strong commitment to the conservation of particular species is evident on the part of at least one range state, it may serve to galvanise the efforts of others: one interesting recent proposal envisages the appointment of a voluntary 'champion' for each species brought within this procedure,[232] which may indeed assist in maximising its potential.

iii) 'Co-operative Actions' for Appendix II species

At the fifth meeting of the CoP in 1997, it was agreed that a parallel procedure should be applied to Appendix II species, since, although many urgently required co-operation for their conservation, no Article IV ancillary agreement was currently in sight.[233] The corncrake,[234] the European quail (*Coturnix coturnix coturnix*) and the black-necked swan were the first to be brought under the ambit of this procedure, which is

[228] For details, see UNEP/CMS/Conf.9.14/Rev.1.

[229] At Djerba, Tunisia, in February 1998 and at Agadir, Morocco, in May 2003. A third meeting was scheduled for 2009.

[230] For the plan itself, see Conservation Measures for Sahelo-Saharan Antelopes: Action Plan and Status Report (CMS Technical Series Publication No. 4, 1999).

[231] Recommendation 5.1, for example, formally endorses the action plans devised by BirdLife International and Wetlands International for numerous avian species, several of which have been brought within the Concerted Actions process.

[232] See the '2005 Synthesis', para. 37. [233] Recommendation 5.2.

[234] See also Recommendation 4.3.

known as Co-operative Actions. It was considerably expanded in 1999 to embrace all albatrosses and several species of petrel,[235] eighteen species of sturgeon,[236] various South American dolphins, and the whale shark (*Rhincodon typus*), African elephant[237] and African penguin (*Spheniscus demersus*). Further species have been added at later meetings.[238] It is doubtless premature to assess the effectiveness of the Co-operative Actions procedure as yet, though it will be apparent from the examples given that the designation of species for this purpose has in several cases already served as a stepping-stone towards the adoption of more elaborate conservation measures via an instrument under Article IV(3) or (4) of the Convention. This has enabled the removal of these species from the Co-operative Actions catalogue,[239] which currently embraces some forty-two species.[240]

iv) Financial and technical support

Apart from co-operation amongst range states themselves, another crucial element for effective conservation action, as national reports amply confirm,[241] is the availability of external financial and technical support for such activities. Although the Bonn Convention itself contains no specific provision for financial assistance, there developed the practice of earmarking a modest sum from within its Trust Fund for the support of conservation and research projects, and between 1997 and 2005 some US$1.5 million was distributed in grants of this kind, numbering around fifty in total.[242] However, although the current Strategic Plan envisages the continuation of direct project funding for developing countries and transitional economies,[243] financial constraints have seen the budgetary

235 See now the 2001 Agreement on the Conservation of Albatrosses and Petrels, discussed in Chapter 7 above.

236 Resolution 7.7(d) called for the development of an appropriate instrument concerning sturgeons, and for closer co-operation between the CMS and CITES for their conservation.

237 See Recommendations 6.5, 9.5 and Resolution 7.7(l).

238 See Recommendations 7.1 and 8.28.

239 E.g. albatrosses and petrels following the entry into force of ACAP. Also, the listing of the African elephant is now restricted to the Central African population following the adoption of the MoU covering West Africa.

240 A full list is appended to Resolution 9.1.

241 Almost all reporting parties outside the EU note the need for such assistance in order to tackle conservation problems faced by migratory species; see the 2005 Analysis, para. 8.

242 For more detailed information, see Overview of the Status of Small-Scale Projects Financed by the CMS Trust Fund, CMS/ScC.13/Doc.4.

243 This is conditional upon them attracting at least 50 per cent matching funding; see Operational Principles 4–6, Logical Framework Table, Resolution 8.2, Annex.

allocation fixed at only token levels,[244] sufficient in fact to fund only six of eighteen proposed small-scale projects in the last triennium.[245] This turn of events prompted serious expressions of concern at the 2008 CoP.[246] Although both financial support and scientific or technical assistance for the conservation of migratory species will doubtless continue to be available from other sources,[247] the ability of CMS to generate such benefits from within its own resources will rightly be seen as an important indicator of its operational effectiveness into the future.

7. Relationship with other agreements

The relationship of the Bonn Convention with other agreements is fairly complex, requiring consideration of several distinct categories.[248]

a) Major global and regional conservation treaties

Article XII(2) of the Bonn Convention stipulates that its provisions in no way affect any rights or obligations deriving from existing agreements, and the text as a whole contains various indications of an intent not to encroach upon the domain of other such regimes.[249] Thus it avoids the issue of international trade entirely, leaving that to be regulated under CITES, while also aiming at conformity with the Whaling Convention in relation to subsidiary agreements concerning cetaceans.[250] As noted above, the exceptions it allows from the strict protection of Appendix I also have much in common with the ICRW, though here there is a risk of incompatibility with other regimes with which the Bonn Convention arguably overlaps more extensively, such as those established by the Bern

[244] The annual allocation for 'Conservation Grants and Projects' was €42,000 for the triennium 2006–8, and €57,000 for 2009–2011.

[245] See Item 4 of the Report of the 15th Meeting of the Scientific Council. Recipients were Bolivia, Peru, Uruguay, Mongolia and India.

[246] See the Report of the Ninth Meeting, paras. 280–1.

[247] At recent CoPs, parties have reported receiving financial or other assistance from such diverse sources as the GEF, the UNDP, the World Bank, UNESCO, the EU, the Ramsar SGF, the WWF, the IUCN, the RSPB, BirdLife International, Wetlands International and other NGOs, along with numerous individual countries or government agencies. See the 2005 Analysis, paras. 25–7; 2008 Analysis, p. 29.

[248] See further N. Matz, 'Chaos or Coherence?' (2005) 65 *ZaöRV* 197.

[249] See, e.g., Article 12(1), which disclaims any intention to prejudice the codification and development of the law of the sea.

[250] Note especially Article V(4)(f).

Convention and the EU Birds Directive.[251] An attempt in the AEWA to avoid similar incongruity may have created significant legal problems.[252]

The Bonn Convention itself is generally left intact by later conservation treaties, including, most importantly, the Biodiversity Convention.[253] However, the very scope and prominence of the CBD inevitably impacts upon the overall direction of policy and practice under earlier biodiversity-related conventions, and the 2002 Johannesburg Summit called for enhanced co-operation within this network of agreements with a view to reducing the rate of biodiversity loss by the year 2010. This call has been echoed in recent CMS resolutions, as well as in the current Strategic Plan.[254] The CMS Secretariat duly participates in the Biodiversity Liaison Group (BLG) established by the executive secretary of the CBD, alongside its counterparts from CITES, Ramsar and the World Heritage and Plant Genetic Resources Conventions.[255] As noted above, the Secretariats of these various treaties also commonly attend meetings of each other's treaty bodies.

Co-operation in this context may take various forms.[256] On the procedural side, important steps have already been taken regarding the harmonisation amongst key treaties both of reporting procedures[257] and of the usage of nomenclature.[258] There is also scope for collaboration in substantive conservation matters through joint programmes of work, several of which have been initiated in recent years. A 1997 MoU between the CMS and Ramsar, for example, has spawned a trilateral programme with AEWA, focusing on the importance of wetland sites for migratory waterbird conservation.[259] Linkages between CMS and the CBD were consolidated by CMS Resolution 8.18, which established a Joint Work Programme to develop guidance upon the integration of migratory species into national biodiversity strategies, action plans and work programmes.

[251] See section 4(c)(ii) above. [252] See section 7(b) below.
[253] See Article 22(1) CBD and, for discussion, Chapter 17 below.
[254] See Resolutions 8.7, 8.11, 9.2 and Target 4.3 respectively.
[255] For further information on the activities of the Group, see UNEP/CMS/Conf.9.12.
[256] For an overview of current arrangements, see UNEP/CMS/Conf.9.23 and, for the future programme, Resolution 9.6.
[257] For a report of the UNEP-WCMC Workshop, Towards the Harmonisation of National Reporting to Biodiversity-Related Treaties, held in Haasrode, Belgium, during September 2004, see www.unep-wcmc.org/conventions/harmonization/workshop04/Workshop_report.pdf.
[258] Particularly with CITES: see Resolution 9.6.
[259] See www.ramsar.org/wn/w.n.cms_aewa_jwp.htm.

b) *CMS 'daughter' agreements*

Naturally, however, the Bonn Convention's closest normative and institutional relationships lie within the CMS family itself, which comprises the various instruments concluded under Article IV. Since the Bonn Convention has itself 'given birth' to these instruments, they inevitably bear its stamp,[260] and it maintains ongoing vigilance over them through the exercise of its supervisory and facilitative functions.[261] The Secretariats of AEWA and EUROBATS are housed alongside the CMS Secretariat in Bonn, allowing for the closest possible co-operation, whilst a formal merger of the CMS and ASCOBANS Secretariats was agreed on an experimental basis in 2006.[262] The various MoUs concluded under Article IV(4) are generally administered by the CMS Secretariat itself, though Marine Turtles-IOSEA has its own independently funded Secretariat based at the UNEP regional office in Bangkok. The authorities in Abu Dhabi (United Arab Emirates) have, moreover, recently offered to finance a co-ordinating unit for the MoUs concerning raptors and dugongs, as well as the north-western area of IOSEA.

The formal legal relationship between CMS and its offspring is largely straightforward, though potential difficulty arises from the drafting of certain provisions of AEWA. As explained in Chapter 7 above, this Agreement strictly regulates the exploitation of various categories of waterbirds,[263] including all those listed in CMS Appendix I.[264] Paragraph 2.1.3 of the Action Plan permits the granting of exceptions from these controls, where there is no other satisfactory solution, for the following purposes:

(a) to prevent serious damage to crops, water and fisheries;
(b) in the interests of air safety or other overriding public interests;
(c) for the purpose of research and education, of re-establishment and for the breeding necessary for these purposes;

260 Consider, for example, Articles I–III of ACAP, which derive unmistakably from the parent Convention.
261 See, e.g., Articles VII(5)(d)–(f); VIII(5)(a) and (d); and IX(4)(b), (g), (h).
262 The ACCOBAMS Secretariat is located in Monaco, while the Seals Agreement is administered by the Wadden Sea Secretariat. Given its original southern hemisphere focus, ACAP's base was established in Canberra, Australia.
263 See Article III(2)(a), and the Action Plan, paras. 2.1.1 and 2.1.2. Note that the Plan is declared to be 'an integral part' of the Agreement itself: Article I(4), AEWA.
264 Table 1, Column A, Category 1(a).

(d) to permit under strictly supervised conditions, on a selective basis and to a limited extent, the taking and keeping or other judicious use of certain birds in small numbers; and
(e) for the purpose of enhancing the propagation or survival of the populations concerned.

Though not identically worded, these exceptions are noticeably closer in content to those of the Bern Convention and the EU Birds Directive than to those of the CMS itself: in particular, there is no reference in the latter to the taking or judicious use of birds in small numbers. This is certainly no oversight, since the power to grant exemptions under AEWA is expressly conferred 'irrespective of the provisions of Article III, paragraph 5 of the [Bonn] Convention'. The intention would therefore seem to be that AEWA overrides the parent convention in this respect[265] – a surprising conclusion, but one that might be explained by the desire to achieve consistency amongst arrangements for avian conservation within the European region especially. Although Article XI(1) of AEWA asserts that its provisions 'do not affect' the rights and obligations of any party deriving from existing treaties, which prima facie would include the CMS itself, the specific stipulation of the Action Plan should arguably be taken to prevail over this more generally worded provision, operating as an exception to it.[266] On the other hand, Article IV of AEWA states that the Plan specifies actions to be taken '*consistent with* the general conservation measures specified in Article III', paragraph 2(a) of which requires '*the same* strict protection for endangered migratory species in the Agreement Area *as is provided for under Article III, paragraphs 4 and 5, of the [parent] Convention*'.[267] Article III(5) of CMS is, of course, the very provision which establishes the ban on taking, and the permissible exceptions to it, for CMS Appendix I-listed species. The correct interpretation of these provisions is therefore far from clear, providing further testimony to the difficulty of achieving complete coherence in the drafting of international treaties.

c) *Protection of migratory species outside the CMS family*

The Bonn Convention is not the only vehicle for the conservation of migratory species. In addition to the long-standing arrangements which

[265] As to which, see the Vienna Convention on the Law of Treaties, Article 30(2)–(4).
[266] In accordance with the principle of interpretation that specific provisions prevail over general ones.
[267] Emphasis added.

the United States has maintained with its immediate neighbours, a number of bilateral treaties were concluded in response to the call at the UNCHE for enhanced protection, particularly amongst countries of the Pacific Rim (several of whom remain outside the CMS system). Most of these have concerned migratory birds,[268] and are discussed more fully in Chapter 7 above. Until recently, there had been minimal interaction between this group of treaties and the Bonn Convention, but Recommendation 7.7 called for increased co-operation amongst range states along the America–Pacific Flyway (whether CMS parties or not), while acknowledging the value of existing arrangements, especially the Western Hemisphere Shorebird Reserve Network. Subsequently, Resolution 9.2 created a specialist working group under the Scientific Council's aegis to develop action plans for all the world's major waterbird flyways. A few months earlier, a potentially seminal institutional development occurred with the opening of a CMS regional office in Washington, in premises generously provided by the US Fish and Wildlife Service.

8. Conclusions

The Bonn Convention undoubtedly got off to a shaky start, and by the time of the Second Meeting of the CoP in 1988, attended by only thirteen parties and the EC, the air of despondency over its future was palpable.[269] None of the handful of ancillary agreements under negotiation had been finalised and no new ones were proposed.[270] The Secretariat rarely had sufficient funds to attend meetings and the Convention was being kept alive largely through correspondence.[271] In recent years, however, its progress has been much more in keeping with its aspirations, although a great deal remains to be accomplished. The total number of parties has certainly increased, though the continuing absence of key players presents a major challenge. In particular, it gravely undermines the value of Appendix I listing, even if the species concerned receive some

[268] Though not all; see, e.g., the 1987 Agreement on the Conservation of the Porcupine Caribou Herd, *Can TS* 1987/31 (US/Canada); N. D. Bankes, 'Migratory Caribou Convention' (1980) 18 *Can YBIL* 285. Note also the North American Monarch Conservation Plan, viewable at www.cec.org, and endorsed in 2007 by the Trilateral Committee for Wildlife and Ecosystem Conservation and Management (Canada/Mexico/US).

[269] See, e.g., the welcoming address at pp. 7–8 of the Proceedings of the Second Meeting.

[270] Ibid., Agenda Items 4 and 5, pp. 36–7. [271] Ibid., Agenda Item 11, p. 13.

degree of protection from measures adopted outside the CMS framework. Significant developments can now be recorded regarding the conclusion of instruments for the conservation of Appendix II species, due partly to imaginative exploitation of the flexibility offered by Article IV(4). This represents arguably the most innovative and productive feature of the CMS system to date, though there is a need to ensure that further planned instruments are expeditiously brought to fruition.[272] In the realms of implementation, the submission record for national reports leaves much to be desired, and current attempts to improve compliance with this obligation must be urgently pursued. Whilst the emergence of the Concerted and Co-operative Actions procedures is to be commended, there is scope for improving their effectiveness. The continued dissemination of information and best practice remains vital, while attention must also be paid to the Convention's remaining financial and institutional problems. In particular, the optimum administrative structure for managing such a heterogeneous family of conservation instruments needs to be speedily determined. All in all the record is mixed, though there is at last room for a degree of cautious optimism.

Recommended further reading

C. de Klemm, 'The Problem of Migratory Species in International Law' (1994) *Green Globe Yearbook* 67

J. Ebbeson, '*Lex Pernis Apivorus*: An Experiment of Environmental Law Methodology' (2003) 15 *JEL* 153

J. Frazier (ed.), 'Special Issue: International Instruments and Marine Turtle Conservation' (2002) 5 *JIWLP*, Nos. 1–2

L. Glowka, 'Complementarities between the Convention on Migratory Species and the Convention on Biological Diversity' (2000) 3 *JIWLP* 205

N. Matz, 'Chaos or Coherence?' (2005) 65 *ZaöRV* 197

R. Vagg, *CMS Family Guide: The Encyclopaedia of the Convention* (UNEP/CMS, 3rd ed., 2009)

[272] Note in this regard the opening for signature in February 2010 of an MoU on the Conservation of Migratory Sharks, heralded as the first global CMS instrument concerning commercially exploited species.

PART V

Biological diversity: a new perspective on wildlife regulation

Chapter 17

The Biodiversity Convention and Biosafety Protocol

1. Background

Biological diversity is an umbrella term referring to the degree of nature's variety. The concept is often used loosely to indicate the total number of species in a given area, or even to highlight particular endangered species such as the African rhinoceros, the blue whale, or the spotted owl. More specifically, it is understood to refer to the existence of diversity or variety at various key levels of biological organisation.[1] Scientists tend to differ as to the number of levels they choose to identify for the purpose, though a minimum of three are commonly specified, namely (a) diversity of ecosystems (or habitat diversity), (b) diversity of species and (c) genetic diversity (within species). This threefold classification is the one adopted in the 1992 Biodiversity Convention, which defines 'biological diversity' as 'the variability among living organisms from all sources including, inter alia, terrestrial, marine and other aquatic ecosystems and the ecological complexes of which they are a part: this includes diversity within species, between species, and of ecosystems' (Article 2).

It is not possible precisely to determine the total number of species on Earth, because new species are being discovered all the time – about 1.7 million have been identified and named, including not only animals and plants but also life forms which are sometimes overlooked in the 'biodiversity count', such as micro-organisms. The total is estimated at anywhere from 5 million to 100 million. Nor is diversity uniform across the planet, but rather varies greatly from place to place. Variation in diversity is partly a question of latitude, with lower latitudes exhibiting higher diversity (contrast the lack of diversity on the continent of Antarctica

[1] See, generally, M. Bowman and C. Redgwell (eds.), *The Conservation of Biological Diversity* (Kluwer, 1996), Introduction.

with the rich diversity of the Brazilian rainforest). What *is* known is that certain species have already become extinct, while many others are at risk: nearly one-quarter of all known mammal species are under threat of extinction, and nearly one-third of fish species, especially freshwater fish. Species extinction is, of course, a natural part of the evolutionary process; however, due to human activities, species and ecosystems are more threatened today than at any time in recorded history. Calculations at the time of the conclusion of the Biodiversity Convention put the rate of extinction at between 1,000 and 10,000 times the natural rate[2] – a trend which has, if anything, accelerated in the intervening eighteen years. The human impact on biodiversity is fourfold and arises principally from: (i) intentional hunting and harvesting; (ii) disruption and/or elimination of habitat particularly in consequence of urbanisation and more intensive forms of agriculture; (iii) introduction of new parasites, predators or competitors of species;[3] and (iv) pollution of the environment. The IUCN estimates that over 75 per cent of extinctions which have occurred since the year 1600 have been caused by human beings, with tropical deforestation now the single highest contributory factor.[4] On one estimate, the worldwide rate of extinction is 50,000 species per annum, resulting in a loss of up to 10 per cent of all species alive today within the next quarter-century.[5]

Certain organisms are particularly vital to the maintenance of the functions of ecosystems and the biosphere – so-called 'keystone species' which carry out functions not performed by any other species. The current rate of species extinction thus has broader implications for the health of ecosystems as a whole. But this is not only an environmental tragedy; there are also profound implications for economic and social development given that at least 40 per cent of the economy and 80 per cent of the food, clothing and fuel needs of the poor are derived, directly or indirectly, from biological resources. There are at least six reasons for saving endangered species:[6]

[2] M.-A. Hermitte, 'La Convention Sur La Diversité Biologique' (1992) 38 *AFDI* 844.

[3] Today the definition of pollution includes the introduction of alien species; see Article 1 of the 1982 Law of the Sea Convention, for example.

[4] The IUCN Red List of Threatened Species reports more than 11,000 species threatened with extinction: 25 per cent of mammal species, 12 per cent of bird species and more than 30 per cent of listed reptiles, amphibians and fish. See further www.iucn.org.

[5] Hermitte, *supra* n. 2.

[6] As the CBD Secretariat observes, 'the variety of life is our insurance policy' – *About the Convention on Biological Diversity* (CBD Secretariat, 2002). For further detail of the

(1) their genetic characteristics;
(2) possible chemical and medicinal uses;[7]
(3) the development of new crops and products;[8]
(4) indigenous peoples' uses for food, shelter, fuel, clothing and medicine;
(5) use for pollution control;[9] and
(6) tourism, especially ecotourism.[10]

Quite apart from these instrumental and anthropocentric justifications for preserving biological diversity, a broader ethical or moral justification may be found.[11]

In 1980, IUCN/UNEP/WWF formulated a comprehensive programme for preserving biodiversity in their World Conservation Strategy (WCS),[12] which, with its underlying theme of sustainable development, set the 'real foundation' for the biodiversity concept in international law. To be sure, there had been some prior brief reference to safeguarding the natural resources of the Earth, especially representative samples of natural ecosystems, in Principle 2 of the 1972 Stockholm Declaration on the Human Environment and, in Principle 4, to humankind's 'special responsibility to safeguard and wisely manage the heritage of wildlife and its habitat which are now gravely imperilled by a combination of adverse factors'. There is, however, little sign of the biodiversity concept as such at Stockholm. The World Conservation Strategy, by contrast, does make explicit reference to such in establishing three fundamental objectives of living-resources conservation, namely (a) to maintain essential ecological processes and life-support systems, (b) to

reasons which follow, see D. B. Botkin and E. A. Keller, *Environmental Science* (Wiley, 7th ed., 2009), Chapter 7.

7 For example, digitalis, an important heart medication, is derived from the purple foxglove, native to Europe and Morocco; aspirin is a derivative of willow bark; steroids were derived from the Mexican yam; and anti-cancer drugs have been developed using the rosy periwinkle, indigenous to Madagascar.

8 A study of the Peruvian tropical rainforest found 275 species, seventy-two of which yield products of distinct economic value. Botkin and Keller, *supra* n. 6.

9 Aquatic filter-feeding animals aid in purifying water; rainforests function as carbon sinks as well as providing habitat rich in biodiversity.

10 Ecotourism is particularly important for states such as Kenya, South Africa and Ecuador.

11 Hermitte, *supra* n. 2, suggests that this dimension played a particularly important role for non-governmental organisations at the 1992 Rio Conference on Environment and Development, where the Convention was opened for signature. See further discussion above, Chapter 3.

12 World Conservation Strategy: Living Resource Conservation for Sustainable Development (1980), prepared by the International Union for the Conservation of Nature (IUCN), with UNEP, the WWF, the FAO and UNESCO.

preserve genetic diversity and (c) to ensure the sustainable utilisation of species and ecosystems. The second of these three objectives, the preservation of genetic diversity, as it is further defined in the WCS, captures the essence of the biodiversity concept later developed. Indeed, the WCS was revised in 1991 and explicitly calls for the protection of biodiversity as an important element in sustainable living.[13]

This is echoed in the 1982 World Charter for Nature,[14] which provides, inter alia, for the maintenance of the 'genetic viability' of the Earth, the conservation of unique areas, representative samples of ecosystems and habitats of rare or endangered species. Also stressed is the need for human management of ecosystems to achieve and maintain optimum sustainable productivity, with planning taking into account environmental impacts. Explicit linkage of biodiversity and legal principle is made in the 1987 Report of the World Commission on Environment and Development,[15] the Legal Experts Group of which proposed Legal Principles for Environmental Protection and Sustainable Development,[16] the third of which provides: 'States shall maintain ecosystems and ecological processes essential for the functioning of the biosphere, shall preserve biological diversity, and shall observe the principles of optimum sustainable yield in the use of living natural resources and ecosystems.'

Another striking feature of the WCS is the emphasis upon the practical, utilitarian values of wildlife conservation, seeking to demonstrate that environmental protection and economic development are not only reconcilable but that the former is a prerequisite for the latter.[17] As was indicated above, economic development is dependent on the continued viability of natural systems and the availability of resources, especially consumables. In other words, sustainable development, the rapprochement of environment and development at the heart of the 1992 Rio Conference at which the CBD was opened for signature, is therefore at the heart of the CBD.

[13] *Caring for the Earth: A Strategy for Sustainable Living* (IUCN/UNEP/WWF, 1991).
[14] Framed in the context of UNGA Resolution 37/7, 28 October 1982, adopted by a vote of 111 in favour, eighteen abstentions, and one vote against (the United States), text at (1983) 23 *ILM* 455.
[15] WCED, *Our Common Future* (Oxford University Press, 1987).
[16] G. Munro and D. Lammers (eds.), *Environmental Protection and Sustainable Development* (London, 1986).
[17] *Supra* n. 12.

2. Negotiating a biodiversity convention

In 1989 UNEP's Governing Council initiated the drafting of a convention on the conservation of biological diversity,[18] which was subsequently brought within the mandate of the United Nations Conference on Environment and Development scheduled for Rio in June 1992.[19] Amongst other things, this imposed serious time constraints on the negotiations if a text was to be ready for signature at Rio. Thus the advantage of UNEP's co-ordination was offset by the need for speed, leading some commentators to conclude that the resulting Convention had a 'rushed and unsatisfactory nature'.[20] Indeed, when the United States made a declaration upon the adoption of the Nairobi Final Act, the final paragraph explicitly condemned the negotiating procedure:

> Procedurally, we believe that the hasty and disjointed approach to the preparation of this Convention has deprived delegations of the ability to consider the text as a whole before adoption. Further, it has not resulted in a text that reflects well on the international treaty-making process in the environmental field.[21]

In particular, a number of controversial provisions were deleted between the fifth negotiating draft concluded in Nairobi in May 1992[22] and the final text adopted in Rio in June 1992, with negotiations on substantive issues still taking place at Rio.[23] Notably, the precautionary

[18] Resolution 15/34 of the UNEP Governing Council, while recognising the need for co-ordinated and effective implementation of existing legal instruments and agreements, also endorsed the adoption of a further legal instrument which might be in the form of a framework convention for the global conservation of biological diversity.

[19] See UNGA Resolution 44/228.

[20] A. E. Boyle, 'The Convention on Biological Diversity', in L. Campiglio, L. Pineschi, D. Siniscalco and T. Treves (eds.) *The Environment after Rio* (Kluwer, 1994), at p. 35; Hermitte, *supra* n. 2, refers to the conclusion of a Convention in 1992 'que ne satisfait vraiment personne'.

[21] Para. 6. Under the Bush administration the United States failed to sign the CBD at Rio owing to a variety of concerns, most notably the treatment of intellectual property rights, finance, technology transfer and biotechnology. The Clinton administration moved to sign in 1993; at the time of writing the United States had still not ratified the Convention and it appears unlikely to do so in the foreseeable future.

[22] In total, seven substantive working sessions of the Intergovernmental Negotiation Committee (INC) were held prior to the adoption of the Nairobi Final Act of the Conference for the Adoption of an Agreed Text on the Convention on Biological Diversity.

[23] See Boyle, *supra* n. 20; see also V. Koester, 'The Biodiversity Convention Negotiating Process: Some Comments on the Outcome' (1997) 27 *EPL* 175.

principle, found in Principle 15 of the Rio Declaration, is transferred in the final text to the preamble (ninth recital). A provision on responsibility for damage to biodiversity, which would have held those responsible for activities threatening or damaging biodiversity responsible for the costs of avoiding or remedying the damage, is deleted. Article 14(2) now merely provides that the Conference of the Parties will – at some unspecified point – examine the issue of liability and redress for damage to biodiversity, where more than merely an internal matter. Admittedly, the retention of a substantive liability provision would have been exceptional; much more common is to defer the matter by making provision for future negotiation of liability issues,[24] if indeed the matter is addressed at all. A global listing of protected areas and species, a technique employed under the World Heritage Convention, was dropped in favour of reliance on each state party to select and manage protected areas and species.[25] A measure of the controversy over such deletions is found in the declarations made by states on the adoption of the Nairobi Final Act, and upon signature and ratification of the CBD. For example, in mirror image portions of their declarations/understandings on adoption, Sudan and India stated that the issue of liability and compensation for damage to biological diversity in Article 14(2) is not a priority area; rather, compensation for harm arising from genetically modified organisms and acid rain should be. France refused initially to sign the Nairobi Final Act in protest against the omission of a global list of protected areas and species. In the event all three states have become parties to the CBD.

3. Scope and objectives of the Convention[26]

Along with the 1992 Framework Convention for Climate Change, the 1992 Convention on Biological Diversity (CBD) was opened for

[24] See, for example, the 1991 Environmental Protocol to the 1959 Antarctic Treaty (discussed in Chapter 11 above) and the 2000 Cartagena Protocol (discussed further below).

[25] See further discussion of Article 8 on *in situ* conservation, below.

[26] On the CBD see, generally, Boyle, *supra* n. 20; F. McConnell, *The Biodiversity Convention: A Negotiating History* (Kluwer, 1996); Hermitte, *supra* n. 2; F. Burhenne-Guilmin and S. Casey-Lefkowitz, 'The New Law of Biodiversity' (1992) 3 *Yb. Int'l Env. L.* 43; the *Convention on Biological Diversity Handbook* (CBD Secretariat, 1996) available at www.biodiv.org; L. Glowka et al., *A Guide to the Convention on Biological Diversity* (CBD Secretariat, 1994), IUCN Environmental Law and Policy Paper No. 30; C. de Klemm and C. Shine, *Biological Diversity Conservation and Law: Legal Mechanisms for Conserving Species and Ecosystems*, IUCN Environmental Policy & Law Paper Series No.

signature at Rio during the 1992 United Nations Conference on Environment and Development (UNCED). Not only was the text concluded very swiftly, as observed above, but the Convention itself entered into force only eighteen months after UNCED, on 29 December 1993, upon the thirtieth ratification of the Convention, by Mongolia. All EU member states, and the European Community itself, are parties to the Convention.[27] With the accession of Somalia on 10 December 2009, the Convention now enjoys virtually universal participation with an impressive 193 parties. The United States (a signatory since 1993) remains the only major state not a party to the Convention.[28]

The Convention is the first international treaty explicitly to address all aspects of biodiversity, ranging from conservation of biological diversity and sustainable use of biological resources[29] to access to biotechnology[30] and the safety of activities related to modified living organisms.[31] Its breadth is revealed in both the preamble and its substantive provisions, with reference, inter alia, to combating deforestation and desertification, planning and management of land resources, managing fragile ecosystems on land and at sea and promoting sustainable utilisation of all living resources. Furthermore, as its parties have observed, it 'ushers in a new era' concerning access to genetic resources governed by the

29 (IUCN, 1993); C. Redgwell, 'The Protection of Biological Diversity', in K. Koufa (ed.), *Protection of the Environment for the New Millennium*, Thesaurus Acroasium, Volume XXXI (Sakkoulas Publications, 2002), 355–96; and two special issues of the *Review of European Community and International Environmental Law* (1997, Volume 6(3) and 2002, Volume 11(1)). For wider background see, generally, Bowman and Redgwell, *supra* n. 1.

27 See Council Decision 93/626/EEC of 25 October 1993 concerning the conclusion of the Convention on Biological Diversity, OJ 1993 L309/1. Article 34 on ratification, acceptance or approval of the Convention explicitly recognises that 'regional economic integration organizations' may become contracting parties to the Convention and any subsequent protocols. Such organisations must make a declaration of the extent of their competence with respect to the matters governed by the Convention and any subsequent protocol. Furthermore, Article 31(2) addresses the right to vote of regional economic integration organisations and their members.

28 The list of non-participants is now very short indeed: the United States, Andorra and the Holy See. See www.biodiv.org, under 'participation'.

29 Defined in Article 2 to include 'genetic resources, organisms or parts thereof, populations, or any other biotic component of ecosystems with actual or potential use or value for humanity'.

30 Defined in Article 2 as 'any technological application that uses biological systems, living organisms, or derivatives thereof, populations, or any other biotic component of ecosystems with actual or potential use or value for humanity'.

31 As is described further below, in 2000 a Protocol to the Convention on living modified organisms was concluded, known as the Cartagena or Biosafety Protocol.

Convention.[32] The CBD thus adds a comprehensive, global approach to the protection of Earth's biodiversity previously lacking in international law, and does so by reaching within as well as beyond national jurisdiction. It supplements the ad hoc approach to 'rational' or 'wise' use of common property or shared resources such as fish and marine mammals,[33] the protection of migratory species and their habitats or of particular habitat types, and preventing the overexploitation of certain species of wildlife through trade addressed in instruments reviewed in previous chapters on the World Heritage, CITES and Bonn Conventions. It also supplements treaties addressed to specific ecosystems such as Ramsar, the Antarctic 1991 Environmental Protocol to the Antarctic Treaty, and marine ecosystems under the law of the sea. All contribute to the conservation of biological diversity, but only in a piecemeal fashion. The Convention clearly illustrates the extent to which biological diversity is an issue that cuts across these species and habitat instruments in particular, which together constitute a web of biodiversity-related treaties.[34] Indeed, this is one reason for the framework character of the Convention, which does not start from a blank slate but rather seeks to fill the 'biodiversity gaps' in existing regulation. It is 'framework' also in the sense that it 'lays down various guiding principles at the international level which states parties are required to take into account in developing national law and policy to implement its objectives, but to which can also be added subsequent ad hoc protocols on related issues',[35] as provided for in Article 28. However, to date only a protocol on biosafety, specifically trailed in Article 19(3), has been adopted. This is notwithstanding calls for a protocol to address the problem of invasive species,[36] a cross-cutting issue under the CBD, with Guiding Principles adopted in 2002 (Decision VI/23) to

[32] Statement from the Conference of the Parties to the Convention on Biological Diversity to the Commission on Sustainable Development at its third session, Annex to Decision 1/8, paras. 9–10.

[33] See further discussion in Chapters 5 and 6 above.

[34] See section 8 below for discussion of the relationship between the CBD and other agreements.

[35] P. W. Birnie, A. E. Boyle and C. J. Redgwell, *International Law and the Environment* (Oxford University Press, 2009), p. 616.

[36] Glowka and de Klemm, 26 EPL (1996) 247; see also the discussion in R. Rayfuse, 'Biological Resources', in D. Bodansky, J. Brunnee and E. Hey (eds), *The Oxford Handbook of International Environmental Law* (Oxford University Press, 2007), Chapter 16, p. 386.

address the introduction and mitigation of impacts of alien species that threaten ecosystems, habitats or species.[37]

The Convention recognises that states have sovereign rights over their natural resources (preamble, Articles 3 and 15) and the sovereign right to exploit their resources pursuant to their own environmental policies (Article 3). The preamble also affirms that the conservation of biological diversity is the 'common concern of humankind',[38] but this falls far short of any internationalisation of biological resources either in their ownership or in their control.[39] It also recognises that states are responsible for conserving their biological diversity and for using their biological resources in a sustainable manner, which, it has been argued, forms a critical link between sovereign rights, on the one hand, and common concern, on the other.[40] Thus the conservation of biodiversity is not a matter exclusively of national concern nor are sovereign rights free of responsibilities, specifically the responsibility for conserving biological diversity and ensuring sustainable use thereof, within national jurisdiction.

The jurisdictional scope of the Convention encompasses both components of biological diversity within the limits of national jurisdiction and processes and activities carried out under a state's jurisdiction and control regardless of where the effects occur and whether within or beyond the limits of national jurisdiction (Article 4). This provision has thus far proved unproblematic, meriting no direct attention from the CoP. 'National jurisdiction' clearly encompasses the exclusive economic zone; thus the CBD regulates the conservation of the diversity of marine biological resources to the extent that this is not inconsistent 'with the rights and obligations of States under the law of the sea' (Article 22(2)).

[37] For discussion of the fragmented character of current international regulation of invasive alien species, see Birnie, Boyle and Redgwell, *supra* n. 35; see also CBD CoP Decision IX/4 (2008), which includes identification of 'gaps and inconsistencies in the international regulatory framework' based on the work of an Ad Hoc Technical Expert Group on the subject.

[38] This is also the approach of the 1992 Framework Convention on Climate Change, which likewise avoids 'common heritage of mankind' terminology. For an excellent discussion of 'common concern' and 'common heritage' terminology, see A. E. Boyle in R. R. Churchill and D. Freestone (eds.), *International Law and Global Climate Change* (Kluwer, 1991). On the legal implications of common concern, see further Birnie, Boyle and Redgwell, *supra* n. 35, pp. 97–9.

[39] Contrast, for example, the resources of the deep seabed which are the 'common heritage of mankind' subject to international management by the International Seabed Authority under the 1982 United Nations Law of the Sea Convention, as read in the light of the 1994 Implementation Agreement.

[40] Glowka et al., *supra* n. 26, at p. 10.

Indeed, at its second meeting in Jakarta in 1995 the CoP adopted the Jakarta Mandate on Marine and Coastal Biodiversity, which addresses the sustainable use of marine and coastal biodiversity in the context of five thematic issues. In addition, the CoP is addressing processes and activities beyond national jurisdiction in its ongoing review of prospective exploitation of the deep seabed and, inter alia, bioprospecting of genetic resources there.[41] The offshore application of the CBD has been relied on in domestic litigation. In seeking standing for judicial review of the United Kingdom Secretary of State's decision to offer offshore blocks for petroleum licensing in the North East Atlantic region, Greenpeace relied successfully upon EEC Directive 92/43 on the Conservation of Natural Habitats and of Wild Fauna and Flora as influenced by, inter alia, the CBD, in arguing that the Secretary of State had failed to take account of the impact of petroleum activities upon coral and cetaceans in the area.[42]

The principal objectives of the Convention are set forth in Article 1[43] and may be summarised as: (a) the conservation of biological diversity;[44] (b) the sustainable use of its components;[45] and (c) fair and equitable sharing of the benefits arising out of the utilisation of genetic resources, including by appropriate access to genetic resources,[46] transfer of relevant technologies, taking into account all rights over those resources,[47] and funding.[48] Each is pursued in further detail in the body of the CBD, the language of which, as de Klemm has observed, is generally couched in terms of goal-setting objectives rather than concrete obligations,[49]

41 For example, the SBSTTA prepared a report on bioprospecting of genetic resources of the deep seabed in response to CoP Decision II/10. Doc. UNEP/CBD/SBSTTA/8/INF/3/Rev.1, 22 February 2003. For further discussion see T. Scovazzi, 'Bioprospecting on the Deep Seabed: A Legal Gap Requiring to be Filled', in F. Francioni and T. Scovazzi (eds.), *Biotechnology and International Law* (Hart Publishing, 2006).

42 *R. v Secretary of State for Trade and Industry, ex parte Greenpeace Ltd.*, [2000] 2 *CMLR* 94 (Q. B. Div.), also reprinted in A. Palmer and C. Robb (eds.), *International Environmental Reports*, Volume IV: *International Environmental Law in National Courts* (Cambridge University Press, 2004), p. 462.

43 The objectives have been referred to by Boyle as a trade-off between conservation and economic equity unusual for an international environmental agreement. Boyle, *supra* n. 20 at p. 38; see also D. M. McGraw, 'The CBD – Key Characteristics and Implications for Implementation' (2002) 11(1) *RECIEL* 17.

44 Addressed further in Articles 6–9, 11 and 14 of the Convention.

45 Addressed in Articles 6, 10 and 14 of the Convention.

46 Article 15 addresses access to genetic resources.

47 See in particular Articles 16 and 19 of the Convention.

48 Set forth in Articles 20 and 21 of the Convention.

49 C. de Klemm, 'International Instruments, Processes and Non-indigenous Species Introduction: Is a Protocol Necessary?' (1996) 26 *EPL* 247, at p. 252.

confirming its framework character.[50] Provisions are addressed to general measures for conservation and sustainable use of biological diversity;[51] the identification and monitoring of the components of biological diversity;[52] *in situ*[53] and *ex situ*[54] conservation of these components and incentive measures for their conservation and sustainable use;[55] research and training in measures for the identification, conservation and sustainable use of components of biological diversity,[56] as well as promoting public education and awareness of the importance of, and measures required for, the conservation of biological diversity;[57] impact assessment and minimising adverse effects on biological diversity;[58] regulating access to genetic resources;[59] access to and transfer of technology;[60] exchange of information[61] and technical and scientific co-operation;[62] and financial support and incentives for national activities intended to achieve the objectives of the Convention.[63]

Of the key concepts in the CBD, 'conservation' is not defined at all, evidently purposely since it is employed in both a broad and a narrow sense in the Convention.[64] 'Sustainable use', on the other hand, is defined in Article 2 as 'the use of components of biological diversity in a way and at a rate that does not lead to the long-term decline of biological diversity, thereby maintaining its potential to meet the needs and aspirations of present and future generations'.[65] At CoP V (2002, Decision V/24), sustainable use was adopted as a cross-cutting issue under the Convention, and at CoP VII (2004) the Addis Ababa Principles and Guidelines for the Sustainable Use of Biodiversity were adopted.[66] Drafted in general terms, the principles are intended as a 'framework for advising Governments, resource managers, indigenous and local communities, the private sector and other stakeholders about how they

50 Birnie, Boyle and Redgwell, *supra* n. 35, p. 617. 51 Article 6. 52 Article 7.
53 Article 8. 54 Article 9. 55 Article 11. 56 Article 12. 57 Article 13.
58 Article 14. 59 Article 15. 60 Article 16. 61 Article 17. 62 Article 18.
63 Article 20. 64 Glowka et al., *supra* n. 26, p. 4.
65 For in-depth discussion of the concept of 'sustainable use' and its ambiguities, see S. Johnston, 'Sustainability, Biodiversity and International Law', in Bowman and Redgwell, *supra* n. 1.
66 There are fourteen 'interdependent practical principles', each with a stated rationale and operational guidelines; a 'fundamental assumption' is that these are set within the context of the ecosystem approach reflected in CoP Decision V/6 (see further section 4(b) below). *Addis Ababa Principles and Guidelines for the Sustainable Use of Biodiversity* (CBD Secretariat, 2004).

can ensure that their use of the components of biological diversity will not lead to the long-term decline of biological diversity'.[67]

The reference to 'sustainable use' of the components of biological diversity is a clear indicator that this Convention is not concerned primarily with the preservation of biodiversity but 'assumes human use and benefit' as an important reason for conserving biodiversity, 'limited only by the requirement of sustainability and the need to benefit future generations'.[68] In this sense, the Convention is 'philosophically closer' to environmental treaties concerned with conservation to permit sustainable human use (e.g. fisheries and migratory species) than to the preservationist concept evidenced in the Protocol to the Antarctic Treaty on Environmental Protection and in the moratorium on commercial whaling under the International Convention for the Regulation of Whaling.[69] Nonetheless, the Convention constitutes an important milestone in its recognition of the intrinsic value of biodiversity and of the conservation of biodiversity as a 'common concern of humankind'.

Another major objective set forth in Article 1 is fair and equitable sharing of the benefits arising from the utilisation of genetic resources. This is further elaborated upon in Article 15 on access to genetic resources, as well as in Article 16 on access to and transfer of technology, discussed further below. Thus while the Convention does not envisage biological resources as common property subject to an international management regime, it does provide for the equitable sharing of the benefits of the exploitation of such resources, albeit with the country of origin rather than with a broader category of, for example, less-developed countries.[70] Indeed, the balancing of developed- and developing-state interests is another fundamental objective of the Convention.

[67] Ibid., p. 5, para. 1.

[68] Boyle, *supra* n. 20, at p. 115. See also Addis Ababa Principle 10 on the ecosystem approach, which states, 'The ecosystem approach should seek the appropriate balance between, and integration of, conservation and use of biological diversity', available at www.cbd.int/ecosystem/principles.shtml.

[69] Boyle, *supra* n. 20.

[70] That is, there are no provisions comparable to those contained in the 1982 United Nations Convention on the Law of the Sea regarding the sharing of proceeds of the exploitation of the resources of the deep seabed, and of the resources of the continental margin beyond 200 nautical miles.

4. Key provisions of the Convention

a) In situ *and* ex situ *conservation*

The Convention places particular emphasis upon *in situ* conservation, defined in Article 2 as 'the conservation of ecosystems and natural habitats and the maintenance and recovery of viable populations of species in their natural surroundings and, in the case of domesticated or cultivated species, in the surroundings where they have developed their distinctive properties'. The preamble refers to 'the fundamental requirement' for the conservation of biodiversity *in situ*, with *ex situ* conservation also having 'an important role to play'.[71] *Ex situ* conservation is defined as 'the conservation of components of biological diversity outside their natural habitats', for example in zoos or botanical gardens. This greater emphasis upon *in situ* conservation is reflected in the body of the Convention, with Article 8 setting forth thirteen obligations of contracting parties for *in situ* conservation as compared with five for *ex situ* conservation in Article 9. Measures for *ex situ* conservation are also expressed to be 'predominantly for the purpose of complementing in situ measures'.

With *in situ* conservation the primary method for biodiversity conservation, there is inevitably increased emphasis on the need for national measures to be taken to implement the Convention. Indeed, it is only *in situ* conservation which is appropriate for the five levels of the biodiversity hierarchy, all of which are addressed by the Convention, namely (1) whole systems such as landscapes or ecosystems, (2) assemblages such as associations or communities, (3) species, (4) populations and (5) genes.[72] *Ex situ* conservation is presently only able to address variability between species; that is, levels 3–5 in the hierarchy.[73] On the other hand, the complementarity of *in situ* and *ex situ* measures is widely accepted and, indeed, in certain instances (captive breeding of wild species threatened with extinction, for example) *ex situ* conservation measures may be designed to permit the augmentation of wild populations.

[71] While the Convention separates conservation into these two categories of *in situ* and *ex situ*, the World Conservation Strategy employed three categories: on site; off site, part of the organism; and off site, the whole organism. See WCS, *supra* n. 12, para. 1.4.

[72] L. M. Warren, 'The Role of Ex Situ Measures in the Conservation of Biodiversity', in Bowman and Redgwell, *supra* n. 1, citing M. E. Soulé, 'Conservation: Tactics for a Constant Crisis' (1991) 253 *Science* 744–50.

[73] Warren, *supra* n. 72.

It is, of course, possible that an ecosystem or assemblage, or the species or populations of species themselves, will range across international boundaries, whether land or maritime. Equally, actions in one state may harm biodiversity in another, or in the area beyond national jurisdiction. While the Convention addresses the transboundary impact on biodiversity of harmful activities in Article 14, there is no explicit recognition of the need for transboundary co-operation in conservation activities apart from the preamble[74] and the more general duty to co-operate 'in respect of areas beyond national jurisdiction and on other matters of mutual interest' found in Article 5. Moreover, the treatment of transboundary harm in Article 14(c) is less than robust, and arguably weaker even than the language contained in Article 19 of the Rio Declaration.[75]

The chief *in situ* conservation obligations are contained in Article 8 of the Convention, which obliges states in fulfilling the objectives of the conservation of biological diversity and the sustainable use of its components, 'as far as possible and as appropriate', to:

(i) establish a protected-areas system;
(ii) develop guidelines for their selection;
(iii) regulate or manage biological resources important for the conservation of biodiversity within and without protected areas;
(iv) promote the protection of ecosystems and natural habitats, and the maintenance of viable populations of species;
(v) promote what are in essence buffer zones around protected areas to enhance their protection;
(vi) rehabilitate and restore degraded ecosystems and promote the recovery of threatened species through, inter alia, plans or other management strategies;

[74] The relevant recital states, '*Stressing* the importance of, and the need to promote, international, regional and global cooperation among States and intergovernmental organizations and the non-governmental sector for the conservation of biological diversity and the sustainable use of its components'.

[75] While Article 14(c) of the Convention merely calls upon states to 'promote, on the basis of reciprocity, notification, exchange of information and consultation' and to incorporate such requirements within bilateral, regional and multilateral arrangements as appropriate, Article 19 of the Rio Declaration on Environment and Development obliges States to 'provide prior and timely notification and relevant information to potentially affected States on activities that may have a significant adverse transboundary effect and shall consult those States at an early stage and in good faith'. As the IUCN *Guide* (Glowka et al., *supra* n. 26, p. 74) points out, 'The obligation merely to "promote" transfrontier cooperation "by encouraging" arrangements is considerably less stringent than in other international agreements or even under general international law.'

(vii) control the risks associated with the use and release of living modified organisms likely to have adverse environmental impact;[76]
(viii) prevent the introduction of, eradicate, or control, alien species threatening ecosystems, habitat or species;[77]
(ix) 'endeavour to provide' the conditions necessary for compatibility between present use, conservation and sustainable use;
(x) respect, preserve and maintain knowledge of indigenous peoples relevant to conservation and sustainable use of biodiversity, and promote the equitable sharing of the benefits arising from promoting their wider application, with their approval and involvement, subject to national legislation;[78]
(xi) legislate for the protection of threatened species and populations;
(xii) regulate activities determined to have significant adverse effect on biodiversity; and
(xiii) co-operate in providing financial support for the above, especially for developing states.

Many of these measures are reflected in existing international conservation treaties such as CITES, Ramsar and the Bern and Bonn Conventions, as well as in many other regional conventions (e.g. the 1985 ASEAN Convention on the Conservation of Nature and Natural Resources and the 1991 Environmental Protocol to the 1959 Antarctic Treaty) and other instruments. Others require the adoption of a thematic approach

[76] This is closely linked with Article 19 concerning the handling of biotechnology and distribution of its benefits, and the 2000 Cartagena Protocol, discussed further below.

[77] The introduction of alien species into the environment and the concomitant threat to biological diversity is addressed in Article 8(h) and has been one particular focus of activity under the CBD, with CoP IV formally adopting it as a cross-cutting issue. 'Guiding Principles for the Prevention, Introduction and Mitigation of Impacts of Alien Species' were adopted at CoP VI (Decision VI/23), and include the precautionary and ecosystem approaches. CoP IX conducted an in-depth review of invasive species which endorsed, inter alia, the continuing application of these principles (Decision IX/4). It also highlighted gaps and inconsistencies in the international regulatory framework and the need to work closely with, inter alia, the International Plant Protection Convention (ibid.). See also, as part of the clearing-house mechanism and in co-operation with other organisations and instruments (e.g. the FAO and CITES), the 'Global Invasive Species Programme' at www.gisp.org.

[78] 'Traditional knowledge, innovations and practices' is one of the cross-cutting issues under the CBD with a Working Group on Article 8(j) and Related Provisions carrying out a programme of work and reporting regularly to, as well as being guided by, the CoP. See, e.g., CoP Decision IX/13.

because of the interlinkage between Article 8 and other provisions of the Convention – traditional and indigenous knowledge, for example.[79]

The centrality of Article 8 to achieving the objectives of the CBD is underscored by the attention paid to the elaboration of its themes by the CoP. Apart from biosafety and traditional knowledge, each of which has been the subject of consideration by an Open Ended Ad Hoc Working Group under the Convention (and with the former, a Protocol adopted in 2000), *in situ* conservation is addressed at the international level largely within an ongoing programme of work established by the CoP. It sets out particular thematic areas and cross-cutting issues. The thematic areas were initially fivefold: (1) marine and coastal biodiversity, (2) agricultural biodiversity, (3) forest biodiversity, (4) inland waters biodiversity and (5) dry and subhumid lands biodiversity, to which have since been added (6) mountain biodiversity and, most recently, (7) island biodiversity.[80] Collectively these correspond to major biomes on the planet. Bearing in mind the framework character of the CBD, co-operation with organisations and treaties active in these areas is encouraged – for example, with the FAO in respect of agricultural biodiversity and with the Ramsar Secretariat in respect of the biodiversity of inland waters.[81]

Further subdivision occurs within each thematic work programme. For example, the Jakarta Mandate on Marine and Coastal Biodiversity adopted at CoP II in 1995 identifies five thematic issues for actions aimed at the conservation and sustainable use of such biodiversity: (i) integrated marine and coastal-area management, (ii) marine and coastal protected areas, (iii) sustainable use of marine and coastal living resources, (iv) mariculture and (v) alien species. There is clear overlap not

[79] Traditional knowledge is also addressed in Article 10(c) (contracting parties to protect and encourage customary use of biological resources compatible with conservation and sustainable use of such resources), Article 15 (access to genetic resources), Article 16 (intellectual property rights), Article 17(2) (exchange of information) and Article 18(4) (scientific and technical co-operation).

[80] For analysis of the thematic areas and their development under the Convention, see the *Convention on Biological Diversity Handbook, Including Its Cartagena Protocol on Biosafety* (CBD Secretariat, 3rd ed., 2005), available at www.cbd.int/handbook; see also the links at www.cbd.int/programmes. See also Chapter 18 below on desert, mountain and forest ecosystems.

[81] The latter has included a joint work programme between the CBD and Ramsar, the second of which was concluded at CoP V with the specific commendation that this serve as a useful example for co-operation with other environmental conventions (Decision V/21). See further section 8 below.

only with Article 8 themes (e.g. Article 8(a)–(c) on protected areas; Article 8(h) on alien species), but also with a number of cross-cutting themes identified for action by the CoP on the basis that these are issues of relevance to all seven thematic areas. Essentially these correspond with Articles 6–20 CBD and include access to genetic resources, intellectual property rights, traditional knowledge, alien species and sustainable use.[82]

b) The ecosystem approach

All CBD activities are carried out within the 'fundamental paradigm' of the ecosystem approach, which is one of eighteen cross-cutting issues identified under the Convention. 'Ecosystem' is defined in Article 2 as meaning 'a dynamic complex of plant, animal and micro-organism communities and their non-living environment interacting as a functional unit'. At CoP II in 1995 the parties adopted this approach as the framework for analysis and implementation of the objectives of the Convention and at CoP V adopted Decision V/6 on the ecosystem approach, annexes to which contain operational guidance and twelve common principles, with the requirement to integrate these principles within national plans and priorities. Implementation guidelines for each principle were adopted at CoP VII.[83] The ecosystem approach is

> a strategy for the integrated management of land, water and living resources that promotes conservation and sustainable use in an equitable way. Thus the application of the ecosystem approach will help to reach a balance of the three objectives of the Convention: conservation; sustainable use; and the fair and equitable sharing of the benefits arising out of the utilization of genetic resources.[84]

A key feature of the ecosystem approach is its flexibility and complementarity:

> The ecosystem approach does not preclude other management and conservation approaches, such as biosphere reserves, protected areas, and single-species conservation programmes, as well as other approaches carried out under existing national policy and legislative frameworks, but could, rather, integrate all these approaches and other methodologies

[82] Biosafety was also identified as a cross-cutting theme but is now addressed in the 2000 Cartagena Protocol.

[83] See Annex I to CoP Decision VII/11. An ecosystem sourcebook was also established to facilitate information sharing and capacity-building: see www.cbd.int/ecosystem/sourcebook.

[84] Decision V/10, Annex A, para. 1.

> to deal with complex situations. There is no single way to implement the ecosystem approach, as it depends on local, provincial, national, regional or global conditions. Indeed, there are many ways in which ecosystem approaches may be used as the framework for delivering the objectives of the Convention in practice.[85]

National implementation is thus a perpetual theme: the CBD's provisions neither compel uniformity nor create collective powers to mandate measures at the international level.[86]

c) *Identification and monitoring*

Closely linked to the activities required of states for *in situ* biodiversity conservation under Article 8[87] is Article 7, which is concerned with identification and monitoring. Clearly the measures required of states under Article 8 require a sound information base on which to build. Thus Article 7 obliges each contracting party, again, 'as far as possible and appropriate', to identify components of biological diversity important for its conservation and sustainable use. Further guidance is given in a brief Annex I. Once identified, these components are to be monitored, which includes identifying and monitoring the effects of processes and activities having or likely to have significant adverse impact upon them. These data are to be maintained and organised.[88] Neither of these identification and monitoring processes is required under the Convention to be carried out by independent inspectors, as is the case, for example, with the independent inspection of sites and facilities under the Environmental Protocol to the Antarctic Treaty, or the inspection system of the Whaling Convention or the Convention for the Conservation of

[85] Ibid. para. 5. Principle 5, 'Conservation of ecosystem structure and functioning, in order to maintain ecosystem services, should be a priority target of the ecosystem approach', explicitly recognises this complementarity or 'additionality' which biodiversity conservation brings to species conservation: 'Ecosystem functioning and resilience depends on a dynamic relationship within species, among species and between species and their abiotic environment, as well as the physical and chemical interactions within the environment. The conservation and, where appropriate, restoration of these interactions and processes is of greater significance for the long-term maintenance of biological diversity than simply protection of species.' See further description at www.cbd.int/ecosystem.

[86] Boyle, *supra* n. 20, p. 43.

[87] And Articles 9 and 10, which address *ex situ* conservation and the sustainable use of components of biological diversity respectively.

[88] Data comprising identification of important components of diversity, regular monitoring thereof, identification of potentially or actually harmful processes and activities, and monitoring of the effects of these activities on the components.

Antarctic Marine Living Resources. This is a potential weakness in the Convention, which no doubt reflects its main field of application, viz., to biological diversity *within* states.

d) Impact assessment and minimising adverse impacts

Article 14 addresses impact assessment and minimising adverse impact on biological diversity. As with many of the provisions already examined, the obligation to introduce environmental impact assessment (EIA) applies only 'as far as possible and as appropriate'. Moreover, the threshold of anticipated harm which is the trigger for the obligation to conduct EIA is set very high: where proposed projects are likely to have significant adverse effects on biological diversity.[89] Article 14 avoids express mention of the precautionary approach, which is found only in the preambular exhortation that 'where there is a threat of significant reduction or loss of biodiversity, lack of full scientific certainty should not be used as a reason for postponing measures to avoid or minimize such threat'. Moreover, there is no transboundary element to the EIA obligation (Article 14(1)(c) merely requires states to promote exchange of information and to enter into arrangements 'as appropriate') and public participation is only 'where appropriate'. When contrasted with other recent environmental agreements, most notably the regional 1991 Espoo Convention on Environmental Impact Assessment in a Transboundary Context and the EIA provisions of the Environmental Protocol to the Antarctic Treaty, the CBD has less detail and higher thresholds. The duty to notify of transboundary harm (Article 14(1)(d)) does little more than restate the customary-law obligation.[90] Similarly, Article 14(2) is all that remains of earlier drafts regarding responsibility and liability issues.[91] It merely calls on the CoP, following studies, to 'examine . . . the issue of liability and redress, including restoration and compensation, for damage to biodiversity except where such liability is a purely internal matter'. No decision has been taken on a common approach to liability and redress under the Convention. Rather, study of the issues commenced at CoPs IV and V with calls for information on national

[89] A more precautionary formulation of the trigger would be 'possible adverse effects', for example. See Boyle, *supra* n. 20, at p. 41.

[90] See P. Okowa, 'Procedural Obligations in International Environmental Agreements' (1996) 71 *BYIL* 275.

[91] As noted above, the responsibility clause of the fifth draft was dropped from the final text of the CBD.

and international practice; this information was then considered by a group of legal and technical experts which,[92] after some delay, reported to CoP VIII, which called on parties to contribute national experience and case studies. These are contained in a synthesis report produced by the CBD executive secretary for CoP IX.[93] Further work on liability and redress is to be determined at CoP X when the Strategic Plan for implementation of the Convention is to be revised.[94]

e) Access to genetic resources

Fair and equitable sharing of the benefits arising out of the utilisation of genetic resources is one of the fundamental objectives of the CBD highlighted in Article 1.[95] Article 15 specifically elaborates upon access to genetic resources, a topic also the focus of the Working Group on Access and Benefit Sharing established at CoP V.[96] A key pillar of the CBD, Article 15 starts with a reaffirmation of the sovereign rights of states over their resources and the consequence that it is for national governments to determine access to their genetic resources and to regulate such access by national legislation. The importance of this provision should not be overlooked: the report of the executive secretary of the CBD to the CSD in 1997 (as part of the five-year review of Agenda 21) points out that naturally occurring genetic material was often by default considered a public good before the CBD, without regulated or controlled access. The CBD allows a 'gatekeeper' to be posted controlling (and even in certain circumstances prohibiting) access. Thus it is a vital bargaining chip to ensure 'that those rich in biological resources have the ability to negotiate terms of access which reflect the true value of the resources'.[97] Whilst Article 15(2) obliges states 'to endeavour to create conditions to

[92] CoP VI, Decision VI/11, sets out in detail the remit of the group, in whose work non-state actors may participate as observers.

[93] 'Synthesis report on technical information relating to damage to biological diversity and approaches to valuation and restoration of damage to biological diversity, as well as information on national/domestic measures and experience', UNEP/CBD/COP/9/20/Add.1.

[94] And in developing the next multiyear programme of work for 2011–2020. See Decision IX/23.

[95] See, generally, R. V. Anuradha, 'In Search of Knowledge and Resources: Who Sows? Who Reaps?' (1997) 6(3) *RECIEL* 263.

[96] Decision V/26 (2000). At the time of writing it had met on nine occasions, most recently in July 2010. See www.cbd.int/wgabs8. The WGABS is presently working on an 'international regime for access and benefit-sharing' as mandated by CoP VII (Decision VII/19), to be considered at CoP X in 2010.

[97] E/CN.17/1997/11, para. 29, 25 February 1997.

facilitate access', the CBD neither creates nor recognises any right of 'free' access by third states. In addition, in respect of conditions for access, the default rule under the CBD is prior informed consent (PIC) for access unless otherwise determined by the party providing the genetic resources (Article 15(5)). Where granted, access is to be on mutually agreed terms (MAT). This strongly suggests negotiated agreements will be the primary vehicle for obtaining access to genetic resources and for sharing the resulting benefits, including technology.[98]

This provision is clearly seeking to redress a potential knowledge imbalance and improve the position of the party providing the genetic resources. This resonates with the marine scientific research consent provisions of the 1982 United Nations Convention on the Law of the Sea,[99] as well as the PIC provisions of the 1989 Basel Convention on the Transboundary Movement of Hazardous Wastes and their Disposal, the 1998 Rotterdam Convention on the Prior Informed Consent Procedure for Certain Hazardous Chemicals and Pesticides in International Trade, and, of course, the Biosafety Protocol to the CBD (which refers to 'advanced informed agreement').[100] Article 15(7) highlights a further crucial issue, which is 'sharing in a fair and equitable way the results of research and development and the benefits arising from the commercial and other utilization of genetic resources with the contracting Party'. This is to be effected through legal, administrative or policy measures; immediate steps after the entry into force of the CBD focused on promoting the development of measures to facilitate access and benefit-sharing and in gathering national/regional information regarding such measures.[101] Access has two dimensions: the party in question is either the country of origin of the resource or, in the case of certain *ex situ* collections, the party supplying the genetic resources which have been acquired abroad but in accordance with the CBD. However, the legal effect of Article 15(3) is to exclude from the purview of this article resources which were collected prior to the entry into force of the Convention for a particular party.[102]

98 UNEP/CBD/COP/2/13, p. 6 para. 20.

99 Especially the EEZ provisions. See Boyle, *supra* n. 20, p. 39.

100 Stoll observes that the AIA of the Protocol is 'very much in line with' the PIC procedure of the Basel and Rotterdam Conventions. P.-T. Stoll, 'Controlling the Risks of Genetically Modified Organisms: The Cartagena Protocol on Biosafety and the SPS Agreement' (1999) 10 *Yb. Int'l Env. L* 82, p. 91.

101 The CHM website contains copies of reports and case studies in this connection: see www.biodiv.org.chm.

102 This is the legal consequence of the words 'in accordance with the CBD'.

State practice varies considerably regarding access. The IUCN's analysis of national implementation has revealed several categories of access legislation:[103]

(1) general framework environmental laws;[104]
(2) framework sustainable development, nature conservation or biodiversity laws;[105]
(3) specific laws or decrees on access to genetic resources;[106]
(4) modification of existing laws;[107]
(5) regional action.

An interesting case study of this last category – regional action – is provided by the Common Regime on Access to Genetic Resources adopted on 2 July 1996 by the Andean Pact comprising Bolivia, Ecuador, Peru and Venezuela – thus including three of the twelve most biologically diverse countries in the world. Agreement on regional action was motivated by the desire for holistic regulation of an eco-regime of outstanding importance; this would prevent harmful undermining of their bargaining position by bioprospectors playing states off against each other, with the result that one state might allow access on unduly favourable terms and thereby diminish potential returns for neighbouring countries. Thus there were both economic and ecological imperatives towards co-operation. International co-operation is evident in the International Undertaking on Plant Genetic Resources under FAO auspices, now replaced by the 2001 International Treaty on Plant Genetic Resources for Food and Agriculture.[108] This was welcomed by CBD CoP VI, which urged CBD parties to ratify it.[109]

Article 15 is addressed to states; that is, to the countries of origin of the genetic resources in question or contracting parties who have acquired them in accordance with the CBD. As already indicated, the latter encompasses *ex situ* collections such as zoos, gene banks and botanical gardens. It will be recalled that Article 9 imposes an obligation upon contracting parties to adopt measures for the *ex situ* conservation of

[103] L. Glowka, 'Emerging Legislative Approaches to Implement Article 15 of the Convention on Biological Diversity' (1997) 6(3) *RECIEL* 249.
[104] Examples cited include Gambia, Kenya and South Korea.
[105] Costa Rica, Fiji and Peru are cited as examples. [106] A rare example is the Philippines.
[107] Nigeria and the United States, for example.
[108] For further information on the FAO Treaty, see H. D. Cooper, 'The International Treaty on Plant Genetic Resources for Food and Agriculture' (2002) 11(1) *RECIEL* 1.
[109] Decision VI/26.

components of biological diversity but expresses a preference for this to be done in the country of origin of such components. Pursuant to Article 15, access to these genetic resources may be regulated by domestic law, though if they are in private hands and not previously regulated, this may give rise to various internal legal problems, such as the unlawful taking of a property right. In practice, however, *ex situ* collections have responded to the CBD by developing their own policy on access to genetic resources and benefit sharing 'to honour the letter and spirit of the Convention on Biological Diversity, Convention on International Trade in Endangered Species, and other international, regional and national laws and policies concerning biodiversity'.[110] These may entail a commitment to making 'reasonable efforts' to obtain the prior informed consent of the country providing the genetic resources and of stakeholders (i.e. a public or private person or organisation affected by or with an interest in the activities at stake – this might range from local public authorities to landowners, indigenous peoples, local communities and private NGOs) as required by the law in the country in question and according to best practice, and to share the benefits arising from the use of genetic resources. For this purpose, a contractual arrangement (material transfer agreement) may be required, especially where collecting permits (issued by the state of origin) do not clarify benefit-sharing or other arrangements. This seeks to remedy contractually any defects or loopholes in the domestic local law.

Whether *in situ* or *ex situ* conservation, two key questions for national implementation are: (1) who decides upon access to and utilisation of genetic resources, and (2) who has the right to receive payment? The issue of rights over resources within contracting parties is not specifically addressed in the CBD but is left for national law to determine. A further issue is, whose knowledge is being appropriated? Here Article 15 becomes closely linked with other provisions of the CBD, including Article 8(j) on indigenous knowledge. While Article 15 itself is largely directed at the state in whose territory the resources are situated, Article 8(j) refers to promoting the wider application of the knowledge, innovations and practices of indigenous and local communities with their approval and involvement, and to encouraging equitable sharing of the benefits of

[110] So states the Policy on Access to Genetic Resources and Benefit-Sharing of the Royal Botanical Gardens, Kew, UK, effective from 1 January 1998. See K. ten Kate, (1997) 6:3 *RECIEL* 46.

utilisation arising therefrom.[111] Thus economic equity under the CBD has not only an inter-state but also an intra-state dimension. With respect to the latter, this is not without its tensions. For example, the fifth draft of the CBD (pre-final text) included a preambular reference to biodiversity as 'the common concern of all peoples', but this was amended to read 'common concern of humankind' following Brazilian objections that this might be viewed as conferring rights on indigenous peoples. In practice various agreements have been entered into between bioprospectors or commercial interests on the one hand, and indigenous peoples on the other. For example, 'know-how agreements' have been entered into between Searle, the pharmaceutical arm of Monsanto, and the Aguaruna people of Peru in acknowledgement of the commercial benefits of exploiting traditional knowledge.[112] An annual know-how licence fee is paid, with established 'milestone' payments, which reside in a trust fund for a board representing the present and future interests of the Aguaruna peoples to administer. The agreement is non-exclusive, and sidesteps any legal difficulties which might arise regarding ownership of the biological resources in question since such legal title is not a precondition for the know-how agreements in question.[113]

f) Intellectual property rights

A further important element of Article 8(j) is the issue of intellectual property (IP) rights obtained over subject matter developed after using traditional knowledge. This was a key sticking point during negotiation of the CBD. Natural genetic resources are not necessarily patentable or a source of legally protected rights. In other words, the traditional IP regime does not generally afford direct legal protection for traditional knowledge. Patentable rights may arise for a new process for isolating and developing substances, or for new uses for existing substances. IP issues also arise under the transfer-of-technology provisions of Article 16 CBD, since this expressly contemplates transfer of patented technology,

[111] See also ILO Convention 169 concerning Indigenous and Tribal Peoples in Independent Countries, which likewise safeguards the rights of such peoples to the natural resources pertaining to their lands and their rights to participate in the use, management and conservation of these resources: (1989) 28 *ILM* 1382.

[112] In addition to the examples found on the Biodiversity website at www.biodiv.org, see K. ten Kate and S. Laird, *The Commercial Use of Biodiversity: Access to Genetic Resources and Benefit-Sharing* (Earthscan, 1999).

[113] For critical analysis of a number of case studies, including several available from the Biodiversity Clearing House Mechanism website (www.biodiv.org/chm), see G. Dutfield, *Intellectual Property Rights, Trade and Biodiversity* (Earthscan, 2000).

although Article 16(2) stresses that access and transfer 'shall be provided on terms which recognize and are consistent with the adequate and effective protection of intellectual property rights'. The strength of this guarantee may be judged by the initial refusal of the United States even to sign the CBD; on the other hand, Malaysia made a declaration on adoption of the Nairobi Final Act stating that 'the terms of the transfer of technology referred to in Article 16, para. 2, do not fully reflect the position of [Malaysia] which requires that such transfer should be specifically on concessional and preferential terms'. That Article 16(2) does not so provide is evidence of the careful balance it strives to achieve, with the negotiators of the CBD well aware of the controversy surrounding transfer-of-technology provisions in other agreements such as the 1982 Law of the Sea Convention. Stumbling blocks include government reluctance to compel private actors to transfer technology which may not be commercially available, objection to the terms of transfer particularly if not at fair market value, and the question of intellectual property rights lost if transfer is required. Article 16(2) addresses these issues by providing that transfers must be on 'fair and most favourable terms' – preferential and concessional terms are not mandated but rather will only apply where mutually agreed; that is, these must be negotiated. Article 16(4) requires states to ensure that the private sector facilitates access, joint development and transfer of technology through appropriate legislative, administrative or policy measures.

5. The Biosafety Protocol

a) Background

In addition to its concerns regarding technology transfer, IP, financing and access to resources, the US and its biotechnology industry also lobbied in favour of a biosafety programme built on existing laws and regulations, rather than a separate protocol. This last issue was addressed in Article 19(3) CBD, which contemplates the possibility of a protocol setting out appropriate procedures, including advanced informed agreement to ensure the safe transfer, handling and use of any living modified organism resulting from biotechnology that may have adverse effect on the conservation and sustainable use of biodiversity. Article 19 also requires states to provide contracting parties, especially developing countries, with the opportunity to participate in biotechnical research where they have provided the genetic resources and 'to promote and advance priority access on a fair and equitable basis' by contracting parties, especially developing countries, to the benefits arising therefrom on mutually agreed terms.[114]

Pursuant to these provisions, an Open-Ended Ad Hoc Group of Experts was established at CoP I to consider the need for, and modalities of, a protocol regulating transfer and use of living modified organisms (LMOs).[115] This was followed at CoP II with the establishment of a Working Group – the Biosafety Working Group – to prepare a draft protocol based on these experts' recommendations. Following much deliberation, the Cartagena Protocol was duly adopted on 29 January 2000 and opened for signature on 15 May 2000.[116] It entered into force on 11 September 2003 and currently has 157 parties, including the EC.

b) *Key provisions of the Protocol*

The focus of the Cartagena Protocol is upon the transboundary movement of LMOs which may have adverse effects on biological diversity and human health. 'Living modified organism' is defined as 'any living organism that possesses a novel combination of genetic material obtained through the use of modern biotechnology'.[117] In fact the Protocol addresses two general categories of LMO: (i) those intended for release into the environment (e.g. seeds for cultivation or animal breeding stock), and (ii) those intended for use in food or feed, or for processing (e.g. corn, cotton and soy). The latter is of particular concern to the United States as the chief exporter of genetically modified crops.[118] In the event the Protocol distinguishes between these

[114] Article 19(1) and (2).

[115] McGraw, *supra* n. 43, p. 19, refers to criticisms of this choice as reflecting an absence of 'sound science' – why not a Protocol on traditional knowledge or on alien species, for example? See also C. Redgwell, 'Biosafety and Biodiversity' (2005) *CLP* 246.

[116] 2000 Cartagena Protocol on Biosafety to the Convention on Biological Diversity, reproduced at (2000) 39 *ILM* 1027. For coverage of the final negotiating session see (2000) 9(137) *ENB* 1–11; see also www.iisd.ca/biodiv.html for the full negotiating history through the *ENB*. On the Protocol generally, see P. E. Hagen and J. B. Weiner, 'The Cartagena Protocol on Biosafety: New Rules for International Trade in Living Modified Organisms' (2000) 12 *Georgetown ELR* 697; and S. W. Burgiel, 'The Cartagena Protocol on Biosafety: Taking the Steps from Negotiation to Implementation' (2002) 11 (1) *RECIEL* 53.

[117] Article 3(f).

[118] See further Hagen and Weiner, *supra* n. 116. Although not a party to the CBD the United States participated in the negotiation of the Protocol, which, notwithstanding the compromises contained in, inter alia, Article 11, it is unlikely to participate in for the foreseeable future.

categories, subjecting organisms intended for direct use as food or feed, or for processing, to a less onerous regime (Article 11) than that applicable to LMOs intended for direct release into the environment (Articles 7–10).

A marked feature of the Protocol is its overtly precautionary approach, with Article 1 making express reference to Principle 15 of the Rio Declaration and with implicit reference in the phrase '*may* have an adverse effect' on biodiversity and/or human health. The chief regulatory technique employed is the advanced informed agreement (AIA) procedure set out in Article 7, which is designed to ensure that contracting parties are provided with the information necessary to make informed decisions before agreeing to the import of LMOs into their territory. AIA marks the Protocol out from the prior informed consent procedures of the 1989 Basel and 1998 Rotterdam Conventions,[119] which are based on prior multilateral agreement on the hazardous substances to be regulated, which are set out in annexes. The primary purpose of the Cartagena Protocol, by contrast, is to facilitate early assessment by each individual contracting party of the potential risks in accordance with the Protocol. As Stoll observes, the Cartagena Protocol's 'unique combination between import State control and risk assessment results from the fact that it does not contain an agreed definition of materials that the importing State may refuse without condition or even an agreement that the substances that it regulates are "undesirable"'.[120] Indeed, the flexibility of the rules under the Protocol has led to suggestions that it represents a form of 'treaty-based environmental unilateralism' and that it is a 'prototype of minimum harmonization legislation'.[121]

[119] Stoll, *supra* n. 100. The 1998 Rotterdam Convention on Prior Informed Consent expressly excludes LMOs from its scope, thus eliminating the possibility of conflict arising between the two treaties.

[120] Stoll, *supra* n. 100, p. 91.

[121] R. Pavoni, 'Assessing and Managing Biotechnology Risk under the Cartagena Protocol on Biosafety' (2000) 10 *Italian YIL* 113, pp. 115–16. It should be noted that Article 14 expressly provides for bilateral, regional and multilateral agreements and arrangements regarding intentional movement of LMOs so long as such arrangements do not provide a lower level of protection than that provided for by the Protocol – either equal protection or in fact a form of bilateral and/or multilateral upward derogation, and certainly precluding 'contracting out' of the Protocol's level of protection. Article 24 also envisages such agreements being concluded between contracting parties and non-parties to the Protocol.

The Article 7 AIA procedure is buttressed by Articles 8–10, which address notification[122] and decision[123] procedures. Article 10(6) stresses that lack of scientific certainty due to insufficient information regarding the potential negative effects of LMOs on biodiversity, including taking into account risks to human health, will not prevent the importing/receiving state from taking decisions in respect of LMOs in order to avoid or minimise potential adverse effects. Decisions must be taken in accordance with the risk assessment procedure stipulated in Article 15 and Annex III. Upward derogation is provided for in Article 2(4) in the sense that it permits action more protective of biodiversity than is provided for in the Protocol, so long as such action is consistent both with the Protocol and with that party's other obligations under international law (e.g. trade obligations).[124] The socioeconomic impact of LMOs on biodiversity, especially its value to indigenous and local communities, may also be taken into account by contracting parties, at least to the extent consistent with their international obligations.[125]

Several of the above provisions have a clear potential for conflict with other international obligations, most notably trade-related obligations (see Chapter 19). The precautionary approach, such a key feature of the Protocol,[126] allows importing countries to ban imports because of lack of scientific certainty. Unlike under the Agreement on the Application of Sanitary and Phytosanitary Measures (the SPS Agreement), there is no obligation to seek further information to enable a more objective, informed assessment of the risk and to review the SPS measure within a reasonable time. Thus a trade-restrictive measure under the Cartagena Protocol may be of unlimited duration, or at least until the importing country decides that scientific certainty exists regarding the effects of products on biodiversity and human health.[127]

[122] Confidentiality may be preserved in accordance with Article 21.

[123] The import may be approved, with or without conditions, or prohibited, or additional information may be requested (Article 10(3)). Silence in response to an initial notification from the party of export does not imply consent to transboundary movement (Article 9(4)). There is also provision for review of decisions in the light of new scientific information regarding the potential adverse effects of the LMO (Article 12).

[124] See also Article 14 (multilateralised upward derogation). [125] Article 26.

[126] In addition to the preambular provisions and Article 1 cited above, see Articles 10(6) and 11(8).

[127] See S. Zarilli, 'International Trade in GMOs and Multilateral Negotiations: A New Dilemma for Developing Countries', in F. Francioni (ed.), *Environment, Human Rights & International Trade* (Hart Publishing, 2001), Chapter 3, pp. 57–64. See also Hagen and Weiner, *supra* n. 116; and G. L. Gaston and R. S. Abate, 'The Biosafety Protocol and the World Trade Organisation: Can the Two Co-exist?' (2000) 12 *Pace Int'l L. Rev.* 107.

The Protocol does address its relationship with trade agreements – a contentious issue during negotiations – in the preamble,[128] which repeats nearly verbatim the preambular language of the 1998 Rotterdam Convention on Prior Informed Consent.[129] Specifically, it begins by recognising that trade and environment agreements should be mutually supportive with a view to achieving sustainable development. It then emphasises that 'this Protocol shall not be interpreted as implying a change in rights and obligations of a Party under any existing international agreements', whilst immediately asserting that this recital 'is not intended to subordinate this Protocol to other international agreements'. There is an obvious contradiction between asserting on the one hand no change in rights and obligations yet on the other rejecting any hierarchy between agreements in the event of conflict. The answers are far from clear and have been the subject of much discussion, though such conflict will only materialise in fact when the Protocol enters into force and a decision taken thereunder is challenged as trade-restrictive.

As for the remaining provisions of the Protocol,[130] the AIA procedures must be read with the risk management provisions for the safe use, handling and transboundary movement of LMOs;[131] emergency measures in the event of unintentional release of LMOs;[132] and provisions on handling, transport, packaging and identification.[133] To facilitate information exchange each contracting party must designate a national focal point for liaison with the Secretariat and a competent national authority to perform the administrative tasks required in implementing an AIA procedure.[134] Monitoring and reporting, so common in international environmental agreements, are also required.[135] The Protocol 'piggybacks' on the institutions established under the CBD, but does also

[128] For thorough analysis see Stoll, *supra* n. 100; see also Gaston and Abate, *supra* n. 127.

[129] As Kummer observes, '[c]ontroversy on this point appears to be inherent in multilateral environmental negotiations addressing transboundary transfer of potentially hazardous substances, since they deal with the interface of trade and environment considerations'. K. Kummer, 'Prior Informed Consent for Chemicals in International Trade: The 1998 Rotterdam Convention' (1999) 8(3) *RECIEL* 322, p. 323.

[130] See also Articles 22 (capacity building) and 23 (public awareness and participation).

[131] Article 16. [132] Article 17. [133] Article 18.

[134] Article 19. The Protocol relies on the institutions established under the CBD, including the Secretariat (Article 31); the CoP, which serves as the Meeting of the Parties to the Protocol (Article 29); and any subsidiary bodies under the Convention which the MoP determines may also serve the Protocol (Article 30). It also shares the financial mechanism of the CBD (Article 28).

[135] Article 33. There is also provision for a five-year assessment of the effectiveness of the Protocol five years after its entry into force (Article 35).

establish its own Biosafety Clearing House to facilitate the exchange of scientific, technical, environmental and legal information.[136] Unlike the CBD, it also includes provisions on liability[137] and non-compliance[138] (both discussed in section 7 below). Illegal transboundary movements are regulated by Article 25, which includes a 'take-back' provision where the country of origin may be requested to dispose of the LMO at its own expense.

6. Institutional arrangements

Institutionally, the Convention provides for a Conference of the Parties,[139] a Secretariat,[140] a Clearing House Mechanism 'to promote and facilitate technical and scientific cooperation',[141] and a multidisciplinary Subsidiary Body on Scientific, Technical and Technological Advice (SBSTTA) to provide the CoP 'with timely advice relating to the implementation of [the CBD]'.[142] There are presently also four working groups operational under the Convention, on access and benefit sharing, on Article 8(j) (indigenous knowledge), on the review of implementation, and on protected areas. Dispute settlement is addressed in Article 27, which obliges states to seek solution of any disputes concerning the interpretation or application of the Convention by negotiation, leaving the further choice of arbitration pursuant to Annex II of the Convention, or recourse to the International Court of Justice, to be indicated by express declaration by each contracting party.[143] No reservations to the Convention are permitted – though given the pervasiveness of qualifying language throughout the Convention text ('as far as possible, and as appropriate', 'in accordance with particular conditions and capabilities') such unilateral differentiation would in many instances be unnecessary.[144]

[136] Article 20. For the pilot phase of the BCH, see www.bch.biodiv.org. [137] Article 27.
[138] Article 34.
[139] Article 23. The CoP is expressly empowered, inter alia, to establish further subsidiary bodies particularly to provide scientific and technical advice deemed necessary for the implementation of the Convention (Article 23(4)(g)).
[140] Article 24. [141] Article 18(3). [142] Article 25. [143] Article 27(3).
[144] On the use of unilateral and multilateralised forms of differentiation in environmental treaty-making, see C. Redgwell, 'Multilateral Environmental Treaty-Making', in V. Gowlland-Debbas (ed.), *Multilateral Treaty-Making: The Current Status of Challenges to and Reforms Needed in the International Legislative Process* (Kluwer, 2000).

The Convention's governing body is the Conference of the Parties (CoP) established under Article 22. Its key function is to keep the Convention's implementation under review. This and other functions are set out in Article 23 and include reviewing scientific and other sources of advice, adopting protocols and amendments to the Convention and its annexes, and considering further annexes. It can also establish such subsidiary bodies as are deemed necessary to implement the Convention, and (through the Secretariat) contact executive bodies of conventions dealing with similar issues in order to establish 'appropriate forms' of co-operation with them, discussed further in section 8 below. To date there have been nine meetings of the CoP,[145] though attendance has been low, especially by developing-country parties. In response, special voluntary trust funds have been established to encourage attendance at CoP and MoP meetings, especially by least-developed and small-island developing states.

Pursuant to Article 24 of the Convention, a Secretariat (SCBD) based in Montreal, Canada, was established to support the goals of the Convention. Its primary functions are to organise meetings, prepare reports, assist member governments in the implementation of the various programmes of work, co-ordinate with other international organisations and collect and disseminate information. Administratively it has five divisions, one of which, the Office of the Executive Secretary, is responsible for overall management of the Secretariat. There is a Social, Economic and Legal Affairs Division (SEL) which supports the work of parties, stakeholders and partner organisations in providing positive incentives for conservation and sustainable use and diminishing the threat to biodiversity conservation posed by 'misguided' social, economic and legal measures and policies. It is this division which, for example, works with the WTO to ensure that the Convention and Protocol, and trade rules, are applied in a mutually supportive fashion, and which is working on issues of liability and redress for transboundary damage to biodiversity. The Scientific, Technical and Technological Matters (STTM) Division supports work on the thematic areas and cross-cutting issues identified above, and provides support for the work of the

[145] CoP I (1994) Nassau, Bahamas; CoP II (1995), Jakarta, Indonesia; CoP III (1996) Buenos Aires, Argentina; CoP IV (1998) Bratislava, Slovakia; CoP V (2000) Nairobi, Kenya; CoP VI (2002) The Hague, Netherlands; CoP VII (2004) Kuala Lumpur, Malaysia; CoP VIII (2006) Curitiba, Brazil; CoP IX (2008) Bonn, Germany. CoP X is scheduled for October 2010 in Nagoya, Japan.

Subsidiary Body on Scientific, Technical and Technological Advice (SBSTTA). The Biosafety Division services the Cartagena Protocol and hosts the Biosafety Clearing House (BCH) created pursuant to Article 20 of the Protocol. The Division for Implementation and Technical Support buttresses the national implementation provisions of the CBD, including national strategies and action plans, reporting, the Convention's Clearing House Mechanism (CHM), financial resources and the financial mechanism, and interagency and programme co-ordination. This division is instrumental in the communication, education and public awareness initiative resulting from CoP VI (Decision VI/19) and works with major groups, namely business,[146] parliamentarians, local authorities and civil society (NGOS, children and youth, women). 'Greening of the SCBD' includes planting trees to offset carbon emissions from staff travel, pursuant to a 16 November 2006 MoU between the CBD and the Green Belt Movement.

7. Implementation

a) National implementation

The CBD is strongly reliant on national implementation. It is up to individual contracting parties to determine the manner of implementation of their obligations, with the Convention setting out broad policy goals and objectives which individual states are expected to concretise and implement. Article 6, described as 'one of the most far-reaching articles in the Convention',[147] places particular emphasis on such national action and priority setting. It provides that, in accordance with its particular conditions and capabilities, each contracting party shall:

> (a) Develop national strategies, plans or programmes for the conservation and sustainable use of biological diversity or adapt for this purpose existing strategies, plans or programmes which shall reflect, *inter alia*, the measures set out in this convention relevant to the Contracting Party concerned; and
>
> (b) Integrate, as far as possible and as appropriate, the conservation and sustainable use of biological diversity into relevant sectoral or cross-sectoral plans, programmes and policies.

[146] The first CoP decision to focus exclusively on business was Decision VIII/17 (business participation in the Convention process).

[147] IUCN Guide, *supra* n. 26, at p. 29. For assessment of National Biodiversity Strategies and Action Plans, see P. Herkenrath, 'The Implementation of the Convention on Biological Diversity: A Non-government Perspective Ten Years On' (2002) 11(1) *RECIEL* 29.

National implementation is thus more than a one-stage process; indeed, though Article 6 does not explicitly state it, the reference to strategies, plans and programmes could be seen as sequential in the implementation process.[148] The link between this article and Article 8 (*in situ* conservation) is clear. On adoption of the treaty text, the Nordic countries (Denmark, Finland, Sweden and Norway) made a joint declaration stressing the need for, inter alia, strong national commitments to render the CBD effective. The first reporting deadline set under the Convention was for contracting parties to report on their implementation of Article 6 by 1 January 1998 (prior to CoP IV); there have been two subsequent reporting deadlines. In addition, parties are encouraged to exchange information and share implementation experiences via the Clearing-House Mechanism (CHM) established pursuant to Article 18(3).[149]

b) Compliance

This national emphasis may also serve to explain the absence from the CBD of a non-compliance procedure of the kind found in the 1987 Montreal Protocol to the 1985 Ozone Convention, the 1997 Kyoto Protocol to the 1992 Framework Convention on Climate Change, and the 2000 Cartagena Protocol to the CBD itself.[150] Writing in 1995, the then vice-president of the CBD's Conference of the Parties, Mr Veit Koester, observed,

> If we are wondering whether the Parties to the Convention are going to comply with the obligations of the Convention and how we can ensure compliance in the long run, my answer would be to forget about this concern: first, because the Convention was never designed with this question in mind. Second, its philosophy differs in many respects from the thinking behind most nature conventions.[151]

Non-compliance procedures are associated with concrete obligations, compliance with which may be measured in some fashion.[152] The

[148] IUCN Guide, *supra* n. 26, at p. 29. [149] See www.biodiv.org.

[150] For general discussion of non-compliance procedures, see M. Fitzmaurice and C. Redgwell, 'Non-compliance Procedures and Environmental Agreements' (2000) 31 *NYIL* 35; and, on the Protocol, C. Ragni, 'Procedures and Mechanisms on Compliance under the 2000 Protocol on Biosafety to the 1992 Convention on Biological Diversity', in T. Treves et al. (eds.), *Non-compliance Procedures and Mechanisms and the Effectiveness of International Environmental Agreements* (Kluwer, 2009).

[151] *Bulletin on Biological Diversity* (CBD, 1995).

[152] Fitzmaurice and Redgwell, *supra* n. 150.

broad scope of the CBD's provisions and the problem of ascertaining the fulfilment of concrete obligations, alongside the emphasis upon national implementation and general principles of co-operation, militates against the development of a non-compliance procedure. Implementation and enforcement in respect of the conservation of biological diversity within states is, *strictu sensu*, a matter for national law, whilst overviewing compliance with Convention obligations in areas beyond national jurisdiction will fall within the competence of various existing international and regional bodies.[153] Although there is no institutional body charged with formal oversight of implementation or compliance issues under the CBD, there is a Working Group on Review of Implementation of the Convention.[154] Thus, whilst Article 26 obliges contracting parties to report on measures taken for the implementation of the provisions of the Convention and their effectiveness in meeting its objectives, at the present time such reports are to be submitted directly to the Conference of the Parties.[155] This provides an opportunity for the CoP, and any committees it might duly establish to overview these reports, to comment on any weaknesses or failures of parties in this respect. Article 27 CBD provides for classic dispute settlement procedures, with Annex II setting out arbitration procedures, but in common with most environmental (and many other) agreements such mechanisms are not compulsory, apart from the obligation to negotiate contained in Article 27(1).[156]

In contrast, Article 34 of the Cartagena Protocol explicitly envisaged the establishment of a compliance procedure, and at the first meeting of the CoP/MoP in 2004 Decision BS/7 created an ad hoc Compliance

[153] Birnie, Boyle and Redgwell, *supra* n. 35, p. 637. Responsibility for overviewing compliance with the Convention's requirements in areas beyond national jurisdiction will generally fall within the competence, if any, of appropriate international and regional bodies, and Article 5 requires parties to co-operate 'as far as possible and appropriate', with other parties directly or through competent international organisations, in respect of these areas on matters of mutual interest, presumably including on compliance matters.

[154] Which has met three times to date, in 2005, 2007 and 2009.

[155] This does not, of course, rule out the subsequent establishment of a subsidiary implementation review body by the CoP, in accordance with the powers conferred by Article 23(4)(g) of the Convention. Thus this supervisory role in respect of implementation could be extended, if the parties so agree, as has been done under certain other treaty instruments such as the Ramsar Convention and the Montreal Protocol to the Ozone Convention.

[156] Article 27 also extends to the 2000 Cartagena Protocol, with the crucial distinction that the latter also contemplates – without prejudice to the operation of Article 27 – a non-compliance procedure (Article 34), discussed immediately below.

Committee, put on a firm footing with Rules of Procedure agreed by CoP/MoP IV (Decision IV/36). It comprises fifteen members elected by the CoP/MoP (three members from each of the five regional groups of the UN) and serving in their personal capacity. Triggered only by the parties themselves (i.e. by the non-complying or another party),[157] the process is non-adversarial and is designed principally to assist parties in implementing the Protocol, to identify circumstances and causes of individual cases of non-compliance, and to make recommendations with a view to assisting states to comply. The sliding scale of responses, recommended by the Committee but decided upon by the CoP/MoP, ranges from financial and technical assistance to issuing a caution, publishing cases of non-compliance on the BCHM (Biosafety Clearing House Mechanism) and, in the case of repeated non-compliance, further action by the CoP/MoP.[158] The latest, sixth, meeting of the Compliance Committee (2009) considered general issues of compliance arising from the national reports, and expressed concern regarding the low national reporting rate under the Protocol.[159]

The Convention also addresses incentives aimed at inducing compliance. Article 11 requires that each contracting party shall 'as far as possible and appropriate', 'adopt economically and socially sound measures that act as incentives for the conservation and sustainable use of components of biological diversity'. It does not provide guidance concerning what these incentives might or should be. The CoP, however, having affirmed that implementation of incentive measures, in a broad social, cultural and economic context, is of central importance to the realisation of the three objectives of the Convention, resolved that such measures would be included ('as appropriate') on the CoP's agenda and integrated into the sectoral and thematic items

[157] In the event of allegations of non-compliance received from non-party sources – e.g. NGOs – the Committee has reiterated that this is beyond its mandate, but will nonetheless invite the party concerned to indicate whether it wishes the Committee to consider the information received. See, for example, Report of the Compliance Committee under the Cartagena Protocol on Biosafety on the Work of its Fifth Meeting, UNEP/CBD/BS/CC/5/4, 21 November 2008, para. 25.

[158] At CoP/MoP IV (2007) the parties decided to postpone consideration of measures to address such cases 'until such time as experience may justify the need for developing and adopting such measures'. Decision BS-IV/1, Report of the Compliance Committee, para. 3.

[159] See Report of the Compliance Committee under the Cartagena Protocol on Biosafety on the Work of its Sixth Meeting, UNEP/CBD/BS/CC/6/4, 27 November 2009.

under its medium-term work programme. It also encouraged parties to review their existing legislation and economic policies; identify and promote incentives for conservation and sustainable use, stressing the importance of taking appropriate action on incentives that threaten biological diversity; and to incorporate market and non-market values of biological diversity into policies, programmes, national accounting systems and investment strategy (such plans etc. being required in Article 6). Otherwise the CoP relies on promotion of such other methods advocated in the Convention as development of training and capacity-building programmes (Article 12), public education and awareness (Article 13), impact assessment (Article 14), exchange of information (Article 17) and co-operation. Parties are invited to 'share their experiences on these incentive measures with and make available case studies to the Secretariat' with a view to the Secretariat providing guidance to the parties on designing and implementing incentive measures.

c) *Liability and responsibility*

The perfunctory treatment of transboundary issues in the CBD has already been noted above, with Article 14(1) doing little more than restate the customary-law obligation to notify of transboundary harm. There is little remaining in the final text of the CBD relating to responsibility and liability issues, a contentious issue during negotiations, with Article 14(2) merely calling on the parties to 'examine ... the issue of liability and redress, including restoration and compensation, for damage to biodiversity except where such liability is purely an internal matter'. A working group of legal and technical experts was established to consider the issue, but little headway has been made. In contrast, Article 27 of the Biosafety Protocol calls for the elaboration of rules and procedures in the field of liability and redress for damage resulting from transboundary movements of LMOs, and an Open-Ended Ad Hoc Working Group of Legal and Technical Experts on Liability and Redress established at CoP/MoP I (Decision BS-I/8) has made some progress. A draft text for a supplementary protocol on liability and redress to the Biosafety Protocol, adopted by Decision BS-IV/12 as the basis for further work, may be finalised in the near future – though whether it takes the form of a supplementary protocol is left ultimately for the CoP/MoP to determine and with many key issues, such as the definition of damage (operational text 6), yet to be finally agreed.[160]

d) Financial and technical assistance

The obligations under Articles 7 and 8, even where a state is party to a range of existing conservation treaties, are potentially quite onerous. This is no doubt one reason for employing qualifying language like 'as far as possible and as appropriate' and 'in accordance with its particular conditions and capabilities' in respect of these obligations. It is also one of the reasons for leaving to national implementation the fulfilment of the objectives of the Convention rather than relying on, inter alia, prescriptive targets or lists. Nonetheless the sheer range of matters addressed in Article 8, combined with the requirements for identification and monitoring in Article 7, require significant resources, both financial and technical, for implementation. These are addressed in the Convention in, for example, Articles 12 (research and training), 16 (transfer of technology) and 20 (financial resources), with particular regard to developing states.

Articles 20 and 21 CBD address financial resources and the financial mechanism respectively. Article 39 underscores the interim character of the GEF (UNDP/UNEP/IBRD) as the relevant institutional mechanism, subject to restructuring. The GEF was initially designated the interim financial mechanism owing primarily to developing-country concerns regarding its governance, an issue addressed in Article 21 CBD. Developed-country concerns focused on the language of Article 21(1) and whether this could give rise to an open-ended financial commitment: this provision states that the amount of resources needed is to be decided periodically by the CoP. A common declaration by nineteen developed countries – and individual declarations confirmed on ratification e.g. by the United Kingdom – stresses that Article 21(1) is confined to a determination of the amount of resources needed and not to the extent or nature and form of the contribution by individual contracting parties.

In the event, restructuring of the governance structure of the GEF duly took place, and the GEF has continued to serve as the funding

[160] A Group of the Friends of the Co-chairs on Liability and Redress was established by Decision BS-IV/12 to continue the negotiations process, with meetings in February 2009 and February 2010. The draft text is annexed to this Decision.

mechanism under the CBD.[161] It comprises thirty-two members representative of the participating states. Under Article 20, developed countries undertake to provide 'new and additional financial resources to enable developing countries to meet the agreed full incremental cost of implementing the obligations of the Convention'. Indeed, Article 20(4) arguably makes the extent of effective implementation of developing-state commitments under the CBD dependent upon effective implementation by developed states of commitments relating to financial resources and transfer of technology, 'taking fully into account the fact that economic and social development and eradication of poverty are the first and overriding priority of the developing country Parties'. This provision mirrors UNFCCC Article 4(7) and Montreal Protocol Article 10 (where the MoP has competence to deal with complaints regarding non-transfer of resources).

The financial mechanism functions under the authority and guidance of the CoP, to which the GEF reports.[162] As required under Article 21(2), comprehensive guidance was issued at CoP I and at each subsequent CoP this guidance has been refined and augmented. For example, Decision V/13 at CoP V lists fourteen areas for GEF support, including projects utilising the ecosystem approach or implementing the Convention's programme of work on agriculture, forestry and drylands biodiversity. GEF has four operational programmes on biodiversity: arid and semi-arid ecosystems; coastal, marine and freshwater ecosystems; forest ecosystems; and mountain ecosystems.[163] In addition, the GEF has been requested, inter alia, to facilitate urgent implementation of Article 6 (national plans), as well as to assist with the preparation of national reports under the reporting obligations of Article 26. The effectiveness of the financial mechanisms is also subject to review by the CoP pursuant to Article 21(3). The first review was carried out at CoP IV, with a three-year review cycle initiated thereafter.

8. Relationship with other agreements

The Conference of the Parties has consistently recognised the need for co-operation with other conventions and this has been a regular subject

[161] For further details see www.gefweb.com.
[162] An MoU has been entered into between the CoP and the GEF Council (CoP III, 1997).
[163] See further details at www.gefweb.com.

of CoP decisions.[164] It is a key element in the Strategic Plan, Goal 1 of which states, 'The Convention is fulfilling its leadership role in international biodiversity issues.' The Secretariats of the Rio Conventions co-operate through the Joint Liaison Group and the CBD takes the lead in the Biodiversity Liaison Group, which also includes the World Heritage Convention and the Ramsar, CITES and Bonn Conventions.[165] These conventions share the goals of conservation and sustainable use, and employ complementary approaches for their implementation. The CBD has entered into memoranda of co-operation or understanding, and/or joint programmes of work, with these instruments and a host of others, including, for example, an MoC concluded in 2008 with the Alps and Carpathian Conventions.[166]

The legal relationship of the CBD[167] with these other treaties is addressed in Article 22 CBD, which provides that the 'provisions of the Convention shall not affect the rights and obligations of any Contracting Party deriving from any existing international agreement except where the exercise of those rights and obligations would cause a serious damage or threat to biological diversity'.[168] This formulation permits less inconsistency between treaties than would be the case if the residual rules of the VCLT applied,[169] with the safeguard that the core of the CBD is preserved through satisfaction of the 'no serious damage or threat to biological diversity' test. Of course, given that the CBD was negotiated expressly to fill the 'biodiversity gap', with UNEP initially speaking of consolidation rather than new regulation, it is unlikely that serious issues

164 Most recently, CoP IX Decision IX/27.

165 In 2005 the secretariats produced a note setting out the options for co-operation amongst the five biodiversity-related conventions. UNEP/CBD/WG-RI/1/7/Add.2, 14 July 2005.

166 There are presently 132 entries on its partnership agreements site (www.cbd.int/partnerships), which includes other conventions, a consortium of scientific partners, and other organisations and stakeholders.

167 On the relationship of the Cartagena Protocol with other agreements, see section 5 above, and Chapter 19 below.

168 Article 22(2) further stipulates that the 'Contracting Parties shall implement this Convention with respect to the marine environment consistently with the rights and obligations of States under the law of the sea.' Presumably direct reference was not made to the LOSC to ensure (a) that Article 22(2) would encompass both treaty and customary international law, and (b) that its phrasing reflected the fact that the LOSC had not then entered into force. It did so on 16 November 1994 when the sixtieth ratification took effect.

169 Under the VCLT, it will be recalled, Articles 30 and 59 provide that earlier treaties relating to the same subject matter will continue to apply to the extent that their provisions are 'compatible' with the later treaty.

of inconsistency will arise with environmental treaties.[170] However, the Colombian declaration on ratification objects to Article 22 on the basis that the matter is regulated by Article 30 VCLT,[171] whilst a number of declarations address the relationship with the Agreement on Trade-Related Aspects of Intellectual Property Rights (TRIPS).[172]

The intellectual property rights protection embodied in Article 16(2) is qualified by Article 16(5), which requires parties to ensure that patents and IP rights in national and international law are supportive of, and do not run counter to, the CBD's objectives. This could be interpreted as respect for IP rights but only in so far as they assist, rather than hinder, implementation of the CBD. At CoP V, in Decision V/26, the WTO is invited to 'acknowledge' the provisions of the CBD and to take into account the fact that TRIPS and the CBD are interrelated and to further explore this interrelationship. This invitation was transmitted both to the WTO and to WIPO, and includes renewal of the request for the Executive Secretary of the CBD to apply for observer status on the TRIPS Council.[173] The relationship between the CBD and the WTO, including TRIPS, is explored further in Chapter 19 below.

9. Conclusion

Initial reaction to the CBD was mixed, ranging from hailing it as a landmark in the field to harsh criticism of its text as rushed, ambiguous

[170] For discussion of the potential for conflict between obligations under the CBD and the operation of the Convention on the Conservation of Antarctic Marine Living Resources, see C. Redgwell, 'Protection of Ecosystems under International Law: Lessons from Antarctica', in A. E. Boyle and D. Freestone (eds.), *International Law and Sustainable Development* (Oxford University Press, 1999).

[171] It also objects to the reference in Article 22(2) to what it terms another legal instrument that, in 1992, had not yet entered into force.

[172] The Declaration on ratification by the Government of Argentina, for example, asserts the full consistency of the CBD with TRIPS. At CoP II, the Executive Secretary of the CBD was requested to liaise with the WTO especially in respect of TRIPS, and with WIPO. This exhortation has been reiterated at subsequent CoPs, e.g. at CoP VI, Decisions VI/15 and VI/20. The former reiterates the complementarity between trade and environmental agreements in achieving sustainable development, a point stressed in the Doha Ministerial Declaration of the WTO adopted on 14 November 2001 as well as reiterated in the 2000 Cartagena Protocol. Article 16(5) CBD requires the contracting parties to co-operate to ensure the compatibility of the patents and other intellectual property rights with the objectives of the CBD. CoP decisions have reinforced the need for co-operation with TRIPS and with WIPO, as well as with WTO Committees on Technical Barriers to Trade, Sanitary and Phyto-sanitary Matters, and Trade and Environment (e.g. Decision VI/20).

[173] See also Decision VI/20.

and haphazard.[174] As the above discussion has demonstrated, the real test of the CBD is in its implementation, particularly given its strong national orientation. It has been in force for nearly seventeen years, with considerable activity at the international and national levels in its implementation. The international community's approach to biodiversity has continued to evolve, with conservation of biological diversity now considered an essential part of efforts to eradicate poverty and achieve sustainable development. In the immediate run-up to the 2002 World Summit on Sustainable Development (WSSD) in Johannesburg, the 2002 Hague Ministerial Declaration of the Conference of the Parties to the CBD recognised

> that biodiversity underpins sustainable development in many ways; poverty eradication, food security, provision of fresh water, soil conservation and human health all depend directly upon maintaining and using the world's biological diversity and therefore sustainable development cannot be achieved without the conservation and sustainable use of biological diversity.[175]

Recommendation 1B of the WSSD accordingly recognises the contribution of the CBD to the sustainable-development process, and to poverty eradication in particular. The need to integrate the objectives of the CBD in global, regional and national sectoral and cross-sectoral programmes and policies – the 'mainstreaming of biodiversity' – is seen both as contributing to the sustainable-development process and as ensuring full implementation of the Convention.[176]

However, the very breadth of its activities has led to concerns that the CBD has not been able sufficiently to focus on key issues and is dissipating its energy across too wide a range of issues.[177] This problem has been widely perceived, with the adoption at CoP VI (2002) of a Strategic Plan for the Convention, a technique used by other conventions such as Ramsar, designed in part to address this problem.[178] Undoubtedly 'the conservation of biological diversity ... presents greater regulatory

[174] See, for example, the range of responses canvassed in McGraw, *supra* n. 43 and in Koester, *supra* n. 23.

[175] Para. 5. The Declaration calls upon the World Summit on Sustainable Development to recognise and to promote these strong linkages (see para. 15(c)).

[176] Contribution of the Convention on Biological Diversity to Implementing the Outcomes of the Johannesburg Summit, Report of the [CBD] Executive Secretary to the Commission on Sustainable Development. The marginalisation of biodiversity issues is perceived as one of the principal obstacles to full implementation of the CBD (para. 6).

[177] McGraw, *supra* n. 43, p. 23.

[178] The Strategic Plan will be revised at CoP X in 2010.

challenges to international law than any other environmental issue',[179] and it is not for the CBD alone to address these – other species and conservation treaties are part of this wider regulatory challenge. Indeed Koester, in his analysis of the five global biodiversity-related conventions, concludes that 'they are in reasonably good shape' and suggests that the pertinent question to ask is, 'What would be the condition of our biodiversity if these conventions did not exist?'[180]

One of the achievements the CBD cites is a doubling in the past twenty years of terrestrial protected-areas coverage, to about 13 per cent of the Earth's land surface.[181] Yet such quantitative statistics obscure the real indicator of effectiveness in conserving biological diversity, which is reducing and eliminating species extinction. Crucial to this is the protection of 'biodiversity hotspots';[182] that is, areas of high species endemism with high species and ecosystem diversity as well. The absence of effective conservation measures for hotspots located particularly in developing countries (only two-fifths of the world's eco-regions reach the 10 per cent benchmark) and in high-seas areas (less than 0.5 per cent of marine areas area covered) led to the adoption in 2002 of strategic targets for terrestrial and marine areas by 2010 (also designated the Year of Biodiversity) and 2012 respectively. Progress in meeting these targets is difficult to assess in the absence of agreed, comprehensive global-scale measures. It is unlikely, however, that these targets will be met, owing to a host of institutional, financial and capacity constraints.[183] For high-seas areas, effective conservation of high-seas biodiversity will require resolution of the relationship between the CBD and the LOSC and of the question whether a new legal instrument is required.[184] The second edition of the CBD's Global Biodiversity Outlook identifies a common, cautiously optimistic, message: 'biodiversity is in decline at all levels and geographical scales, but targeted response options – whether through protected areas, or resource management and pollution prevention programmes – can reverse this trend for specific habitats or species'.[185]

[179] P. Sands, *Principles of International Environmental Law* (Cambridge University Press, 2nd ed., 2003), p. 450.

[180] V. Koester, 'The Five Biodiversity-Related Conventions' (2001) 31 *EPL* 151.

[181] Global Biodiversity Outlook 2, at www.cbd.int/2010-target/implementation/achievements.shtml. At the time of writing, GBO3 is under preparation: see www.cbd.int/gbo3.

[182] See, for example, N. Meyers, 'The Biodiversity Challenge: Expanded Hot-Spot Analysis' (1990) 10 *Environmentalist* 243.

[183] So concurs Rayfuse, supra n. 36, p. 382. [184] Ibid. p. 383.

[185] Available at www.cbd.int/2010-target/implementation/achievements.shtml.

Recommended further reading

A. E. Boyle, 'The Convention on Biological Diversity', in L. Campiglio, L. Pineschi, D. Siniscalco and T. Treves (eds.), *The Environment after Rio* (Kluwer, 1994)

L. Glowka et al., *A Guide to the Convention on Biological Diversity* (CBD Secretariat, 1994)

P. E. Hagan and J. B. Weiner, 'The Cartagena Protocol on Biosafety: New Rules for International Trade in Living Modified Organisms' (2000) 12 *Georgetown ELR* 697

F. McConnell, *The Biodiversity Convention: A Negotiating History* (Kluwer, 1996)

R. Rayfuse, 'Biological Resources', in D. Bodansky, J. Brunnee and E. Hey (eds.), *The Oxford Handbook of International Environmental Law* (Oxford University Press, 2007)

Chapter 18

Deserts, forests and mountains

1. Introduction

It was hoped that the Rio process would bring about not only a convention conserving biodiversity but also conventions on desertification and forests. From 1975 onwards, the UN, UNEP, and various conferences of concerned international organisations and bodies had drawn attention to the increasingly serious environmental and economic consequences of the expansion of arid lands and destruction of forests, especially tropical forests. Various recommendations[1] emerged from these and were promoted by, inter alia, UNEP, UNESCO, and the FAO, but action lagged until the spread and severity of desertification and rate of destruction of forests led to intensified demands for action. This was inhibited, however, by the insistence of some states that the issues involved fell wholly within their national sovereignty. Thus, although some progress was made on definitional aspects, the goal of concluding conventions on these topics was not attained at UNCED, though Agenda 21 did define and draw attention to desertification,[2] and a non-binding statement of principles relating to forests was adopted.[3] It was not until 1994 that a Convention to Combat Desertification was adopted; to date, no global agreement on binding standards for the protection of forests has been reached.

Agenda 21 also called for regional legal and other instruments to protect fragile mountain ecosystems,[4] with a step in this direction

[1] See discussion in P. Sands, *Principles of International Environmental Law* (Cambridge University Press, 2nd ed., 2003), Chapter 11.

[2] Chapter 12, 'Managing Fragile Ecosystems: Combating Desertification and Drought', *Agenda 21: Earth's Action Plan* (Oceana Publications, 2002).

[3] 'Non-legally Binding Authoritative Statement of Principles for a Global Consensus on the Management, Conservation and Sustainable Development of All Types of Forest', Annex III to the Report of the United Nations Conference on Environment and Development, UN Doc A/CONF.151/26 (Vol. III), 14 August 1992.

[4] Chapter 13, 'Managing Fragile Ecosystems: Sustainable Mountain Development' *Agenda 21*, *supra* n. 2.

taken the previous year with the conclusion of the 1991 Alps Convention in Europe. This was the first international treaty to address mountain ecosystem protection; in 2003, the Convention on the Protection and Sustainable Development of the Carpathians was concluded and several other areas – the Caucasus, Central Asia and the Andes – may follow suit in the near future.[5] As discussed in the previous chapter, all three ecosystems – desert, forest and mountain – are recognised thematic areas under the CBD; all three constitute critically important habitat for wildlife. It is the purpose of this chapter to consider each of these in turn, to the extent that they are addressed beyond the CBD framework.[6] The existence of concern for desert, forest and mountain ecosystems is evidence of the growing recognition of the importance of protection at the level of ecosystem which, with the notable exception of the Ramsar Convention, had previously only been implicitly recognised, if at all.[7]

2. Deserts

Deserts comprise unique ecosystems with millennia-old natural habitats, as well as being of significant cultural and landscape importance.[8] Less biologically diverse, and certainly less studied,[9] than tropical rainforests, drylands contain significant numbers of species including several of the largest land animals on the planet. In particular, the native plant, animal and microbial species inhabiting drylands have developed special coping strategies to deal with low and sporadic rainfall and variations in temperature that may be of global importance in adapting to climate change.[10]

The spur for the conclusion of a treaty came from Agenda 21, and it was following a recommendation made in Chapter 12 therein that the

[5] See www.alpconv.org for discussion of its precedential impact.

[6] This is not to suggest that there is not a degree of co-ordination and synergy between the CBD and the instruments discussed in this chapter, as the following sections detail.

[7] On the growth of the ecosystem approach and its importance to wildlife and habitat conservation, see D. Tarlock, 'Ecosystems', in D. Bodansky, J. Brunnee and E. Hey (eds.) *The Oxford Handbook of International Environmental Law* (Oxford University Press, 2007).

[8] See, generally, UNEP, *Global Environmental Outlook for Deserts* (UNEP, 2006).

[9] A recent report notes that 'the status of wild animal and plant species diversity is poorly documented, apart from IUCN Red Lists records on endangered species'. See the Global Drylands Partnership (CIDA, UNSO, UNDP/GEF, IIED, IUCN, WWF, NEF), *Biodiversity in Drylands: Challenges and Opportunities for Conservation and Sustainable Use* (IUCN, 2004), p. 3. See also www.fao.org/ag/agl/agll/drylands/biodiversity.htm.

[10] Global Drylands Partnership, *supra* n. 9, at p. 4.

UNGA initiated negotiation of a convention focusing particularly on African states experiencing serious drought.[11] States were, however, anxious to avoid conflict and overlap with existing conventions, such as those on climate change and biodiversity. Problems also arose concerning the conclusion and status of specific regional instruments, which it was agreed should be an integral part of the convention.

A Convention to Combat Desertification (UNCCD) was eventually concluded in 1994, with four annexes covering Africa, Latin America and the Caribbean, Asia, and the Northern Mediterranean.[12] It entered into force on 26 December 1996 and, as of January 2010, had 193 parties.[13] It thus enjoys virtually universal participation but unfortunately this has not yet translated into an effective regime for drylands conservation, not least because the Convention is weak on specific commitments. In 1999 a permanent Secretariat was established in Bonn and, in 2003, the GEF was formally designated a financial mechanism for the Convention. There have been nine meetings of the Conference of the Parties to date, most recently in the autumn of 2009. In addition to being served by the standing Committee on Science and Technology (CST) established under the Convention, the CoP in 2001 created a subsidiary body, the Committee for Review of Implementation of the Convention (CRIC) which was recently elevated to a standing body of the CoP.[14] There is also a Group of Experts (GoE) to provide expert advice to the CST on matters such as benchmarks and indicators, traditional knowledge and early warning systems; it has also commented on reports submitted to the CRIC by state parties and international organisations. A further subsidiary body is the Global Mechanism, envisaged by Article 21 of the

[11] UNGA Res. 47/188 (1992); text in (1993) 23 *EPL* 43–6.

[12] For reports on the difficulties experienced in negotiations, see (1993) 23 *EPL* 202–3; (1994) 24 *EPL* 36; on the CoPs, (1996) 26 *EPL* 462; (1997) 27 *EPL* 80 and 169; (1998) 28 *EPL* 46; (2000) 30 *EPL* 32–3. See generally M. Bekhechi, 'Une nouvelle étape dans le développement de droit international de l'environnement: la Convention sur la desertification' (1997) 101 *RGDIP* 32; and W. C. Burns, 'International Convention to Combat Desertification: Drawing a Line in the Sand' (1994–5) 16 *Mich. J Int'l L* 831.

[13] Iraq is not a party, nor is it a signatory to the Convention.

[14] Decision 11/COP. 9. Para. 14 establishes the focus of the CRIC's work between CoPs as undertaking an assessment of national implementation against performance indicators (every two years) and impact indicators (every four years) and disseminating best practice on, and financial flows for, implementation of the Convention. One of the achievements of CoP 9 was to agree two minimum impact indicators for national reports – the proportion of population in affected areas living above the poverty line, and land cover status – with additional optimal impact indicators. See further Decisions 13 and 17/CoP. 9.

Convention, which is tasked with mobilising 'substantial financial resources, including for the transfer of technology' by building effective partnerships with national and international actors, including the GEF.[15]

The Convention, as in the case of the Biodiversity Convention, confines provisions touching on controversial issues to its Preamble: human beings are recognised as being at the centre of concerns to combat desertification and mitigate drought. The 'urgent concern of the international community' about the adverse impacts of these problems is 'reflected' in the text, though as the problems are stated to be of 'global dimensions in that they affect all regions of the world', it is 'acknowledged' that joint action of that community is needed to combat them. Stress is laid on the prevalence of developing states in the areas and the need both to resolve the economic and social problems of the areas concerned and to achieve sustainable economic growth. The parties reaffirm Rio Declaration Principle 2 concerning the right to pursue their own developmental as well as environmental policies and assert that national governments play a crucial role in combating the problems involved, but they also draw attention to the accompanying need for 'new and additional funding' and access to technology, without which, they state, it will be difficult for them to comply with their treaty obligations. They do, however, recognise the relationship between desertification and other global environmental problems and 'bear in mind' the contribution that combating desertification will make to achieving their objectives under the Climate Change and Biological Diversity Conventions.[16] They also note that it will be necessary to base strategies on rigorous scientific knowledge if they are to be effective, and stress the urgent need to improve 'the effectiveness and co-ordination of international co-operation'. The need to take 'appropriate action' against desertification and drought for the benefit of present and future generations is acknowledged but the precautionary approach is not mentioned.

'Desertification' is defined in Article 1 as meaning 'land degradation in arid, semi-arid and dry humid areas resulting from various factors',

[15] For the four-year plan of work of the Global Mechanism (GM) proposed within the context of the present ten-year strategy (2008–2018) see ICCD/CRIC(7)/2/Add 3, 27 August 2008. Despite being the subject of extensive discussion, including at the recent CoP 9, the relationship between the distinct entitles of the GM and the Secretariat has not finally been resolved. See, inter alia, Decision 6/CoP. 9 'Joint Inspection Unit Report on the Assessment of the Global Mechanism'.

[16] The CBD's SBSTTA has recommended improving synergies between the CBD and UNCCD regarding dry and subhumid lands biodiversity: CBD CoP 8 (2006).

including climatic variations and human activities; 'combating' it includes activities aimed at (i) prevention or reduction of land degradation, (ii) rehabilitation of partly degraded land and (iii) reclamation of desertified land.[17] The substantive articles are weak on positive commitment. As in the case of the Biodiversity Convention, reference is made in the Preamble to the Rio Declaration's goal-setting principles, such as sustainable development and accounting for the interests of future generations, but much development of the implementing measures required will depend on the degree of technology transfer and financial support, invoked in other articles, so far as the many developing countries in the desertified areas are concerned.

One of the key mechanisms for implementation of the Convention is the ongoing development of national, subregional and regional action programmes by state parties affected by desertification in Africa, Asia, Latin America, the Caribbean and the Northern Mediterranean. As Rayfuse notes,[18] the Convention is characterised both by a 'bottom-up' approach[19] – 'treating desertification as a local management issue' – and by reliance on participatory mechanisms for such management rather than on the protected-areas approach of other instruments such as the CBD. Developed-country parties have the obligation to support affected countries through the provision of additional financial resources and by facilitating access to technology, knowledge and know-how.[20] Developed-country national reports under the Convention indicate support – both financial and technical – for sustainable land-use development, sustainable production systems and conservation programmes. Less attention is given by such parties, however, to sustainable use of range lands, the development and use of early warning systems and desertification monitoring and assessment. Yet it is in relation to these last two, particularly in the development of baseline data, that developing-country implementation has been slow.[21] Indeed, the

[17] Drought is a 'natural hazard' while desertification involves degradation of land resources. M. Kassas, 'Desertification: A General Review' (1995) 30(2) *J. of Arid Environments* 115.

[18] R. Rayfuse, 'Biological Resources', in D. Bodansky, J. Brunnee and E. Hey (eds.), *The Oxford Handbook of International Environmental Law* (Oxford University Press, 2007) 362, at p. 383.

[19] See K. W. Danish, 'International Environmental Law and the "Bottom-up" Approach: A Review of the Desertification Convention' (1995) *3 Ind. J. Global Legal Stud.* 1; and H. Iles, 'The Desertification Convention: A Deeper Focus on Social Aspects of Environmental Degradation' (1995) 36 *Harv. ILJ* 207.

[20] Articles 6 and 20 CSD.

[21] See, for example, the GoE's synthesis and analysis of national reports to the CRIC3 available at www.unccd.int/science/groupofexperts/synthesis-cric3.pdf.

GoE has pointed out that lack of standardisation in reporting format, varying understanding of the questions posed and significant gaps in baseline data monitoring render it difficult to assess compliance with the Convention in terms of drylands protection and conservation.[22] This is echoed in an IUCN report which concludes,

> Drylands have been neglected in both conservation and sustainable use efforts. It is therefore difficult to provide a definitive picture of biodiversity status and trends . . . following the precautionary principle, and until such time as additional data proves otherwise, it is safe to say that habitat degradation is an imminent and immediate problem affecting biodiversity loss in drylands.[23]

Current efforts are focused on enhancing the implementation of the Convention, which is at an early stage. The designation of 2006 as the UN International Year of Deserts and Desertification was intended, inter alia, to give greater impetus to the implementation of the Convention. Institutional partners for this purpose include UNEP, the UNDP, IFAD, the World Bank, UNESCO, the GEF and the FAO, while linkages have also been established with the CBD. Within the framework of a ten-year strategic plan (2008–18) agreed at CoP 8 to enhance implementation of the Convention, CRIC is to consider progress in implementation of several key strategic objectives including improvement of the condition of affected ecosystems based on the work undertaken by the CST. At CoP 9 some steps were taken to specify impact indicators and to improve reporting procedures and mechanisms.[24] However, though the Convention has now been in force for over a decade, political support remains weak notwithstanding the large number of parties, and political and institutional wrangles persist.[25] Despite the great need to combat the problems of desertification and aridity, the Convention has failed to engender the urgent and positive action required. Financial mechanisms have been problematic, with a significant step being the acknowledgement of the need for facilitative finance for, inter alia, baseline

[22] Ibid. [23] Global Drylands Partnership, *supra* n. 9.

[24] See, for example, Decision 13/CoP. 9, 'Improving the procedures for communication of information as well as the quality and format of reports to be submitted to the [CoP]'; and Decision 17/CoP. 9, 'Advice on how best to measure progress on strategic objectives 1, 2 and 3 of The Strategy'.

[25] See the summary and analysis of CoP 9 in (2009) 4(229) *ENB* (5 October 2009), available at www.iisd.ca/desert/cop9. For example, decision on the contentious issue of the relationship between the Global Mechanism and the Secretariat was postponed to CoP 10.

monitoring activities.[26] The Land Degradation Assessment in Drylands (LADA) programme, GEF-funded and administered by the FAO, is intended – like the CBD'S GTI – to plug this knowledge gap. In addition, like the other UNCED and post-UNCED instruments, progress on the implementation of the CCD is periodically subject to review by the UN, the CSD, and UNEP.[27]

3. Forests

Forests[28] have value as an exploitable reservoir of timber and fuel, as a source of food, as a habitat rich in wildlife, and as a major reservoir of biodiversity.[29] In addition, they act as sinks for the absorption of carbon.[30] Despite the high profile given to deforestation, little has been done to control this problem internationally and the instruments adopted to date are weak. A new International Tropical Timber Agreement was concluded in 2006,[31] replacing earlier agreements.[32] The 2006 Agreement, though paying greater attention to sustainable development, is still effectively little more than a commodity market adjustment among consumer and producer states, with a commitment to increase international trade in tropical timber from sustainably managed and legally harvested forests. Some forests are also protected to some extent by the World Heritage Convention[33] and wood products by CITES.[34] A number of regional and subregional treaties contain general provisions on rational or sustainable use of tropical forests, such as

[26] Land degradation was first added to the GEF portfolio in 2002. The Global Mechanism under the CCD continues to seek co-finance of project elements outside the GEF mandate.

[27] See www.csd.org.

[28] See, generally, R. Tarasofsky, *The International Forest Regime: Legal and Policy Issues* (IUCN, 1995); D. König, in R. Wolfrum (ed.), *Enforcing International Environmental Standards: Economic Mechanisms as Viable Means* (Springer, 1996); Canadian Council on International Law, *Global Forests and International Environmental Law* (CCIL, 1996).

[29] Recognition of the importance of and wide variety of uses for forests resources and forest lands, including as habitats for wildlife, is found in para. 2(b) of the Non-legally Binding Forest Principles; para. 4 recognises their role in ecological processes and importance as 'rich storehouses of biological diversity and biological resources'. *Supra* n 3.

[30] For discussion of flora and fauna and climate change, see Chapter 21 below.

[31] Text available at www.itto.int.

[32] In particular the 1983 agreement as subsequently revised.

[33] Chapter 14 above; and *Commonwealth of Australia v State of Tasmania*, (1983) *ALR* 46, 625; see also IUCN, *A Global Overview of Forest Protected Areas on the World Heritage List* (IUCN, 1997).

[34] For example, export permits are required under CITES for bigleaf mahogany logs, sawn wood, veneer and plywood (but furniture and furniture parts are not covered). The CITES permitting system has been described as a '"passport" for sustainable and legal

the 1993 Central American Convention on Management and Conservation of Natural Forest Ecosystems and Forest Plantation Development and the 1978 Treaty for Amazonian Co-operation.[35] Article 4 of the latter affirms the exclusive sovereignty of each state over its own forests, but also promotes co-operation in forest management. The (non-binding) 1989 Declaration of San Francisco adopted by the parties recognises, inter alia, the importance of the Amazonian ecosystem for biodiversity, the need for joint preservation policies and the rational use of forest resources. Of all the regional forest instruments in place, only the 1985 ASEAN Convention[36] requires a serious commitment to forest protection in a broader environmental context (Article 6), a reflection perhaps of the IUCN's role in drafting the treaty. However, it is not in force.

As Sand has pointed out,[37] responsibility for forest conservation is divided uneasily among several institutions, including the FAO's Committee on Forestry (COFO); UNCTAD's International Tropical Timber Organization and the open-ended Inter-Governmental Forum on Forests (IFF), whose work is overseen by the Commission on Sustainable Development. None is located in the same country and co-ordination has proved difficult. Attempts at Rio to negotiate an International Convention on Conservation and Development of Forests were blocked by the irreconcilable concerns of developed and developing states, the latter led especially by Brazil and Malaysia. Instead, the curiously entitled Non-legally Binding Authoritative Statement of Forest Principles was adopted, which fell far short of providing a basis for the protection of the world's forests. The failure of the negotiations at UNCED was partly attributable to the fact that developed states did not propose to submit their own boreal forests to criteria for sustainable utilisation and the European Community attempted to trade developed states' agreement to a desertification convention as a quid pro quo for developing states' acceptance of a forest treaty.[38] The resulting

trade': see discussion by the International Wood Products Association at www.iwpa-wood.org.

35 1993 Central American Convention on Management and Conservation of Natural Forest Ecosystems and Forest Plantation Development: www.ecolex.org; 1978 Treaty for Amazonian Co-operation: (1978) 17 *ILM* 1045.

36 1985 ASEAN Agreement on the Conservation of Nature and Natural Resources, discussed further in Chapter 12 above.

37 P. H. Sand, 'Institution-Building to Assist Compliance with International Environmental Law: Perspectives' (1996) 56 *ZaöRV* 774.

38 A point made by P. W. Birnie, A. E. Boyle and C. J. Redgwell, *International Law and the Environment* (Oxford University Press, 3rd ed., 2009), p. 695. As they note, however,

polarisation and sensitivity over sovereignty issues still inhibits conclusion of a comprehensive global convention despite the accelerating destruction of tropical forests. Thus, in contrast with the successful completion of a new International Tropical Timber Agreement noted above, the UN Forum on Forests has since the year 2000 sought to strengthen the International Agreement on Forests, but without success.[39] As Forner relates, there is currently no consensus on how to achieve the goals agreed, namely reversal of loss of forest cover worldwide, enhancement of 'forest-based benefits', a significant increase in the area of protected forest, and a reversal in the decline in official development assistance for sustainable forestry management.[40] Forests have also been the subject of negotiation in the Conference of the Parties to the Kyoto Protocol on Climate Change and they could potentially be addressed, perhaps along the lines of the ASEAN model,[41] by a protocol to the Biological Diversity Convention where forest biodiversity is one of its five thematic areas. The parties to the CBD have no present intentions to do so, however.

4. Mountains

Chapter 13 of Agenda 21, on sustainable mountain development, recognises the need for mountain-area conservation,[42] and the contribution which mountain ecosystems make to biological diversity.[43] 'Mighty but frail', mountain ecosystems are considered one of the world's most vulnerable geographical domains, encompassing heterogeneous habitats which are often the 'last bastion of wild nature' constituting 'vertical ecological islands' amongst densely populated, biologically degraded,

since then the EU has promulgated a co-ordinated forest strategy to secure recognition of European forests' diversity; see (1999) 29 *EPL* 48.

39 In 2009 the secretariats of the UNFF and CBD signed a MoU to strengthen joint action to ensure sustainable management of forests.

40 Forner (2007) 16 *YBIEL* 488.

41 A suggestion in Birnie, Boyle and Redgwell, *supra* n. 38.

42 See, generally, T. Treves, L. Pineschi and A. Fodella (eds.), *International Law and the Protection of Mountain Areas* (Giuffrè Editore, 2002); T. Treves, L. Pineschi and A. Fodella (eds.), *Protection of Mountain Areas in International Law: Rio, Johannesburg and Beyond* (Giuffrè Editore, 2004); the Report of the Secretary-General, Sustainable Mountain Development, UN Doc A/62/292, 23 August 2007; and, for national developments, FAO, Mountains and the Law: Emerging Trends (2006).

43 *Agenda 21*, *supra* n. 2. Mountain ecosystems can also constitute biodiversity 'hot spots', as defined by N. Myers, 'The Biodiversity Challenge: Expanded Hot-Spot Analysis' (1990) 10 *Environmentalist* 243.

lowlands.[44] Mountain ecosystems are one of the thematic areas under the CBD upon which parties are required regularly to report.[45] As part of the conservation and sustainable use of biological diversity, the protection of native plants and animals is thus an integral part of the protection accorded mountain ecosystems from the Andes to the Himalayas.[46] The main threats to mountain species arise from illegal logging; poaching of wild plants and animals; and destruction of habitat through human interference such as unsustainable grazing and agricultural encroachment, poorly designed infrastructure projects, mining and quarrying activities and tourism.[47]

a) The 1991 Alps Convention

In addition to general protection of mountain ecosystems under the CBD, in 1991 a mountain-specific regional agreement was concluded, the 1991 Alpine Convention.[48] In force and with nine parties,[49] the aim

44 *Operational Program Number 4: Mountain Ecosystems* (GEF, 2000), para. 4.1.

45 See, for example, Australia's report on the Australian Alps. Because this geographic area spans three territories - New South Wales, the Australian Capital Territory and Victoria - and its protection also requires Commonwealth regulation, a memorandum of understanding was concluded in 1986 among ministers responsible for nature conservation at each level. This MoU, which agrees to co-operate to manage the area for the protection of, inter alia, native plants and animals and cultural values, is the only MoU of its type in Australia. It has been held up as 'a leading international example of effective conservation planning and management across jurisdictions' and is recognised by the IUCN 'as the best example of its kind in the world': Environment Australia, State of the Environment Report (2001), p. 82.

46 See further M. Bowman, 'International Law and the Conservation of Biological Diversity in Mountain Ecosystems', in Treves, Pineschi and Fodella, *International Law and the Protection of Mountain Areas*, *supra* n. 42, pp. 95–131.

47 *Mountain Ecosystems*, *supra* n. 44.

48 The official website for the Convention is www.alpconv.org. A convention was called for as early as 1952 in the documents founding the International Commission for the Protection of Alpine Regions (CIPRA), a grouping of four alpine states (Austria, France, Italy and Switzerland), German nature organisations and the IUCN. In the year 2000 the Council of Ministers of the Council of Europe considered, but did not adopt, a European Outline Convention on Mountain Regions, and in 2003 the Congress of Local and Regional Authorities of the Council of Europe recommended the adoption of a non-binding European Charter for Mountains.

49 The Convention was concluded on 17 November 1991 in Salzburg, Austria, and entered into force in 1995 following ratification by Austria, Liechtenstein and Germany, with the remainder following by 1999. Austria is the depositary, with German, Italian, French and Slovene the equally authentic languages of the text. The non-authentic English version of the text relied upon here is taken from the EC translation: europa.eu/legislation_summaries/environment/nature_and_biodiversity/l28161_fn.htm. Price has highlighted the linguistic

of the Convention is the long-term protection of the natural ecosystem of the Alps and sustainable development of the Alpine region. The geographic scope of the Convention covers a territory of 190,600 square kilometres distributed among eight Alpine states (Austria, France, Germany, Italy, Liechtenstein, Slovenia, Switzerland and the Principality of Monaco, all of whom are parties to the Convention, as is the EC) embracing eighty-three regions and 5,800 towns. It grew out of concerns to conserve this biogeographic region rich in flora and fauna from increased human exploitation threatening its natural diversity, whilst at the same time recognising its economic importance.

Accordingly, the objective of the Convention is the long-term protection of the natural Alps ecosystem and sustainable development of the area, taking into account the economic interests of its inhabitants. From a wildlife perspective, the preamble recognises, inter alia, that the Alps 'are one of the largest continuous unspoilt natural areas in Europe ... with ... outstanding unique and diverse natural habitat' and that they 'constitute an essential habitat and last refuge for many endangered species of plants and animals'. Whilst human impact is viewed as endangering these natural-habitat values, the Convention recognises the transport, cultural and general economic importance of the area and thus 'the need for economic interests to be reconciled with ecological requirements'. This balancing of environmental and economic requirements reflects the sustainable-development theme of the Rio Conference, which was convened only a few months after the Alps Convention was concluded. The latter anticipates and reflects the provisions of Chapter 13 of Agenda 21 on managing fragile mountain ecosystems.[50] The Convention thus imposes obligations on the parties directly to conserve species and habitat, together with obligations indirectly fostering this objective through requirements of sustainable transport,[51] tourism, farming and forestry.

Article 2(1) sets forth the general objective of the Convention to preserve and protect the Alps through the application of the principles

harmonisation problems which have arisen, especially where protocols have been negotiated in a working language which is not always rendered into the four equally authentic languages prior to signature and ratification. M. F. Price, 'The Alpine Convention: A Model for Other Mountain Regions?' (2000) 20(2) *Mountain Research and Development* 192.

50 See, generally, Permanent Secretariat of the Alpine Convention, Alpine Signals 2: The Alpine Convention Is Taking Shape (2004).

51 Article 2(2)(j) provides, inter alia, 'the objective is to reduce the volume and dangers of inter-Alpine and trans-Alpine traffic to a level which is not harmful to humans, animals and plants and their habitats'.

of prevention, polluter-pays, and transborder co-operation (but not, note, the precautionary principle). It then identifies in Article 2(2) twelve areas of activity under the Convention,[52] in respect of which subsequent protocols are envisaged.[53] Eight such protocols have currently been concluded, all becoming effective on 18 December 2002.[54] The Protocols are central to the effectiveness of the Convention, which is framework in character and relies on the Protocols for further elaboration of the parties' obligations. Their conclusion led to the establishment from 2003 of the permanent Secretariat[55] envisaged by Article 9 of the Convention and a shift in focus to implementation issues, with a six-year programme (Multi-Annual Work Programme of the Alpine Conference – MAP) of work agreed in 2004.[56] Two of these protocols, on conservation of nature and the countryside (1994) and mountain forests (1996), are of particular relevance for wildlife protection.[57] Indirect protection is also found in the prevention of air pollution, with the stated object of drastically reducing 'the emission of pollutants and pollution problems in the Alpine region, together with inputs of harmful substances from outside the region, to a level which is not harmful to man, animals and plants', though as yet no protocol on air pollution has been agreed under the Convention.

As indicated, the guiding principles of the Convention are prevention, polluter-pays and transborder co-operation. In addition, there are provisions for co-operation in research and regional monitoring (Article 3),

[52] In addition to areas discussed in the text, these are: regional planning, mountain farming, soil conservation, tourism and recreation, energy, transport, prevention of air pollution, water management, population and culture, and waste management.

[53] The Convention explicitly envisages that protocols 'laying down details for the implementation of the Convention' will be concluded (Article 2(3)).

[54] The 2004 MAP envisages completion of Protocols for the four remaining areas identified in Article 2, namely 'Population and Culture', 'Protection of the Air Quality', 'Water Management' and 'Waste Management'. As for the main framework treaty, three ratifications are necessary for a protocol to enter into force (Article 11). A ninth protocol has been concluded on dispute settlement which, unusually in an environmental instrument, provides for binding arbitration.

[55] Decision VII/2 of the Alpine Conference. The Permanent Secretariat is based in Innsbruck, with a branch office in Bolzano/Bozen in Italy responsible for technical and operational aspects of administering the Convention, in particular the system for observation and information about the Alps (SOIA).

[56] Text available at www.alpconv.org/NR/rdonlyres/26C9672B-98A8-4808-95A9-515AC4D79F7E/0/MAP_E_GESAMT.pdf.

[57] The preamble to the 1996 Mountain Forests Protocol acknowledges, inter alia, the importance of Alpine forests as habitat for a variety of plant and animal species. The 1994 Protocol is discussed in more detail below.

and in legal, scientific, economic and technical matters (Article 4). As a framework instrument the Alps Convention initially took a light touch regarding institution building, establishing a conference of the parties – the Alpine Conference – which meets every two years or so at ministerial level. The tenth Alpine Conference was held in 2009. There are now a dozen official observers in the work of the Convention, ranging from representation of UNEP's regional European office and the IUCN to ISCAR (International Scientific Committee on Research in the Alps) and the Comunità di Lavoro delle Città delle Alpi.

Particularly germane to wildlife conservation is the 1994 Protocol on Nature, which six states have ratified to date, but with Italy, Switzerland and the EC yet to do so. Certain key principles are evident in the Preamble, which recognises that the ways and intensity of use of Alpine territory have caused irrecoverable loss of landscape, biotopes and species worth saving, and will continue to do so if perpetuated. It stresses the importance of Alpine landscape (meadows, forests and waterways) as habitat for a wide variety of flora and fauna and the need for 'correction' of the ecological balance. Indeed, the Preamble explicitly states that ecological considerations should prevail over economic ones 'if this were necessary for maintaining the fundamentals of natural life'. Protection of existing habitat and restoration of degraded areas are both reflected in the fundamental commitments of the parties set forth in Article 2, as is sustainable use:

> In accordance with this Protocol, each Contracting Party undertakes to adopt the measures necessary to ensure the protection, care and, to the extent necessary, the restoring of nature and the landscape of the Alpine territory, together with the wild animal and plant species, their diversity and their habitat, while also considering the possibility of their ecologically tolerable usage.

The Protocol requires international co-operation for the systematic identification and management of a network of protected areas for the conservation of Alpine nature,[58] coupled with assessment of impacts and

[58] This has been reinforced by the work programme agreed at the eighth session of the Alpine Conference in 2004 for the 2005–10 period which identifies four priority areas, one of which is 'nature, agriculture and forestry, cultural landscape', where one of the key issues identified is 'maintaining landscapes, habitats and species (keeping the landscape open, cultivation, biodiversity, protected areas, biotope networks, soil protection, etc.)'. See MAP, *supra* n. 54, p. 11. A priority for the next six years is improving the cross-border network of protected areas.

the requirement to provide offsetting nature conservation where irreparable harm to the conservation of nature might occur.[59] The principle of integration is reflected in Article 4, which requires nature protection to be factored into the implementation of the other subject areas (such as energy and transport) set forth in Article 2 of the Alps Convention. Moreover, it is expressly contemplated that international co-operation to agree limits on these other uses will take place, reflecting the ecological priority of the Protocol. As indicated above, 'unavoidable impairments' must be offset by conservation measures elsewhere; impairment which cannot be compensated is to be permitted only if the conservation needs are not dominant (Article 10). At first blush this is in accordance with the preambular recognition that, in the event of conflict between ecological and other values, the former should prevail; however, it is expressly subject to the limitation 'in accordance with national law'. Inventories of the state of nature conservation in the Alpine region are to be completed within three years of the entry into force of the Protocol, with at most ten-yearly inventories thereafter. A list of factors to be inventoried is contained in Annex I and includes the legal and policy framework as well as the physical state of the environment.

In addition to these provisions on habitat protection, the Protocol also addresses species protection, requiring the identification, within two years of the entry into force of the Protocol, of specifically threatened species needing special protection measures (Article 14). Article 15 addresses removal of, and trade in, flora and fauna. Parties are to

> prohibit the capture, possession, injuring and killing of certain animal species, and disturbing them particularly during their periods of reproduction, growth and wintering, and also any destruction, removal or collecting of eggs coming from nature, and the possession, offer, purchase or sale of specimens of the same, or parts of them, taken from nature.[60]

Parallel provisions exist for flora. These are subject to strictly limited exceptions, including for scientific purposes and for nature conservation purposes. The Protocol encourages regulated reintroduction of indigenous species (Article 16),[61] while limiting the introduction of alien species to instances where such introduction is 'necessary' and would not result in negative environmental impact. A very high threshold is set for the release of genetically modified organisms in the environment,

[59] See Part II, 'Specific Measures', Article 6 et seq. [60] Article 15(1).

[61] On problems of transboundary co-operation regarding wolf reintroduction, see the 9th session of the Alpine Conference (2005).

which shall only take place when, on the basis of a 'formal evaluation', such release 'will not lead to *any* risk for man and the environment' (Article 17, emphasis added).[62]

Regular reports on measures taken under the Protocol, and their effectiveness, are to be forwarded to the Standing Committee, which is charged with monitoring state parties' compliance with the Protocol. It may request further information from the state party, and from 'other information sources' (such as NGOs). The Standing Committee is charged with the preparation of a report to the Alpine Conference on compliance with the Protocol, while it is the Alpine Conference that may make recommendations with respect to non-compliance revealed by the report (Article 23). Linked with national reports on the effectiveness of implementation is review of effectiveness of the provisions of the Protocol, a process in which regional and local authorities shall, and non-governmental organisations may, play a part (Article 24).

Established by Decision VII/4 of the Alpine Conference, the Compliance Committee presented its first report to the tenth meeting of the Alpine Conference in 2009.[63] Compliance information is drawn from national reports and the inventories of the state of nature conservation in the Alpine region which were to be completed within three years of the entry into force of the Protocol. In addition, two State of the Alps reports have been produced under the Convention, the first on transport and mobility (2007) and the second on water and water management issues (2009). The Compliance Committee's 2009 review identifies gaps in implementation of the Convention, potential areas of conflict and incomplete responses. A number of observers participated in the meetings of the Committee, CIPRA International most assiduously. Very little emerges in this first report with respect to compliance with Convention Article 2(2)(f) (conservation of nature and the countryside), though the practice of Monaco and Switzerland in preparing comprehensive inventories of their biodiversity is strongly commended:

> Monaco et la Suisse sont les premiers États au monde à avoir recensé leur biodiversité. Dans le cadre de la surveillance de la biodiversité réalisée en Suisse (BDM), près de 200 biologistes recensent régulièrement les

[62] See discussion of GMOs in Chapter 17 above.

[63] For analysis see L. Pineschi, 'The Compliance Mechanism of the 1991 Convention on the Protection of the Alps and its Protocols', in T. Treves et al. (eds.), *Non-compliance Procedures and Mechanisms and the Effectiveness of International Environmental Agreements* (T.M.C. Asser Press, 2009), Chapter 12.

> animaux et les plantes sur le terrain. Ils prélèvent des échantillons à des endroits définis, répartis de manière uniforme sur l'ensemble du territoire suisse. Ces données constituent une base importante pour la future politique de protection de la nature. Un centre de coordination a pour mission d'informer le public sur les résultats et les motivations du programme.[64]

With respect to the effectiveness of measures put in place for implementation of the 1994 Protocol, practice has varied. Germany reported no difficulties (and this appears to have been accepted at face value), but Austria and Switzerland have indicated that it is not yet possible fully to evaluate effectiveness (the former noting the contribution Natura 2000[65] is making to redressing the information deficit). As a later adherent to the Protocol, Slovenia is still putting in place the necessary legal measures for effective implementation.[66] Other shortcomings are that Liechtenstein does not have a system of protected areas in place under the Convention 'owing to lack of space', Monaco has not complied with Article 11 of the Protocol, and Switzerland is still examining the possibility of transboundary protected areas as required under Article 12. Despite these problems, no verified instance of non-compliance with the Convention or Protocols was raised, though this possibility is explicitly provided for in the decision of the Alpine Conference establishing the compliance review mechanism.[67] Indeed, the tenor of the report is one of facilitation and co-operation rather than sanction.[68] Under Decision VII/4, paragraph II.2.5, it is open to the Compliance Committee to make recommendations and it has done so. Amongst other things, it calls on the parties to improve steps to reduce air pollution causing damage to forest ecosystems, and to examine methods for reconciling competing uses such as the impact of forestry and hunting on nature conservation measures.[69]

The importance of the Alps Convention as an 'ecosystem-oriented treaty' is linked to the effectiveness of the implementation measures, particularly under the Protocols, which flesh out the general obligations of the framework Convention. As Tarlock recently observed, 'it is a work in progress' offering '[t]he hope ... that reporting requirements might

[64] Compliance Report (2009), p. 12.
[65] Discussed in detail in Chapter 7 above.
[66] Compliance Report (2009), p. 27.
[67] See Decision VII/4, para. II.2.3.
[68] Compliance Report (2009), p. 53. This facilitative approach is provided for in the decision of the Alpine Conference establishing the compliance review mechanism; see Decision VII/4, para. II.2.3.
[69] Compliance Report (2009), 'Conclusions', p. 54.

ultimately produce consistent and coordinated national ecosystem protection measures and standards' such that the framework convention 'will have evolved into a coordinated large-scale ecosystem mechanism'.[70]

b) The Carpathian Convention

The Carpathians[71] are Europe's largest reserve of untouched forest and are an important reservoir for biodiversity.[72] They are 'Europe's last refuge for large mammals: brown bear, wolf, and lynx, home to populations of European bison, moose, wildcat, chamois, golden eagle, eagle owl, black grouse, plus many unique insect species'.[73] With the assistance of UNEP's Regional Office for Europe, and spurred on by 2002 as UN Year of the Mountains, seven Carpathian region states[74] concluded a framework Convention on the Protection and Sustainable Development of the Carpathians the following year. It entered into force on 4 January 2006, with all seven mountain states of the region party by 2008. A Protocol on Conservation and Sustainable Use of Biological and Landscape Diversity was adopted at the same time, but has not yet come into force. It builds on many of the core principles already identified with respect to the Alps Convention, including designation of national and transboundary protected areas (the Planned Carpathian Network of Protected Areas).[75] The framework character of the Convention means much remains to be fleshed out, including the geographic scope of its application, since 'the Carpathian region' used throughout the text has been left for a subsequent CoP to define further. Given the very short period for which this instrument has enjoyed full

[70] D. Tarlock, 'Ecosystems', in Bodansky, Brunnee and Hey, *supra* n. 18, p. 591.

[71] For background to the Carpathian Convention see J. Fall, 'Designing Framework Conventions to Promote and Support Transboundary Protected Areas: Theory and Practice from the Carpathian Convention', in G. Tamburelli (ed.), *Biodiversity and Protected Areas: The Evolution of the Italian and Ukrainian Legislation* (Giuffrè Editore, 2006); and E. Samce, *The Carpathians: Existing Instruments and Programmes and a Background Sector Analysis* (UNEP, 2002).

[72] Sustainable Mountain Development, *supra* n. 42, p. 15.

[73] Introduction to the Carpathian Convention at www.carpathianconvention.org/index.htm.

[74] Namely the Czech Republic, Hungary, Poland, Romania, Serbia and Montenegro, Slovakia and Ukraine.

[75] The first transboundary protected area was established in 1991 under the Association of Carpathian National Parks; see Fall, *supra* n. 71, who claims that the Carpathian Convention is the first instrument explicitly to provide for *transboundary* protected areas in its text.

participation by its range states at the time of writing, it is far too soon to evaluate the effectiveness of this Convention. However, like the Alps Convention, it will be able to build on the legal frameworks already in place for species and habitat conservation under EU law[76] and under the aegis of the UNECE and of the Council of Europe.

5. Conclusion

The legal frameworks emerging with respect to desert, forest and mountain ecosystems demonstrate some features which distinguish them from the other instruments considered in this volume. Essentially products of the post-UNCED process, there is a decided emphasis on sustainable development and a detectable anthropocentric thrust. Forests constitute one end of the continuum, with weak substantive commitments and a robust statist approach; while the CCD, on the other hand, adopts a 'bottom-up' approach. The Alps Convention accords a degree of priority to ecological interests and allows both indigenous populations and NGOs a significant participatory role. However, in respect of all three ecosystems there remains a lack of baseline data which renders it difficult effectively to evaluate progress with species and habitat conservation. As the IUCN report on desert biodiversity makes clear, operating from a red list of species endangerment in the absence of better baseline data falls far short of good environmental management practice. Even in the case of the Alps Convention, covering a closely knit European region in which significant environmental integration has already occurred, problems of effective implementation persist. This may be attributed in part to continuing tensions, evident also under the CCD, between environmental protection and economic development.[77]

Recommended further reading

W. C. Burns, 'International Convention to Combat Desertification: Drawing a Line in the Sand' (1994–5) 16 *Mich. J. Int'l L* 831

[76] Such as the Habitats Directive; see above, Chapter 17.

[77] See the summary of CoP 9 CCD outcomes, *supra* n. 25; Price, *supra* n. 49, notes that the Swiss federal government had to reach financial accommodation with the cantons – concerned about the perceived conservation bias of the Alps Convention and impediments to economic development – before Switzerland was able to ratify the Convention.

K. W. Danish, 'International Environmental Law and the "Bottom-up" Approach: A Review of the Desertification Convention' (1995) 3 *Ind. J. Global Legal Stud.* 1

T. Treves, L. Pineschi and A. Fodella (eds.), *International Law and the Protection of Mountain Areas* (Giuffrè Editore, 2002)

T. Treves, L. Pineschi and A. Fodella (eds.), *Protection of Mountain Areas in International Law: Rio, Johannesburg and Beyond* (Giuffrè Editore, 2004)

PART VI

Cross-sectoral issues in wildlife regulation

Chapter 19

Wildlife and trade

1. Introduction

Over the past two decades the interrelationship between multilateral environmental agreements (MEAs) containing trade-related environmental measures (TREMs) and trade agreements has received considerable attention. The purpose of this chapter is not to revisit this wider, and well-documented, 'trade and environment debate',[1] but rather to locate the international wildlife law and practice discussed here within it. That such treatment is pertinent is obvious given that some of the treaties considered in this volume directly employ TREMs as a regulatory tool.[2] One of the earliest examples is the 1916 Convention for the Protection of Migratory Birds, which prohibited trade in such birds falling within its scope, or in their eggs, during the close season.[3] Today international trade in wildlife is governed primarily by CITES,[4] where the potential for conflict with trade law may arise in consequence of CITES listing. Reeve points out that in 1997 Zimbabwe apparently considered WTO challenge of Appendix I listing of the elephant, to compensate for loss of ivory markets. This course was not taken because CoP 10 downlisted

1 The debate is encapsulated in the contributions by E. B. Weiss, 'Environment and Trade as Partners in Sustainable Development: A Commentary', and T. Schoenbaum, 'Free International Trade and Protection of the Environment: Irreconcilable Conflict?', in (1992) 86(4) *AJIL* 700. For a good overview of an abundant literature, see P. W. Birnie, A. E. Boyle and C. J. Redgwell, *International Law and the Environment* (Oxford University Press, 2009), Chapter 14; and generally, A. Goyal, *The WTO and International Environmental Law: Towards Conciliation* (Oxford University Press, 2006).

2 The origins of concern for trade in wildlife have already been discussed in Chapter 1 above.

3 39 Stat 1702; *USTS* 628, Article 4, discussed further in Chapter 7 above.

4 See also the regulation of the transboundary movement of living modified organisms under the Cartagena Protocol to the 1992 CBD, discussed in Chapter 17 above; and, generally, G. L. Gaston and R. S. Abate, 'The Biosafety Protocol and the World Trade Organisation: Can the Two Co-Exist?' (2000) 12 *Pace Int'l L. Rev.* 107.

Zimbabwe's elephant population to Appendix II, and permitted limited trade in stockpiled ivory.[5]

Yet the direct nexus with trade does not stop here, as CITES also serves to illustrate. Trade – or, more accurately, suspending trade – may also be employed as a compliance tool.[6] As of 2009 there were thirty-two trade suspensions in effect under CITES, for failure to provide the required annual report on illegal trade, for failure properly to implement CITES in domestic law and for significant trade in Appendix II species.[7] This total includes trade suspensions against four states which are not parties to CITES (Bahrain, Haiti, Iraq and Tajikistan), two of which are WTO members (Bahrain and Haiti). This is not to suggest that such suspensions would necessarily be challenged; yet it should be noted that Russia apparently considered a GATT complaint when its trading privileges were suspended for non-compliance with the 1987 Montreal Protocol to the 1985 Vienna Convention on the Protection of the Ozone Layer, the first MEA to adopt a compliance mechanism.[8] The question of the compatibility of CITES trade measures with WTO rules has not arisen in practice, with some commentators viewing such a prospect as 'largely hypothetical'.[9] Far less hypothetical is challenge of trade measures adopted as one means of combatting IUU fishing, such as under ICCAT in 2002. The EC–Chile swordfish dispute illustrates the potential for fishing-conservation TREMs to be challenged

[5] R. Reeve, *Policing International Trade in Endangered Species: The CITES Treaty and Compliance* (Earthscan, 2002), p. 307 n. 17, citing D. Brack, 'Environmental Treaties and Trade: Multilateral Environmental Agreements and the Multilateral Trading System', in G. P. Sampson and W. B. Chambers (eds.), *Trade, Environment and the Millennium* (UN University, 2nd ed., 2001), n. 8.

[6] See S. Biniaz, 'Remarks about the CITES Compliance Regime', in U. Beyerlin, P. T. Stoll and R. Wolfrum (eds.), *Ensuring Compliance with Multilateral Environmental Agreements* (Martinus Nijhoff, 2006), 89; and, more generally, M. Fitzmaurice and C. Redgwell, 'Environmental Non-compliance Procedures and International Law' (2000) 31 *NYIL* 35; and T. Treves et al. (eds.), *Non-compliance Procedures and Mechanisms and the Effectiveness of International Environmental Agreements* (T.M.C. Asser Press, 2009).

[7] The thirty-two suspensions are in effect against twenty-four states, four of which are non-parties (where only the last, trade with CITES parties in Appendix-protected species, is applicable).

[8] See J. Werksman, 'Compliance and Transition: Russia's Non-compliance Tests the Ozone Regime' (1996) 56 *ZaöRV* 750.

[9] E. Milano, 'The Outcomes of the Procedure and Their Legal Effects', in T. Treves et al., *supra* n. 6, pp. 412–13; and P. H. Sand, 'Sanction in Case of Non-compliance and State Responsibility: *Pacta Sunt Servanda* – Or Else?', in Beyerlin, Stoll and Wolfrum, *supra* n. 6, p. 267.

under the WTO.[10] Indeed, the EC has proposed TREMs to combat IUU fishing under CCAMLR, based on the ICCAT model, but thus far unsuccessfully, with some members opposed owing to perceived conflict with WTO rules.[11]

Trade and wildlife may also conflict in a more diffuse sense in that increasing globalisation and liberalisation of trade lead to increased pressures upon and threats to species endangered by (illegal) trade and to adverse effects on ecosystems and habitats,[12] such as through the introduction of invasive alien species transported in ships' ballast.[13] These are trade impacts which, if addressed, are done so under separate environmental and standards-setting instruments (for example, the CBD's working group on invasive species, and the 2004 IMO Convention on Ballast Water).[14]

2. The GATT/WTO

a) Introduction

Tension between wildlife protection and trade may arise in consequence of national implementation of TREMs authorised by wildlife treaties. More likely, however, given the flexibility in implementation of most instruments, is the potential for trade-distorting effects of measures taken unilaterally in pursuance of domestic environmental policies, whether directly or indirectly giving effect to internationally agreed TREMs. The environmentally inimical approach to the balancing of trade and environment of the pre-WTO GATT dispute settlement panels, in particular, gave rise to concerns exacerbated by the 'centrifugal pull' of the WTO's compulsory dispute settlement mechanism.[15] The leading cases are *Tuna–Dolphin I* and *II* (both pre-WTO), *US Gasoline* and *Shrimp–Turtle*.[16] Of particular relevance for wildlife law is the fact that both *Tuna–Dolphin* and *Shrimp–Turtle* involved unilateral national

[10] See n. 18 below; the ICCAT measures are discussed in Chapter 5 above.

[11] See recent discussion in the 2009 CCAMLR Report, paras. 12.94–12.105.

[12] Compare OECD, *The Environmental Effects of Trade* (OCED, 1994); and GATT, *Trade and Environment* (GATT, 1991).

[13] R. Rayfuse, 'Biological Resources', in D. Bodansky, J. Brunnee and E. Hey (eds.), *The Oxford Handbook of International Environmental Law* (Oxford University Press, 2007), p. 386.

[14] See Chapter 17 above; and www.imo.org, respectively.

[15] Schoenbaum, *supra* n. 1.

[16] *United States – Restrictions on Import of Tuna*, 3 September 1991, *BISD* 39S/155, reproduced at (1991) 30 *ILM* 1594 (not adopted); *US – Restrictions on Imports of Tuna II*, circulated on 16 June 1994, DS29/R, reproduced at (1994) 33 *ILM* 839 (not

measures for species protection, in the latter case against the backdrop of CITES.

While it is important to trace the evolution of the case law to understand precisely why concerns have been raised regarding trade and wildlife issues, it is important to underscore two points at the outset. The first is that no GATT/WTO dispute settlement body has ruled directly on the compatibility of a wildlife (or any other environmental) treaty with the covered agreements.[17] Indeed, the 1982 LOSC remains the only agreement with environmental provisions whose relationship with WTO law has been raised before an international tribunal.[18] In *Shrimp–Turtle*, the Appellate Body acknowledged the right of WTO members to legislate for the protection of natural resources – including fish and sea turtle conservation – beyond national jurisdiction, so long as giving effect to a multilateral conservation agreement.[19] However, it is unclear from WTO jurisprudence whether only the parties to the dispute must be party to the relevant agreement (in *Shrimp–Turtle* it so happened that all parties to the dispute were also parties to CITES) or whether *all* WTO member states must also be party to the treaty in question. The latter would only be satisfied by wildlife treaties of very widespread participation. The Panel in *EC-Biotech* declined to apply the CBD and the Cartagena Protocol, interpreting 'rules of international law applicable' to mean only treaties applicable between all parties.[20] The illustration at the outset of CITES trade suspensions impacting on four non-party states illustrates the difficulties which might arise

adopted); *US – Standards for Reformulated and Conventional Gasoline*, adopted 20 May 1996, WT/DS2/9, Report of the Panel reproduced at (1996) 35 *ILM* 274, Report of the Appellate Body reproduced at (1996) 35 *ILM* 603; *US – Import Prohibition of Certain Shrimp and Shrimp Products*, adopted on 6 November 1998, WT/DS58/AB/R (Appellate Body), WT/DS58R (Panel), reproduced at (1999) 38 *ILM* 118 and (1998) 37 *ILM* 832 respectively.

[17] The most pertinent of which for wildlife purposes are GATT 1994, the Agreement on Sanitary and Phytosanitary Measures (SPS), the Agreement on Technical Barriers to Trade (TBT), and the Agreement on the Trade-Related Aspects of Intellectual Property Rights (TRIPs). All contain specific environmental exceptions.

[18] See *Case Concerning the Conservation and Sustainable Exploitation of Swordfish Stocks in the South-Eastern Pacific Ocean* (Chile–EC), ITLOS No. 7, Order No. 2000/3 (discontinued 16 December 2009), and EC–Chile, *Measures Affecting the Transit and Importation of Swordfish* (WTO, 2000), WT/DS193 (withdrawn 13 December 2007).

[19] At paras. 171–2.

[20] Panel Report, *EC – Measures Affecting the Approval and Marketing of Biotech Products*, WT/DS291/R, WT/DS292/R, WT/DS292/R, adopted 21 November 2006, paras. 7.70–7.95. On this point see M. Young, 'The EC–Biotech Case and the Law of Treaties' (2007) 56 *ICLQ* 907.

with such a restrictive approach to interpreting the 'rules of international law applicable'.

The second point is that, since the 1991 *Tuna–Dolphin I* case, there has been increased rapprochement between trade and environmental principles and fora: for example, the need to reconcile trade and environment acknowledged in Principle 12 of the Rio Declaration, the 1994 WTO Agreement with its preambular recognition of sustainable development, and the creation of the WTO Committee on Trade and Environment with observer participation by the secretariats of major wildlife treaties such as the CBD and CITES.[21] So, important though the historical journey is to understand where we stand today with respect to trade and wildlife, these points should be borne in mind.

b) The GATT/WTO case law

National environmental measures have been challenged under the compulsory GATT/WTO dispute settlement procedures as contrary to the GATT, in particular Article I (most-favoured nation treatment), Article III (non-discrimination or national treatment standard) and Article XI (elimination of quantitative restrictions).[22] The exceptions which may be relied upon to justify violation of these principles are found in Article XX, the relevant provisions of which state:

> Subject to the requirement that such measures are not applied in a manner which would constitute a means of arbitrary or unjustifiable discrimination between countries where the same conditions prevail, or a disguised restriction on international trade, nothing in this Agreement shall be construed to prevent the adoption or enforcement by any contracting party of measures:
>
> . . .
>
> (b) necessary to protect human, animal or plant life or health;
>
> . . .
>
> (g) relating to the conservation of exhaustible natural resources if such measures are made effective in conjunction with restrictions on domestic production or consumption.

Despite a last-minute Austrian proposal that 'environment' be inserted before 'human' in Article XX(b), Article XX remained untouched by the

[21] The work of the Committee is considered further below.

[22] Article XI(2) includes a narrow exception, inter alia, for import restrictions on agricultural or fish products that are necessary for the enforcement of certain governmental measures.

Uruguay round of trade negotiations, with GATT 1994 reflecting the language of GATT 1947 in this respect.[23]

In *Tuna–Dolphin I*,[24] Mexico challenged regulations pursuant to the Marine Mammal Protection Act, which prohibited the import into the US of fish or fish products caught using fishing technologies which led to incidental mortality or injury to marine mammals (dolphins) in excess of those permitted under US law.[25] Violation of Articles III, XI and XIII (non-discriminatory administrative or quantitative restrictions) were alleged. The US response was that, should such measures fall foul of one or more of these provisions, such measures were justified under the exceptions permitted under Article XX(b) or (g) set out above. The Panel held that Article XI.1 had been violated and that such measures could not be justified under either of the Article XX exceptions relied upon. In particular, the Panel stressed the need to interpret narrowly the Article XX exceptions to the basic principles under the GATT.[26] Moreover, in response to the US argument that such measures were intended to protect a common property resource on the global commons, the Panel expressed doubt that Article XX(b) might be invoked to allow extraterritorial jurisdiction for the protection of life and health. In any event, were Article XX(b) to be so interpreted there would nonetheless be the additional requirement of satisfying the 'necessary' requirement,[27] which the US measures failed to do. All options reasonably available to it had neither been fully explored nor exhausted.[28] In particular the Panel stressed that the US had failed vigorously to pursue multilateral negotiations aimed at dolphin conservation; that in essence there had been insufficient efforts to multilateralise unilateral trade measures for

[23] MTN/GNG/NG7/W/75 (1 November 1990); see, generally, S. Charnovitz, 'Exploring the Environmental Exceptions in GATT Article XX' (1991) 25(5) *JWT* 37.

[24] *United States – Restrictions on Import of Tuna*, 3 September 1991, *BISD* 39S/155, reproduced at (1991) 30 *ILM* 1594 (not adopted).

[25] Mexico also challenged the 'dolphin-friendly' labelling scheme under the Dolphin Protection Consumer Information Act. This allowed producers to market tuna in the US with such a label so long as the US authorities were satisfied that the tuna had been caught in a manner which did not unnecessarily endanger the lives of dolphins. Arguments that this breached Article I (most-favoured nation) failed, with the Panel holding that the requirements of the Act would apply to any state desiring to fish in the Eastern Tropical Pacific and market its tuna in the US.

[26] *Supra* n. 24, para. 5.22.

[27] For recent discussion of the 'necessary' requirement in the GATT, SPS and TBT Agreements, see G. Kapterian, 'A Critique of the WTO Jurisprudence on Necessity' (2010) 59 *ICLQ* 89.

[28] *Supra* n. 24, paras. 5.28–5.29.

environmental protection (a point also raised in the *Shrimp–Turtle* case discussed below).

Similarly restrictive reasoning was employed in respect of the Article XX(g) exception, the conditions of which the US had likewise failed to meet, even should the provision be held to have 'extra-jurisdictional' effect. The Panel relied on a previous ruling, *Canada – Measures Affecting Exports of Unprocessed Herring and Salmon*,[29] in which 'measures relating to the conservation of exhaustible resources' was interpreted as measures 'primarily aimed at' such conservation, and held that the US measures failed to satisfy this test. Of particular concern was the fact that the permissible taking rate for dolphins was pegged to the taking rate actually recorded by the US tuna fishery, giving rise to problems of legal certainty:

> Consequently, the Mexican authorities could not know whether, at a given point of time, their conservation policies conformed to the United States conservation standards. The Panel considered that a limitation on trade based on such unpredictable conditions could not be regarded as primarily aimed at the conservation of dolphins.[30]

This case provoked significant controversy because of the specific outcome (though the US and Mexico reached a negotiated compromise on the fisheries issue)[31] and because of the restrictive approach which the Panel took to interpreting Article XX exceptions. Rather than a level playing field for the application of rules of horizontal equivalence, the approach was to subordinate environment to trade concerns. Of particular wildlife concern was the finding that the US could not ban tuna based solely on the production method used nor could it use trade measures to protect natural resources outside its own territorial jurisdiction.

[29] BISD 35S/98. [30] *Supra* n. 24, para. 5.33.

[31] In the event, an International Dolphin Conservation Programme (IDCP) between countries that fish for tuna in the eastern tropical Pacific was concluded in 1998 pursuant to the 1992 Agreement to Reduce Dolphin Mortality in the Eastern Tropical Pacific Fishery, available at (1994) 33 *ILM* 936. This does not prohibit the use of purse seine nets but does stipulate mortality limits and other conservation measures. The US developed a dolphin-friendly label and qualification system based on the provisions of the Agreement, anticipated in the International Dolphin Conservation Program Act (105 Public Law 42). This provides for a fast-track procedure for exemption where monitoring of commitments under a binding international agreement is accepted. That is, the US based domestic regulation on the satisfaction of negotiated international standards. On 12 April 2000, the decade-long embargo on Mexican yellowfin tuna imports was lifted in acknowledgement of Mexico's bona fide implementation of the IDCP.

Subsequent cases have added important glosses to these conclusions of significance for wildlife protection. More immediately, in *Tuna–Dolphin II*, the Panel concluded that 'it could see no valid reason supporting the conclusion that the provisions of Article XX(g) apply only ... to the conservation of exhaustible natural resources located within the territory of the contracting party' invoking the exception, although of course extraterritorial enforcement would be reliant on jurisdictional grounds other than territoriality, such as nationality.[32] Article XX(b) and (g) thus could be interpreted to permit national measures to protect extraterritorial resources, such as fish stocks or highly migratory species on the high seas. Indeed the Appellate Body in *Shrimp–Turtle* acknowledged such extraterritorial scope, although there the highly migratory species (sea turtle) spent part of its life cycle within US waters.

In addition, the Panel articulated a three-stage test of compatibility under each provision. In respect of Article XX(g), it stated:[33]

1. It had to be determined whether the policy in respect of which these provisions were invoked fell within the range of policies to conserve exhaustible natural resources;[34]
2. It had to be determined whether the measure for which the exception was being invoked – that is, the particular trade measure inconsistent with the obligations under the General Agreement – was 'related to' the conservation of exhaustible natural resources, and whether it was made effective 'in conjunction' with restrictions on domestic production or consumption;[35]
3. It had to be determined whether the measure was applied in conformity with the requirement set out in the preamble to Article XX, namely that the measure not be applied in a manner which would constitute a means of arbitrary or unjustifiable discrimination between countries where the same conditions prevail or in a manner

[32] *US – Restrictions on Imports of Tuna* (1994) 33 *ILM* 839, para. 5.20. This dispute arose from the same measures complained of by Mexico; here the EC and the Netherlands challenged the US intermediary nation embargo sanctioned under the Marine Mammals Protection Act.

[33] Ibid., paras. 5.11–5.12.

[34] The Panel found that the policy to conserve dolphins in the eastern tropical Pacific Ocean so qualified: ibid., paras. 5.13–5.22.

[35] Using the 'primarily aimed at' test the Panel found that the measures were not primarily aimed at conservation of exhaustible natural resources nor at rendering restrictions on domestic production or consumption more effective; rather, the measures were taken so as to force other countries to change their policies. Ibid., paras. 5.21–5.26.

which would constitute a disguised restriction on international trade.[36]

In both *Tuna–Dolphin I* and *II* the measures cleared the first hurdle, but fell at the second, without the necessity therefore to consider compatibility with the requirements set forth in the preamble or chapeau to Article XX as reflected in the third stage of the Panel's analysis. This combination of the interpretation of the Article XX(g) wording 'related to' as 'primarily aimed at' and of the Article XX(b) word 'necessary' as 'least inconsistent with'[37] set a high threshold for satisfaction of these exceptions, fuelling the perception that the GATT was prioritising trade over environment in the event of conflict between them.

A further element of controversy was introduced by the 'like' product requirement and process and production methods (PPMs) which do not affect the product produced. So, for example, pesticides used on food crops or hormones in feed for beef cattle result in products contaminated by these methods, which are covered under the SPS and TBT Agreements. But tuna caught in a purse seine with significant dolphin fatality, or shrimp harvested by methods resulting in sea turtle by-catch, are production methods and processes which do not alter the end product, i.e. its physical characteristics, as such. In both *Tuna–Dolphin I* and *II* the US measure targeting tuna harvesting methods and designed to reduce dolphin mortality (and prevent (foreign) dolphin-unfriendly tuna from entering the US market alongside (US) dolphin-friendly tuna) was found to be discrimination between 'like' products (though a labelling requirement was permissible).

The perception of the GATT/WTO as inimical to environmental concerns was initially reinforced by the first trade and environment case to arise under the new WTO Dispute Settlement Understanding, the *US Gasoline* case.[38] There the Appellate Body concluded that clean air was an exhaustible natural resource the conservation of which the measures in question were 'primarily aimed at' securing.[39] Thus for the first time the third stage in the process outlined in *Tuna–Dolphin* was

[36] Not considered by the Panel since step 2 was not satisfied.

[37] See also *EC – Measures Affecting Asbestos and Asbestos-Containing Products* WT/DS135/AB/R (2001), paras. 164–75.

[38] *US – Standards for Reformulated and Conventional Gasoline*, adopted 20 May 1996, WT/DS2/9, Report of the Panel reproduced at (1996) 35 *ILM* 274, Report of the Appellate Body reproduced at (1996) 35 *ILM* 603.

[39] Report of the Appellate Body, (1996) 35 *ILM* 603, p. 22.

reached, namely the requirements of the preamble to Article XX. In the *Gasoline* case the Appellate Body emphasised two stages of analysis: 'first, provisional justification by reason of characterization of the measures under Article XX(g); second, further appraisal of the same measure under the introductory clause of Article XX'.[40] However, the Gasoline Rule failed to meet the standard set forth in the preamble – the application of the measure *did* result in unjustifiable discrimination and constituted a disguised restriction on trade.[41]

The Appellate Body's approach to interpretation of the preamble to Article XX was revisited in the *Shrimp–Turtle* case.[42] Here India, Malaysia, Pakistan and Thailand complained of a US measure pursuant to the Endangered Species Act of 1973 which prohibited the import of shrimp harvested with technology posing a risk to sea turtles which have protected status under the legislation as a threatened or endangered species. In this instance the legislation required the exporting state to impose comparable requirements on their shrimp fishery before import into the US would be permitted. The key measure was Section 609, which, in addition to calling for the initiation of negotiations for possible bilateral and multilateral agreements with other states regarding the protection and conservation of sea turtles, also provided for an import ban on shrimp harvested with commercial fishing technology which may adversely affect sea turtles. Harvesting nations could escape the ban through a certification process further specified in subsequent guidelines. In essence these required the demonstration that a regulatory programme comparable to the US programme was in place regarding the incidental taking of sea turtles, and that the average rate of incidental taking of sea turtles was comparable to that in the US. In other words, an obligation of result was imposed, inter alia, as a method of determining the effectiveness of harvesting states' regulations.

The US measures were challenged as contrary to Articles I, XI and XIII GATT; the Panel found violation of Article XI without saving by Article XX. In interpreting the chapeau to Article XX the Panel placed considerable emphasis on protection of the world trading system in considering whether measures of this type, if adopted by other WTO members, 'would threaten the security and predictability' of that system. As in

[40] Ibid. [41] Ibid. pp. 22–9.

[42] *US – Import Prohibition of Certain Shrimp and Shrimp Products*, adopted on 6 November 1998, WT/DS58/AB/R (Appellate Body), WT/DS58R (Panel), reproduced at (1999) 38 *ILM* 118 and (1998) 37 *ILM* 832 respectively.

the *Tuna–Dolphin* cases, the US legislation was operating in the absence of multilateral rules agreed for the protection of the species in question. The Panel in *Shrimp–Turtle* was at pains to address the wildlife law context, in essence stressing the need 'to reach co-operative agreement on integrated conservation strategies . . . taking into account the specific conditions of the different geographical areas concerned'. Sustainable development, one of the objectives of the WTO set forth in the preamble, is expressly referred to by the Panel in exhorting such multilateral co-operation in order to protect sea turtles 'in a manner consistent with WTO objectives'. Furthermore, it observed that[43]

> general international law and international environmental law clearly favour the use of negotiated instruments rather than unilateral measures when addressing transboundary or global environmental problems, particularly when developing countries are concerned. Hence a negotiated solution is clearly to be preferred, both from a WTO and an international environmental law perspective.

In its ruling the Panel comes perilously close to suggesting that not only is protection of the multilateral trading system at the core of the Panel's concern, but that it will be the rare unilateral measure indeed which satisfies not only the conditions of Article XX(b) and (g) but also (as interpreted by the Panel) the preamble. This lack of balance in addressing trade and environment issues was severely criticised.[44]

The US appealed against the Panel's decision, affording the Appellate Body the opportunity to reconsider the balance between trade and environment within the GATT. In particular, it took the opportunity to review the rules of general international law relating to treaty interpretation and their application by the Panel in the instant case. In wording drawn implicitly from the Vienna Convention on the Law of Treaties[45] the Appellate Body stated the relevant rules to require an 'examination of the ordinary meaning of the words of a treaty, read in

[43] Ibid., Panel report, para. 7.61.

[44] See, for example, R. Howse, 'The Turtles Panel: Another Environmental Disaster in Geneva' (1998) 32 *JWT* 73.

[45] Article 31(1) VCLT expresses the general rule of interpretation, which is that '[a] treaty shall be interpreted in good faith in accordance with the ordinary meaning to be given to the terms of the treaty in their context and in the light of its object and purpose'. Article 3.2 of the Dispute Settlement Understanding requires the application of 'customary rules of interpretation of public international law', of which this provision is a general reflection.

their context and in the light of the object and purpose of the treaty involved'.[46]

The Appellate Body reversed the Panel's finding that Section 609 fell outside the scope of measures permitted under Article XX and thus found it necessary (i) to consider whether the US could claim justification for Section 609 under Article XX(g) and then (ii) to test such justification, if made, by the conditions of the preamble.[47] In so doing, the Appellate Body determined that living natural resources constitute 'exhaustible natural resources' relying on, inter alia, the WCED's acknowledgement in *Our Common Future* of the widespread reality of depletion, exhaustion and extinction of such resources as a result of human activities.[48] Thus 'living resources are just as "finite" as petroleum, iron ore and other non-living resources'.[49] The Appellate Body adopted an evolutive approach[50] to interpretation of Article XX, reading its provisions 'in the light of contemporary concerns of the community of nations about the protection and conservation of the environment'.[51] Reference was made to the Rio Declaration, the CMS, the CBD, LOSC and CITES.

Though Article XX was not amended in the Uruguay Round, the Appellate Body drew inspiration for this evolutive approach from the preamble to the WTO Agreement (which applies to the GATT 1994 as well as to other covered agreements), which refers, inter alia, to 'the objective of sustainable development, seeking both to protect and preserve the environment and to enhance the means for doing so' – which, in their view, demonstrates that the state parties to the WTO Agreement were 'fully aware of the importance and legitimacy of environmental protection as a goal of national and international policy'.[52] Such language 'demonstrates a recognition by WTO negotiators that optimal use of the world's resources should be made in accordance with the objective of sustainable development'.[53] In addition, the Appellate Body noted the creation of the WTO Committee on Trade and Environment (CTE) at

[46] Appellate Body report, *supra* n. 42, para. 114.
[47] Article XX(b) was also invoked by the US, but only in the alternative should the Article XX(g) justification fail.
[48] *Our Common Future* (Oxford University Press, 1987), p. 13.
[49] Appellate Body report, *supra* n. 42, para. 128.
[50] Ibid., para. 130. The Appellate Body explicitly refers to its approach as 'evolutionary', citing general international law sources.
[51] Ibid., para. 129. [52] Ibid. [53] Ibid., para. 153.

Marrakesh in 1994. The preamble to the Decision on Trade and Environment adopted by Ministers at Marrakesh states, inter alia, that

> there should not be, nor need be, any policy contradiction between upholding and safeguarding an open, non-discriminatory and equitable multilateral trading system on the one hand, and acting for the protection of the environment, and the promotion of sustainable development, on the other . . .[54]

Moreover, there was no evidence of the intention of the original drafters of Article XX to exclude living resources from the ambit of Article XX(g).[55] Turning to the specific issue of whether the sea turtles in particular are 'exhaustible', the Appellate Body swiftly concluded that they are, not least because all seven species of sea turtle are listed in Appendix I of CITES, i.e. as species threatened with extinction which are, or may be, affected by trade. All of the participants in the appeal were parties to CITES.[56] Whether there is any jurisdictional limitation on the scope of Article XX (g) was *not* expressly considered since sea turtles are highly migratory species and occur, inter alia, within US waters, over which it clearly has jurisdiction.

The Appellate Body then examined the question whether the measure sought to be justified relates to the conservation of exhaustible natural resources: 'In making this determination, the treaty interpreter essentially looks into the relationship between the measure at stake and the legitimate policy of conserving exhaustible natural resources.'[57] The widespread participation in CITES of all states, including the participants in the present dispute, underscored the legitimacy of the concern, and the Appellate Body found '[t]he means and end relationship between Section 609 and the legitimate policy of conserving an exhaustible, and in fact, endangered species, is observably a close and real one'.[58] It also determined that such measures were made effective in conjunction with restrictions on US shrimp trawl vessels ('in principle, Section 609 is an even-handed measure'), thus leaving only the hurdle of satisfaction of the preamble conditions for the US measure to be a justifiable exception under Article XX.

54 Reproduced in (1994) 34 *ILM* 445.

55 Appellate Body report, *supra* n. 42, para. 131, n. 114. The Appellate Body also notes earlier jurisprudence holding fish to be an exhaustible natural resource within the meaning of Article XX(g).

56 At the time of the Appellate Body's decision, there were 144 states party to CITES.

57 *Supra* n. 36, para. 135. 58 Ibid., para. 141.

The measure fell at this final hurdle, with the Appellate Body holding that in its application Section 609 had 'intended an actual coercive effect on the specific policy decisions made by foreign governments, Members of the WTO'. Any flexibility intended in the primary legislation was swept aside by the 1996 Guidelines under the Endangered Species Act and the practical administration of the certification scheme which required a demonstration that the regulatory programme requires the use of a turtle extractor device or a requirement falling within the extremely limited exceptions available to US shrimp trawlers – 'other measures the harvesting nation undertakes to protect sea turtles' referred to in the Guidelines are of little relevance in administrative practice. Thus the *application* of the measure requires other WTO members to demonstrate that a regulatory scheme is in place that is essentially the same as in the US, described by the Appellate Body as a 'rigid and unbending standard'.

The final obstacle to success in meeting the conditions of the preamble was the evidence that even states complying with the regulatory conditions of the scheme, i.e. shrimp caught using methods identical to those in the US, would be subject to the import ban if the shrimp were caught in the waters of a non-certified state. This suggested to the Appellate Body

> that this measure, in its application, is more concerned with effectively influencing WTO members to adopt essentially the same comprehensive regulatory regime as that applied by the United States to its domestic shrimp trawlers, even though many of those Members may be differently situated.[59]

Coupled with the failure to respond vigorously to the exhortation in the legislation to seek bilateral and multilateral agreements for sea turtle conservation,[60] the Appellate Body had little difficulty in determining that the measure had been applied in an unjustifiably discriminatory fashion. It also found the discrimination to be arbitrary, thus depriving the measure of Article XX protection and rendering unnecessary

[59] Ibid., para. 165.

[60] Only one agreement had been concluded, the 1996 Inter-American Convention for the Protection and Conservation of Sea Turtles. Article IV(1) requires each party to 'take appropriate and necessary measures, in accordance with international law and on the basis of the best scientific evidence, for the protection, conservation and recovery of sea turtle populations and their habitats'. See further www.seaturtle.org.

consideration of the final limb of the preamble (disguised restriction on trade).

Both the language and methodology of the Appellate Body are a striking departure from the wording and the approach of the Panel Report, and demonstrate a willingness to strike a more even balance between trade and wildlife concerns. Of particular note is the acceptance of an unsolicited NGO brief, a move consonant with general measures within the WTO to improve transparency and access for, if not the direct participation of, NGOs.[61] The reliance on general principles of international law, including general principles of international environmental law, is heartening. Most telling is the Appellate Body's awareness of its wider audience, for it concludes, inter alia, with what the appeal has *not* decided:

> We have *not* decided that the protection and preservation of the environment is of no significance to the Members of the WTO. Clearly, it is. We have *not* decided that the sovereign nations that are Members of the WTO cannot adopt effective measures to protect endangered species, such as sea turtles. Clearly, they can and should. And we have *not* decided that sovereign states should not act together bilaterally, plurilaterally or multilaterally, either within the WTO or in other international fora, to protect endangered species or otherwise protect the environment. Clearly, they should and do.[62]

The DSB has also recognised that the process of international negotiation may be a painstaking and time-consuming one. Thus it refused to find the US in non-compliance with its ruling when in the year 2000 Malaysia, one of the original complainants in the *Shrimp–Turtle* dispute, argued that the US had failed to lift the import prohibition and had not taken 'the necessary measures to allow the importation of certain shrimp and shrimp products in an unrestrictive manner'.[63] The US stressed, inter alia, its continuing efforts to secure agreement with governments in the Indian Ocean region on the protection of sea turtles in that region.

3. SPS and TBT Agreements

National food safety and animal and plant health measures fell for consideration under the general provisions of the GATT until the

[61] As part of this initiative see www.wto.org/wto/ngo/contact.htm. The CTE has about twenty observers which are inter-governmental organisations, including, as already noted, representatives of the Secretariats of the CBD and CITES.

[62] *Supra* n. 36, para. 185, original emphases.

[63] Para. 1(16), Overview of the State-of-Play of WTO Disputes, WTO, 27 October 2000.

adoption in 1994 of the Agreement on the Application of Sanitary and Phytosanitary Measures (SPS Agreement)[64] which 'essentially seeks to spell out in a limited area the principles of Article XX(b) of the GATT'.[65] The Agreement applies to 'additives, contaminants, toxins and disease-carrying organisms in food, beverages and feedstuffs'.[66] Amongst other things, it recognises that if an import restriction is based on scientific findings which are incorporated into a widely accepted international standard, and the importing state conforms to that standard, the import restriction should be deemed 'necessary to protect human, animal or plant life or health' and hence compatible with GATT and the SPS Agreement.[67] It explicitly recognises the right of states to take precautionary provisional measures in the face of scientific uncertainty, whilst seeking further information.

Of the several cases which have arisen under the SPS Agreement with environment and/or human health dimensions, the most significant is the *Beef Hormones* case.[68] There the US alleged violation of, inter alia, Article 5.1 SPS Agreement, on risk assessment. This aspect of the complaint, accepted by the Panel, was upheld by the Appellate Body, which did not consider that the EC ban on beef containing growth hormones was 'based on' a risk assessment within the meaning of Article 5.1. This provision, held the Appellate Body, requires a 'rational' or 'objective' relationship between the measure and the risk assessment. It agreed with the Panel that the precautionary principle – which it did not consider to be customary law – overrode the provisions of Articles 5.1 and 5.2 of the SPS Agreement.[69] It did not, however, support the Panel's finding of a breach of Article 3.1 (where it held that the import ban was not based on international standards and was imposed without adequate scientific justification, contrary to Article 3.3). The Appellate Body considered that Article 5.1 allows for more stringent national standards than the

[64] See commentary by J. Scott, *The WTO Agreement on Sanitary and Phytosanitary Measures: A Commentary* (Oxford University Press, 2007).

[65] A. F. Lowenfeld, *International Economic Law* (Oxford University Press, 2nd ed., 2008), p. 399.

[66] Birnie, Boyle and Redgwell, *supra* n. 1, p. 779. The Agreement on Technical Barriers to Trade (TBT Agreement) and SPS Agreement are mutually exclusive, with the former applicable to all other product standards.

[67] Article 3.2.

[68] *European Communities – Measures Affecting Meat and Meat Products*, Panel (WT/DS48/R/Can) and Appellate Body (WT/DS48/AB/R), adopted 13 February 1998.

[69] Appellate Body Report, paras. 124–5. Article 5.2 risk assessment criteria include 'ecological and environmental conditions'.

prevailing international standards where human health is at stake and where there is a scientific justification for doing so. This must then be tested against the provisions of Article 5.5 (similar to the preamble to Article XX in its reference to no arbitrary discrimination and not a disguised restriction on trade). In addition it held that the evidentiary burden falls on the complainants in cases under the SPS Agreement to establish a prima-facie case of the inconsistency of an SPS measure with the SPS Agreement (this is consistent with the approach to violations of the GATT 1994 and Article XX justifications).[70]

Under the TBT Agreement, states are not to use technical regulations so as to create 'unnecessary obstacles to international trade. For this purpose, technical regulation shall not be more restrictive than necessary to fulfil a legitimate objective.'[71] 'Legitimate objective' is defined broadly to include 'protection of ... animal, plant life or health, or the environment'.[72] This leaves the level of protection to the member state to determine, including a high level of protection for animal and plant life or health, without the obligation to apply international standards (if any). Moreover, if such standards are 'ineffective or inappropriate' for the fulfilment of legitimate objectives, and a strict level of environmental protection is chosen, states may employ stricter standards than international technical requirements.[73]

International standards thus have an important role to play under both the SPS and TBT Agreements, acting as a benchmark for national regulation. Indeed, there is a clear link between national sanitary and phytosanitary measures and national CITES implementation, and with the technical barriers to trade especially in the regulation of transport of live specimens and standard-setting for animal welfare. CITES co-operates with IATA's Live Animals and Perishables Board and the Board of the Animal Transportation Association (AATA), and seeks stronger links with the International Animal Health Organisation (OIE) and the International Plant Protection Convention (IPPC).[74]

4. Committee on Trade and Environment

The difficulty clearly remains of the gravitational pull of the institutional and normative centralisation of the GATT/WTO and the absence of

[70] See M. Du, 'The Standard of Review under the SPS Agreement after EC–Hormones II' (2010) 59 *ICLQ* 441.

[71] Article 2(2). [72] Ibid. [73] Birnie, Boyle and Redgwell, *supra* n. 1, p. 781.

[74] See CITES Resolution Conf. 10.21, CoP 14.

realistic institutional alternatives for the playing out of such trade and wildlife disputes. This has caused attention to focus on the WTO and its institutions for resolution of the trade and environment conflict. In this connection, since 1995 the WTO Committee on Trade and Environment (CTE) has been working to a ten-point agenda based on the Marrakesh Ministerial Decision on Trade and Environment of 15 April 1994.[75]

In 2001, in the Ministerial Declaration adopted at the Doha Conference, member states agreed to negotiations 'without prejudging their outcome' on the relationship between existing WTO rules and the specific trade obligations set out in multilateral environmental agreements.[76] The CTE's output has been meagre, with its annual reports notable principally for their brevity.[77] However, Charnovitz notes the institutional impact of the CTE, bringing 'environmental issues into WTO processes' and attitudinal changes ('socialization') through meetings between trade officials and representatives of selected MEAs such as CITES.[78]

5. Relationship with other agreements

It has been observed that the relatively more transparent and participatory international environmental treaty framework has had some impact on WTO processes, with the admission of amicus briefs and observer status for the IUCN and increased co-operation between the WTO and environmental treaty secretariats.[79] Some wildlife treaty secretariats have observer status in the CTE; for example, both the CBD and CITES Secretariats are permanent observers to regular sessions of the CTE

[75] Report (1996) of the WTO Committee on Trade and Environment to the WTO Ministerial Conference in Singapore, December 1996 (PRESS/TE 014, 18 November 1996).

[76] Adopted 14 November 2001, para. 31, WT/MIN(01)/DEC/1 (20 November 2001). In particular, the relationship between the CBD and the WTO Agreement on Trade-Related Aspects of Intellectual Property was one of the topics for the newly created CTE identified in the Doha Declaration. Where disputes might arise is with respect to access to genetic resources, and patentability. Article 27(2) TRIPS allows members to exclude from patentability inventions that endanger human, animal or plant life or health, or the environment where such exclusion is 'necessary' for such purpose. Naturally occurring plants and animals are not patentable, a point underscored in Article 27(3), which allows the exclusion of plants, animals and biological resources. See further Chapter 17 above.

[77] Birnie, Boyle and Redgwell, *supra* n. 1, p. 763.

[78] S. Charnovitz, 'The WTO's Environmental Progress' (2007) 10 *JIEL* 685.

[79] Ibid.

and are seeking observer status in other key WTO committees, including the SPS and TBT Committees. Both CITES[80] and the CBD have explored the possibility of concluding MoUs with the WTO, but in the event have pursued less formal avenues of co-operation.[81]

6. Conclusion

While the case law of the GATT/WTO has thus far focused exclusively upon the relationship between domestic environmental measures and WTO rules, the potential for conflict between the latter and international measures has been heightened in consequence of increased consideration of TREMs as a regulatory technique and for enhancing compliance with wildlife agreements. Indeed, this may be viewed as part of a wider trend in environmental regulation, a 'paradigm shift' from safety-focused to trade-related approaches.[82] While there has been some assessment of the likely compatibility of these mechanisms with the GATT,[83] there is much work still to be done in providing detailed analysis of both the potential for conflict between trade and wildlife norms, and the appropriate dispute settlement mechanism. Moreover, the spheres of operation of domestic and international wildlife regulation are interlinked, both through national implementation measures pursuant to wildlife treaty obligations and through unilateral domestic action to achieve broader goals, such as species conservation, in the absence of internationally agreed rules. The use by states of unilateral trade restrictions in furtherance of domestic conservation policies with extraterritorial effect is well illustrated by the GATT *Tuna–Dolphin* dispute. While Mexico succeeded in its challenge to the extraterritorial effect of US environmental

80 CITES conducts national wildlife trade policy reviews, while, pursuant to the Doha Development Agenda, CITES training is part of trade capacity building.

81 See CITES, 'Cooperation with the World Trade Organization', fifty-eighth meeting of the Standing Committee, Geneva, 6–10 July 2009, SC58 Doc.12, p. 2.

82 H.-W. Micklitz, 'International Regulation on Health, Safety and the Environment – Trends and Challenges' (2000) 23 *JCP* 3.

83 For analysis of seven agreements – CITES, the Montreal Protocol, the Basel Convention, the CBD, the FCCC, the Rotterdam Convention on the Prior Informed Consent Procedure for Certain Hazardous Chemicals and Pesticides in International Trade (the PIC Convention) and the 2000 Cartagena Biosafety Protocol – see *Environment and Trade: A Handbook* (UNEP/IISD, 2000) with an updated Web version reproduced at both www.unep.ch/etu and www.iisd.ca/trade/handbook. See also D. Goldberg, R. Housman, B. Van Dyke and D. Zaelke (eds.), *The Use of Trade Measures in Selected Multilateral Environmental Agreements* (UNEP Trade Monograph 10, 1995).

policy through the mechanism of the GATT, the panel decision raised acutely the tension between trade rules and environmental protection, particularly where domestic environmental measures seek, inter alia, to protect common property resources in the global commons. While the practical outcome of the dispute was the adoption of international measures for the conservation of dolphin in the Eastern Tropical Pacific tuna fishery, and the alignment of US domestic policy with the international rules, it is a far from straightforward task to negotiate such international standards, notwithstanding the emphasis placed on such a solution in recent WTO jurisprudence.

This discussion takes place against the backdrop of the inadequacy of the general principles of treaty law such as a *lex superior* and a *lex specialis* prevailing to resolve normative conflict.[84] Which is *lex generalis* – trade or wildlife law? Are trade and wildlife treaties 'relating to the same subject matter' within the meaning of Article 30 VCLT such that the later in time prevails in the event of conflict? Article 30 'will not operate to give general WTO rules adopted in 1994 priority as treaty law over earlier, more specific trade restrictions' found in wildlife treaties such as CITES, for example.[85] In any event, given the evolutive and dynamic character of wildlife treaties, with significant subsequent developments such as non-compliance procedures or subsequent protocols or amendments, a straightforward chronology of 'earlier' and 'later' may be difficult to map out. Of course it is always open to the parties to provide expressly for the relationship between agreements, though this is rare in wildlife treaties and raising the issue of compatibility with WTO rules has been shown to be 'near deal-breaking'.[86] Under the WTO there are also legal mechanisms which would immunise wildlife treaties from challenge such as waiver pursuant to Article IX(3), but this has hardly ever been used, and never for an environmental instrument. The example of the 1992 North American Free Trade Agreement is instructive, Article 104 of which provides that certain named agreements, including CITES, prevail over the trade obligations of the parties (subject to certain conditions

[84] See discussion in A. Boyle, 'Relationship between International Environmental Law and Other Branches of International Law', in D. Bodansky, J. Brunnee and E. Hey (eds.), *The Oxford Handbook of International Environmental Law* (Oxford University Press, 2007), Chapter 7, at pp. 132–6; and, more generally, J. Pauwelyn, *Conflict of Norms in Public International Law* (Cambridge University Press, 2003).

[85] Boyle, *supra* n. 84.

[86] *Environment and Trade, supra* n. 83, p. 62. Contrast Article 22 CBD with the difficulty in drafting the Cartagena Protocol.

being fulfilled such as non-discrimination).[87] But there is no sign of any of these approaches being adopted.[88] Indeed, while it remains at least doubtful whether TREMs relating to PPMs that discriminate between parties and non-parties and are extraterritorial in application are compatible with trade law, the process has been one of accommodation rather than 'grand synthesis' of trade and wildlife concerns.[89]

Recommended further reading

P. W. Birnie, A. E. Boyle and C. J. Redgwell, *International Law and the Environment* (Oxford University Press, 2009), Chapter 14

S. Charnovitz, 'Exploring the Environmental Exceptions in GATT Article XX' (1991) 25(5) *JWT* 37

S. Charnovitz, 'The WTO's Environmental Progress' (2007) 10 *JIEL* 685

A. Goyal, *The WTO and International Environmental Law: Towards Conciliation* (Oxford University Press, 2006)

J. Scott, *The WTO Agreement on Sanitary and Phytosanitary Measures: A Commentary* (Oxford University Press, 2007)

[87] However, adding further agreements to this provision requires the agreement of all three states parties.

[88] Other possibilities under the WTO are amendment to, or an agreed collective interpretation of, the GATT Article XX exceptions, but each would require a special majority vote (Articles 11 and 12): see, generally, Birnie, Boyle and Redgwell, *supra* n. 1, pp. 768–9.

[89] Ibid., p. 810.

Chapter 20

Wildlife and welfare

1. Introduction

While the principal focus of this work is upon the conservation of wildlife populations, the philosophical arguments canvassed in Chapter 3 above suggest that the intrinsic value exhibited by each autopoietic entity embraces not only the good-of-its-kind, but also the good-of-its-own: consequently, any sound ethical policy should additionally have regard to the extent to which *individual* organisms are permitted to flourish in accordance with their biological nature. Accordingly, insofar as such arguments merit credence in the realm of international affairs, it might be expected that a body of rules would also have emerged for the protection of individual wildlife specimens, seen not only as representatives of their kind but as legitimate objects of moral concern on their own account. The need for such measures, moreover, is plainly most acute in the case of sentient animals, whose capacity for pain and suffering generates a particularly cogent case for protection.

Formal recognition of these points may be found in the revised version of the World Conservation Strategy, *Caring for the Earth*,[1] which proclaims,

> Every form of life warrants respect independently of its worth to people. Human development should not threaten the integrity of nature or the survival of other species. People should treat all creatures decently, and protect them from cruelty, avoidable suffering and unnecessary killing.

Yet the Strategy represents a policy prescription rather than a normative document, and it is accordingly necessary to examine the extent to which such principles have actually been translated into international law. Ordinarily, the quest for evidence of such developments might begin

[1] IUCN/UNEP/WWF, *Caring for the Earth: A Strategy for Sustainable Living* (IUCN, 1991). See also Respect and Care for the Community of Life – the first of nine interrelated and mutually supporting principles for a sustainable society.

with an examination of the material sources of international law – judicial decisions and the writings of publicists – but such an approach seems unpromising in this context, since issues concerning animal welfare seldom impact directly upon *inter-governmental* relations as such, and are therefore unlikely to find reflection in the mainstream of international discourse. Rather, such matters have typically been addressed at the national level, and may consequently become almost invisible when viewed through the prism of international legal doctrine or jurisprudence.[2] For similar reasons, when considering the formal sources of law, compelling evidence for the existence of any *customary* principle concerning welfare should probably not be expected, since state practice regarding the protection of animals is almost invariably attributable to *domestic* standards and sensibilities rather than to any sense of *international legal obligation*, rendering proof of *opinio juris* extremely difficult. Insofar as the welfare question has been addressed at all on the international plane, this will generally have occurred through the medium of specialised treaty arrangements, and the most fertile source of evidence will therefore lie in the texts of such agreements and the body of practice they have generated. Much of this chapter is accordingly devoted to an examination of such material. Nevertheless, treaties and custom do not constitute the only formal sources of international law, and, given that welfare issues are characteristically addressed at the national level, it becomes relevant to explore whether the 'general principles of law recognised by civilised nations' represent a mechanism through which such considerations might have become established in the international legal order.

2. General principles of law

a) The role of general principles

The juridical nature and function of general principles of law within the international legal system were explained in Chapter 2 above. Although they have most commonly been invoked in relation to ancillary, procedural issues in litigation, rather than as an independent source of primary, substantive obligations, there is no reason in principle why they should not also serve the latter function.[3] This might, however, be judged

[2] S. R. Harrop, 'The Dynamics of Wild Animal Welfare Law' (1997) 9 *JEL* 287.

[3] Note especially the analysis of Judge Weeramantry in the *Gabcikovo-Nagymaros Project* case (discussed below), concerning sustainable development, and of Judge Tanaka in the *South-West Africa Cases (Second Phase)*, (1966) *ICJ Rep* 6, regarding human rights.

to require stronger endorsement, drawn from a more extensive survey of national legislation, than has been deemed sufficient in relation to the procedural questions which have hitherto predominated. Yet even if this were considered necessary, adequate support could probably be found, since the World Society for the Protection of Animals,[4] which enjoys consultative status with both the UN and the Council of Europe, affirms that 'many states already have a system of legal protection for animals both domestic and wild'.[5] In relation to hunting, for example, one end-of-millennium survey suggested that the use of steel-jaw traps had been outlawed in some eighty-eight countries,[6] while commentators have adverted to specific welfare provisions in the hunting laws of states as diverse as Brazil, China, Ireland, Japan, Lithuania, Malaysia, New Zealand, Norway, Poland and the US.[7] More generally, examples of recent legislation for the protection of animals can be found across the entire international community from Mexico to Malawi to Myanmar,[8] with major overhauls of domestic legislation having been undertaken in numerous countries, including Australia, Korea, Latvia, Malta, the Philippines, Taiwan, the UK and the UAE.[9] The Latvian legislation, which addresses a wide range of welfare issues, is particularly noteworthy for the carefully considered ethical perspective disclosed in its preamble:

> The ethical obligation of humankind is to ensure the welfare and protection of all species of animals, because every unique being is itself of value. A human being has a moral obligation to honour every creature, to treat animals with empathic understanding and to protect them. Without a

[4] WSPA is a federation of some 900 member societies in over 150 countries. For information on its activities, see www.wspa.org.uk.

[5] Preamble, Universal Declaration for the Welfare of Animals, as to which see section 4 below.

[6] C. Liss, 'Trapping', in M. Bekoff and C. A. Meaney (eds.), *Encyclopedia of Animal Rights and Animal Welfare* (Fitzroy Dearborn, 1998).

[7] See A. Gillespie, 'Humane Killing: A Recognition of Universal Common Sense in International Law' (2003) 6 *JIWLP* 1, pp. 9–12.

[8] See, e.g., Official Emergency Standard NOM-EM-136-ECOL-2002 of January 2002, Specifications for the Preservation of Marine Mammals in Captivity (Mexico); National Parks and Wildlife Act, No. 11 of 1992, esp. Part IX (Malawi); Animal Health and Development Law, No.17/93 of November 1993 (Myanmar).

[9] See the Australian Animal Welfare Act, Act No. 63 of 1993; Korean Animal Protection Law, of 7 May 1991; Latvian Animal Protection Law, of 1 December 1999; Maltese Animal Welfare Act, Act No. XXV of 2001; Philippines' Animal Welfare Act, Republic Act No. 8485 of 1998; Taiwanese Animal Protection Law, of 4 November 1998; British Animal Welfare Act, 2006; UAE's Ministerial Decision on Animal Welfare, of 27 September 2004.

> substantiated reason, no one is permitted to kill an animal, to cause it pain, create suffering or otherwise harm it.

In some countries, recognition of the importance of the protection of animals is evident in legislative instruments of the highest level. The Constitution of Sri Lanka not only recognises obligations on the part of citizens and the state to safeguard natural habitats and wildlife, but imposes a duty on everyone to 'value all forms of life',[10] while the 1998 Costa Rican Law on Biodiversity proclaims that 'all living things have the right to life, regardless of their economic value, actual or potential'.[11]

Although these provisions might be read as reflecting concern for the species rather than the organism,[12] others proclaim unequivocal commitments to animals as individuals; thus the Indian Constitution recognises the duty of every citizen not only to protect the natural environment, including wildlife, but 'to have compassion for living creatures'.[13] Similarly, Article 225 of the Brazilian Constitution exhorts the government to protect flora and fauna against all practices 'which represent a risk to their ecological function, cause the extinction of species or subject animals to cruelty'. Recent amendments to the French Civil Code[14] and to the German Constitution[15] respectively (i) distinguish animals from all other forms of property and (ii) create specific duties to defend them, while the Swiss Constitution contains comprehensive provision regarding both conservation and animal welfare and, following an amendment in 1992, explicit recognition of the individual dignity and value of non-human creatures.[16]

On one view, a comprehensive review of national legislation may not even be necessary. According to Judge Weeramantry in the *Gabcikovo-Nagymaros* case,[17] general principles as a source of law should be understood to embrace not only those common to all the major legal systems today, but also certain 'pristine and universal values which command international recognition',[18] as evidenced by their acceptance by all the principal cultures and civilisations throughout history. The normative concept specifically under consideration was that of sustainable development, but the values in question were frequently expressed in terms

[10] See Articles 52(6), 53(6). See also Article 3 of the Constitution of Bhutan.
[11] Ley No. 7788, Article 9(1).
[12] See also Article 15, 1991 Constitution of Bulgaria; Article 20, 1999 Constitution of Nigeria.
[13] Article 51(A), 1949 Constitution of India, as amended.
[14] 1999 Amendment to Articles 24, 25. [15] 2002 Amendment to Article 20(a).
[16] See Articles 77–80, 120(2). [17] (1997) ICJ Rep 7. [18] See esp. ibid., pp. 105–6,

which evinced a more general respect and concern for nature,[19] as reflected especially in his treatment of Buddhist perspectives:[20]

> The notion of not causing harm to others and hence *sic utere tuo ut alienum non laedas* was a central notion of Buddhism ... '*Alienum*' in this context would be extended by Buddhism to future generations as well, and to other component elements of the natural order beyond man himself, for the Buddhist concept of duty had an extremely long reach.

Thus the forest water tanks which formed part of the ancient Sri Lankan irrigation system were also intended 'to provide water to wild animals'.[21] Contemporary chronicles confirm that these works were undertaken not only for human benefit but 'out of compassion for all living creatures',[22] which is, indeed, known as the 'First Precept' of Buddhism.[23]

b) *Animal welfare in cultural and religious tradition*

Buddhism is, moreover, certainly not unique in insisting upon the need for care and compassion on the part of humans in their dealings with animals. A similar spirit is evident within Baha'ism, Confucianism, Hinduism, Sikhism, Shintoism, Taoism, Zoroastrianism and – despite the doubts which have sometimes been expressed[24] – within the Abrahamic tradition, embracing Judaism, Christianity and Islam.[25] Indeed, various commentators refer to the formulation of principles concerning animal rights by Islamic scholars over seven centuries ago.[26] Equally, within Judaism, Old Testament references to animal welfare are strongly supported by other elements of religious doctrine; thus the principle referred to as *tsa'ar ba'aley haim* (recently invoked by the Israeli courts in support of their ban on the production of pâté de foie

[19] Ibid. [20] Ibid., p. 99. [21] Ibid., p. 96. [22] Ibid., p. 98.

[23] See, e.g., D. Keown (ed.), *Contemporary Buddhist Ethics* (Curzon, 2000), esp. Chapter 4.

[24] See especially L. White Jr, 'The Historical Roots of Our Ecologic Crisis' (1967) 155 *Science* 1203.

[25] For helpful overviews of this issue, see Bekoff and Meaney, *supra* n. 6, pp. 283–300; J. Beversluis, *Sourcebook of the World's Religions* (New World Library, 3rd ed., 2000); P. Morgan and M. Braybrooke (eds.), *Testing the Global Ethic* (CoNexus, 1998). See further J. R. Engel and J. G. Engel (eds.), *Ethics of Environment and Development* (Belhaven, 1990); A. L. Peterson, *Being Human* (University of California Press, 2001); R. D. Ryder, *Animal Revolution* (Berg, rev. ed., 2000).

[26] See A. A. Baqader et al., *Environmental Protection in Islam* (IUCN, 2nd ed., 1994); A. O. Naseef, 'The Muslim Declaration on Nature', in H. A. Haleem, *Islam and the Environment* (Ta-Ha, 1998), p. 14.

gras)[27] forbids the causing of unwarranted suffering to any living creature.[28] Universal compassion arguably reaches its apotheosis in Jainism, one of the world's oldest religions, which emphasises that all life is mutually supportive and upholds non-violence (*ahimsa*) as the highest commitment.[29] Realistically, however, it should be acknowledged that most religious traditions display considerable ambivalence towards animals, with compassion representing merely one strand in a complex skein of ideas, in which humans are almost always accorded exalted status. Accordingly, the exploitation of animals is seldom excluded, but recognition of the need for sensitivity and restraint represents at the very least a strong, recurrent subsidiary theme which is encountered almost universally.

The point was confirmed in 1993 by the Council for a Parliament of the World's Religions, in their document Towards a Global Ethic: An Initial Declaration.[30] Its preamble declared that the global ethic formulated was based upon a 'common set of core values' found in the teachings of the world's major religions, and included the assertion that:

> We are interdependent. Each of us depends upon the well-being of the whole, and so we have respect for the community of living beings, for people, animals and plants, and for the preservation of the Earth, the air, water and soil.

Furthermore, various delegates expressly confirmed that the first of its major commitments – to a culture of non-violence and respect for life – was understood to apply not only to humans but to all forms of life.[31]

Additional support for this view can be found in the belief systems of the tribal, or 'chthonic',[32] communities which preceded the emergence of organised religion and which survive in many places even to this day. The case for subsuming these traditions within the rubric of general

27 '*Noah' v Attorney-General et al.* [2002–3] *Isr SC* 215 (HCJ 9232/01); translation viewable at www.animallaw.info/nonus/cases/cas_pdf/Israel2003case.pdf.

28 W. Clark, 'The Range of Mountains Is His Pasture', in Engel and Engel, *supra* n. 25; S. P. Toperoff, *The Animal Kingdom in Jewish Thought* (Jason Aronson, 1995), pp. xxiii–xxviii.

29 See A. T. Salgia, 'Jainism: A Portrait', in Beversluis, *supra* n. 25.

30 Text reproduced in Beversluis, *supra* n. 25, pp. 174–82.

31 See generally Morgan and Braybrooke, *supra* n. 25. For subsequent inter-faith efforts to pursue this commitment, note the report of the 5th Klingenthal Symposium, organised by Pax Christi in July 2001, at http://storage.paxchristi.net/DE13E01.pdf.

32 Meaning 'of or pertaining to the land' (from the Greek *khthonos*, meaning 'land'). See further H. P. Glenn, *Legal Traditions of the World* (Oxford University Press, 2000), Chapter 3.

principles of law is greatly strengthened by the widespread recent recognition of the need to harness the wisdom of such cultures as part of the process of reconstructing humanity's relations with the natural world.[33] Within such communities, nature is commonly seen as sacred and there is no notion of human supremacy.[34] Exploitation of wildlife is, of course, essential for survival, but hunting activities are commonly preceded by elaborate rituals aimed at expiation of any wrongdoing involved,[35] and wanton killing is generally excluded.

That is not to say that the concern exhibited by such cultures would necessarily have involved fine attention to the *welfare* of target animals: to the contrary, many traditional hunting methods would doubtless appear exceptionally brutal to contemporary sensibilities. Human life itself may be extremely harsh in such communities, however, and it is unrealistic to expect that animals will be accorded any special exemption from suffering. Where circumstances permit, however, their welfare may receive greater attention, as recent developments within the International Whaling Commission amply confirm. Specifically, aboriginal whalers from Greenland, Russia and the US agreed at a historic first meeting in 2006 that, within the constraints imposed by the techniques available to subsistence hunters and the paramount need to ensure their own safety, achieving a humane death for the whale represented the highest priority.[36]

c) *Reflections in international law*

There are therefore ample grounds for recognising concern for animal welfare both as a principle widely reflected in national legal systems and as a universal value, in the broader sense indicated by Judge Weeramantry. Yet given the absence of reference to this matter in standard contemporary accounts of international law, it would be wise to ensure, before declaring it to be a general principle of law, that it has in

[33] Rio Declaration, Principle 22; Biodiversity Convention, 12th preambular recital and Articles 8(j), 10(c).

[34] Bekoff and Meaney, *supra* n. 6, pp. 251–5. See further J. Hope, *The Secret Language of the Soul* (Chronicle Books, 1997), pp. 80–105; A. M. Josephy Jr, *The Indian Heritage of America* (1968), esp. Chapter 3.

[35] J. Frazer, *The Golden Bough* (1922; Wordsworth ed., 1993), Chapter 53; C. Cullinan, *Wild Law* (Siber Ink, 2003), Chapter 7; Ryder, *supra* n. 25, Chapter 2.

[36] See the Report of the Workshop on Whale Killing Methods and Associated Welfare Issues, IWC/58/ Rep 7, Item 4.1 and Appendix 4.

addition attracted some element of formal recognition in the international legal context.[37] Within the European region, this is certainly the case. As long ago as 1961, the Consultative Assembly of the Council of Europe declared that 'the humane treatment of animals is one of the hallmarks of Western civilisation',[38] a conviction which prompted the subsequent adoption of various supra-national legal measures in this field.[39] While these apply mainly to domesticated animals, a number are relevant to wild animals as well. Recent Council of Europe agreements confirm that 'man has a moral obligation to respect all living creatures',[40] and call for 'due consideration for their capacity for suffering and memory'.[41] Finally, Article 13 of the consolidated Treaty on the Functioning of the European Union,[42] recognising that animals are sentient beings, requires that full regard be paid to their welfare requirements across a range of areas of shared competence.[43]

This growing preoccupation with animal welfare issues is also discernible at the global level. An early example can be found in a resolution adopted at the 1958 UN Conference on the Law of the Sea which requested states

> to prescribe, by all means available to them, those methods for the capture and killing of marine life, especially of whales and seals, which will spare them suffering to the greatest extent possible.[44]

Subsequently, the matter has been pursued on a broader front, as indicated above, through elaboration of the issue in the World Charter for Nature and the revised version of the World Conservation Strategy. The 2002 Johannesburg Declaration on Sustainable Development[45] envisioned a

[37] 'Recognition' for this purpose obviously need not be manifest in hard-law (e.g. customary) form, since, if it were, it would be unnecessary to resort to general principles at all.

[38] Recommendation 287 (1961).

[39] See generally D. B. Wilkins, *Animal Welfare in Europe* (Kluwer, 1997); M. Radford, *Animal Welfare Law in Britain* (Oxford University Press, 2001).

[40] See the preambles to the 1986 European Convention for the Protection of Vertebrate Animals Used for Experimental and Other Scientific Purposes, *ETS* 123; and the 1987 European Convention for the Protection of Pet Animals, *ETS* 125.

[41] The 1986 Convention, *supra* n. 40.

[42] OJ 2008 C115/47 (i.e. the Treaty of Rome, as amended by the 2007 Lisbon Reform Treaty).

[43] This provision consolidates reforms first introduced by the 1997 Treaty of Amsterdam. See T. Camm and D. Bowles, 'Animal Welfare and the Treaty of Rome' (2000) 12 *JEL* 197.

[44] Resolution 5, on the Humane Killing of Marine Life, 1958 UN Conference on the Law of the Sea, Official Records, Vol. II, Doc. A/CONF.13/38, Annexes.

[45] See www.un.org/esa/sustdev/documents/WSSD_POI_PD/English/POI PD.htm.

'*humane*, equitable, caring global society', and accordingly reaffirmed human responsibility 'to one another, *to the greater community of life* and to our children'.[46] In similar vein, the Addis Ababa Principles and Guidelines for the Sustainable Use of Biodiversity, adopted under the CBD in 2004, call for the 'more efficient, ethical and humane use'[47] of the components of biodiversity.[48] These general expressions of concern have, moreover, already been particularised and actualised through a host of more specific treaty commitments, discussed in section 3 below.

Given the pervasiveness of international concern for animal welfare, and the wealth of recent formal expressions of commitment to that objective, it may indeed now be plausible to discern a convergence upon a general principle of law to that effect in the sense conveyed by Article 38 of the ICJ Statute.

d) The significance of a general principle of law concerning animal welfare

Even if that claim can be accepted, however, the precise legal specification and significance of any such principle remain to be determined. In particular, are states now formally obliged to ensure the observance of specific welfare standards in their treatment of animals? On balance this seems unlikely, particularly if the appropriate analogy for the realisation of animal welfare as a general principle of international law is that of sustainable development. In that regard, certain leading commentators remain unconvinced that international law yet demands, in a substantive sense, that all development endeavours be sustainable. A more plausible argument, they suggest, is that decisions in this field must be the outcome of a process which promotes sustainable development.[49]

On this view, its function is primarily *procedural*, rendering national decisions amenable to some form of international institutional review while reserving ultimate discretion to governments in respect of concrete application. Thus in the *Gabcikovo* case itself the parties were required to 'look afresh' at the environmental consequences of their arrangements

[46] Paras. 2 and 6 (emphasis added).

[47] Decision VII/12, Annex II, Practical Principle 11, Operational Guidelines.

[48] See further the Earth Charter (especially Principles 1(a), 2 and 15), an NGO project published in 2000 and subsequently endorsed by IUCN and UNESCO, text in Beversluis, *supra* n. 25, p. 303.

[49] P.W. Birnie, A.E. Boyle and C.J. Redgwell, *International Law and the Environment* (Oxford University Press, 3rd ed., 2009), pp. 126–7.

and to implement such monitoring and abatement measures as they judged to be necessary in the light of considerations of sustainable development.[50] This approach seems equally applicable in relation to animal protection, so that, even in the absence of specific customary or treaty-based obligations, national (or indeed international) organs which fail to pay due regard to welfare considerations when formulating or implementing policies and projects might simply be called upon to reconsider.[51]

Notions such as sustainable development and animal welfare can, moreover, be accorded some measure of *substantive* legal significance in the form of what has been described as a 'meta-principle', i.e. one relevant to the interpretation and amplification of norms established by other means.[52] Article 31(3)(c) of the Vienna Convention on the Law of Treaties specifically requires, for treaty interpretation purposes, that account be taken of 'any relevant rules of international law applicable in the relations between the parties', and it seems that the evolutionary character of such rules must also be borne in mind.[53] Thus references in nature conservation treaties to the regulation of methods of capture, or to the culling of exotic species, might be understood to permit (or indeed require) scrutiny on grounds of welfare considerations, while the need to put severely injured animals out of their misery might be read as an implied exception to the rules prohibiting the killing of specimens of endangered species.[54] Even beyond the realms of wildlife law, the protection of animal welfare might have to be considered as an aspect of general public policy or morality, potentially justifying restrictions on treaty-based guarantees protecting free trade or human rights, for example.

There are, however, two key limitations to this approach. The first is that the *precise* content of international obligations regarding animal welfare cannot currently be specified by this means: national legislation is sure to vary widely in terms of coverage, rigour and detail. The second is

[50] Ibid. See further A. E. Boyle and D. A. C. Freestone (eds.), *International Law and Sustainable Development* (Oxford University Press, 1999), 'Introduction', esp. pp. 16–18.

[51] For a broadly similar approach to the interpretation of Constitutional provisions regarding the natural world discussed above, see the Indian Supreme Court decision in *Shri Sachidanand Pandey and Another v State of West Bengal* (1987) *AIR* SC 1109, pp. 1114–15; C. M. Abraham, *Environmental Jurisprudence in India* (Hotei, 1999), p. 124.

[52] V. Lowe, Chapter 2, in Boyle and Freestone, *supra* n. 50. Established examples of such principles include good faith, proportionality and reciprocity.

[53] A. Aust, *Modern Treaty Law and Practice* (Cambridge University Press, 2000), p. 195.

[54] See section 4(d) below.

that, since the superimposition of such concerns at the international level would occur essentially as an aspect of the interpretation of duties deriving from other sources, such considerations could be excluded entirely by express provision. Consequently, the generation of precisely specified, free-standing norms regarding wild-animal welfare will more effectively be secured through incorporation in the substantive provisions of relevant treaties, and their supporting 'soft-law' codes of practice, to which we must now turn.

3. Treaty provisions concerning wild-animal welfare

In fact, welfare issues affecting wildlife have been addressed in a surprisingly wide range of treaty commitments, and especially those concerning removal from the wild.

a) Removal from the wild

The regulation of this process has long been a feature of international legal instruments.[55] Typically, this has involved the control or outright prohibition of particular techniques, especially the use of poisons, explosives, dazzling lights, nets, traps or snares, vehicles or aircraft, and (semi-) automatic weapons.[56] These have doubtless been regarded as objectionable principally on account of their *indiscriminate* nature, and hence their threat to conservation, but the proscription of such methods will plainly have produced incidental welfare benefits in many cases.[57]

In some instances, moreover, such as prohibition of the use of blinded or mutilated decoys,[58] the prevention of cruelty would appear to be the *primary* goal of regulation, while occasionally express reference is made to welfare as an objective. Thus Article 5 of the 1950 Convention for the Protection of Birds requires the prohibition of techniques which are likely 'to result in the mass killing or capture of birds or to cause them

[55] See Gillespie, *supra* n. 7, Part 6.

[56] See, e.g., the 1900, 1933 and 1968 African Conventions, the 1902 Convention for the Protection of Birds Useful to Agriculture, and other agreements discussed below. More recent requirements include the fitting of 'turtle excluder devices' to fishing nets; see the special issue on Marine Turtles, (2002) 5(1/2) *JIWLP*.

[57] Poison, for example, may produce a painful, lingering death in animals that ingest it.

[58] See, e.g., the 1950 Convention for the Protection of Birds, Article 5; 1979 Bern Convention on the Conservation of European Wildlife and Natural Habitats, Appendix IV.

unnecessary suffering'. Similar references are now commonly encountered in relation to other species.

i) Marine mammals

Thus the resolution adopted at the 1958 UN Conference, referred to above, was implemented in various later instruments, including several concerning sealing. The 1972 Convention on the Conservation of Antarctic Seals, for example, specifies permitted methods of capture in an Annex, which are to be periodically reviewed in the interests of, inter alia, the 'rational and *humane* use of seal resources'.[59] Paragraph 7(a) of the Annex itself authorises the making of recommendations designed to ensure 'that the killing or capturing of seals is quick, painless and efficient'. Under paragraph 7(b), moreover, the taking of seals in the water is to be prohibited, except in limited numbers for research purposes, which are to include the refinement of sealing methods from the viewpoint of humane treatment, indicating that welfare is seen as fundamental to the whole process.

The concern for humane killing has also become a prominent, if controversial, feature in the history of the Whaling Convention.[60] Recent information regarding the Greenland hunt, for example, has shown that the time taken for the larger whales to die from the moment of being struck has occasionally extended to twelve hours.[61] While whaling states have traditionally maintained that welfare issues fall outside the formal competence of the IWC,[62] the UK, Germany and New Zealand have been prominent in arguing that the Commission has a moral responsibility to consider such matters.[63] Although the Convention contains no overt reference to welfare, the matters to be regulated by the Schedule include both methods of whaling and types of apparatus and appliances which may be used,[64] thereby opening the

[59] See Articles 2, 3 (emphasis added). See also the 1976 Amendment to the 1957 Fur Seals Convention, *TIAS* no. 8368.

[60] Note especially IWC Resolution 2004–3. See further S. R. Harrop, 'From Cartel to Conservation and on to Compassion: Animal Welfare and the International Whaling Commission' (2003) 6 *JIWLP* 79; Gillespie, *supra* n. 7, pp. 21–8.

[61] See the data submitted by Denmark in Annex G, 'Chairman's Report', Annual Report of the International Whaling Commission, 2004.

[62] Most whaling nations have nevertheless provided relevant data on a voluntary basis.

[63] For recent discussion, see the Chairman's Report on the Workshop on Whale Killing Methods and Associated Welfare Issues, Document IWC/58/18 (2006).

[64] Article 5(e) and (f).

door to it indirectly.[65] Furthermore, the Convention's avowed objective regarding 'the orderly development of the whaling industry' arguably renders it legitimate to address any matter which might prove prejudicial to good order, as perceived cruelty (or the response to it) plainly could.[66] Finally, if there is indeed a general principle of law regarding animal welfare, Article 31(3)(c) of the Vienna Convention creates not merely a moral but a legal responsibility to address such issues.

The first concrete measure to be adopted in this regard involved the prohibition, in 1981, of the 'cold-grenade' harpoon for commercial purposes.[67] From that time, it was necessary to use harpoons which exploded upon impact,[68] thereby increasing the chances of rapid death.[69] Following the imposition of the moratorium, welfare issues remained relevant in relation to any whaling which continued, i.e. by states which had registered objections to the moratorium resolution, such as Norway, as well as scientific and aboriginal activities. Humane killing accordingly remained on the agenda, not least because even the exploding harpoon is scarcely an ideal weapon from a welfare perspective.[70] A Working Group was established in 1982,[71] and five workshops on killing methods have been held since 1992.[72] The ongoing pressure has secured further reforms, including the introduction of a more powerful explosive, penthrite, increased efficiency of triggering devices, and better training of operatives. Secondary killing methods have also been addressed, with the use of rifles encouraged in preference to the 'electric

[65] It has certainly been actively debated since the 1930s. For a survey of the early literature, see E. D. Mitchell et al., Bibliography of Whale Killing Techniques (IWC Special Issue No. 7, 1986).

[66] Harrop, *supra* n. 60, pp. 95–8. The point is arguably conceded implicitly by IWC Resolutions 2006–2 and 2007–2: see M. J. Bowman, '"Normalizing" the International Convention for the Regulation of Whaling' (2008) 29 *Michigan JIL* 293, pp. 434–6.

[67] The minke whale was briefly exempted; also, Japan and Norway initially registered objections to the ban, but later withdrew them.

[68] The cold-grenade harpoon is powered by explosives but has no charge for detonation upon impact.

[69] See J. Cherfas, *The Hunting of the Whale* (Penguin, 1989), p. 142. Whalers had originally opposed the change, as such weapons destroy more meat.

[70] It depends upon the whale's vital organs being destroyed in the blast: if death is not instantaneous, suffering is likely to be acute. Harrop, *supra* n. 60, p. 92, notes an instance during the 1993 Norwegian hunt where a whale took fifty-five minutes to die.

[71] The Working Group on Humane Killing, later renamed the Working Group on Whale Killing Methods and Associated Welfare Problems. See para. 9.2, Chairman's Report, IWC Annual Report, 1999.

[72] For the report of the most recent (in 2006), see Document IWC/58/18. A workshop on welfare issues associated with entanglement is scheduled for April 2010.

lance', which administers a lethal shock to the whale, but is notoriously inefficient and has sometimes to be applied repeatedly. Overall, there is no doubt that welfare improvements have been achieved, particularly by Norway, but the present situation remains far from ideal and it may be doubted whether the killing of such large creatures under such difficult circumstances can realistically be achieved in an acceptable, humane fashion.[73]

Particular problems are generated by aboriginal whaling activities, where the very factor which minimises their impact from a conservation perspective – primitiveness of technique – may inherently serve to aggravate welfare problems. Even here, the IWC has called upon whalers to cause the least possible pain and distress to hunted whales, and this has led to the adoption of more modern and humane methods of killing in some cases. The recent declaration by aboriginal whalers of commitment to the welfare principle has already been noted.[74] Political pressure has also led to modification of the methods used to hunt small cetaceans, in the Faeroe Islands, for example.[75]

ii) Terrestrial species

Various provisions designed to mitigate cruelty in relation to the taking of protected terrestrial species have already been noted. A further, more recent, example is provided by Article 3(6) of Annex II to the 1991 Antarctic Environmental Protocol, which requires that the taking of animals on the Antarctic landmass be accomplished 'in a manner that involves the least degree of pain and suffering practicable'.

If, however, the prohibition of cruelty constitutes a moral imperative in its own right, it should be applicable to the hunting of *any* species, regardless of conservation status, including even those that are prolific or considered pests. The question is therefore potentially relevant to all treaty provisions which permit the taking or culling of wildlife populations, for whatever reason.[76] Occasionally, the need for such activities to

[73] For recent developments, see the IWC Annual Report, 2008, Annex G, and Revised Chair's Report of the 60th Annual Meeting, Section 5; Document IWC/61/Rep6 (2009).

[74] See section 2(b) above. [75] For elaboration, see Gillespie, *supra* n. 7, pp. 25–6.

[76] See, e.g., the Biodiversity Convention, Article 8(h); Bern Convention, Articles 2, 9, 11(2)(b); Bonn Convention, Article 3(4)(c), 3(5); the Whaling Convention, Article 8; the Polar Bears Convention, Article 3.

be conducted humanely is expressly stipulated, but such a requirement might arguably be implied in any event by virtue of the 'meta-principle' regarding animal welfare referred to above.[77] Interestingly, the Bern Convention's Standing Committee has indicated that methods used to eradicate introduced alien species should be 'as selective, ethical and without cruelty as possible, consistent with the aim of permanently eliminating the invasive species'.[78] Equally, welfare assurances have been sought or given with regard to both the eradication of particular exotics[79] and the culling of wild animals for reasons of public health.[80]

iii) The Agreement on Humane Trapping Standards

Utilisation of the leg-hold trap has attracted particular condemnation, since animals caught in such devices may suffer a lingering death in extreme pain from broken limbs, severed tendons and ligaments or the onset of gangrene. Such injuries are commonly exacerbated, moreover, by the animal's own attempts to escape, which sometimes entail chewing or wringing off the disabled limb. Accordingly, the prohibition of such traps has become increasingly common in national legislation,[81] though resistance to reform has tended to persist in areas with strong trapping traditions, especially North America and Russia. Measures adopted within the EC in 1991 controversially sought to prohibit not only the use of such traps throughout the Community,[82] but also the importation of specified pelts unless the country of origin had itself banned such traps or established a regime that met internationally agreed humane trapping standards. However, concern at the prospect of a challenge within the WTO caused the import ban to be postponed while a negotiated solution was sought.[83] In the case of Canada and Russia, this ultimately

[77] See section 4(d) below.

[78] Recommendation No. 77 (1999), preamble. The question is not addressed, however, in the earlier general guidelines on the subject appended to Recommendation 57 (1997), which are essentially ecological in orientation.

[79] Report of the 17th Meeting of the Standing Committee, Agenda Item 6.2, concerning eradication of the North American ruddy duck (*Oxyura jamaicensis*) in the UK.

[80] Report of the 19th Meeting (1999), Agenda Items 6.1, 6.2.

[81] See section 2(a) above.

[82] Regulation 3254/91 prohibiting the use of leg-hold traps, etc., OJ 1991 L308/1.

[83] Though the Netherlands decided to implement it unilaterally. See generally A. Nollkaemper, 'The Legality of Moral Crusades Disguised in Trade Laws' (1996) 8 *JEL* 237.

materialised in the form of the 1997 Agreement on Humane Trapping Standards,[84] a modified version of which was also agreed informally with the United States.[85]

The Agreement, which is not self-executing,[86] seeks to balance trade and humanitarian concerns. It applies to the trapping of specified animals, including otters, beavers, martens, bobcats and wolves,[87] for such purposes as wildlife conservation or management, pest control, and the acquisition of fur, skin or meat.[88] Each party undertakes to establish certification procedures for traps to ensure that trapping is conducted in conformity with stipulated standards, which are to be the subject of ongoing development. It must also require manufacturers to identify certified traps and provide instructions for their safe operation and maintenance.[89]

Article 10 authorises the granting of individual derogations from the core obligations for specified purposes, including the protection of property, public health or safety, research or education, repopulation and wildlife protection, and the use of traditional wooden traps essential for preserving the cultural heritage of indigenous communities. However, these may not be applied so as to undermine the Agreement's objectives, and must be justified to the Joint Management Committee which it establishes.[90] Significantly, no party may impose trade-restrictive measures on fur or fur products originating from any other party, though this prohibition is without prejudice to the dispute settlement provisions of Article 15 (which allow for arbitration) or the 'relevant provisions' of CITES.[91] Parties may, however, request a certificate of origin that fur to be imported has been obtained from animals caught or farmed in the territory of another,[92] since otherwise there could be no assurance of compliance with the standards established.

[84] OJ 1998 L042, approved by Council Decision 98/142. In force 22 June 2008. Pending ratification by Russia, the Agreement had been applied provisionally between the EU and Canada since 1 June 1999. See further S. R. Harrop, 'The Agreements on International Humane Trapping Standards' (1998) 1 *JIWLP* 387, and 'The International Regulation of Animal Welfare' (2000) 12 *JEL* 333.

[85] See the Agreed Minute on humane trapping standards, OJ 1998 L219, approved in Council Decision 98/487, and now in effect. The US was unwilling to conclude a formal treaty as regulation of trapping is regarded as a matter for state and tribal authorities.

[86] Article 17(3).

[87] Section 4 of the Annex lists nineteen species in all (some extremely common), and allows also for future additions.

[88] Article 3. [89] Articles 7–9.

[90] See Article 14. The Committee's first meeting, involving representatives from all four participants, took place in October 2009.

[91] Article 13(1). [92] Article 13(2).

The standards themselves are contained in Annex I of the Agreement and aim to ensure a sufficient, and improving, level of welfare for trapped animals.[93] Welfare is assessed by reference to specified indicators, including the occurrence of particular injuries (e.g. fracture, severe internal organ damage, ocular damage, spinal cord injury or death) or behaviours (e.g. self-mutilation or excessive immobility). Threshold requirements are then established by sections 2 and 3 in relation to trapping methods designed for restraint and killing respectively. Thus a restraining method is considered acceptable only if data from at least twenty individuals of the target species demonstrate that at least 80 per cent display *none* of these indicators. As regards killing methods, acceptable time limits to unconsciousness (which must be determined by scientifically proven means) range from 45 to 300 seconds for different species, though early re-evaluation of the upper limit is envisaged, with a view to its reduction to 180 seconds.[94] Parties are allowed up to five years from the Agreement's entry into force to acquire the relevant data, and a further three to prohibit methods that do not comply. They may, however, continue to permit their interim usage pending the identification of replacement methods.[95] Plainly, this timescale may entail lengthy postponement of the elimination of ethically unacceptable techniques. Extensive guidelines are established regarding the testing of traps and research on the ongoing development of trapping methods.[96]

The Agreement does not guarantee any fundamental, immediate advance towards the elimination of animal suffering, but it has at least served to consolidate the place of animal welfare on the international agenda, and the institutions it establishes may offer the prospect of further progress in the future.[97]

b) Transportation

Quite apart from welfare implications, the transboundary movement of animals has long been a matter of international concern on account of the management problems it generates for transport undertakings and the risk of transmission of disease from one country to another. Such

[93] Section 1.1. [94] Section 3.3. [95] Section 4.2, Implementation Schedule.

[96] See Parts 3 and 4 of the Schedule.

[97] For a damning appraisal of the standards proposed in 2004 for implementation of the Agreement in Europe, see S. Harris et al., *Trapped by Bad Science: The Myths behind the Humane Trapping Standards* (IFAW/EUROGROUP for Animal Welfare, 2005).

problems led to the adoption of a series of international treaties dating from the 1920s, though these did not always prove particularly effective and were in any event focused primarily on domesticated animals.[98] Arguably the first significant step was the Council of Europe's 1968 Convention for the Protection of Animals during International Transport,[99] which again predominantly concerned domesticated animals, though Chapter V extended to wild mammals and birds,[100] while Chapter VI made cursory provision for all cold-blooded animals. Growing dissatisfaction with the realities of animal transportation in the region led eventually, however, to the adoption of updated measures within the EU,[101] and a revised version of the Council of Europe Convention in 2003.[102] With the exception of transportation entirely within the EU (to be governed by its own regime), the Convention covers almost all international movements of vertebrate animals.[103] The substantive principles governing transportation are not greatly changed from 1968, though they are structured differently and implementation arrangements are much improved.[104] In particular, *all* parties are now invested with supervisory responsibilities, rather than merely the state of despatch. Furthermore, the 2003 revision is designed as a framework Convention, allowing for the adoption of technical protocols governing such matters as space allowances and provisioning through a multilateral consultation process.[105] In addition, certain general principles are now

98 For an overview of these developments, see M. J. Bowman, 'The Protection of Animals under International Law' (1989) 4 *Connecticut JIL* 487, pp. 488–90.

99 788 *UNTS* 195; *ETS* 65. The Convention attracted twenty-four parties in all, eight of which have since denounced it following acceptance of its 2003 successor. On early transportation arrangements within the European region generally, see Wilkins, *supra* n. 39, Chapter 1.

100 Chapters II–IV of the Convention deal with specified categories of domestic animals and birds, while Chapter V is headed 'Other Mammals and Birds'.

101 Council Regulation 1/2005 on the protection of animals during transport and related operations, OJ 2005 L3/1, which amends various earlier provisions and repeals, from 5 January 2007, Directive 91/628 and Regulation 411/98.

102 *CETS* 193. The Convention entered into force during March 2006 and currently has ten parties (Bulgaria, Estonia, Germany, Greece, Luxembourg, Netherlands, Norway, Romania, Sweden and Switzerland) and a further nine signatories, including the EU. Upon acceptance, parties must denounce the 1968 Agreement (Article 37(2)).

103 Journeys of less than fifty kilometres are excluded, while only minimal provision applies to accompanied pets and other single attended animals (Articles 1, 2). The parties may, however, adopt stricter domestic measures than the Convention establishes (Article 4).

104 See Articles 3–5 and the Explanatory Report, which accompanies the Convention.

105 See Articles 31–5. General questions of interpretation may also be considered at such events.

established,[106] requiring that animals be transported in a manner which safeguards their health and welfare, and as far as possible without delay. They are to be given priority over other consignments at control points and only detained where necessary for their own welfare or for disease control, and even then proper arrangements must be made for their care. More detailed provisions then follow,[107] with Article 7 placing an increased emphasis on journey planning. Finally, specific obligations are established regarding particular modes of transport,[108] including express provision for conveyance in vehicles transported on roll-on roll-off ferries.[109]

Another regime concerning the international transportation of wild animals, this time potentially of global application though limited substantively to species listed in its Appendices, has been established under CITES.[110] Its significance stems in part from the Convention's very wide definition of 'trade',[111] embracing virtually any consignment of a listed specimen across international borders.[112] CITES controls begin when such consignments are initially authorised. Before granting a permit, the relevant Management Authority must be 'satisfied that any living specimen will be so prepared and shipped as to minimize the risk of injury, damage to health or cruel treatment'.[113] To facilitate implementation of these obligations, the CITES Guidelines for Transport and Preparation for Shipment of Live Animals and Plants were elaborated in 1980.[114] The first section comprises guidance to carriers, addressing various aspects of the animals' welfare, transit arrangements and accommodation, while the second, much longer, section consists of nineteen sets of copiously illustrated packer's guidelines, each concerning different kinds of animal and addressing such matters as general welfare, advance arrangements for transportation, construction and labelling of containers, installation of animals within them and accompanying documentation. The final

[106] Article 4. [107] Articles 6–25.

[108] Articles 26–30. Obligations were deliberately restructured around the mode of transport adopted, rather than the species transported, since this was seen as the key determinant of applicable standards (Explanatory Report, 'General Considerations', para. 4). It may also simplify negotiations with transport authorities.

[109] Article 29.

[110] See generally M. J. Bowman, 'Conflict or Compatibility? The Trade, Conservation and Animal Welfare Dimensions of CITES' (1998) 1 *JIWLP* 9.

[111] See Article 1(c). [112] The principal exclusions are established by Article 7.

[113] See respectively Articles 3(2)(c), 4(2)(c), 5(2)(b), 3(4)(b) and 4(5)(b), and, for marginally modified versions, Articles 4(6)(b) and 7(7)(c).

[114] See Plen. 2.6(Rev.), Agenda Item XIX.

section briefly addresses the transportation of plants, providing a welcome reminder that they too have a good of their own, and may either flourish or perish as a result of the treatment they receive.

Following further negotiations with the airlines' organisation IATA, however, it was agreed that the latter's Live Animals Regulations should be deemed to satisfy CITES requirements and that they might be implemented by parties in place of its own Guidelines.[115] In 2007, the CoP also commended the much more recently promulgated OIE guidelines regarding transport by sea and air.[116] None of these sets of standards is of itself legally binding, though CITES Conference Resolution 10.21 does urge the parties to promote the use of the Transport Guidelines,[117] and to incorporate the IATA Regulations into domestic legislation.[118] CITES also encourages the provision of animal-holding facilities at designated ports[119] and the inspection of shipments where possible, especially during extended stopovers, but more sophisticated mechanisms for monitoring and improving compliance with welfare standards have either been rejected or abandoned as unduly onerous.[120] The parties have also been reluctant[121] to undertake the burden of collecting detailed information concerning morbidity and mortality rates of traded specimens,[122] and the past performance of particular carriers and consignors in that regard, despite the fact that these would seem to be prerequisites to the performance in good faith of their certification responsibilities under the Convention.[123]

115 See Resolutions Conf. 4.20 and, currently, Conf. 10.21, para.(d).

116 Decision 14.58. On the work of the OIE, see section 4 below.

117 See originally Resolution Conf. 3.16.

118 See originally Resolution Conf. 5.18. IATA claimed during 2004 that 'many countries' had by then incorporated its Regulations into national legislation – see Doc. 13.21, para. 16. Decision 14.58 cautions against both duplication and inconsistency between national, regional or international regimes.

119 See Article 8(3), discussed below.

120 Thus the various welfare checklists established by Resolutions Conf. 6.24, para.(b), and 7.13, para.(c), were omitted from the subsequent consolidating Resolution Conf. 9.23. For discussion, see Bowman, *supra* n. 110, pp. 18–19.

121 UK and US constitute honourable exceptions here. See 'Transport of Live Specimens', Doc. 8.36, para. 7(b).

122 This task was imposed by Resolution Conf. 10.21, consolidating earlier measures to similar effect, but relaxed by Decision 13.89, following a reasonably encouraging (albeit sketchy) Secretariat survey, which revealed mortality rates for twelve sample species of around 1.25 per cent. See 'Transport of Live Animals', Doc. 12.25.

123 Article 2(4) provides that the parties 'shall not allow' trade in listed specimens other than in accordance with Articles 3–5.

The welfare precondition to the authorisation of trade is reinforced by a specific duty to ensure adequate protection during the *actual process of transportation*. Thus Article 8(3), a provision commonly overlooked in this context,[124] states that:

> As far as possible, the Parties shall ensure that specimens pass through any formalities required for trade with a minimum of delay ... The Parties shall ensure further that all living specimens, during any period of transit, holding or shipment, are properly cared for so as to minimize the risk of injury, damage to health or cruel treatment.

This duty is ostensibly not limited, moreover, to the state that originally authorised the transaction, but applies to *any* party under whose jurisdiction or control the specimens fall during the course of transportation. Nor is there anything to exclude its application even in situations where normal permit requirements have been relaxed by virtue of Article 7. Although this provision would seem to require not only the enactment but the rigorous enforcement of appropriate domestic legislation regarding animal welfare, such commitment is as yet by no means guaranteed in all countries.[125]

In general, ensuring compliance with welfare standards has proved a major challenge for CITES,[126] and significantly increased effort is required if this matter is to be accorded the attention it deserves.

c) *Management of captive wildlife*

There are numerous situations where wild animals are maintained outside their natural habitat under human control. They may be bred in captivity, possibly for ultimate reintroduction into the wild, or utilised in scientific experiments, either in connection with conservation programmes or for medical or other purposes. They are also kept as pets, or for public entertainment in zoos, circuses or dolphinaria. Various

[124] Article 8(3) is seldom mentioned in resolutions or deliberations concerning the welfare issue: one notable exception, Resolution Conf. 4.21, is now repealed.

[125] Decisions 14.27 and 14.59 instruct the Secretariat to prepare an analysis of existing legislation on this (and other) matters for the next CoP. For an ingenious, though probably underutilised, alternative solution, see Resolution Conf. 12.3, Annex 1(n), and Doc. 8.19(Rev.), Sect. 6(A).

[126] See, e.g., the devastating early reports prepared by the Environmental Investigation Agency: Injury, Damage to Health and Cruel Treatment (1985) and The Trade in Live Wildlife (1987). For details of current cases, see the *Traffic Bulletin*, published by the World Conservation Monitoring Centre.

species are farmed for their fur, meat or other products. Finally, illegally traded specimens may be confiscated by the authorities and held for disposal. Welfare problems may arise in all these contexts, and effective legal regulation is not necessarily guaranteed. Within the European region, protective standards established primarily for the benefit of domesticated animals may sometimes be applicable,[127] though the use of wild animals for experimentation or companionship, especially if they have actually been removed from the wild, is actively discouraged by the treaties in question.[128]

Where CITES-listed specimens are imported for such purposes, appropriate documentation will be required. In the case of Appendix I species, commercial transactions are in general prohibited, but consignments may be authorised for scientific or educational purposes. Amongst the conditions of which the relevant authority will have to be satisfied is that the 'proposed recipient of a living specimen is suitably equipped to house and care for it',[129] which should ensure that some attention at least is given to its welfare needs. Of course, this is linked with conservation considerations: given that the species is by definition endangered, the fate of every individual becomes a matter of heightened concern.

In certain situations where wildlife specimens are held in custody, however, more specific welfare obligations may apply.

i) Treatment of confiscated specimens

The enforcement of international conservation obligations may frequently entail the confiscation by national authorities of specimens which have been illegally acquired or traded,[130] but few treaties make detailed provision for what should then happen to them. CITES is a notable exception, however, and the procedures agreed offer guidance for other conventions. Article 8(4) requires that such specimens be entrusted to the Management Authority, which may either return them to the state of export at that state's expense, or send them to a rescue

[127] See (i) the 1976 Convention for the Protection of Animals Kept for Farming Purposes, *ETS* 87, as amended by the 1992 Protocol, *ETS* 145, under which specific standards of husbandry have been agreed for ratites (ostriches, emus etc.), fur-bearing animals and muscovy ducks; (ii) the 1986 Convention on the Protection of Vertebrate Animals Used for Experimental and Other Scientific Purposes, *ETS* 123; and (iii) the 1987 Convention for the Protection of Pet Animals, *ETS* 125.

[128] See, e.g., the Pets Convention, preamble and Article 4(3); Experimentation Convention, Article 21.

[129] Article 3(3)(b), (5)(b).

[130] CITES, Article 8(1)(b), for example, specifically endorses such confiscation.

centre or other appropriate place. More comprehensive guidelines were established by Conference Resolution 10.7,[131] which emphasises, inter alia, the need for suitable training, funding and allocation of functions to enable such authorities to discharge these responsibilities effectively. The evaluation of options for disposal (i.e. captivity, return to the wild or euthanasia) must commence immediately following seizure, and balance three key objectives, namely

(i) maximising the conservation value of the specimens without endangering the health, behavioural repertoire or conservation status of wild or captive populations;
(ii) discouraging further illegal or irregular trade; and
(iii) providing a humane solution.

Given the practical problems involved, euthanasia will often be the preferred solution (especially for Appendix II specimens), even though it is not mentioned specifically in the Convention itself.

ii) Captive breeding and associated activities

Captive-breeding programmes designed to augment depleted wild-living populations are recognised as an important supplement to *in situ* conservation efforts and have accordingly been initiated under various conventions. Since such activities are generally undertaken by accredited scientific institutions, the welfare of individual specimens will normally be accorded high priority in order to maximise the project's chances of success. Wild animals may also be bred, however, for purely commercial purposes, where their welfare needs are less likely to be prioritised.[132] Under CITES, however, the approval of any captive-breeding operation – and, indeed, of 'ranching' animals in their natural habitat[133] – is to be made conditional upon assurances that 'the operation shall be carried out at all stages in a humane (i.e. non-cruel) manner',[134] which the Secretariat may monitor through requests for data concerning mortality rates. Captive-bred specimens are generally exempted from the usual permits for transportation abroad,[135] but Appendix I specimens bred for

[131] Consolidating earlier resolutions on the matter.
[132] Even operations of this kind may assist conservation, provided they reduce (rather than stimulate) the demands upon wild populations.
[133] For this distinction, and further discussion, see Chapter 15 above.
[134] See respectively Resolutions Conf. 12.10, Annex 1, para. 19, and Conf. 11.16, para. (c)(iii).
[135] Article 7(5).

commercial purposes will require the documentation normally appropriate to Appendix II.[136]

iii) Research and experimentation

Wildlife treaties commonly encourage the conduct of research into conservation issues, and sometimes create exemptions from the basic protective regime to accommodate such work. Although research itself is capable of posing threats to ecological processes, to conservation or to the welfare of individual organisms, it is relatively unusual for such matters to be addressed in the text of the treaty itself. They are, however, sometimes addressed through the formulation of recommendations or codes of practice by treaty institutions. EUROBATS Resolution 4.6, for example, calls for the licensing of research activities in order to minimise disturbance to bat populations. While the primary concern here is conservation, the proposed research should also 'take account of the welfare of individual bats'.[137] Accordingly, methods of capture involving techniques or devices likely to cause them injury or suffering should be prohibited,[138] while licence holders are specifically required to comply with any national legislation regarding animal experimentation or welfare.

Within the European region, moreover, animal experimentation is comprehensively regulated under the 1986 Council of Europe Convention.[139] Although it envisages the use of purpose-bred animals for the most part, it covers wild animals to the limited extent that they are used for general research purposes. It also contains some provisions which are of specific relevance to conservation-based research. Article 12, for example, provides that animals may be 'set free' if the experiment so requires, as where wild animals are fitted with sensors to monitor their movements or physiological condition.[140] Since such release inevitably excludes the normal handling and accommodation obligations which the Convention establishes,[141] it is stipulated instead that the maximum practicable care be taken in such circumstances to safeguard the animal's wellbeing. Furthermore, release is not permitted solely for educational or training purposes.[142]

[136] Article 7(4). [137] See the Guidance Note to para. 1.
[138] See EUROBATS.MoP4.Record.Annex9a.
[139] *ETS* 123. As of January 2010, there were twenty parties, including the EU, and a further seven signatories.
[140] See the Explanatory Report to the Convention, para. 48.
[141] Under Articles 5, 11(3) and Appendix A.
[142] See on this point the Explanatory Report, para. 49.

d) *Animal welfare as a defence*

Human concern for animal welfare is manifest in treaty provisions not only in the form of positive duties for their protection, but also sometimes in a different guise, namely as a *justification for failure to comply with a legal obligation*. This function bears some similarities to the notion of *distress*, an established defence to breach of obligation in international law generally.[143] Although the International Law Commission has asserted that the defence of distress is limited to cases where human life is at stake,[144] it is unlikely to have had the case of non-human animals in mind. In particular, where the obligation in question is designed specifically for the benefit of animals, proof that any specific instance of non-compliance was attributable to the need to protect animal lives, or avoid their suffering, seems like an eminently plausible defence. In that vein, the Explanatory Report to the Bern Convention explains the absence of such provision from Article 9, where various justifications for non-compliance are specified, on the basis that

> It was considered that the taking or killing of protected fauna for humane or humanitarian reasons was an accepted practice that *did not require a specific provision in the convention* . . .[145]

For the avoidance of doubt, however, it may be preferable to provide expressly for such a defence, as occurred in the 2001 Agreement on the Conservation of Albatrosses and Petrels. Having prohibited deliberate taking or harmful interference with such birds, Article 3 goes on to exclude the humane killing of injured or moribund specimens by duly authorised persons in order to end their suffering.[146]

The pervasiveness of concern for animal welfare suggests, moreover, that it may manifest itself through the provision of such defences in treaties far beyond the realm of wildlife conservation or animal protection specifically. Thus examples of such references may be found in trade

[143] See Article 24 of the International Law Commission's Articles on the Responsibility of States for Internationally Wrongful Acts (2001), published with commentary in Report of the 53rd Session of the ILC (2001), UN Doc A/56/10. See further J. Crawford, *The International Law Commission's Articles on State Responsibility: Introduction, Text and Commentaries* (Cambridge University Press, 2002).

[144] ILC Report, *supra* n. 143, p. 192. Cf., however, the *Rainbow Warrior* arbitration (1990) 82 *ILR* 499.

[145] See para. 39 (emphasis added).

[146] See further para. 1.4.2 of Annex 2 to the appended Action Plan. For similar provision, see the Wadden Sea Seals Agreement, Articles 6(1), (2).

liberalisation agreements such as the 1957 Treaty of Rome and the 1994 GATT. As to the former, Article 36 of the Treaty on the Functioning of the European Union currently allows for the imposition of trade restrictions on various grounds, including public morality, policy or security, and the protection of the health and life of humans, animals or plants. Broadly similar allowance is made in the global trade regime by virtue of GATT Article 20. These exceptions are, however, customarily given a restrictive interpretation, which arguably goes beyond the legitimate need to ensure that welfare measures are not used as a means of arbitrary discrimination or disguised restrictions upon trade. A heavy onus of justification will be imposed upon the state invoking the exception, and purely unilateral measures are unlikely to survive this scrutiny process.[147]

Finally, animal welfare may in appropriate circumstances operate as a legitimate constraint upon the exercise of freedoms guaranteed by human rights conventions. Under the European Convention on Human Rights, for example, the 'protection of morals' is widely recognised as a permissible justification for such restriction,[148] and, given the Council of Europe's long-standing recognition of the humane treatment of animals as a hallmark of Western civilisation, it would be surprising if that were not reflected in the interpretation of the relevant provisions. In *Friend, and Countryside Alliance and Others v UK*,[149] the European Court of Human Rights duly confirmed the legitimacy under this rubric of domestic measures 'designed to eliminate the hunting and killing of animals for sport in a manner which the legislature judged to cause suffering and to be morally and ethically objectionable'. It therefore rejected the appellants' claims as inadmissible, essentially endorsing the view of the UK courts[150] that no breach of human rights resulted from the ban on hunting with dogs imposed by the Hunting Act 2004.[151]

147 See generally A. Vedder (ed.), *The WTO, and Concerns regarding Animals and Nature* (Nijmegen, 2003).

148 See para. 2 of Articles 8, 9, 10 and 11 respectively.

149 Application Nos. 16072/06, 27809/08. See also *Cha'are Shalom Ve Tsedek v France*, Application No. 27417/95.

150 [2008] 2 *All ER* 95.

151 The applicants invoked various combinations of Articles 8, 9, 11 and 14, and Article 1 of the 1st Protocol. No interference was found with any of these, except arguably the last, and even there it could be justified on the grounds indicated above.

4. Animal welfare – the way ahead

The developments outlined above confirm that the welfare of individual animals (whether wild or domesticated) is emerging as a significant and pervasive concern of the international community, albeit one which has not yet attracted the level of attention or consistency of response achieved by the issue of species conservation. In particular, the problem has thus far been addressed in an ad hoc and piecemeal fashion, predominantly at the regional level and without the benefit of clear theoretical foundations. In that respect, it arguably mirrors the state of conservation law prior to the Stockholm Conference. In order to develop a more coherent and co-ordinated regime, certain reforms appear desirable, including the establishment of an acceptable global forum for the elaboration and harmonisation of appropriate welfare standards. This would seem to require, as a minimum, the identification of a suitable inter-governmental institution to undertake responsibility for this task, or, more ambitiously, the negotiation of an overarching legal instrument to replicate the role of the Biodiversity Convention in the conservation field.[152]

Happily, significant developments can be reported on both fronts, specifically (i) the recent expansion of the remit of the World Organisation for Animal Health (OIE) – an institution created in 1924 to address problems associated with contagious diseases of livestock[153] – to embrace a general Animal Welfare Mandate,[154] and (ii) the support attracted by the World Society for the Protection of Animals (WSPA) for its non-binding Universal Declaration on Animal Welfare.[155] The

[152] For an unofficial early attempt to devise a viable model for such an instrument, note the draft International Convention for the Protection of Animals, and its five associated protocols, discussed by Bowman, *supra* n. 98, pp. 496–9, and by D. S. Favre, Chapter 13, in D. E. Blackman, P. N. Humphreys and P. Todd (eds.), *Animal Welfare and the Law* (Cambridge University Press, 1989).

[153] For its constituent instrument, see the 1924 International Agreement for the Creation of an International Office for Epizootics, 57 *LNTS* 135. The OIE currently boasts 175 members. For further information, see its website at www.oie.int/eng/en_index.htm.

[154] Resolution No. XIV (2002). For recent reaffirmation of this mandate, see Resolution No. 23 (2009), adopted at the 77th General Session of OIE. Note also Resolution No. XVII (2004), on the creation of a World Animal Health and Welfare Fund. A permanent Working Group on Animal Welfare has been established, meeting for the eighth time in 2009.

[155] The declaration was endorsed by the EC Commission and by twenty-one (predominantly European and Asian) governments at a conference in Manila in 2003. Subsequently, governmental recruitment has expanded and an international steering

preamble to this Declaration asserts that 'animals are living, sentient beings and therefore deserve due consideration and respect', and commends for governmental consideration both the 'five freedoms' of animal husbandry and the 'three Rs' of animal experimentation.[156] Key substantive provisions are that animals should be treated in a 'humane and sustainable manner', regardless of economic, religious or cultural differences, and that all appropriate steps should be taken to prevent cruelty and reduce suffering. The OIE has already devised detailed guidelines concerning the transport of animals by land, sea and air; the killing of animals for human consumption and disease control; and the control of stray-dog populations, and has organised two global conferences on animal welfare, the most recent (held in Cairo in October 2008) focusing on the implementation of these standards. It has also recently established a co-operative agreement with WSPA and endorsed in principle the formal adoption of the Universal Declaration under its own aegis.[157] These developments offer some hope for the rationalisation and consolidation of the at present rather desultory and disjointed state of welfare provision.

Recommended further reading

M. Bekoff and C. A. Meaney (eds.), *Encyclopedia of Animal Rights and Animal Welfare* (Fitzroy Dearborn, 1998)

M. J. Bowman, 'Conflict or Compatibility: The Trade, Conservation and Animal Welfare Dimensions of CITES' (1998) 1 *JIWLP* 9

A. Gillespie, 'Humane Killing: A Recognition of Universal Common Sense in International Law' (2003) 6 *JIWLP* 1

S. R. Harrop, 'The Dynamics of Wild Animal Welfare Law' (1997) 9 *JEL* 287

S. R. Harrop, 'From Cartel to Conservation and on to Compassion: Animal Welfare and the International Whaling Commission' (2003) 6 *JIWLP* 79

J. Webster, *Animal Welfare: Limping towards Eden* (Blackwell, 2005)

committee has been formed with a view to securing ultimate adoption by the UN. For further information, see www.wspa-international.org/wspawork/udaw/Default.aspx.

[156] 'Five freedoms': freedom from hunger, thirst and malnutrition; freedom from fear and distress; freedom from physical and thermal discomfort; freedom from pain, injury and disease; and freedom to express normal patterns of behaviour. 'Three Rs': reduction in numbers, refinement of methods and replacement with non-animal techniques. See generally J. Webster, *Animal Welfare: Limping towards Eden* (Blackwell, 2005).

[157] See Resolutions Nos. IX and XIV (2007) and, most recently, No. XXIII (2009).

Chapter 21

Wildlife and pollution

1. Background

The impact of pollution on wildlife is all too apparent. Many coral reefs have, for example, suffered from bleaching due to increases in seawater temperatures as a result of climate change. Additionally, the impact of oil pollution on the marine environment is potentially dramatic as shown by numerous high-profile oil pollution instances since the *Torrey Canyon* spill in 1967. More recently, the impact of anthropogenic noise sources on marine wildlife has been raised as a particular concern. Whilst international legal regimes designed specifically to protect wildlife and related ecosystems understandably provide the focus of this book,[1] it is also important to appreciate that these regimes form just a part of the body of laws that make up international environmental law. International rules directly pertaining to wildlife conservation should not be regarded as acting in isolation from other international environmental treaty regimes. Regimes not specifically designed to conserve wildlife, but instead to prevent, minimise and eliminate pollution, also have an important part to play in the conservation of fauna, flora and associated habitats. This chapter provides examples of some of the key forms of pollution which threaten biodiversity, without aiming to be totally comprehensive in coverage. A brief introduction will also be provided to some of the most important treaties established to address these pollutants. The initial focus of discussion in this chapter is the significant threat posed by climate change, followed by the consequences of ozone layer depletion, acid precipitation and oil pollution. In addition coverage is given to the impact of chemicals, pesticides and heavy metals, and of anthropogenic sources of noise pollution on biodiversity.

[1] Some of these regimes directly address the issue of pollution; see, for example, discussion of Article 3(2) Bern Convention in Chapter 10 above, and Articles VI(3) and VII(1) of the revised 2003 African Convention addressed in Chapter 9 above.

2. Climate change

The 2007 Fourth Report of the Intergovernmental Panel on Climate Change (IPCC) indicated that the 'globally averaged net effect of human activities since 1750 has been one of warming'.[2] Significantly, this determination by the world's leading scientists in the field as to the influence of humans on the planet's climate was one of 'very high confidence'.[3] Carbon dioxide is the main greenhouse gas. Concentrations in the atmosphere have increased by 35 per cent since pre-industrial days, mainly as a result of the burning of fossil fuels and forest clearance.[4] Methane and nitrous oxide are two other key greenhouse gases. Methane concentrations have risen by 148 per cent during this time, and nitrous oxide by 18 per cent.[5] Increases in methane concentrations are 'very likely' to be due to 'anthropogenic activities, predominantly agriculture and fossil fuel use',[6] whilst the rise in nitrous oxide levels has been particularly influenced by agricultural activities, such as the use of fertilisers.

The current rate of warming over the last fifty years is almost double that of the last hundred years,[7] and the warming effect is 'now evident from observations of increases in global average air and ocean temperatures, widespread melting of snow and ice, and rising global average sea level'.[8] Over the last 150 years global temperature has on average risen by approximately 0.6 degrees Celsius, and could rise by 1.4–5.8 degrees Celsius by the year 2100.[9] Such a dramatic rise in temperature is likely to lead to more rain and flooding in South East Asia and countries with temperate climates; a reduction in rainfall and the resultant greater likelihood of droughts in Africa, Central Asia, the Mediterranean region and Australasia; and the continued melting of sea ice in the Arctic and Antarctic.[10]

The impacts for wildlife, as for humans, are potentially catastrophic. Climate change can impact upon the geographical location of ecosystems, and also influence the type and blend of species within a given ecosystem;[11] species may well be unable to tolerate changes in climate

[2] IPCC, *Climate Change 2007: The Physical Science Basis, Working Group I* (Cambridge University Press, 2007) (summary for policy-makers), p. 5.

[3] Ibid., where it is also indicated that 'very high confidence' represented 'a 9 out of 10 chance of being correct'.

[4] Ibid., p. 2. [5] Ibid., p. 4. [6] Ibid. [7] Ibid., p. 5. [8] Ibid.

[9] Secretariat to the CBD, Biodiversity and Climate Change (2007), p. 5. [10] Ibid., p. 6.

[11] IPCC, The Regional Impacts of Climate Change: An Assessment of Vulnerability (1997) (summary for policy-makers), p. 2.

and therefore seek to migrate towards the polar areas. A recent report underlines the susceptibility of ecosystems to climate change as evidenced 'by the changes in distribution of various bird, plant, lichen, insect, spider and fungi species that have already been observed in Europe and other parts of the world'.[12] Furthermore, the same report indicates the 'alteration of species ranges is especially relevant because species will not move to the same extent or at the same rate'.[13] For example, some species and types of forest may not be able to migrate quickly enough and may therefore not survive at all. While, for example, mosses are highly adaptable as they 'enjoy easy dispersal, through light windborne spores, and can rapidly colonize suitable new habitat',[14] trees by contrast migrate at a much slower rate.[15] The migration rate of trees is known to be between four and two hundred kilometres in every hundred years but in mid-latitude regions 'an average warming of 1–3.5 degrees Celsius over the next 100 years would be equivalent to a poleward shift of the present bands of similar temperatures ... [by] approximately 150–550 km'.[16] Certain types of forest could therefore cease to exist, the land quite possibly becoming inhabited by different species establishing a quite different ecosystem.[17] There is, for instance, concern that white spruce trees in Canada will be unable to migrate at a rate which would guarantee that population's survival.[18]

The likely increased frequency of fires, heatwaves, droughts, surges and storms brought about by changes in the Earth's climate may well impact upon particular ecosystems and the mix of species therein.[19] There is very real potential for harm to particularly fragile ecosystems and vulnerable species:

> Natural systems at risk include glaciers, coral reefs and atolls, mangroves, boreal and tropical forests, polar and alpine ecosystems, prairie wetlands, and remnant native grasslands. While some species may increase in abundance or range, climate change will increase existing risks of extinction of some vulnerable species and loss of biodiversity. It is

[12] EEA, Vulnerability and Adaptation to Climate Change in Europe (2006), Technical Report No. 7/2005, p. 54.
[13] Ibid.
[14] M. Bowman, 'Global Warming and the International Legal Protection of Wildlife', in R. R. Churchill and D. Freestone (eds.), *International Law and Global Climate Change* (Kluwer, 1991), p. 129.
[15] Ibid. [16] IPCC, *supra* n. 11, p. 3. [17] Ibid.
[18] Secretariat to the CBD, *supra* n. 9, p. 24.
[19] For a comprehensive assessment see IPCC, *supra* n. 11. A useful insight is also provided in Bowman, *supra* n. 14, pp. 127–45.

> well-established that the geographical extent of the damage or loss, and the number of systems affected, will increase with the magnitude and rate of climate change.[20]

By way of illustration, it is estimated that Arctic ecosystems are particularly susceptible to change, with perhaps as much as half of the tundra being 'replaced by boreal forests under a 1.3–3.8 degrees Celsius rise in global average temperature'.[21] Average air temperature in the Arctic has increased far more than the global average.[22] Continued melting of the sea ice, an important habitat for several Arctic mammals, will increase pressures on native animals such as polar bears and seals. Anticipated permafrost thawing 'would lead to lowered water tables in some areas and would flood thaw lakes in others, altering current wetland ecosystem types'.[23] Wildlife in Antarctica is, however, likely to undergo less change, although 'there may be species shifts' and 'in the sea, marine ecosystems will move poleward'.[24] In desert regions temperatures will become more intense, which may well present difficulties for wildlife as 'many organisms in the deserts already are near their tolerance levels, and some may not be able to adapt further under hotter conditions'.[25] In dryland areas reduced rainfall is likely to lead to more outbreaks of fires, thereby placing biodiversity under greater pressure.[26]

Biodiversity situated in or around coastal regions and island biodiversity will also come under increased pressure. Mangroves in small island states can be susceptible to rises in sea level as their 'natural capacity ... to adapt and migrate landward ... is expected to be reduced by coastal land loss and the presence of infrastructure in the coastal zone'.[27] The landward migration of mangroves in tropical Asia may also be limited, 'constrained by human infrastructure and human activities'.[28] Coral reefs deserve particular attention as they represent habitat for around 25 per cent of marine species.[29] The Great Barrier Reef, for example, suffered bleaching episodes in 1998, and again in 2002 when 'between 60 and 95 per cent of reefs were affected. Most of these recovered well but a small percentage (less than 5%) suffered high mortality, losing between

[20] IPCC, Climate Change 2001: Synthesis Report, Working Group 2 (summary for policy-makers), at para. 2.3.
[21] EEA, *supra* n. 12, p. 55. [22] Secretariat to the CBD, *supra* n. 9, p. 12.
[23] IPCC, *supra* n. 11, p. 10. [24] Ibid., p. 8. [25] Ibid., p. 6.
[26] Secretariat to the CBD, *supra* n. 9, p. 21. [27] IPCC, *supra* n. 11, p. 15. [28] Ibid., p. 3.
[29] Secretariat to the CBD, *supra* n. 9, p. 36.

50 and 90 per cent of their corals.'[30] Rising carbon dioxide emissions have led to ocean acidification and subsequent strains on marine ecosystems.[31] Biodiversity located on low-level islands also faces an obvious threat. On the Maldives, for example, '50% to 80% of land area is less than one metre above sea level'.[32] Wildlife situated on such low-level islands faces eradication as sea levels continue to rise.

The 1992 UN Framework Convention on Climate Change (Climate Change Convention)[33] and its 1997 Kyoto Protocol[34] represent the key legal response to climate change. With an 'ultimate objective' to 'achieve . . . stabilization of greenhouse gas concentration in the atmosphere at a level that would prevent dangerous anthropogenic interference with the climate system',[35] the Climate Change Convention is framework in nature and a tentative first step to tackle the problem. No emission reduction timetable was politically possible in 1992. However, the treaty established key principles and a framework for co-operation within which it has become possible to adopt the Kyoto Protocol. Not all industrialised countries are currently within the Protocol's regime – most notably the US.

Importantly, the Climate Change Convention noted that 'the developed country parties should take the lead in combating climate change and the adverse effects thereof'.[36] As such, the principle of common but differentiated responsibilities has been endorsed, taking into account the fact that the industrialised world is in large part responsible for the release of greenhouse emissions over the last century. The principle of common but differentiated responsibility also plays a key part in the 1997 Kyoto Protocol. Under the Kyoto Protocol emission reduction commitments only apply to developed countries, and not to the developing world. The reductions are to be met by the 2008–12 period and, if

[30] World Heritage Committee, The Impacts of Climate Change on World Heritage Properties (2006), Doc. WHC-06/30.COM/7.1, p. 27, citing Greg Terrill, assistant secretary, Heritage Division, Australian Department of Environment and Heritage.

[31] IPCC, *Climate Change 2007: Synthesis Report* (IPCC, 2007), para. 3.3.4.

[32] Secretariat to the CBD, *supra* n. 9, p. 32.

[33] In force 21 March 1994, (1992) 31 *ILM* 849. See D. Bodansky, 'The United Nations Framework Convention on Climate Change: A Commentary' (1993) 18 *Yale JIL* 451–558.

[34] In force 16 February 2005, (1998) 37 *ILM* 22. See D. Freestone and C. Streck, *Legal Aspects of Implementing the Kyoto Protocol Mechanisms: Making Kyoto Work* (Oxford University Press, 2005); and M. Grubb, D. Brack and C. Vrolijk, *The Kyoto Protocol: A Guide and Assessment* (Royal Institute of International Affairs, 1999).

[35] Article 2. [36] Article 3(1).

signatories were to comply with their individual targets, would produce a decrease in greenhouse gas emissions of just over 5 per cent compared to 1990 emissions.[37] Reductions are certainly not all to be made at home, as the Protocol endorsed the 'flexible mechanisms': the project-specific Joint Implementation (JI) and Clean Development Mechanism (CDM); and also the notion of greenhouse gas emissions trading between industrialised countries. The JI and the CDM both allow for investment in an emission-reducing project abroad to partially offset required domestic emission reductions. More controversially, emissions trading allows an industrialised country effectively to sell surplus greenhouse emissions to another industrialised state which is in danger of failing to meet its individual Kyoto Protocol target.

In addition to action within the regime established by the Climate Change Convention, a variety of wildlife treaties have drawn attention to the growing problem. The World Heritage Committee in 2005 called on UNESCO's World Heritage Centre to establish a working group of experts on the impacts of climate change on World Heritage after concern had been raised as to its impact upon Sagarmatha National Park (Nepal), Huascaran National Park (Peru), the Great Barrier Reef (Australia) and the Belize Barrier Reef Reserve System (Belize).[38] The report of the working group highlighted threats to several World Heritage sites,[39] and the World Heritage Committee subsequently called on state parties to implement the strategy endorsed by the working group to protect sites from the impact of climate change.[40] In relation to migratory species, the CMS Conference of the Parties has requested its Scientific Committee to 'afford climate change high priority in its future programme of activities' and called on range state parties and non-parties to 'implement, as appropriate, adaptation measures that would help the foreseeable adverse effects of climate change on Appendix I species'.[41] Additionally, the 10th Meeting of the Parties of Ramsar in

[37] Reductions cover a basket of six greenhouse gases: carbon dioxide, methane, nitrous oxides and also hydrofluorocarbons, perfluorocarbons and sulphur hexafluoride.

[38] World Heritage Committee, Decision 29COM 7B.a (2005).

[39] See World Heritage Committee, The Impacts of Climate Change on World Heritage properties (2006), Doc. WHC-06/30.COM/7.1, which incorporates the working group's findings.

[40] World Heritage Committee, Decision 30COM 7.1 (2006). Note also UNESCO, Policy Document on the Impact of Climate Change on World Heritage Properties (2008).

[41] UNEP/CMS Resolution 8.13 (Nairobi, 20–5 November 2005). See also UNEP/CMS Secretariat, Migratory Species and Climate Change: Impacts of a Changing Environment on Wild Animals (2006).

2008 urged parties to 'manage wetlands wisely to reduce the multiple pressures they face and thereby increase their resilience to climate change'.[42] Furthermore, the 2008 CBD Conference of the Parties encouraged parties to implement a range of activities to promote further co-operation between key actors within the legal regimes established under the three Rio conventions and also established an Ad Hoc Technical Expert group on Biodiversity and Climate Change.[43]

3. Ozone layer depletion

The ozone layer in the Earth's stratosphere absorbs a degree of the UV-B radiation emitted by the Sun. In this way the ozone layer acts as a natural filter reducing the amount of harmful radiation that reaches the Earth's surface. Scientific research in the 1970s revealed that certain substances deplete the amount of stratospheric ozone and hence this filtering effect. In humans, raised exposure to UV-B increases the risk of skin cancer and cataracts and also reduces immunity. In relation to wildlife, it can be detrimental to the growth of some plants and harmful to marine ecosystems, and also impacts upon biogeochemical cycles. The effect of increased UV-B on phytoplankton is particularly important. Inhabiting the surface areas of the oceans, phytoplankton is a key element of the aquatic food chain and UV-B is known to have a negative impact on growth and reproduction. Additionally, corals are also known to be susceptible to increased exposure to UV-B.[44]

The Vienna Convention for the Protection of the Ozone Layer was adopted in March 1985.[45] The treaty failed to impose reductions in the consumption and production of ozone-depleting substances but did establish a framework within which such reductions have subsequently been negotiated. Shortly after the treaty was opened for signature, Dr Joe Farman published the findings of his British Antarctic Survey team, drawing attention to the hole in the ozone layer which opened up over Antarctica in springtime. Added momentum was given to negotiations

[42] 10th Meeting of the Parties, Resolution X.24 (Changwon, 28 October–4 November 2008).

[43] CBD CoP 9, Decision IX/16 (Bonn, Germany, 19–30 May 2008).

[44] See generally UNEP, Environmental Effects of Ozone Depletion: 1998 Assessment (1998).

[45] In force 22 September 1988, (1987) 26 *ILM* 1529. On the legal regime see R. Benedict, *Ozone Diplomacy* (Harvard University Press, 1998) and also the UNEP Ozone Secretariat website at ozone.unep.org.

for a legally binding protocol detailing an emission reduction timetable and the Montreal Protocol on Substances that Deplete the Ozone Layer was signed in September 1987.[46] Although it was not altogether clear whether chlorofluorocarbons (CFCs) were contributing to the thinning effect, precautionary action was taken under the Protocol. Since that time the Meetings of the Parties to the Montreal Protocol have made a number of 'adjustments' bringing forward phase-out dates, and 'amendments' which have either introduced new substances to the Protocol or imposed a licensing system for trade in ozone-depleting substances.

The production and consumption of the majority of ozone-depleting substances has now been phased out in the developed world under the Protocol. For example, with the exception of certain essential uses, the consumption and production of CFCs, carbon tetrachloride, methyl chloroform and HBFCs (hydrobromofluorocarbons) have been banned in industrialised countries since 1 January 1996. Work is under way to phase out hydrochlorofluorocarbons (HCFCs), a substitute for CFCs but now also known to contribute to the problem. Endorsing a common but differentiated approach, the Montreal Protocol has established a delayed phase-out period for developing countries (known as Article 5 countries). Article 5 states are also eligible to obtain funds from the Multilateral Fund established by the parties. The establishment of this fund proved a key incentive to both India's (1992) and China's (1991) decision to ratify the Protocol as it allows Article 5 countries to meet the 'incremental costs' incurred in phasing out depleting substances including the cost of technology conversion and of substitutes. Very considerable progress has certainly been made under this legal regime since the original treaty was adopted in 1985. However, the recovery of the ozone layer is only expected after 2050 due to the fact that ozone-depleting substances take a considerable time to break down once in the atmosphere.

4. Acid precipitation

Sulphur dioxide released in the burning of fossil fuels in power stations and other heavy industrial plants is a key contributor to the acid rain problem. Nitrogen oxide is also produced in these processes and in the operation of motor vehicles, shipping and aircraft. Once emitted into the atmosphere, sulphur dioxide and nitrogen oxides can be taken by the winds and travel considerable distances. These pollutants, released either

[46] In force 1 January 1989, (1987) 26 *ILM* 1550.

by wet deposition (commonly known as 'acid rain') or as dry deposition, can have considerable impact upon the balance of soils and have led to the decimation of forest areas. In addition, acidity levels in some rivers and lakes have risen as a consequence to such a point that these fresh waters are no longer capable of sustaining fish life.

The key instrument in the field is the regional 1979 Convention on Long-Range Transboundary Air Pollution (the LRTAP Convention).[47] Open to signature by all members of the UN's Economic Commission for Europe, the treaty was ratified by European countries as well as the USA, Canada and the Russian Federation. More recently, Azerbaijan, Kazakhstan and Kyrgyzstan have also become parties, extending the reach of the treaty into Central Asia and the number of parties to over fifty. Although the LRTAP Convention is regional in nature, it in fact applies to a significant portion of the industrialised world. Like the treaties that apply to climate change and the ozone layer, the 1979 LRTAP Convention is framework in nature with broad obligations that most countries would have no hesitation in agreeing to. No emission reductions are specifically detailed, Article 2 merely stipulating in vague terms that parties will 'endeavour to limit and, as far as possible, gradually reduce and prevent air pollution including long-range transboundary air pollution'. However, having ensured maximum participation in the legal regime by not alienating the heaviest polluters, it was anticipated by at least some of LRTAP's parties that protocols would later be adopted detailing clear emission reduction timetables when political will allowed. There are now in fact eight protocols.

Crucial in the dynamic evolution of the LRTAP regime has been the broad and general obligations included in LRTAP which have provided a framework within which protocols have been negotiated. These obligations include provisions providing for information exchange and co-operative arrangements between parties, as well as the promotion of research and monitoring within the Co-operative Programme for the Monitoring and Evaluation of the Long-Range Transmission of Air Pollutants in Europe (EMEP). The role of scientific research and the work of EMEP have been particularly influential. The then West

[47] In force 16 March 1983, (1979) 18 *ILM* 1442. See www.unece.org/env/lrtap. Sulphur and nitrogen oxide emissions from shipping have also been limited to an extent by Annex VI of the International Convention for the Prevention of Pollution from Ships, 1973, as amended by the Protocol of 1978 relating thereto (MARPOL 73/78). MARPOL 73/78 entered into force on 2 October 1983, (1978) 17 *ILM* 546. Annex VI entered into force on 19 May 2005; see further www.imo.org. Amendments to Annex VI were adopted in October 2008 but are not in force at the time of writing.

Germany was initially reluctant to agree to emission reductions to reduce acid rain but changed its viewpoint when it became clear that acidification was having a major impact on German forests. As the causes of acid rain and of its impact on the environment have grown more certain, more parties have been willing to negotiate protocols establishing timetabled reductions within the Executive Body of LRTAP.

LRTAP has undoubtedly played a role in achieving reductions in emissions of acidifying substances in the UN ECE area, although other factors, such as the impact of regional European Community regulation and the restructuring of Eastern European industry, should also not be underestimated. Since 1980 sulphur dioxide emissions in Europe have been reduced by more than 50 per cent, and nitrogen oxide emissions declined by 15 per cent in the 1980–98 period.[48] Several of LRTAPs protocols aim to reduce sulphur dioxide and nitrogen oxide emissions.[49] The most recent of these is the multipollutant 1999 Gothenburg Protocol, which seeks to reduce sulphur dioxide emissions by 63 per cent and nitrogen oxide emissions by 41 per cent when compared to 1990 levels. Despite these developments, a recent report on the state of Europe's environment notes that '[i]n 2004 more than 23% of trees assessed in 31 countries were classified as damaged as a result of acidification, although defoliation varies greatly between species and regions'.[50]

5. Oil pollution

The impact of oil pollution on the marine environment, and on aquatic and terrestrial (near-shore) species and habitat in particular, can be severe. For example, the spillage of over 40 million litres of crude oil from the *Exxon Valdez* into Prince William Sound, Alaska in 1989

[48] Secretariat for the Convention on Long-Range Transboundary Air Pollution, 2000 Review of Strategies and Policies for Air Pollution Abatement (2000), pp. 2–3 (Executive Summary).

[49] The 1985 Protocol on the Reduction of Sulphur Emissions or Their Transboundary Fluxes by at least 30%; the 1988 Protocol Concerning the Control of Emissions of Nitrogen Oxides or Their Transboundary Fluxes; the 1994 Protocol on Further Reduction of Sulphur Emissions; and the 1999 Gothenberg Protocol to Abate Acidification, Eutrophication and Ground-Level Ozone. Copies of all these protocols are available at www.unece.org/env/lrtap.

[50] European Environment Agency (EEA), *Europe's Environment: The Fourth Assessment* (EEA, 2007), p. 184.

affected nearly 2,000 kilometres of coastline and had an immediate effect on wildlife:

> [M]ass mortalities of 1000 to 2800 sea otters and unprecedented numbers of seabird deaths estimated at 250,000 were documented during the days after the spill. An estimated 302 harbor seals . . . were killed not by oiled pelage but likely from inhalation of toxic fumes leading to brain lesions, stress and disorientation.[51]

The detrimental impact on biodiversity was not confined to the days after the *Exxon Valdez* ran aground on Bligh Reef in Prince William Sound. Research has documented the continuing harm caused to specific species (fish, seabirds and marine mammals) and also to coastal habitats over a decade after the spill.[52] The potential impact of this type of oil pollution on wildlife has been underlined by the Conference of the Parties to the Bonn Convention, which has invited 'all relevant international, regional and national organizations and bodies to cooperate with CMS in efforts to prevent oil pollution and to minimise the negative impacts on migratory species of the release of crude and refined oils into the environment'.[53]

The main global instrument preventing oil pollution of the marine environment is Annex I of the International Convention for the Prevention of Pollution from Ships, 1973, as amended by the Protocol of 1978 relating thereto (MARPOL 73/78).[54] Standards have also been adopted under the 1974 International Convention for the Safety of Life at Sea as amended (SOLAS).[55] Annex I of MARPOL 73/78 stipulates a variety of construction requirements and equipment standards for oil tankers. These include the requirement introduced after the *Exxon Valdez* incident that all new tankers delivered on or after 6 July 1996 must be fitted with double hulls.[56] Existing tankers previously had to

[51] C. H. Peterson, S. D. Rice, J. W. Short, D. Esler, J. L. Bodkin, B. E. Bellachey and D. B. Irons, 'Long-Term Ecosystem Response to the Exxon Valdez Oil Spill' (2003) 302 *Science* 2082–6, at p. 2082.

[52] Ibid., p. 2085. [53] CMS Resolution 7.3 (2002).

[54] MARPOL 73/78 entered into force on 2 October 1983, (1978) 17 *ILM* 546. Annex I has been revised on several occasions. The most recent revision was introduced by virtue of the International Maritime Organisation's Marine Environment Protection Committee Resolution MEPC.117 (52) adopted on 15 October 2004. The revised Annex came into force on 1 January 2007. See generally www.imo.org. On details of activities to reduce oil pollution under regional seas programmes see www.unep.org/regionalseas/Programmes/default.asp.

[55] 1184 *UNTS* 2; into force 25 May 1980. SOLAS has been amended several times; see www.imo.org.

[56] Annex I, Regulation 19.

comply with this requirement within thirty years of their delivery but, in the light of the *Erika* disaster off the Brittany coast in late 1999, the time within which this requirement must be fulfilled has been brought forward to 2010.[57] A more recent requirement stipulates that pump-rooms of oil tankers constructed on or after 1 January 2007 must be provided with a double bottom.[58] Additionally, the 1990 International Convention on Oil Pollution Preparedness, Response and Cooperation (OPRC Convention) obliges parties to take measures to prepare for and respond to oil pollution incidents.[59] Obligations include the need for all ships to have on board an emergency plan for oil pollution.[60]

The 1969 Convention on Civil Liability for Oil Pollution Damage (1969 Civil Liability Convention)[61] and the 1971 Convention on the Establishment of an International Fund for Compensation for Oil Pollution Damage (1971 Fund Convention)[62] established a system of civil liability in relation to oil pollution from ships. The 1969 Civil Liability Convention is being replaced by a protocol adopted in 1992, and a further 1992 protocol replaces the 1971 Fund Convention.[63] The Civil Liability Convention as amended by the 1992 Protocol allows for the liability of the owner of a ship causing 'pollution damage' defined as including compensation for environmental impairment covering 'reasonable measures of reinstatement actually undertaken or to be undertaken'.[64]

This section has addressed the issue of oil pollution but it is important to note that run-off of pollutants (such as chemicals, pesticides and heavy metals, which are addressed in the next section) from land-based sources actually provides a more significant threat to the marine environment than that posed by oil spillage.[65]

6. Chemicals, pesticides and heavy metals

Many persistent organic pollutants (POPs) have been used as pesticides, including DDT, chlordane, aldrin, mirex and dieldrin. Others are

57 Annex I, Regulation 20. 58 Annex I, Regulation 22.

59 30 *ILM* 733 (1991), in force 13 May 1995. See P. Sands, *Principles of International Environmental Law* (Cambridge University Press, 2nd ed., 2003), 451–2.

60 Article 3. 61 973 *UNTS* 3. 62 (1972) 11 *ILM* 284,

63 See www.imo.org/conventions.

64 Article 1(6)(a) of the treaty as amended by the 1992 Protocol.

65 P. W. Birnie, A. E. Boyle and C. J. Redgwell, *International Law and the Environment* (Oxford University Press, 3rd ed., 2009), p. 380.

industrial chemicals (including PCBs), whilst some are by-products of industrial processes such as dioxins and furans from incinerators, and polycyclic aromatic hydrocarbons (PAHs) from the combustion of fossil fuels. The presence of POPs in the environment is believed to have a number of negative impacts. DDT, for example, is responsible for 'reduced fertility and eggshell thinning in birds',[66] and PCBs are thought to have a detrimental effect on the immune system.[67] POPs accumulate in fatty tissue and, as such, 'their adverse effects are compounded by their bioaccumulation in species at the head of food chains, such as marine mammals, birds of prey, and humans'.[68]

Under LRTAP's 1998 Protocol on Persistent Pollutants,[69] the parties agree to a variety of measures. The production and use of a range of POPs is prohibited. It is envisaged that other POPs, such as DDT and PCBs, will be eradicated in the future and in the meantime their use is restricted. In addition, emissions of substances including furans, dioxins and PAHs must be reduced below the level of emissions in 1990 (or another year between 1985 and 1995). Importantly, parties are also obliged to identify POPs in waste and ensure such waste is destroyed or disposed of in an environmentally sound way.

LRTAP is of course only a regional treaty, but the successful adoption of the 1998 POP Protocol gave added momentum to calls for a global treaty to tackle POPs. In 2001 the Stockholm Convention on Persistent Organic Compounds[70] (Stockholm Convention) was adopted and, subject to certain specific exemptions, places parties under an obligation to eliminate the production and use of Annex A chemicals, and to restrict the use of the Annex B chemical DDT. The unintentional production of Annex C chemicals (including PCBs and HCBs) from industrial processes (waste incineration, cement kilns and the production of pulp) is made subject to action intended to reduce and, where possible, eliminate such releases. Restrictions are also to be placed on the import and export of Annex A and Annex B substances.

The Stockholm Convention has already attracted ratification by over 160 parties. An Ad Hoc Joint Working Group has also been established to enhance co-ordination and co-operation between the Stockholm

[66] R. M. Harrison (ed.), *Pollution: Causes, Effects and Control* (Royal Society of Chemistry, 4th ed., 2001), p. 454.
[67] Ibid., p. 453. [68] Ibid., p. 451. [69] (1998) 37 *ILM* 505, in force 23 October 2003.
[70] (2001) 40 *ILM* 532, in force 17 May 2004. See www.pops.int and also P. L. Lallas, 'The Stockholm Convention on Persistent Organic Compounds' (2001) 95(3) *AJIL* 692.

Convention, the 1989 Basel Convention on the Control of Transboundary Movements of Hazardous Wastes and Their Disposal[71] (Basel Convention) and the 1998 Rotterdam Convention on the Prior Informed Consent Procedure for Certain Hazardous Chemicals and Pesticides in International Trade (Rotterdam Convention).[72] The Basel Convention regulates the movement, management and disposal of hazardous and other wastes, whilst the Rotterdam Convention seeks to implement the Prior Informed Consent Procedure (PIC) which is a system under which a party's decision whether or not to receive certain chemicals listed in the Convention's Annex III is obtained and circulated.

Heavy metals also have an adverse impact on wildlife and ecosystems. For example, mercury is known to have a detrimental impact on the ability of fish to reproduce and is thought to be a source of neurological problems in birds.[73] LRTAP's 1998 Protocol on Heavy Metals regulates emissions of cadmium, lead and mercury by obliging parties to reduce their emissions below 1990 levels (or those of another year between 1985 and 1995).[74] Other measures include phasing out lead in petrol, and the reduction of emissions from industrial processes.

In the context of pollution of the marine environment by chemicals and other harmful substances, it is important to note that MARPOL 73/78 seeks to prevent pollution by noxious substances and their impact on marine ecosystems and species.[75] Other instruments additionally seek to do so, including SOLAS,[76] the 1972 Convention on the Prevention of Marine Pollution by Dumping of Wastes as amended[77] (the London

[71] (1989) 28 *ILM* 657, in force 24 May 1992. See K. Kummer, *International Management of Hazardous Wastes: The Basel Convention and Related Legal Rules* (Clarendon Press, 1995), and Sands, *supra* n. 59, pp. 691–5. See also www.basel.int.

[72] (1999) 38 *ILM* 1, in force 24 February 2004. See www.pic.int; and Sands, *supra* n. 59, pp. 635–6.

[73] L. Schweiger, F. Stadler and C. Bowes, *Poisoning Wildlife: The Reality of Mercury Pollutants* (National Wildlife Federation, 2006), pp. 6–8.

[74] In force 29 December 2003.

[75] MARPOL Annex II – Regulations for the Control of Pollution by Noxious Liquid Substances in Bulk. See also MARPOL Annex III in relation to the prevention of pollution by harmful substances in packaged form. See www.imo.org.

[76] SOLAS Chapter VII – Carriage of Dangerous Goods. See www.imo.org.

[77] The 1996 Protocol to the 1972 Convention on the Prevention of Marine Pollution by Dumping of Wastes and other Matter replaced the 1972 London Convention, (1997) 36 *ILM* 1. It adopts a precautionary approach and endorses the polluter-pays principle (Article 3). It bans the dumping of waste at sea apart from certain materials on an approved list in Annex 1 (Article 4). Additionally, incineration of waste at sea is expressly prohibited (Article 5). See www.imo.org.

Convention) and a number of regional seas programmes.[78] Moreover, the OPRC Convention's 2000 Protocol on Preparedness, Response and Cooperation to Pollution Incidents by Hazardous and Noxious Substances[79] (OPRC-HNS Protocol) places the onus on parties to introduce measures to prepare for and respond to pollution incidents involving hazardous and noxious substances. Necessary measures include the need for vessels to carry pollution emergency plans on board to deal with pollution by such substances.[80]

The accumulation of POPs and heavy metals in cetacean blubber exemplifies the threat to wildlife. For some time the International Whaling Commission (IWC) has been aware of the issue and its ongoing POLLUTION 2000+ programme is investigating the impact of pollutants. Cetaceans in the Mediterranean appear to be particularly susceptible to contamination, as evidenced by the high levels of organochlorines and heavy metals in striped dolphins.[81] In the year 2000 the IWC encouraged parties to sign and ratify LRTAP's 1998 POPs and Heavy Metals Protocols, noting that 'organic contaminants and heavy metals are seriously polluting the environment and its living resources including whales, and may have a significant negative health effect on consumers of marine mammal products'.[82] A similar resolution was approved the following year, encouraging parties to sign the then newly adopted Stockholm Convention.[83]

7. Anthropogenic sources of noise

A matter of growing concern in recent years has been the impact of anthropogenic noise sources on marine wildlife, especially marine mammals.[84] High noise levels are often, for example, emitted by oil tankers,

[78] See, for example, the 1992 Convention for the Protection of the Marine Environment of the North East Atlantic (OSPAR Convention) – in force 25 March 1998, (1993) 32 *ILM* 1068; note in particular OSPAR's Annex I (prevention and elimination of pollution from land-based sources), Annex II (prevention and elimination of pollution by dumping and incineration) and Annex III (prevention and elimination of pollution from offshore sources). Details of activities under other regional seas programmes can be obtained at www.unep.org/regionalseas/Programmes/default.asp.

[79] In force on 14 June 2007. [80] Article 3.

[81] A. Aguilar, 'Population Biology, Conservation Threats and Status of Mediterranean Striped Dolphins' (2000) 2(1) *Journal of Cetacean Research and Management* 17–26.

[82] IWC Resolution 2000-6. [83] IWC Resolution 2001-10.

[84] See generally K. N. Scott, 'International Regulation of Undersea Noise' (2004) 53 *ICLQ* 287–324.

bulk carriers and hovercraft, and significant noise pollution is known to take place in the application of sonar by submarines and other naval vessels.[85] Such naval activity is believed to contribute to some whale strandings.[86] Excessive noise from sonar, shipping and drilling can lead to cetaceans changing course and even leaving areas, and '[w]here individuals do not withdraw from noisy areas, noticeable changes in cycles of feeding and respiration have been documented'.[87] Additionally, noise from seismic surveying used in energy resource exploration may well have a negative impact on marine wildlife.

Although the international regulation of undersea noise is to date underdeveloped, the issue has been addressed to an extent in a number of regimes. The IWC, for example, in 1993 called on its Scientific Committee to give priority to research on the impact of environmental change on whales, and in 1994 one of the five factors identified in this process was the impact of noise. In 1996 the IWC called on the Scientific Committee through its Standing Working Group on Environmental Concerns to consider the impact of noise on cetaceans.[88] Recent subsequent deliberations have indeed addressed the impact of acoustic output from seismic surveys on cetaceans. The fifth meeting of ASCOBANS parties also addressed this particular issue in calling on parties to introduce guidelines for seismic surveys to minimise risk to small cetaceans.[89] Furthermore, it called for further research on the impact of noise on small cetaceans from a range of sources, including high-speed ferries, acoustic devices and wind farms, and for parties to develop mitigation measures (including impact assessments) to reduce disturbance to small cetaceans.[90] ACCOBAMS has additionally called for action in underlining the importance of the need for parties to 'take special care and, if appropriate, to avoid any use of man made noise in habitats of vulnerable species and in areas where marine mammals or endangered species may be concentrated'.[91]

8. Conclusion

Those pollutants discussed in this chapter are not the only sources of pollution which impact negatively on wildlife and their habitats. However, they do reflect some of the key hazards. Substantial progress

[85] Ibid., pp. 288–92. [86] Ibid., p. 290. [87] Ibid., p. 291. [88] IWC Resolution 1996-8.
[89] ASCOBANS Resolution No. 4, 5th Meeting of the Parties. [90] Ibid.
[91] ACCOBAMS Resolution 2.16, 2nd Meeting of the Parties.

has already been made to reduce the impact of ozone layer depletion and acid rain, although it must be noted that in relation to acid deposition the 1979 LRTAP Convention is only regional in nature and, in particular, excludes from its remit most countries in Asia. Efforts are continuing to prevent oil spills, particularly under the MARPOL regime, and in recent years the international community has set out to address the problem of environmental degradation caused by chemicals, pesticides and heavy metals. Even more recently, some regimes have tentatively begun to address the impact on the marine environment of anthropogenic noise. However, of all the dangers posed to wildlife the threat of climate change remains the most significant and provides the biggest environmental challenge still to be addressed effectively. It is therefore particularly disappointing to note that the parties to the Climate Change Convention failed at Copenhagen in December 2009 to reach agreement on legally binding measures to reduce greenhouse gas emissions beyond the Kyoto Protocol's commitment period (2008–12), or on additional measures to be taken to mitigate the effects of climate change.

Recommended further reading

R. Benedict, *Ozone Diplomacy* (Harvard University Press, 1998)

R. R. Churchill, G. Kutting and L. Warren, 'The 1994 UN ECE Sulphur Protocol' (1995) 7(2) *JEL* 169

D. Freestone and C. Streck, *Legal Aspects of Implementing the Kyoto Protocol Mechanisms: Making Kyoto Work* (Oxford University Press, 2005)

M. Grubb, D. Brack and C. Vrolijk, *The Kyoto Protocol: A Guide and Assessment* (Royal Institute of International Affairs, 1999)

P. L. Lallas, 'The Stockholm Convention on Persistent Organic Compounds' (2001) 95(3) *AJIL* 692

K. N. Scott, 'International Regulation of Undersea Noise' (2004) 53 *ICLQ* 287

PART VII

Conclusion

Chapter 22

Final reflections

The analysis of international regulatory activity for the conservation, protection and management of nature and natural resources which has been presented above indicates that international wildlife law has come a very long way since its emergence in the latter stages of the nineteenth century. The intervening periods have witnessed an extraordinary proliferation of protective measures, frequently concluded in legally binding treaty form, and displaying ever greater indications of sophistication, adaptability and mutual coherence. In particular, this has been achieved through the incorporation of dedicated institutional arrangements which have sustained and enhanced the capacity of these treaties to clarify and advance their stated goals, and to work collaboratively to that end. The active participation of non-governmental actors – especially the scientific and technical communities and the various campaigning organisations and other representatives of civil society – has proved crucial in maximising the potential of these institutional arrangements. While the basic foundations for this elaborate edifice of twenty-first-century international wildlife law and institutions had already been laid by the publication of the original edition of this work in 1985, they have been both deepened and strengthened, and significantly built upon, in the interim. There is, accordingly, little serious risk of the modern generation of international conservation agreements ultimately sharing the fate suffered by so many of their forebears – namely gradual but inexorable consignment to that forlorn category of 'sleeping treaties', to utilise Simon Lyster's own evocative phrase. A key element underlying this building process has been the substantial raising of consciousness regarding the fundamental importance of nature conservation, both within the circles of government and on the part of the public at large. The decision of the UN to designate the year 2010 as the International Year of Biodiversity amply demonstrates the extent to which such issues have now consolidated their place on the international political agenda.

Yet, for all this, there is little cause for either celebration or relaxation. For however marked have been the advances in international regulatory principles, procedures and techniques during the modern era of conservation, the seemingly relentless acceleration of both the direct exploitationary pressures and the casual, collateral destructiveness associated with contemporary human lifestyles threatens ultimately to outstrip the capacity of either natural or regulatory systems to control or counteract their effects. 2010 was also, after all, the year which had been earmarked at the 2002 Johannesburg Summit for achieving 'a significant reduction of the current rate of biodiversity loss', a target which has since 2007 been formally integrated into the Millennium Development Goals. In Europe, meanwhile, the still more ambitious objective had been set of halting such loss entirely. But it is surely now clear that the international community will not even come close to attaining such targets, and that revised aspirations, approaches and attitudes will therefore be required.[1]

To illustrate the point, a report prepared by UNEP for the Johannesburg Summit itself revealed that, globally, over 11,000 species of flora and fauna were known to be facing a high risk of extinction.[2] These included 1,130 species of mammal (24 per cent of the total) and 1,183 species of bird (12 per cent of the total). Alongside them were some 5,611 species of plant, though since only around 4 per cent of the world's known flora had then been properly evaluated the true number of species at risk is certain to have been very much higher. Indeed, beyond a few well-studied and comprehensively documented biological taxa, the paucity of relevant data regarding conservation status has long been a pervasive problem. Biologists are, of course, engaged in a continuous struggle to expand the catalogue of available information, but more recently compiled data has not made encouraging reading, with some commentators assessing contemporary extinction rates as being perhaps a thousandfold higher than the norm throughout environmental history.[3]

In this vein, the first comprehensive survey of amphibians, for example, revealed them to be at significantly greater risk of extinction than

[1] For a brief editorial overview to that effect, see M. Fisher, '2010 and All That – Looking Forward to Biodiversity Conservation in 2011 and Beyond' (2009) 43(4) *Oryx* 449.

[2] UNEP, Global Environment Outlook-3 (Geo-3) (2002).

[3] The most recent major survey, completed by an international team of experts assembled by the Stockholm Environment Institute, confirms an increase of between 100 and 1000 times the background rate of extinction during the period since the Industrial Revolution, with a further projected tenfold increase during the present century: J. Rockström, W. Steffen et al., 'Planetary Boundaries: Explaining the Safe Operating Space for Humanity' (2009) 14 *Ecology & Society* 32.

either birds or mammals.[4] Indeed, almost one-third of all known species were found to be under threat, with 427 (over 7 per cent) judged 'critically endangered'. Subsequently, the Millennium Ecosystem Assessment, a global inventory of natural resources compiled by over 1,300 scientists in ninety-five countries published early in 2005,[5] provided irrefutable confirmation of a world living far beyond its ecological means. Key findings include an assessment that around 60 per cent of the planet's ecosystem services are being degraded or used unsustainably. Human destruction or transformation of the natural landscape through such activities as logging or conversion to agriculture has led to unprecedented losses of natural biomes, with forest cover reduced by more than 90 per cent in some twenty-nine countries and all but eradicated in a further twenty-five. Some 35 per cent of mangroves and 27 per cent of coral reefs have also been lost in the last few decades. Furthermore, the combined effect of ecosystem degradation and population movement has recently been reflected in alarming increases in the incidence of fire- and flood-related disasters. Then, in 2008, the Living Planet Index prepared on behalf of WWF,[6] which tracks nearly 4,000 different wildlife populations, revealed an overall decline of 27 per cent since 1970, with marine species particularly badly affected. Finally, the November 2009 update to the IUCN's Red List of Threatened Species, published the previous year, served only to corroborate the sorry tale. Indeed, of 47,677 species evaluated, an aggregate of 17,291 were found to be threatened with extinction. This total included 28 per cent of reptiles so far assessed, 37 per cent of freshwater fish, 35 per cent of invertebrates and 70 per cent of plants. Given the acute limitations of existing botanical knowledge in particular, the likelihood is that numerous floral species will become extinct before ever having been discovered, let alone formally described or evaluated for their potential benefits to humankind. Of course, the theoretical potential of such statistics to exaggerate the seriousness of the current position must always be recognised, since research into the conservation status of wildlife species tends inevitably to be focused on those already believed to be at risk: great care must accordingly be taken not to overextrapolate from these figures. Unfortunately, overall survival

[4] S. N. Stuart et al., 'Status and Trends of Amphibian Declines and Extinctions Worldwide' (2004) 306 *Science* 1783.

[5] This was followed in January 2006 by the publication of four 'foundation' reports on which the assessment was based; see generally www.millenniumassessment.org/en/products.aspx.

[6] Accessible via http://assets.panda.org/downloads/living_planet_report_2008.pdf.

prospects are scarcely more encouraging for taxa which have been *comprehensively* assessed, where the proportion of threatened species currently stands at 12 per cent for birds, 21 per cent for mammals, and 30 per cent for amphibians.

Plainly, therefore, those engaged in organising events for the International Year of Biodiversity should be concentrating their efforts more upon the continued enhancement of ecological awareness than upon indulgence in celebration or mutual congratulation. Yet consciousness-raising endeavours alone are most unlikely to prove sufficient to reverse current trends of species decline, since experience suggests that even individuals who are relatively well informed about conservation goals, and support them in principle, often seem unable or unwilling actually to modify their behaviour in order to align it more effectively with such aspirations.[7] Consequently, renewed commitment to the development of techniques and approaches that are calculated to bring about such behavioural change is a key priority. As several of the major conservation agreements have already recognised, this will entail placing a much heavier emphasis than hitherto on the effective *implementation* of treaty obligations and associated soft-law commitments. In addition, the transfer of expertise and resources from the developed to the developing world will surely have to be intensified, though greater attention may need to be paid in future to the practical productivity of such transfers.[8]

Perhaps the most urgent priority of all, however, should be the more enlightened and efficacious *integration* of conservation principles and practices into the mainstream of governmental activity, and especially into the particular channels of energy, trade, transport, security and finance. Amongst the many instances of interaction between wildlife law and other areas of regulation, the interface between trade and the environment presents particular cause for concern, especially in view of the forensic predominance of the WTO Agreement's dispute settlement mechanism in this area. There is an urgent need for more serious and effective functional co-operation between trade and environmental institutions globally, and scope still for achieving a more appropriate

[7] For a recent formal study to that effect, see K. A. Waylen et al., 'Ecotourism Positively Affects Awareness and Attitudes but Not Conservation Behaviours' (2009) 43(3) *Oryx* 343.

[8] For current perspectives on these issues, see, e.g., V. Kapos et al., 'Outcomes, Not Implementation, Predict Conservation Success' (2009) 43(3) *Oryx* 336; S. Milne and E. Niesten, 'Direct Payments for Biodiversity Conservation in Developing Countries' (2009) 43(4) *Oryx* 530.

substantive reconciliation of their respective concerns in the light of sustainable-development principles, notwithstanding the modestly progressive jurisprudence of the WTO Appellate Body in that regard. More generally, the earnest endeavours of conservation treaty institutions over many decades risk being marginalised entirely unless a host of 'contamination' problems associated with human activities – and especially the threats posed by pollution, greenhouse gas emission and the destructive dispersion of exotic life forms – are urgently and effectively addressed.

The place of nature itself within the network of national and international regimes for compensating environmental harm also demands attention. Wildlife will, after all, continue to be treated as a free resource to the extent that compensation systems fail to make due allowance for harm to the environment per se, while the systemic shortcomings of purely economic approaches to the evaluation of environmental loss must also be effectively addressed or circumvented in this context. As seen in Chapter 3, the recent formulations of principle by the International Law Commission in relation both to state responsibility and to civil liability offer new opportunities for overcoming these problems, but it remains unclear to what extent these will be embraced either by governments themselves or by the various adjudicative tribunals to which they have entrusted the task of resolving environmental disputes. Perhaps the International Court of Justice will grasp this particular nettle in currently pending litigation, though its decision in the *Pulp Mills* case certainly does not give much cause for optimism in that regard.[9]

The scale, severity and intractability of these various problems remain a major impediment to the goal of reversing current declines in biological diversity worldwide. International wildlife law has indeed travelled far from its humble beginnings, but the journey ahead appears longer and harder than ever.

[9] See the discussion of the cases in question in Chapter 2 above.

INDEX